Mastering
VMware vSphere™ 4

Scott Lowe

WILEY

Wiley Publishing, Inc.

Acquisitions Editor: Agatha Kim
Development Editor: Jennifer Leland
Technical Editor: Rick J. Scherer
Production Editor: Christine O'Connor
Copy Editor: Kim Wimpsett
Editorial Manager: Pete Gaughan
Production Manager: Tim Tate
Vice President and Executive Group Publisher: Richard Swadley
Vice President and Publisher: Neil Edde
Book Designer: Maureen Forys, Happenstance Type-O-Rama; Judy Fung
Proofreader: Sheilah Ledwidge, Word One New York
Indexer: Nancy Guenther
Project Coordinator, Cover: Lynsey Stanford
Cover Designer: Ryan Sneed
Cover Image: © Pete Gardner/Digital Vision/Getty Images

Library of Congress Cataloging-in-Publication Data

Lowe, Scott, 1970-
  Mastering VMware vSphere 4 / Scott Lowe. – 1st ed.
    p. cm.
  Summary: "Update to the bestselling book on VMWare Infrastructure This update to the bestselling book on VMWare Infrastructure 3, Mastering VMware TBD will prove to be indespensible to anyone using the market-leading virtualization software. As part of the highly acclaimed Mastering series from Sybex, this guide offers a comprehensive look at VMware technology, how to implement it, and how to make the most of what it offers. Shows how VMware Infrastructure saves on hardware costs while maximizing capacity Demonstrates how to work with virtual machines, reducing a company's carbon footprint within its data center Helps maximize the technology Reinforces understanding of VMware Infrastructure through real-world examples Now that virtualization is a key cost-saving strategy, Mastering VMware is the strategic guide you need to maximize the opportunities"–Provided by publisher.
  ISBN 978-0-470-48138-7 (pbk.)
  1. VMware. 2. Virtual computer systems. I. Title.
  QA76.9.V5L67 2009
  005.4'3–dc22
                          2009027781

Dear Reader,

Thank you for choosing *Mastering VMware vSphere 4*. This book is part of a family of premium-quality Sybex books, all of which are written by outstanding authors who combine practical experience with a gift for teaching.

Sybex was founded in 1976. More than 30 years later, we're still committed to producing consistently exceptional books. With each of our titles, we're working hard to set a new standard for the industry. From the paper we print on, to the authors we work with, our goal is to bring you the best books available.

I hope you see all that reflected in these pages. I'd be very interested to hear your comments and get your feedback on how we're doing. Feel free to let me know what you think about this or any other Sybex book by sending me an email at nedde@wiley.com. If you think you've found a technical error in this book, please visit http://sybex.custhelp.com. Customer feedback is critical to our efforts at Sybex.

Best regards,

Neil Edde
Vice President and Publisher
Sybex, an Imprint of Wiley

First and foremost, this book is dedicated to my Lord and Savior, whose strength makes all things possible (Philippians 4:13). Without Him, this book would never have been completed. I'd also like to dedicate this book to my kids: Summer, Johnny, Michael, Elizabeth, Rhys, Sean, and Cameron. To each of you, thank you for your support, your understanding, and your willingness to pitch in and help out all those nights when I was glued to my laptop. You're finally getting Daddy back! I love each and every one of you. Finally, I dedicate this book to my loving wife, Crystal, who believed in me enough to tell me, "Go for it, honey!" Thanks for always supporting me and helping to make this dream a reality.

Acknowledgments

There are so many people to acknowledge and thank for their contributions to this book that I'm not sure where to begin. Although my name is the only name on the cover, this book is the work of many individuals.

I'd like to start with a special thanks to Chad Sakac of EMC, who thought enough of me to extend the offer to write this book. Thanks for your help in getting me in touch with the appropriate resources at VMware and EMC, and thanks for the incredible contributions about VMware vSphere's storage functionality. Without your input and assistance, this book wouldn't be what it is.

Thanks to the product managers and product teams at VMware for working with me, even in the midst of deadlines and product releases. The information you were willing to share with me has made this book better. And thanks to VMware as a whole for creating such a great product.

To all of the people at Sybex, thank you. Agatha, thanks for taking a chance on a first-time author — I hope I have managed to meet and exceed your expectations! Jennifer, thank you for helping me keep my writing clear and concise and constantly reminding me to use active voice. I also appreciate your patience and putting up with all the last-minute revisions. To Christine and the rest of the production team — thanks for your hard work. To Kim Wimpsett, the copy editor, and Sheilah Ledwidge, the proofreader, thanks for paying attention to the details. I'd also like to thank Nancy Guenther, Pete Gaughan, Jay Lesandrini, and Neil Edde. This is my first published book, and I do have to say that it has been a pleasure working with the entire Sybex team. Who's up for another one?

Thanks also to Steve Beaver for his assistance. Steve, your input and help has been tremendous. I couldn't have asked for more. I appreciate you as a colleague and as a friend.

Thanks to Rick Scherer, my technical editor, for always keeping me straight on the details. Thanks for putting up with the odd questions and the off-the-wall inquiries. I know that you invested a lot of time and effort, and it shows. Thank you.

Thank you to Matt Portnoy for reviewing the content and providing an objective opinion on what could be done to improve it. I appreciate your time and your candor.

Finally, thanks to the vendors who supplied equipment to use while writing the book: Hewlett-Packard, Dell, NetApp, EMC, and Cisco. Without your contributions, building labs to run VMware vSphere would have been almost impossible. I appreciate your support.

About the Author

Scott Lowe is an author, consultant, and blogger focusing on virtualization, storage, and other enterprise technologies. As the national technical lead for the virtualization practice at ePlus Technology, Scott has been involved in planning, designing, deploying, and troubleshooting VMware virtualization environments for a range of companies both large and small. He also provides technical leadership and training for the entire virtualization practice at a national level. Scott has provided virtualization expertise to companies such as BB&T, NetApp, PPD, Progress Energy, and more.

Scott's experience also extends into a number of other technologies, such as storage area networks (SANs), directory services, and Ethernet/IP networking. His list of industry certifications and accreditations include titles from VMware, Microsoft, and NetApp, among others. In addition, Scott was awarded a VMware vExpert award for his role in the VMware community, one of only 300 people worldwide to have been recognized by VMware for their contributions.

As an author, Scott has contributed to numerous online magazines focused on VMware and related virtualization technologies. He is regularly quoted as a virtualization expert in virtualization news stories. This is his first published book.

Scott is perhaps most well known for his acclaimed virtualization blog at `http://blog` `.scottlowe.org`. VMware, Microsoft, and other virtualization industry leaders regularly refer to content on his site. It is here that Scott shares his love of technology and virtualization with his readers through a wide selection of technical articles.

About the Contributors

The following individuals also contributed significantly to this book.

Chad Sakac is a principal engineer and VP of the VMware Technical Alliance. Chad is responsible for all of EMC's VMware-focused activities, including the overall strategic alliance, joint engineering projects, joint reference architectures and solutions validation, joint services, and joint marketing activity and sales engagement across global geographies. Chad was also awarded a VMware vExpert award in 2009 for his work in the VMware virtualization community. Chad maintains a public blog at http://virtualgeek.typepad.com and has been a popular speaker at major conferences such as VMworld and EMC World.

Chad brings more than 18 years of engineering, product management, and sales experience to EMC. Before joining EMC via acquisition, Chad held various positions, most recently director of systems engineering at Allocity. There, he was focused on working with customers to develop software that automatically configured storage subsystems to tune for key applications (Exchange, SQL Server, Oracle, and VMware) and on the development of a novel distributed iSCSI target using commodity x86 hardware. Allocity delivered solutions focused on making provisioning, tuning, and backup and recovery simpler and more effective in application-focused environments.

Chad has an undergraduate degree in electrical engineering/computer science from the University of Western Ontario, Canada.

Steve Beaver is the coauthor of two books on virtualization, *Essential VMware ESX Server* and *Scripting VMware Power Tools: Automating Virtual Infrastructure Administration*. In addition, he is the technical editor of *VMware ESX Server: Advanced Technical Design Guide* and a contributing author to *How to Cheat at Configuring VMware ESX Server*. A respected pundit on virtualization technology, Steve is a frequently requested speaker at venues such as VMworld, the VMware Virtualization Forum, and the VMware Healthcare Forum. Steve is an active community expert in VMware's weekly online show, ''VMware Communities Roundtable'', and is one of the most active participants and a moderator on the VMware Communities forum. In fact, Steve was recently named a 2009 VMware vExpert, an award given to individuals who have significantly contributed to the community of VMware users and who have helped spread the word about virtualization over the past year.

Prior to joining Tripwire, Steve was a systems engineer with one of the largest private hospitals in the United States, Florida Hospital in Orlando, Florida, where he was responsible for the entire virtualization life cycle — from strategic planning to design and test, integration, and deployment to operation management. Prior to Florida Hospital, Steve served as a senior engineer at the law firm Greenberg Traurig where he designed and deployed the firm's virtual infrastructure worldwide. He has also held posts at Lockheed Martin, the State of Nebraska, and the World Bank.

Contents at a Glance

Introduction . . . . *xvii*

Chapter 1 • Introducing VMware vSphere 4 1

Chapter 2 • Planning and Installing VMware ESX and VMware ESXi 17

Chapter 3 • Installing and Configuring vCenter Server 57

Chapter 4 • Installing and Configuring vCenter Update Manager 103

Chapter 5 • Creating and ManagingVirtual Networks 139

Chapter 6 • Creating and Managing Storage Devices 215

Chapter 7 • Creating and Managing Virtual Machines 317

Chapter 8 • Migrating and Importing Virtual Machines 361

Chapter 9 • Configuring and Managing VMware vSphere Access Controls 385

Chapter 10 • Managing Resource Allocation 411

Chapter 11 • Ensuring High Availability and Business Continuity 455

Chapter 12 • Monitoring VMware vSphere Performance 519

Chapter 13 • Securing VMware vSphere 555

Chapter 14 • Automating VMware vSphere 587

Appendix A • The Bottom Line 611

Appendix B • Frequently Used Commands 637

Appendix C • VMware vSphere Best Practices 645

Index *653*

Contents

Introduction . . . . *xvii*

Chapter 1 • Introducing VMware vSphere 4 . . . . **1**
Exploring VMware vSphere 4 1
   VMware ESX and ESXi 2
   VMware Virtual Symmetric Multi-Processing 3
   VMware vCenter Server 4
   VMware vCenter Update Manager 5
   VMware vSphere Client 6
   VMware VMotion and Storage VMotion 6
   VMware Distributed Resource Scheduler 7
   VMware High Availability 8
   VMware Fault Tolerance 9
   VMware Consolidated Backup 10
   VMware vShield Zones 10
   VMware vCenter Orchestrator 10
Licensing VMware vSphere 12
Why Choose vSphere? 14
The Bottom Line 15

Chapter 2 • Planning and Installing VMware ESX and VMware ESXi **17**
Planning a VMware vSphere 4 Deployment 17
   Selecting VMware ESX or VMware ESXi 18
   Choosing a Server Platform 19
   Determining a Storage Architecture 21
   Integrating with the Network Infrastructure 21
Deploying VMware ESX 23
   Partitioning the Service Console 23
   Installing from DVD 27
   Performing an Unattended ESX Installation 37
Deploying VMware ESXi 40
   Deploying VMware ESXi Installable 40
   Deploying VMware ESXi Embedded 43
Installing the vSphere Client 44
Performing Post-installation Configuration 45
   Changing the Service Console/Management NIC 45
   Adjusting the Service Console Memory (ESX Only) 49
   Configuring Time Synchronization 51
The Bottom Line 54

Chapter 3 • Installing and Configuring vCenter Server **57**

Introducing vCenter Server 57
    Centralizing User Authentication 59
    Providing an Extensible Framework 60
Planning and Designing a vCenter Server Deployment 61
    Sizing Hardware for vCenter Server 61
    Choosing a Database Server for vCenter Server 63
    Planning for vCenter Server Availability 64
    Running vCenter Server in a VM 66
Installing vCenter Server 67
    Configuring the vCenter Server Back-End Database Server 67
    Running the vCenter Server Installer 73
Installing vCenter Server in a Linked Mode Group 77
Exploring vCenter Server 79
    The vCenter Server Home Screen 80
    The Navigation Bar 81
Creating and Managing a vCenter Server Inventory 81
    Understanding Inventory Views and Objects 81
    Adding and Creating Inventory Objects 83
Exploring vCenter Server's Management Features 86
    Understanding Basic Host Management 86
    Using Scheduled Tasks 88
    Using Events View in vCenter Server 89
    Using vCenter Server's Maps 91
    Working with Host Profiles 92
Managing vCenter Server Settings 94
    Custom Attributes 94
    vCenter Server Settings 95
The Bottom Line 101

Chapter 4 • Installing and Configuring vCenter Update Manager **103**

Overview of vCenter Update Manager 103
Installing vCenter Update Manager 104
    Configuring the Separate Database Server 104
    Creating the Open Database Connectivity Data Source Name 107
    Installing VUM 108
    Configuring the VUM Services 111
    Installing the vCenter Update Manager Plug-In 113
Configuring vCenter Update Manager 113
    Baselines and Groups 114
    Configuration 117
    Events 120
    Patch Repository 120
Patching Hosts and Guests 121
    Attaching and Detaching Baselines 121
    Performing a Scan 124

Staging Patches 126
Remediating Hosts 127
Remediating the Guest Operating Systems 129
Upgrading the VMware Tools 131
Upgrading Virtual Machine Hardware 132
Upgrading ESX/ESXi Hosts with vCenter Update Manager 133
Performing an Orchestrated Upgrade 136
The Bottom Line 137

Chapter 5 • Creating and Managing Virtual Networks **139**
Putting Together a Virtual Network 139
Working with vNetwork Standard Switches 142
Comparing Virtual Switches and Physical Switches 143
Understanding Ports and Port Groups 144
Understanding Uplinks 144
Configuring Service Console Networking 147
Configuring VMkernel Networking 153
Configuring Management Networking (ESXi Only) 156
Configuring Virtual Machine Networking 157
Configuring VLANs 160
Configuring NIC Teaming 164
Traffic Shaping 177
Bringing It All Together 178
Working with vNetwork Distributed Switches 182
Creating a vNetwork Distributed Switch 182
Configuring dvPort Groups 188
Managing Adapters 194
Setting Up Private VLANs 196
Installing and Configuring the Cisco Nexus 1000V 200
Installing the Cisco Nexus 1000V 201
Configuring the Cisco Nexus 1000V 204
Configuring Virtual Switch Security 207
Promiscuous Mode 207
MAC Address Changes and Forged Transmits 208
The Bottom Line 212

Chapter 6 • Creating and Managing Storage Devices **215**
The Importance of Storage Design 215
Shared Storage Fundamentals 216
Common Storage Array Architectures 220
RAID Technologies 223
Midrange and Enterprise Storage Design 226
Protocol Choices 228
Making Basic Storage Choices 247
VMware Storage Fundamentals 249
Core VMware Storage Concepts 249

VMFS version 3 Datastores 249
Creating a VMFS Datastore 252
NFS Datastores 258
Raw Device Mapping 270
Virtual Machine-Level Storage Configuration 272
New vStorage Features in vSphere 4 277
Thin Provisioning 278
VMFS Expansion 282
VMFS Resignature Changes 282
Hot Virtual Disk Expansion 284
Storage VMotion Changes 284
Paravirtualized vSCSI 290
Improvements to the Software iSCSI Initiator 291
Binding the iSCSI Initiator to Multiple Interfaces 293
Storage Management Improvements 298
VMDirectPath I/O and SR-IOV 301
vStorage APIs for Multipathing 303
vStorage APIs for Site Recovery Manager 308
Leveraging SAN and NAS Best Practices 309
The Bottom Line 314

Chapter 7 • Creating and Managing Virtual Machines **317**
Creating a Virtual Machine 317
Installing a Guest Operating System 330
Installing VMware Tools 335
Managing and Modifying Virtual Machines 340
Creating Templates and Deploying Virtual Machines 351
The Bottom Line 358

Chapter 8 • Migrating and Importing Virtual Machines **361**
Setting Up the Conversion Tools 361
Installing VMware vCenter Converter 361
Installing the Guided Consolidation Service 364
Using Guided Consolidation 367
Using vCenter Converter to Perform P2V Migrations 371
Performing Hot Migrations 373
Performing Cold Migrations 378
Importing Virtual Appliances 380
The Bottom Line 382

Chapter 9 • Configuring and Managing VMware vSphere Access Controls . . **385**
Managing and Maintaining ESX/ESXi Host Permissions 385
Creating Custom Roles 387
Granting Permissions 389
Using Resource Pools to Assign Permissions 390
Removing Permissions 391

Identifying Permission Usage 391
Editing and Removing Roles 392
Managing and Maintaining vCenter Server Permissions 393
Understanding vCenter Server's Hierarchy 394
Understanding vCenter Server's Roles 397
Working with vCenter Server Roles 399
Understanding vCenter Server Privileges 399
Combining Privileges, Roles, and Permissions in vCenter Server 401
Managing Virtual Machines Using the Web Console 405
The Bottom Line 409

Chapter 10 • Managing Resource Allocation **411**
Allocating Virtual Machine Resources 411
Allocating Virtual Machine Memory 412
Understanding ESX/ESXi Advanced Memory Technologies 413
Controlling Memory Allocation 414
Setting a Custom Memory Reservation 415
Setting a Custom Memory Limit 417
Setting a Custom Memory Shares Value 419
Addressing Memory Overhead 419
Allocating Virtual Machine CPU Capacity 420
Default CPU Allocation 421
Setting a Custom CPU Reservation 422
Setting a Custom CPU Limit 422
Assigning a Custom CPU Shares Value 423
Using Resource Pools 425
Configuring Resource Pools 426
Understanding Resource Allocation with Resource Pools 429
Exploring VMotion 432
Examining VMotion Requirements 435
Performing a VMotion Migration 438
Investigating Clusters 441
Exploring VMware DRS 443
Manual Automation Behavior 443
Partially Automated Behavior 444
Fully Automated Behavior 444
DRS Rules 445
Ensuring VMotion Compatibility 448
Per-Virtual Machine CPU Masking 448
Enhanced VMotion Compatibility 450
The Bottom Line 452

Chapter 11 • Ensuring High Availability and Business Continuity **455**
Clustering Virtual Machines 455
Microsoft Clustering 455
Virtual Machine Clustering Scenarios 458

Examining Cluster-in-a-Box Scenarios 459
Examining Cluster-Across-Boxes Configurations 460
Examining Physical to Virtual Clustering 469
Implementing VMware High Availability 470
Understanding HA 471
Configuring HA 474
Implementing VMware Fault Tolerance 490
Recovering from Disasters 495
Backing Up with VMware Consolidated Backup 496
Using Backup Agents in a Virtual Machine 497
Using VCB for Full Virtual Machine Backups 498
Using VCB for Single VMDK Backups 504
Using VCB for File-Level Backups 505
Restoring with VMware Consolidated Backup 508
Restoring a Full Virtual Machine Backup 509
Restoring a Single File from a Full Virtual Machine Backup 511
Restoring VCB Backups with VMware Converter Enterprise 513
Implementing VMware Data Recovery 514
Implementing an Office in a Box 515
Replicating SANs 516
The Bottom Line 517

Chapter 12 • Monitoring VMware vSphere Performance 519
Overview of Performance Monitoring 519
Using Alarms 520
Understanding Alarm Scopes 521
Creating Alarms 522
Managing Alarms 528
Working with Performance Graphs 529
Overview Layout 530
Advanced Layout 531
Working with Command-Line Tools 541
Using esxtop 541
Using resxtop 543
Monitoring CPU Usage 543
Monitoring Memory Usage 546
Monitoring Network Usage 548
Monitoring Disk Usage 550
The Bottom Line 552

Chapter 13 • Securing VMware vSphere . . . . • 555
Overview of vSphere Security 555
Securing ESX/ESXi Hosts 556
Working with ESX Authentication 556
Controlling Secure Shell Access 561
Using TCP Wrappers 563

Configuring the Service Console Firewall 564
Auditing Service Console Files 567
Securing ESXi Hosts 569
Keeping ESX/ESXi Hosts Patched 570
Securing vCenter Server 570
Leveraging Active Directory 571
Understanding the vpxuser Account 572
Securing Virtual Machines 573
Configuring Network Security Policies 573
Keeping Virtual Machines Patched 574
Providing Virtual Network Security with vShield Zones 574
Installing vShield Zones 574
Using vShield Zones to Protect Virtual Machines 580
Understanding VMsafe 583
The Bottom Line 584

Chapter 14 • Automating VMware vSphere **587**
Why Use Automation? 587
Using Workflows with vCenter Orchestrator 588
Configuring vCenter Orchestrator 588
Using an Orchestrator Workflow 595
Automating with PowerShell and PowerCLI 597
Installing PowerCLI 597
Working with Objects 599
Running Some Simple PowerCLI Scripts 601
Using Shell Scripts with VMware ESX 605
Creating VMkernel Interfaces with Jumbo Frames Enabled 606
Mounting NFS Datastores via the esxcfg-nas Command 607
Enabling a VMkernel Interface for VMotion 607
The Bottom Line 608

Appendix A • The Bottom Line **611**
Chapter 1: Introducing VMware vSphere 4 611
Chapter 2: Planning and Installing VMware ESX and VMware ESXi 612
Chapter 3: Installing and Configuring vCenter Server 613
Chapter 4: Installing and Configuring vCenter Update Manager 615
Chapter 5: Creating and Managing Virtual Networks 617
Chapter 6: Creating and Managing Storage Devices 619
Chapter 7: Creating and Managing Virtual Machines 623
Chapter 8: Migrating and Importing Virtual Machines 625
Chapter 9: Configuring and Managing VMware vSphere Access Controls 627
Chapter 10: Managing Resource Allocation 628
Chapter 11: Ensuring High Availability and Business Continuity 629
Chapter 12: Monitoring VMware vSphere Performance 631
Chapter 13: Securing VMware vSphere 632
Chapter 14: Automating VMware vSphere 634

Appendix B • Frequently Used Commands **637**

Navigating, Managing, and Monitoring Through the Service Console 637

Managing Directories, Files, and Disks in the Service Console 638

Using the esxcfg-* Commands 638

Using the vicfg-* Commands 641

Appendix C • VMware vSphere Best Practices **645**

ESX/ESXi Installation Best Practices 645

vCenter Server Best Practices 646

Virtual Networking Best Practices 648

Storage Management Best Practices 649

Virtual Machine Best Practices 650

Disaster Recovery and Business Continuity Best Practices 651

Monitoring and Troubleshooting Best Practices 652

Index *653*

Introduction

Virtualization! It's everywhere in the information technology community recently. Every vendor has a product that is somehow tied to virtualization, and existing products and technologies are suddenly getting renamed so as to associate them with virtualization. But what is virtualization, anyway? And why is it so incredibly pertinent and important to today's information technology professional?

I define *virtualization* as the abstraction of one computing resource from another computing resource. Consider storage virtualization; in this case, you are abstracting servers (one computing resource) from the storage to which they are connected (another computing resource). This holds true for other forms of virtualization, too, such as application virtualization (abstracting applications from the operating system). However, when most information technology professionals think of virtualization, they think of hardware virtualization: abstracting the operating system from the underlying hardware upon which it runs and thus enabling multiple operating systems to run simultaneously on the same physical server. And synonymous with this form of virtualization is the company that, for all intents and purposes, invented the market: VMware.

VMware's enterprise-grade virtualization solution has revolutionized how organizations manage their datacenters. Prior to the introduction of VMware's powerful virtualization solution, organizations bought a new server every time a new application needed to be provisioned. Over time, datacenters became filled with servers that were all using only a fraction of their overall capacity. Even though these servers were operating at only a fraction of their total capacity, organizations still had to pay to power them and to dissipate the heat they generated.

Now, using virtualization, organizations can run multiple operating systems and applications on their existing hardware, and new hardware needs to be purchased only when capacity needs dictate. No longer do organizations need to purchase a new physical server whenever a new application needs to be deployed. By stacking workloads together using virtualization, organizations derive greater value from their hardware investments. Organizations also reduce operational costs by reducing the number of physical servers and associated hardware in the datacenter, in turn reducing power usage and reducing cooling needs in the datacenter. In some cases, these operational cost savings can be quite significant.

Virtualization would be of limited value, though, if all it had to offer was hardware reduction. VMware has continued to extend the value of virtualization by adding features such as the ability to quickly and easily provision new instances of operating systems and the ability to move entire operating system instances from one physical server to a different physical server *with no downtime*.

In 2006, VMware further revolutionized virtualization by adding even more functionality, such as dynamic workload optimization and automated high availability for virtualized operating system instances. Since its introduction in 2006, the industry has widely and aggressively adopted VMware Infrastructure 3. In fact, according to VMware, 100 percent of the Fortune 100, 98 percent of the Fortune 500, and 96 percent of the Fortune 1000 use VMware Infrastructure.

In 2009, VMware is set to revolutionize the virtualization industry again with the introduction of its next-generation virtualization solution, named VMware vSphere 4. Built upon the technologies perfected in previous generations, VMware vSphere brings new levels of scalability, security, and availability to virtualized environments.

This book provides all the details you, as an information technology professional, need to design, deploy, configure, manage, and monitor a dynamic virtualized environment built on this next-generation product, VMware vSphere 4.

What Is Covered in This Book

This book was written with a start-to-finish approach to installing, configuring, managing, and monitoring a virtual environment using the VMware vSphere product suite. The book begins by introducing the vSphere product suite and all of its great features. After introducing all of the bells and whistles, this book details how to install the product and then moves into configuration. This includes configuring VMware vSphere's extensive networking and storage functionality. Upon completion of the installation and configuration, the book moves into virtual machine creation and management and then into monitoring and troubleshooting. You can read this book from cover to cover to gain an understanding of the vSphere product suite in preparation for a new virtual environment. If you're an IT professional who has already begun your virtualization, you can use this book to complement your skills with the real-world tips, tricks, and best practices you'll find in each chapter.

This book, geared toward aspiring and practicing virtualization professionals, provides information to help implement, manage, maintain, and troubleshoot an enterprise virtualization scenario. As an added benefit, I have included three appendixes: one that offers solutions to the "Master it" problems, another that details common Linux and ESX commands, and another that describes best practices for VMware vSphere 4.

Here is a glance at what's in each chapter:

Chapter 1: Introducing VMware vSphere 4   I begin with a general overview of all the products that make up the VMware vSphere product suite. This chapter also covers VMware vSphere licensing and pricing, and it provides some examples of benefits that an organization might see from adopting VMware vSphere as its virtualization solution.

Chapter 2: Planning and Installing VMware ESX and VMware ESXi   This chapter looks at selecting the physical hardware, choosing VMware ESX or VMware ESXi, planning your installation, and actually installing VMware ESX/ESXi, both manually and in an unattended fashion.

Chapter 3: Installing and Configuring vCenter Server   In this chapter, I dive deep into planning your vCenter Server environment. vCenter Server is a critical management component of VMware vSphere, so this chapter discusses the proper design, planning, installation, and configuration for vCenter Server.

Chapter 4: Installing and Configuring vCenter Update Manager   This chapter describes what is involved in planning, designing, installing, and configuring vCenter Update Manager. You'll use vCenter Update Manager to keep your ESX/ESXi hosts, virtual machines, and virtual appliances patched and up-to-date.

Chapter 5: Creating and Managing Virtual Networks   The virtual networking chapter covers the design, management, and optimization of virtual networks, including new features such as the vNetwork Distributed Switch and the Cisco Nexus 1000V. In addition, it initiates discussions and provides solutions on how to integrate the virtual networking architecture with the physical network architecture while maintaining network security.

Chapter 6: Creating and Managing Storage Devices   This in-depth chapter provides an extensive overview of the various storage architectures available for VMware vSphere. This chapter discusses Fibre Channel, iSCSI, and NAS storage design and optimization techniques as well as the new advanced storage features such as thin provisioning, multipathing and round-robin load balancing, NPIV, and Storage VMotion.

Chapter 7: Creating and Managing Virtual Machines   This chapter introduces the practices and procedures involved in provisioning virtual machines through vCenter Server. In addition, you'll be introduced to timesaving techniques, virtual machine optimization, and best practices that will ensure simplified management as the number of virtual machines grows larger over time.

Chapter 8: Migrating and Importing Virtual Machines   In this chapter I continue with more information about virtual machines but with an emphasis on performing physical-to-virtual (P2V) and virtual-to-virtual (V2V) migrations in the VMware vSphere environment. This chapter provides a solid, working understanding of VMware Guided Consolidation and VMware vCenter Converter and offers real-world hints at easing the pains of transitioning physical environments into virtual realities.

Chapter 9: Configuring and Managing vSphere Access Controls   Chapter 9 covers the security model of VMware vSphere and shows you how to manage user access for environments with multiple levels of system administration. The chapter shows you how to use Windows users and groups in conjunction with the VMware vSphere security model to ease the administrative delegation that comes with enterprise-level deployments.

Chapter 10: Managing Resource Allocation   In this chapter I provide a comprehensive look at managing resource utilization. From individual virtual machines to resource pools to clusters of ESX/ESXi hosts, this chapter explores how resources are consumed in VMware vSphere. In addition, you'll get details on the configuration, management, and operation of VMotion, VMware Distributed Resource Scheduler (DRS), and Enhanced VMotion Compatibility (EVC).

Chapter 11: Ensuring High Availability and Business Continuity   This exciting chapter covers all of the hot topics regarding business continuity and disaster recovery. I'll provide details on building highly available server clusters in virtual machines as well as multiple suggestions on how to design a backup strategy using VMware Consolidated Backup and other backup tools. In addition, this chapter discusses the use of VMware High Availability (HA) and the highly anticipated VMware Fault Tolerance (FT) as ways of providing failover for virtual machines running in a VMware vSphere environment.

Chapter 12: Monitoring VMware vSphere Performance   In Chapter 12 I take a look at some of the native tools in VMware vSphere that allow virtual infrastructure administrators the ability to track and troubleshoot performance issues. The chapter focuses on monitoring CPU, memory, disk, and network adapter performance across ESX/ESXi hosts, resource pools, and clusters in vCenter Server 4.0.

Chapter 13: Securing VMware vSphere   Security is an important part of any implementation, and in this chapter I cover different security management aspects, including managing direct ESX/ESXi host access and integrating VMware ESX with Active Directory. I'll also touch upon VMware vShield Zones, a new security product from VMware, as well as discuss some techniques for incorporating security through the VMware vSphere environment.

Chapter 14: Automating VMware vSphere   Many tasks VMware vSphere administrators face are repetitive tasks, and here automation can help. In Chapter 14 I discuss several different ways to bring automation to your VMware vSphere environment, including vCenter Orchestrator, PowerCLI, and ESX shell scripts.

Appendix A: The Bottom Line   This appendix offers solutions to the "Master It" problems at the end of each chapter.

Appendix B: Frequently Used Commands   To help build your proficiency with command-line tasks, this appendix focuses on navigating through the Service Console command line and performing management, configuration, and troubleshooting tasks.

Appendix C: VMware vSphere Best Practices   This appendix serves as an overview of the design, deployment, management, and monitoring concepts discussed throughout the book. It is designed as a quick reference for any of the phases of a virtual infrastructure deployment.

The Mastering Series

The Mastering series from Sybex provides outstanding instruction for readers with intermediate and advanced skills in the form of top-notch training and development for those already working in their field and provides clear, serious education for those aspiring to become pros. Every Mastering book includes the following:

- ◆ Real-World Scenarios, ranging from case studies to interviews, that show how the tool, technique, or knowledge presented is applied in actual practice

- ◆ Skill-based instruction, with chapters organized around real tasks rather than abstract concepts or subjects

- ◆ Self-review test questions, so you can be certain you're equipped to do the job right

The Hardware Behind the Book

Because of the specificity of the hardware for installing VMware vSphere 4, it might be difficult to build an environment in which you can learn by implementing the exercises and practices detailed in this book. It is possible to build a practice lab to follow along with the book; however, the lab will require very specific hardware and might be quite costly. Be sure to read Chapters 2 and 3 before attempting to construct any type of environment for development purposes.

For the purpose of writing this book, I used the following hardware components:

- ◆ Four Hewlett-Packard (HP) DL385 G2 servers

- ◆ One HP ML350 G4 server

- ◆ Four Dell PowerEdge 1950 servers

- ◆ Two Dell PowerEdge R805 servers

- ◆ Two Dell PowerEdge 2950 servers

◆ Several models of Fibre Channel host bus adapters (HBAs), including QLogic 23xx dual-port 4Gbps HBAs and Emulex LP10000 HBAs

◆ A number of different storage arrays, including the following:

   ◆ NetApp FAS940 unified storage array

   ◆ Atrato Velocity 1000 Fibre Channel array

   ◆ EMC CX4-240 CLARiiON Fibre Channel array

◆ For additional NFS and iSCSI testing, the EMC Celerra Virtual Storage Appliance (VSA) running DART 5.6.43.18

◆ Several models of Fibre Channel switches, including Cisco MDS 9124, Brocade 200e, and Brocade Silkworm 3800 Fibre Channel switches

A special thanks goes to Hewlett-Packard, Dell, NetApp, EMC, and Cisco for their help in supplying the equipment used during the writing of this book.

Who Should Buy This Book

This book is for IT professionals looking to strengthen their knowledge of constructing and managing a virtual infrastructure on VMware vSphere 4. Although the book can be helpful for those new to IT, there is a strong set of assumptions made about the target reader:

◆ A basic understanding of networking architecture

◆ Experience working in a Microsoft Windows environment

◆ Experience managing DNS and DHCP

◆ A basic understanding of how virtualization differs from traditional physical infrastructures

◆ A basic understanding of hardware and software components in standard x86 and x64 computing

How to Contact the Author

I welcome feedback from you about this book or about books you'd like to see from me in the future. You can reach me by writing to scott.lowe@scottlowe.org or by visiting my blog at http://blog.scottlowe.org.

Chapter 1

Introducing VMware vSphere 4

VMware vSphere 4 builds upon previous generations of VMware virtualization products, becoming an even more robust, scalable, and reliable server virtualization product. With dynamic resource controls, high availability, unprecedented fault tolerance features, distributed resource management, and backup tools included as part of the suite, IT administrators have all the tools they need to run an enterprise environment ranging from a few servers up to thousands of servers.

In this chapter, you will learn to:

◆ Identify the role of each product in the vSphere product suite

◆ Recognize the interaction and dependencies between the products in the vSphere suite

◆ Understand how vSphere differs from other virtualization products

Exploring VMware vSphere 4

The VMware vSphere product suite includes a number of products and features that together provide a full array of enterprise virtualization functionality. These products and features in the vSphere product suite include the following:

◆ VMware ESX and ESXi

◆ VMware Virtual Symmetric Multi-Processing

◆ VMware vCenter Server

◆ VMware vCenter Update Manager

◆ VMware vSphere Client

◆ VMware VMotion and Storage VMotion

◆ VMware Distributed Resource Scheduler

◆ VMware High Availability

◆ VMware Fault Tolerance

◆ VMware Consolidated Backup

◆ VMware vShield Zones

◆ VMware vCenter Orchestrator

Rather than waiting to introduce these products and features in their own chapters, I'll introduce each product or feature in the following sections. This will allow me to explain how each product or feature affects the design, installation, and configuration of your virtual infrastructure. After I cover the features and products in the vSphere suite, you'll have a better grasp of how each of them fits into the design and the big picture of virtualization.

Certain products outside the vSphere product suite extend the vSphere product line with new functionality. Examples of these additional products include VMware vCenter Lifecycle Manager, VMware vCenter Lab Manager, VMware vCenter Stage Manager, and VMware vCenter Site Recovery Manager. Because of the size and scope of these products and because they are developed and released on a schedule separate from VMware vSphere, they will not be covered in this book.

VMware ESX and ESXi

The core of the vSphere product suite is the hypervisor, which is the virtualization layer that serves as the foundation for the rest of the product line. In vSphere, the hypervisor comes in two different forms: VMware ESX and VMware ESXi. Both of these products share the same core virtualization engine, both can support the same set of virtualization features, and both are considered bare-metal installations. VMware ESX and ESXi differ in how they are packaged.

TYPE 1 AND TYPE 2 HYPERVISORS

Hypervisors are generally grouped into two classes: type 1 hypervisors and type 2 hypervisors. Type 1 hypervisors run directly on the system hardware and thus are often referred to as *bare-metal* hypervisors. Type 2 hypervisors require a host operating system, and the host operating system provides I/O device support and memory management. VMware ESX and ESXi are both type 1 bare-metal hypervisors. Other type 1 bare-metal hypervisors include Microsoft Hyper-V and products based on the open source Xen hypervisor like Citrix XenServer and Oracle VM.

VMware ESX consists of two components that interact with each other to provide a dynamic and robust virtualization environment: the Service Console and the VMkernel.

The Service Console, for all intents and purposes, is the operating system used to interact with VMware ESX and the virtual machines that run on the server. The Linux-derived Service Console includes services found in traditional operating systems, such as a firewall, Simple Network Management Protocol (SNMP) agents, and a web server. At the same time, the Service Console lacks many of the features and benefits that traditional operating systems offer. This is not a deficiency, though. In this particular case, the Service Console has been intentionally stripped down to include only those services necessary to support virtualization, making the Service Console a lean, mean virtualization machine.

The second installed component is the VMkernel. While the Service Console gives you access to the VMkernel, the VMkernel is the real foundation of the virtualization process. The VMkernel manages the virtual machines' access to the underlying physical hardware by providing CPU scheduling, memory management, and virtual switch data processing. Figure 1.1 shows the structure of VMware ESX.

VMware ESXi, on the other hand, is the next generation of the VMware virtualization foundation. Unlike VMware ESX, ESXi installs and runs without the Service Console. This gives ESXi an ultralight footprint of only 32MB. ESXi shares the same underlying VMkernel as VMware ESX and supports the same set of virtualization features that will be described shortly, but it does not rely upon the Service Console.

FIGURE 1.1
Installing VMware ESX installs two interoperable components: the Linux-derived Service Console and the virtual machine-managing VMkernel.

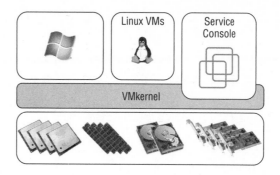

Compared to previous versions of ESX/ESXi, VMware has expanded the limits of what the hypervisor is capable of supporting. Table 1.1 shows the configuration maximums for this version of ESX/ESXi as compared to the previous release.

TABLE 1.1:   VMware ESX/ESXi 4.0 Maximums

COMPONENT	VMWARE ESX 4 MAXIMUM	VMWARE ESX 3.5 MAXIMUM
Number of virtual CPUs per host	256	128
Number of cores per host	64	32
Number of logical CPUs (hyperthreading enabled)	64	32
Number of virtual CPUs per core	20	8 (increased to 20 in Update 3)
Amount of RAM per host	1TB	128GB (increased to 256GB in Update 3)

Where appropriate, each chapter will include additional values for VMware ESX/ESXi 4 maximums for NICs, storage, virtual machines, and so forth.

Because VMware ESX and ESXi form the foundation of the vSphere product suite, I'll touch on various aspects of ESX/ESXi throughout the book. I'll go into more detail about the installation of both VMware ESX and ESXi in Chapter 2, "Planning and Installing VMware ESX and VMware ESXi." In Chapter 5, "Creating and Managing Virtual Networks," I'll more closely examine the networking capabilities of ESX/ESXi. Chapter 6, "Creating and Managing Storage Devices," describes the selection, configuration, and management of the storage technologies supported by ESX/ESXi, including the configuration of VMware vStorage VMFS datastores.

VMware Virtual Symmetric Multi-Processing

The VMware Virtual Symmetric Multi-Processing (vSMP, or Virtual SMP) product allows virtual infrastructure administrators to construct virtual machines with multiple virtual processors. VMware Virtual SMP is *not* the licensing product that allows ESX/ESXi to be installed on servers with multiple processors; it is the technology that allows the use of multiple processors *inside* a virtual machine. Figure 1.2 identifies the differences between multiple processors in the ESX/ESXi host system and multiple virtual processors.

FIGURE 1.2
VMware Virtual SMP allows virtual machines to be created with two or four processors.

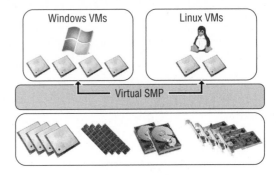

With VMware Virtual SMP, applications that require and can actually use multiple CPUs can be run in virtual machines configured with multiple virtual CPUs. This allows organizations to virtualize even more applications without negatively impacting performance or being unable to meet service-level agreements (SLAs).

In Chapter 7, "Creating and Managing Virtual Machines," I'll discuss how to build virtual machines with multiple virtual processors.

VMware vCenter Server

Stop for a moment to think about your current network. Does it include Active Directory? There is a good chance it does. Now imagine your network without Active Directory, without the ease of a centralized management database, without the single sign-on capabilities, and without the simplicity of groups. That is what managing VMware ESX/ESXi hosts would be like without using VMware vCenter Server. Now calm yourself down, take a deep breath, and know that vCenter Server, like Active Directory, is meant to provide a centralized management utility for all ESX/ESXi hosts and their respective virtual machines. vCenter Server is a Windows-based, database-driven application that allows IT administrators to deploy, manage, monitor, automate, and secure a virtual infrastructure in an almost effortless fashion. The back-end database (Microsoft SQL Server or Oracle) that vCenter Server uses stores all the data about the hosts and virtual machines.

VCENTER SERVER FOR LINUX

At the time this book was written, VMware had just released a technology preview of a Linux version of vCenter Server. A Linux version of vCenter Server would remove the requirement to have a Windows-based server present in the environment in order to support VMware vSphere, something that Linux- and UNIX-heavy organizations have long desired.

In addition to its configuration and management capabilities—which include features such as virtual machine templates, virtual machine customization, rapid provisioning and deployment of virtual machines, role-based access controls, and fine-grained resource allocation controls—vCenter Server provides the tools for the more advanced features of VMware VMotion, VMware Distributed Resource Scheduler, VMware High Availability, and VMware Fault Tolerance.

In addition to VMware VMotion, VMware Distributed Resource Scheduler, VMware High Availability, and VMware Fault Tolerance, using vCenter Server to manage ESX/ESXi hosts also enables a number of other features:

◆ Enhanced VMotion Compatibility (EVC), which leverages hardware functionality from Intel and AMD to enable greater CPU compatibility between servers grouped into VMware DRS clusters

◆ Host profiles, which allow administrators to bring greater consistency to host configurations across larger environments and to identify missing or incorrect configurations

◆ vNetwork Distributed Switches, which provide the foundation for cluster-wide networking settings and third-party virtual switches

vCenter Server plays a central role in any sizable VMware vSphere implementation. Because of vCenter Server's central role, I'll touch on aspects of vCenter Server's functionality throughout the book. For example, in Chapter 3, "Installing and Configuring vCenter Server," I discuss planning and installing vCenter Server, as well as look at ways to ensure its availability. Chapters 5 through 12 all cover various aspects of vCenter Server's role in managing your VMware vSphere environment. As an integral part of your VMware vSphere installation, it's quite natural that I discuss vCenter Server in such detail.

vCenter Server is available in three editions:

◆ vCenter Server Essentials is integrated into the vSphere Essentials edition for small office deployment.

◆ vCenter Server Standard provides all the functionality of vCenter Server, including provisioning, management, monitoring, and automation.

◆ vCenter Server Foundation is like vCenter Server Standard but is limited to managing three ESX/ESXi hosts.

You can find more information on licensing and product editions for VMware vSphere in the section "Licensing VMware vSphere."

VMware vCenter Update Manager

vCenter Update Manager is a plug-in for vCenter Server that helps users keep their ESX/ESXi hosts and select virtual machines patched with the latest updates. vCenter Update Manager provides the following functionality:

◆ Scans to identify systems that are not compliant with the latest updates

◆ User-defined rules for identifying out-of-date systems

◆ Automated installation of patches for ESX/ESXi hosts

◆ Full integration with other vSphere features like Distributed Resource Scheduler

◆ Support for patching Windows and Linux operating systems

◆ Support for patching select Windows applications inside virtual machines

Chapter 4, "Installing and Configuring vCenter Update Manager," features more extensive coverage of vCenter Update Manager.

VMware vSphere Client

The VMware vSphere Client is a Windows-based application that allows you to manage ESX/ESXi hosts, either directly or through a vCenter Server. You can install the vSphere Client by browsing to the URL of an ESX/ESXi host or vCenter Server and selecting the appropriate installation link. The vSphere Client is a graphical user interface (GUI) used for all the day-to-day management tasks and for the advanced configuration of a virtual infrastructure. Using the client to connect directly to an ESX/ESXi host requires that you use a user account residing on that host, while using the client to connect to a vCenter Server requires that you use a Windows account. Figure 1.3 shows the account authentication for each connection type.

FIGURE 1.3
The vSphere Client manages an individual ESX/ESXi host by authenticating with an account local to that host; however, it manages an entire enterprise by authenticating to a vCenter Server using a Windows account.

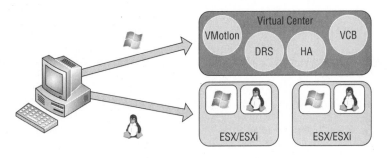

Almost all the management tasks available when you're connected directly to an ESX/ESXi host are available when you're connected to a vCenter Server, but the opposite is not true. The management capabilities available through a vCenter Server are more significant and outnumber the capabilities of connecting directly to an ESX/ESXi host.

VMware VMotion and Storage VMotion

If you have read anything about VMware, you have most likely read about the extremely unique and innovative feature called VMotion. VMotion, also known as *live migration*, is a feature of ESX/ESXi and vCenter Server that allows a running virtual machine to be moved from one physical host to another physical host without having to power off the virtual machine. This migration between two physical hosts occurs with no downtime and with no loss of network connectivity to the virtual machine.

VMotion satisfies an organization's need for maintaining SLAs that guarantee server availability. Administrators can easily initiate VMotion to remove all virtual machines from an ESX/ESXi host that is to undergo scheduled maintenance. After the maintenance is complete and the server is brought back online, VMotion can again be utilized to return the virtual machines to the original server.

Even in normal day-to-day operations, VMotion can be used when multiple virtual machines on the same host are in contention for the same resource (which ultimately is causing poor performance across all the virtual machines). VMotion can solve the problem by allowing an administrator to migrate any of the running virtual machines that are facing contention to another ESX/ESXi host with greater availability for the resource in demand. For example, when two virtual machines are in contention with each other for CPU power, an administrator can eliminate the contention by performing a VMotion of one of the virtual machines to an ESX/ESXi host that has more available CPU. More details on the VMware VMotion feature and its requirements are provided in Chapter 10, "Managing Resource Allocation."

Storage VMotion builds on the idea and principle of VMotion, further reducing planned downtime with the ability to move a virtual machine's storage while the virtual machine is still running. Deploying VMware vSphere in your environment generally means that lots of shared storage—Fibre Channel or iSCSI SAN or NFS—is needed. What happens when you need to migrate from an older storage array to a newer storage array? What kind of downtime would be required?

Storage VMotion directly addresses this concern. Storage VMotion moves the storage for a running virtual machine between datastores. Much like VMotion, Storage VMotion works without downtime to the virtual machine. This feature ensures that outgrowing datastores or moving to a new SAN does not force an outage for the affected virtual machines and provides administrators with yet another tool to increase their flexibility in responding to changing business needs.

VMware Distributed Resource Scheduler

Now that I've piqued your interest with the introduction of VMotion, let me introduce VMware Distributed Resource Scheduler (DRS). If you think that VMotion sounds exciting, your anticipation will only grow after learning about DRS. DRS, simply put, is a feature that aims to provide automatic distribution of resource utilization across multiple ESX/ESXi hosts that are configured in a cluster. The use of the term *cluster* often draws IT professionals into thoughts of Microsoft Windows Server clusters. However, ESX/ESXi clusters are not the same. The underlying concept of aggregating physical hardware to serve a common goal is the same, but the technology, configuration, and feature sets are different between ESX/ESXi clusters and Windows Server clusters.

AGGREGATE CAPACITY AND SINGLE HOST CAPACITY

Although I say that a DRS cluster is an implicit aggregation of CPU and memory capacity, it's important to keep in mind that a virtual machine is limited to using the CPU and RAM of a single physical host at any given time. If you have two ESX/ESXi servers with 32GB of RAM each in a DRS cluster, the cluster will correctly report 64GB of aggregate RAM available, but any given virtual machine will not be able to use more than approximately 32GB of RAM at a time.

An ESX/ESXi cluster is an implicit aggregation of the CPU power and memory of all hosts involved in the cluster. After two or more hosts have been assigned to a cluster, they work in unison to provide CPU and memory to the virtual machines assigned to the cluster. The goal of DRS is twofold:

- ◆ At startup, DRS attempts to place each virtual machine on the host that is best suited to run that virtual machine at that time.

- ◆ While a virtual machine is running, DRS seeks to provide that virtual machine with the required hardware resources while minimizing the amount of contention for those resources in an effort to maintain good performance levels.

The first part of DRS is often referred to as *intelligent placement*. DRS can automate the placement of each virtual machine as it is powered on within a cluster, placing it on the host in the cluster that it deems to be best suited to run that virtual machine at that moment.

DRS isn't limited to operating only at virtual machine startup, though. DRS also manages the virtual machine's location while it is running. For example, let's say three servers have been configured in an ESX/ESXi cluster with DRS enabled. When one of those servers begins to experience a high contention for CPU utilization, DRS uses an internal algorithm to determine which virtual machine(s) will experience the greatest performance boost by being moved to another server with less CPU contention.

DRS performs these on-the-fly adjustments without any downtime or loss of network connectivity to the virtual machines. Does that sound familiar? It should, because the behind-the-scenes technology used by DRS is VMware VMotion, which I described previously. In Chapter 10, "Managing Resource Allocation," I'll dive deeper into the configuration and management of DRS on an ESX/ESXi cluster.

FEWER BIGGER SERVERS OR MORE SMALLER SERVERS?

Remember from Table 1.1 that VMware ESX/ESXi supports servers with up to 64 CPU cores and up to 1TB of RAM. With VMware DRS, though, you can combine multiple smaller servers together for the purpose of managing aggregate capacity. This means that bigger, more powerful servers may not be better servers for virtualization projects. These larger servers are generally significantly more expensive than smaller servers, and using a greater number of smaller servers may provide greater flexibility than a smaller number of larger servers. The key thing to remember here is that a bigger server isn't necessarily a better server!

VMware High Availability

In many cases, high availability (HA)—or the lack of high availability—is the key argument used against virtualization. The most common form of this argument more or less sounds like this: "Before virtualization, the failure of a physical server affected only one application or workload. After virtualization, the failure of a physical server will affect many more applications or workloads running on that server at the same time. We can't put all our eggs in one basket!"

VMware addresses this concern with another feature present in ESX/ESXi clusters called VMware High Availability (HA). Once again, by nature of the naming conventions (clusters, high availability), many traditional Windows administrators will have preconceived notions about this feature. Those notions, however, are premature in that VMware HA does not function like a high-availability configuration in Windows. The VMware HA feature provides an automated process for restarting virtual machines that were running on an ESX/ESXi host at a time of complete server failure. Figure 1.4 depicts the virtual machine migration that occurs when an ESX/ESXi host that is part of an HA-enabled cluster experiences failure.

FIGURE 1.4
The VMware HA feature will power on any virtual machines that were previously running on an ESX server that has experienced server failure.

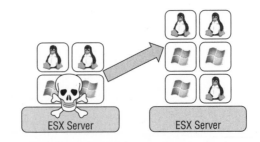

The VMware HA feature, unlike DRS, does not use the VMotion technology as a means of migrating servers to another host. In a VMware HA failover situation, there is no anticipation of failure; it is not a planned outage, and therefore there is no time to perform a VMotion. VMware HA is intended to address unplanned downtime because of the failure of a physical ESX/ESXi host.

By default VMware HA does not provide failover in the event of a guest operating system failure, although you can configure VMware HA to monitor virtual machines and restart them automatically if they fail to respond to an internal heartbeat. For users who need even higher levels of availability, VMware Fault Tolerance (FT), which is described in the next section, can satisfy that need.

Chapter 11, "Ensuring High Availability and Business Continuity," explores the configuration and working details of VMware High Availability and VMware Fault Tolerance.

VMware Fault Tolerance

For users who require even greater levels of high availability than VMware HA can provide, VMware vSphere introduces a new feature known as VMware Fault Tolerance (FT).

VMware HA protects against unplanned physical server failure by providing a way to automatically restart virtual machines upon physical host failure. This need to restart a virtual machine in the event of a physical host failure means that some downtime—generally less than three minutes—is incurred. VMware FT goes even further and eliminates any downtime in the event of a physical host failure. Using vLockstep technology, VMware FT maintains a mirrored secondary VM on a separate physical host that is kept in lockstep with the primary VM. Everything that occurs on the primary (protected) VM also occurs simultaneously on the secondary (mirrored) VM, so that if the physical host on which the primary VM is running fails, the secondary VM can immediately step in and take over without any loss of connectivity. VMware FT will also automatically re-create the secondary (mirrored) VM on another host if the physical host on which the secondary VM is running fails, as illustrated in Figure 1.5. This ensures protection for the primary VM at all times.

FIGURE 1.5
VMware FT provides protection against host failures with no downtime to the virtual machines.

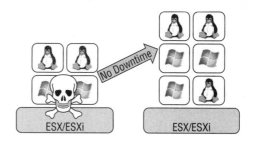

In the event of multiple host failures—say, the hosts running both the primary and secondary VMs failed—VMware HA will reboot the primary VM on another available server, and VMware FT will automatically create a new secondary VM. Again, this ensures protection for the primary VM at all times.

VMware FT can work in conjunction with VMotion, but it cannot work with DRS, so DRS must be manually disabled on VMs that are protected with VMware FT.

Chapter 10 provides more information on how to disable DRS for specific VMs. Chapter 11 provides more information on VMware FT.

VMware Consolidated Backup

One of the most critical aspects to any network, not just a virtualized infrastructure, is a solid backup strategy as defined by a company's disaster recovery and business continuity plan. VMware Consolidated Backup (VCB) is a set of tools and interfaces that provide both LAN-free and LAN-based backup functionality to third-party backup solutions. VCB offloads the backup processing to a dedicated physical or virtual server and provides ways of integrating third-party backup solutions like Backup Exec, TSM, NetBackup, or others. VCB takes advantage of the snapshot functionality in ESX/ESXi to mount the snapshots into the file system of the dedicated VCB server. After the respective virtual machine files are mounted, entire virtual machines or individual files can be backed up using third-party backup tools. VCB scripts integrate with several major third-party backup solutions to provide a means of automating the backup process. Figure 1.6 details a VCB implementation.

FIGURE 1.6
VCB is a LAN-free online backup solution that uses a Fibre Channel or iSCSI connection to expedite and simplify the backup process.

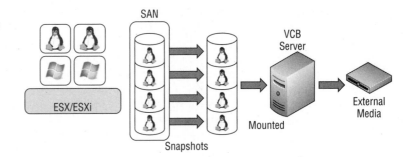

In Chapter 11, you'll learn how to use VCB to provide a solid backup and restore process for your virtualized infrastructure.

VMware vShield Zones

VMware vSphere offers some compelling virtual networking functionality, and vShield Zones builds upon vSphere's virtual networking functionality to add virtual firewall functionality. vShield Zones allows vSphere administrators to see and manage the network traffic flows occurring on the virtual network switches. You can apply network security policies across entire groups of machines, ensuring that these policies are maintained properly even though virtual machines may move from host to host using VMware VMotion and VMware DRS.

You can find more information on VMware vShield Zones in Chapter 13, "Securing VMware vSphere."

VMware vCenter Orchestrator

VMware vCenter Orchestrator is a workflow automation engine that is automatically installed with every instance of vCenter Server. Using vCenter Orchestrator, vSphere administrators can build automated workflows to automate a wide variety of tasks available within vCenter Server. The automated workflows you build using vCenter Orchestrator range from simple to complex. To get an idea of the kind of power available with vCenter Orchestrator, it might help to know that VMware vCenter Lifecycle Manager, a separate product in the vCenter virtualization management family of products, is completely built on top of vCenter Orchestrator.

Chapter 14, "Automating VMware vSphere," provides more information on vCenter Orchestrator and other automation technologies and tools.

 **Real World Scenario**

VMWARE VSPHERE COMPARED TO HYPER-V AND XENSERVER

It's not really possible to compare some virtualization solutions to other virtualization solutions because they are fundamentally different in approach and purpose. Such is the case with VMware ESX/ESXi and some of the other virtualization solutions on the market.

To make accurate comparisons between vSphere and other virtualization solutions, one must include only type 1 ("bare-metal") virtualization solutions. This would include ESX/ESXi, of course, and Microsoft Hyper-V and Citrix XenServer. It would not include products such as VMware Server or Microsoft Virtual Server, both of which are type 2 ("hosted") virtualization products. Even within the type 1 hypervisors, there are architectural differences that make direct comparisons difficult.

For example, both Microsoft Hyper-V and Citrix XenServer route all the virtual machine I/O through the "parent partition" or "dom0." This typically provides greater hardware compatibility with a wider range of products. In the case of Hyper-V, for example, as soon as Windows Server 2008—the general-purpose operating system running in the parent partition—supports a particular type of hardware, then Hyper-V supports it also. Hyper-V "piggybacks" on Windows' hardware drivers and the I/O stack. The same can be said for XenServer, although its "dom0" runs Linux and not Windows.

VMware ESX/ESXi, on the other hand, handles I/O within the hypervisor itself. This typically provides greater throughput and lower overhead at the expense of slightly more limited hardware compatibility. In order to add more hardware support or updated drivers, the hypervisor must be updated because the I/O stack and device drivers are in the hypervisor.

This architectural difference is fundamental. Nowhere is this architectural difference more greatly demonstrated than in ESXi, which has a very small footprint yet provides a full-featured virtualization solution. Both Citrix XenServer and Microsoft Hyper-V require a full installation of a general-purpose operating system (Windows Server 2008 for Hyper-V, Linux for XenServer) in the parent partition/dom0 in order to operate.

In the end, each of the virtualization products has its own set of advantages and disadvantages, and large organizations may end up using multiple products. For example, VMware vSphere might be best suited in the large corporate datacenter, while Microsoft Hyper-V or Citrix XenServer might be acceptable for test, development, or branch-office deployment. Organizations that don't require VMware vSphere's advanced features like VMware DRS, VMware FT, or Storage VMotion may also find that Microsoft Hyper-V or Citrix XenServer is a better fit for their needs.

As you can see, VMware vSphere offers some pretty powerful features that will change the way you view the resources in your datacenter. Some of these features, though, might not be applicable to all organizations, which is why VMware has crafted a flexible licensing scheme for organizations of all sizes.

Licensing VMware vSphere

With the introduction of VMware vSphere, VMware introduces a number of new licensing tiers and bundles that are intended to provide a good fit for every market segment. In this section, I'll explain the different licensing tiers—called *editions*—and how the various features that I've discussed so far fit into these editions.

Six editions of VMware vSphere are available:

◆ VMware vSphere Essentials

◆ VMware vSphere Essentials Plus

◆ VMware vSphere Standard

◆ VMware vSphere Advanced

◆ VMware vSphere Enterprise

◆ VMware vSphere Enterprise Plus

Each of these six editions features a different combination of features and products included. Table 1.2 lists the different editions and which features and products are included in each edition.

The vSphere Essentials and vSphere Essentials Plus editions are not licensed per CPU; these two editions are licensed for up to three physical servers. The cost for VMware vSphere Essentials is $995 and includes one year of subscription; support is optional and available on a per-incident basis. vSphere Essentials Plus is $2,995.

On all editions of VMware vSphere except Essentials, Support and Subscription (SnS) is sold separately. At least one year of SnS is required for each license. Subscription—but not support—is bundled with vSphere Essentials.

Also, it's important to note that all editions of VMware vSphere include support for thin provisioning, vCenter Update Manager, the VMsafe APIs, and the vStorage APIs. I did not include them in Table 1.2 because they are supported in all editions. I've specified only the list price for all editions; discounts may be available through a value-added reseller or VMware partner.

Looking carefully at Table 1.2, you may also note that VMware has moved away from licensing per pair of CPUs to licensing per CPU. With the advent of multicore processors, it's far more common to see physical servers with only a single physical CPU. To reflect this trend, VMware is licensing vSphere on a per-CPU basis.

In addition to all the editions listed in Table 1.2, VMware also offers a free edition of ESXi, named ESXi Free. ESXi Free includes the ESXi hypervisor and support for thin provisioning, but it cannot be managed by vCenter Server and does not support any of the other advanced features listed in Table 1.2. Customers can, though, go from ESXi Free to vSphere Standard, Advanced, or Enterprise simply by applying the appropriate license to an ESXi Free installation. This provides a great upgrade path for smaller organizations as they grow.

Now that you have an idea of how VMware licenses vSphere, I'd like to briefly review why an organization might choose to use vSphere and what benefits that organization could see as a result.

TABLE 1.2:   Overview of VMware vSphere Product Editions

	ESSENTIALS	ESSENTIALS PLUS	STANDARD	ADVANCED	ENTERPRISE	ENTERPRISE PLUS
vCenter Server compatibility	vCenter Server for Essentials	vCenter Server for Essentials	vCenter Server Foundation and Standard	vCenter Server Foundation and Standard	vCenter Server Foundation and Standard	vCenter Server Foundation and Standard
Cores/CPU	6	6	6	12	6	12
vSMP support	4-way	4-way	4-way	4-way	4-way	8-way
RAM/Server	256GB	256GB	256GB	256GB	256GB	No license limit
VMware HA	✓	✓	✓	✓	✓	✓
vCenter Data Recovery		✓		✓	✓	✓
VM Hot Add				✓	✓	✓
VMware FT				✓	✓	✓
VMotion				✓	✓	✓
Storage VMotion					✓	✓
VMware DRS					✓	✓
vNetwork Distributed Switch						✓
Host profiles						✓
Third-party multipathing						✓
List price per CPU			$795	$2245	$2875	$3495

Source: "VMware vSphere Pricing, Packaging and Licensing Overview" white paper published by VMware, available at www.vmware.com

Why Choose vSphere?

Much has been said and written about the total cost of ownership (TCO) and return on investment (ROI) for virtualization projects involving VMware virtualization solutions. Rather than rehashing that material here, I'll instead focus, very briefly, on why an organization should choose VMware vSphere as their virtualization platform.

ONLINE TCO CALCULATOR

VMware offers a web-based TCO calculator that helps you calculate the total cost of ownership and return on investment for a virtualization project using VMware virtualization solutions. This calculator is available online at www.vmware.com/go/calculator.

You've already read about the various features that VMware vSphere offers. To help understand how these features can benefit your organization, I'll apply them to the fictional XYZ Corporation. I'll walk through several different scenarios and look at how vSphere helps in these scenarios:

Scenario 1 XYZ Corporation's IT team has been asked by senior management to rapidly provision six new servers to support a new business initiative. In the past, this meant ordering hardware, waiting on the hardware to arrive, racking and cabling the equipment once it arrived, installing the operating system and patching it with the latest updates, and then installing the application. The timeframe for all these steps ranged anywhere from a few days to a few months and was typically a couple of weeks. Now, with VMware vSphere in place, the IT team can use vCenter Server's templates functionality to build a virtual machine, install the operating system, and apply the latest updates, and then rapidly clone—or copy—this virtual machine to create additional virtual machines. Now their provisioning time is down to hours, likely even minutes. Chapter 7 will discuss this functionality in more detail.

Scenario 2 Empowered by the IT team's ability to quickly respond to the needs of this new business initiative, XYZ Corporation is moving ahead with deploying updated versions of a line-of-business application. However, the business leaders are a bit concerned about upgrading the current version. Using the snapshot functionality present in ESX/ESXi and vCenter Server, the IT team can take a "point-in-time picture" of the virtual machine so that if something goes wrong during the upgrade, it's a simple rollback to the snapshot for recovery. Chapter 7 discusses snapshots.

Scenario 3 XYZ Corporation is really impressed with the IT team and vSphere's functionality and is now interested in expanding their use of virtualization. In order to do so, however, a hardware upgrade is needed on the servers currently running ESX/ESXi. The business is worried about the downtime that will be necessary to perform the hardware upgrades. The IT team uses VMotion to move virtual machines off one host at a time, upgrading each host in turn without incurring any downtime to the company's end users. Chapter 10 discusses VMotion in more depth.

Scenario 4 After the great success it's had virtualizing its infrastructure with vSphere, XYZ Corporation now finds itself in need of a new, larger shared storage array. vSphere's support for Fibre Channel, iSCSI, and NFS gives XYZ room to choose the most cost-effective storage solution available, and the IT team uses Storage VMotion to migrate the virtual machines without any downtime. Chapter 6 discusses Storage VMotion.

These scenarios begin to provide some idea of the benefits that organizations see when virtualizing with an enterprise-class virtualization solution like VMware vSphere.

The Bottom Line

Identify the role of each product in the vSphere product suite. The VMware vSphere product suite contains ESX and ESXi and vCenter Server. ESX and ESXi provide the base virtualization functionality and enable features like Virtual SMP. vCenter Server provides management for ESX/ESXi and enables functionality like VMotion, Storage VMotion, VMware Distributed Resource Scheduler (DRS), VMware High Availability (HA), and VMware Fault Tolerance (FT). VMware Consolidated Backup is a backup framework that allows for the integration of third-party backup solutions into a vSphere implementation.

Master It Which products are licensed features within the VMware vSphere suite?

Recognize the interaction and dependencies between the products in the vSphere suite. VMware ESX and ESXi form the foundation of the vSphere product suite, but some features require the presence of vCenter Server. Features like VMotion, Storage VMotion, VMware DRS, VMware HA, and VMware FT require both ESX/ESXi as well as vCenter Server.

Master It Name three features that are supported only when using vCenter Server along with ESX/ESXi.

Understand how vSphere differs from other virtualization products. VMware vSphere's hypervisor, ESX/ESXi, uses a type 1 bare-metal hypervisor that handles I/O directly within the hypervisor. This means that a host operating system, like Windows or Linux, is not required in order for ESX/ESXi to function. Although other virtualization solutions are listed as "type 1 bare-metal hypervisors," most other type 1 hypervisors on the market today require the presence of a "parent partition" or "dom0," through which all virtual machine I/O must travel.

Master It One of the administrators on your team asked whether he should install Windows Server on the new servers you purchased for ESX. What should you tell him, and why?

Chapter 2

Planning and Installing VMware ESX and VMware ESXi

Now that you've taken a closer look at VMware vSphere 4 and its suite of applications in Chapter 1, it's easy to see that VMware ESX 4 and VMware ESXi 4 are the foundation of vSphere. The deployment, installation, and configuration of VMware ESX and VMware ESXi require adequate planning for a successful, VMware-supported implementation.

In this chapter, you will learn to:

◆ Understand the differences among VMware ESX, VMware ESXi Installable, and VMware ESXi Embedded

◆ Understand VMware ESX/ESXi compatibility requirements

◆ Plan a VMware ESX/ESXi deployment

◆ Install VMware ESX and VMware ESXi Installable

◆ Perform post-installation configuration of VMware ESX and VMware ESXi

◆ Install the vSphere Client

Planning a VMware vSphere 4 Deployment

Deploying VMware vSphere 4 is more than just virtualizing servers. A vSphere deployment affects storage and networking in equally significant ways as the physical servers themselves. As a result of this broad impact on numerous facets of your organization's information technology (IT), the process of planning the vSphere deployment becomes even more important. Without the appropriate planning, your vSphere implementation runs the risk of configuration problems, incompatibilities, and diminished financial impact.

Your planning process for a vSphere deployment involves answering a number of questions:

◆ Will I use VMware ESX or VMware ESXi?

◆ What types of servers will I use for the underlying physical hardware?

◆ What kinds of storage will I use, and how will I connect that storage to my servers?

◆ How will the networking be configured?

In some cases, the answers to these questions will in turn determine the answers to other questions. After you have answered these questions, you can then move on to more difficult questions that must also be answered. These questions center on how the vSphere deployment will impact your staff, your business processes, and your operational procedures. I'm not going to try to help you answer those sorts of questions here; instead, let's just focus on the technical issues.

In the next few sections, I'll discuss the four major questions that I outlined previously that are a key part of planning your vSphere deployment.

Selecting VMware ESX or VMware ESXi

One of the first major decisions that you must make when planning to deploy VMware vSphere 4 is whether to use VMware ESX or VMware ESXi. If you choose ESXi, you must also choose between ESXi Installable and ESXi Embedded. To make this decision, though, you must first understand some of the architectural differences between ESX and ESXi.

ESX and ESXi share the same 64-bit, bare-metal hypervisor at their cores (commonly known as *VMkernel*). Both ESX and ESXi can be managed by vCenter Server, and both ESX and ESXi support advanced virtualization functionality such as VMotion, Storage VMotion, VMware Distributed Resource Scheduler (DRS), VMware High Availability (HA), and VMware Fault Tolerance (FT).

VMware ESX incorporates a customized 64-bit management interface, known as the Service Console, which provides an interface for administrators to use to interact with the hypervisor. This built-in service console, based on Linux, provides a place for third-party applications or agents to execute and allows vSphere administrators to run command-line configuration tools and custom scripts.

VMKERNEL'S DUAL PERSONALITY

Remember that the *hypervisor* is the software that runs on the bare metal and provides the virtualization functionality. Although VMkernel is commonly used as the name for VMware's bare-metal hypervisor found in both ESX and ESXi, two distinct components are actually involved. VMkernel manages physical resources, process creation, I/O stacks, and device drivers. The virtual machine monitor (VMM) is responsible for actually executing commands on the CPUs, performing binary translation (BT) or programming VT/SVM hardware, and so on, and is instanced—meaning that a separate VMM exists for each virtual machine. Although these two components are indeed separate and distinct, for the sake of simplicity I'll continue to refer to both of them as *VMkernel* unless there is a clear need to distinguish them.

VMware ESXi omits the Service Console. Instead, ESXi is a hypervisor-only deployment that requires just 32MB of space. By omitting the Service Console, ESXi also eliminates the potential security vulnerabilities that are contained within that customized Linux environment, as well as dramatically shrinks its footprint. This minimized footprint is what enables ESXi to be distributed in two different versions: ESXi Installable, which can be installed onto a server's hard drives; and ESXi Embedded, which is intended to run from a Universal Serial Bus (USB)–based flash device. Aside from their intended deployment model, ESXi Installable and ESXi Embedded are the same; they share the same underlying architecture and code. I'll just refer to both of them as ESXi except where it's necessary to distinguish between ESXi Installable and ESXi Embedded.

Although ESX enjoys much broader support from third-party tools like backup or monitoring tools, VMware has made no secret that the future of its bare-metal hypervisor lies with ESXi. Therefore, when evaluating ESX vs. ESXi for your deployment, be sure to consider ESXi support if you plan to use third-party tools in your deployment.

 **Real World Scenario**

PREVIOUS EXPERIENCE PLAYS A ROLE, TOO

Aside from the technical factors that play a role when choosing to use VMware ESX or VMware ESXi, the nontechnical factors should not be dismissed. The previous experience, expertise, and knowledge that you and your IT staff has are a significant deciding factor.

A customer of mine rolled out a server virtualization using blades. The customer chose VMware ESX as their virtualization platform. Ownership of the virtualization infrastructure fell, as it often does, to the group within IT responsible for managing Windows-based servers. This group enlisted the help of the Linux group within the organization to create unattended installation scripts (more on that later in this chapter) so that the installation of VMware ESX was fast, simple, and easy. As a result of this work, the administrators managing the deployment could deploy a new VMware ESX server in just minutes.

Even so, the Windows administrators who were now responsible for managing the virtualization infrastructure were uncomfortable with the Linux-based Service Console in VMware ESX. The Service Console was an unknown entity. Not too far along into their consolidation effort, the organization switched from VMware ESX to VMware ESXi. The reason? Their administrators felt more comfortable with the way ESXi operated. Because ESXi has no Linux-based Service Console, there was no concern over having to learn new skills or cope with new technologies about which the administrators knew very little. Even though both ESX and ESXi are managed by vCenter Server—a Windows-based application—the Windows team thought ESXi was a better fit for their skill set, previous experience, and expertise.

When you are choosing between ESX and ESXi, be sure to keep not only the technical reasons in mind but also the nontechnical reasons.

Choosing a Server Platform

The second major decision to make when planning to deploy VMware vSphere 4 is choosing a hardware platform. Compared to "traditional" operating systems like Windows or Linux, ESX and ESXi have more stringent hardware restrictions. ESX and ESXi won't necessarily support every storage controller or every network adapter chipset available on the market. VMware ESXi Embedded, in particular, has a very strict list of supported hardware platforms. Although these hardware restrictions do limit the options for deploying a supported virtual infrastructure, they also ensure the hardware has been tested and will work as expected when used with ESX/ESXi. Although not every vendor or white-box configuration can play host to ESX/ESXi, the list of supported hardware platforms continues to grow and change as VMware tests newer models from more vendors.

You can check for hardware compatibility using the searchable Hardware Compatibility List (HCL) available on VMware's website at `www.vmware.com/resources/compatibility/search.php`. A quick search returns dozens of systems from major vendors such as Hewlett-Packard (HP), IBM, Sun Microsystems, and Dell. For example, at the time of this writing, searching the HCL for *HP* returned 129 different server models, including blades and traditional rack-mount servers. Within the major vendors, it is generally not too difficult to find a tested and supported platform upon which to run ESX/ESXi.

> **THE RIGHT SERVER FOR THE JOB**
>
> Selecting the appropriate server is undoubtedly the first step in ensuring a successful vSphere deployment. In addition, it is the only way to ensure VMware will provide the necessary support. Remember the discussion from Chapter 1, though—a bigger server isn't necessarily a better server!

Finding a supported server is only the first step. It's also important to find the right server—the server that strikes the correct balance of capacity and affordability. Do you use larger servers, such as a server that supports up to four physical CPUs and 128GB of RAM? Or would smaller servers, such as a server that supports dual physical CPUs and 64GB of RAM, be a better choice? There is a point of diminishing returns when it comes to adding more physical CPUs and more RAM to a server. Once you pass the point of diminishing returns, the servers get more and more expensive to acquire and support, but the number of virtual machines the servers can host doesn't increase enough to offset the increase in cost. The challenge, therefore, is finding server models that provide enough expansion for growth and then fitting them with the right amount of resources to meet your needs.

Fortunately, a deeper look into the server models available from a specific vendor, such as HP, reveals server models of all types and sizes (see Figure 2.1), including the following:

◆ Half-height C-class blades, such as the BL460c and BL465c

◆ Full-height C-class blades, such as the BL685c

◆ Dual-socket 1U servers, such as the DL360

◆ Dual-socket 2U servers, such as the DL380 and the DL385

◆ Quad-socket 4U servers, such as the DL580 and DL585

FIGURE 2.1
Servers on the compatibility list come in various sizes and models.

Partner Name	Model	CPU Model	CPU Series	Supported Releases
HP	ProLiant BL20p G2	Second-Generation AMD Opteron Processor Model 2220	Dual-core AMD Opteron 2200 series	ESX 3.5 U4, ESX 3.5 U3, ESX 3.5 U2, ESX 3.5 U1, ESX 3.5, ESXi 3.5 Installable U1, ESX 3.0.3, ESX 3.0.2 U1, ESX 3.0.2, ESX 3.0.1
HP	ProLiant BL20p G3	Dual-core Intel Xeon 7040	Dual-core Intel Xeon 7000 series	ESX 3.5 U4, ESX 3.5 U3, ESX 3.5 U2, ESX 3.5 U1, ESX 3.5, ESX 3.0.3, ESX 3.0.2 U1, ESX 3.0.2, ESX 3.0.1, ESX 3.0
HP	ProLiant BL20p G4	Quad-core Intel Xeon 5300 Series	Quad-core Intel Xeon 5300 series	ESX 3.5 U4[1], ESX 3.5 U3[1], ESX 3.5 U2[1], ESX 3.5 U1[1], ESX 3.5[1], ESXi 3.5 Installable U1, ESX 3.0.3[1], ESX 3.0.2 U1[1], ESX 3.0.2[1]
HP	ProLiant BL20p G4	Quad-core Intel Xeon X5355	Quad-core Intel Xeon 5300 series	ESX 3.5 U4[1], ESX 3.5 U3[1], ESX 3.5 U2[1], ESX 3.5 U1[1], ESX 3.5[1], ESXi 3.5 Installable U1, ESX 3.0.3[1], ESX 3.0.2 U1[1], ESX 3.0.2[1], ESX 3.0.1
HP	ProLiant BL20p G4	Dual-core Intel Xeon 5100 Series	Dual-core Intel Xeon 5100 series	ESX 3.5 U4[1], ESX 3.5 U3[1], ESX 3.5 U2[1], ESX 3.5 U1[1], ESX 3.5[1], ESXi 3.5 Installable U1, ESX 3.0.3[1], ESX 3.0.2 U1[1], ESX 3.0.2[1]
HP	ProLiant BL20p G4	Quad-core Intel Xeon 5300 Series	Quad-core Intel Xeon 5300 series	ESX 3.5 U4[1], ESX 3.5 U3[1], ESX 3.5 U2[1], ESX 3.5 U1[1], ESX 3.5[1], ESXi 3.5 Installable U1, ESX 3.0.3[1], ESX 3.0.2 U1[1], ESX 3.0.2[1]
HP	ProLiant BL20p G4	Quad-core Intel Xeon X5355	Quad-core Intel Xeon 5300 series	ESX 3.5 U4[1], ESX 3.5 U3[1], ESX 3.5 U2[1], ESX 3.5 U1[1], ESX 3.5[1], ESX 3.0.3[1], ESX 3.0.2 U1[1], ESX 3.0.2[1]
HP	ProLiant BL20p G4	Quad-core Intel Xeon 5100 Series	Quad-core Intel Xeon 5100 series	ESX 3.5 U4[1], ESX 3.5 U3[1], ESX 3.5 U2[1], ESX 3.5 U1[1], ESX 3.5[1], ESXi 3.5 Installable U1, ESX 3.0.3[1], ESX 3.0.2 U1[1], ESX 3.0.2[1]
HP	ProLiant BL20p G4	Dual-core Intel Xeon 5120	Dual-core Intel Xeon 5100 series	ESX 3.5 U4[1], ESX 3.5 U3[1], ESX 3.5 U2[1], ESX 3.5 U1[1], ESX 3.5[1], ESX 3.0.3[1], ESX 3.0.2 U1[1], ESX 3.0.2[1], ESX 3.0.1, ESX 3.0
HP	ProLiant BL20p G4	Quad-core Intel Xeon 5365	Quad-core Intel Xeon 5300 series	ESX 3.5 U4[1], ESX 3.5 U3[1], ESX 3.5 U2[1], ESX 3.5 U1[1], ESX 3.5[1], ESXi 3.5 Installable U1, ESX 3.0.3[1], ESX 3.0.2 U1[1], ESX 3.0.2[1]
HP	ProLiant BL20p G4	Dual-core Intel Xeon 5080	Dual-core Intel Xeon 5000 series	ESX 3.5 U4, ESX 3.5 U3, ESX 3.5 U2, ESX 3.5 U1, ESX 3.5, ESX 3.0.3, ESX 3.0.2 U1, ESX 3.0.2, ESX 3.0.1, ESX 3.0

Which server is the right server? The answer to that question depends on many factors. The number of CPU cores is often used as a determining factor, but you should also be sure to consider the total number of RAM slots. A higher number of RAM slots means that you can use lower-cost, lower-density RAM modules and still reach high memory configurations. You should also consider server expansion options, such as the number of available Peripheral Component Interconnect (PCI) or Peripheral Component Interconnect Express (PCIe) buses, expansion slots, and the types of expansion cards supported in the server.

Determining a Storage Architecture

Selecting the right storage solution is the third major decision that you must make before you proceed with your vSphere deployment. The lion's share of advanced features within vSphere—features like VMotion, VMware DRS, VMware HA, and VMware FT—depend upon the presence of a shared storage architecture, making it equally as critical a decision as the choice of the server hardware upon which to run ESX/ESXi.

THE HCL ISN'T JUST FOR SERVERS

VMware's HCL isn't just for servers. The searchable HCL also provides compatibility information on storage arrays and other storage components. Be sure to use the searchable HCL to verify the compatibility of your host bus adapters (HBAs) and storage arrays to ensure the appropriate level of support from VMware.

Fortunately, vSphere supports a number of storage architectures out of the box and has implemented a modular, plug-in architecture that will make supporting future storage technologies easier. vSphere supports Fibre Channel–based storage, iSCSI-based storage, and storage accessed via Network File System (NFS). In addition, vSphere supports the use of multiple storage protocols within a single solution so that one portion of the vSphere implementation might run over Fibre Channel, while another portion runs over NFS. This provides a great deal of flexibility in choosing your storage solution.

When determining the correct storage solution, you must consider the following questions:

◆ What type of storage will best integrate with my existing storage or network infrastructure?

◆ Do I have existing experience or expertise with some types of storage?

◆ Can the storage solution provide the necessary throughput to support my environment?

◆ Does the storage solution offer any form of advanced integration with vSphere?

The procedures involved in creating and managing storage devices is discussed in detail in Chapter 6, "Creating and Managing Storage Devices."

Integrating with the Network Infrastructure

The fourth major decision that you need to make during the planning process is how your vSphere deployment will integrate with the existing network infrastructure. In part, this decision is driven by the choice of server hardware and the storage protocol.

For example, an organization selecting a blade form factor may run into limitations on the number of network interface cards (NICs) that can be supported in a given blade model. This affects how the vSphere implementation will integrate with the network. Similarly, organizations choosing to use iSCSI or NFS instead of Fibre Channel will typically have to deploy more NICs in their VMware ESX hosts to accommodate the additional network traffic. Organizations also need to account for network interfaces for VMotion and VMware FT.

In most vSphere deployments, ESX/ESXi hosts will have a minimum of six NICs and often will have eight, 10, or even 12 NICs. So, how do you decide how many NICs to use? We'll discuss some of this in greater detail in Chapter 5, "Creating and Managing Virtual Networks," but here are some general guidelines:

◆ The Service Console needs at least one NIC. Ideally, you'd also want a second NIC for redundancy.

◆ VMotion needs a NIC. Again, a second NIC for redundancy would be ideal. This NIC should be at least Gigabit Ethernet.

◆ VMware FT, if you will be utilizing that feature, needs a NIC. A second NIC would provide redundancy. This should be at least a Gigabit Ethernet NIC, preferably a 10 Gigabit Ethernet NIC.

◆ For deployments using iSCSI or NFS, at least one more NIC, preferably two, is needed. Gigabit Ethernet or 10 Gigabit Ethernet is necessary here.

◆ Finally, at least two NICs would be needed for traffic originating from the virtual machines themselves. Gigabit Ethernet or faster is strongly recommended for VM traffic.

This adds up to 10 NICs per server. For this sort of deployment, you'll want to ensure that you have enough network ports available, at the appropriate speeds, to accommodate the needs of the vSphere deployment.

 Real World Scenario

HOW ABOUT 18 NICS?

Lots of factors go into designing how a vSphere deployment will integrate with the existing network infrastructure. For example, I was involved in a deployment of VMware ESX in a manufacturing environment that had seven subnets—one for each department within the manufacturing facility. Normally, in a situation like that, I recommend using VLANs and VLAN tagging so that the VMware ESX servers can easily support all the current subnets as well as any future subnets. This sort of configuration is discussed in more detail in Chapter 5.

In this particular case, though, the physical switches into which these ESX servers would be connected were configured in such a way that each subnet had a separate physical switch. The switch into which you plugged your Ethernet cable determined which subnet you used. Additionally, the core network switches didn't have the necessary available ports for us to connect the ESX servers directly to them. These factors, taken together, meant that we would need to design the ESX servers to have enough NICs to physically connect them to each of the different switches.

With 7 subnets, plus connections for the Service Console and VMotion, the final design ended up with 18 NICs connected in pairs to nine different physical switches. Fortunately, the servers that had been selected to host this environment had enough expansion slots to hold the four quad-port NICs and two Fibre Channel HBAs that were necessary to support the required network connectivity.

Deploying VMware ESX

You've gone through the planning process. You've decided on VMware ESX as your platform, you've selected a supported server model and configuration, you've determined how you're going to handle the storage requirements, and you have an idea how you'll integrate everything into your existing network infrastructure. Now comes the time to install.

To be honest, installing ESX is the easy part. Installing ESX can be done in a graphical mode or a text-based installation, which limits the intricacy of the screen configuration during the installation. The graphical mode is the more common of the two installation modes. The text mode is reserved for remote installation scenarios where the wide area network is not strong enough to support the graphical nature of the graphical installation mode.

VMware ESX offers both a DVD-based installation and an unattended installation that uses the same kickstart file technology commonly used for unattended Linux installations. In the following sections, I'll start by covering a standard DVD installation, and then I'll transition into an automated ESX installation.

Partitioning the Service Console

Before you install VMware ESX, you need to complete one more planning task, and that is planning your Service Console partitions.

Remember from earlier that ESX uses a Linux-based Service Console (also referred to as the *console operating system*, *console OS*, or *COS*) as the interface to the user. The core hypervisor, VMkernel, is not Linux-based but uses the Linux-based Service Console to provide a means whereby users can interact with the hypervisor. Because it is based on Linux, it uses Linux conventions for partitioning.

Unlike Windows, Linux (and by derivation, the ESX Service Console) doesn't use drive letters to correspond to partitions on the physical disks. Windows uses a *multiroot file system*, whereby each partition has its own root. Think of C:\ and D:\—each drive letter represents its own partition, and each partition has its own "top-level" directory at the root of the drive.

Linux, on the other hand, uses a *single-root file system*, where there is only one root. This root is denoted with a slash (/). All other partitions are grafted into this single namespace through mount points. A *mount point* is a directory (like /opt) that is associated with a partition on the physical disk. So, in a Linux environment, every directory starts at the same root. This creates paths like /usr/local/bin, /usr/sbin, or /opt/vmware. Any directory that isn't a mount point becomes part of the same partition as the root directory, so if there isn't a partition mounted at /home/slowe, then that directory is stored in the same partition as the root directory (/).

With a Windows-based server, what happens when the C: drive runs out of space? Bad things. We all know that bad things happen when the C: drive of a Windows computer runs out of space. So, Windows administrators create additional partitions (D:, E:) to prevent the C: drive from filling up.

The same is true for VMware ESX. Of course, ESX, as noted earlier, doesn't use drive letters. Instead, everything hangs off the root (/) directory. Like Windows, if the root (/) partition runs out of space, bad things happen. So, to protect the root partition from filling up, Linux administrators create additional partitions, and they mount those partitions as directories under the root directory. Likewise, ESX administrators will create additional partitions to protect the root partition from filling up.

NOT SO DIFFERENT AFTER ALL

One thing that Windows and the VMware ESX Service Console share in common is the limitation to a maximum of four partitions. The x86 architecture only allows for a maximum of three primary partitions and an extended partition that contains multiple logical partitions.

Figure 2.2 compares Windows disk partitioning and notation against the Linux disk partitioning and notation methods.

FIGURE 2.2
Windows and Linux represent disk partitions in different ways. Windows, by default, uses drive letters, while Linux uses mount points.

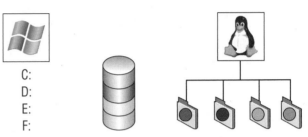

C:
D:
E:
F:

Now that we've explored why the Service Console partitioning is important—to protect the root partition from filling up—let's look at the default partitions in VMware ESX. Table 2.1 shows the default partitioning strategy for ESX.

TABLE 2.1:   Default VMware ESX Partition Scheme

MOUNT POINT NAME	TYPE	SIZE
/boot	Ext3	250MB
/	Ext3	5000MB (5GB)
(none)	Swap	600MB
/var/log	Ext3	2000MB (2GB)
(none)	Vmkcore	100MB

THE /BOOT PARTITION

The /boot partition, as its name suggests, stores all the files necessary to boot VMware ESX. The boot partition is created by default during the installation of ESX, setting aside 250MB of space. What's interesting is that the ESX installation program does not expose the boot partition or allow the user to modify the boot partition during installation. This is a big change from previous versions of ESX. If you are interested, you can see information on the boot partition on the installation summary screen toward the end of the ESX installation. Because the user has no ability to modify the boot partition in any way, I've included it here only for the sake of completeness.

THE ROOT (/) PARTITION

The root (/) partition is the "top" of the Service Console operating system. As stated earlier, the Service Console uses a single-rooted file system where all other partitions attach to a mount point under the root partition. I have already alluded to the importance of the root of the file system and why you don't want to let the root partition run out of space. Is 5GB enough for the root partition? One might say that 5GB must be enough if that is what VMware chose as the default. The minimum size of the root partition is 2.5GB, so the default is twice the size of the minimum. So, why change the size of the root partition? Keep in mind that any directory on which another partition is not mounted is stored in the root partition. If you anticipate needing to store lots of files in the /home directory but don't create a separate partition for /home, this space comes out of the root partition.

As you can imagine, 5GB can be used rather quickly. Because resizing a partition after it has been created is difficult and error-prone, it's best to plan for future growth. To avoid this situation, you should plan for a root partition with plenty of space to grow. Many consultants often recommend that the root partition be given more than the default 5GB of space. It is not uncommon for virtualization architects to suggest root partition sizes of 20GB to 25GB. However, the most important factor is to choose a size that fits your comfort for growth and that fits into the storage available in your chosen server platform and configuration.

THE SWAP PARTITION

The swap partition, as the name suggests, is the location of the Service Console swap file. This partition defaults to 600MB. As a general rule, swap files are created with a size equal to at least two times the memory allocated to the operating system. The same holds true for VMware ESX. The installation process allocates a default amount of 300MB of memory for the Service Console; therefore, the default swap partition size would be 600MB.

It might be necessary to increase the amount of memory granted to the Service Console. This could be for any number of reasons. If additional third-party software packages are needed to run in the Service Console—perhaps to provide monitoring or management functionality—then more memory may need to be dedicated to the Service Console. The Service Console can be granted up to 800MB of memory. Instructions on how to accomplish this are provided in the "Performing Post-Installation Configuration" section of this chapter.

With 800MB as the maximum of RAM dedicated to the Service Console, the recommended swap partition size becomes 1600MB (2 × 800MB). To accommodate for the possibility that the Service Console's memory allocation may need to be increased, it's recommended to increase the size of the swap partition to 1600MB.

THE /VAR/LOG PARTITION

The /var/log partition is where the Service Console creates log files during the normal course of operation. This partition is created with a default size of 2000MB, or 2GB of space. This is typically a safe value for this partition. However, I recommend that you make a change to this default configuration. VMware ESX uses the /var directory during patch management tasks. Because the default partition is /var/log, this means that the /var partition is still under the root partition. Therefore, space consumed in /var is space consumed in root. For this reason, I recommend that you change the mount point to /var instead of /var/log and that you increase the space to a larger value like 10GB or 15GB. This alteration provides ample space for patch management without jeopardizing the root partition and still providing a dedicated partition to store log data.

THE VMKCORE PARTITION

The vmkcore partition is the dump partition where VMware ESX writes information about a system halt. We are all familiar with the infamous Windows blue screen of death (BSOD) either from experience or from the multitude of jokes that arose from the ever-so-frequent occurrences. When ESX crashes, it, like Windows, writes detailed information about the system crash. This information is written to the vmkcore partition. Unlike Windows, an ESX server system crash results in a purple screen of death (PSOD) that many administrators have never seen. Like the boot partition, the vmkcore partition is hidden from the user during the installation process and cannot be modified or changed. It's included here for the sake of completeness.

THE /OPT PARTITION

The default partitions do not include the /opt partition. Like version 3.5 of VMware ESX, many additional components of vSphere install themselves into the /opt directory structure, including the vCenter Agent and the VMware HA Agent. I recommend creating an /opt partition with enough size to hold these components as well as any other third-party products that may need to be installed into the Service Console. Examples may include hardware management agents or backup agents. By creating an /opt partition and installing software into the /opt directory structure, you are further protecting the root partition from running out of space.

ALL THAT SPACE AND NOTHING TO DO

Although local disk space is often useless in the face of a dedicated storage area network, there are ways to take advantage of local storage rather than let it go to waste. LeftHand Networks (www.lefthandnetworks.com), now part of HP, has developed a virtual storage appliance (VSA) that presents local VMware ESX storage space as an iSCSI target. In addition, this space can be combined with other local storage on other servers to provide data redundancy. And the best part of being able to present local storage as virtual shared storage units is the availability of VMotion, DRS, and HA. This can be an inexpensive way to provide shared storage for test and evaluation environments, but I don't recommend using it for production workloads.

Table 2.2 provides a customized partitioning strategy that offers strong support for any future needs in a VMware ESX installation. I've removed the boot and vmkcore partitions from this list because they are not visible and cannot be modified during the installation process.

TABLE 2.2:   Custom VMware ESX Partition Scheme

MOUNT POINT NAME	TYPE	SIZE
/	Ext3	20,000MB (20GB)
(none)	Swap	1,600MB (1.6GB)
/var	Ext3	15,000MB (15GB)
/opt	Ext3	10,000MB (10GB)

LOCAL DISKS, REDUNDANT DISKS

The availability of the root file system, vmkcore, Service Console swap, and so forth, is critical to a functioning VMware ESX host. For the safety of the installed Service Console and the hypervisor, always install ESX on a hardware-based RAID array. Unless you intend to use a product like a VSA, there is little need to build a RAID 5 array with three or more large hard drives. A RAID 1 (mirrored) array provides the needed reliability while minimizing the disk requirements. The custom partition scheme presented in Table 2.2 will easily fit into a RAID 1 mirror of two 72GB hard drives.

WHAT ABOUT A VIRTUAL MACHINE FILE SYSTEM PARTITION?

If you're familiar with previous versions of VMware ESX, you may note that the recommended partition scheme in Table 2.2 does not include a Virtual Machine File System (VMFS) partition. This is for a very good reason.

In ESX 4, the Service Console continues its evolution toward becoming completely encapsulated by the underlying hypervisor. This process started in ESX 3, when VMware removed the need to dedicate a NIC to the Service Console and allowed the Service Console to use a NIC under the control of the hypervisor. In ESX 4, that evolution continues in that users no longer set aside space for a VMFS version 3 (VMFS 3) partition along with Service Console partitions; instead, users now set aside space for Service Console partitions on a VMFS 3 partition.

VMware ESX now treats all local storage as a VMFS 3 partition (or datastore). During the installation of ESX and the configuration of the Service Console partitions, users are instead carving space out of an underlying VMFS3 datastore to grant to the Service Console. Whatever is not granted to the Service Console is left in the VMFS3 partition for use by other virtual machines. This makes the Service Console much more like a virtual machine than in the past. This will become clear in Chapter 6 when I discuss storage in more detail.

Installing from DVD

If you've already done VMware ESX installs, you are probably wondering what I could be talking about in this section given that the installation can be completed by simply clicking the Next button until the Finish button shows up. This is true to a certain extent, although there are some significant decisions to be made during the installation—decisions that affect the future of the ESX deployment as well as decisions that could cause severe damage to company data. For this reason, it is important for both the experienced administrator and the newbie to read this section carefully and understand how best to install ESX to support current and future needs.

WARNING! YOU MIGHT LOSE DATA IF YOU DON'T READ THIS

If storage area network (SAN)–based storage has already been presented to the server being installed, it's possible to initialize SAN LUNs during the installation process. If these LUNs contain production data, *that data will be lost!* As a precaution, it is strongly recommended that you disconnect the server from the SAN or ensure LUN masking has been performed to prevent the server from accessing LUNs.

Access to the SAN is required during installation only if a boot from SAN configuration is required.

Perform the following steps to install VMware ESX from a DVD:

1. Disconnect the server from the SAN, configure the server to boot from the optical drive, insert the ESX DVD, and reboot the computer.

2. Select the graphical installation mode by pressing the Enter key at the boot options screen, shown in Figure 2.3. If no other options are selected, then the ESX installation will automatically continue in graphical mode after 30 seconds.

FIGURE 2.3
VMware ESX 4 offers both a graphical installation mode and a text-based installation mode. The graphical mode is selected by default unless you select another option.

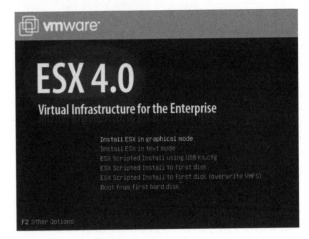

3. Click the Next button on the Welcome To The ESX Installer screen.

4. Read through the end user license agreement (EULA), click the I Accept The Terms Of The License Agreement box, and then click the Next button.

5. Select the U.S. English keyboard layout, or whichever is appropriate for your installation, as shown in Figure 2.4. Then click the Next button.

FIGURE 2.4
ESX 4 offers support for numerous keyboard layouts.

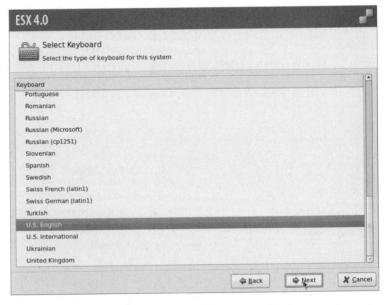

6. If any custom drivers need to be installed, click the Add button to add them, as shown in Figure 2.5. When you are finished adding custom drivers or if there are no custom drivers

to be added, click the Next button. When prompted to confirm loading the system drivers, click Yes.

FIGURE 2.5
Users have the option of adding custom drivers to be loaded during the ESX 4 installation.

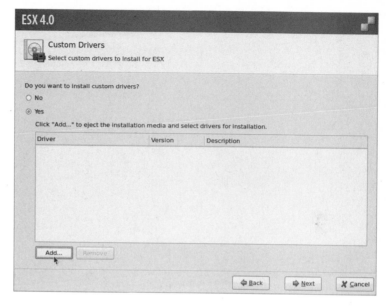

7. When the system drivers have been loaded, click the Next button to proceed.

8. Enter a serial number for this installation, or click to enter a serial number later, as illustrated in Figure 2.6. If you will be using vCenter Server to manage your VMware ESX hosts, the latter option is the option to use. Then click Next.

FIGURE 2.6
ESX 4 can be licensed during installation or after installation. As indicated, users with vCenter Server can configure the serial number later.

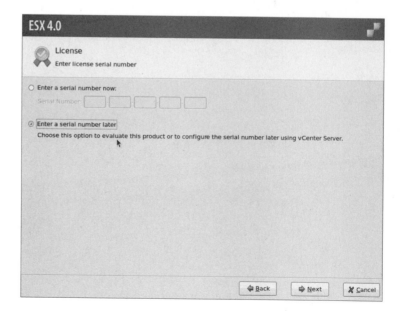

9. Select the NIC that should be used for system tasks. This NIC supports the Service Console interface. If a VLAN ID needs to be specified, select the box labeled This Adapter Requires A VLAN ID (Leave Unchecked If Not Sure), and specify the VLAN ID, as shown in Figure 2.7. Click Next when you are ready to continue.

FIGURE 2.7
You must select a NIC for the Service Console interface and specify a VLAN ID if necessary.

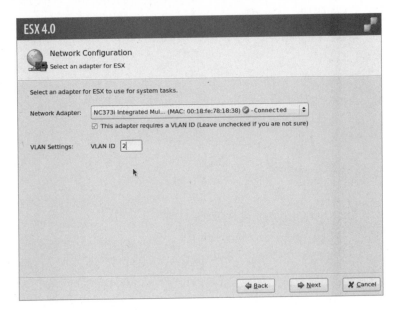

10. If the Service Console interface will be configured via Dynamic Host Configuration Protocol (DHCP), then click Next; otherwise, select the option labeled Use The Following Network Settings, and enter the IP address, subnet mask, default gateway, DNS servers, and fully qualified host name before clicking Next. If you want to test the settings, there is a Test These Settings button to ensure that the network configuration is working as expected, as shown in Figure 2.8.

11. The next screen prompts you for either Standard Setup or Advanced Setup, as shown in Figure 2.9. If you want the option to customize the ESX partitions, select Advanced Setup. Click Next.

12. The next screen asks you to confirm the storage device to which it will install ESX, as shown in Figure 2.10. Click Next.

    If you selected Standard Setup in the previous step, you can go directly to step 15.

13. If you selected Advanced Setup in step 11, the next screen will ask for the name to be assigned to the VMFS datastore that will be created on the storage device selected in the previous step. The default is Storage1. Enter the desired name, as shown in Figure 2.11, and click Next.

FIGURE 2.8
Specify the TCP/IP network configuration parameters for the Service Console interface.

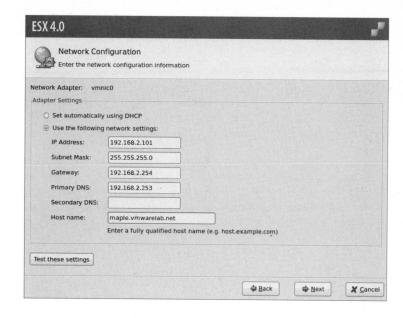

FIGURE 2.9
Choose Advanced Setup if you want to customize the ESX partitions.

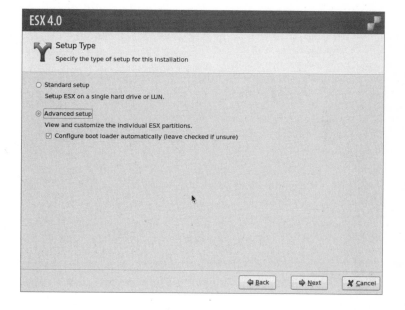

FIGURE 2.10
You need to select a
storage device for the
installation of ESX 4.

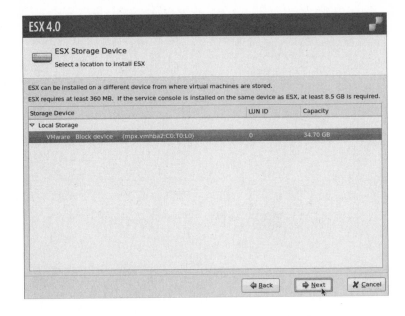

FIGURE 2.11
When you select
Advanced Setup, you
must assign a name to
the VMFS partition cre-
ated during installation.

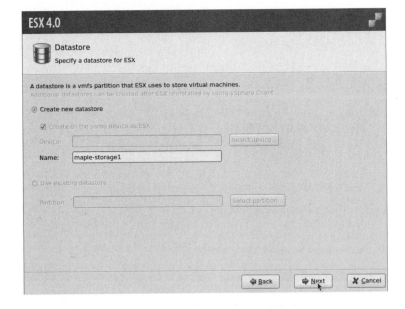

14. If you chose Advanced Setup, the next screen presents the default Service Console
partition layout and offers the opportunity to customize the partition layout. To edit an
existing partition—for example, to modify the size of the swap partition to 1600MB, as
recommended—select the partition, and click Edit. To add a new partition, such as the
/opt partition, click the New button. When the partitions are configured as desired, click

Next to continue. Figure 2.12 shows the default partition layout; Figure 2.13 shows the customized partition layout.

FIGURE 2.12
The ESX 4 default partition layout creates a 5GB root partition, a 600MB swap partition, and a 2GB partition for /var/log.

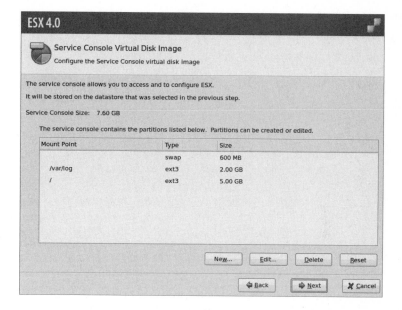

FIGURE 2.13
This customized ESX 4 partition layout has separate partitions for /var, /opt, and /tmp plus a larger swap partition.

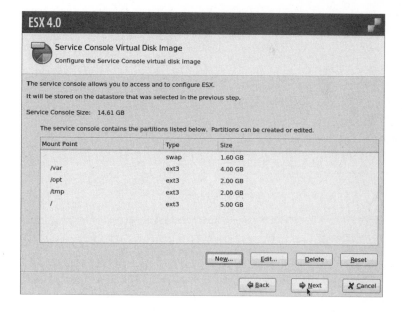

15. Select the correct time zone by clicking the nearest city in your time zone, as shown in Figure 2.14; then click Next. For example, users on the eastern coast of the United States might choose New York.

FIGURE 2.14
ESX 4 is configured
with time-zone sup-
port for many differ-
ent time zones.

16. The next screen offers you the option to configure time either via Network Time Protocol
(NTP) or manually, as shown in Figure 2.15. To configure time via NTP, enter the name or
IP address of an NTP server that is accessible from this server. Otherwise, make the date
and time selection at the bottom, and click Next. Note if you choose manual time configuration, you can always switch to NTP later, if desired.

FIGURE 2.15
You can set the date
and time in ESX 4 via
NTP or manually.

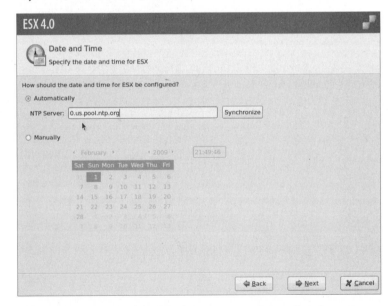

17. Enter a root password twice to confirm. On the same screen, you have the option of creating additional users. For ease of access to the server via Secure Shell (SSH), I recommend

creating at least one additional user during installation, as depicted in Figure 2.16. Click Next when ready.

FIGURE 2.16
Each ESX 4 host needs a root user and password set during installation. Additional users can also be created during installation.

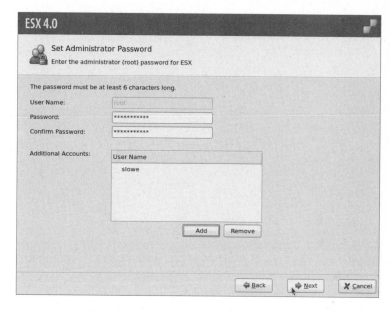

18. At the installation summary screen, shown in Figure 2.17, review the selections that were made. If there are any corrections to be made, use the Back button to return to the appropriate step in the installation and make the necessary changes. If everything looks acceptable, click Next to begin the installation.

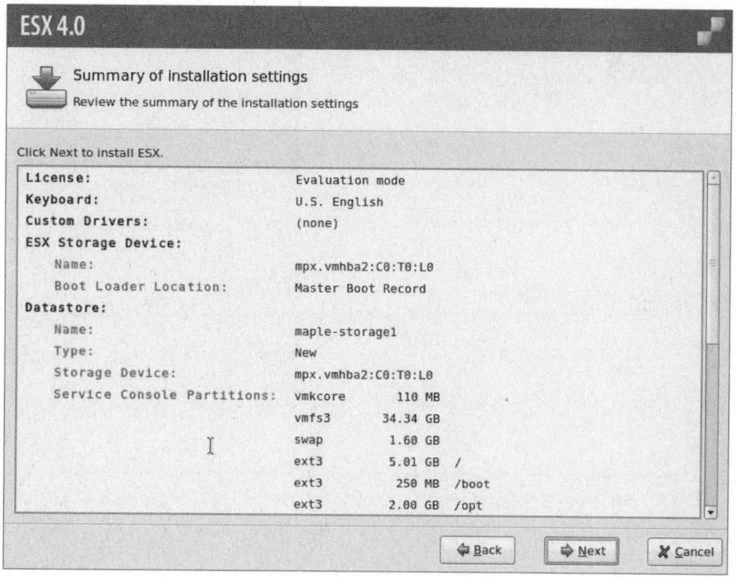

FIGURE 2.17
The summary of installation settings offers a final chance to double-check the server configuration and make changes if needed.

19. As shown in Figure 2.18, the installation will begin. Upon completion, click Next to continue.

FIGURE 2.18
A progress meter shows the status of the ESX 4 installation.

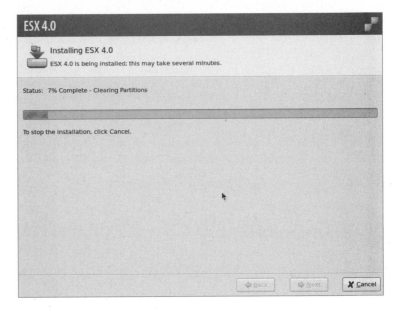

20. On the final screen, click Finish to reboot the server into ESX.

21. Upon completion of the server reboot, the console session displays the information for accessing the server from a remote computer, as shown in Figure 2.19.

FIGURE 2.19
After reboot, ESX 4 displays information on how to access the server.

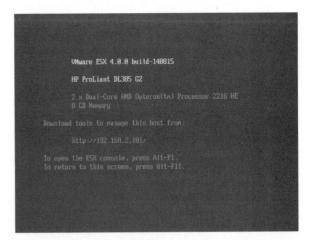

WHAT IF I CHOOSE THE WRONG NIC DURING INSTALLATION?

Compared to previous versions of ESX, ESX 4 is much friendlier with regard to helping you properly identify which NIC should be associated with the Service Console interface during installation. As you saw in Figure 2.7, the installation at least provides some information about the vendor and model of the NICs involved.

If, for whatever reason, the wrong NIC gets selected, access to the server via SSH, a web page, or the vSphere Client will fail. As part of the "Performing Post-Installation Configuration" section of this chapter, I will detail how to recover if you select the wrong NIC during the installation wizard. This fix requires direct access to the console or an out-of-band management tool like HP's integrated Lights-Out (iLO).

Despite the ease with which ESX can be installed, it is still not preferable to perform manual, attended installations of a bulk number of servers. Nor is it preferable to perform manual, attended installation in environments that are rapidly deploying new ESX hosts. To support large numbers or rapid-deployment scenarios, ESX can be installed in an unattended fashion.

Performing an Unattended ESX Installation

Unattended ESX installations help speed the installation process and help ensure consistency in the configuration of multiple servers, a key factor in helping to ensure stability and functionality in an ESX server farm.

The unattended installation procedure involves booting the computer, reading the installation files, and reading the unattended installation script. The destination host can be booted from a DVD, a floppy, or a Preboot Execution Environment (PXE) boot server and then directed to the location of the installation files and answer files. The installation files and/or answer script can be stored and accessed from any of the following locations:

- An HTTP URL
- An NFS export
- An FTP directory
- A DVD (install files only)

Table 2.3 outlines the various methods and the boot options required for each option set. The boot option is typed at the installation screen shown previously in Figure 2.3.

TABLE 2.3:   Unattended Installation Methods

IF THE COMPUTER BOOTS FROM...	AND THE MEDIA IS STORED ON A...	AND THE ANSWER FILE IS STORED ON A...	THEN THE BOOT OPTION IS...
PXE	(Media) URL	(Answer) URL	esx ks=<answer URL> method=<media URL> ksdevice=<NIC>
CD	CD	URL	esx ks=<answer URL> ksdevice=<NIC>

Regardless of the method used to access the installation files or the answer file, one of the first tasks that you must accomplish is creating the answer file, known as a *kickstart file*. The kickstart file derives its name from the Red Hat Linux kickstart file, which is used to automate the installation of Red Hat Linux. Although the ESX kickstart file uses some of the same commands as a Red Hat Linux kickstart file, the two formats are not compatible.

When editing kickstart files, be aware of differences between how Windows marks the end of a line and how Linux marks the end of a line. It's safe to edit kickstart files in WordPad on Windows, because WordPad will preserve the proper line endings. You should not use Notepad to edit kickstart scripts. If you use a Linux or Mac OS X system to edit the kickstart scripts, just be sure that the text editor of choice uses the correct line endings (LF instead of CR/LF).

The kickstart file does help automate the installation of ESX, but the kickstart script does not provide a way of generating unique information for multiple installations. Each install will require a manually created (or adjusted) kickstart file that is specific to that installation, particularly around the configuration of static information such as IP address and hostname.

Listing 2.1 shows a simple kickstart script that you can use to perform an unattended installation when the installation files are located on a DVD. The kickstart script itself could be located on a USB key or a network URL.

LISTING 2.1:   Automating the Installation of VMware ESX

```
#root Password
rootpw Password123
# Authconfig
authconfig --enableshadow --enablemd5
# BootLoader (Use grub by default.)
bootloader --location=mbr
# Timezone
timezone America/New_York
#Install
install cdrom
#Network install type
network --device=vmnic0 --bootproto=static --ip=192.168.2.102
--netmask=255.255.255.0 --nameserver=192.168.2.253
--gateway=192.168.2.254 --addvmportgroup=0
--hostname=birch.virtlab.net --vlanid=2
#Keyboard
keyboard us
#Reboot after install?
reboot
# Clear partitions
clearpart --firstdisk=local
# Partitioning
part /boot --fstype=ext3 --size=250 --onfirstdisk
part birch-storage1 --fstype=vmfs3 --size=20000 --grow --onfirstdisk
part None --fstype=vmkcore --size=100 --onfirstdisk
# Create the vmdk on the cos vmfs partition.
virtualdisk cos --size=15000 --onvmfs=birch-storage1
# Partition the virtual disk.
part / --fstype=ext3 --size=5000 --grow --onvirtualdisk=cos
```

```
part swap --fstype=swap --size=1600 --onvirtualdisk=cos
part /var --fstype=ext3 --size=4000 --onvirtualdisk=cos
part /opt --fstype=ext3 --size=2000 --onvirtualdisk=cos
part /tmp --fstype=ext3 --size=2000 --onvirtualdisk=cos
# VMware Specific Commands
accepteula
```

Perform the following for an unattended installation using a DVD for the installation files and a USB key for the kickstart script:

1. Boot the target server from the ESX 4 DVD with the USB device containing the kickstart script plugged into an available USB port.

2. At the installation mode screen, as shown previously in Figure 2.3, use the arrow keys to highlight ESX Scripted Install Using USB Ks.cfg. To see the options that are added to the bootstrap menu, press F2. The Boot Options command at the bottom of the screen should look something like this:

```
initrd=initrd.img vmkopts=debugLogToSerial:1 mem=512M ks=usb quiet
```

Figure 2.20 illustrates this.

FIGURE 2.20
The installation mode screen offers different unattended installation options, including the option to use a scripted installation on a USB device.

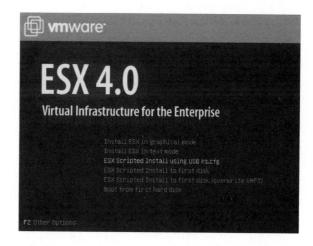

3. Press Enter. The installation should start and continue until the final reboot.

It's also possible to perform an unattended installation using a DVD for the installation files and a network location for the kickstart script.

Perform the following steps for an unattended installation with the kickstart script located on an HTTP server:

1. Boot the target server from the ESX 4 DVD.

2. At the installation mode screen, as shown previously in Figure 2.3, use the arrow keys to highlight ESX Scripted Install Using USB Ks.cfg, but do not press Enter to select that menu item.

3. Press F2 to edit the Boot Options command so it looks like this, substituting the correct IP address and path for the location of the `ks.cfg` file:

```
initrd=initrd.img vmkopts=debugLogToSerial:1 mem=512M
ks=http://192.168.2.151/esx4/ks.cfg ksdevice=vmnic0
```

4. Press Enter. The installation should start and continue until the final reboot.

The process for using an FTP server or an NFS server would look essentially the same, substituting the correct URL for the `ks=` parameter shown previously.

Although HTTP and NFS are acceptable options for the location of the kickstart file, be aware that a Windows file share is not an option. This makes it a bit more difficult to get the kickstart script to the correct location. Free tools like Veeam FastSCP (www.veeam.com) or WinSCP (www.winscp.com) are useful in copying the kickstart file to the HTTP server, FTP server, or NFS server. After the file is in place on the network server, you can launch the unattended installation.

KICKSTART CUSTOMIZATIONS

Although the kickstart script included earlier in this section did not perform any post-installation customizations, kickstart files can be edited to configure numerous post-installation customizations. These customizations can include Service Console NIC corrections, creation of virtual switches and port groups, storage configuration, and even modifications to Service Console config files for setting up external time servers. The command-line syntax for virtual networking and storage is covered in Chapters 5 and 6.

Deploying VMware ESXi

As stated earlier in this chapter, VMware ESXi comes in two different flavors, VMware ESXi Installable and VMware ESXi Embedded. Although these two versions of VMware ESXi share the same architecture, the way in which they are deployed is quite different.

Deploying VMware ESXi Installable

The installation of ESXi Installable begins by ensuring that the computer system is configured to boot from the CD-ROM drive. To do this, insert the ESXi Installable installation CD into the drive, and power on the system. You can download the installation files from VMware's website at www.vmware.com/downloads. The installation files for ESXi are listed separately from ESX. After the server is powered on and boots from the CD, the VMware VMvisor Boot Menu screen displays, as shown in Figure 2.21. To make changes to the installation parameters, press the Tab key. The default parameters show beneath the boot menu.

After you accept the license agreement, you will have the opportunity to select the hard drive onto which you want to install ESXi. The available logical disks are listed, as shown in Figure 2.22. ESXi Installable requires local hard drives to be available for the installation. The local hard drives can be Serial ATA (SATA), Small Computer System Interface (SCSI), or Serial Attached SCSI (SAS) as long as they are connected to a controller that is listed on the HCL for VMware ESXi. The size of the hard drives is practically irrelevant because enterprise deployments of vSphere will most commonly place all virtual machines, templates, and ISOs on a shared storage device. Be sure to keep that in mind when you are in the process of identifying hardware specifications for new servers that you intend to use as thin virtualization clients with ESXi Installable; there's no sense in purchasing large disk arrays for local storage on ESXi hosts. The smallest hard drives available in a RAID 1 configuration will provide ample room and redundancy for the installation of ESXi.

FIGURE 2.21
ESXi Installable has a different installation routine than ESX.

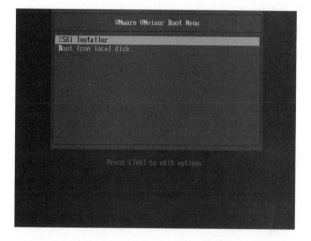

FIGURE 2.22
You can install ESXi on SATA, SCSI, or SAS drives.

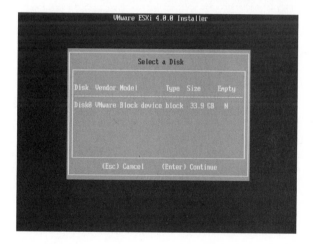

If the disk you select for the installation has existing data, you will receive a warning message about the data being overwritten with the new installation, as shown in Figure 2.23. Before answering Continue to this prompt, be sure there isn't any critical data on this disk, because answering Continue to this prompt will erase all the data on the selected disk. Move any critical data on this disk to a different server before proceeding with installation.

After the installation process begins, it takes only a few minutes to load the thin hypervisor. Upon completion, the server requires a reboot and is configured by default to obtain an IP address via DHCP. Depending upon the network configuration, you might find that ESXi will not be able to obtain an IP address via DHCP. Later in this chapter I'll discuss how to correct networking problems after installing ESXi.

FIGURE 2.23
Disks with existing data will be overwritten during the ESXi installation procedure.

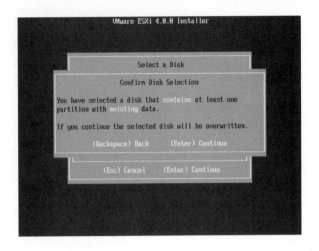

Perform the following steps to install ESXi:

1. Insert the ESXi Installable installation CD into the server's CD-ROM drive.

2. Boot the computer from the installation CD.

3. Allow the eight-second automatic boot timer to expire before beginning the ESXi Installer option selected on the VMware VMvisor Boot Menu screen.

4. The setup process loads the VMware ISO and VMkernel components, as shown in Figure 2.24.

FIGURE 2.24
The ESXi Installable ISO loads the VMkernel components to begin the installation.

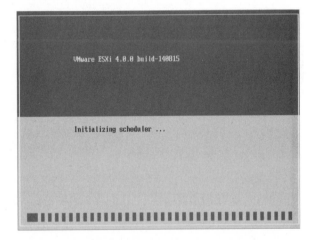

5. After the components are loaded and the Welcome To The VMware ESXi 4.0.0 Installation screen displays, as shown in Figure 2.25, press Enter to perform the installation.

6. Press the F11 key to accept the license agreement and to continue the installation.

7. Select the appropriate disk onto which you will install ESXi, and press the Enter key to continue.

FIGURE 2.25
Installing ESXi on
a local disk

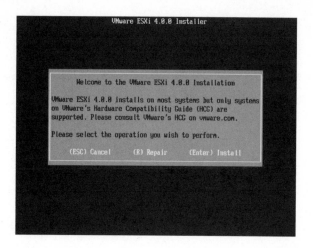

8. If you receive a warning about existing data, press Enter to continue only after verifying that the data loss will not be of concern.

9. Press the F11 key to complete the installation.

Deploying VMware ESXi Embedded

VMware ESXi Embedded refers to the original equipment manufacturer (OEM) installation of VMware ESXi onto a persistent storage device inside the qualified hardware. This is an exciting option that will save administrators the time of performing any type of installation. The embedded hypervisor truly allows for the plug-and-play hardware-type atmosphere. You can see that major server manufacturers are banking on this idea because their server designs include an internal USB port. Perhaps eventually the ESXi hypervisor will move from USB flash drive on an internal port to some type of flash memory built right onto the motherboard.

When you purchase a system with ESXi Embedded, you only need to rack the server, connect the networking cables, and power on. The ESXi embedded on the persistent storage will obtain an IP address from a DHCP server to provide immediate access via the console, vSphere Client, or vCenter Server.

The server set to run ESXi Embedded must be configured to boot from the appropriate device. Take, for example, a HP server with a USB flash drive with ESXi Embedded connected to an internal (or external) USB port. To run the thin hypervisor, the server must be configured to boot from the USB device. Figure 2.26 shows the BIOS of an HP ProLiant DL385 G2 server.

Because ESXi Embedded is installed on and running from the internal USB device, no local hard drives are necessary in this sort of configuration. Customers deploying ESXi Embedded can be servers without hard drives, removing another potential point of failure in the datacenter and further reducing power consumption and heat generation. Additionally, because ESXi Embedded is already "installed" on the USB device, there is no installation of which to speak. Once the server is configured to boot from the persistent storage device and ESXi Embedded is up and running, it is managed and configured in the same fashion as ESXi Installable. This makes it incredibly easy to deploy additional servers in a very rapid fashion.

Although ESXi Embedded is intended for use by OEMs, it's possible to create your own "ESXi Embedded" edition by putting ESXi Installable onto a USB drive. This is a great way to test ESXi Embedded, but keep in mind that VMware does not support this sort of configuration.

FIGURE 2.26
To run ESXi Embedded, you must configure the server to boot from the persistent storage device.

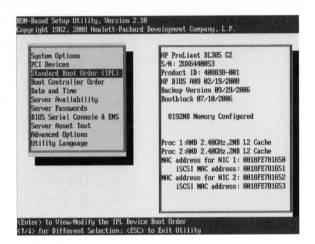

Installing the vSphere Client

The vSphere Client is a Windows-only application that allows for connecting directly to an ESX/ESXi host or to a vCenter Server installation. The only difference in the tools used is that connecting directly to an ESX/ESXi host requires authentication with a user account that exists on that specific host, while connecting to a vCenter Server installation relies on Windows users for authentication. Additionally, some features of the vSphere Client—such as initiating VMotion, for example—are available when connecting to a vCenter Server installation.

You can install the vSphere Client as part of a vCenter Server installation or with the vCenter Server installation media. However, the easiest installation method is to simply connect to the Web Access page of an ESX/ESXi host or vCenter Server and choose to install the application right from the web page.

If you're having problems connecting to the Web Access page of your newly installed ESX/ESXi host, it might be because of an incorrect Service Console/management network configuration. Jump ahead to the "Performing Post-installation Configuration" section for more information on how to correct this problem; then return here for the installation of the vSphere Client.

Perform the following steps to install the vSphere Client from an ESX/ESXi host's Web Access page:

1. Open an Internet browser (such as Internet Explorer or Firefox).

2. Type in the IP address or fully qualified domain name of the ESX/ESXi host from which the vSphere Client should be installed.

3. On the ESX/ESXi host or vCenter Server home page, click the link labeled Download vSphere Client.

4. You can save the application to the local system by clicking the Save button, or if the remote computer is trusted, it can be run directly from the remote computer by clicking the Run button.

5. Click the Run button in the Security Warning box that identifies an unverified publisher, as shown in Figure 2.27.

FIGURE 2.27
The vSphere Client might issue a warning about an unverified publisher.

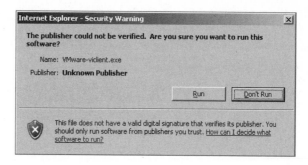

6. Click the Next button on the welcome page of the Virtual Infrastructure Client Wizard.

7. Click the radio button labeled I Accept the Terms in the License Agreement, and then click the Next button.

8. Specify a username and organization name, and then click the Next button.

9. Configure the destination folder, and then click the Next button.

10. Click the Install button to begin the installation.

11. Click the Finish button to complete the installation.

64-BIT VS. 32-BIT

Although the vSphere Client can be installed on 64-bit Windows operating systems, the vSphere Client itself remains a 32-bit application and runs in 32-bit compatibility mode.

Performing Post-installation Configuration

Whether you are installing from a DVD or performing an unattended installation of ESX, once the installation is complete, there are several post-installation changes that either must be done or are strongly recommended. Among these configurations are changing the physical NIC used by the Service Console/management network, adjusting the amount of RAM allocated to the Service Console, and configuring an ESX/ESXi host to synchronize with an external NTP server. I'll discuss these tasks in the following sections.

Changing the Service Console/Management NIC

During the installation of ESX, the NIC selection screen creates a virtual switch—also known as a *vSwitch*—bound to the selected physical NIC. The tricky part, depending upon your server hardware, can be choosing the correct physical NIC connected to the physical switch that makes up the logical IP subnet from which the ESX host will be managed. I'll talk more about the reasons why ESX must be configured this way in Chapter 5, but for now just understand that this is a requirement for connectivity.

Although the ESX 4 installation program makes it a little bit easier to distinguish between NICs, Figure 2.28 shows that there is still room for confusion.

ESXi doesn't even give the user the option to select the NIC that should be used for the management network, which is ESXi's equivalent to the Service Console in ESX. This makes it very possible for the wrong NIC to be selected for the management network. In either situation, if the wrong NIC is selected, the server will be inaccessible via the network. Figure 2.29 shows the structure of the virtual networking when the wrong NIC is selected and when the correct NIC is selected.

FIGURE 2.28
The ESX installation still makes it possible to choose the wrong NIC to be bound to the Service Console.

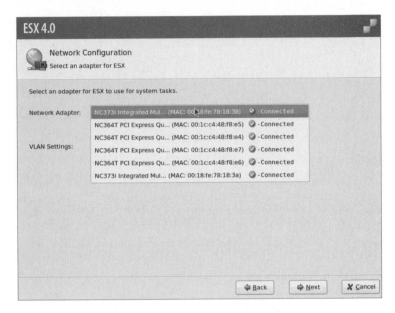

FIGURE 2.29
The virtual switch that the Service Console uses must be associated with the physical switch that makes up the logical subnet from which the Service Console will be managed.

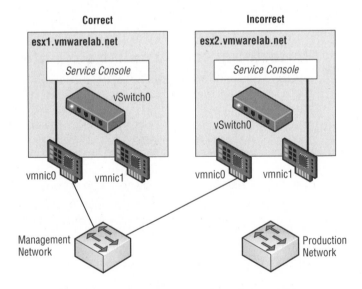

The simplest fix for this problem is to unplug the network cable from the current Ethernet port in the back of the server and continue trying the remaining ports until the web page is accessible.

The problem with this solution is that it puts a quick end to any type of documented standard that dictates the physical connectivity of the ESX/ESXi hosts in a virtual environment.

Is there a better fix? Absolutely! Of course, if you like installations, go for it, but I prefer a simpler solution. First I'll talk about fixing ESX using the Service Console, and then I'll show how you'd go about fixing ESXi.

FIXING THE SERVICE CONSOLE NIC IN ESX

Perform the following steps to fix the Service Console NIC in ESX:

1. Log in to the console of the ESX host using the root user account. If the server supports a remote console, such as HP iLO, that is acceptable as well.

2. Review the PCI addresses of the physical NICs in the server by typing the following command:

   ```
   esxcfg-nics -l
   ```

BEWARE OF CASE SENSITIVITY

Remember that the ESX Service Console holds its roots in Linux, and therefore almost all types of command-line management or configuration will be case sensitive. This means, for example, that `esxcfg-vswitch -x` (lowercase x) and `esxcfg-vswitch -X` (uppercase X) are two different commands and perform two different functions.

---

3. The results, as shown in Figure 2.30, list identifying information for each NIC. Note the PCI addresses and names of each adapter.

FIGURE 2.30
The `esxcfg-nics` command provides detailed information about each network adapter in an ESX host.

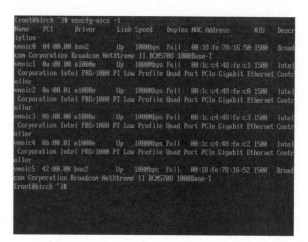

4. Review the existing Service Console configuration by typing the following command:

   ```
   esxcfg-vswitch -l
   ```

5. The results, as shown in Figure 2.31, display the current configuration of the Service Console port association.

FIGURE 2.31

The esxcfg-vswitch command provides information about the current virtual switch configuration, which affects the Service Console.

6. To change the NIC association, the existing NIC must be unlinked by typing the following command:

   ```
   esxcfg-vswitch -U vmnic# vSwitch#
   ```

   In this example, the appropriate command would be as follows:

   ```
   esxcfg-vswitch -U vmnic0 vSwitch0
   ```

7. Use the following command to associate a new NIC with the vSwitch0 used by the Service Console:

   ```
   esxcfg-vswitch -L vmnic# vSwitch#
   ```

   If you're still unsure of the correct NIC, try each NIC listed in the output from step 2. For this example, to associate vmnic1 with a PCI address of 08:07:00, the appropriate command is as follows:

   ```
   esxcfg-vswitch -L vmnic1 vSwitch0
   ```

8. Repeat steps 6 and 7 until a successful connection is made to the Web Access page of the VMware ESX host.

FIXING THE MANAGEMENT NIC IN ESXI

Because there is no Service Console in ESXi, fixing an incorrect assignment of the NIC assigned to the management network is handled quite differently than in ESX. Fortunately, VMware anticipated this potential problem and provided a menu-driven system whereby you can fix it.

Perform the following steps to fix the management NIC in ESXi:

1. Access the console of the ESXi host, either physically or via a remote console solution such as HP iLO.

2. On the ESXi home screen, shown in Figure 2.32, press F2 to customize the system. If a root password has been set, enter that root password.

3. From the System Customization menu, select Configure Management Network, and press Enter.

4. From the Configure Management Network menu, select Network Adapters, and press Enter.

5. Use the spacebar to toggle which network adapter or adapters will be used for the system's management network, as shown in Figure 2.33. Press Enter when finished.

FIGURE 2.32
The ESXi home screen provides options for customizing the system and restarting or shutting down the server.

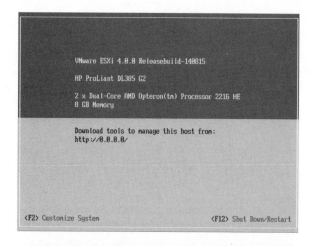

FIGURE 2.33
In the event the incorrect NIC is assigned to ESXi's management network, you can select a different NIC.

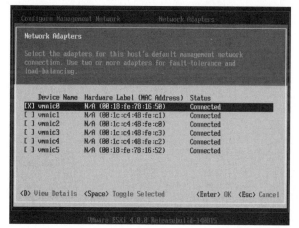

6. Press Esc to exit the Configure Management Network menu. When prompted to apply changes and restart the management network, press Y.

7. Press Esc to log out of the System Customization menu and return to the ESXi home screen.

After the correct NIC has been assigned to the ESXi management network, the System Customization menu provides a Test Management Network option to verify network connectivity.

Adjusting the Service Console Memory (ESX Only)

Because ESXi omits the Service Console, this section applies only to ESX. Adjusting the amount of memory given to the Service Console is not mandatory but is strongly recommended if you have to install third-party applications into the Service Console. These third-party applications will consume memory available to the Service Console. As noted earlier, the Service Console is granted 300MB of RAM by default, as shown in Figure 2.34, with a hard-coded maximum of 800MB.

FIGURE 2.34
The Service Console is allocated 300MB of RAM by default.

The difference of 500MB is, and should be, negligible in relation to the amount of memory in an ESX host. Certainly an ESX host in a production network would not have less than 8GB of memory, and more likely it would have 32GB, 64GB, or even 128GB. So, adding 500MB of memory for use by the Service Console does not place a significant restriction on the number of virtual machines a host is capable of running because of a lack of available memory.

Perform the following steps to increase the amount of memory allocated to the Service Console:

1. Use the vSphere Client to connect to an ESX host or a vCenter Server installation.

2. Select the appropriate host from the inventory tree on the left, and then select the Configuration tab from the details pane on the right.

3. Select Memory from the Hardware menu.

4. Click the Properties link.

5. As shown in Figure 2.35, enter the amount of memory to be allocated to the Service Console in the text box, and then click the OK button. The value entered must be between 256 and 800.

FIGURE 2.35
You can increase the amount of memory allocated to the Service Console to a maximum of 800MB.

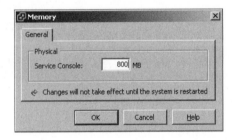

6. Reboot the ESX host.

Best practices call for the ESX swap partition to be twice the size of the available RAM, which is why I recommended earlier in this chapter to set the size of the swap partition to 1600MB (twice the maximum amount of RAM available to the Service Console). If you didn't size the swap partition appropriately, you can create a swap file on an existing Service Console partition.

Perform the following steps to create a swap file:

1. Create a new swap file on an existing Service Console partition using the dd command. This command will create a 1.5GB file:

```
dd if=/dev/zero of=/path/to/swap.file bs=1024 count=1572864
```

2. Use this command to turn this file into a usable swap file:

```
mkswap /path/to/swap.file
```

3. Enable the swap file with this command:

```
swapon /path/to/swap.file
```

Given the ease with which you can simply reinstall VMware ESX, especially if you are using an unattended installation script, I don't recommend creating a swap file in this manner. Instead, simply rebuild the ESX host, and set the Service Console partitions to the recommended sizes during installation.

Configuring Time Synchronization

Time synchronization in ESX/ESXi is an important configuration because the ramifications of incorrect time run deep. While ensuring ESX/ESXi has the correct time seems trivial, time synchronization issues can affect features such as performance charting, SSH key expirations, NFS access, backup jobs, authentication, and more. After the installation of ESX/ESXi Installable or during an unattended installation of ESX using a kickstart script, the host should be configured to perform time synchronization with a reliable time source. This source could be another server on your network or a time source located on the Internet. For the sake of managing time synchronization, it is easiest to synchronize all your servers against one reliable internal time server and then synchronize the internal time server with a reliable Internet time server.

The simplest way to configure time synchronization for ESX/ESXi involves the vSphere Client, and the process is the same for both ESX and ESXi.

Perform the following steps to enable NTP using the vSphere Client:

1. Use the vSphere Client to connect directly to the ESX/ESXi host or to a vCenter Server installation.

2. Select the hostname from the inventory tree on the left, and then click the Configuration tab in the details pane on the right.

3. Select Time Configuration from the Software menu.

4. Click the Properties link.

5. For ESX only, in the Time Configuration dialog box, be sure to select the box labeled NTP Client Enabled. The option to enable the NTP client is grayed out (unavailable) in ESXi.

6. Still in the Time Configuration dialog box, click the Options button.

7. Select the NTP Settings option in the left side of the NTP Daemon (Ntpd) Options dialog box, and add one or more NTP servers to the list, as shown in Figure 2.36.

8. Check the box marked Restart NTP Service To Apply Changes; then click OK.

9. Click OK to return to the vSphere Client. The Time Configuration area will update to show the new NTP servers.

Because the Service Console in ESX also includes a firewall that manages both inbound and outbound connections, you'll note that using the vSphere Client to enable NTP this way also automatically enables NTP traffic through the firewall. You can verify this by clicking Security Profile under the Software menu and seeing that NTP Client is listed under Outgoing Connections.

FIGURE 2.36
Specifying NTP servers allows ESX/ESXi to automatically keep time synchronized.

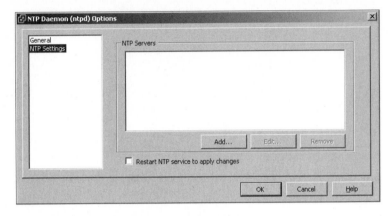

In the event that the Service Console firewall did not get automatically reconfigured, you can manually enable NTP traffic. Perform these steps to manually enable NTP client traffic through the Service Console firewall:

1. Use the vSphere Client to connect directly to the ESX host or to a vCenter Server installation.

2. Select the hostname from the inventory tree on the left, and then click the Configuration tab in the details pane on the right.

3. Select Security Profile from the Software menu.

4. Enable the NTP Client option in the Firewall Properties dialog box, as shown in Figure 2.37.

5. Alternatively, you could enable the NTP client using the following command in the Service Console:

   ```
   esxcfg-firewall -e ntpClient
   ```

   Type the following command to apply the changes made to the Service Console firewall:

   ```
   service mgmt-vmware restart
   ```

In ESX, it's also possible to configure NTP from the command line in the Service Console, but this method is more error-prone than using the vSphere Client. There is no equivalent way to configure time with ESXi; you must use the vSphere Client.

Perform the following steps to configure the ntp.conf and step-tickers files for NTP time synchronization on an ESX host:

1. Log in to a console or SSH session with root privileges. Because root access via SSH is normally denied, it may be best to use a remote console functionality like HP iLO or the equivalent. If using SSH, log in with a standard user account, and use the su – command to elevate to the root user privileges and environment.

2. Create a copy of the ntp.conf file by typing the following command:

   ```
   cp /etc/ntp.conf /etc/old.ntpconf
   ```

FIGURE 2.37
You can enable the
NTP Client through
the security profile of
a VMware ESX host.

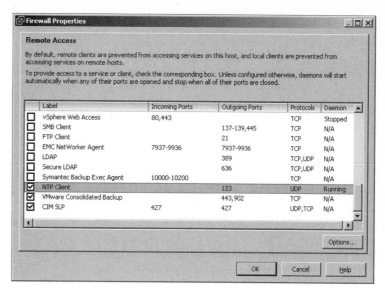

3. Type the following command to use the nano editor to open the ntp.conf file:

   `nano -w /etc/ntp.conf`

4. Replace the following line:

   `restrict default ignore`

   with this line:

   `restrict default kod nomodify notrap noquery nopeer`

5. Uncomment the following line:

   `#restrict mytrustedtimeserverip mask 255.255.255.255 nomodify notrap noquery`

   Edit the line to include the IP address of the new time server. For example, if the time server's IP address is 172.30.0.111, the line would read as follows:

   `restrict 172.30.0.111 mask 255.255.255.255 nomodify notrap noquery`

6. Uncomment the following line:

   `#server mytrustedtimeserverip`

   Edit the line to include the IP address of the new time server. For example, if the time server's IP address is 172.30.0.111, the line would read as follows:

   `server 172.30.0.111`

   Save the file by pressing Ctrl+X. Click Y to accept.

7. Create a backup of the step-tickers file by typing the following command:

   `cp /etc/ntp/step-tickers /etc/ntp/backup.step-tickers`

8. Type the following command to open the step-tickers file:

   `nano -w /etc/ntp/step-tickers`

9. Type the IP address of the new time server. For example, if the time server's IP address is 172.30.0.111, the single entry in the step-tickers would read as follows:

   172.30.0.111

10. Save the file by pressing Ctrl+X. Click Y to accept.

WINDOWS AS A RELIABLE TIME SERVER

You can configure an existing Windows Server as a reliable time server by performing these steps:

1. Use the Group Policy Object editor to navigate to Administrative Templates ➤ System ➤ Windows Time Service ➤ Time Providers.

2. Enable the Enable Windows NTP Server Group Policy option.

3. Navigate to Administrative Templates ➤ System ➤ Windows Time Service.

4. Double-click the Global Configuration Settings option, and select the Enabled radio button.

5. Set the AnnounceFlags option to 4.

6. Click the OK button.

The Bottom Line

Understand the differences among VMware ESX, VMware ESXi Installable, and VMware ESXi Embedded.   Although ESX, ESXi Installable, and ESXi Embedded share the same core hypervisor technology, there are significant differences among the products that may lead organizations to choose one over the other. ESX uses a Linux-based Service Console, for example, while ESXi does not have a Service Console and therefore doesn't have a command-line interface.

Master It   You're evaluating ESX and ESXi as part of a vSphere deployment within your company. What are some of the factors that might lead you to choose ESX over ESXi, or vice versa?

Understand VMware ESX/ESXi compatibility requirements.   Unlike traditional operating systems like Windows or Linux, both ESX and ESXi have much stricter hardware compatibility requirements. This helps ensure a stable, well-tested product line that is able to support even the most mission-critical applications.

Master It   You'd like to run ESXi Embedded, but your hardware vendor doesn't have a model that includes ESXi Embedded. Should you go ahead and buy the servers anyway, even though the hardware vendor doesn't have a model with ESXi Embedded?

Plan a VMware ESX/ESXi deployment.   Deploying ESX or ESXi will affect many different areas of your organization—not only the server team but also the networking team, the storage team, and the security team. There are many decisions that must be considered, including server hardware, storage hardware, storage protocols or connection types, network topology, and network connections. Failing to plan properly could result in an unstable and unsupported implementation.

Master It   Name three areas of networking that must be considered in a vSphere design.

Install VMware ESX and VMware ESXi Installable.   ESX and ESXi Installable can be installed onto any supported and compatible hardware platform. Because of the architectural differences between ESX and ESXi, the installation routines are quite different.

>   **Master It**   Your manager asks you to provide him with a copy of the unattended installation script that you will be using when you roll out ESXi Installable. Is this something you can give him?

Perform post-installation configuration of VMware ESX and VMware ESXi.   Following the installation of ESX/ESXi, there may be some additional configuration steps that are required. If the wrong NIC is assigned to the Service Console/management network, then the server won't be accessible across the network.

>   **Master It**   You've installed ESX on your server, but the Web Access page is inaccessible, and the server doesn't respond to ping. What could be the problem?

Install the vSphere Client.   ESX, ESXi Installable, and ESXi Embedded are all managed using the vSphere Client, a Windows-only application that provides the functionality to manage the virtualization platform. The easiest way to install the vSphere Client is to download it directly from the Web Access page on one of the installed ESX/ESXi hosts.

>   **Master It**   List three ways by which you can install the vSphere Client.

Chapter 3

Installing and Configuring vCenter Server

In the majority of today's information systems, the client-server architecture is king. This emphasis is because the client-server architecture has the ability to centralize management of resources and to provide end users and client systems with access to those resources in a simplified manner. Imagine, or recall if you can, the days when information systems existed in a flat, peer-to-peer model ... when user accounts were required on every system where resource access was needed and when significant administrative overhead was needed simply to make things work. That is how managing a large infrastructure with many ESX/ESXi hosts feels without vCenter Server. vCenter Server brings the advantages of the client-server architecture to the ESX/ESXi host and to virtual machine management.

In this chapter, you will learn to:

◆ Understand the features and role of vCenter Server

◆ Plan a vCenter Server deployment

◆ Install and configure a vCenter Server database

◆ Install and configure vCenter Server

◆ Use vCenter Server's management features

Introducing vCenter Server

As the size of a virtual infrastructure grows, the ability to manage the infrastructure from a central location becomes significantly more important. vCenter Server is a Windows-based application that serves as a centralized management tool for ESX/ESXi hosts and their respective virtual machines. vCenter Server acts as a proxy that performs tasks on the individual ESX/ESXi hosts that have been added as members of a vCenter Server installation. Although vCenter Server is licensed and sold as an "optional" component in the vSphere product suite, it is required in order to leverage some features of the vSphere product line, and I strongly recommend including it in your environment.

Specifically, vCenter Server offers core services in the following areas:

◆ Resource management for ESX/ESXi hosts and virtual machines

◆ Template management

◆ Virtual machine deployment

◆ Virtual machine management

◆ Scheduled tasks

◆ Statistics and logging

◆ Alarms and event management

◆ ESX/ESXi host management

Figure 3.1 outlines the core services available through vCenter Server.

FIGURE 3.1
vCenter Server is
a Windows-based
application that
provides a full spectrum
of virtualization
management functions.

Most of these core services are discussed in later chapters. For example, Chapter 7, "Creat-ing and Managing Virtual Machines," discusses virtual machine deployment, virtual machine management, and template management. Chapter 10, "Managing Resource Allocation," deals with resource management for ESX/ESXi hosts and virtual machines, and Chapter 12, "Moni-toring VMware vSphere Performance," discusses alarms. In this chapter, I'll focus primarily on ESX/ESXi host management, but I'll also discuss scheduled tasks, statistics and logging, and event management.

There are two other key items about vCenter Server that you can't really consider core services. Instead, these underlying features support the core services provided by vCenter Server. In order to more fully understand the value of vCenter Server in a vSphere deployment, you need to take a closer look at the centralized user authentication and extensible framework that vCenter Server provides.

Centralizing User Authentication

Centralized user authentication is not listed as a core service of vCenter Server, but it is essential to how vCenter Server operates, and it is essential to the reduction of management overhead that vCenter Server brings to a VMware vSphere implementation. In Chapter 2, I discussed a user's authentication to an ESX/ESXi host under the context of a user account created and stored locally on that host. Without vCenter Server, you would need a separate user account on each ESX/ESXi host for each administrator who needed access to the server. As the number of ESX/ESXi hosts and the number of administrators who need access to those hosts grows, the number of accounts to manage grows exponentially.

In a virtualized infrastructure with only one or two ESX/ESXi hosts, administrative effort is not a major concern. Administration of one or two servers would not incur incredible effort on the part of the administrator, and the creation of user accounts for administrators would not be too much of a burden.

In situations like this, vCenter Server might not be missed from a management perspective, but it will certainly be missed from a feature set viewpoint. In addition to its management capabilities, vCenter Server provides the ability to perform VMware VMotion, configure VMware Distributed Resource Scheduler (DRS), establish VMware High Availability (HA), and use VMware Fault Tolerance (FT). These features are not accessible using ESX/ESXi hosts without vCenter Server. Without vCenter Server, you also lose key functionality like vNetwork Distributed Switches, host profiles, and vCenter Update Manager. I consider vCenter Server a requirement for any enterprise-level virtualization project.

VCENTER SERVER REQUIREMENT

Strictly speaking, vCenter Server is not a requirement for a vSphere deployment. However, to utilize the advanced features of the vSphere product suite—features such as Update Manager, VMotion, VMware DRS, VMware HA, vNetwork Distributed Switches, host profiles, or VMware FT—vCenter Server must be licensed, installed, and configured accordingly.

But what happens when the environment grows? What happens when there are 10 ESX/ESXi hosts and five administrators? Now, the administrative effort of maintaining all these local accounts on the ESX/ESXi hosts becomes a significant burden. If a new account is needed to manage the ESX/ESXi hosts, you must create the account on 10 different hosts. If the password to an account needs to change, you must change the password on 10 different hosts.

vCenter Server addresses this problem. vCenter Server installs on a Windows Server–based operating system and uses standard Windows user accounts and groups for authentication. These users and groups can reside in the local security accounts manager (SAM) database for that specific Windows-based server, or the users and groups can belong to the Active Directory domain to which the vCenter Server computer belongs. With vCenter Server in place, you can use the vSphere Client to connect to vCenter Server using a Windows-based account or to connect to an ESX/ESXi host using a local account.

Although the vSphere Client supports authenticating to both vCenter Server and ESX/ESXi hosts, organizations should use a consistent method for provisioning user accounts to manage their vSphere infrastructure because local user accounts created on an ESX/ESXi host are not reconciled or synchronized with the Windows or Active Directory accounts that vCenter Server uses.

For example, if a user account named Shane is created locally on an ESX/ESXi host named esx05.vmwarelab.net and the user account is granted the permissions necessary to manage the host, Shane will not be able to utilize the vSphere Client connected to vCenter Server to perform his management capabilities. The inverse is also true. If a Windows user account named Elaine is granted permissions through vCenter Server to manage an ESX/ESXi host named esx04.vmwarelab.net, then Elaine will not be able to manage the host by using the vSphere Client to connect directly to that ESX/ESXi host.

VSPHERE CLIENT

Logging on to an ESX/ESXi host using the vSphere Client requires the use of an account created and stored locally on that host. Using the same vSphere Client to connect to vCenter Server requires the use of a Windows user account. Keep in mind that vCenter Server and ESX/ESXi hosts do not make any attempt to reconcile the user accounts in their respective account databases.

Using the vSphere Client to connect directly to an ESX/ESXi host that is currently being managed by vCenter Server can cause negative effects in vCenter Server. A successful logon to a managed host results in a pop-up box that warns you of this potential problem.

Providing an Extensible Framework

Like centralized authentication, I don't include vCenter Server's extensible framework as a core service. Rather, this extensible framework provides the foundation for vCenter Server's core services and enables third-party developers to create applications built around vCenter Server. Figure 3.2 shows some of the components that revolve around the core services of vCenter Server.

FIGURE 3.2
Other applications can extend vCenter Server's core services to provide additional management functionality.

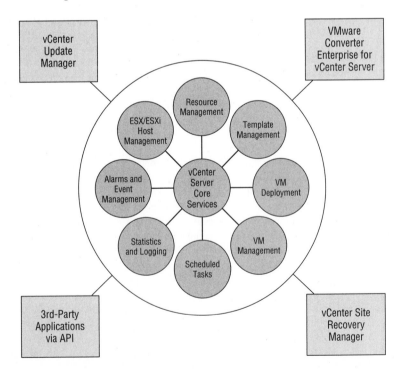

A key aspect for the success of virtualization is the ability to allow third-party companies to provide additional products that add value, ease, and functionality to existing products. By building vCenter Server in an extensible fashion and providing an application programming interface (API) to vCenter Server, VMware has shown its interest in allowing third-party software developers to play an integral part in virtualization. The vCenter Server API allows companies to develop custom applications that can take advantage of the virtual infrastructure created in vCenter Server. For example, Vizioncore's vRanger Pro is a simplified backup utility that works off the exact inventory created inside vCenter Server to allow for advanced backup options of virtual machines. Other third-party applications use the vCenter Server APIs to provide management, monitoring, lifecycle management, or automation functionality.

Some of the functionality vCenter Server provides is covered in other chapters where it makes more sense. For example, Chapter 7 provides a detailed look at templates along with virtual machine deployment and management, and Chapter 9, "Configuring and Managing VMware vSphere Access Controls," goes deeper into vCenter Server's access controls. Chapter 10 discusses resource management, while Chapter 12 offers an in-depth look at ESX/ESXi host and virtual machine monitoring as well as alarms.

You're almost ready to take a closer look at installing, configuring, and managing vCenter Server. First, however, I'll discuss some of the planning and design considerations that have to be addressed before you actually install vCenter Server.

Planning and Designing a vCenter Server Deployment

vCenter Server is a critical application for managing your virtual infrastructure. Its implementation should be carefully designed and executed to ensure availability and data protection. When discussing the deployment of vCenter Server, some of the most common questions include the following:

◆ How much hardware do I need to power vCenter Server?

◆ Which database server should I use with vCenter Server?

◆ How do I prepare vCenter Server for disaster recovery?

◆ Should I run vCenter Server in a virtual machine?

A lot of the answers to these questions are dependent upon each other. Still, I have to start somewhere, so I'll start with the first topic: figuring out how much hardware you need for vCenter Server.

Sizing Hardware for vCenter Server

The amount of hardware required by vCenter Server is directly related to the number of hosts and virtual machines it will be managing. As a starting point, the vCenter Server minimum hardware requirements are as follows:

◆ 2GHz processor or faster

◆ 2GB of RAM or more

◆ 1GB of free disk space (2GB recommended)

◆ A network adapter (Gigabit Ethernet strongly recommended)

◆ Windows Server 2003 Service Pack 1 or Service Pack 2 (x86 or x64), Windows Server 2003 R2 with or without Service Pack 2 (x86 or x64), or Windows Server 2008 (x86 or x64)

LOCAL DISKS ON VCENTER SERVER

Disk storage allocation is of minimal concern when planning a vCenter Server installation because the data is stored in an SQL Server or Oracle database on a remote server.

Keep in mind these are *minimum* system requirements. Large enterprise environments with many ESX/ESXi hosts and virtual machines must scale the vCenter Server system accordingly. In addition, these requirements do not account for running a database server, which vCenter Server requires. Although vCenter Server is the application that performs the management of your ESX/ESXi hosts and virtual machines, vCenter Server uses a separate database for storing all of its configuration, permissions, statistics, and other data. Figure 3.3 shows the relationship between vCenter Server and the separate database server.

FIGURE 3.3
vCenter Server acts as a proxy for managing ESX/ESXi hosts, but all of the data for vCenter Server is stored in an external database.

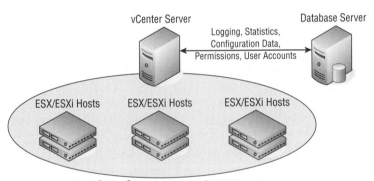

When answering the question of how much hardware vCenter Server requires, you have to address not only the computer running vCenter Server but also the computer running the database server. Although you can run vCenter Server and the database server on the same machine, it's not recommended because it creates a single point of failure for two key aspects of your virtual infrastructure.

Throughout this chapter, I'll use the term *separate database server* to refer to a database server application that is separately installed and managed. Although it might reside on the same computer, it is still considered a separate database server because it is managed independently of vCenter Server. You'll also see the term *back-end database*, which refers to the actual database that vCenter Server uses on the separate database server.

Without considering the separate database server, VMware suggests a system configured with two CPU cores and 3GB of RAM to support up to 100 ESX/ESXi hosts and 2,000 virtual machines. An environment of that size is much larger than a typical environment might be, so it's feasible to simply scale the specifications back to meet your needs. For example, a server with two CPU cores and 2GB of RAM should suffice for up to 50 ESX/ESXi hosts and 1,000 virtual machines. Though it helps to have a good starting point for the deployment of vCenter Server, you can always alter the specifications to achieve adequate performance levels.

CPU CORES

Most modern physical servers ship by default with quad-core CPUs. vCenter Server is able to leverage some of the additional processing power but won't fully utilize all four CPU cores. It's for this reason that our discussion on sizing vCenter Server focuses more on RAM than on CPU capacity.

Should you choose to run the separate database server on the same physical computer as vCenter Server, you'll need to consult the documentation for whatever database server you choose to use. That brings me to the next topic: choosing which database server to use.

Choosing a Database Server for vCenter Server

In light of the sensitive and critical nature of the data in the vCenter Server database, VMware supports vCenter Server issues only with back-end databases on enterprise-level database servers. vCenter Server officially supports the following database servers:

- ◆ Oracle 10*g*
- ◆ Oracle 11*g*
- ◆ Microsoft SQL Server 2005 Express Edition (comes bundled with vCenter Server)
- ◆ Microsoft SQL Server 2005 with Service Pack 2 (x86 or x64)
- ◆ Microsoft SQL Server 2008 (x86 or x64)

IBM DB2 v9.5 is experimentally supported for use with vCenter Server, but not for any other components of VMware vSphere such as vCenter Update Manager or other plug-ins that require database support.

For smaller environments, users have the option of using Microsoft SQL Server 2005 Express Edition. Users should use SQL Server 2005 Express Edition only when their vSphere deployment will be limited in size; otherwise, users should plan on using a separate database server. If you are starting out with a small environment that will work with SQL Server 2005 Express Edition, note that it is possible to upgrade to a more full-featured version of SQL Server at a later date. More information on upgrading SQL Server 2005 Express is available on the Microsoft website (www.microsoft.com).

USING SQL SERVER 2005 EXPRESS EDITION

With the introduction of VirtualCenter 2.5, SQL Server 2005 Express Edition became the minimum database available as a back end to vCenter Server. SQL Server 2005 Express Edition replaced the MSDE option for demo or trial installations.

Microsoft SQL Server 2005 Express Edition, like MSDE, has physical limitations that include the following:

- ◆ One CPU maximum
- ◆ 1GB of maximum of addressable RAM
- ◆ 4GB database maximum

Large virtual enterprises will quickly outgrow these SQL Server 2005 Express Edition limitations. Therefore, you might assume that any virtual infrastructures using SQL Server 2005 Express Edition are smaller deployments with little projections, if any, for growth. VMware suggests using SQL Server 2005 Express Edition only for deployments with 5 or fewer hosts and 50 or fewer virtual machines.

Because the separate database server is independently installed and managed, some additional configuration is required. Later in this chapter, the section "Installing vCenter Server" provides detailed information about working with separate database servers and the specific configuration that is required for each.

So, how does an organization go about choosing which separate database server to use? The selection of which database server to use with vCenter Server is typically a reflection of what an organization already uses or is already licensed to use. Organizations that already have Oracle may decide to continue to use Oracle for vCenter Server; organizations that are predominantly based on Microsoft SQL Server will likely choose to use SQL Server to support vCenter Server. You should choose the database engine with which you are most familiar and that will support both the current and projected size of the virtual infrastructure.

With regard to the hardware requirements for the database server, the underlying database server will largely determine those requirements. VMware provides some general guidelines around Microsoft SQL Server in the white paper "VirtualCenter Database Performance for Microsoft SQL Server 2005," available on VMware's website at www.vmware.com/files/pdf/vc_database_performance.pdf. Although written with VirtualCenter 2.5 in mind, this information applies to vCenter Server 4.0 as well. In a typical configuration with standard logging levels, an SQL Server instance with two CPU cores and 4GB of RAM allocated to the database application should support all but the very largest or most demanding environments.

If you are planning on running the database server and vCenter Server on the same hardware, you should adjust the hardware requirements accordingly.

Appropriately sizing hardware for vCenter Server and the separate database server is good and necessary. Given the central role that vCenter Server plays in a VMware vSphere environment, though, you must also account for availability.

Planning for vCenter Server Availability

Planning for a vCenter Server deployment is more than just accounting for CPU and memory resources. You must also create a plan for business continuity and disaster recovery. Remember, features such as VMware VMotion, VMware Storage VMotion, and VMware DRS—but not VMware HA, as you'll see in Chapter 11, "Ensuring High Availability and Business Continuity"—stop functioning when vCenter Sever is unavailable. While vCenter Server is down, you won't be able to clone virtual machines or deploy new virtual machines from templates. You also lose centralized authentication and role-based administration of the ESX/ESXi hosts. Clearly, there are reasons why you might want vCenter Server to be highly available.

Keep in mind, too, that the heart of the vCenter Server content is stored in a back-end database on Oracle or SQL Server. Any good disaster recovery or business continuity plan must also include instructions on how to handle data loss or corruption in the back-end database, and the separate database server should be designed and deployed in a resilient and highly available fashion. This is especially true in larger environments.

There are a few different ways to approach this concern. First, I'll discuss how to protect vCenter Server, and then I'll talk about protecting the separate database server.

First, VMware vCenter Server Heartbeat—a product that VMware released for VirtualCenter/vCenter Server 2.5 to provide high availability with little or no downtime—will be available with support for vCenter Server 4.0 upon the release of VMware vSphere or shortly thereafter. Using vCenter Server Heartbeat will automate both the process of keeping an active and passive vCenter Server instance synchronized and the process of failing over from one to another (and back again). The VMware website at www.vmware.com/products/vcenter-server-heartbeat has more information on vCenter Server Heartbeat.

If the vCenter Server computer is a physical server, one way to provide availability is to create a standby vCenter Server system that you can turn on in the event of a failure of the online vCenter Server computer. After failure, you bring the standby server online and attach it to the existing SQL Server database, and then the hosts can be added to the new vCenter Server computer. In this approach, you'll need to find mechanisms to keep the primary and secondary/standby vCenter Server systems synchronized with regard to file system content and configuration settings.

A variation on that approach is to keep the standby vCenter Server system as a virtual machine. You can use physical-to-virtual (P2V) conversion tools to regularly "back up" the physical vCenter Server instance to a standby VM. This method reduces the amount of physical hardware required and leverages the P2V process as a way of keeping the two vCenter Servers synchronized.

As a last resort for recovering vCenter Server, it's possible to just reinstall the software, point to the existing database, and connect the host systems. The installation of vCenter Server is not a time-consuming process. Ultimately, the most important part of the vCenter Server recovery plan is to ensure that the database server is redundant and protected.

For high availability of the database server supporting vCenter Server, you can configure the back-end database on an SQL Server cluster. Figure 3.4 illustrates using an SQL Server cluster for the back-end database. This figure also shows a standby vCenter Server system. Methods used to provide high availability for the database server are in addition to whatever steps you might take to protect vCenter Server itself. Other options might include using SQL log shipping to create a database replica on a separate system. If using clustering or log shipping/database replication is not available or is not within fiscal reach, you should strengthen your database backup strategy to support easy recovery in the event of data loss or corruption. Using the native SQL Server tools, you can create a backup strategy that combines full, differential, and transaction log backups. This strategy allows you to restore data up to the minute when loss or corruption occurred.

The suggestion of using a virtual machine as a standby system for a physical computer running vCenter Server naturally brings me to the last topic: should you run vCenter Server in a virtual machine? That's quite a question, and it's one that I'll answer next.

VIRTUALIZING VCENTER SERVER

Another option for vCenter Server is to install it into a virtual machine. Though you might hesitate to do so, there are really some great advantages to doing this. The most common concern is the misconception that losing the vCenter Server computer causes a domino effect resulting in losing the functionality of VMware HA. The truth, however, is that HA is an advantage to virtualizing the vCenter Server machine because VMware HA continues to function even if vCenter Server is unavailable. In addition to taking advantage of the HA feature, vCenter Server installed as a virtual machine offers increased portability, snapshot functionality, and cloning functionality (though not in the traditional sense).

Although there are advantages to installing vCenter Server in a virtual machine, you should also understand the disadvantages. Features such as cold migration, cloning, and editing hardware are not available for the virtual machine running vCenter Server.

FIGURE 3.4
A good disaster recovery plan for vCenter Server should include a quick means of regaining the user interface as well as ensuring the data is highly available and protected against damage.

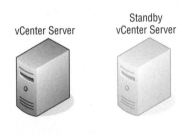
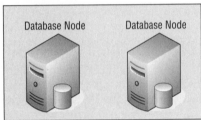

Running vCenter Server in a VM

Instead of running a standby clone of vCenter Server as a virtual machine, you also have the option of skipping a physical server entirely and running vCenter Server as a virtual machine from the beginning. This gives you several advantages, including snapshots, VMotion, and VMware HA.

Snapshots are a feature I'll discuss in greater detail in Chapter 7. At a high level, snapshot functionality gives you the ability to return to a specific point in time for your virtual machine, in this case, your vCenter Server virtual machine, specifically. VMotion gives you the portability required to move the server from host to host without experiencing server downtime. VMware HA restarts the vCenter Server automatically if the physical host on which it is running fails. But what happens when a snapshot is corrupted or the virtual machine is damaged to the point it will not run? With vCenter Server as your virtual machine, you can make regular copies of the virtual disk file and keep a "clone" of the server ready to go in the event of server failure. The clone will have the same system configuration used the last time the virtual disks were copied. Given that the bulk of the data processing by vCenter Server ends up in a back-end database running on a different server, this should not be very different. Figure 3.5 illustrates the setup of a manual cloning of a vCenter Server virtual machine.

By now, you have a good understanding of the importance of vCenter Server in a large enterprise environment and some of the considerations that go into planning for a vCenter Server deployment. You also have a good idea of the features, functions, and role of vCenter Server. With this information in mind, let's install vCenter Server.

FIGURE 3.5

If vCenter Server is a virtual machine, its virtual disk file can be copied regularly and used as the hard drive for a new virtual machine, effectively providing a point-in-time restore in the event of complete server failure or loss.

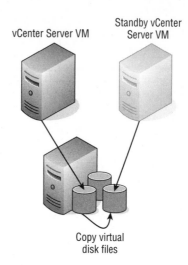

vCenter Server VM

Standby vCenter Server VM

Copy virtual disk files

Installing vCenter Server

Depending upon the size of the environment to be managed, installing vCenter Server can be simple. In small environments, the vCenter Server installer can install and configure all the necessary components. For larger environments, installing vCenter Server in a scalable and resilient fashion is a bit more involved and requires a few different steps. For example, supporting more than 200 ESX/ESXi hosts or more than 3,000 virtual machines requires installing multiple vCenter Server instances in a Linked Mode group, a scenario that I'll discuss later in this chapter. Additionally, you know that the majority of vCenter Server deployments need a separate database server installed and configured to support vCenter Server. The exception would be the very small deployments in which SQL Server 2005 Express Edition is sufficient.

VCENTER SERVER PRE-INSTALLATION TASKS

Before you install vCenter Server, you should ensure that the computer has been updated with the latest updates from the Microsoft Windows Update site. This will ensure updates like Windows Installer 3.1 and all required .NET components are installed.

Depending upon the database engine you will use, different configuration steps are required to prepare the database server for vCenter Server, and these steps must be completed before you can actually install vCenter Server. If you are planning on using SQL Server 2005 Express Edition—and you're aware of the limitations of using SQL Server 2005 Express Edition, as described earlier in the sidebar "Using SQL Server 2005 Express Edition"—you can skip ahead to the section "Running the vCenter Server Installer." Otherwise, let's take a closer look at working with a separate database server and what is required.

Configuring the vCenter Server Back-End Database Server

As noted earlier, vCenter Server stores the majority of its information in a back-end database, usually using a separate database server. It's important to realize that the back-end database is a key component to this infrastructure. The back-end database server should be designed and deployed accordingly. Without the back-end database, you will find yourself rebuilding an entire infrastructure.

VCENTER SERVER BUSINESS CONTINUITY

Losing the server that runs vCenter Server might result in a small period of downtime; however, losing the back-end database to vCenter Server could result in days of downtime and extended periods of rebuilding.

On the back-end database server, vCenter Server requires specific permissions on its database. After that database is created and configured appropriately, connecting vCenter Server to its back-end database requires that an Open Database Connectivity (ODBC) data source name (DSN) be created on the vCenter Server system. The ODBC DSN should be created under the context of a database user who has full rights and permissions to the database that has been created specifically for storing vCenter Server data.

In the following sections, we'll take a closer look at working with the two most popular database servers used in conjunction with vCenter Server: Oracle and Microsoft SQL Server. Although other database servers are experimentally supported for use with vCenter Server, Oracle and SQL Server are officially supported and account for the vast majority of all installations.

USING A 32-BIT DATA SOURCE NAME ON 64-BIT SYSTEMS

Even though vCenter Server is supported on 64-bit Windows Server operating systems, you will need to create a 32-bit DSN for vCenter Server's use. Use the 32-bit ODBC Administrator application to create this 32-bit DSN.

WORKING WITH ORACLE DATABASES

Perhaps because Microsoft SQL Server was designed as a Windows-based application, like vCenter Server, working with Oracle as the back-end database server involves a bit more effort than using Microsoft SQL Server.

To use Oracle 10g or 11g, you need to install Oracle and create a database for vCenter Server to use. Although it is supported to run Oracle on the same computer as vCenter Server, it is not a configuration I recommend. Still, in the event you have valid business reasons for doing so, I'll walk through the steps for configuring Oracle to support vCenter Server both locally (on the same computer as vCenter Server) and remotely (on a different computer than vCenter Server). Both of these sets of instructions assume that you have already created the database you are going to use.

SPECIAL PATCHES NEEDED FOR ORACLE 10G RELEASE 2

First, you must apply patch 10.2.0.3.0 to both the client and the Oracle database server. Then apply patch 5699495 to the client.

Perform the following steps to prepare Oracle for vCenter Server if your Oracle database resides on the same computer as vCenter Server:

1. Log on with SQL*Plus to the database with the database owner account (the default is sys), and run the following query:

```
CREATE TABLESPACE "VC" DATAFILE `C:\Oracle\ORADATA\VC\VC.DAT'
SIZE 1000M AUTOEXTEND ON NEXT 500K;
```

2. Now you need to assign a user permission to this newly created tablespace. While you are still connected to SQL*Plus, run the following query:

```
CREATE USER "vpxadmin" PROFILE "DEFAULT" IDENTIFIED BY "vcdbpassword"
DEFAULT TABLESPACE
"VC" ACCOUNT UNLOCK;
grant connect to VPXADMIN;
grant resource to VPXADMIN;
grant create view to VPXADMIN;
grant create sequence to VPXADMIN;
grant create table to VPXADMIN;
grant execute on dbms_lock to VPXADMIN;
grant execute on dbms_job to VPXADMIN;
grant unlimited tablespace to VPXADMIN;
```

3. Install the Oracle client and the ODBC driver.

4. Create the ODBC DSN.

5. Modify the TNSNAMES.ORA file to reflect where your Oracle database is located:

```
VC=
(DESCRIPTION=
(ADDRESS_LIST=
(ADDRESS=(PROTOCOL=TCP)(HOST=localhost)(PORT=1521))
)
(CONNECT_DATA=
(SERVICE_NAME=VC)
)
)
HOST=
```

6. After you complete the vCenter Server installation, copy the Oracle JDBC driver (ojdbc13.jar) to the tomcat\lib folder under the VMware vCenter Server installation folder.

For larger enterprise networks where the Oracle 10g or 11g database server is a separate computer, you need to perform the following tasks on the computer running vCenter Server:

1. Log on with SQL*Plus to the database with the database owner account (the default is sys), and run the following query:

```
CREATE SMALLFILE TABLESPACE "VC" DATAFILE `/PATH/TO/ORADATA/VC/VC.DAT'
SIZE 1G AUTOEXTEND ON NEXT 10M MAXSIZE UNLIMITED LOGGING EXTENT
```

```
MANAGEMENT LOCAL SEGMENT
SPACE MANAGEMENT AUTO;
```

2. While you are still connected to SQL*Plus, run the following query to assign a user permission to this tablespace:

```
CREATE USER "vpxadmin" PROFILE "DEFAULT" IDENTIFIED BY "vcdbpassword"
DEFAULT TABLESPACE
"VC" ACCOUNT UNLOCK;
grant connect to VPXADMIN;
grant resource to VPXADMIN;
grant create view to VPXADMIN;
grant create sequence to VPXADMIN;
grant create table to VPXADMIN;
grant execute on dbms_lock to VPXADMIN;
grant execute on dbms_job to VPXADMIN;
grant unlimited tablespace to VPXADMIN;
```

3. Install the Oracle client and the ODBC driver.

4. Create the ODBC DSN.

5. Modify your TNSNAMES.ORA file as follows:

```
VC=
(DESCRIPTION=
(ADDRESS_LIST=
(ADDRESS=(PROTOCOL=TCP)(HOST=oracle.vmwarelab.net)(PORT=1521))
)
(CONNECT_DATA=
(SERVICE_NAME=VC)
)
)
HOST=
```

6. After you complete the vCenter Server installation, copy the Oracle JDBC driver (ojdbc13.jar) to the tomcat\lib folder under the VMware vCenter Server installation folder.

After the Oracle database is created and configured appropriately and the ODBC DSN is established, then you're ready to install vCenter Server.

VCENTER SERVER AND ORACLE

You can find all the downloadable files required to make vCenter Server work with Oracle on Oracle's website at www.oracle.com/technology/software/index.html.

WORKING WITH MICROSOFT SQL SERVER DATABASES

In light of the existing widespread deployment of Microsoft SQL Server 2005 and Microsoft SQL Server 2008, it is most common to find SQL Server as the back-end database for vCenter Server.

This is not to say that Oracle does not perform as well or that there is any downside to using Oracle. Microsoft SQL Server just happens to be implemented more commonly than Oracle and therefore is a more common database server for vCenter Server.

Connecting vCenter Server to a Microsoft SQL Server database, like the Oracle implementation, requires a few specific configuration tasks, as follows:

◆ Unlike previous versions of VirtualCenter/vCenter Server, version 4.0 of vCenter Server does not require the SQL Server instance to be configured for Mixed Mode authentication. Instead, vCenter Server 4.0 supports both Windows and Mixed Mode authentication. Be aware of which authentication type the SQL Server is using, because this setting will affect other portions of the vCenter Server installation.

◆ You must create a new database for vCenter Server. Each vCenter Server computer— remember that there may be multiple instances of vCenter Server running in a Linked Mode group—will require its own SQL database.

◆ You must create a SQL login that has full access to the database you created for vCenter Server. If the SQL Server is using Windows authentication, this login must be linked to a domain user account; for Mixed Mode authentication, the associated domain user account is not required.

◆ You must set the appropriate permissions for this SQL login by mapping the SQL login to the dbo user on the database created for vCenter Server. In SQL Server 2005, you do this by right-clicking the SQL login, selecting Properties, and then going to User Mapping.

◆ The SQL login must not only have dbo (db_owner) privileges on the database created for vCenter Server, but the SQL login must also be set as the owner of the database. Figure 3.6 shows a new SQL database being created with the owner set to the vCenter Server SQL login.

◆ Finally, the SQL login created for use by vCenter Server must also have dbo (db_owner) privileges on the MSDB database, but only for the duration of the installation process. This permission can and should be removed after installation is complete.

If you have an existing SQL Server 2005 database that needs to be used as the back end for vCenter Server, you can use the sp_changedbowner stored procedure command to change the database ownership accordingly. For example, EXEC sp_changedbowner @loginame=`vcdbuser`, @map=`true` would change the database owner to a SQL login named vcdbuser.

You need to take these steps prior to creating the ODBC DSN to the SQL Server database.

SQL SERVER 2005 PERMISSIONS

Not only will most database administrators cringe at the thought of overextending privileges to a SQL Server computer, it is not good practice to do so. As a best and strong security practice, it is best to minimize the permissions of each account that access the SQL Server computer. Therefore, in the case of the vCenter Server installation procedure, you will need to grant a SQL Server user account the db_owner membership on the MSDB database. However, after the installation is complete, this role membership can and should be removed. Normal day-to-day operation of and access to the vCenter Server database does not require this permission. It is a temporary requirement needed for the installation of vCenter Server.

FIGURE 3.6
SQL Server 2005 databases that vCenter Server uses must be owned by the account vCenter Server uses to connect to the database.

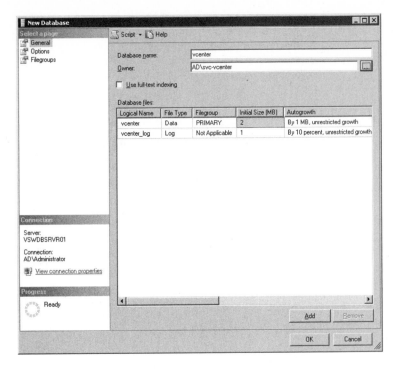

After your database is set up, you can create the ODBC DSN to be used during the vCenter Server installation wizard. SQL Server 2005 and SQL Server 2008 require the use of the SQL Native Client. If you do not find the SQL Native Client option while creating the ODBC DSN, you can download it from Microsoft's website or install it from the SQL Server installation media.

After the SQL Native Client has been installed—if it wasn't installed already—then you are ready to create the ODBC DSN that vCenter Server uses to connect to the SQL Server instance hosting its database. This ODBC DSN must be created on the computer where vCenter Server will be installed.

Perform the following steps to create an ODBC DSN to a SQL Server 2005 database:

1. Log into the computer where vCenter Server will be installed later. You need to log in with an account that has administrative permissions on that computer.

2. Open the Data Sources (ODBC) applet from the Administrative Tools menu.

3. Select the System DSN tab.

4. Click the Add button.

5. Select the SQL Native Client from the list of available drivers, and click the Finish button. If the SQL Native Client is not in the list, it can be downloaded from Microsoft's website or installed from the SQL Server installation media. Go back and install the SQL Native Client.

6. The Create New Data Source To SQL Server dialog box opens. In the Name text box, type the name you want to use to reference the ODBC DSN. Make note of this name—this is the name you will give to vCenter Server during installation to establish the database connection.

7. In the Server drop-down list, select the SQL Server 2005 computer where the database was created, or type the name of the computer running SQL Server 2005 that has already been prepared for vCenter Server.

8. Click the Next button.

9. Choose the correct authentication type, depending upon the configuration of the SQL Server instance. If you are using SQL Server authentication, you also need to supply the SQL login and password created earlier for use by vCenter Server. Click Next.

10. If the default database is listed as Master, select the Change The Default Database To check box, and then select the name of the vCenter Server database as the default. Click Next.

11. None of the options on the next screen—including the options for changing the language of the SQL Server system messages, regional settings, and logging options—need to be changed. Click Finish to continue.

12. On the summary screen, click the Test Data Source button to test to the ODBC DSN. If the tests do not complete successfully, double-check the SQL Server and SQL database configuration outlined previously.

13. Click OK to return to the ODBC Data Source Administrator, which will now have the new System DSN you just created listed.

At this point, you are now ready to actually install vCenter Server.

Running the vCenter Server Installer

With the database in place and configured, you can now install vCenter Server. After you've done that, you can add servers and continue configuring your virtual infrastructure, including adding vCenter Server instances in a Linked Mode group.

USE THE LATEST VERSION OF VCENTER SERVER

Remember that the latest version of vCenter Server is available for download from www.vmware.com/download. It is often best to install the latest version of the software to ensure the highest levels of compatibility, security, and simplicity.

The vCenter Server installation takes only a few minutes and is not administratively intensive, assuming you've completed all of the pre-installation tasks. You can start the vCenter Server installation by double-clicking autorun.exe inside the vCenter Server installation directory.

The VMware vCenter Installer, shown in Figure 3.7, is the central point for a number of installations:

◆ vCenter Server

◆ vCenter Guided Consolidation Service

◆ vSphere Client

◆ vCenter Update Manager

◆ vCenter Converter

FIGURE 3.7
The VMware vCenter Installer offers options for installing several different components.

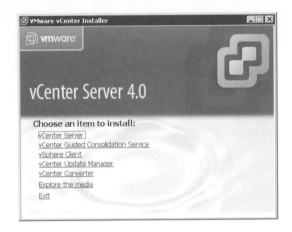

Some of these installation types are new features of vCenter Server. Chapter 4, "Installing and Configuring vCenter Update Manager," provides more detail on vCenter Update Manager. Chapter 8, "Migrating and Importing Virtual Machines," provides more detail on vCenter Guided Consolidation and vCenter Converter. You've already installed the vSphere Client in Chapter 2. For now, I'll focus just on vCenter Server.

If you will be using Windows authentication with a separate SQL Server database server, there's an important step here before you go any farther. For the vCenter Server services to be able to connect to the SQL database, these services need to run in the context of the domain user account that was granted permission to the database. Unfortunately, the vCenter Server installer doesn't let you choose which account you'd like to have the vCenter Server services run as; it just uses whatever account the user is currently logged in as. So, in order to have the vCenter Server services run in the context of the correct user account, you need to log in as the domain user account that has been granted permissions to the SQL database. For example, if you created a domain user account called *vcenter* and granted that account permissions to the SQL database as outlined previously, you need to log on as that user to the computer that will run vCenter Server. You will probably find it necessary to grant this domain user account administrative permissions on that computer because administrative permissions are required for installation.

VCENTER ORCHESTRATOR ICONS WILL BE MISSING

The vCenter Server installation wizard will create icons for vCenter Orchestrator, a workflow engine installed with vCenter Server. However, these icons are placed on the Start Menu for the currently logged-on user, not for all users. If you log on as a specific account because you are using Windows authentication with a separate SQL Server database server, the vCenter Orchestrator icons will only appear on the Start Menu for that specific user.

If you are using SQL authentication, then the user account used to install vCenter Server doesn't matter.

I'll assume that you will use integrated Windows authentication. After you've logged on as the correct user to the computer that will run vCenter Server, then start the vCenter Server installation process by clicking the link for vCenter Server in the VMware vCenter Installer, shown previously in Figure 3.13. After you select a language for the installation, you arrive at the installation wizard for vCenter Server.

Perform the following steps to install vCenter Server:

1. Click Next to begin the installation wizard.

2. Click I Agree To The Terms In The License Agreement, and click Next.

3. Supply a username, organization name, and license key. If you don't have a license key yet, you can continue installing vCenter Server in evaluation mode.

4. At this point you must select whether to use SQL Server 2005 Express Edition or a separate database server. If the environment will be small (a single vCenter Server with fewer than 5 hosts or less than 50 virtual machines), then using SQL Server 2005 Express is acceptable. For all other deployments, select Use An Existing Supported Database, and select your ODBC DSN from the drop-down list.

   For the rest of this procedure, I'll assume that you are using an existing supported database. Select the correct ODBC DSN, and click Next.

ODBC TO DB

An ODBC DSN must be defined, and the name must match in order to move past the database configuration page of the installation wizard. Remember to set the appropriate authentication strategy and user permissions for an existing database server. If you receive an error at this point in the installation, revisit the database configuration steps. Remember to set the appropriate database ownership and database roles.

5. If you are using SQL authentication, then the next screen prompts for the SQL login and password that has permissions to the SQL database created for vCenter Server. Login information is not required if you are using Windows authentication, so you can just leave these fields blank.

   If the SQL Server Agent service is not running on the SQL Server computer, you receive an error at this step and won't be able to proceed. Make sure the SQL Server Agent service is running.

6. Unless you have specifically configured the database server differently than the default settings, a dialog box pops up warning you about the Full recovery model and the possibility that transaction logs may grow to consume all available disk space.

IMPLICATIONS OF THE SIMPLE RECOVERY MODEL

If your SQL Server database is configured for the Full recovery model, the installer suggests reconfiguring the vCenter Server database into the Simple recovery model. What the warning does not tell you is that doing this means that you will lose the ability to back up transaction logs for the vCenter Server database. If you leave the database set to Full recovery, be sure to work with the database administrator to routinely back up and truncate the transaction logs. By having transaction log backups from a database in Full recovery, you have the option to restore to an exact point in time should any type of data corruption occur. If you alter the recovery model as suggested, be sure you are taking consistent full backups of the database, but understand that you will be able to recover only to the point of the last full backup because transaction logs will be unavailable.

7. The next screen prompts for account information for the vCenter Server services.

    If you are using Windows authentication with a SQL database, then you should already be logged in as the correct user, and that username should populate in the username field. The "correct user" in this context is the domain user account granted permissions on the SQL database. If you are using SQL authentication, then the account information is not as important, although if you want to run the vCenter Server services under an account other than the SYSTEM account, you need to run the installer while logged in as that account. This was described previously.

8. Select the directory where you want vCenter Server to be installed, and click Next.

9. If this is the first vCenter Server installation in your environment, then select Create A Standalone VMware vCenter Server Instance. Click Next.

    I'll cover the other option later in this chapter when I discuss installing into a Linked Mode group.

VCENTER SERVER AND IIS

Despite that vCenter Server is accessible via a web browser, it is not necessary to install Internet Information Services on the vCenter Server computer. vCenter Server access via a browser relies on the Apache Tomcat web service that is installed as part of the vCenter Server installation. IIS should be uninstalled because it can cause conflicts with Apache Tomcat.

---

10. The next screen provides the option for changing the default TCP and UDP ports on which vCenter Server operates. Unless you have specific reason to change them, I recommend accepting the defaults. The ports listed on this screen include the following:

    ◆ TCP ports 80 and 443 (HTTP and HTTPS)

    ◆ UDP port 902

    ◆ TCP ports 8080 and 8443

    ◆ TCP ports 389 and 636

11. Click Install to begin the installation.

12. Click Finish to complete the installation.

    Upon completion of the vCenter Server installation, browsing to vCenter Server's URL (http://<server name> or http://<server ip address>) will turn up a page that allows for the installation of the vSphere Client or the use of a web-based tool for managing the individual virtual machines hosted by the ESX/ESXi hosts within the vCenter Server inventory. Chapter 9 describes the web-based virtual machine management tool, vSphere Web Access.

The vSphere Client connected to vCenter Server should be the primary management tool for managing ESX/ESXi hosts and their respective virtual machines. As I've mentioned on several occasions already, the vSphere Client can connect directly to ESX/ESXi hosts under the context of a local user account defined on each ESX/ESXi host, or it can connect to a vCenter Server instance under the context of a Windows user account defined in Active Directory or the local SAM of the vCenter Server computer. Using vCenter Server along with Active Directory user accounts is the recommended deployment scenario.

After the installation of vCenter Server, there will be a number of new services installed to facilitate the operation of vCenter Server. These services include the following:

◆ VMware Mount Service for Virtual Center is used to support vCenter Server integration with VMware Consolidated Backup (VCB).

◆ VMware vCenter Orchestrator Configuration supports the Orchestrator workflow engine, which I'll describe briefly in Chapter 14, "Automating VMware vSphere."

◆ VMware VirtualCenter Management Webservices is used to allow browser-based access to the vCenter Server application.

◆ VMware VirtualCenter Server is the core of vCenter Server and provides centralized management of ESX/ESXi hosts and virtual machines.

◆ VMwareVCMSDS is the Microsoft Active Directory Application Mode (ADAM) instance that supports multiple vCenter Server instances in a Linked Mode group.

As a virtual infrastructure administrator, you should be familiar with the default states of these services. In times of troubleshooting, check the status of the services to see whether they have changed. Keep in mind the dependencies that exist between vCenter Server and other services on the network. For example, if the vCenter Server service is failing to start, be sure to check that the system has access to the SQL Server (or Oracle) database. If vCenter Server cannot access the database because of a lack of connectivity or the database service is not running, then it will not start.

As additional features and extensions are installed, additional services will also be installed to support those features. For example, installing vCenter Update Manager will install an additional service called VMware Update Manager Service. You'll learn more about vCenter Update Manager in Chapter 4.

Your environment may be one that requires only a single instance of vCenter Server running. If that's the case, you're ready to get started managing ESX/ESXi hosts and virtual machines. However, for those of you with very large virtual environments, you'll need more than one vCenter Server, so I'll show you how to install additional vCenter Server instances in a Linked Mode group.

Installing vCenter Server in a Linked Mode Group

If your environment exceeds the recommended limits of a single vCenter Server instance, then vCenter Server 4.0 allows you to install multiple instances of vCenter Server and have those instances share inventory and configuration information for a centralized view of all the virtualized resources across the enterprise.

Table 3.1 shows the maximums for a single instance of vCenter Server. Using a Linked Mode group is necessary if you need to manage more than the number of ESX/ESXi hosts or virtual machines listed in Table 3.1.

TABLE 3.1: Maximum Number of Hosts or VMs per vCenter Server

ITEM	MAXIMUM
ESX/ESXi hosts per vCenter Server	200
Virtual machines per vCenter Server	3,000

vCenter Server Linked Mode uses Microsoft ADAM to replicate information between the instances. The replicated information includes the following:

◆ Connection information (IP addresses and ports)

◆ Certificates and thumbprints

◆ Licensing information

◆ User roles

In a Linked Mode environment, there are multiple vCenter Server instances, and each of the instances has its own set of hosts, clusters, and virtual machines. However, when a user logs into a vCenter Server instance using the vSphere Client, that user sees all the vCenter Server instances where they have permissions assigned. This allows a user to perform actions on any ESX/ESXi host managed by any vCenter Server within the Linked Mode group.

Before you install additional vCenter Server instances, you must verify the following prerequisites:

◆ All computers that will run vCenter Server in a Linked Mode group must be members of a domain. The servers can exist in different domains only if a two-way trust relationship exists between the domains.

◆ DNS must be operational. Also, the DNS name of the servers must match the server name.

◆ The servers that will run vCenter Server cannot be domain controllers or terminal servers.

Each vCenter Server instance must have its own back-end database, and each database must be configured as outlined earlier with the correct permissions. The databases can all reside on the same database server, or each database can reside on its own database server.

MULTIPLE VCENTER SERVER INSTANCES WITH ORACLE

If you are using Oracle, you'll need to make sure that each vCenter Server instance has a different schema owner or use a dedicated Oracle server for each instance.

After you have met the prerequisites, installing vCenter Server in a Linked Mode group is straightforward. You follow the steps outlined earlier in "Installing vCenter Server" until you get to step 9. In the previous instructions, you installed vCenter Server as a stand-alone instance in step 9. This sets up a master ADAM instance used by vCenter Server to store its configuration information.

This time, however, at step 9 you simply select the option Join A VMware vCenter Server Group Using Linked Mode To Share Information.

When you select to install into a Linked Mode group, the next screen also prompts for the name and port number of a remote vCenter Server instance. The new vCenter Server instance uses this information to replicate data from the existing server's ADAM repository.

After you've provided the information to connect to a remote vCenter Server instance, the rest of the installation follows the same steps described previously.

After the additional vCenter Server is up and running, logging in via the vSphere Client displays all the linked vCenter Server instances in the inventory view, as you can see in Figure 3.8.

FIGURE 3.8
In a Linked Mode environment, the vSphere Client shows all the vCenter Server instances for which a user has permission.

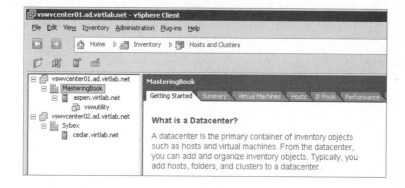

Installing vCenter Server is just the beginning. Before you're ready to start using vCenter Server in earnest, you must first become a bit more familiar with the user interface and how to create and manage objects in vCenter Server.

Exploring vCenter Server

You access vCenter Server via the vSphere Client, which you installed previously. The vSphere Client is installed either through the home page of an ESX/ESXi host or through the home page of a vCenter Server instance. When you launch the vSphere Client, you are prompted to enter the IP address or name of the server to which you will connect, along with security credentials. vCenter Server 4.0 supports pass-through authentication, enabled by the check box Use Windows Session Credentials. When this check box is selected, the username and password are grayed out, and authentication to the vCenter Server is handled using the currently logged-on account.

The first time that you connect to a vCenter Server instance, you receive a Security Warning dialog box. This security warning is the result of the fact that the vSphere Client uses HTTP over Secure Sockets Layer (HTTPS) to connect to vCenter Server while the vCenter Server is using a Secure Sockets Layer (SSL) certificate from an "untrusted" source.

To correct this error, you have the following two options:

◆ You can select the box Install This Certificate And Do Not Display Any Security Warnings For *server.domain.com*. This option installs the SSL certificate locally so that the system running the vSphere Client will no longer consider it to be an untrusted certificate.

◆ You can install your own SSL certificate from a trusted certification authority on the vCenter Server.

After the vSphere Client connects to vCenter Server, you will notice a Getting Started tab that facilitates the construction of a new datacenter. The starting point for the vCenter Server inventory is the vCenter Server itself, while the building block of the vCenter Server inventory is called a *datacenter*. I'll discuss the concept of the datacenter and building out your vCenter Server inventory in the section "Creating and Managing a vCenter Server Inventory."

REMOVING THE GETTING STARTED TABS

If you'd prefer not to see the Getting Started tabs in the vSphere Client, you can turn them off. From the vSphere Client menu, select Edit ➢ Client Settings, and deselect the box Show Getting Started Tabs.

Clicking the Create A Datacenter link allows you to create a datacenter. The Getting Started Wizard would then prompt you to add an ESX/ESXi host to vCenter Server, but before you do that, you should acquaint yourself with the vSphere Client interface when it's connected to vCenter Server.

The vCenter Server Home Screen

So far, you've seen only the Hosts And Clusters view of inventory. This is where you manage ESX/ESXi hosts, VMware DRS/HA clusters, and virtual machines. To see the rest of what vCenter Server has to offer, click the Home button on the navigation bar; you'll see a screen something like the screen shown in Figure 3.9.

FIGURE 3.9
The vCenter Server home screen shows the full selection of features within vCenter Server.

The home screen lists all the various features that vCenter Server has to offer in managing ESX/ESXi hosts and virtual machines:

◆ Under Inventory, vCenter Server offers several views, including Hosts And Clusters, VMs And Templates, Datastores, and Networking.

◆ Under Administration, vCenter Server has screens for managing roles, viewing and managing current sessions, licensing, viewing system logs, managing vCenter Server settings, and viewing the status of the vCenter Server services.

◆ Under Management, there are areas for scheduled tasks, events, maps, host profiles, and customization specifications.

A lot of these features are explored in other areas. For example, networking is discussed in Chapter 5, "Creating and Managing Virtual Networks," and datastores are discussed in Chapter 6, "Creating and Managing Storage Devices." Chapter 7 discusses templates and customization specifications, and Chapter 9 discusses roles and permissions. A large portion of the rest of this chapter is spent just on vCenter Server's Inventory view.

From the home screen, you can click any of the icons shown there to navigate to that area. But vCenter Server and the vSphere Client also have another way to navigate quickly and easily, and that's called the *navigation bar*.

The Navigation Bar

Across the top of the vSphere Client, just below the menu bar, is the navigation bar. The navigation bar shows you exactly where you are in the various screens that vCenter Server provides.

If you click any portion of the navigation bar, a drop-down menu appears. The options that appear illustrate a key point about the vSphere Client and vCenter Server: the menu options and tabs that appear within the application are context sensitive, meaning they change depending upon what object is selected or active. You'll learn more about this topic throughout the chapter.

Of course, you can also use the menu bar, where the View menu will be the primary method whereby you would switch between the various screens that are available to you. The vSphere Client also provides numerous keyboard shortcuts, making it even easier to flip quickly from one area to another with very little effort.

Now you're ready to get started creating and managing the vCenter Server inventory.

Creating and Managing a vCenter Server Inventory

As a VMware vSphere administrator, you will spend a pretty significant amount of time using the vSphere Client. Out of that time, you will spend a great deal of it working with the various inventory views available in vCenter Server, so I think it's quite useful to spend a little bit of time first explaining the inventory views in vCenter Server.

Understanding Inventory Views and Objects

Every vCenter Server has a root object, the datacenter, which serves as a container for all other objects. Prior to adding an object to the vCenter Server inventory, you must create a datacenter object. The objects found within the datacenter object depend upon which inventory view is active. The navigation bar provides a quick and easy reminder of which inventory view is currently active. In the Hosts And Clusters inventory view, you will work with ESX/ESXi hosts, VMware

HA/DRS clusters, resource pools, and virtual machines. In the VMs And Templates view, you will work with folders, virtual machines, and templates. In the Datastores view, you will work with datastores; in the Networking view, you'll work with vNetwork Standard Switches and vNetwork Distributed Switches.

VCENTER SERVER INVENTORY DESIGN

If you are familiar with objects used in a Microsoft Windows Active Directory (AD), you may recognize a strong similarity in the best practices of AD design and the design of a vCenter Server inventory. A close parallel can even be drawn between a datacenter object and an organizational unit because both are the building blocks of their respective infrastructures.

You organize the vCenter Server inventory differently in different views. The Hosts And Clusters view is primarily used to determine or control where a virtual machine is executing or how resources are allocated to a virtual machine or group of virtual machines. You would not, typically, create your logical administrative structure in Hosts And Clusters inventory view. This would be a good place, though, to provide structure around resource allocation or to group hosts into clusters according to business rules or other guidelines.

In VMs And Templates inventory view, though, the placement of VMs and templates within folders is handled irrespective of the specific host on which that virtual machine is running. This allows you to create a logical structure for VM administration that remains independent of the physical infrastructure upon which those VMs are running.

The naming strategy you provide for the objects in vCenter Server should mirror the way that network management is performed. For example, if you have qualified IT staff at each of your three datacenters across the country, then you would most likely create a hierarchical inventory that mirrors that management style. On the other hand, if your IT management was most profoundly set by the various departments in your company, then the datacenter objects might be named after each respective department. In most enterprise environments, the vCenter Server inventory will be a hybrid that involves management by geography, department, server type, and even project title.

The vCenter Server inventory can be structured as needed to support a company's IT management needs. Folders can be created above and below the datacenter object to provide higher or more granular levels of control that can propagate to lower-level child objects. Figure 3.10 shows a Hosts And Clusters view of a vCenter Server inventory that is based on a geographical management style.

FIGURE 3.10

Users can create folders above the datacenter object to grant permission at a level that can propagate to multiple datacenter objects or to create folders beneath a datacenter to manage the objects within the datacenter object.

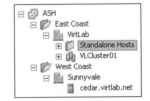

Should a company use more of a departmental approach to IT resource management, then the vCenter Server inventory can be shifted to match the new management style. Figure 3.11 reflects a Hosts And Clusters inventory view based on a departmental management style.

FIGURE 3.11

A departmental vCenter Server inventory allows the IT administrator to implement controls within each organizational department.

In most enterprise environments, the vCenter Server inventory will be a hybrid of the different topologies. Perhaps one topology might be a geographical top level, followed by departmental management, followed by project-based resource configuration.

The Hosts And Clusters inventory view is just one view of the inventory, though. In addition to building your inventory structure in the Hosts And Clusters view, you also build your inventory structure in VMs And Templates. Figure 3.12 shows a sample VMs And Templates inventory view that organizes virtual machines by department.

FIGURE 3.12

The structure of the VMs And Templates inventory is separate from the Hosts And Clusters inventory.

These inventory views are completely separate. For example, the Hosts And Clusters inventory view may reflect a geographical focus, while the VMs And Templates inventory view may reflect a departmental or functional focus. Because permissions are granted based on these structures, organizations have the ability to build inventory structures that properly support their administrative structures. Chapter 9 will describe the security model of vCenter Server that will work hand in hand with the management-driven inventory design. In addition, in Chapter 9, I'll spend a bit more time explaining the vCenter Server hierarchy.

With that basic understanding of vCenter Server inventory views and the hierarchy of inventory objects behind you, it's now time for you to actually build out your inventory structure and start creating and adding objects in vCenter Server.

Adding and Creating Inventory Objects

Before you can really build your inventory—in either Hosts And Clusters view or VMs And Templates view—you must first get your ESX/ESXi hosts into vCenter Server. And before you can get your ESX/ESXi hosts into vCenter Server, you need to have a datacenter object. You may have created the datacenter object as part of the Getting Started Wizard, but if you didn't, you must create one now. Don't forget that you can have multiple datacenter objects within a single vCenter Server instance.

Perform the following steps to add a datacenter object:

1. Launch the vSphere Client, if it is not already running, and connect to a vCenter Server instance.

2. From the View menu, select Inventory ➤ Hosts And Clusters, or press the Ctrl+Shift+H keyboard hotkey.

3. Right-click the vCenter Server object, and select Add Datacenter.

4. Type in a name for the new datacenter object. Press Enter, or click anywhere else in the window when you are finished.

If you already have a datacenter object, then you are ready to start adding ESX/ESXi hosts to vCenter Server.

Perform the following steps to add an ESX/ESXi host to vCenter Server:

1. Launch the vSphere Client, if it is not already running, and connect to a vCenter Server instance.

2. From the View menu, select Inventory ➤ Hosts And Clusters, or press the Ctrl+Shift+H keyboard hotkey.

3. Right-click the datacenter object, and select Add Host.

4. In the Add Host Wizard, supply the IP address or fully qualified hostname and user account information for the host being added to vCenter Server. This will typically be the root account.

    Although you supply the root password when adding the host to the vCenter Server inventory, vCenter Server uses the root credentials only long enough to establish a different set of credentials for its own use moving forward. This means that you can change the root password without worrying about breaking the communication and authentication between vCenter Server and your ESX/ESXi hosts. In fact, regular changes of the root password are considered a security best practice.

 Real World Scenario

MAKE SURE NAME RESOLUTION IS WORKING

Name resolution—the ability for one computer to match the hostname of another computer to its IP address—is a key component for a number of ESX/ESXi functions. I have witnessed a number of problems that were resolved by making sure that name resolution was working properly.

I strongly recommend you ensure that name resolution is working in a variety of directions. You will want to do the following:

◆ Ensure that the vCenter Server computer can resolve the hostnames of each and every ESX/ESXi host added to the inventory.

◆ Ensure that each and every ESX/ESXi host can resolve the hostname of the vCenter Server computer by which it is being managed.

◆ Ensure that each and every ESX/ESXi host can resolve the hostnames of the other ESX/ESXi hosts in the inventory, especially if those hosts may be combined into a VMware HA cluster.

Although I've seen some recommendations about using the /etc/hosts file to hard-code the names and IP addresses of other servers in the environment, I don't recommend it. Managing the /etc/hosts file on every ESX host gets cumbersome very quickly and is error-prone. In addition, ESXi doesn't support the /etc/hosts file. For the most scalable and reliable solution, ensure your Domain Naming System (DNS) infrastructure is robust and functional, and make sure that the vCenter Server computer and all ESX/ESXi hosts are configured to use DNS for name resolution. You'll save yourself a lot of trouble later by investing a little bit of effort in this area now.

5. When prompted to decide whether to trust the host and an SHA1 fingerprint is displayed, click Yes.

Strictly speaking, security best practices dictate that you should verify the SHA1 fingerprint before accepting it as valid. VMware ESX requires that you run a command from within the Service Console to verify the SHA1 fingerprint; VMware ESXi provides the SHA1 fingerprint in the View Support Information screen at the console.

6. The next screen displays a summary of the ESX/ESXi host being added, along with information on any virtual machines currently hosted on that server. Click Next.

7. Figure 3.13 shows the next screen, where you need to assign a license to the host being added. The option to add the host in evaluation mode is also available. Choose evaluation mode, or assign a license; then click Next.

FIGURE 3.13
Licenses can be assigned to an ESX/ESXi host as they are added to vCenter Server or at a later time.

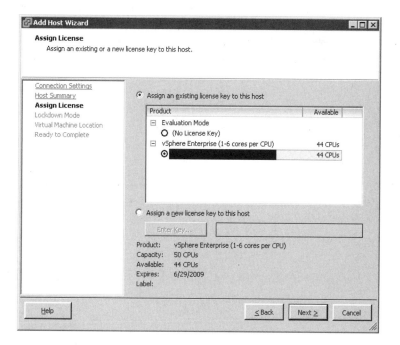

8. If the host is an ESXi host, the next screen offers the option to enable lockdown mode. Lockdown mode ensures that the management of the host occurs via vCenter Server, not through the vSphere Client connected directly to the ESXi host. Click Next.

9. Choose a location for this host's virtual machines, and click Next.

10. Click Finish at the summary screen.

Now compare the tabs in the pane on the right of the vSphere Client for the vCenter Server, datacenter, and host objects. You can see that the tabs presented to you change depending upon the object selected in the inventory tree. This is yet another example of how vCenter Server's user interface is context sensitive and changes the options available to the user depending upon what is selected.

Adding ESX/ESXi hosts to vCenter Server enables you to manage them with vCenter Server. You'll explore some of vCenter Server's management features in the next section.

Exploring vCenter Server's Management Features

After your ESX/ESXi hosts are managed by vCenter Server, you can take advantage of some of vCenter Server's management features. In this section, you'll take a quick look at the following:

◆ Basic host management tasks in Hosts And Clusters inventory view

◆ Scheduled tasks

◆ Events

◆ Maps

◆ Host profiles

In the next few sections, you'll examine each of these areas in a bit more detail.

Understanding Basic Host Management

A great deal of the day-to-day management tasks for ESX/ESXi hosts in vCenter Server occurs in the Hosts And Clusters inventory view. From this area, the right-click context menu for an ESX/ESXi host shows some of the options available:

◆ Create A New Virtual Machine

◆ Create A New Resource Pool

◆ Create A New vApp

◆ Disconnect From The Selected ESX/ESXi Host

◆ Enter Maintenance Mode

◆ Add Permission

◆ Manage Alarms For The Selected ESX/ESXi Host

◆ Shut Down, Reboot, Power On, Or Place The ESX/ESXi Host Into Standby Mode

◆ Produce Reports

◆ Remove The ESX/ESXi Host From vCenter Server

The majority of these options are described in later chapters. Chapter 7 describes creating virtual machines, and Chapter 10 discusses resource pools. Chapter 9 covers permissions, and Chapter 10 discusses alarms and reports. Of the remaining actions—shutting down, rebooting, powering on, standing by, disconnecting, and removing from vCenter Server—are self-explanatory and do not need any additional explanation.

Additional commands may appear on this right-click menu as extensions are installed into vCenter Server. For example, after you install vCenter Update Manager, several new commands appear on the context menu for an ESX/ESXi host.

In addition to the context menu, the tabs across the top of the right side of the vSphere Client window also provide some host management features. Figure 3.14 shows some of the tabs; note the left/right arrows that allow you to scroll through the tabs when they don't all fit in the window.

FIGURE 3.14
When a host is selected in inventory view, the tabs across the top of the right side of the window also provide host management features.

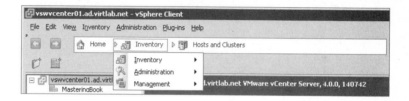

For the most part, these tabs correspond closely to the commands on the context menu. Here are the tabs that are displayed when a host is selected in the inventory view, along with a brief description of what each tab does:

Summary   The Summary tab gathers and display information about the underlying physical hardware, the storage devices that are configured and accessible, the networks that are configured and accessible, and the status of certain features such as VMotion and VMware FT. In addition, the Commands area of the Summary tab provides links to commonly performed host management tasks.

Virtual Machines   The Virtual Machines tab lists the virtual machines currently running on that host. The list of virtual machines also provides summary information on the VM's status, provisioned vs. used space, and how much CPU and RAM the VM is actually using.

Performance   The Performance tab displays performance information for the host, such as overall CPU utilization, memory utilization, disk I/O, and network throughput. I'll discuss this area in more detail in Chapter 10.

Configuration   The Configuration tab is where you will make configuration changes to the host. Tasks such as configuring storage, configuring network, changing security settings, configuring hardware, and so forth, are all performed here.

Tasks & Events   All tasks and events related to the selected host are displayed here. The Tasks view shows all tasks, the target object, what account initiated the task, what vCenter Server was involved, and the result of the task. The Events view lists all events related to the selected host.

Alarms   The Alarms tab shows either triggered alarms or alarm definitions. If a host is using almost all of its RAM or if a host's CPU utilization is very high, you may see some triggered alarms. The Alarms Definition section allows you to define your own alarms.

Permissions   The Permissions tab shows permissions on the selected host. This includes permissions inherited from parent objects/containers as well as permissions granted directly to the selected host.

Maps   The Maps tab shows a graphical topology map of resources and VMs associated with that host. vCenter Server's maps functionality is described in more detail later in this chapter.

Storage Views   The Storage Views tab brings together a number of important storage-related pieces of information. For each VM on the selected host, the Storage Views tab shows the current multipathing status, the amount of disk space used, the amount of snapshot space used, and the current number of disks.

Hardware Status   The Hardware Status tab displays sensor information on hardware components such as fans, CPU temperature, power supplies, network interface cards (NICs) and NIC firmware, and more.

As you can see, vCenter Server provides all the tools that most administrators will need to manage ESX/ESXi hosts. Although these host management tools are visible in the Hosts And Clusters inventory view, vCenter Server's other management features are found in the Management view, accessible from the View ➤ Management menu.

Using Scheduled Tasks

Selecting View ➤ Management ➤ Scheduled Tasks displays the Scheduled Tasks area of vCenter Server. You can also use the Ctrl+Shift+T keyboard shortcut.

From here, you can create jobs to run based on a defined logic. The list of tasks that can be scheduled include the following:

- You can change the power state of a virtual machine.

- You can clone a virtual machine.

- You can deploy a virtual machine from a template.

- You can move a virtual machine with VMotion.

- You can move a virtual machine's virtual disks with Storage VMotion.

- You can create a virtual machine.

- You can make a snapshot of a virtual machine.

- You can add a host.

- You can change resource settings for a resource pool or virtual machine.

- You can check compliance for a profile.

As you can see, vCenter Server supports quite a list of tasks you can schedule to run automatically. Because the information required for each scheduled task varies, the wizards are different for each of the tasks. Let's take a look at one task that you might find quite useful to schedule: adding a host.

Why might you want to schedule a task to add a host? Perhaps you know that you will be adding a host to vCenter Server, but you want to add the host after hours. You can schedule a task to add the host to vCenter Server later tonight, although keep in mind that the host must be reachable and responding when the task is created.

Perform the following steps to create a scheduled task to add a host to vCenter Server:

1. Launch the vSphere Client, if it is not already running, and connect to a vCenter Server instance.

2. After you connect to vCenter Server, navigate to the Scheduled Tasks area by selecting View ➢ Management ➢ Scheduled Tasks. You can also click the Scheduled Tasks icon on the vCenter Server home screen, or you can press Ctrl+Shift+T.

3. Right-click the blank area of the Scheduled Tasks list, and select New Scheduled Task.

4. From the list of tasks to schedule, select Add A Host.

5. The Add Host Wizard starts. Select the datacenter or cluster to which this new host will be added.

6. Supply the hostname, username, and password to connect to the host, just as if you were adding the host manually.

7. When prompted to accept the host's SHA1 fingerprint, click Yes.

8. The next three or four steps in the wizard—three steps for ESX, four steps for ESXi—are just like you were adding the host manually. You will click Next after each step until you come to the point of scheduling the task.

9. Supply a task name, task description, frequency of the task, and schedule for the task. For adding a host, the frequency option doesn't really make sense.

10. Select if you want to receive email notification of the scheduled task when it completes and supply an email address. Note that vCenter Server must be configured with the name of an SMTP server it can use.

In my mind, scheduling the addition of an ESX/ESXi host is of fairly limited value. However, the ability to schedule tasks such as powering off a group of virtual machines, moving their virtual disks to a new datastore, and then powering them back on again is quite powerful.

Using Events View in vCenter Server

The Events view in vCenter Server brings together all the events that have been logged by vCenter Server. Figure 3.15 shows the Events view with an event selected.

You can view the details of an event by simply clicking it in the list. Any text highlighted in blue is a hyperlink; clicking that text will take you to that object in vCenter Server. You can search through the events using the search box in the upper-right corner of the vSphere Client window, and just below the navigation bar is a button to export the events to a text file. Figure 3.16 shows the dialog box for exporting events.

FIGURE 3.15
vCenter Server's Events
view lets you view event
details, search events,
and export events.

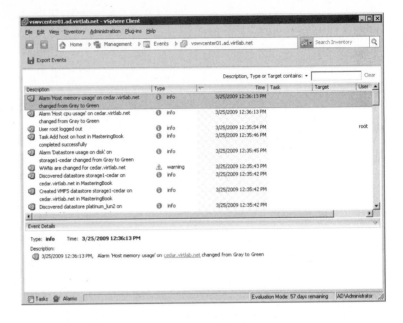

FIGURE 3.16
Users have a number of
options when exporting
events out of vCenter
Server to a text file.

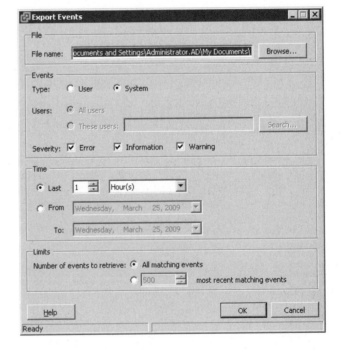

Using vCenter Server's Maps

The Maps feature of vCenter Server is a great tool for quickly reviewing your virtual infrastructure. Topology maps graphically represent the relationship that exists between different types of objects in the virtual infrastructure. The maps can display any of the following relationships:

◆ Host to virtual machine

◆ Host to network

◆ Host to datastore

◆ Virtual machine to network

◆ Virtual machine to datastore

In addition to defining the relationships to display, you can include or exclude specific objects from the inventory. Perhaps you are interested only in the relationship that exists between the virtual machines and the networks on a single host. In this case, you can exclude all other hosts from the list of relationships by deselecting their icons in the vCenter Server inventory on the left side of the window. Figure 3.17 shows a series of topology maps defining the relationships for a set of objects in the vCenter Server inventory. For historical purposes or further analysis, you can save topology maps as JPG, BMP, PNG, GIF, TIFF or EMF file formats.

FIGURE 3.17
vCenter Server's Maps feature is a flexible, graphical utility that helps identify the relationships that exist between the various objects in the virtual infrastructure.

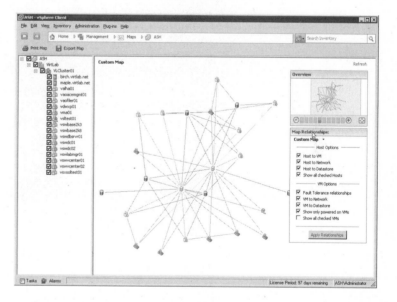

Topology maps are available from the menu by selecting View ➢ Management ➢ Maps, by using the navigation bar, or by using the Ctrl+Shift+M keyboard shortcut. You can also select an inventory object and then select the Maps tab. Figure 3.17 showed the Maps feature from the vCenter Server menu, and Figure 3.18 shows the Maps tab available for each inventory object (in this case, an ESX host). In either case, the depth of the relationship can be identified by enabling or disabling options in the list of relationships on the right side of the maps display.

The Maps button on the menu allows for the scope of the relationship to be edited by enabling and disabling objects in the vCenter Server inventory. By selecting an inventory object and then viewing the topology map, the focus is limited to just that object. In both cases, the Overview mini-window lets you zoom in to view specific parts of the topology map or zoom out to view the whole topology map.

FIGURE 3.18
The Maps tab for inventory objects limits the scope of the map to the selected object.

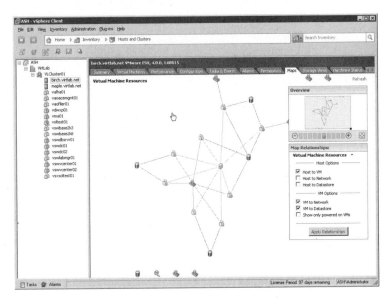

Working with Host Profiles

Host profiles are an exciting new feature of vCenter Server. As you'll see in coming chapters, there can be quite a bit of configuration involved in setting up an ESX/ESXi host. Although vCenter Server and the vSphere Client make it easy to perform these configuration tasks, it's easy to overlook something. Additionally, making all these changes manually for multiple hosts can be time-consuming and even more error-prone. That's where host profiles can help.

A host profile is essentially a collection of all the various configuration settings for an ESX/ESXi host. This includes settings such as Service Console memory, NIC assignments, virtual switches, storage configuration, date and time settings, and more. By attaching a host profile to an ESX/ESXi host, you can then compare the compliance of that host with the settings outlined in the host profile. If the host is compliant, then you know its settings are the same as the settings in the host profile. If the host is not compliant, then you can enforce the settings in the host profile to make it compliant. This provides administrators with a way not only to verify consistent settings across ESX/ESXi hosts but also with a way to quickly and easily apply settings to new ESX/ESXi hosts.

To work with host profiles, select View ➤ Management ➤ Host Profiles, or use the Ctrl+Shift+P keyboard shortcut. Figure 3.19 shows the Host Profiles view in vCenter Server, where two different host profiles have been created.

As you can see in Figure 3.19, there are four toolbar buttons across the top of the window, just below the navigation bar. These buttons allow you to create a new host profile, edit an existing host profile, delete a host profile, and attach a host or cluster to a profile.

To create a new profile, you must either create one from an existing host or import a profile that was already created somewhere else. Creating a new profile from an existing host requires that you only select the reference host for the new profile. vCenter Server will then compile the host profile based on that host's configuration.

FIGURE 3.19

Host profiles provide a mechanism for checking and enforcing compliance with a specific configuration.

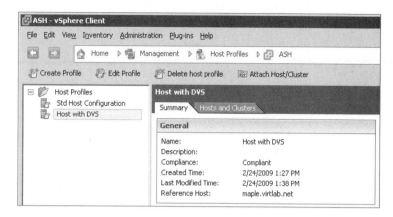

After a profile is created, you can edit the profile to fine-tune the settings contained in it. For example, you might need to change the IP addresses of the DNS servers found in the profile because they've changed since the profile was created.

Perform the following steps to edit the DNS server settings in a host profile:

1. If the vSphere Client isn't already running, launch it and connect to a vCenter Server instance.

2. From the menu, select View ➢ Management ➢ Host Profiles.

3. Right-click the host profile to be edited, and select Edit Profile.

4. From the tree menu on the left side of the Edit Profile window, navigate to Networking ➢ DNS Configuration. Figure 3.20 shows this area.

FIGURE 3.20

To make changes to a number of ESX/ESXi hosts at the same time, put the settings into a host profile, and attach the profile to the hosts.

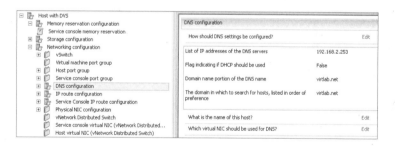

5. Click the blue Edit link to change the values shown in the host profile.

6. Click OK to save the changes to the host profile.

Host profiles don't do anything until they are attached to ESX/ESXi hosts. Click the Attach Host/Cluster toolbar button just below the navigation bar in the vSphere Client to open a dialog box that allows you to select one or more ESX/ESXi hosts to which the host profile should be attached.

After a host profile has been attached to an ESX/ESXi host, checking for compliance is as simple as right-clicking that host on the Hosts And Clusters tab and selecting Check Compliance Now.

If an ESX/ESXi host is found noncompliant with the settings in a host profile, you can then place the host in maintenance mode and apply the host profile. When you apply the host profile, the settings found in the host profile are enforced on that ESX/ESXi host to bring it into compliance. Note that some settings, such as changing the Service Console memory on an ESX host, require a reboot in order to take effect.

To truly understand the power of host profiles, consider this scenario: you have a group of hosts in a cluster. As you'll learn later in the book, hosts in a cluster need to have consistent settings. With a host profile that captures those settings, adding a new host to the cluster is a simple two-step process:

1. Add the host to vCenter Server and to the cluster.

2. Attach the host profile and apply it.

That's it. The host profile will enforce all the settings on this new host that are required to bring it into compliance with the settings on the rest of the servers in the cluster. This is a huge advantage for larger organizations that need to be able to quickly deploy new ESX/ESXi hosts.

At this point, you have installed vCenter Server, added at least one ESX/ESXi host, and explored some of vCenter Server's features for managing settings on ESX/ESXi hosts. Now I'll cover how to manage some of the settings for vCenter Server.

Managing vCenter Server Settings

To make it easier for vSphere administrators to be able to find and change the settings that affect the behavior or operation of vCenter Server, VMware centralized these settings into a single area within the vSphere Client user interface. This single area, found on the Administration menu in vCenter Server, allows for post-installation configuration of vCenter Server. In fact, it even contains configuration options that are not provided during installation. The Administration menu contains the following items:

◆ Custom Attributes

◆ vCenter Server Settings

◆ Role

◆ Session

◆ Edit Message Of The Day

◆ Export System Logs

Of these commands on the Administration menu, the Custom Attributes commands and the vCenter Server Settings are particularly important, so I'll review those two areas first. I'll start with Custom Attributes.

Custom Attributes

The Custom Attributes option lets you define custom identification or information options for virtual machines, hosts, or both (global). This is a pretty generic definition; perhaps a more concrete example will help. Say that you want to add metadata to each virtual machine to identify whether it is an application server, an infrastructure server (that is, DHCP server, DNS server), or a domain controller.

To accomplish this task, you could add a custom virtual machine attribute named VMRole. To add this custom attribute, select Administration ➢ Attributes. This opens the Custom Attributes dialog box, and from there you can click Add to create a new custom attribute. You can create a custom attribute that is global in nature or that applies only to ESX/ESXi hosts or virtual machines.

After you've created this VMRole custom attribute, you can edit the attribute data on the Summary tab of the object. After the custom attribute is added, it appears in the Annotations section of the object. You can use the Edit button to open the Custom Attributes window and add the required metadata, as shown in Figure 3.21.

FIGURE 3.21
You can add metadata to objects by editing the values of the custom attributes.

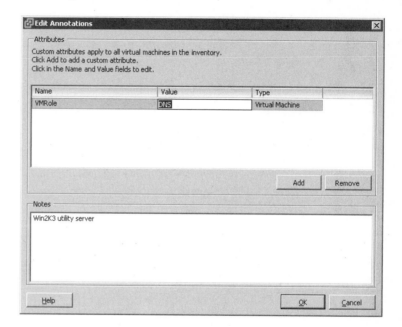

With the metadata clearly defined for various objects, you can then search based on that data. Figure 3.22 shows a custom search for all virtual machines with a VM role equal to DNS.

Using custom attributes to build metadata around your ESX/ESXi hosts and virtual machines is quite powerful, and the integration with the vSphere Client's search functionality makes managing very large inventories much more manageable.

But the Administration menu is about more than just custom attributes and metadata, it's also about configuring vCenter Server itself. The vCenter Server Settings command on the Administration menu gives you access to change the settings that control how vCenter Server operates, as you'll see in the next section.

vCenter Server Settings

The vCenter Server Settings dialog box contains 13 vCenter Server settings:

◆ Licensing

◆ Statistics

◆ Runtime Settings

◆ Active Directory

◆ Mail

◆ SNMP

◆ Web Service

◆ Timeout Settings

◆ Logging Options

◆ Database

◆ Database Retention Policy

◆ SSL Settings

◆ Advanced Settings

FIGURE 3.22
After you've defined the data for a custom attribute, you can use it as search criteria for quickly finding objects with similar metadata.

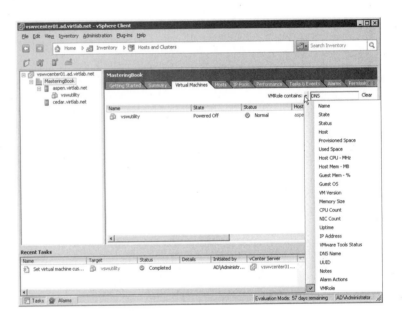

Each of these settings controls a specific area of interaction or operation for vCenter Server that I briefly discuss next.

Licensing The Licensing configuration page of the vCenter Server Settings dialog box, shown in Figure 3.23, provides the parameters for how vCenter Server is licensed. The options include using an evaluation mode or applying a license key to this instance of vCenter Server. If this vCenter Server instance will also manage ESX 3.x hosts, then this dialog box provides an option for specifying the license server those hosts should use.

When an evaluation of vSphere and vCenter Server is no longer required and the appropriate licenses have been purchased, you must deselect the evaluation option and add a license key.

FIGURE 3.23
Licensing vCenter Server is managed through the vCenter Server Settings dialog box.

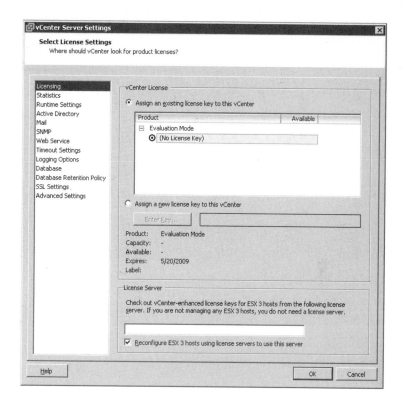

Statistics   The Statistics page, shown in Figure 3.24, offers the ability to configure the collection intervals and the system resources for accumulating statistical performance data in vCenter Server. In addition, it also provides a database-sizing calculator that can estimate the size of a vCenter Server database based upon the configuration of statistics intervals. By default, the following four collection intervals are available:

◆ Past day: 5 minutes per sample at statistics level 1

◆ Past week: 30 minutes per sample at statistics level 1

◆ Past month: 2 hour per sample at statistics level 1

◆ Past year: 1 day per sample at statistics level 1

By selecting an interval from the list and clicking the Edit button, you can customize the interval configuration. You can set the interval, how long to keep the sample, and what statistics level (Level 1 through Level 4) vCenter Server will use.

FIGURE 3.24
You can customize statistics collection intervals to support broad or detailed logging.

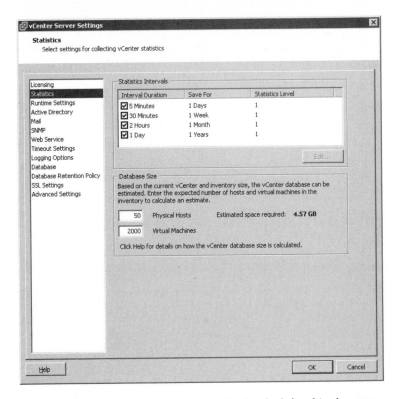

The Statistics Collection level offers the following four collection levels defined in the user interface:

Level 1 Basic metrics for average usage of CPU, Memory, Disk, and Network. It also includes data about system uptime, system heartbeat, and DRS metrics. Statistics for devices are not included.

Level 2 Includes all the average, summation, and rollup metrics for CPU, Memory, Disk, and Network. It also includes system uptime, system heartbeat, and DRS metrics. Maximum and minimum rollup types as well as statistics for devices are not included.

Level 3 Includes all metrics for all counter groups, including devices, except for minimum and maximum rollups. Maximum and minimum rollup types are not included.

Level 4 Includes all metrics supported by vCenter Server.

DATABASE ESTIMATES

By editing the statistics collection configuration, you can see the estimated database size change accordingly. For example, by reducing the one-day collection interval to one minute as opposed to five minutes, the database size jumps from an estimated 4.81GB to an estimated 8.93GB. Similarly, if the collection samples taken once per day are kept for five years instead of one year, the database size jumps from an estimated 4.81GB to an estimated 10.02GB. The collection intervals and retention durations should be set to a level required by your company's audit policy.

Runtime Settings   The Runtime Settings area lets you configure the vCenter Server Unique ID, the IP address used by vCenter Server, and the server name of the computer running vCenter Server. The unique ID will be populated by default, and changing it requires a restart of the vCenter Server service. These settings would normally require changing only when running multiple vCenter Server instances in the same environment. It is possible conflicts might exist if not altered.

Active Directory   This page includes the ability to set the Active Directory timeout value, a limit for the number of users and groups returned in a query against the Active Directory database, and the validation period (in minutes) for synchronizing users and groups used by vCenter Server.

Mail   The Mail page might be the most commonly customized page because its configuration is crucial to the sending of alarm results, as you'll see in Chapter 12. The mail SMTP server name or IP address and the sender account will determine the server and the account from which alarm results will be sent.

SNMP   The SNMP configuration page is where you would configure vCenter Server for integration with a Systems Network Management Protocol (SNMP) management system. The receiver URL should be the name or IP address of the server with the appropriate SNMP trap receiver. The SNMP port, if not configured away from the default, should be set at 162, and the community string should be configured appropriately (public is the default). vCenter Server supports up to four receiver URLs.

Web Service   The Web Service page is used to configure the HTTP and HTTPS ports used by the vCenter Server Web Access feature.

Timeout Settings   This area, the Timeout Settings area, is where you configure client connection timeouts. The settings by default allow for a 30-second timeout for normal operations or 120 minutes for long operations.

Logging Options   The Logging Options page, shown in Figure 3.25, customizes the level of detail accumulated in vCenter Server logs. The logging options include the following:

- None (Disable logging)
- Errors (Errors only)
- Warning (Errors and warnings)
- Information (Normal logging)
- Verbose (Verbose)
- Trivia (Trivia)

By default, vCenter Server stores its logs at `C:\Documents and Settings\All Users\Application Data\VMware\VMware VirtualCenter\Logs`.

Database   The Database page lets you configure the maximum number of connections to the back-end database.

Database Retention Policy   To limit the growth of the vCenter Server database, you can configure a retention policy. vCenter Server offers options for limiting the length of time that both tasks and events are retained in the back-end database.

SSL Settings   This page includes the ability to configure a certificate validity check between vCenter Server and the vSphere Client. If enabled, both systems will check the trust of the SSL certificate presented by the remote host when performing tasks such as adding a host to inventory or establishing a remote console to a virtual machine.

Advanced Settings   The Advanced Settings page provides for an extensible configuration interface.

FIGURE 3.25
vCenter Server offers several options for configuring the amount of data to be stored in vCenter Server logs.

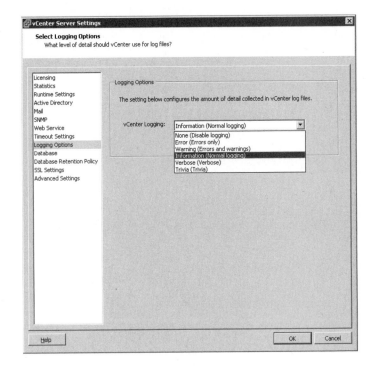

ROLES

After the vCenter Server Settings command on the Administration menu is the Roles command.

The Roles option from the Administration menu is available only when the view is set to Administration and the Roles tab is selected. This menu works like a right-click context menu that offers the ability to add, edit, rename, or remove roles based on what object is selected.

Chapter 9 describes vCenter Server's roles in detail.

SESSIONS

The Sessions menu option is available only when the view is set to Administration ➢ Sessions. The Sessions view allows for terminating all sessions and editing the text that makes up the message of the day (MOTD). The currently used session identified by the status "This Session" cannot be terminated.

EDIT MESSAGE OF THE DAY

As the name suggests, this menu item allows for editing the MOTD. The MOTD is displayed to users each time they log in to vCenter Server. This provides an excellent means of distributing information regarding maintenance schedules or other important information.

As extensions are added to vCenter Server—such as vCenter Update Manager or Guided Consolidation—additional commands may appear on the Administration menu.

The next chapter discusses one such extension to vCenter Server, and that is vCenter Update Manager.

The Bottom Line

Understand the features and role of vCenter Server. vCenter Server plays a central role in the management of ESX/ESXi hosts and virtual machines. Key features such as VMotion, Storage VMotion, VMware DRS, VMware HA, and VMware FT are all enabled and made possible by vCenter Server. vCenter Server provides scalable authentication and role-based administration based on integration with Active Directory.

> **Master It** Specifically with regard to authentication, what are three key advantages of using vCenter Server?

Plan a vCenter Server deployment. Planning a vCenter Server deployment includes selecting a back-end database engine, choosing an authentication method, sizing the hardware appropriately, and providing a sufficient level of high availability and business continuity. You must also decide whether you will run vCenter Server as a virtual machine or on a physical system.

> **Master It** What are some of the advantages and disadvantages of running vCenter Server as a virtual machine?

Install and configure a vCenter Server database. vCenter Server supports several enterprise-grade database engines, including Oracle and Microsoft SQL Server. IBM DB2 is also experimentally supported. Depending upon the database in use, there are specific configuration steps and specific permissions that must be applied in order for vCenter Server to work properly.

> **Master It** Why is it important to protect the database engine used to support vCenter Server?

Install and configure vCenter Server. vCenter Server is installed using the VMware vCenter Installer. You can install vCenter Server as a stand-alone instance or join a Linked Mode group for greater scalability. vCenter Server will use a predefined ODBC DSN to communicate with the separate database server.

> **Master It** When preparing to install vCenter Server, are there any concerns about which Windows account should be used during the installation?

Use vCenter Server's management features. vCenter Server provides a wide range of management features for ESX/ESXi hosts and virtual machines. These features include scheduled tasks, topology maps, host profiles for consistent configurations, and event logging.

> **Master It** Your manager has asked you to prepare an overview of the virtualized environment. What tools in vCenter Server will help you in this task?

Chapter 4

Installing and Configuring vCenter Update Manager

Software patches are, unfortunately, a fact of life in today's IT departments. Most organizations recognize that it is impossible to create 100 percent error-free code and that software patches will be necessary to correct problems or flaws or to add new features. Fortunately, VMware offers a tool to help automate this process for vSphere. This tool is called vCenter Update Manager (VUM).

In this chapter, you will learn to:

- ◆ Install VUM and integrate it with the vSphere Client

- ◆ Determine which ESX/ESXi hosts or virtual machines need to be patched or upgraded

- ◆ Use VUM to upgrade virtual machine hardware or VMware Tools

- ◆ Apply patches to ESX/ESXi hosts

- ◆ Apply patches to Windows guests

Overview of vCenter Update Manager

VUM is a tool designed to help VMware administrators automate and streamline the process of applying updates—which could be patches or upgrades to a new version—to their vSphere environment. VUM is fully integrated within vCenter Server and offers the ability to scan and remediate ESX/ESXi hosts, virtual appliances, virtual machine templates, and online and offline virtual machines running certain versions of Windows, Linux, and some Windows applications. VUM can also upgrade VMware Tools and upgrade virtual machine hardware. Further, VUM is the vehicle used to install and update the Cisco Nexus 1000V third-party distributed virtual switch. The Cisco Nexus 1000V is covered in Chapter 5, "Creating and Managing Virtual Networks."

VUM also does the following:

- ◆ Integrates with VMware Distributed Resource Scheduler (DRS) for nondisruptive updating of ESX/ESXi hosts. Here "updating" means both applying software patches, as well as upgrading to new versions of ESX/ESXi.

- ◆ Can apply snapshots prior to updating VMs to enable rollback in the event of a problem

- ◆ Identifies VMs with outdated VMware Tools and assists in upgrading them

- ◆ Fully integrates configuration and administration into VMware vCenter and the vSphere Client

To help keep ESX/ESXi hosts and guest operating systems patched and up-to-date, VUM communicates across your company's Internet connection to download information about available updates, the products to which those updates apply, and the actual updates themselves. Based on rules and policies that are defined and applied by the VMware administrator using the vSphere Client, VUM will then apply updates to hosts and guest operating systems. The installation of updates can be scheduled, and even offline virtual machines can have updates applied to the guest operating systems installed on them.

Putting VUM to work in your vSphere deployment involves installing and configuring VUM, setting up baselines, scanning hosts and guest operating systems, and applying patches.

Installing vCenter Update Manager

VUM installs from the vCenter Server Installer and requires that at least one vCenter Server instance is already installed. You will find that installing VUM is much like installing vCenter Server, which you saw in the previous chapter.

Perform the following general steps to install VUM:

1. Configure the separate database server for VUM.

2. Create an Open Database Connectivity (ODBC) data source name (DSN) for VUM.

3. Install VUM.

4. Configure the VUM services to support Windows authentication.

5. Install the VUM plug-in for the vSphere Client.

INSTALLING UPDATE MANAGER DOWNLOAD SERVICE IS AN OPTIONAL STEP

An additional optional step in the deployment of VUM is the installation of the Update Manager Download Service (UMDS). UMDS provides a centralized download service. Installing UMDS is especially useful in two situations. First, UMDS is beneficial when you have multiple VUM servers; using UMDS prevents the updates and update metadata from being separately downloaded by each of the VUM servers, thus consuming more bandwidth. UMDS will download the updates and update metadata once, and multiple VUM servers can leverage the centralized UMDS repository. The second situation in which UMDS is beneficial is in environments where the VUM servers do not have direct Internet access. Since Internet access is required to download the updates and update metadata, you can use UMDS to download and distribute the information to the individual VUM servers.

Let's examine each of these steps in a bit more detail.

Configuring the Separate Database Server

Like vCenter Server, VUM requires a separate database server. Where vCenter Server uses the separate database server to store configuration and performance statistics, VUM uses the separate database server to store patch metadata. As in Chapter 3, I'll use the term *separate database server* simply to refer to a database application that is configured and managed independently of any of the VMware vCenter products.

SUPPORTED DATABASE SERVERS

VUM's support of separate database servers is identical to vCenter Server, with the exception of DB2. Although DB2 is experimentally supported by vCenter Server, DB2 is not supported at all by VUM. Refer to Chapter 3 for more information on the specific versions of Oracle and SQL Server that are supported by vCenter Server; these versions are also supported by VUM.

For small installations, up to 5 hosts and 50 virtual machines, VUM can use an instance of SQL Server 2005 Express Edition. SQL Server 2005 Express Edition is included on the VMware vCenter media, and the VUM installation will automatically install and configure this SQL Server 2005 Express instance appropriately. No additional work is required outside of the installation routine. However, as you learned from my discussion of vCenter Server in Chapter 3, SQL Server 2005 Express Edition does have some limitations, so plan accordingly. For the rest of my discussion here, I'll assume that you are not using SQL Server 2005 Express Edition. If you do plan on using SQL Server 2005 Express Edition, you can skip ahead to the section "Installing vCenter Update Manager."

If you've decided against using SQL Server 2005 Express Edition, you must now make another decision: where do you put the VUM database? Although it is possible for VUM to use the same database as vCenter Server, it is strongly recommended that you use a separate database, even if you will keep both databases on the same physical computer. For environments with fewer than 30 hosts, it's generally safe to keep these databases on the same computer, but moving beyond 30 hosts or 300 virtual machines, it's recommended to separate the vCenter Server and VUM databases onto different physical computers. When you move beyond 100 hosts or 1,000 virtual machines, you should be sure to use separate database servers for both the vCenter Server database and the VUM database as well as separate servers for vCenter Server and the VUM server software. Other factors, such as high availability or capacity, may also affect this decision. Aside from knowing which database server you'll use, the decision to use a single computer vs. multiple computers won't affect the procedures described in this section.

In either case, whether hosting the VUM database on the same computer as the vCenter Server database or not, there are specific configuration steps that you'll need to follow, just as you did when installing vCenter Server. You'll need to create the database, assign ownership, and grant permissions to the MSDB database. Be sure to complete these steps before trying to install VUM, because this information is required during installation.

Perform the following steps to create and configure an SQL Server 2005 database for use with VUM:

1. Launch the SQL Server Management Studio application. When prompted to connect to a server, connect to the appropriate server running SQL Server 2005 SP2 or later. Select Database Engine as the server type.

2. From the Object Explorer on the left side, expand the server node at the top level, and then expand the Databases node.

3. Right-click the Databases node, and select New Database.

4. In the New Database window, specify a database name. Use a name that is easy to identify, like VUM or vCenterUM.

5. Set the owner of the new database.

   If you are using Windows authentication, you'll need to set the owner of the database to an Active Directory user account created for the purpose of running VUM. If you are using SQL authentication, set the owner to be an SQL login that's already been created. The decision that you make here will affect other tasks later during the VUM installation, as you'll see.

   Figure 4.1 shows a new database being created with an Active Directory account set as the owner; this is the configuration to use for Windows authentication.

FIGURE 4.1
Be sure to set the owner of the database correctly according to the type of authentication you're using.

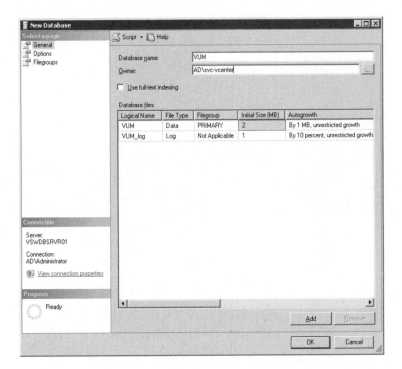

6. For ideal performance, set the location of the database and log files so they are on different physical disks than the operating system and the patch repository. Figure 4.2 shows where the database and log files are stored on a separate drive from the operating system.

7. After the settings are done, click OK to create the new database.

MSDB PERMISSIONS DON'T NEED TO PERSIST

VUM requires dbo permissions on the MSDB database. You can and should remove the dbo permissions on the MSDB database after the installation of VUM is complete. They are not needed after installation, similar to vCenter Server.

FIGURE 4.2
Place the database and log files for vCenter Update Manager on different physical drives than the operating system and patch repository.

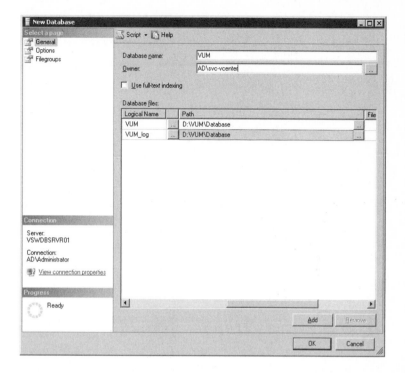

As with the vCenter Server database, the login that VUM will use to connect to the database server must have dbo permissions on the new database as well as on the MSDB database. You should remove the permissions on the MSDB database after installation is complete.

Creating the Open Database Connectivity Data Source Name

After you configure the separate database server, you must create an ODBC DSN to connect to the back-end database. You'll need to have the ODBC DSN created before you start VUM installation.

Perform the following steps to create an ODBC DSN for the VUM database:

1. From the Start menu, select Administrative Tools, and then select Data Sources (ODBC).

2. Select the System DSN tab.

3. Click the Add button.

4. From the list of available drivers, select the correct driver for the database server you're using. As with vCenter Server, you will need to ensure the correct ODBC driver is installed for the database server hosting the VUM database. For SQL Server 2005, select the SQL Native Client.

5. On the first screen of the Create A New Data Source Wizard, fill in the name of the DSN, a description, and the name of the server to which this DSN will connect. Be sure to make a note of the DSN name; you'll need this information later. Click Next when you're finished.

6. On the next screen you'll need to supply an authentication type and credentials to connect to the separate database server.

   The option that you select here must match the configuration of the database. To use Windows authentication, a Windows account must be set as the owner of the database; to use SQL authentication, an SQL login must be set as the owner of the database.

   Select With Integrated Windows Authentication, and click Next.

7. Click Next two more times; there is no need to change any of the settings on the next two screens.

8. Click Finish.

9. In the ODBC Microsoft SQL Server Setup dialog box, click the Test Data Source connection to verify the settings. If the results say the tests completed successfully, click OK twice to return to the ODBC Data Source Administrator window. If not, go back to double-check and correct the settings.

With the database created and the ODBC connection defined, you're now ready to proceed with installing VUM.

Installing VUM

Now that you have met all the prerequisites—at least one instance of vCenter Server running and accessible across the network, a separate database server running and configured appropriately, and an ODBC DSN defined to connect to the preconfigured database—you can start the VUM installation. Before you begin, make sure that you have a note of the ODBC DSN you defined earlier and, if using SQL authentication, the username and password configured for access to the database.

The VUM installation differs from the vCenter Server installation here with regard to the use of Windows authentication. When installing vCenter Server, you needed to log in as the user under whose context the vCenter Server services should run. In other words, if the vCenter Server services should run in the context of the user *vcenter*, then you needed to log in as *vcenter* when you ran the installation. This is not the case with VUM. Instead, if you are using Windows authentication, you'll need to manually switch the account under which the services run after installation.

Perform the following steps to install VUM:

1. Insert the vCenter Server DVD into the computer. The VMware vCenter Installer runs automatically; if it does not, simply double-click the DVD drive in My Computer to invoke AutoPlay.

2. Select vCenter Update Manager.

3. Choose the correct language for the installation, and click OK.

4. On the Welcome To The InstallShield Wizard For VMware vCenter Update Manager screen, click Next to start the installation.

5. Accept the terms in the license agreement, and click Next.

6. Fill out the next screen with the correct IP address or hostname, HTTP port, username, and password for the vCenter Server instance to which this VUM server will be associated. Click Next when the information is complete.

7. Select to either install an SQL 2005 Express instance or to use an existing database instance. If you are using a supported separate database server, select the correct DSN from the list, and click Next.

As described previously, using a supported database instance requires that you have already created the database and ODBC DSN. If you haven't created the ODBC DSN yet, you'll need to exit the installation, create the DSN, and restart the installation.

8. The next screen prompts for user credentials to connect to the database specified in the DSN and configured for use by VUM.

Depending upon the configuration of the separate database server, you may or may not need to specify any credentials here. For SQL authentication, supply a username and password. For integrated Windows authentication, leave the username and password fields blank, as shown in Figure 4.3.

FIGURE 4.3
When using Windows authentication with a separate database server, leave the username and password fields blank.

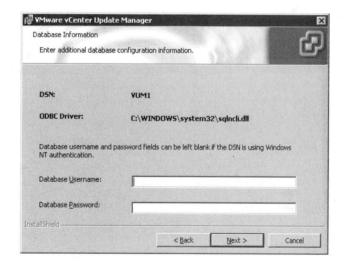

9. If the SQL Server database is set to the Full recovery model (the default), a dialog box pops up warning you about the need for regular backups.

Click OK to dismiss the dialog box and continue with the installation, but be sure to arrange for regular backups of the database. Otherwise, the database transaction logs could grow to consume all available space.

10. Unless there is a need to change the default port settings, leave the default settings, as shown in Figure 4.4. If there is a proxy server that controls access to the Internet, click the check box labeled Yes, I Have Internet Connection And I Want To Configure Proxy Settings Now. Otherwise, if there isn't a proxy or if you don't know the correct proxy configuration, leave the box deselected, and click Next.

CONFIGURING PROXY SETTINGS DURING INSTALLATION

If you forget to select the box to configure proxy settings during installation, fear not! All is not lost. After you install VUM, you can use the vSphere Client to set the proxy settings accordingly. Just be aware that VUM's first attempt to download patch information will fail because it can't access the Internet.

FIGURE 4.4
The vCenter Update Manager installation provides the option to configure proxy settings, if a proxy server is present. If there is no proxy, leave the box deselected.

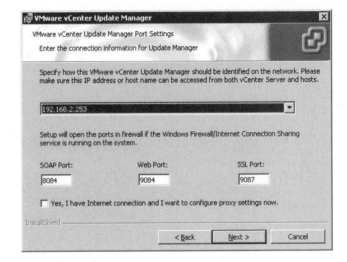

11. VUM downloads patches and patch metadata from the Internet and stores them locally for use in remediating hosts and guests.

   The next screen allows you to specify where to install VUM as well as where to store the patches, as shown in Figure 4.5. Use the Change button to modify the location of the patches to a location with sufficient storage capacity.

   In Figure 4.6, you can see where I've selected a different drive than the system drive to store the downloaded patches.

12. If you select a drive or partition with less than 20GB, a dialog box will pop up warning you to be sure you have sufficient space to download the appropriate patches. Click OK to proceed.

13. Click Install to install VUM.

14. Click Finish when the installation is complete.

At this point, VUM is installed, but it is not quite ready to run. If you've been following the steps in this section, you've configured VUM to use Windows authentication. Before you can actually use VUM, you must first configure the VUM services and the user account under which those services will run.

FIGURE 4.5
The default settings for vCenter Update Manager place the application files and the patch repository on the system drive.

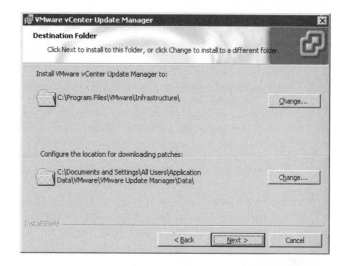

FIGURE 4.6
Moving the downloaded patches to a drive other than the system drive and with more available space.

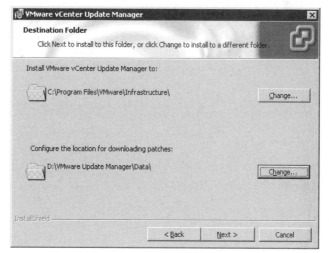

Configuring the VUM Services

As I noted earlier, VUM supports using either SQL authentication or Windows authentication for connecting to the separate database server. In environments using SQL authentication, the VUM installer prompts for SQL credentials, and upon the completion of installation, VUM is ready to use. In environments using Windows authentication, there's an additional step. You must specify the user account under which the VUM services will run. If you do not, these services will run as the LocalSystem account. The LocalSystem account, however, has no way of authenticating across the network, and therefore VUM will fail to operate because it cannot authenticate to the separate database server. To prevent this situation, you must change the user account under which the services run. Before you begin this procedure, be sure you know the username and password of the account under which the services should run (this should be the same account that was configured for ownership of the database).

Perform the following steps to change the configuration of the VUM services to support Windows authentication:

1. Log on to the computer where VUM was installed as an administrative user. In many cases, VUM is installed on the same computer as vCenter Server.

2. From the Start menu, select Run, and enter this command:

    ```
    services.msc
    ```

3. Click OK to launch the Services console.

4. Scroll down to the VMware Update Manager Service, and if it is running, stop it.

5. Right-click the VMware Update Manager Service, and select Properties.

6. Click the Log On tab.

7. Select the This Account radio button, and supply the username and password of the account under which the VUM services should run, as illustrated in Figure 4.7. This should be the same account configured for ownership of the VUM database.

FIGURE 4.7
To use Windows authentication with VMware Update Manager, you must change the user account under which the services run.

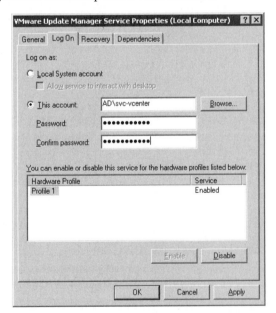

8. Click OK. If you receive a message indicating that the account has been granted the Log On As A Service right, click OK.

9. Restart the VMware Update Manager Service.

At this point, VUM is installed, but you have no way to manage it. In order to manage VUM, you must install the VUM plug-in for vCenter Server and the vSphere Client, as discussed in the next section.

Installing the vCenter Update Manager Plug-In

The tools to manage and configure VUM are implemented as vCenter Server plug-ins and are completely integrated into vCenter Server and the vSphere Client. However, to access these tools, you must first install and register the plug-in in the vSphere Client. This enables the vSphere Client to manage and configure VUM by adding an Update Manager tab and some extra context menu commands to objects in the vSphere Client. vSphere Client plug-ins are managed on a per-client basis; that is, each installation of the vSphere Client needs to have the plug-in installed in order to access the VUM administration tools.

Perform the following steps to install the VUM plug-in for each instance of the vSphere Client:

1. Launch the vSphere Client if it isn't already running, and connect to the appropriate vCenter Server instance.

2. From the vSphere Client's Plug-ins menu, select Manage Plug-Ins.

3. Find the vCenter Update Manager extension, and click the Download And Install link, as shown in Figure 4.8.

FIGURE 4.8
Installing the vSphere Client plug-in is done from within the vSphere Client.

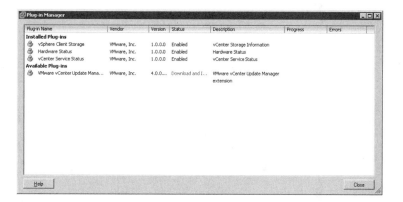

4. Run through the installation of the vCenter Update Manager extension, selecting the language, agreeing to the license terms, and completing the installation.

5. After the installation is complete, the status of the plug-in is listed as Enabled. Click Close to return to the vSphere Client.

The VUM plug-in is now installed into this instance of the vSphere Client. Remember that the VUM plug-in is per instance of the vSphere Client, so you need to repeat this process on each installation of the vSphere Client. After that is done, you are ready to configure VUM for your environment.

Configuring vCenter Update Manager

After you have installed and registered the plug-in with the vSphere Client, a new Update Manager icon appears on the vSphere Client home page. In addition, when in the Hosts And Clusters or VMs And Templates inventory view, a new tab labeled Update Manager appears on objects in the vSphere Client. From this Update Manager tab, you can scan for patches, create and attach baselines, stage patches to hosts, remediate hosts and guests, and perform all the other tasks involved in configuring and managing VUM.

Clicking the Update Manager icon at the vSphere Client home page takes you to the main VUM administration screen. Figure 4.9 shows that this area is divided into four main sections: Baselines And Groups, Configuration, Events, and Patch Repository.

FIGURE 4.9
There are four main tabs in the vCenter Update Manager Administration area within the vSphere Client.

These four tabs comprise the four major areas of configuration for VUM, so let's take a closer look at each of these areas in more detail.

Baselines and Groups

Baselines are a key part of how VUM works. In order to keep ESX/ESXi hosts and guest operating systems updated, VUM uses *baselines*.

VUM uses several different types of baselines. First, baselines are divided into host baselines, designed to be used in updating ESX/ESXi hosts, and VM/VA baselines, which are designed to be used to update virtual machines and virtual appliances. Baselines are further subdivided into patch baselines and upgrade baselines. Patch baselines define lists of patches to be applied to an ESX/ESXi host or guest operating system; upgrade baselines define how to upgrade an ESX/ESXi host or virtual appliance. Because of the broad differences in how various guest operating systems are upgraded, there are no upgrade baselines for guest operating systems. There are upgrade baselines for virtual appliances (VAs) and for other VM-related items, as you will see shortly.

Finally, baselines are divided once again into dynamic baselines or fixed baselines. Dynamic baselines can change over time ("all the patches released since January 1, 2009, for Windows XP Professional"), but fixed baselines remain constant ("include .NET Framework 3.5 Service Pack 1").

WHEN SHOULD YOU USE DYNAMIC VS. FIXED BASELINES?

Fixed baselines are best used to apply a specific fix to a group of hosts or guest operating systems. For example, let's say that VMware released a specific fix for ESX/ESXi that you wanted to be sure that all your hosts had installed. By creating a fixed baseline that included just that patch and attaching that baseline to your hosts, you could ensure that your hosts had that specific fix installed. Another use for fixed baselines is to establish the approved set of patches that you have tested and are now ready to deploy to the environment as a whole.

Dynamic baselines, on the other hand, are best used to keep systems current with the latest sets of patches. Because these baselines evolve over time, attaching them to your hosts or guest operating systems can help you understand just how current your systems are (or aren't!).

VMware provides a few baselines with VUM when it's installed. The baselines that are present upon installation include the following:

◆ Two host patch baselines named Critical Host Patches and Non-Critical Host Patches

◆ Two VM patch baselines named Critical VM Patches and Non-Critical VM Patches

◆ Four VM/VA upgrade baselines named VMware Tools Upgrade to Match Host, VM Hardware Upgrade to Match Host, VA Upgrade to Latest, and VA Upgrade to Latest Critical

Although these baselines provide a good starting point, many users will need to create additional baselines that better reflect their organizations' specific patching policy or procedures. For example, organizations may want to ensure that ESX/ESXi hosts are kept fully patched with regard to security patches, but not necessarily critical nonsecurity patches. This can be accomplished by creating a custom dynamic baseline.

Perform the following steps to create a new dynamic baseline for security-related ESX/ESXi host patches:

1. Launch the vSphere Client, and connect to the vCenter Server instance with which VUM is registered.

2. In the vSphere Client, navigate to the Update Manager Administration area, and click the Baselines And Groups tab.

3. Just under the tab bar, you need to select the correct baseline type, Host or VM/VA. In this case, select Host.

4. Click the Create link in the top-right area of the window. This launches the New Baseline Wizard.

5. Supply a name and description for the new baseline, and select Host Patch as the baseline type. Click Next.

6. Select Dynamic, and click Next.

7. On the next screen you define the criteria for the patches to be included in this baseline. Select the correct criteria for the baseline you are defining, and then click Next.

   Figure 4.10 shows a sample selection set—in this case, all security-related ESX patches.

8. Click Finish to create the baseline.

You can now use this baseline to determine which ESX/ESXi hosts are not compliant with the latest security patches by attaching it to one or more hosts, a procedure you'll learn later in this chapter in the section "Patching Hosts and Guests."

Groups, or baseline groups, are simply combinations of nonconflicting baselines. You might use a baseline group to combine multiple dynamic patch baselines, like the baseline group shown in Figure 4.11. In that example, a baseline group is defined that includes the built-in Critical Host Patches and Non-Critical Host Patches baselines. By attaching this baseline group to your ESX/ESXi hosts, you would be able to ensure that your hosts had all available patches installed.

Figure 4.12 shows another example of a host baseline group. In this example, I used a baseline group to combine dynamic baselines and fixed baselines. For example, there might be a specific fix for your ESX/ESXi hosts, and you want to ensure that all your hosts have all the critical patches—easily handled by the built-in Critical Host Patches dynamic baseline—as well as the specific fix. To do this, create a fixed baseline for the specific patch you want included, and then combine it in a baseline group with the built-in Critical Host Patches dynamic baseline.

FIGURE 4.10
Dynamic baselines contain a set of criteria that determine which patches are included in the baseline and which patches are not included in the baseline.

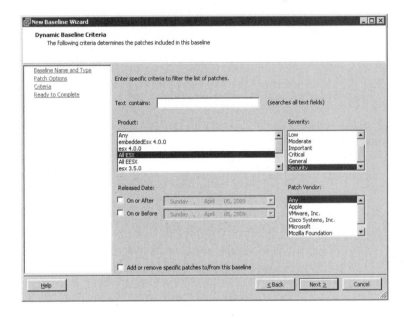

FIGURE 4.11
Combining multiple dynamic baselines into a baseline group provides greater flexibility in managing patches.

FIGURE 4.12
Use baseline groups to combine dynamic and fixed baselines.

Perform the following steps to create a host baseline group combining multiple host baselines:

1. Launch the vSphere Client if it isn't already running, and connect to the vCenter Server instance with which VUM is registered.

2. Navigate to the Update Manager Administration area.

3. In the lower-left corner of the Update Manager Administration area, click the link to create a new baseline group. This starts the New Baseline Group Wizard.

4. Type in a name for the new baseline group, and select Host Baseline Group as the baseline type. Click Next.

Each baseline group can include one of each type of upgrade baseline. For a host baseline group, there is only one type of upgrade baseline—a host upgrade. For VM/VA upgrade baselines, there are multiple types: VA Upgrades, VM Hardware Upgrades, and VM Tools Upgrades.

5. Select None, and click Next to skip attaching an upgrade baseline to this host baseline group.

6. Place a check mark next to the individual baseline to include in this baseline group, as shown in Figure 4.13.

FIGURE 4.13
A baseline group combines multiple individual baselines for more comprehensive patching capability.

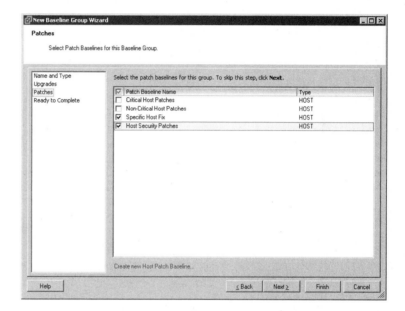

7. On the summary screen, review the settings, and click Finish to create the new baseline group.

The new baseline group you just created is now listed in the list of baseline groups, and you can attach it to ESX/ESXi hosts or clusters to identify which of them are not compliant with the baseline.

You'll see more about host upgrade baselines later in this chapter in the section "Upgrading ESX/ESXi Hosts with vCenter Update Manager."

Configuration

The bulk of the configuration of VUM is performed on the Configuration tab. From here, users can configure the full range of VUM settings, including network connectivity, patch download settings, patch download schedule, virtual machine settings, ESX/ESXi host settings, and vApp settings. These are some of the various options that you can configure:

Network Connectivity Under Network Connectivity, you can change the ports on which VUM communicates. In general, there is no need to change these ports, and you should leave them at the defaults.

Patch Download Settings The Patch Download Settings area allows you to configure what types of patches VUM will download and store. If you want to use VUM primarily as a mechanism for patching ESX/ESXi hosts but not virtual machines, you can save bandwidth and disk storage by deselecting the patch sources for virtual machines. You can also add custom URLs to download third-party patches. Figure 4.14 shows the patch sources for Windows and Linux VMs deselected so that VUM will not download patches from those sources.

FIGURE 4.14
vSphere administrators can deselect patch sources so that vCenter Update Manager downloads only certain types of patches.

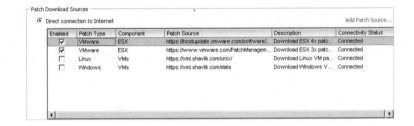

Enabled	Patch Type	Component	Patch Source	Description	Connectivity Status
✓	VMware	ESX	https://hostupdate.vmware.com/software/...	Download ESX 4x patc...	Connected
✓	VMware	ESX	https://www.vmware.com/PatchManagem...	Download ESX 3x patc..	Connected
☐	Linux	VMs	https://xml.shavlik.com/unix/	Download Linux VM pa...	Connected
☐	Windows	VMs	https://xml.shavlik.com/data	Download Windows V...	Connected

---

USING vCENTER UPDATE MANAGER ONLY FOR ESX/ESXi HOSTS

VUM is flexible and supports a variety of different deployment scenarios.

Using VUM only for applying patches to ESX/ESXi hosts is one fairly common configuration. Many organizations already have patch management solutions in place for scanning and patching Windows and Linux VMs. Rather than trying to replace these existing solutions with VUM, these organizations can simply tailor VUM to handle only the ESX/ESXi hosts and leave the existing patch management solutions to handle the guest operating systems inside the virtual machines.

Another fairly common configuration is using VUM for virtual machine scanning, but not remediation. You can use VUM to determine the status of updates for virtual machines without needing to switch to a different application.

The Patch Download Settings area is also where you would set the proxy configuration, if a proxy server is present on your network. VUM needs access to the Internet in order to download the patches and patch metadata, so if a proxy server controls Internet access, you must configure the proxy settings here in order for VUM to work.

Note that VUM does support a distributed model in which a single patch repository downloads patches, and multiple VUM servers all access the shared repository. Setting VUM to use a centralized download server is done with the Use A Shared Repository radio button.

Patch Download Schedule The Patch Download Schedule area allows you to control the timing and frequency of patch downloads. Click the Edit Patch Downloads link in the upper-right corner of this area to open the Schedule Update Download Wizard, which allows you to specify the schedule for patch downloads as well as gives you the opportunity to configure email notifications.

EMAIL NOTIFICATIONS REQUIRE SMTP SERVER CONFIGURATION

To receive any email notifications that you might configure in the Schedule Update Download Wizard, you must also configure the SMTP server in the vCenter Server settings, accessible from the Administration menu of the vSphere Client.

Virtual Machine Settings   Under Virtual Machine Settings, vSphere administrators configure whether to use virtual machine snapshots when applying patches to virtual machines. As you'll see in Chapter 7, "Creating and Managing Virtual Machines," snapshots provide the ability to capture a virtual machine's state at a given point in time and then roll back to that captured state if so desired. Having the ability, via a snapshot, to undo the installation of a series of patches is incredibly valuable. How many times have you run into the situation where applying a patch broke something else? By allowing VUM to integrate snapshots into the patching process, you are providing yourself with a built-in way to undo the patching operation and get back to a known good state.

Figure 4.15 shows the default settings that enable snapshots.

FIGURE 4.15
By default, virtual machine snapshots are enabled for use with vCenter Update Manager.

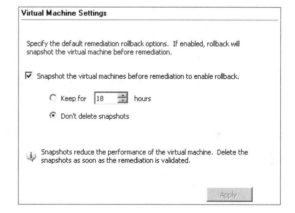

ESX Host Settings   The ESX Host Settings area provides controls for fine-tuning how VUM handles maintenance mode operations. Before an ESX/ESXi host is patched or upgraded, it is first placed into maintenance mode. When the ESX/ESXi host is part of a cluster that has VMware Distributed Resource Scheduler (DRS) enabled, this will also trigger automatic VMotions of virtual machines to other hosts in the cluster. These settings allow you to control what happens if a host fails to go into maintenance mode and how many times VUM retries the maintenance mode operation. The default settings specify that VUM will retry three times to place a host in maintenance mode.

vApp Settings   The vApp Settings allow you to control whether VUM's "smart reboot" feature is enabled for vApps. vApps are teams, if you will, of virtual machines. Consider a multitier application that consists of a front-end web server, a middleware server, and a back-end database server. These three different virtual machines and their respective guest operating systems could be combined into a vApp. The smart reboot feature simply restarts the different virtual machines within the vApp in a way that accommodates inter-VM dependencies. For example, if the database server has to be patched and rebooted, then it is quite likely that the web server and the middleware server will also need to be rebooted, and they shouldn't be restarted until after the database server is back up and available again. The default setting is to leverage smart reboot.

Events

The Events tab lists the events logged by VUM. As shown in Figure 4.16, the Events tab lists actions taken by administrators as well as automatic actions taken by VUM. Administrators can sort the list of events by clicking the column headers, but there is no functionality to help users filter out only the events they want to see. There is also no way to export events from here.

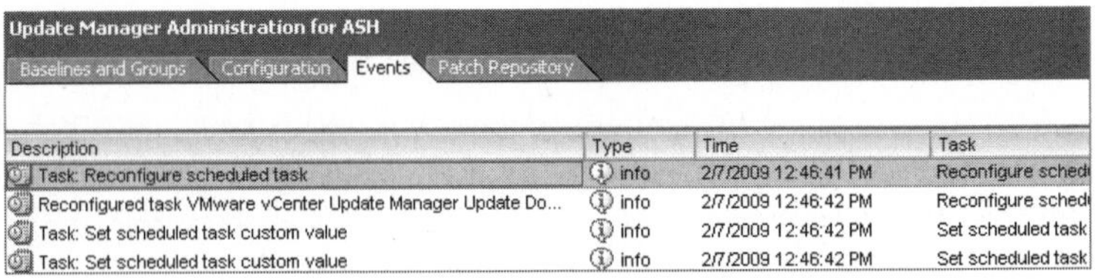

FIGURE 4.16
The Events tab lists events logged by vCenter Update Manager during operation and can be a good source of information for troubleshooting.

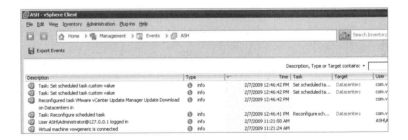

However, you can also find the events listed here in the Management ➤ Events area of vCenter Server, and that area does include some filtering functionality as well as the ability to export the events, as shown in Figure 4.17.

FIGURE 4.17
Events from vCenter Update Manager are also included in the Management area of vCenter Server, where information can be exported or filtered.

I discussed the functionality of the Management ➤ Events area of vCenter Server in detail in Chapter 3.

Patch Repository

The Patch Repository tab shows all the patches that are currently in VUM's patch repository. From here, you can also view the details of any specific patch by right-clicking the patch and selecting Show Patch Detail. Figure 4.18 shows the additional information displayed about a patch when you select Show Patch Detail from the right-click context menu.

This particular item shown in Figure 4.18 is the Virtual Ethernet Module for the Cisco Nexus 1000V, a third-party distributed virtual switch that I discuss in detail in Chapter 5.

FIGURE 4.18
The Patch Repository tab also offers more detailed information about each of the items in the repository.

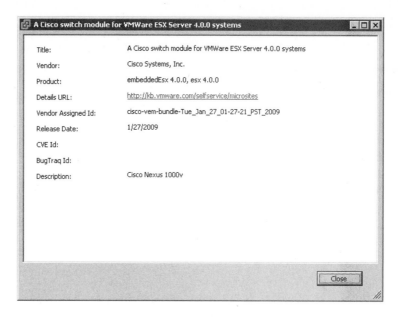

The Patch Repository tab also allows you to see in what baselines a particular patch might be included. The Show link to the far right of each entry in the patch repository link shows all the baselines that include that particular patch.

Let's now take a look at actually using VUM to patch ESX/ESXi hosts and guest operating systems.

Patching Hosts and Guests

VUM uses the term *remediation* to refer to the process of applying patches to an ESX/ESXi host or guest operating system instance. As described in the previous section, VUM uses baselines to create lists of patches based on certain criteria. By attaching a baseline to a host or guest operating system and performing a scan, VUM can determine whether that host or guest operating system is compliant or noncompliant with the baseline. Compliant with the baseline means that the host or guest operating system has all the patches included in the baseline currently installed and is up-to-date; noncompliant means that one or more patches are missing and the target is not up-to-date.

After compliance with one or more baselines or baseline groups has been determined, the vSphere administrator can remediate—or *patch*—the hosts or guest operating system. Optionally, the administrator also has the option of staging patches to ESX/ESXi hosts before remediation.

Attaching—or detaching—baselines is the first step, then, to patching ESX/ESXi hosts or guest operating systems. Let's start by taking a closer look at how to attach and detach baselines.

Attaching and Detaching Baselines

Before you patch a host or guest, you must determine whether a host or guest operating system is compliant or noncompliant with one or more baselines or baseline groups. Defining a baseline or baseline group alone is not enough. To determine compliance, the baseline or baseline group must be attached to a host or guest operating system. After it is attached, the baseline or baseline group becomes the "measuring stick" that VUM uses to determine compliance with the list of patches included in the attached baselines or baseline groups.

Attaching and detaching baselines is performed in one of vCenter Server's Inventory views. To attach or detach a baseline or baseline groups for ESX/ESXi hosts, you need to be in the Hosts And Clusters view; for guest operating systems, you need to be in the VMs And Templates view. In both cases, you'll use the Update Manager tab to attach or detach baselines or baseline groups.

In both views, baselines and baseline groups can be attached to a variety of objects. In the Hosts And Clusters view, baselines and baseline groups can be attached to datacenters, clusters, or individual ESX/ESXi hosts. In VMs And Templates view, baselines and baseline groups can be attached to datacenters, folders, or specific virtual machines. Because of the hierarchical nature of the vCenter Server inventory, a baseline attached at a higher level will automatically apply to eligible child objects as well. You may also find yourself applying different baselines or baseline groups at different levels of the hierarchy; for example, there may be a specific baseline that applies to all hosts in the environment but another baseline that applies only to a specific subset of hosts.

Let's look at attaching a baseline to a specific ESX/ESXi host. The process is much the same, if not identical, for attaching a baseline to a datacenter, cluster, folder, or virtual machine.

Perform the following steps to attach a baseline or baseline group to an ESX/ESXi host:

1. Launch the vSphere Client if it is not already running, and connect to a vCenter Server instance.

   Because VUM is integrated with and depends upon vCenter Server, you cannot manage, attach, or detach VUM baselines when connected directly to an ESX/ESXi host.

2. From the menu, select View ≻ Inventory ≻ Hosts And Clusters, or press the Ctrl+Shift+H keyboard shortcut.

3. In the inventory tree on the left, select the ESX/ESXi host to which you want to attach a baseline or baseline group.

4. From the pane on the right, use the double-headed arrows to scroll through the list of tabs until you can see the Update Manager tab, and then select it.

   The screen shown in Figure 4.19 shows the Update Manager tab for a specific ESX/ESXi that has no baselines or baseline groups attached.

5. Click the Attach link in the upper-right corner; this link opens the Attach Baseline Or Group dialog box.

6. Select the baselines or baseline groups that you want to attach to this ESX/ESXi host, and then click Attach.

The steps for attaching a baseline or baseline group to a virtual machine with a guest operating system installed are similar, but let's walk through the process anyway. This time I want to point out a very useful baseline named VMware Tools Upgrade to Match Host. This baseline is a default baseline that is defined upon installation of VUM, and its purpose is to help you identify which guest operating systems are running outdated versions of the VMware Tools. As you'll see in Chapter 7, the VMware Tools are an important piece of optimizing your guest operating systems to run in a virtualized environment, and it's great that VUM can help identify which guest operating systems don't have the current version of the VMware Tools installed.

FIGURE 4.19
The Update Manager tab of an ESX/ESXi host shows what baselines and baseline groups, if any, are currently attached.

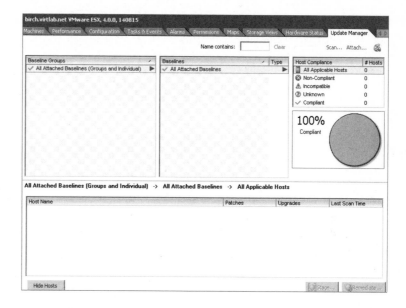

Perform the following steps to attach a baseline to a datacenter so that it applies to all the objects under the datacenter:

1. Launch the vSphere Client if it is not already running, and connect to a vCenter Server instance.

2. Switch to the VMs And Templates inventory view by selecting View ➢ Inventory ➢ VMs And Templates, by using the navigation bar, or by using the Ctrl+Shift+V keyboard shortcut.

3. Select the datacenter object from the inventory on the left.

4. From the contents pane on the right, click the Update Manager tab.

5. Right-click a blank area of the list of baselines or baseline groups, and select Attach from the right-click context menu. This opens the Attach Baseline Or Group dialog box.

6. Click to select the VMware Tools Upgrade To Match Host upgrade baseline, and then click Attach.

After you attach this baseline, you'll see the screen change to show that VUM is unsure about whether the systems to which this baseline has been applied are in compliance with the baseline. The screen will look something like Figure 4.20.

To determine compliance or noncompliance with a baseline or baseline group, you need to perform a scan.

FIGURE 4.20
vCenter Update Manager is unsure if the objects to which the baseline has been attached are in compliance with the baseline.

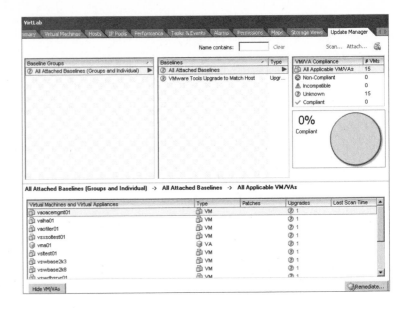

Performing a Scan

The next step after attaching a baseline is to perform a scan. The purpose of a scan is to determine the compliance—or noncompliance—of an object with the baseline. If the object being scanned matches what's defined in the baseline, then the object—be it an ESX/ESXi host or guest operating system instance—is compliant. If there's something missing from the host or guest OS, then it's noncompliant. You may perform scans on ESX/ESXi hosts, online virtual machines with a guest operating system installed, offline virtual machines with a guest operating system installed, and some powered-on virtual appliances.

Perform the following steps to initiate a scan of an ESX/ESXi host after a baseline is attached:

1. Launch the vSphere Client if it is not already running, and connect to a vCenter Server instance.

2. Go to the Hosts And Clusters inventory view by selecting View ➢ Inventory ➢ Hosts And Clusters, by using the navigation bar, or by pressing the Ctrl+Shift+H keyboard shortcut.

3. Select an ESX/ESXi host from the inventory tree on the left.

4. From the content pane on the right, scroll through the list of tabs, and select the Update Manager tab.

5. Click the Scan link in the upper-right corner.

6. Select whether you want to scan for patches, upgrades, or both, and then click Scan.

When the scan is complete, the Update Manager tab will update to show whether the object is compliant or noncompliant. Compliance is measured on a per-baseline basis. In Figure 4.21, you can see that the selected ESX/ESXi host is compliant with the Critical Host Patches baseline but noncompliant with the Non-Critical Host Patches baseline. Because the host is noncompliant with at least one attached baseline, the host is considered noncompliant overall.

FIGURE 4.21
When multiple baselines are attached to an object, compliance is reflected on a per-baseline basis.

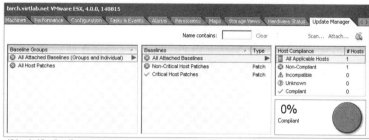

When you are viewing the Update Manager tab for an object that contains other objects, like a datacenter, cluster, or folder, then compliance might be mixed. That is, some objects might be compliant, while other objects might be noncompliant. Figure 4.22 shows a cluster with mixed compliance reports.

FIGURE 4.22
vCenter Update Manager can show partial compliance when viewing objects that contain other objects.

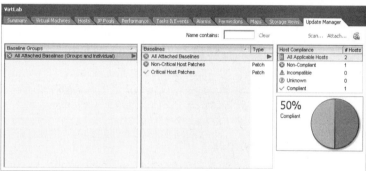

Depending upon the type of scan you are performing, scans can be fairly quick. Scanning a large group of virtual machines for VMware Tools upgrades or VM hardware upgrades is fairly quick. Scanning a large group of virtual machines for patches, on the other hand, may be more time-consuming and more resource intensive. For this reason, VUM has limits on how many operations it will sustain at a given time, as shown in Table 4.1.

CALCULATING VCENTER UPDATE MANAGER LIMITS

Use the limits in Table 4.1 cautiously. When running different sorts of tasks at the same time, VUM doesn't combine the limits. So, if you were running both powered-on and powered-off Windows VM scans, the limit would be 6 per ESX/ESXi host, not 12 per host.

After the scanning is complete and compliance is established, you are ready to fix the noncompliant systems. Before we discuss remediation, let's first look at staging patches to ESX/ESXi hosts.

TABLE 4.1: Limits for vCenter Update Manager

VUM OPERATION	MAXIMUM TASKS PER ESX/ESXi HOST	MAXIMUM TASKS PER VUM SERVER
VM remediation	5	48
Powered-on Windows VM scan	6	72
Powered-off Windows VM scan	6	10
Powered-on Linux VM scan	6	72
Host scan	1	72
Host remediation	1	48
VMware Tools scan	145	145
VM hardware scan	145	145
VMware Tools upgrade	145	145
VM hardware upgrade	145	145
Host upgrade	1	48

Source: "VMware vCenter Update Manager Performance and Best Practices" white paper available on VMware's website at www.vmware.com

Staging Patches

If the target of remediation—that is, the object within vCenter Server that you are trying to remediate and make compliant with a baseline—is an ESX/ESXi host, an additional option exists. VUM offers the option of staging patches to ESX/ESXi hosts. Staging a patch to an ESX/ESXi host copies the files across to the host to speed up the actual time of remediation. Staging is not a required step; you can update hosts without staging the updates first, if you prefer.

Perform the following steps to stage patches to an ESX/ESXi host using VUM:

1. Launch the vSphere Client if it is not already running, and connect to a vCenter Server instance.

2. Navigate to the Hosts And Clusters view by selecting View ➤ Inventory ➤ Hosts And Clusters, by using the Ctrl+Shift+H keyboard shortcut, or by using the navigation bar.

3. From the inventory list on the left, select an ESX/ESXi host.

4. From the content pane on the right, scroll through the tabs, and select the Update Manager tab.

5. Click the Stage button, or right-click the host and select Stage Patches. Either method activates the Stage Wizard.

6. Select the baselines for the patches you want to be staged, and click Next to proceed.

7. The next screen allows you to deselect any specific patches you do not want to be staged. If you want all the patches to be staged, leave them all selected, and click Next.

8. Click Finish at the summary screen to start the staging process.

After the staging process is complete, the Tasks pane at the bottom of the vSphere Client reflects this, as shown in Figure 4.23.

FIGURE 4.23
The vSphere Client reflects when the process of staging patches is complete.

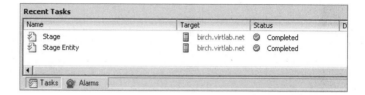

After you stage patches to the ESX/ESXi hosts, you can begin the task of remediating.

Remediating Hosts

After you have attached a baseline to a host, scanned the host for compliance, and optionally staged the updates to the host, you're ready to remediate, or update, the ESX/ESXi host.

Perform the following steps to update an ESX/ESXi host:

1. Launch the vSphere Client if it is not already running, and connect to a vCenter Server instance.

2. Switch to the Hosts And Clusters view by using the navigation bar, by using the Ctrl+Shift+H keyboard shortcut, or by selecting View ➢ Inventory ➢ Hosts And Clusters.

3. Select an ESX/ESXi host from the inventory tree on the left.

4. From the content pane on the right, select the Update Manager tab. You might need to scroll through the available tabs in order to see the Update Manager tab.

5. In the lower-right corner of the window, click the Remediate button. You can also right-click the ESX/ESXi host and select Remediate from the context menu.

6. The Remediate dialog box displays, as shown in Figure 4.24. From here, select the baselines or baseline groups that you want to apply. Click Next.

7. Deselect any patches that you don't want applied to the ESX/ESXi host. This allows you to customize the exact list of patches. Click Next after you've deselected any patches to exclude.

8. Specify a name and description for the remediation task. Also, choose whether you want the remediation to occur immediately or whether it should run at a specific time. Figure 4.25 shows these options. You also have the option of modifying the default settings for how VUM handles ESX/ESXi hosts and maintenance mode.

9. Review the summary screen, and click Finish if everything is correct. If there are any errors, use the Back button to double-check and change the settings.

FIGURE 4.24
The Remediate dialog box allows you to select the baselines or baseline groups against which you would like to remediate an ESX/ESXi host.

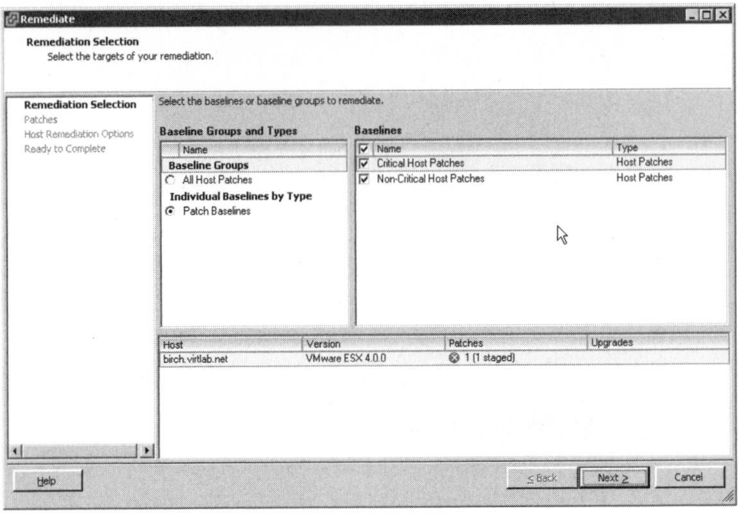

FIGURE 4.25
When remediating a host, you need to specify a name for the remediation task and a schedule for the task. All other parameters are optional.

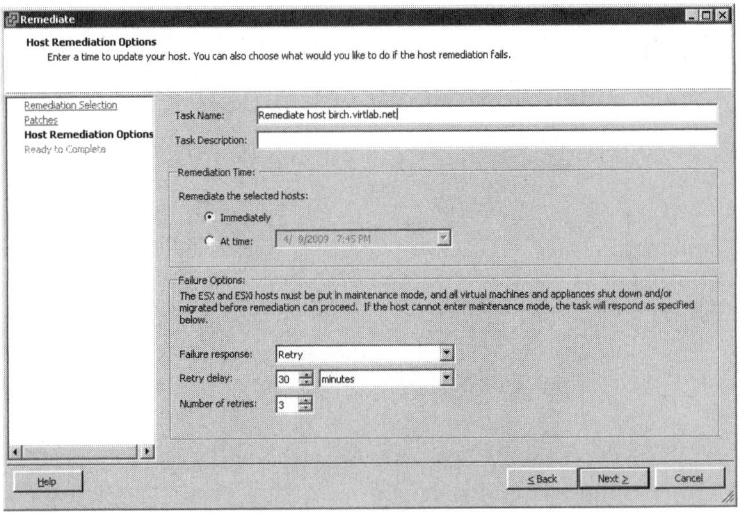

If you selected to have the remediation occur immediately, which is the default setting, VUM initiates a task request with vCenter Server. You'll see this task, as well as some related tasks, in the Tasks pane at the bottom of the vSphere Client.

If necessary, VUM automatically puts the ESX/ESXi host into maintenance mode. If the host is a member of a DRS-enabled cluster, putting the host into maintenance mode will, in turn, initiate a series of VMotion operations to migrate all virtual machines to other hosts in the cluster. After the patching is complete, VUM automatically reboots the host, if necessary, and then takes the host out of maintenance mode.

Remediating hosts is only part of the functionality of VUM. Another major part is remediating your guest operating systems.

🌐 Real World Scenario

KEEPING HOSTS PATCHED IS IMPORTANT

Keeping your ESX/ESXi hosts patched is important. I know that all of you already know this, but too often VMware administrators forget to incorporate this key task into their operations.

Here's an example. During the ESX 3.5 Update 2 timeframe, VMware uncovered a bug that affected environments using Network File System (NFS) for their virtual machine storage. The issue manifested itself as an inability to delete VMware snapshots. A workaround was available that involved disabling NFS locks. Unfortunately, this workaround also had some nasty side effects, such as allowing a virtual machine to be booted up on two different ESX/ESXi hosts at the same time. A patch was made available a short time later, but many VMware administrators who had disabled NFS locks did not apply the patch and were impacted by the side effects of the workaround. Some of them even lost virtual machines or data within the virtual machines. Had these VMware administrators incorporated a regular patching routine into their operational procedures, these data losses might have been avoided.

VUM makes keeping your hosts patched much easier, but you still need to actually do it! Be sure to take the time to establish a regular schedule for applying ESX/ESXi host updates and take advantage of VUM's integration with VMotion, vCenter Server, and VMware Distributed Resource Scheduler (DRS) to avoid downtime for your end users during the patching process.

Remediating the Guest Operating Systems

VUM can scan and remediate not only ESX/ESXi hosts but also virtual machines running Windows and Linux. You follow the same general order of operations for remediating guest operating systems as you did for hosts:

1. Attach one or more baselines or baseline groups.

2. Scan the guest operating systems for compliance with the attached baselines or baseline groups.

3. Remediate the guest operating systems if they are noncompliant.

The procedure for attaching a baseline was described previously in the section "Attaching and Detaching Baselines," and the process of performing a scan for compliance with a baseline was also described previously in the section "Performing a Scan."

If you have attached a baseline to a virtual machine and scanned the guest operating system on that virtual machine for compliance with the baseline, the next step is actually remediating the guest operating system.

Perform the following steps to remediate a guest operating system in a virtual machine:

1. Launch the vSphere Client if it is not already running, and connect to an instance of vCenter Server.

2. Using the menu, navigate to the VMs And Templates area by selecting View ➤ Inventory ➤ VMs And Templates. You can also use the navigation bar or the Ctrl+Shift+V keyboard shortcut.

3. Right-click the virtual machine that you want to remediate, and select Remediate from the context menu. This displays the Remediate dialog box.

4. In the Remediate dialog box, select the baselines or baseline groups that you want to apply, and then click Next.

5. Deselect any patches that you don't want included in the remediation, and click Next. If you just click Next, all the patches defined in the attached baselines or baseline groups are included.

6. Provide a name for the remediation task, and select a schedule for the task. Different schedules are possible for powered-on VMs, powered-off VMs, and suspended VMs, as shown in Figure 4.26.

FIGURE 4.26
vCenter Update Manager supports different schedules for remediating powered-on VMs, powered-off VMs, and suspended VMs.

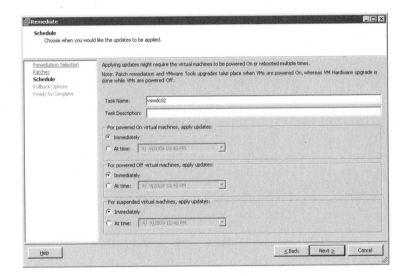

7. Select an appropriate schedule for each of the different classes of virtual machines, and then click Next.

8. If you want to take a snapshot of the virtual machine, supply a name for the snapshot and a description.

   You may also specify a maximum age for the snapshot and whether to snapshot the virtual machine's memory. The default settings, as shown in Figure 4.27, do not provide a maximum age for snapshots (do not delete snapshots) and do not snapshot the virtual machine's memory.

9. Review the information in the summary screen. If anything is incorrect, use the Back button to double-check and change the settings. Otherwise, click Finish to start the remediation.

VUM applies the patches to the guest operating system in the virtual machine and reboots the virtual machine automatically, if necessary. Where multiple virtual machines are joined together in a vApp, VUM and vCenter Server will coordinate restarting the virtual machines within the vApp to satisfy inter-VM dependencies unless you turned off smart reboot in the VUM configuration.

FIGURE 4.27
vCenter Update Manager integrates with vCenter Server's snapshot functionality to allow remediation operations to be rolled back in the event of a problem.

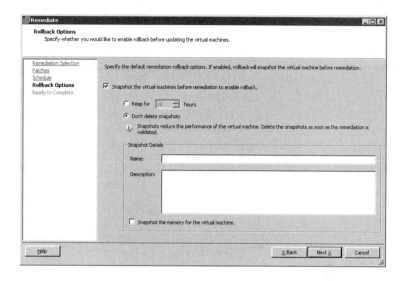

Guest operating system patches are not the only area of keeping virtual machines up-to-date. You also need to consider the VMware Tools and virtual machine hardware.

Upgrading the VMware Tools

The VMware Tools are an important part of your virtualized infrastructure. The basic idea behind the VMware Tools is to provide a set of virtualization-optimized drivers for all the guest operating systems that VMware supports with VMware vSphere. These virtualization-optimized drivers help provide the highest levels of performance for guest operating systems running on VMware vSphere, and it's considered a best practice to keep the VMware Tools up-to-date whenever possible.

To help with that task, VUM comes with a prebuilt upgrade baseline named VMware Tools Upgrade to Match Host. This baseline can't be modified or deleted from within the vSphere Client, and its sole purpose is to help vSphere administrators identify virtual machines that are not running a version of VMware Tools that is appropriate for the host on which they are currently running.

Once again, you follow the same overall procedure to use this functionality within VUM:

1. Attach the baseline.

2. Scan for compliance.

3. Remediate.

In general, a reboot of the guest operating system is required after the VMware Tools upgrade is complete, although that varies from guest OS to guest OS. Most Windows versions require a reboot, so plan accordingly.

You can find a more complete and thorough discussion of the VMware Tools in Chapter 7.

When you are dealing with virtual machines brought into a VMware vSphere environment from earlier versions of VMware Infrastructure, you must be sure to first upgrade VMware Tools to the latest version and then deal with upgrading virtual machine hardware as discussed in the next section. By upgrading the VMware Tools first, you ensure that the appropriate drivers are already loaded into the guest operating system when you upgrade the virtual machine hardware.

Now let's look at upgrading virtual machine hardware and what is involved in the process.

Upgrading Virtual Machine Hardware

So far, I haven't really had the opportunity to discuss the idea of virtual machine hardware. This is a topic I'll cover in greater detail later, but for now suffice it to say that virtual machines brought into a VMware vSphere environment from earlier versions of ESX/ESXi will have outdated virtual machine hardware. In order to use all the functionality of VMware vSphere with these VMs, you will have to upgrade the virtual machine hardware. To help with this process, VUM includes the ability to scan for and remediate virtual machines with out-of-date virtual machine hardware.

VUM already comes with a VM upgrade baseline that addresses this: the VM Hardware Upgrade to Match Host baseline. This baseline is predefined and can't be changed or deleted from within the vSphere Client. The purpose of this baseline is to determine whether a virtual machine's hardware is current. Virtual machine hardware version 7 is the version used by VMware vSphere; previous versions of ESX/ESXi used virtual machine hardware version 4.

To upgrade the virtual machine hardware version, you again follow the same general sequence:

1. Attach the baseline.

2. Perform a scan.

3. Remediate.

To attach the baseline, you follow the same procedures outlined previously in the section "Attaching and Detaching Baselines." Performing a scan is much the same as well; be sure you select the VM Hardware upgrades option when initiating a scan in order for VUM to detect outdated VM hardware. Even if the correct baseline is attached, outdated VM hardware won't be detected during a scan unless you select this box.

PLANNING FOR DOWNTIME

Remediation of virtual machines found to be noncompliant—for example, found to have outdated virtual machine hardware—is again much like the other forms of remediation that I've already discussed. The only important thing to note, as indicated in the text shown in Figure 4.28, is that VM hardware upgrades are done while the VM is powered off. This means you must plan for downtime in the environment in order to remediate this issue.

VUM performs virtual machine hardware upgrades only when the VM is powered off. It's also important to note that VUM doesn't conduct an orderly shutdown of the guest operating system in order to do the VM hardware upgrade. To avoid an unexpected shutdown of the guest operating system when VUM powers off the VM, specify a schedule in the Remediate dialog box, shown in Figure 4.28, that provides you with enough time to perform an orderly shutdown of the guest operating system first.

Depending upon which guest operating system and which version is running inside the virtual machine, the user may see prompts for "new hardware" after the virtual machine hardware upgrade is complete. If you've followed my recommendations and the latest version of the

VMware Tools are installed, then all the necessary drivers should already be present, and the "new hardware" should work without any real issues.

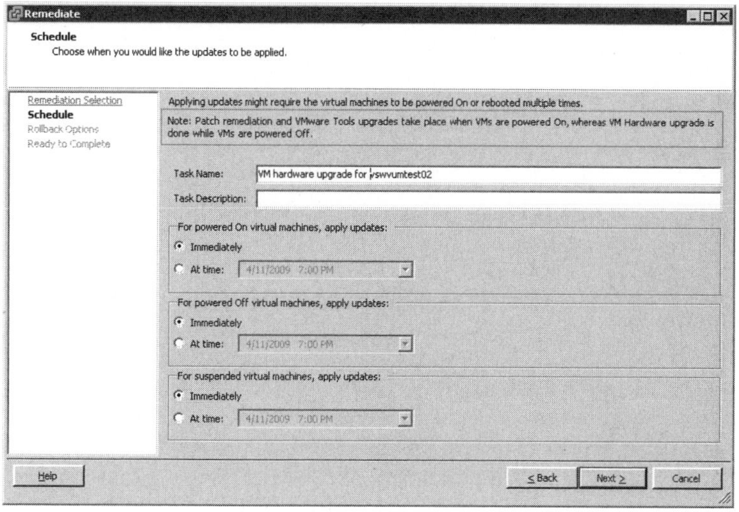

FIGURE 4.28
The Remediate dialog box indicates that VM hardware upgrades are performed while VMs are powered off.

You can find more information on virtual machine hardware and virtual machine hardware versions in Chapter 7.

Now let's look at the last major piece of VUM's functionality: upgrading ESX/ESXi hosts.

Upgrading ESX/ESXi Hosts with vCenter Update Manager

Previously in this chapter I discussed baselines and walked you through creating a baseline. During that process, you saw two different types of host baselines: host patch baselines and host upgrade baselines. I've already discussed the first host baseline type in the previous section, and you know that host patch baselines are used to keep ESX/ESXi hosts patched to current revision levels. Now you'll take a look at host upgrade baselines and how you would use them.

VUM uses host upgrade baselines to help automate the process of upgrading ESX/ESXi hosts from previous versions to version 4.0. Let's start by walking through creating an upgrade baseline.

Perform the following steps to create an upgrade baseline:

1. Launch the vSphere Client if it is not already running, and connect to a vCenter Server instance.

2. Navigate to the Update Manager Administration area by using the navigation bar or by selecting View ➢ Solutions And Applications ➢ Update Manager.

3. Click the Baselines And Groups tab. Make sure the view is set to Hosts, not VMs/VAs. Use the small buttons just below the tab bar to set the correct view.

4. Select the Upgrade Baselines tab.

5. Right-click a blank area of the Upgrade Baselines list, and select New Baseline. The New Baseline Wizard starts.

6. Supply a name for the baseline and an optional description, and note that the vSphere Client has automatically selected the type as Host Upgrade. Click Next to continue.

7. Select the ESX upgrade ISO and the ESXi upgrade ZIP files. You can use the Browse button to find the files on the vCenter Server computer or another location accessible across the network.

8. Click Next to upload the files and continue; note that the file upload might take a few minutes to complete.

9. After the file uploads and file imports have completed, click Next.

10. The next screen asks about where to place the storage for the ESX Service Console.

    As you saw in Chapter 2, the Service Console (referred to here as the COS or the Console OS) resides within a virtual machine disk file (a VMDK file). The upgrade baseline needs to know where to place the VMDK for the COS during the upgrade process.

11. Select Automatically Select A Datastore On The Local Host, and click Next.

12. If the upgrade process fails or if the host is unable to reconnect to vCenter Server, VUM offers the option of automatically rebooting the host and "rolling back" the upgrade.

    The next screen offers the option to disable that feature by deselecting the box marked Try To Reboot The Host And Roll Back The Upgrade In Case Of Failure. You can also specify a post-upgrade script and control the time that the post-upgrade script should be allowed to run.

    Leave this option selected, and don't select to run a post-upgrade script or to specify a timeout for the post-upgrade script, as shown in Figure 4.29.

FIGURE 4.29
Leave the check box selected to allow vCenter Update Manager to reboot the ESX/ESXi host and roll back the upgrade in the event of a failure.

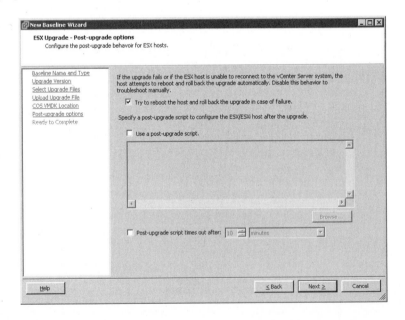

13. Click Next to continue.

14. Review the summary of the options selected in the upgrade baseline. If anything is incorrect, use the Back button to correct it. Otherwise, click Finish.

After you've created a host upgrade baseline, using the host upgrade baseline to upgrade an ESX/ESXi host follows the same basic sequence of steps outlined previously:

◆ Attach the baseline to the ESX/ESXi hosts that you want to upgrade. Refer to the earlier section "Attaching and Detaching Baselines" for a review of how to attach the host upgrade baseline to an ESX/ESXi host.

◆ Scan the ESX/ESXi hosts for compliance with the baseline. Don't forget to select to scan for upgrades when presented with the scan options.

◆ Remediate (for example, upgrade) the host.

The Remediate Wizard is much the same as what you've already seen, but there are enough differences that I'll review the process.

Perform the following steps to upgrade an ESX/ESXi host with a VUM host upgrade baseline:

1. On the first screen, select the host upgrade baseline you want to use for remediating the ESX/ESXi host, and then click Next.

2. Select the check box to accept the license terms, and then click Next.

3. Review the settings specified in the host upgrade baseline. A blue hyperlink next to each setting, as shown in Figure 4.30, allows you to modify the settings. To leave the settings as they were specified in the host upgrade baseline, simply click Next.

FIGURE 4.30
The blue hyperlinks allow you to modify the specific details of the host upgrade baseline.

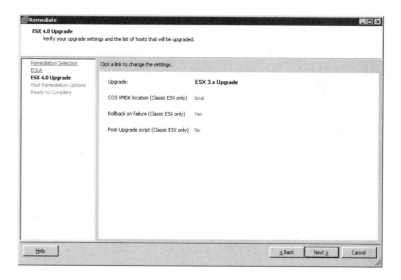

4. Specify a name, description, and a schedule for the remediation task, and then click Next.

5. Review the settings, and use the Back button if any settings need to be changed. Click Finish when the settings are correct and you are ready to proceed with the upgrade.

VUM then proceeds with the host upgrade at the scheduled time (Immediately is the default setting in the wizard). The upgrade will be an unattended upgrade, and at the end of the upgrade the ESX/ESXi host automatically reboots.

CUSTOM SERVICE CONSOLE PARTITIONS ARE NOT HONORED

There is one drawback to using host upgrade baselines to upgrade your ESX hosts: custom Service Console partitions are not honored. (ESXi does not have a user-accessible Service Console, so this doesn't apply.) In Chapter 2 we discussed the need for a custom Service Console partition scheme that protected the root (/) directory from filling up and causing the host to stop functioning.

Unfortunately, vCenter Update Manager and the host upgrade baseline don't honor these partitioning schemes. Although the old partitions are preserved (their contents are kept intact and mounted under the /esx3-installation directory), the new Service Console will have a single partition mounted at the root directory.

If you want your ESX 4.0 hosts to have a custom partition scheme after the upgrade, you need to forgo the use of VUM and host upgrade baselines.

I've discussed a lot of VUM's functionality so far, but there is one more topic that I'll cover in this chapter. By combining some of the different features of VUM, you can greatly simplify the process of upgrading your virtualized infrastructure to VMware vSphere 4 through an orchestrated upgrade.

Performing an Orchestrated Upgrade

Now that I've discussed host upgrade baselines, I can revisit the idea of baseline groups and discuss a specific use case for baseline groups: the *orchestrated upgrade*. An orchestrated upgrade involves the use of a host baseline group and a VM/VA baseline group that, when run sequentially, will help automate the process of moving an organization's environment fully into VMware vSphere.

Consider this sequence of events:

1. You create a host baseline group that combines a host upgrade baseline with a dynamic host patch baseline to apply the latest updates.

2. You create a VM baseline group that combines two different VM upgrade baselines—the VMware Tools upgrade baseline and the virtual machine hardware upgrade baseline—with an optional VM patch baseline to apply the latest updates.

3. You schedule the host baseline group to execute, followed at some point later by the VM baseline group.

4. The host baseline group upgrades the hosts from ESX/ESXi 3.x to ESX/ESXi 4.0 and installs all applicable patches and updates.

5. The VM baseline group upgrades the VMware Tools and then upgrades the virtual machine hardware from version 4 to version 7.

When these two baseline groups have completed, all the hosts and VMs affected by the baselines will be upgraded and patched. Most, if not all, of the tedious tasks surrounding upgrading the VMware Tools and the virtual machine hardware have been automated. Congratulations! You've just simplified and automated the upgrade path for your virtual environment.

Now you're ready to start taking advantage of the new networking and storage functionality available in VMware vSphere. In the next chapter I'll discuss networking, and in Chapter 6, "Creating and Managing Storage Devices," I'll cover storage in detail.

The Bottom Line

Install VUM and integrate it with the vSphere Client. vCenter Update Manager is installed from the VMware vCenter installation media and requires that vCenter Server has already been installed. Like vCenter Server, vCenter Update Manager requires the use of a back-end database server. Finally, you must install a plug-in into the vSphere Client in order to access, manage, or configure vCenter Update Manager.

> **Master It** You have vCenter Update Manager installed, and you've configured it from the vSphere Client on your laptop. One of the other administrators on your team is saying that she can't access or configure vCenter Update Manager and that there must be something wrong with the installation. What is the most likely cause of the problem?

Determine which ESX/ESXi hosts or virtual machines need to be patched or upgraded. Baselines are the "measuring sticks" whereby vCenter Update Manager knows whether an ESX/ESXi host or guest operating system instance is up-to-date. vCenter Update Manager compares the ESX/ESXi hosts or guest operating systems to the baselines to determine whether they need to be patched and, if so, what patches need to be applied. vCenter Update Manager also uses baselines to determine which ESX/ESXi hosts need to be upgraded to the latest version or which virtual machines need to have their virtual machine hardware upgraded. vCenter Update Manager comes with some predefined baselines and allows administrators to create additional baselines specific to their environments. Baselines can be fixed—the contents remain constant—or they can be dynamic, where the contents of the baseline change over time. Baseline groups allow administrators to combine baselines together and apply them together.

> **Master It** In addition to ensuring that all your ESX/ESXi hosts have the latest critical and security patches installed, you also need to ensure that all your ESX/ESXi hosts have another specific patch installed. This additional patch is noncritical and therefore doesn't get included in the critical patch dynamic baseline. How do you work around this problem?

Use VUM to upgrade virtual machine hardware or VMware Tools. vCenter Update Manager can detect virtual machines with outdated virtual machine hardware versions and guest operating systems that have outdated versions of the VMware Tools installed. vCenter Update Manager comes with predefined baselines that enable this functionality. In addition, vCenter Update Manager has the ability to upgrade virtual machine hardware versions and upgrade the VMware Tools inside guest operating systems to ensure that everything is kept up-to-date. This functionality is especially helpful after upgrading your ESX/ESXi hosts to version 4.0 from a previous version.

> **Master It** You've just finished upgrading your virtual infrastructure to VMware vSphere. What two additional tasks would be beneficial to complete?

Apply patches to ESX/ESXi hosts. Like other complex software products, VMware ESX and VMware ESXi need software patches applied from time to time. These patches might be bug fixes or security fixes. To keep your ESX/ESXi hosts up-to-date with the latest patches, vCenter Update Manager can apply patches to your hosts on a schedule of your choosing. In addition, to reduce downtime during the patching process or perhaps to simplify the deployment of patches to remote offices, vCenter Update Manager can also stage patches to ESX/ESXi hosts before the patches are applied.

Master It How can you avoid virtual machine downtime when applying patches (for example, remediating) your ESX/ESXi hosts?

Apply patches to Windows guests. Even though you deal with virtual machines in a VMware vSphere environment, you must still manage the installations of Windows in those virtual machines. These Windows installations need security patches and bug fixes, like the installations on physical systems. vCenter Update Manager has the ability to apply patches to the Windows operating system and select applications within Windows in order to keep both the guest operating system and these select applications updated.

Master It You are having a discussion with another VMware vSphere administrator about keeping hosts and guests updated. The other administrator insists that in order to use vCenter Update Manager to keep ESX/ESXi hosts updated, you must also use vCenter Update Manager to keep guest operating systems updated as well. Is this accurate?

Chapter 5

Creating and Managing Virtual Networks

Eventually, it all comes back to the network. Having servers running VMware ESX/ESXi with virtual machines stored on a highly redundant Fibre Channel SAN is great, but they are ultimately useless if the virtual machines cannot communicate across the network. What good is the ability to run 10 production systems on a single host at less cost if those production systems aren't available? Clearly, virtual networking within ESX/ESXi is a key area for every VMware administrator to understand fully.

In this chapter, you will learn to:

♦ Identify the components of virtual networking

♦ Create virtual switches (vSwitches) and distributed virtual switches (dvSwitches)

♦ Install and perform basic configuration of the Cisco Nexus 1000V.

♦ Create and manage NIC teaming, VLANs, and private VLANs

♦ Configure virtual switch security policies

Putting Together a Virtual Network

Designing and building virtual networks with VMware ESX/ESXi and vCenter Server bears some similarities to designing and building physical networks, but there are enough significant differences that an overview of components and terminology is first warranted. So, I'll take a moment here to define the various components involved in a virtual network, and then I'll discuss some of the factors that affect the design of a virtual network:

vNetwork Standard Switch (vSwitch)   A software-based switch that resides in the VMkernel and provides traffic management for virtual machines. Users must manage vSwitches independently on each ESX/ESXi host.

vNetwork Distributed Switch   A software-based switch that resides in the VMkernel and provides traffic management for virtual machines, the Service Console, and the VMkernel. Distributed vSwitches are shared by and managed across entire clusters of ESX/ESXi hosts. You might see vNetwork Distributed Switch abbreviated as vDS; I'll use the term *dvSwitch* throughout this book.

Port/port group   A logical object on a vSwitch that provides specialized services for the Service Console, the VMkernel, or virtual machines. A virtual switch can contain a Service Console port, a VMkernel port, or a virtual machine port group. On a vNetwork Distributed Switch, these are called *dvPort groups*.

Service Console port   A specialized virtual switch port type that is configured with an IP address to allow access to the Service Console at the respective address. A Service Console port is also referred to as a *vswif*. Service Console ports are available only on VMware ESX because VMware ESXi does not have a Service Console.

VMkernel port   A specialized virtual switch port type that is configured with an IP address to allow VMotion, iSCSI storage access, network attached storage (NAS) or Network File System (NFS) access, or VMware Fault Tolerance (FT) logging. On VMware ESXi, a VMkernel port also provides management connectivity for managing the host. A VMkernel port is also referred to as a *vmknic*.

Virtual machine port group   A group of virtual switch ports that share a common configuration and allow virtual machines to access other virtual machines or the physical network.

Virtual LAN   A logical LAN configured on a virtual or physical switch that provides efficient traffic segmentation, broadcast control, security, and efficient bandwidth utilization by providing traffic only to the ports configured for that particular virtual LAN (VLAN).

Trunk port (trunking)   A port on a physical switch that listens for and knows how to pass traffic for multiple VLANs. It does this by maintaining the VLAN tags for traffic moving through the trunk port to the connected device(s). Trunk ports are typically used for switch-to-switch connections to allow VLANs to pass freely between switches. Virtual switches support VLANs, and using VLAN trunks allows the VLANs to pass freely into the virtual switches.

Access port   A port on a physical switch that passes traffic for only a single VLAN. Unlike a trunk port, which maintains the VLAN identification for traffic moving through the port, an access port strips away the VLAN information for traffic moving through the port.

Network interface card team   The aggregation of physical network interface cards (NICs) to form a single logical communication channel. Different types of NIC teams provide varying levels of traffic load balancing and fault tolerance.

vmxnet adapter   A virtualized network adapter operating inside a guest operating system. The vmxnet adapter is a high-performance, 1Gbps virtual network adapter that operates only if the VMware Tools have been installed. The vmxnet adapter is sometimes referred to as a *paravirtualized* driver. The vmxnet adapter is identified as Flexible in the virtual machine properties.

vlance adapter   A virtualized network adapter operating inside a guest operating system. The vlance adapter is a 10/100Mbps network adapter that is widely compatible with a range of operating systems and is the default adapter used until the VMware Tools installation is completed.

e1000 adapter   A virtualized network adapter that emulates the Intel e1000 network adapter. The Intel e1000 is a 1Gbps network adapter. The e1000 network adapter is most common in 64-bit virtual machines.

Now that you have a better understanding of the components involved and the terminology that you'll see in this chapter, I'll discuss how these components work together to form a virtual network in support of virtual machines and ESX/ESXi hosts.

The answers to the following questions will, in large part, determine the design of your virtual networking:

◆   Do you have or need a dedicated network for management traffic, such as for the management of physical switches?

◆ Do you have or need a dedicated network for VMotion traffic?

◆ Do you have an IP storage network? Is this IP storage network a dedicated network? Are you running iSCSI or NAS/NFS?

◆ How many NICs are standard in your ESX/ESXi host design?

◆ Is there a need for extremely high levels of fault tolerance for VMs?

◆ Is the existing physical network comprised of VLANs?

◆ Do you want to extend the use of VLANs into the virtual switches?

As a precursor to setting up a virtual networking architecture, you need to identify and document the physical network components and the security needs of the network. It's also important to understand the architecture of the existing physical network, because that also greatly influences the design of the virtual network. If the physical network can't support the use of VLANs, for example, then the virtual network's design has to account for that limitation.

Throughout this chapter, as I discuss the various components of a virtual network in more detail, I'll also provide guidance on how the various components fit into an overall virtual network design. A successful virtual network combines the physical network, NICs, and vSwitches, as shown in Figure 5.1.

FIGURE 5.1
Successful virtual networking is a blend of virtual and physical network adapters and switches.

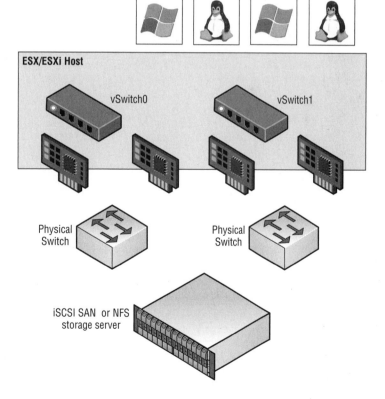

Because the virtual network implementation makes virtual machines accessible, it is essential that the virtual network is configured in a manner that supports reliable and efficient communication around the different network infrastructure components.

Working with vNetwork Standard Switches

The networking architecture of ESX/ESXi revolves around the creation and configuration of virtual switches (vSwitches). These virtual switches are either vNetwork Standard Switches or vNetwork Distributed Switches. In this section, I'll discuss vNetwork Standard Switches, hereafter called vSwitches; I'll discuss vNetwork Distributed Switches in the next section.

You create and manage vSwitches through the vSphere Client or through the VMware ESX Service Console (hereafter called the Service Console, because you know by now that ESXi does not have a Service Console) using the `esxcfg-vswitch` command, but they operate within the VMkernel. Virtual switches provide the connectivity to provide communication:

◆ between virtual machines within an ESX/ESXi host

◆ between virtual machines on different ESX/ESXi hosts

◆ between virtual machines and physical machines on the network

◆ for Service Console access (ESX only), and

◆ for VMkernel access to networks for VMotion, iSCSI, NFS, or fault tolerance logging (and management on ESXi)

Take a look at Figure 5.2, which shows the vSphere Client depicting the virtual switches on a host running ESX 4.0.

FIGURE 5.2
Virtual switches alone can't provide connectivity; they need ports or port groups and uplinks.

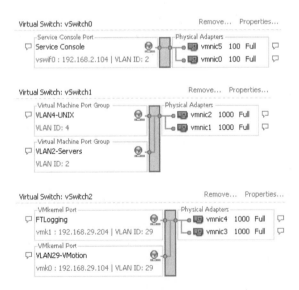

In this figure, the vSwitches aren't depicted alone; they also require ports or port groups and uplinks. Without uplinks, a virtual switch can't communicate with the rest of the network; without

ports or port groups, a vSwitch cannot provide connectivity for the Service Console, the VMkernel, or virtual machines. It is for this reason that most of our discussion about virtual switches centers on ports, port groups, and uplinks.

First, though, let's take a closer look at vSwitches and how they are both similar to, yet different from, physical switches in the network.

Comparing Virtual Switches and Physical Switches

Virtual switches in ESX/ESXi are constructed by and operate in the VMkernel. Virtual switches, or vSwitches, are not managed switches and do not provide all the advanced features that many new physical switches provide. You cannot, for example, telnet into a vSwitch to modify settings. There is no command-line interface (CLI) for a vSwitch. Even so, a vSwitch operates like a physical switch in some ways. Like its physical counterpart, a vSwitch functions at Layer 2, maintains MAC address tables, forwards frames to other switch ports based on the MAC address, supports VLAN configurations, is capable of trunking using IEEE 802.1q VLAN tags, and is capable of establishing port channels. Similar to physical switches, vSwitches are configured with a specific number of ports.

CREATING AND CONFIGURING VIRTUAL SWITCHES

By default every virtual switch is created with 64 ports. However, only 56 of the ports are available, and only 56 are displayed when looking at a vSwitch configuration through the vSphere Client. Reviewing a vSwitch configuration via the esxcfg-vswitch command shows the entire 64 ports. The eight-port difference is attributed to the fact that the VMkernel reserves eight ports for its own use.

After a virtual switch is created, you can adjust the number of ports to 8, 24, 56, 120, 248, 504, or 1016. These are the values that are reflected in the vSphere Client. But, as noted, there are eight ports reserved, and therefore the command line will show 32, 64, 128, 256, 512, and 1,024 ports for virtual switches.

Changing the number of ports in a virtual switch requires a reboot of the ESX/ESXi host on which the vSwitch was altered.

Despite these similarities, vSwitches do have some differences from physical switches. A vSwitch does not support the use of dynamic negotiation protocols for establishing 802.1q trunks or port channels, such as Dynamic Trunking Protocol (DTP) or Port Aggregation Protocol (PAgP). A vSwitch cannot be connected to another vSwitch, thereby eliminating a potential loop configuration. Because there is no possibility of looping, the vSwitches do not run Spanning Tree Protocol (STP). Looping can be a common network problem, so this is a real benefit of vSwitches.

SPANNING TREE PROTOCOL

In physical switches, STP offers redundancy for paths and prevents loops in the network topology by locking redundant paths in a standby state. Only when a path is no longer available will STP activate the standby path.

It is possible to link vSwitches together using a virtual machine with Layer 2 bridging software and multiple virtual NICs, but this is not an accidental configuration and would require some effort to establish.

Some other differences of vSwitches from physical switches include the following:

◆ A vSwitch authoritatively knows the MAC addresses of the virtual machines connected to that vSwitch, so there is no need to learn MAC addresses from the network.

◆ Traffic received by a vSwitch on one uplink is never forwarded out another uplink. This is yet another reason why vSwitches do not run STP.

◆ A vSwitch does not need to perform Internet Group Management Protocol (IGMP) snooping because it knows the multicast interests of the virtual machines attached to that vSwitch.

As you can see from this list of differences, you simply can't use virtual switches in the same way you can use physical switches. You can't use a virtual switch as a transit path between two physical switches, for example, because traffic received on one uplink won't be forwarded out another uplink.

With this basic understanding of how vSwitches work, let's now take a closer look at ports and port groups.

Understanding Ports and Port Groups

As described previously in this chapter, a vSwitch allows several different types of communication, including communication to and from the Service Console, to and from the VMkernel, and between virtual machines. To help distinguish between these different types of communication, ESX/ESXi uses ports and port groups. A vSwitch without any ports or port groups is like a physical switch that has no physical ports; there is no way to connect anything to the switch, and it is, therefore, useless.

Port groups differentiate between the types of traffic passing through a vSwitch, and they also operate as a boundary for communication and/or security policy configuration. Figure 5.3 and Figure 5.4 show the three different types of ports and port groups that you can configure on a vSwitch:

◆ Service Console port

◆ VMkernel port

◆ Virtual Machine port group

Because a vSwitch cannot be used in any way without at least one port or port group, you'll see that the vSphere Client combines the creation of new vSwitches with the creation of new ports or port groups.

As shown in Figure 5.2, though, ports and port groups are only part of the overall solution. The uplinks are the other part of the solution that you need to consider because they provide external network connectivity to the vSwitches.

Understanding Uplinks

Although a vSwitch provides for communication between virtual machines connected to the vSwitch, it cannot communicate with the physical network without uplinks. Just as a physical switch must be connected to other switches in order to provide communication across the network, vSwitches must be connected to the ESX/ESXi host's physical NICs as uplinks in order to communicate with the rest of the network.

FIGURE 5.3
Virtual switches can contain three connection types: Service Console, VMkernel, and virtual machine.

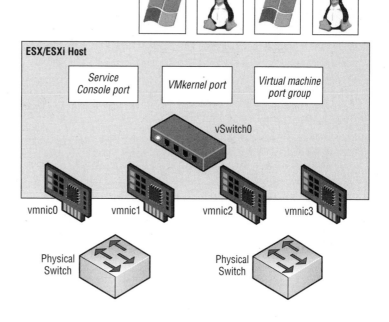

FIGURE 5.4
You can create virtual switches with all three connection types on the same switch.

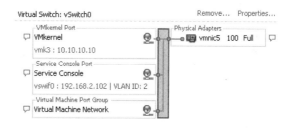

Unlike ports and port groups, uplinks aren't necessarily required in order for a vSwitch to function. Physical systems connected to an isolated physical switch that has no uplinks to other physical switches in the network can still communicate with each other—just not with any other systems that are not connected to the same isolated switch. Similarly, virtual machines connected to a vSwitch without any uplinks can communicate with each other but cannot communicate with virtual machines on other vSwitches or physical systems.

This sort of configuration is known as an *internal-only* vSwitch. It can be useful to allow virtual machines to communicate with each other, but not with any other systems. Virtual machines that communicate through an internal-only vSwitch do not pass any traffic through a physical adapter on the ESX/ESXi host. As shown in Figure 5.5, communication between virtual machines connected to an internal-only vSwitch takes place entirely in software and happens at whatever speed the VMkernel can perform the task.

No Uplink, No VMotion

Virtual machines connected to an internal-only vSwitch are not VMotion capable. However, if the virtual machine is disconnected from the internal-only vSwitch, a warning will be provided, but VMotion will succeed if all other requirements have been met. The requirements for VMotion are covered in Chapter 10.

FIGURE 5.5
Virtual machines communicating through an internal-only vSwitch do not pass any traffic through a physical adapter.

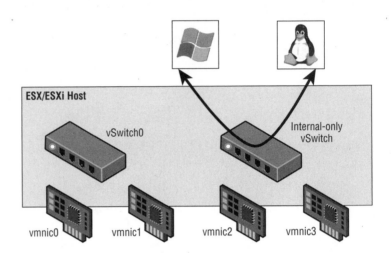

For virtual machines to communicate with resources beyond the virtual machines hosted on the local ESX/ESXi host, a vSwitch must be configured to use at least one physical network adapter, or uplink. A vSwitch can be bound to a single network adapter or bound to two or more network adapters.

A vSwitch bound to at least one physical network adapter allows virtual machines to establish communication with physical servers on the network or with virtual machines on other ESX/ESXi hosts. That's assuming, of course, that the virtual machines on the other ESX/ESXi hosts are connected to a vSwitch that is bound to at least one physical network adapter. Just like a physical network, a virtual network requires connectivity from end to end. Figure 5.6 shows the communication path for virtual machines connected to a vSwitch bound to a physical network adapter. In the diagram, when VM1 on ESX1 needs to communicate with VM2 on ESX2, the traffic from the virtual machine passes through vSwitch0 (via a virtual machine port group) to the physical network adapter to which the vSwitch is bound. From the physical network adapter, the traffic will reach the physical switch (PhySw1). The physical switch (PhySw1) passes the traffic to the second physical switch (PhySw2), which will pass the traffic through the physical network adapter associated with the vSwitch on ESX2. In the last stage of the communication, the vSwitch will pass the traffic to the destination virtual machine VM2.

The vSwitch associated with a physical network adapter provides virtual machines with the amount of bandwidth the physical adapter is configured to support. All the virtual machines will share this bandwidth when communicating with physical machines or virtual machines on other ESX/ESXi hosts. In this way, a vSwitch is once again similar to a physical switch. For example, a vSwitch bound to a network adapter with a 1Gbps maximum speed will provide up to 1Gbps worth of bandwidth for the virtual machines connected to it; similarly, a physical switch with a

1Gbps uplink to another physical switch provides up to 1Gbps of bandwidth between the two switches for systems attached to the physical switches.

FIGURE 5.6
A vSwitch with a single network adapter allows virtual machines to communicate with physical servers and other virtual machines on the network.

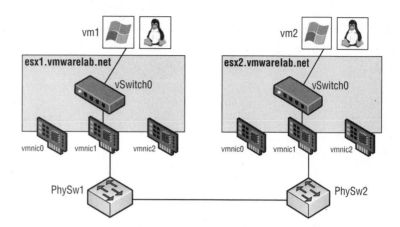

A vSwitch can also be bound to multiple physical network adapters. In this configuration, the vSwitch is sometimes referred to as a *NIC team*, but in this book I'll use the term *NIC team* or *NIC teaming* to refer specifically to the grouping of network connections together, not to refer to a vSwitch with multiple uplinks.

UPLINK LIMITS

Although a single vSwitch can be associated with multiple physical adapters as in a NIC team, a single physical adapter cannot be associated with multiple vSwitches. ESX/ESXi hosts can have up to 32 e1000 network adapters, 32 Broadcom TG3 Gigabit Ethernet network ports, or 16 Broadcom BNX2 Gigabit Ethernet network ports. ESX/ESXi hosts support up to four 10 Gigabit Ethernet adapters.

Figure 5.7 and Figure 5.8 show a vSwitch bound to multiple physical network adapters. A vSwitch can have a maximum of 32 uplinks. In other words, a single vSwitch can use up to 32 physical network adapters to send and receive traffic from the physical switches. Binding multiple physical NICs to a vSwitch offers the advantage of redundancy and load distribution. Later in this chapter, you'll dig deeper into the configuration and workings of this sort of vSwitch configuration.

So, you've examined vSwitches, ports and port groups, and uplinks, and you should have a basic understanding of how these pieces begin to fit together to build a virtual network. The next step is to delve deeper into the configuration of the various types of ports and port groups, because they are so essential to virtual networking.

Configuring Service Console Networking

Recall that the Service Console port is one of three types of ports or port groups you can create on a vSwitch. As shown in Figure 5.9 and Figure 5.10, the Service Console port acts as a passage into the management and monitoring capabilities of the console operating system.

ESXi AND THE MANAGEMENT PORT

Because ESXi lacks a Service Console, most of what is discussed here applies only to ESX. Information specific to ESXi, which uses a management port instead of a Service Console port, is provided in the "Configuring Management Networking (ESXi Only)" section.

FIGURE 5.7
A vSwitch using NIC teaming has multiple available adapters for data transfer. NIC teaming offers redundancy and load distribution.

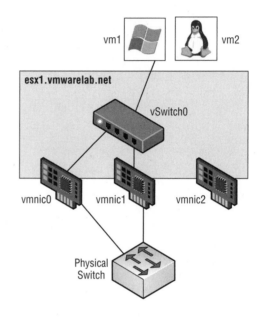

FIGURE 5.8
Virtual switches using NIC teaming are identified by the multiple physical network adapters assigned to the vSwitch.

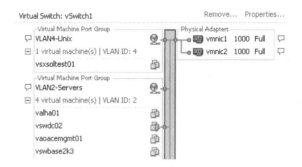

Although the vSphere Client masks most of this complexity, there are actually two different parts to Service Console networking. The first part is the Service Console port on the vSwitch; the second part is the vswif interface.

The Service Console port on the vSwitch defines connectivity information such as the VLAN ID, policy information such as the NIC failover order, and which uplinks the Service Console port may use to communicate with external entities. To display or modify this information, use the `esxcfg-vswitch` command from the Service Console or use the vSphere Client.

FIGURE 5.9
The Service Console port type on a vSwitch is linked to an interface with an IP address that can be used for access to the console operating system.

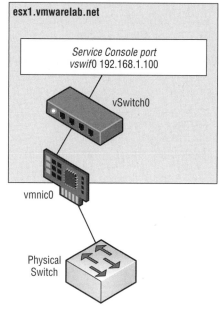

FIGURE 5.10
The vSphere Client shows the Service Console port, the associated vswif interface, the assigned IP address, and the configured VLAN ID.

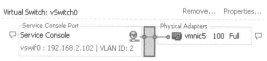

The vswif interface, on the other hand, is the logical network interface that is created within the Linux-based Service Console. The vswif is where the IP address is assigned. Commands like `ifconfig` or `esxcfg-vswif` will display information about the vswif interface.

Technically speaking, the vswif is not the Service Console port, or vice versa. For a vswif interface to exist, there will always be a Service Console port, but in order for a Service Console port to exist, there does not need to be a vswif.

Let's create a Service Console port, first using the vSphere Client and then using the Service Console, to help understand how these different components are so intricately related to one another.

Perform the following steps to create a new Service Console port using the vSphere Client:

1. Use the vSphere Client to establish a connection to a vCenter Server or an ESX host.

2. Click the hostname in the inventory panel on the left, select the Configuration tab in the details pane on the right, and then choose Networking from the Hardware menu list.

3. Click Add Networking to start the Add Network Wizard.

    Here is where the vSphere Client hides some of the complexity of the various components involved. A vSwitch without any ports or port groups is useless because nothing can be connected to the vSwitch. Therefore, the vSphere Client doesn't ask about creating a new vSwitch, but rather what type of port or port group to create, as shown in Figure 5.11.

FIGURE 5.11
The vSphere Client provides options only for creating new ports or port groups.

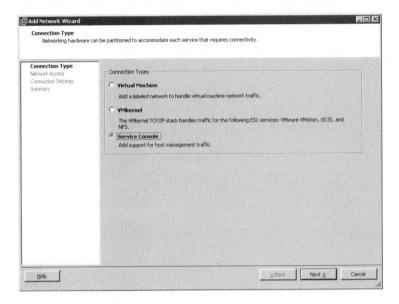

4. Select the Service Console radio button, and click Next.

5. After you select what type of port or port group to create, then you have the option of creating that port or port group on a new vSwitch or on an existing vSwitch.

   If you are adding a new vSwitch and a new Service Console port, select the check box that corresponds to the network adapter to be assigned to the new vSwitch as an uplink, as shown in Figure 5.12. If you are adding a Service Console port to an existing vSwitch, simply select the vSwitch to be used.

   Select Create A New vSwitch, select an available uplink, and then click Next.

6. Type a name for the Service Console port in the Network Label text box. If you know the VLAN ID (more on that later), specify it here. Click Next.

7. Enter an IP address for the new Service Console port. Ensure the IP address is a valid IP address for the network to which the physical NIC from step 5 is connected. You do not need a default gateway for the new Service Console port if a functioning gateway has already been assigned on the Service Console port created during the ESX installation process.

8. Click Next to review the configuration summary, and then click Finish.

During this process, the following three things occurred:

◆ A new vSwitch was created.

◆ A new Service Console port was created on that vSwitch.

◆ A new vswif interface was created, linked to the Service Console port group, and assigned an IP address.

FIGURE 5.12
Creating a new vSwitch
is possible in the
vSphere Client only
while also creating a
new port or port group.

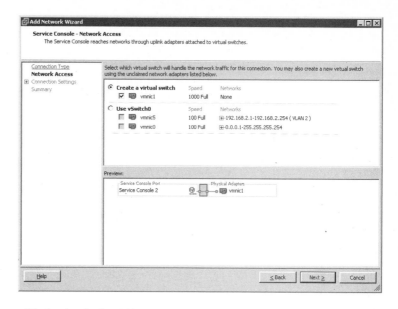

The following steps will help clarify the different components involved:

1. Using PuTTY.exe (Windows), a terminal window (Linux or Mac OS X), or the console session, log in to an ESX host, and enter the su – command to establish root permissions.

DON'T LOG IN REMOTELY AS ROOT!

By default, ESX refuses to allow remote SSH logins as root. This is considered a security best practice. Therefore, you should log in as an ordinary user and then use the su (switch user) command to elevate to root permissions. In Chapter 13, I'll discuss the sudo command, which provides greater flexibility and more granular auditing functionality.

---

2. Enter the following command to list the current vSwitches and ports or port groups (that's a lowercase *L* in the command):

   ```
   esxcfg-vswitch -1
   ```

   Note the output of the command. You should see listed a vSwitch with a Service Console port and a single uplink, as shown in Figure 5.13.

FIGURE 5.13
The output of the
esxcfg-vswitch
command shows the
vSwitches and ports
or port groups.

3. Now enter the `esxcfg-vswif` command (again, that's a lowercase *L* in the command) to list the Service Console interfaces:

```
esxcfg-vswif -l
```

The output of the command should show `vswif0`, the interface created during ESX installation, as well as `vswif1`, the interface created just a few moments ago, as shown in Figure 5.14. The output of the command also shows that each of these interfaces is associated with a Service Console port group that was also included in the output of the previous command.

```
Name     Port Group/DVPort   IP Family IP Address                              N
etmask                                 Broadcast       Enabled   TYPE
vswif0   Service Console     IPv4      192.168.2.104                           2
55.255.255.0                           192.168.2.255   true      STATIC
vswif1   Service Console 2   IPv4      192.168.2.114                           2
55.255.255.0                           192.168.2.255   true      STATIC
```

FIGURE 5.14
The `esxcfg-vswif` command lists the Service Console interfaces and their matching Service Console port groups.

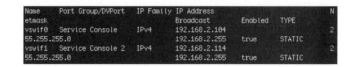

4. Finally, enter the `ifconfig` command to list logical interfaces in the Linux-based Service Console:

```
ifconfig -a
```

As before, the output of the command should show `vswif0` and `vswif1` and the IP addresses assigned to these interfaces, as shown in Figure 5.15.

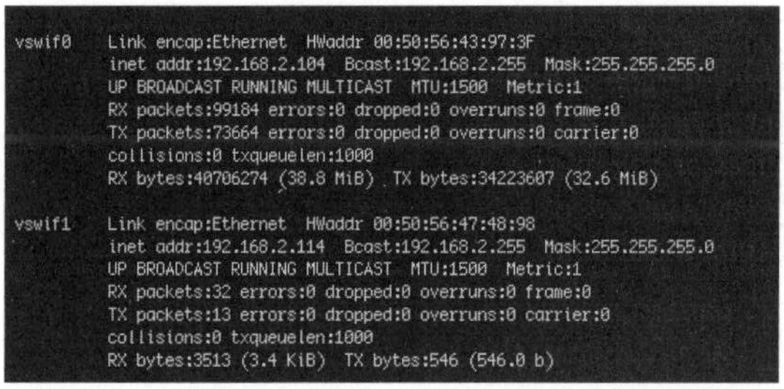

```
vswif0    Link encap:Ethernet  HWaddr 00:50:56:43:97:3F
          inet addr:192.168.2.104  Bcast:192.168.2.255  Mask:255.255.255.0
          UP BROADCAST RUNNING MULTICAST  MTU:1500  Metric:1
          RX packets:99184 errors:0 dropped:0 overruns:0 frame:0
          TX packets:73664 errors:0 dropped:0 overruns:0 carrier:0
          collisions:0 txqueuelen:1000
          RX bytes:40706274 (38.8 MiB)  TX bytes:34223607 (32.6 MiB)

vswif1    Link encap:Ethernet  HWaddr 00:50:56:47:48:98
          inet addr:192.168.2.114  Bcast:192.168.2.255  Mask:255.255.255.0
          UP BROADCAST RUNNING MULTICAST  MTU:1500  Metric:1
          RX packets:32 errors:0 dropped:0 overruns:0 frame:0
          TX packets:13 errors:0 dropped:0 overruns:0 carrier:0
          collisions:0 txqueuelen:1000
          RX bytes:3513 (3.4 KiB)  TX bytes:546 (546.0 b)
```

FIGURE 5.15
The `ifconfig` command lists all network interfaces in the Service Console, including the vswif interfaces.

The fact that there are three components involved here—the vSwitch, the Service Console port, and the Service Console interface (the vswif)—is further underscored by the steps that are required to create a new Service Console interface from the Service Console itself. Although the vSphere Client linked all these tasks together into a single wizard, from the CLI it's easier to see that they are indeed separate (albeit closely linked).

Perform the following steps to create a new vSwitch with a Service Console port using the command line:

1. Using `PuTTY.exe` (Windows), a terminal window (Linux or Mac OS X), or the console session, log in to an ESX host, and enter the `su -` command to establish root permissions.

2. Enter the following command to create a vSwitch named vSwitch5:

```
esxcfg-vswitch -a vSwitch5
```

3. Enter the following command to assign the physical adapter vmnic3 to the new vSwitch:

```
esxcfg-vswitch -L vmnic3 vSwitch5
```

A physical adapter may be linked or assigned to only a single vSwitch at a time.

4. Enter the following command to create a port group named SCX to a vSwitch named vSwitch5:

```
esxcfg-vswitch -A SCX vSwitch5
```

5. Enter the following command to add a Service Console interface named vswif99 with an IP address of 172.30.0.204 and a subnet mask of 255.255.255.0 to the SCX port group created in step 3:

```
esxcfg-vswif --add --ip=172.30.0.204 --netmask=255.255.255.0
--portgroup=SCX vswif99
```

6. Enter the following command to restart the VMware management service:

```
service mgmt-vmware restart
```

If you go back and run through the steps you followed after creating the Service Console port via the vSphere Client, you'll find that—aside from differences in names or the uplink used by the vSwitch—the results are the same.

SERVICE CONSOLE PORT MAXIMUMS

ESX supports up to 16 Service Console ports.

In many cases, you won't need to create a Service Console port. In Chapter 2 we covered how the ESX installer creates the first vSwitch with a Service Console port to allow access to the host after installation. In Chapter 2 we also discussed how to fix it when the wrong NIC was bound to the vSwitch; this underscores the need to be sure that the physical NICs are cabled to the correct switch or switches and that those switches are capable of carrying the correct traffic for managing your ESX hosts.

So, when would it be necessary to create a Service Console port? Creating a second Service Console connection provides redundancy in the form of a multihomed console operating system and, as you'll see in Chapter 11, provides a number of benefits when using VMware HA.

As mentioned earlier, the idea of configuring Service Console networking is unique to ESX and does not apply to ESXi. Before I can discuss how to handle ESXi management traffic, though, I must first discuss VMkernel networking.

Configuring VMkernel Networking

VMkernel ports provide network access for the VMkernel's TCP/IP stack, which is separate and independent from the Service Console TCP/IP stack. As shown in Figure 5.16 and Figure 5.17, VMkernel ports are used for VMotion, iSCSI, NAS/NFS access, and VMware FT. With ESXi, VMkernel ports are also used for management. In later chapters I detail the iSCSI and NAS/NFS configurations, as well as the details of the VMotion process and how VMware FT works. These discussions provide insight into the traffic flow between VMkernel and storage devices (iSCSI/NFS) or other ESX/ESXi hosts (for VMotion or VMware FT). At this point, you should be concerned only with configuring VMkernel networking.

FIGURE 5.16
A VMkernel port is associated with an interface and assigned an IP address for accessing iSCSI or NFS storage devices or for performing VMotion with other ESX/ESXi hosts.

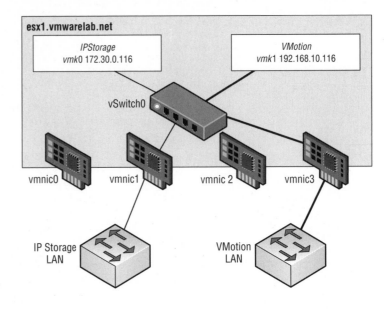

FIGURE 5.17
The port labels for VMkernel ports should be as descriptive as possible.

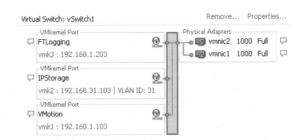

Like a Service Console port, a VMkernel port actually comprises two different components: a port on a vSwitch and a VMkernel network interface, also known as a *vmknic*. And like a Service Console port, creating a VMkernel port using the vSphere Client combines the task of creating the port group and the VMkernel NIC. Unlike a Service Console port, there is no need for administrative access to the IP address assigned to a VMkernel port.

Perform the following steps to add a VMkernel port to an existing vSwitch using the vSphere Client:

1. Use the vSphere Client to establish a connection to a vCenter Server or an ESX/ESXi host.

2. Click the hostname in the inventory panel on the left, select the Configuration tab in the details pane on the right, and then choose Networking from the Hardware menu list.

3. Click Properties for the virtual switch to host the new VMkernel port.

4. Click the Add button, select the VMkernel radio button option, and click Next.

5. Type the name of the port in the Network Label text box.

6. If necessary, specify the VLAN ID for the VMkernel port.

7. Select the various functions that will be enabled on this VMkernel port, and then click Next. For a VMkernel port that will be used only for iSCSI or NAS/NFS traffic, all check boxes should be deselected.

   Select Use This Port Group For VMotion if this VMkernel port will host VMotion traffic; otherwise, leave the check box deselected.

   Similarly, select the Use This Port Group For Fault Tolerance Logging box if this VMkernel port will be used for VMware FT traffic. On ESXi, a third option labeled Use This Port Group For Management Traffic is also available, as illustrated in Figure 5.18.

FIGURE 5.18
VMkernel ports on ESXi also have an option for enabling management traffic on the interface.

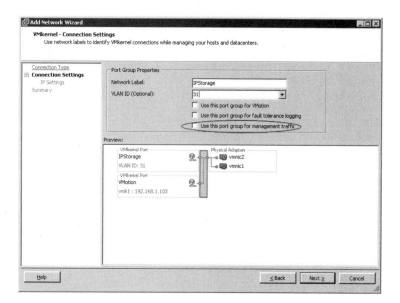

8. Enter an IP address for the VMkernel port. Ensure the IP address is a valid IP address for the network to which the physical NIC is connected. You do not need to provide a default gateway if the VMkernel does not need to reach remote subnets.

9. Click Next to review the configuration summary, and then click Finish.

After you complete these steps, the `esxcfg-vswitch` command on an ESX host shows the new VMkernel port, and the `esxcfg-vmknic` command on an ESX host shows the new VMkernel NIC that was created:

```
esxcfg-vmknic --list
```

To help illustrate the different parts—the VMkernel port and the VMkernel NIC, or vmknic—that are created during this process, let's again walk through the steps for creating a VMkernel port using the Service Console command line. As usual, this procedure applies only to ESX, not ESXi, because ESXi doesn't have a CLI.

Perform the following steps to create a VMkernel port on an existing vSwitch using the command line:

1. Using PuTTY.exe (Windows), a terminal window (Linux or Mac OS X), or the console session, log in to an ESX host, and enter the su – command to establish root permissions.

2. Enter the following command to add a port group named VMkernel to vSwitch0:

   ```
   esxcfg-vswitch -A VMkernel vSwitch0
   ```

3. Enter the following command to assign an IP address and subnet mask to the VMkernel port created in the previous step:

   ```
   esxcfg-vmknic -a -i 172.30.0.114 -n 255.255.255.0 VMkernel
   ```

4. Enter the following command to assign a default gateway of 172.30.0.1 to the VMkernel port:

   ```
   esxcfg-route 172.30.0.1
   ```

5. Enter the following command to restart the VMware management service:

   ```
   service mgmt-vmware restart
   ```

No VMkernel ports are created during installation of ESX/ESXi, so all the VMkernel ports that may be required in your environment will need to be created, either using the vSphere Client or, if you are using ESX, using the Service Console.

Before I cover the last connection type, the virtual machine port group, I'll first discuss management networking with ESXi.

Configuring Management Networking (ESXi Only)

Because ESXi lacks a Linux-based Service Console like ESX, the idea of how management networking works with ESXi is quite different. Instead of using Service Console ports, ESXi uses VMkernel ports. To help distinguish the various types of VMkernel ports, ESXi offers an option to enable management traffic on a VMkernel port. Figure 5.18 illustrates this. To create additional management network interfaces, you would use the procedure described previously for creating VMkernel ports using the vSphere Client, simply enabling the Use This Port Group For Management Traffic option while creating the port.

In the event that the ESXi host is unreachable—and therefore cannot be configured using the vSphere Client—you need to use the ESXi interface to configure the management network.

Perform the following steps to configure the ESXi management network using the ESXi console:

1. At the server's physical console or using a remote console utility such as the HP iLO, press F2 to enter the System Customization menu. If prompted to log in, enter the appropriate credentials.

2. Use the arrow keys to highlight the Configure Management Network option, as shown in Figure 5.19, and press Enter.

3. From the Configure Management Network menu, select the appropriate option for configuring ESXi management networking, as shown in Figure 5.20. You cannot create additional management network interfaces from here; you can only modify the existing management network interface.

FIGURE 5.19
To configure ESXi's equivalent of the Service Console port, use the Configure Management Network option in the System Customization menu.

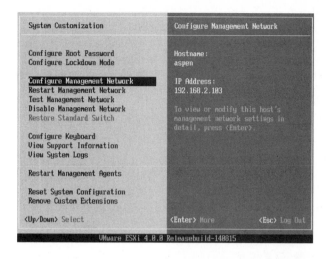

FIGURE 5.20
From the Configure Management Network menu, users can modify assigned network adapters, change the VLAN ID, or alter the IP configuration.

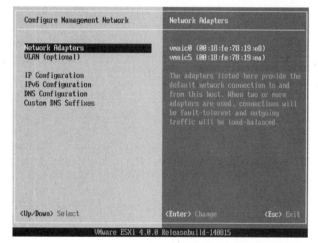

4. When finished, follow the screen prompts to exit the management networking configuration. If prompted to restart the management networking, select Yes; otherwise, restart the management networking from the System Customization menu, as shown in Figure 5.21.

In looking at Figure 5.19 and Figure 5.21, you'll also see options for testing the management network, which lets you be sure that the management network is configured correctly. This is invaluable if you are unsure of the VLAN ID or network adapters that you should use.

Only one type of port or port group remains, and that is a virtual machine port group.

Configuring Virtual Machine Networking

The last connection type (or port group) to discuss is the virtual machine port group. The virtual machine port group is quite different from a Service Console port or a VMkernel port. Both of the other ports have a one-to-one relationship with an interface—each Service Console interface, or vswif, requires a matching Service Console port on a vSwitch, and each VMkernel NIC, or vmknic, requires a matching VMkernel on a vSwitch. In addition, these interfaces require IP addresses that are used for management or VMkernel network access.

FIGURE 5.21
The Restart Management Network option restarts ESXi's management networking and applies any changes that have been made.

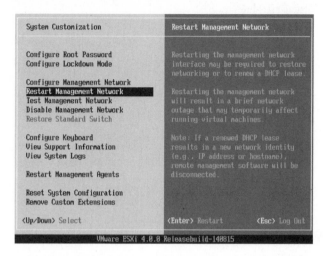

A virtual machine port group, on the other hand, does not have a one-to-one relationship, and it does not require an IP address. For a moment, forget about vSwitches, and consider standard physical switches. When you install an unmanaged physical switch into your network environment, that physical switch does not require an IP address. Adding unmanaged physical switches does not require IP addresses; you simply install the switches and plug in the appropriate uplinks that will connect them to the rest of the network.

A vSwitch created with a Virtual Machine port group is really no different. A vSwitch with a Virtual Machine port group acts just like an additional unmanaged physical switch. You need only plug in the appropriate uplinks—physical network adapters, in this case—that will connect that vSwitch to the rest of the network. As with an unmanaged physical switch, an IP address does not need to be configured for a Virtual Machine port group to combine the ports of a vSwitch with those of a physical switch. Figure 5.22 shows the switch-to-switch connection between a vSwitch and a physical switch.

Perform the following steps to create a vSwitch with a virtual machine port group using the vSphere Client:

1. Use the vSphere Client to establish a connection to a vCenter Server or an ESX/ESXi host.

2. Click the hostname in the inventory panel on the left, select the Configuration tab in the details pane on the right, and then select Networking from the Hardware menu list.

3. Click Add Networking to start the Add Network Wizard.

4. Select the Virtual Machine radio button option, and click Next.

5. Because you are creating a new vSwitch, select the check box that corresponds to the network adapter to be assigned to the new vSwitch. Be sure to select the NIC connected to the switch that can carry the appropriate traffic for your virtual machines.

6. Type the name of the virtual machine port group in the Network Label text box.

7. Specify a VLAN ID, if necessary, and click Next.

8. Click Next to review the virtual switch configuration, and then click Finish.

FIGURE 5.22

A vSwitch with a virtual machine port group uses an associated physical network adapter to establish a switch-to-switch connection with a physical switch.

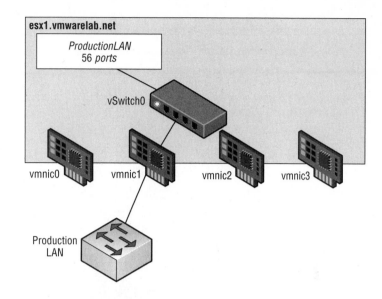

If you are using ESX, you can create a virtual machine port group from the Service Console as well. You can probably guess the commands that are involved from the previous examples, but I'll walk you through the process anyway.

Perform the following steps to create a vSwitch with a virtual machine port group using the command line:

1. Using PuTTY.exe (Windows), a terminal window (Linux or Mac OS X), or the console session, log in to an ESX host, and enter the su – command to establish root permissions.

2. Enter the following command to add a virtual switch named vSwitch1:

   ```
   esxcfg-vswitch -a vSwitch1
   ```

3. Enter the following command to bind the physical NIC vmnic1 to vSwitch1:

   ```
   esxcfg-vswitch -L vmnic1 vSwitch1
   ```

   By binding a physical NIC to the vSwitch, you provide network connectivity to the rest of the network for virtual machines connected to this vSwitch. Again, remember that you can assign a physical NIC to only one vSwitch at a time.

4. Enter the following command to create a virtual machine port group named Production-LAN on vSwitch1:

   ```
   esxcfg-vswitch -A ProductionLAN vSwitch1
   ```

5. Enter the following command to restart the VMware management service:

   ```
   service mgmt-vmware restart
   ```

Of the three different connection types—Service Console port, VMkernel port, and virtual machine port group—vSphere administrators will spend most of their time creating, modifying, managing, and removing virtual machine port groups.

> **PORTS AND PORT GROUPS ON A VIRTUAL SWITCH**
>
> A vSwitch can consist of multiple connection types, or each connection type can be created in its own vSwitch.

Configuring VLANs

Several times so far we've referenced the use of the VLAN ID when configuring a Service Console port, a VMkernel port, or a virtual machine port group. As defined previously in this chapter, a virtual LAN (VLAN) is a logical LAN that provides efficient segmentation, security, and broadcast control while allowing traffic to share the same physical LAN segments or same physical switches. Figure 5.23 shows a typical VLAN configuration across physical switches.

FIGURE 5.23
Virtual LANs provide secure traffic segmentation without the cost of additional hardware.

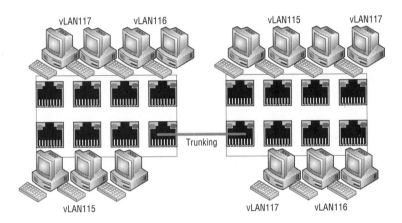

VLANs utilize the IEEE 802.1Q standard for *tagging*, or marking, traffic as belonging to a particular VLAN. The VLAN tag, also known as the VLAN ID, is a numeric value between 1 and 4094, and it uniquely identifies that VLAN across the network. Physical switches such as the ones depicted in Figure 5.23 must be configured with ports to trunk the VLANs across the switches. These ports are known as *trunk* (or *trunking*) ports. Ports not configured to trunk VLANs are known as *access ports* and can carry traffic only for a single VLAN at a time.

> **USING VLAN ID 4095**
>
> Normally the VLAN ID will range from 1 to 4094. In the ESX/ESXi environment, however, a VLAN ID of 4095 is also valid. Using this VLAN ID with ESX/ESXi causes the VLAN tagging information to be passed through the vSwitch all the way up to the guest operating system. This is called *virtual guest tagging* (VGT) and is useful only for guest operating systems that support and understand VLAN tags.

VLANs are an important part of ESX/ESXi networking because of the impact they have on the number of vSwitches and uplinks that are required. Consider this:

◆ The Service Console (or the Management Network in ESXi) needs access to the network segment carrying management traffic.

◆ VMkernel ports, depending upon their purpose, may need access to an isolated VMotion segment or the network segment carrying iSCSI and NAS/NFS traffic.

◆ Virtual machine port groups need access to whatever network segments are applicable for the virtual machines running on the ESX/ESXi hosts.

Without VLANs, this configuration would require three or more separate vSwitches, each bound to a different physical adapter, and each physical adapter would need to be physically connected to the correct network segment, as illustrated in Figure 5.24.

FIGURE 5.24
Supporting multiple networks without VLANs can increase the number of vSwitches and uplinks that are required.

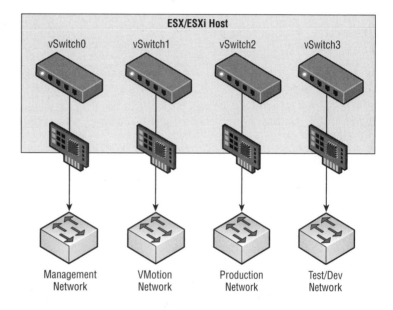

Add in an IP-based storage network and a few more virtual machine networks that need to be supported, and the number of required vSwitches and uplinks quickly grows. And this doesn't even take uplink redundancy, for example NIC teaming, into account!

VLANs are the answer to this dilemma. Figure 5.25 shows the same network as in Figure 5.24, but with VLANs this time.

While the reduction from Figure 5.24 to Figure 5.25 is only a single vSwitch and a single uplink, you can easily add more virtual machine networks to the configuration in Figure 5.25 by simply adding another port group with another VLAN ID. Blade servers provide an excellent example of when VLANs offer tremendous benefit. Because of the small form factor of the blade casing, blade servers have historically offered limited expansion slots for physical network adapters. VLANs allow these blade servers to support more networks than they would be able to otherwise.

NO VLAN NEEDED

Virtual switches in the VMkernel do not need VLANs if an ESX/ESXi host has enough physical network adapters to connect to each of the different network segments. However, VLANs provide added flexibility in adapting to future network changes, so the use of VLANs where possible is recommended.

FIGURE 5.25
VLANs can reduce the number of vSwitches and uplinks required.

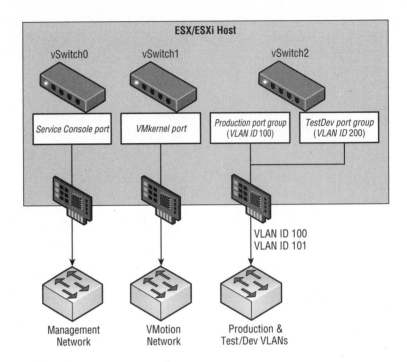

As shown in Figure 5.25, VLANs are handled by configuring different port groups within a vSwitch. The relationship between VLANs is not a one-to-one relationship; a port group can be associated with only one VLAN at a time, but multiple port groups can be associated with a single VLAN. Later in this chapter when I discuss security settings, you'll see some examples of when you might have multiple port groups associated with a single VLAN.

To make VLANs work properly with a port group, the uplinks for that vSwitch must be connected to a physical switch port configured as a trunk port. A trunk port understands how to pass traffic from multiple VLANs simultaneously while also preserving the VLAN IDs on the traffic. Figure 5.26 shows a snippet of configuration from a Cisco Catalyst 3560G switch for a couple of ports configured as trunk ports.

THE NATIVE VLAN

In Figure 5.26, you might notice the `switchport trunk native vlan 999` command. The default native VLAN is VLAN ID 1. If you need to pass traffic on VLAN 1 to the ESX/ESXi hosts, you should designate another VLAN as the native VLAN using this command. I recommend creating a dummy VLAN, like 999, and setting that as the native VLAN. This ensures that all VLANs will be tagged with the VLAN ID as they pass into the ESX/ESXi hosts.

When the physical switch ports are correctly configured as trunk ports, the physical switch passes the VLAN tags up to the ESX/ESXi server, where the vSwitch tries to direct the traffic to a port group with that VLAN ID configured. If there is no port group configured with that VLAN ID, the traffic is discarded.

FIGURE 5.26
The physical switch ports must be configured as trunk ports in order to pass the VLAN information to the ESX/ESXi hosts for the port groups to use.

```
!
interface GigabitEthernet0/6
 switchport trunk encapsulation dot1q
 switchport trunk native vlan 999
 switchport mode trunk
 spanning-tree portfast trunk
!
interface GigabitEthernet0/7
 switchport trunk encapsulation dot1q
 switchport trunk native vlan 999
 switchport mode trunk
 spanning-tree portfast trunk
!
```

Perform the following steps to configure a virtual machine port group using VLAN ID 31:

1. Use the vSphere Client to establish a connection to a vCenter Server or an ESX/ESXi host.

2. Click the hostname in the inventory panel on the left, select the Configuration tab in the details pane on the right, and then select Networking from the Hardware menu list.

3. Click the Properties link for the vSwitch where the new port group should be created.

4. Click the Add button, select the Virtual Machine radio button option, and then click Next.

5. Type the name of the virtual machine port group in the Network Label text box. Embedding the VLAN ID and a brief description into the name of the port group is strongly recommended, so typing something like **VLANXXX-NetworkDescription** would be appropriate, where XXX represents the VLAN ID.

6. Type **31** in the VLAN ID (Optional) text box, as shown in Figure 5.27. You will want to substitute a value that is correct for your network here.

FIGURE 5.27
You must specify the correct VLAN ID in order for a port group to receive traffic intended for a particular VLAN.

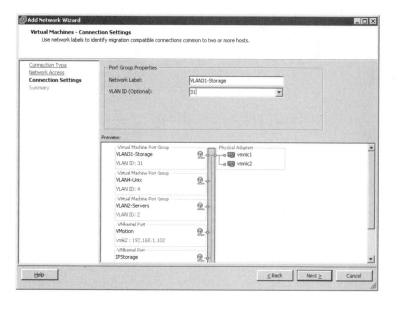

7. Click Next to review the vSwitch configuration, and then click Finish.

For users with ESX, you can use the `esxcfg-vswitch` command in the Service Console to create or modify the VLAN settings for ports or port groups.

Perform the following steps to modify the VLAN ID for a virtual machine port group from the ESX Service Console:

1. Using `PuTTY.exe` (Windows), a terminal window (Linux or Mac OS X), or the console session, log in to an ESX host, and enter the `su -` command to establish root permissions.

2. Run this command to set the VLAN ID of the port group named ProductionLAN on vSwitch1 to 45:

   ```
   esxcfg-vswitch -v 45 -p ProductionLAN vSwitch1
   ```

3. Run this command to remove the VLAN ID, if set, on the port group named TestDev on vSwitch1:

   ```
   esxcfg-vswitch -v 0 -p TestDev vSwitch1
   ```

4. This command lists all the vSwitches, their port groups, and their configured VLAN IDs:

   ```
   esxcfg-vswitch --list
   ```

Although VLANs reduce the costs of constructing multiple logical subnets, keep in mind that VLANs do not address traffic constraints. Although VLANs logically separate network segments, all the traffic still runs on the same physical network underneath. For bandwidth-intensive network operations, the disadvantage of the shared physical network might outweigh the scalability and cost savings of a VLAN.

CONTROLLING THE VLANS PASSED ACROSS A VLAN TRUNK

You might also see the `switchport trunk allowed vlan` command in some Cisco switch configurations as well. This command allows you to control what VLANs are passed across the VLAN trunk to the device at the other end of the link—in this case, an ESX/ESXi host. You will need to ensure that all the VLANs that are defined on the vSwitches are also included in the `switchport trunk allowed vlan` command, or else those VLANs not included in the command won't work.

Configuring NIC Teaming

We know that in order for a vSwitch and its associated ports or port groups to communicate with other ESX/ESXi hosts or with physical systems, the vSwitch must have at least one uplink. An *uplink* is a physical network adapter that is bound to the vSwitch and connected to a physical network switch. With the uplink connected to the physical network, there is connectivity for the Service Console, VMkernel, or virtual machines connected to that vSwitch. But what happens when that physical network adapter fails, when the cable connecting that uplink to the physical network fails, or the upstream physical switch to which that uplink is connected fails? With a single uplink, network connectivity to the entire vSwitch and all of its ports or port groups is lost. This is where NIC teaming comes in.

NIC teaming involves connecting multiple physical network adapters to single vSwitch. NIC teaming provides redundancy and load balancing of network communications to Service Console, VMkernel, and virtual machines.

Figure 5.28 illustrates NIC teaming conceptually. Both of the vSwitches have two uplinks, and each of the uplinks connects to a different physical switch. Note that NIC teaming supports all the different connection types, so it can be used with Service Console networking, VMkernel networking, and networking for virtual machines.

FIGURE 5.28
Virtual switches with multiple uplinks offer redundancy and load balancing.

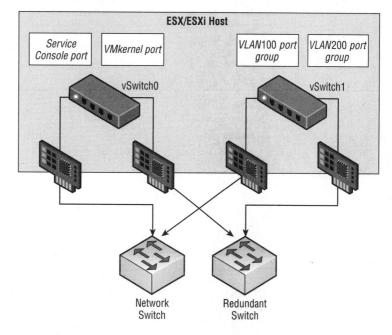

Figure 5.29 shows what NIC teaming looks like from within the vSphere Client. In this example, the vSwitch is configured with an association to multiple physical network adapters (uplinks). As mentioned in the previous section, the ESX/ESXi host can have a maximum of 32 uplinks; these uplinks can be spread across multiple vSwitches or all tossed into a NIC team on one vSwitch. Remember that you can connect a physical NIC to only one vSwitch at a time.

FIGURE 5.29
The vSphere Client shows when multiple physical network adapters are associated to a vSwitch using NIC teaming.

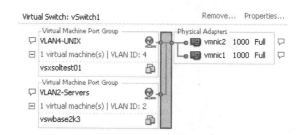

Building a functional NIC team requires that all uplinks be connected to physical switches in the same broadcast domain. If VLANs are used, then all the switches should be configured for VLAN trunking, and the appropriate subset of VLANs must be allowed across the VLAN trunk. In a Cisco switch, this is typically controlled with the `switchport trunk allowed vlan` statement.

In Figure 5.30, the NIC team for vSwitch0 will work, because both of the physical switches share VLAN100 and are therefore in the same broadcast domain. The NIC team for vSwitch1, however, will not work because the physical network adapters do not share a common broadcast domain.

CONSTRUCTING NIC TEAMS

NIC teams should be built on physical network adapters located on separate bus architectures. For example, if an ESX/ESXi host contains two onboard network adapters and a PCI Express-based quad-port network adapter, a NIC team should be constructed using one onboard network adapter and one network adapter on the PCI bus. This design eliminates a single point of failure.

FIGURE 5.30
All the physical network adapters in a NIC team must belong to same Layer 2 broadcast domain.

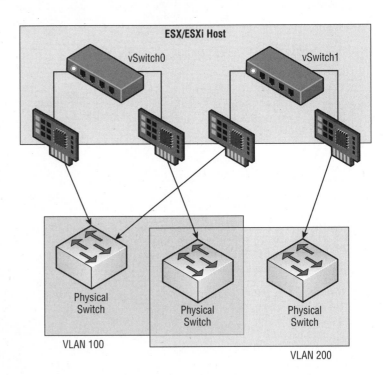

Perform the following steps to create a NIC team with an existing vSwitch using the vSphere Client:

1. Use the vSphere Client to establish a connection to a vCenter Server or an ESX/ESXi host.

2. Click the hostname in the inventory panel on the left, select the Configuration tab in the details pane on the right, and then select Networking from the Hardware menu list.

3. Click the Properties for the virtual switch that will be assigned a NIC team, and select the Network Adapters tab.

4. Click Add and select the appropriate adapter from the Unclaimed Adapters list, as shown in Figure 5.31.

FIGURE 5.31
Create a NIC team using unclaimed network adapters that belong to the same Layer 2 broadcast domain as the original adapter.

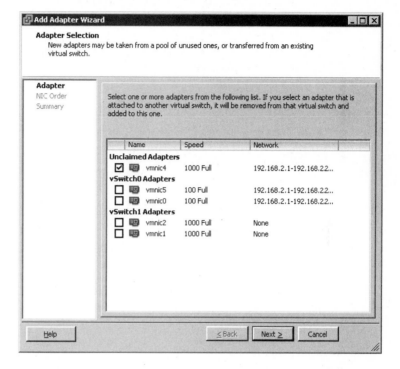

5. Adjust the Policy Failover Order as needed to support an active/standby configuration.

6. Review the summary of the virtual switch configuration, click Next, and then click Finish.

On an ESX host, the process of establishing a NIC team is equally straightforward. Perform the following steps to establish a NIC team using the Service Console on an ESX host:

1. Using PuTTY.exe (Windows), a terminal window (Linux or Mac OS X), or the console session, log in to an ESX host, and enter the su – command to establish root permissions.

2. Run this command to link the physical network adapter labeled vmnic4 to the existing vSwitch named vSwitch2:

   ```
   esxcfg-vswitch –L vmnic4 vSwitch2
   ```

3. This command lists the current vSwitch configuration, including all linked physical network adapters:

   ```
   esxcfg-vswitch --list
   ```

After a NIC team is established for a vSwitch, ESX/ESXi can then perform load balancing for that vSwitch. The load-balancing feature of NIC teaming does not function like the load-balancing feature of advanced routing protocols. Load balancing across a NIC team is not a product of identifying the amount of traffic transmitted through a network adapter and shifting traffic to equalize data flow through all available adapters. The load-balancing algorithm for NIC teams in a vSwitch is a balance of the number of connections—not the amount of traffic. NIC teams on a vSwitch can be configured with one of the following three load-balancing policies:

◆ vSwitch port-based load balancing (default)

◆ Source MAC-based load balancing

◆ IP hash-based load balancing

OUTBOUND LOAD BALANCING

The load-balancing feature of NIC teams on a vSwitch applies only to the outbound traffic.

VIRTUAL SWITCH PORT LOAD BALANCING

The vSwitch port-based load-balancing policy that is used by default uses an algorithm that ties each virtual switch port to a specific uplink associated with the vSwitch. The algorithm attempts to maintain an equal number of port-to-uplink assignments across all uplinks to achieve load balancing. As shown in Figure 5.32, this policy setting ensures that traffic from a specific virtual network adapter connected to a virtual switch port will consistently use the same physical network adapter. In the event that one of the uplinks fails, the traffic from the failed uplink will failover to another physical network adapter.

FIGURE 5.32
The vSwitch port-based load-balancing policy assigns each virtual switch port to a specific uplink. Failover to another uplink occurs when one of the physical network adapters experiences failure.

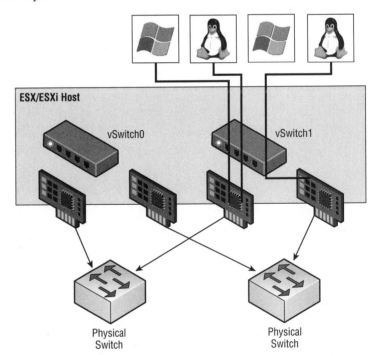

You can see how this policy does not provide load balancing but rather redundancy. Because the port to which a virtual machine is connected does not change, each virtual machine is tied to a physical network adapter until failover occurs regardless of the amount of network traffic that is generated. Looking at Figure 5.32, imagine that the Linux virtual machine and the Windows virtual machine on the far left are the two most network-intensive virtual machines. In this case, the vSwitch port-based policy has assigned both of the ports used by these virtual machines to the same physical network adapter. This could create a situation in which one physical network adapter is much more heavily utilized than some of the other network adapters in the NIC team.

The physical switch passing the traffic learns the port association and therefore sends replies back through the same physical network adapter from which the request initiated. The vSwitch port-based policy is best used when the number of virtual network adapters is greater than the number of physical network adapters. In the case where there are fewer virtual network adapters than physical adapters, some physical adapters will not be used. For example, if five virtual machines are connected to a vSwitch with six uplinks, only five used vSwitch ports will be assigned to exactly five uplinks, leaving one uplink with no traffic to process.

SOURCE MAC LOAD BALANCING

The second load-balancing policy available for a NIC team is the source MAC-based policy, shown in Figure 5.33. This policy is susceptible to the same pitfalls as the vSwitch port-based policy simply because the static nature of the source MAC address is the same as the static nature of a vSwitch port assignment. Like the vSwitch port-based policy, the source MAC-based policy is best used when the number of virtual network adapters exceeds the number of physical network adapters. In addition, virtual machines are still not capable of using multiple physical adapters unless configured with multiple virtual network adapters. Multiple virtual network adapters inside the guest operating system of a virtual machine will provide multiple source MAC addresses and therefore offer an opportunity to use multiple physical network adapters.

FIGURE 5.33
The source MAC-based load-balancing policy, as the name suggests, ties a virtual network adapter to a physical network adapter based on the MAC address.

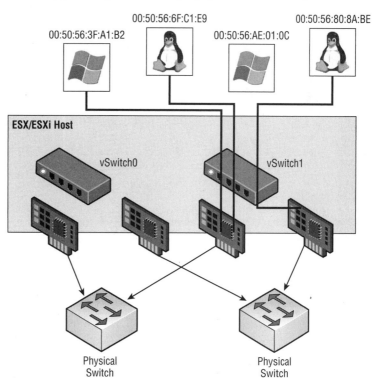

VIRTUAL SWITCH TO PHYSICAL SWITCH

To eliminate a single point of failure, you can connect the physical network adapters in NIC teams set to use the vSwitch port-based or source MAC-based load-balancing policies to different physical switches; however, the physical switches must belong to the same Layer 2 broadcast domain. Link aggregation using 802.3ad teaming is not supported with either of these load-balancing policies.

IP HASH LOAD BALANCING

The third load-balancing policy available for NIC teams is the IP hash-based policy, also called the *out-IP* policy. This policy, shown in Figure 5.34, addresses the limitation of the other two policies that prevents a virtual machine from accessing two physical network adapters without having two virtual network adapters. The IP hash-based policy uses the source and destination IP addresses to determine the physical network adapter for communication. This algorithm then allows a single virtual machine to communicate over different physical network adapters when communicating with different destinations.

BALANCING FOR LARGE DATA TRANSFERS

Although the IP hash-based load-balancing policy can more evenly spread the transfer traffic for a single virtual machine, it does not provide a benefit for large data transfers occurring between the same source and destination systems. Because the source-destination hash will be the same for the duration of the data load, it will flow through only a single physical network adapter.

Unless the physical hardware supports it, a vSwitch with the NIC teaming load-balancing policy set to use the IP-based hash must have all physical network adapters connected to the same physical switch. Some newer switches support link aggregation across physical switches, but otherwise all the physical network adapters will need to connect to the same switch. In addition, the switch must be configured for link aggregation. ESX/ESXi supports standard 802.3ad teaming in static (manual) mode but does not support the Link Aggregation Control Protocol (LACP) or Port Aggregation Protocol (PAgP) commonly found on switch devices. Link aggregation will increase throughput by combining the bandwidth of multiple physical network adapters for use by a single virtual network adapter of a virtual machine.

Figure 5.35 shows a snippet of the configuration of a Cisco switch configured for link aggregation.

Perform the following steps to alter the NIC teaming load-balancing policy of a vSwitch:

1. Use the vSphere Client to establish a connection to a vCenter Server or an ESX/ESXi host.

2. Click the hostname in the inventory panel on the left, select the Configuration tab in the details pane on the right, and then select Networking from the Hardware menu list.

3. Click the Properties for the virtual switch, select the name of virtual switch from the Configuration list, and then click the Edit button.

FIGURE 5.34
The IP hash-based policy is a more scalable load-balancing policy that allows virtual machines to use more than one physical network adapter when communicating with multiple destination hosts.

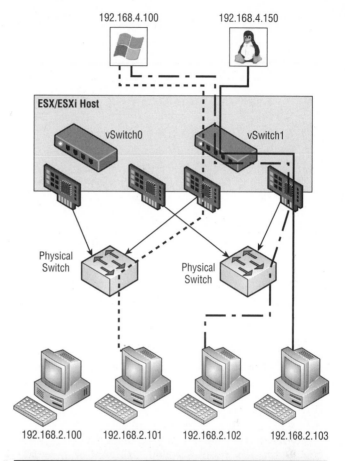

FIGURE 5.35
The physical switches must be configured to support the IP-based hash load-balancing policy.

```
!
interface Port-channel2
 description Link aggregate for ESX server
 switchport trunk encapsulation dot1q
 switchport trunk native vlan 999
 switchport mode trunk
!
interface GigabitEthernet0/1
 switchport trunk encapsulation dot1q
 switchport trunk native vlan 999
 switchport mode trunk
 channel-group 2 mode on
 spanning-tree portfast trunk
!
```

4. Select the NIC Teaming tab, and then select the desired load-balancing strategy from the Load Balancing drop-down list, as shown in Figure 5.36.

5. Click OK, and then click Close.

FIGURE 5.36
Select the load-balancing
policy for a vSwitch on
the NIC Teaming tab.

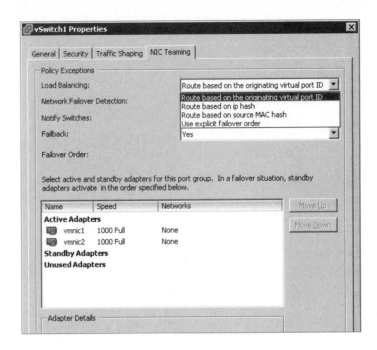

Now that I've explained the load-balancing policies, let's take a deeper look at the failover and failback of uplinks in a NIC team. There are two parts to consider: failover detection and failover policy.

Failover detection with NIC teaming can be configured to use either a link status method or a beacon probing method.

The link status failover detection method works just as the name suggests. Failure of an uplink is identified by the link status provided by the physical network adapter. In this case, failure is identified for events like removed cables or power failures on a physical switch. The downside to the link status failover detection setting is its inability to identify misconfigurations or pulled cables that connect the switch to other networking devices (for example, a cable connecting one switch to an upstream switch.)

OTHER WAYS OF DETECTING UPSTREAM FAILURES

Some network switch manufacturers have also added features into their network switches that assist in the task of detecting upstream network failures. In the Cisco product line, for example, there is a feature known as *link state tracking* that enables the switch to detect when an upstream port has gone down and react accordingly. This feature can reduce or even eliminate the need for beacon probing.

The beacon probing failover detection setting, which includes link status as well, sends Ethernet broadcast frames across all physical network adapters in the NIC team. These broadcast frames allow the vSwitch to detect upstream network connection failures and will force failover when Spanning Tree Protocol blocks ports, when ports are configured with the wrong VLAN, or when a switch-to-switch connection has failed. When a beacon is not returned on a physical network adapter, the vSwitch triggers the failover notice and reroutes the traffic from the failed network adapter through another available network adapter based on the failover policy.

Consider a vSwitch with a NIC team consisting of three physical network adapters, where each adapter is connected to a different physical switch and each physical switch is connected to a single physical switch, which is then connected to an upstream switch, as shown in Figure 5.37. When the NIC team is set to the beacon probing failover detection method, a beacon will be sent out over all three uplinks.

FIGURE 5.37
The beacon probing failover detection policy sends beacons out across the physical network adapters of a NIC team to identify upstream network failures or switch misconfigurations.

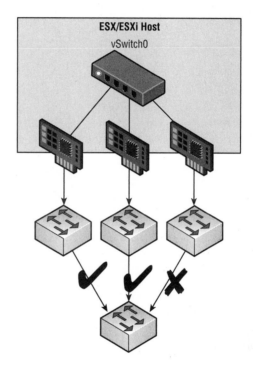

After a failure is detected, either via link status or beacon probing, a failover will occur. Traffic from any virtual machines or any Service Console or VMkernel ports is rerouted to another member of the NIC team. Exactly which member that might be, though, depends primarily upon the configured failover order.

Figure 5.38 shows the failover order configuration for a vSwitch with two adapters in a NIC team. In this configuration, both adapters are configured as active adapters, and either or both adapters may be used at any given time to handle traffic for this vSwitch and all its associated ports or port groups.

Now look at Figure 5.39. This figure shows a vSwitch with three physical network adapters in a NIC team. In this configuration, one of the adapters is configured as a standby adapter. Any adapters listed as standby adapters will not be used until a failure occurs on one of the active adapters, at which time the standby adapters activate in the order listed.

Now take a quick look back at Figure 5.36. You'll see an option there labeled Use Explicit Failover Order. If you select that option instead of one of the other load-balancing options, then traffic will move to the next available uplink in the list of active adapters. If no active adapters are available, then traffic will move down the list to the standby adapters. Just as name of the option implies, ESX/ESXi will use the order of the adapters in the failover order to determine how traffic will be placed on the physical network adapters. Because this option does not perform any sort of load balancing whatsoever, it's generally not recommended, and one of the other options is used instead.

FIGURE 5.38
The failover order helps determine how adapters in a NIC team are used when a failover occurs.

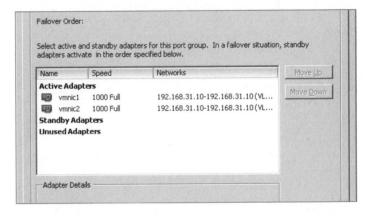

FIGURE 5.39
Standby adapters automatically activate when an active adapter fails.

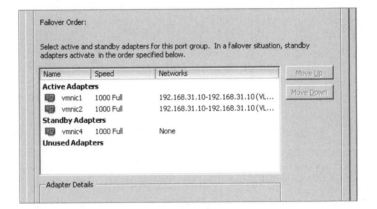

The Failback option controls how ESX/ESXi will handle a failed network adapter when it recovers from failure. The default setting, Yes, indicates the adapter will be returned to active duty immediately upon recovery, and it will replace any standby adapter that may have taken its place during the failure. Setting Failback to No means that the recovered adapter remains inactive until another adapter fails, triggering the replacement of newly failed adapter.

USING FAILBACK WITH VMKERNEL PORTS AND IP-BASED STORAGE

I recommend setting Failback to No for VMkernel ports you've configured for IP-based storage. Otherwise, in the event of a "port flapping" issue—a situation in which a link may repeatedly go up and down quickly—performance is negatively impacted. Setting Failback to No in this case protects performance in the event of port flapping as shown in Figure 5.40.

FIGURE 5.40
By default, a vSwitch using NIC teaming has Failback enabled (set to Yes).

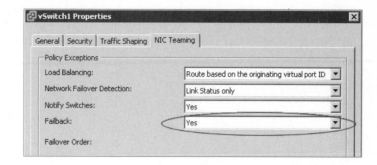

Perform the following steps to configure the Failover Order policy for a NIC team:

1. Use the vSphere Client to establish a connection to a vCenter Server or an ESX/ESXi host.

2. Click the hostname in the inventory panel on the left, select the Configuration tab in the details pane on the right, and then select Networking from the Hardware menu list.

3. Click the Properties for the virtual switch, select the name of virtual switch from the Configuration list, and then click the Edit button.

4. Select the NIC Teaming tab.

5. Use the Move Up and Move Down buttons to adjust the order of the network adapters and their location within the Active Adapters, Standby Adapters, and Unused Adapters lists, as shown in Figure 5.41.

FIGURE 5.41
Failover order for a NIC team is determined by the order of network adapters as listed in the Active Adapters, Standby Adapters, and Unused Adapters lists.

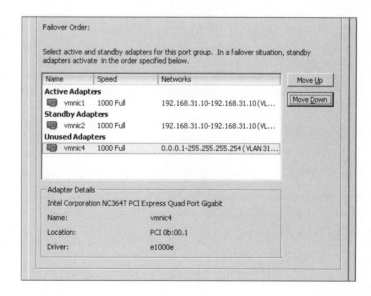

6. Click OK, and then click Close.

When a failover event occurs on a vSwitch with a NIC team, the vSwitch is obviously aware of the event. The physical switch that the vSwitch is connected to, however, will not know immediately. As shown in Figure 5.42, a vSwitch includes a Notify Switches configuration setting, which, when set to Yes, will allow the physical switch to immediately learn of any of the following changes:

◆ A virtual machine is powered on (or any other time a client registers itself with the vSwitch)

◆ A VMotion occurs

◆ A MAC address is changed

◆ A NIC team failover or failback has occurred

TURNING OFF NOTIFY SWITCHES

The Notify Switches option should be set to No when the port group has virtual machines using Microsoft Network Load Balancing (NLB) in Unicast mode.

FIGURE 5.42
The Notify Switches option allows physical switches to be notified of changes in NIC teaming configurations.

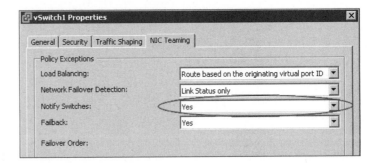

In any of these events, the physical switch is notified of the change using the Reverse Address Resolution Protocol (RARP). RARP updates the lookup tables on the physical switches and offers the shortest latency when a failover event occurs.

Although the VMkernel works proactively to keep traffic flowing from the virtual networking components to the physical networking components, VMware recommends taking the following actions to minimize networking delays:

◆ Disable Port Aggregation Protocol (PAgP) and Link Aggregation Control Protocol (LACP) on the physical switches.

◆ Disable Dynamic Trunking Protocol (DTP) or trunk negotiation.

◆ Disable Spanning Tree Protocol (STP).

VIRTUAL SWITCHES WITH CISCO SWITCHES

VMware recommends configuring Cisco devices to use PortFast mode for access ports or PortFast trunk mode for trunk ports.

Traffic Shaping

By default, all virtual network adapters connected to a vSwitch have access to the full amount of bandwidth on the physical network adapter with which the vSwitch is associated. In other words, if a vSwitch is assigned a 1Gbps network adapter, then each virtual machine configured to use the vSwitch has access to 1Gbps of bandwidth. Naturally, if contention becomes a bottleneck hindering virtual machine performance, NIC teaming will help. However, as a complement to NIC teaming, it is also possible to enable and to configure traffic shaping. Traffic shaping involves the establishment of hard-coded limits for peak bandwidth, average bandwidth, and burst size to reduce a virtual machine's outbound bandwidth capability.

As shown in Figure 5.43, the peak bandwidth value and the average bandwidth value are specified in kilobits per second, and the burst size is configured in units of kilobytes. The value entered for the average bandwidth dictates the data transfer per second across the virtual vSwitch. The peak bandwidth value identifies the maximum amount of bandwidth a vSwitch can pass without dropping packets. Finally, the burst size defines the maximum amount of data included in a burst. The burst size is a calculation of bandwidth multiplied by time. During periods of high utilization, if a burst exceeds the configured value, packets are dropped in favor of other traffic; however, if the queue for network traffic processing is not full, the packets are retained for transmission at a later time.

TRAFFIC SHAPING AS A LAST RESORT

Use the traffic shaping feature sparingly. Traffic shaping should be reserved for situations where virtual machines are competing for bandwidth and the opportunity to add network adapters is removed by limitations in the expansion slots on the physical chassis. With the low cost of network adapters, it is more worthwhile to spend time building vSwitch devices with NIC teams as opposed to cutting the bandwidth available to a set of virtual machines.

FIGURE 5.43
Traffic shaping reduces the outbound bandwidth available to a port group.

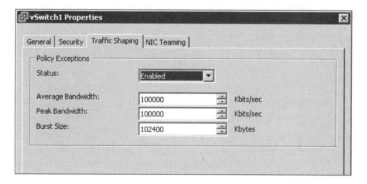

Perform the following steps to configure traffic shaping:

1. Use the vSphere Client to establish a connection to a vCenter Server or an ESX/ESXi host.

2. Click the hostname in the inventory panel on the left, select the Configuration tab in the details pane on the right, and then select Networking from the Hardware menu list.

3. Click the Properties for the virtual switch, select the name of the virtual switch or port group from the Configuration list, and then click the Edit button.

4. Select the Traffic Shaping tab.

5. Select the Enabled option from the Status drop-down list.

6. Adjust the Average Bandwidth value to the desired number of kilobits per second.

7. Adjust the Peak Bandwidth value to the desired number of kilobits per second.

8. Adjust the Burst Size value to the desired number of kilobytes.

Bringing It All Together

By now you've seen how all the various components of ESX/ESXi virtual networking interact with each other—vSwitches, ports and port groups, uplinks and NIC teams, and VLANs. But how do you assemble all these pieces together into a usable whole?

The number and the configuration of the vSwitches and port groups are dependent on several factors, including the number of network adapters in the ESX/ESXi host, the number of IP subnets, the existence of VLANs, and the number of physical networks. With respect to the configuration of the vSwitches and virtual machine port groups, there is no single correct configuration that will satisfy every scenario. It is true, however, to say that the greater the number of physical network adapters in an ESX/ESXi host, the more flexibility you will have in your virtual networking architecture.

 Real World Scenario

WHY DESIGN IT THAT WAY?

During the virtual network design I am often asked a number of different questions, such as why virtual switches should not be created with the largest number of ports to leave room to grow, or why multiple vSwitches should be used instead of a single vSwitch (or vice versa). Some of these questions are easy to answer; others are a matter of experience and, to be honest, personal preference.

Consider the question about why vSwitches should not be created with the largest number of ports. As you'll see in Table 5.1, the maximum number of ports in a virtual switch is 1016, and the maximum number of ports across all switches on a host is 4096. This means that if virtual switches are created with the 1016 port maximum, only 4 virtual switches can be created. If you're doing a quick calculation of 1016 × 4 and realizing it is not 4096, don't forget that virtual switches actually have 8 reserved ports, as pointed out earlier. Therefore, the 1016 port switch actually has 1,024 ports. Calculate 1,024 × 4, and you will arrive at the 4096 port maximum for an ESX/ESXi host.

Other questions aren't necessarily so clear-cut. I have found that using multiple vSwitches can make it easier to shift certain networks to dedicated physical networks; for example, if a customer wants to move their management network to a dedicated physical network for greater security, this is more easily accomplished when using multiple vSwitches instead of a single vSwitch. The same can be said for using VLANs.

In the end, though, many areas of virtual networking design are simply areas of personal preference and not technical necessity. Learning to determine which areas are which will go a long way to helping you understand your virtualized networking environment.

Later in the chapter I'll discuss some advanced design factors, but for now let's stick with some basic design considerations. If the vSwitches created in the VMkernel are not going to be configured with multiple port groups or VLANs, you will be required to create a separate vSwitch for every IP subnet or physical network to which you need to connect. This was illustrated previously in Figure 5.24 in our discussion about VLANs. To really understand this concept, let's look at two more examples.

Figure 5.44 shows a scenario in which there are five IP subnets that your virtual infrastructure components need to reach. The virtual machines in the production environment must reach the production LAN, the virtual machines in the test environment must reach the test LAN, the VMkernel needs to access the IP storage and VMotion LANs, and finally the Service Console must be on the management LAN. In this scenario, without the use of VLANs and port groups, the ESX/ESXi host must have five different vSwitches and five different physical network adapters. (Of course, this doesn't account for redundancy or NIC teaming for the vSwitches.)

FIGURE 5.44

Without the use of port groups and VLANs in the vSwitches, each IP subnet will require a separate vSwitch with the appropriate connection type.

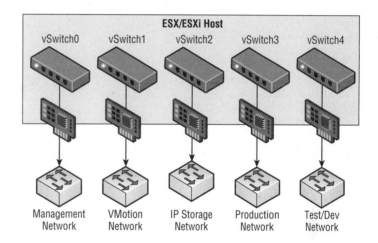

Figure 5.45 shows the same configuration, but this time using VLANs for the Management, VMotion, Production, and Test/Dev networks. The IP storage network is still a physically separate network.

The configuration in Figure 5.45 still uses five network adapters, but this time you're able to provide NIC teaming for all the networks except for the IP storage network.

If the IP storage network had been configured as a VLAN, the number of vSwitches and uplinks could have been even further reduced. Figure 5.46 shows a possible configuration that would support this sort of scenario.

This time, you're able to provide NIC teaming to all the traffic types involved—Service Console/Management traffic, VMotion, IP storage, and the virtual machine traffic—using only a single vSwitch with multiple uplinks.

Clearly, there is a tremendous amount of flexibility in how vSwitches, uplinks, and port groups are assembled to create a virtual network capable of supporting your infrastructure. Even given all this flexibility, though, there are limits. Table 5.1 lists some of the limits of ESX/ESXi networking.

FIGURE 5.45
The use of the physically separate IP storage network limits the reduction in the number of vSwitches and uplinks.

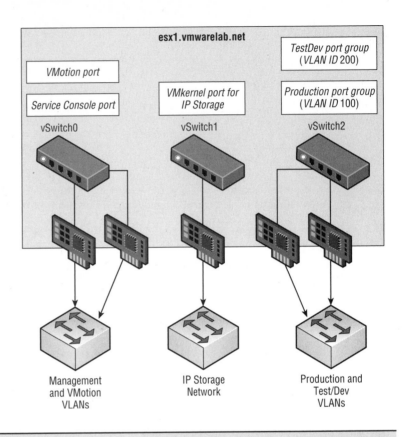

VIRTUAL SWITCH CONFIGURATIONS ... DON'T GO TOO BIG!

Although you can create a vSwitch with a maximum of 1,016 ports (really 1,024), it is not recommended if you anticipate growth. Because ESX/ESXi hosts cannot have more than 4,096 ports, if you create vSwitches with 1,016 ports, then you are limited to only 4 vSwitches (1,024 × 4). With room for only four vSwitches, you may not be able to connect to all the networks that you need. I recommend creating virtual switches with just enough ports to cover existing needs and projected growth. In the event you do run out of ports on an ESX/ESXi host and need to create a new vSwitch, you can reduce the number of ports on an existing vSwitch. That change requires a reboot to take effect, but VMotion allows you to move the VMs to a different host to prevent VM downtime.

With all the flexibility provided by the different virtual networking components, you can be assured that whatever the physical network configuration might hold in store, there are several ways to integrate the virtual networking. What you configure today may change as the infrastructure changes or as the hardware changes. ESX/ESXi provides enough tools and options to ensure a successful communication scheme between the virtual and physical networks.

FIGURE 5.46
With the use of port groups and VLANs in the vSwitches, even fewer vSwitches and uplinks are required.

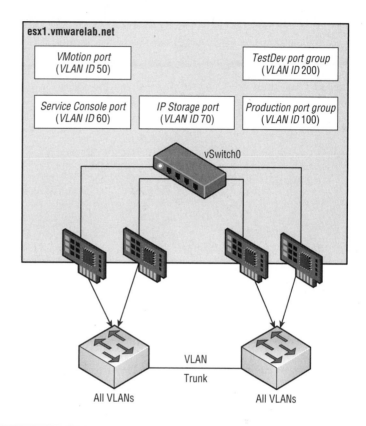

TABLE 5.1: Configuration Maximums for ESX/ESXi Networking Components (vNetwork Standard Switches)

CONFIGURATION ITEM	MAXIMUM
Number of vSwitches	248
Ports per vSwitch	1,016
Ports per host	4,096
Port groups per vSwitch	512
Port groups per host	512
Uplinks per vSwitch	32
Number of Service Console/VMkernel NICs	16
Number of virtual NICs per host	4,096

Working with vNetwork Distributed Switches

So far our discussion has focused solely on vNetwork Standard Switches (just vSwitches). With the release of ESX/ESXi 4.0 and the vSphere product suite, there is now a new option: vNetwork Distributed Switches.

Whereas vSwitches are managed per host, a vNetwork Distributed Switch functions as a single virtual switch across all the associated ESX/ESXi hosts. There are a number of similarities between a vNetwork Distributed Switch and a standard vSwitch:

◆ Like a vSwitch, a vNetwork Distributed Switch provides connectivity for virtual machines, Service Console or Management traffic, and VMkernel interfaces.

◆ Like a vSwitch, a vNetwork Distributed Switch leverages physical network adapters as uplinks to provide connectivity to the external physical network.

◆ Like a vSwitch, a vNetwork Distributed Switch can leverage VLANs for logical network segmentation.

Of course, there are differences as well, but the biggest of these is that a vNetwork Distributed Switch spans multiple servers in a cluster instead of each server having its own set of vSwitches. This greatly reduces complexity in clustered ESX/ESXi environments and simplifies the addition of new servers to an ESX/ESXi cluster.

VMware's official abbreviation for a vNetwork Distributed Switch is vDS. For ease of reference and consistency with other elements in the vSphere user interface, we'll refer to vNetwork Distributed Switches from here on as dvSwitches.

Creating a vNetwork Distributed Switch

The process of creating a dvSwitch is twofold. First, using the vSphere Client, the new dvSwitch is created. After you create the dvSwitch, you add ESX/ESXi hosts to the dvSwitch. You perform both of these tasks from within the vSphere Client.

Perform the following steps to create a new dvSwitch:

1. Launch the vSphere Client, and connect to a vCenter Server instance.

2. On the vSphere Client home screen, select the Networking option under Inventory.

3. Right-click the Datacenter object in the Inventory pane on the left, and select New vNetwork Distributed Switch from the context menu. This launches the Create vNetwork Distributed Switch Wizard.

4. Specify a name for the dvSwitch, and specify the number of dvUplink ports, as illustrated in Figure 5.47. Click Next.

5. On the next screen, you can choose to add hosts to the dvSwitch now or add them later. To add hosts now, select unused physical adapters from each applicable host, and then click Next. These physical adapters will be configured as uplinks connected to a dvUplink port. Figure 5.48 shows a single host being added to a dvSwitch during creation.

6. To create a default dvPort group, leave the box selected labeled Automatically Create A Default Port Group (the default), as shown in Figure 5.49. Click Finish.

FIGURE 5.47
The number of dvUplink ports controls how many physical adapters from each host can serve as uplinks for the distributed switch.

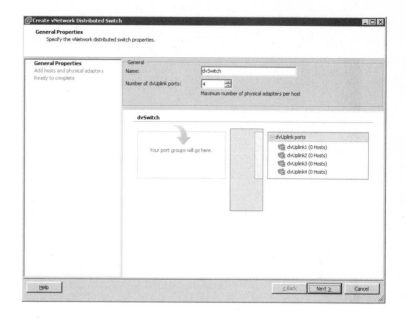

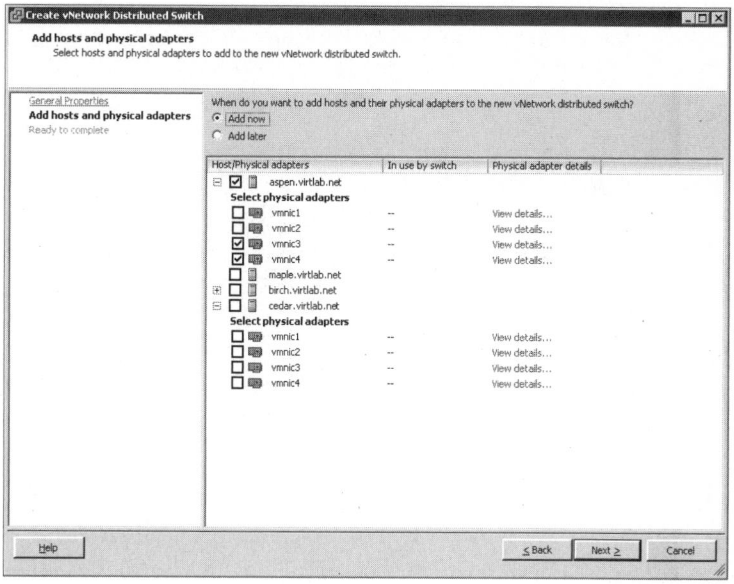

FIGURE 5.48
Users can add ESX/ESXi hosts to a vNetwork Distributed Switch during or after creation.

FIGURE 5.49
By default, a dvPort group is created during the creation of the distributed switch.

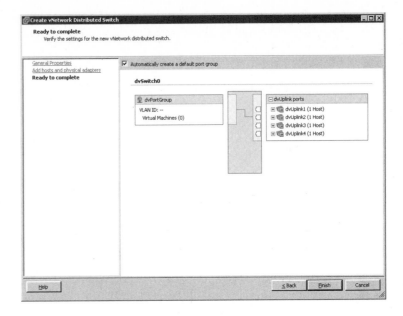

Upon completion of the Create vNetwork Distributed Switch Wizard, a new dvSwitch, a dvPort group for the uplinks, and the default dvPort group will appear in the inventory list. On a host running VMware ESX, the `esxcfg-vswitch` command will show the new vNetwork Distributed Switch and dvPort groups. Because of the shared nature of the dvSwitch, though, configuration of the distributed switch occurs in the vSphere Client connected to vCenter Server.

VNETWORK DISTRIBUTED SWITCHES REQUIRE VCENTER SERVER

This may seem obvious, but it's important to point out that because of the shared nature of a vNetwork Distributed Switch, vCenter Server is required. That is, you cannot have a vNetwork Distributed Switch in an environment that is not being managed by vCenter Server.

After creating a vNetwork Distributed Switch, it is relatively easy to add another ESX/ESXi host. When the additional ESX/ESXi host is created, all of the dvPort groups will automatically be propagated to the new host with the correct configuration. This is the distributed nature of the dvSwitch—as configuration changes are made via the vSphere Client, vCenter Server pushes those changes out to all participating hosts in the dvSwitch. VMware administrators used to managing large ESX/ESXi clusters and having to repeatedly create vSwitches and port groups across all the servers individually will be very pleased with the reduction in administrative overhead that dvSwitches offer.

Perform the following steps to add another host to an existing dvSwitch:

1. Launch the vSphere Client, and connect to a vCenter Server instance.

2. On the vSphere Client home screen, select the Networking option under Inventory.

3. Select an existing vNetwork Distributed Switch in the Inventory pane on the left, click the Summary tab in the pane on the right, and select Add Host from the Commands section. This launches the Add Host To Distributed Virtual Switch Wizard, as shown in Figure 5.50.

FIGURE 5.50
Adding a host to an existing vNetwork Distributed Switch uses the same format as adding hosts during creation of the dvSwitch.

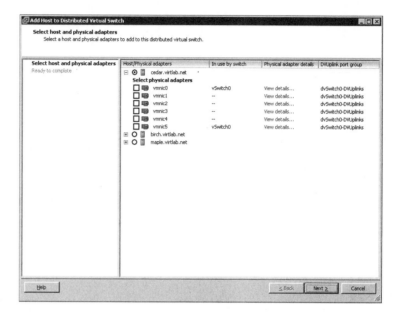

4. Select the physical adapters on the host being added that should be connected to the dvSwitch's dvUplinks port group as uplinks for the distributed switch, and then click Next.

5. At the summary screen, review the changes being made to the dvSwitch—which are helpfully highlighted in the graphical display of the dvSwitch, as shown in Figure 5.51—and click Finish if everything is correct.

DVSWITCH TOTAL PORTS AND AVAILABLE PORTS

With vNetwork Standard Switches, the VMkernel reserved eight ports for its own use, creating a discrepancy between the total number of ports listed in different places. When looking at a dvSwitch, you may think the same thing is true—a dvSwitch with 2 hosts will have a total port count of 136, with only 128 ports remaining. Where are the other eight ports? Those are the ports in the dvUplink port group, reserved for uplinks. For every host added to a dvSwitch, another four ports (by default) are added to the dvUplinks port group. So, a dvSwitch with 3 hosts would have 140 total ports with 128 available, a dvSwitch with 4 hosts would have 144 total ports with 128 available, and so forth. If a value other than 4 was selected as the maximum number of uplinks, then the difference between total ports and available ports would be that value times the number of hosts in the dvSwitch.

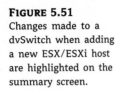

FIGURE 5.51
Changes made to a dvSwitch when adding a new ESX/ESXi host are highlighted on the summary screen.

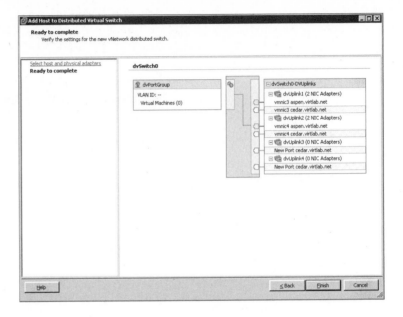

Naturally, you can also remove ESX/ESXi hosts from a dvSwitch. A host can't be removed from a dvSwitch if it still has virtual machines connected to a dvPort group on that dvSwitch. This is analogous to trying to delete a standard vSwitch or a port group while a virtual machine is still connected; this, too, is prevented. To allow the host to be removed from the dvSwitch, all virtual machines will need to be moved to a standard vSwitch or a different dvSwitch.

Perform the following steps to remove an individual host from a dvSwitch:

1. Launch the vSphere Client, and connect to a vCenter Server instance.

2. On the vSphere Client home screen, select the Networking option under Inventory. You can also select the View menu and then choose Inventory ➤ Networking, or you can press the keyboard hotkey (Ctrl+Shift+N).

3. Select an existing vNetwork Distributed Switch in the Inventory pane on the left, and click the Hosts tab in the pane on the right. A list of hosts currently connected to the selected dvSwitch displays.

4. Right-click the ESX/ESXi host to be removed, and select Remove From Distributed Virtual Switch from the context menu, as shown in Figure 5.52.

5. If any virtual machines are still connected to the dvSwitch, the vSphere Client throws an error similar to the one shown in Figure 5.53.

   To correct this error, reconfigure the virtual machine(s) to use a different dvSwitch or vSwitch, or migrate the virtual machines to a different host using VMotion. Then proceed with removing the host from the dvSwitch.

RECONFIGURING VM NETWORKING WITH A DRAG-AND-DROP OPERATION

While in the Networking view (View ➤ Inventory ➤ Networking), you can use drag and drop to reconfigure a virtual machine's network connection. Simply drag the virtual machine onto the desired network, and drop it. vCenter Server reconfigures the virtual machine to use the selected virtual network.

FIGURE 5.52
Use the right-click context menu on the host while in the Networking Inventory view to remove an ESX/ESXi host from a dvSwitch.

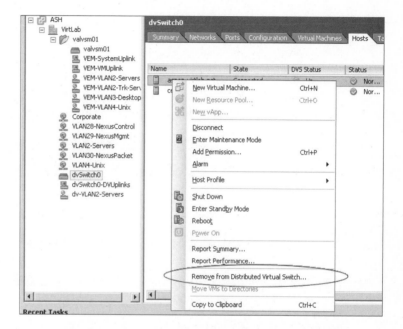

FIGURE 5.53
The vSphere Client won't allow a host to be removed from a dvSwitch if a virtual machine is still attached.

6. If there were no virtual machines attached to the dvSwitch, or after all virtual machines are reconfigured to use a different vSwitch or dvSwitch, the host is removed from the dvSwitch.

Removing the last ESX/ESXi host from a dvSwitch does not remove the dvSwitch itself. If you want to get rid of the dvSwitch entirely, you must remove the dvSwitch and not just remove the hosts from the dvSwitch. When you remove a dvSwitch, it is removed from all hosts and removed from the vCenter Server inventory as well.

Removing a dvSwitch is possible only if no virtual machines have been assigned to a dvPort group on the dvSwitch. Otherwise, the removal of the dvSwitch is blocked with an error message like the one displayed previously in Figure 5.53. Again, you'll need to reconfigure the virtual machine(s) to use a different vSwitch or dvSwitch before the operation can proceed. Refer to Chapter 7 for more information on modifying a virtual machine's network settings.

Perform the following steps to remove the dvSwitch if no virtual machines are using the dvSwitch or any of the dvPort groups on that dvSwitch:

1. Launch the vSphere Client, and connect to a vCenter Server instance.

2. On the vSphere Client home screen, select the Networking option under Inventory. You can also select the View menu and then choose Inventory ➢ Networking, or you can press the keyboard hotkey (Ctrl+Shift+N).

3. Select an existing vNetwork Distributed Switch in the Inventory pane on the left.

4. Right-click the dvSwitch and select Remove, or choose Remove from the Edit menu. A confirmation dialog box like the one shown in Figure 5.54 displays. Select Yes to continue.

FIGURE 5.54
vCenter Server asks the user to confirm the removal of the dvSwitch before proceeding.

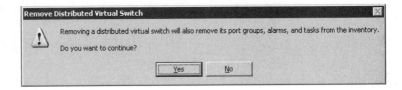

5. The dvSwitch and all associated dvPort groups are removed from the Inventory and from any connected hosts.

The bulk of the configuration for a dvSwitch isn't performed for the dvSwitch itself, but rather for the dvPort groups on that dvSwitch.

Configuring dvPort Groups

With vNetwork Standard Switches, port groups are the key to connectivity for the Service Console, VMkernel, or virtual machines. Without ports and port groups on a vSwitch, nothing can be connected to that vSwitch. The same is true for vNetwork Distributed Switches. Without a dvPort group, nothing can be connected to a dvSwitch, and the dvSwitch is, therefore, unusable. In this section, you'll take a closer look at creating and configuring dvPort groups.

Perform the following steps to create a new dvPort group:

1. Launch the vSphere Client, and connect to a vCenter Server instance.

2. On the vSphere Client home screen, select the Networking option under Inventory. Alternately, from the View menu, select Inventory ➢ Networking.

3. Select an existing vNetwork Distributed Switch in the Inventory pane on the left, click the Summary tab in the pane on the right, and select New Port Group in the Commands section. This launches the Create Distributed Virtual Port Group Wizard, as illustrated in Figure 5.55.

FIGURE 5.55
The Create Distributed Virtual Port Group Wizard allows the user to specify the name of the dvPort group, the number of ports, and the VLAN type.

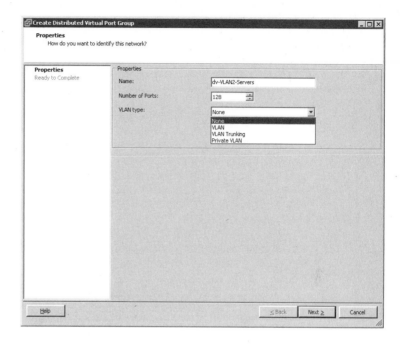

The name of the dvPort group and the number of ports are self-explanatory, but the options under VLAN Type need a bit more explanation:

◆ With VLAN Type set to None, the dvPort group will receive only untagged traffic. In this case, the uplinks must connect to physical switch ports configured as access ports, or they will receive only untagged/native VLAN traffic.

◆ With VLAN Type set to VLAN, you'll then need to specify a VLAN ID. The dvPort group will receive traffic tagged with that VLAN ID. The uplinks must connect to physical switch ports configured as VLAN trunks.

◆ With VLAN Type set to VLAN Trunking, you'll then need to specify the range of allowed VLANs. The dvPort group will pass the VLAN tags up to the guest operating systems on any connected virtual machines.

◆ With VLAN Type set to Private VLAN, you'll then need to specify a Private VLAN entry. Private VLANs are described in detail later in this section.

Specify a descriptive name for the dvPort group, select the appropriate number of ports, select the correct VLAN type, and then click Next.

4. On the summary screen, review the settings, and click Finish if everything is correct.

After a dvPort group has been created, you can select that dvPort group in the virtual machine configuration as a possible network connection, as shown in Figure 5.56.

FIGURE 5.56
A dvPort group is selected as a network connection for virtual machines, just like port groups on a standard vSwitch.

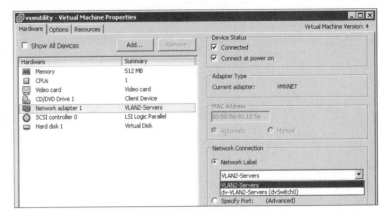

After creating a dvPort group, selecting the dvPort group in the inventory on the left side of the vSphere Client provides you with the option to get more information about the dvPort group and its current state:

◆ The Summary tab provides exactly that—summary information such as the total number of ports in the dvPort group, the number of available ports, any configured IP pools, and the option to edit the settings for the dvPort group.

◆ The Ports tab lists the dvPorts in the dvPort group, their current status, attached virtual machines, and port statistics, as illustrated in Figure 5.57.

FIGURE 5.57
The Ports tab shows all the dvPorts in the dvPort group along with port status and port statistics.

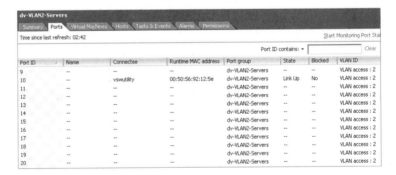

To update the port status or statistics, click the link in the upper-right corner labeled Start Monitoring Port State. That link then changes to Stop Monitoring Port State, which you can use to disable port monitoring.

◆ The Virtual Machines tab lists any virtual machines currently attached to that dvPort group. The full range of virtual machine operations—such as editing virtual machine settings, shutting down the virtual machine, and migrating the virtual machine—is available from the right-click context menu of a virtual machine listed in this area.

◆ The Hosts tab lists all ESX/ESXi hosts currently participating in the dvSwitch that hosts this dvPort group. As with virtual machines, right-clicking a host here provides a context menu with the full range of options, such as creating a new virtual machine, entering maintenance mode, checking host profile compliance, or rebooting the host.

◆ The Tasks & Events tab lists all tasks or events associated with this dvPort group.

◆ The Alarms tab shows any alarms that have been defined or triggered for this dvPort group.

◆ The Permissions tab shows permissions that have been applied to (or inherited by) this dvPort group.

To delete a dvPort group, right-click the dvPort group, and select Delete. If any virtual machines are still attached to that dvPort group, the vSphere Client prevents the deletion of the dvPort group and displays an error message like the one shown in Figure 5.58.

FIGURE 5.58
As long as at least one virtual machine is still using the dvPort group, the vSphere Client won't delete the dvPort group.

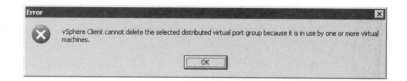

To delete the dvPort group, you first have to reconfigure the virtual machine to use a different dvPort group or a different vSwitch or dvSwitch.

To edit the configuration of a dvPort group, use the Edit Settings link in the Commands section on the dvPort group's Summary tab. This produces a dialog box shown in Figure 5.59. The various options along the left side of the dvPort group settings dialog box allow you to modify different aspects of the dvPort group.

FIGURE 5.59
The Edit Settings command for a dvPort group allows you to modify the configuration of the dvPort group.

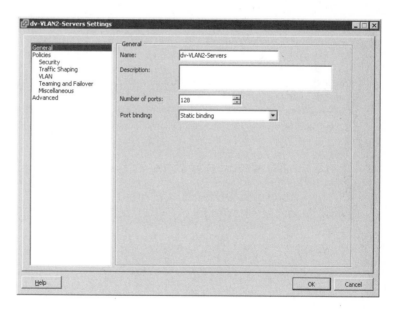

I'll discuss the policy settings for security later in this chapter, so I'll skip over them for now and focus on modifying VLAN settings, NIC teaming, and traffic shaping for the dvPort group.

Perform the following steps to modify the VLAN settings for a dvPort group:

1. Launch the vSphere Client, and connect to a vCenter Server instance.

2. On the vSphere Client home screen, select the Networking option under Inventory. Alternately, from the View menu, select Inventory ➢ Networking.

3. Select an existing dvPort group in the Inventory pane on the left, select the Summary tab in the pane on the right, and click the Edit Settings option in the Commands section.

4. In the dvPort Group Settings dialog box, select the VLAN option under Policies from the list of options on the left.

5. Modify the VLAN settings by changing the VLAN ID or by changing the VLAN Type setting to VLAN Trunking or Private VLAN. Refer to Figure 5.55 earlier in the chapter for the different VLAN configuration options.

6. Click OK when you are finished making changes.

Perform the following steps to modify the NIC teaming and failover policies for a dvPort group:

1. Launch the vSphere Client, and connect to a vCenter Server instance.

2. On the vSphere Client home screen, select the Networking option under Inventory. Alternately, from the View menu, select Inventory ➢ Networking.

3. Select an existing dvPort group in the Inventory pane on the left, select the Summary tab in the pane on the right, and click the Edit Settings option in the Commands section.

4. Select the Teaming And Failover option from the list of options on the left of the dvPort Group Settings dialog box, as illustrated in Figure 5.60.

FIGURE 5.60
The Teaming And Failover item in the dvPort group settings dialog box provides options for modifying how a dvPort group uses dvUplinks.

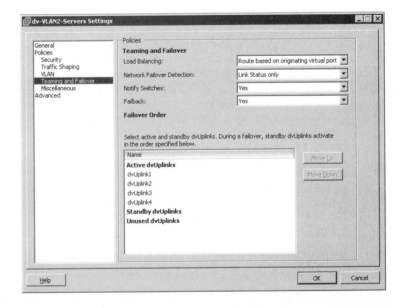

The settings here are described in greater detail previously in this chapter in the section titled "Configuring NIC Teaming."

5. Click OK when you are finished making changes.

Perform the following steps to modify the traffic shaping policy for a dvPort group:

1. Launch the vSphere Client, and connect to a vCenter Server instance.

2. On the vSphere Client home screen, select the Networking option under Inventory. Alternately, from the View menu, select Inventory ➢ Networking.

3. Select an existing dvPort group in the Inventory pane on the left, select the Summary tab in the pane on the right, and click the Edit Settings option in the Commands section.

4. Select the Traffic Shaping option from the list of options on the left of the dvPort group settings dialog box, as illustrated in Figure 5.61.

FIGURE 5.61

You can apply both ingress and egress traffic shaping policies to a dvPort group on a dvSwitch.

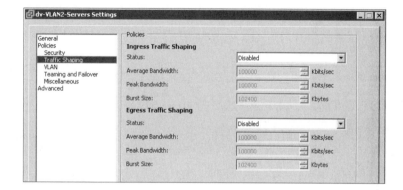

Traffic shaping was described in detail in the section labeled "Traffic Shaping." The big difference here is that with a dvSwitch, you can apply traffic shaping policies to both ingress and egress traffic. With vNetwork Standard Switches, you could apply traffic shaping policies only to egress (outbound) traffic. Otherwise, the settings here for a dvPort group function as described earlier.

5. Click OK when you are finished making changes.

If you browse through the available settings, you might notice a Blocked policy option. This is the equivalent of disabling a group of ports in the dvPort group. Figure 5.62 shows that the Blocked setting is set to either Yes or No. If you set the Blocked policy to Yes, then all traffic to and from that dvPort group is dropped. Don't set the Blocked policy to Yes unless you are prepared for network downtime for all virtual machines attached to that dvPort group!

FIGURE 5.62

The Blocked policy is set to either Yes or No. Setting the Blocked policy to Yes disables all the ports in that dvPort group.

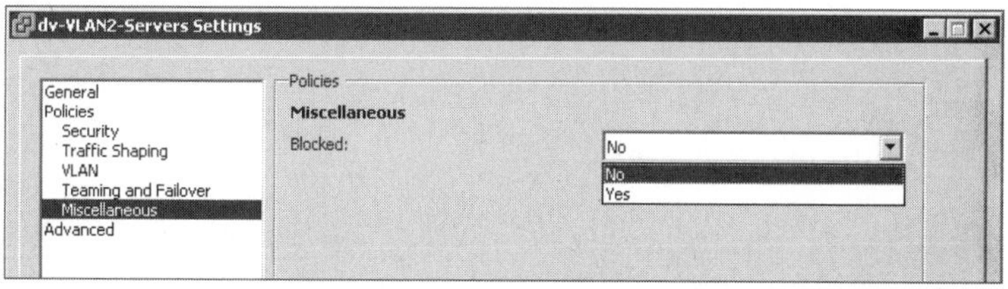

Managing Adapters

With a dvSwitch, managing adapters—both virtual and physical—is handled quite differently than with a standard vSwitch. Virtual adapters are Service Console and VMkernel interfaces, so by managing virtual adapters, I'm really talking about managing Service Console/management traffic and VMkernel traffic on a dvSwitch. Physical adapters are, of course, the physical network adapters that serve as uplinks for the dvSwitch. Managing physical adapters means adding or removing physical adapters connected to ports in the dvUplinks dvPort group on the dvSwitch.

Perform the following steps to add a virtual adapter to a dvSwitch:

1. Launch the vSphere Client, and connect to a vCenter Server instance.

2. On the vSphere Client home screen, select the Hosts And Clusters option under Inventory. Alternately, from the View menu, select Inventory ➢ Hosts And Clusters. The Ctrl+Shift+H hotkey also takes you to the correct view.

3. Select an ESX/ESXi host in the inventory on the left, click the Configuration tab in the pane on the right, and select Networking from the Hardware list.

4. Click to change the view from Virtual Switch to Distributed Virtual Switch, as illustrated in Figure 5.63.

FIGURE 5.63
To manage virtual adapters, switch the Networking view to Distributed Virtual Switch in the vSphere Client.

5. Click the Manage Virtual Adapters link. This opens the Manage Virtual Adapters dialog box, as shown in Figure 5.64.

FIGURE 5.64
The Manage Virtual Adapters dialog box allows users to create Service Console and VMkernel interfaces.

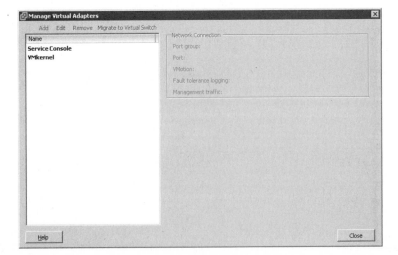

6. Click the Add link. The Add Virtual Adapter Wizard appears, offering you the option to either create a new virtual adapter or migrate existing virtual adapters.

Creating a new virtual adapter involves selecting the type of virtual adapter—Service Console (ESX only) or VMkernel (ESX and ESXi)—and then attaching the new virtual adapter to an existing dvPort group. The wizard also prompts for IP address information because that is required when creating a Service Console or VMkernel interface. Refer to the earlier sections about configuring Service Console/management and VMkernel networking for more information.

In this case, select Migrate Existing Virtual Adapters, and click Next.

7. For each current virtual adapter, select the new destination port group on the dvSwitch. Deselect the box next to the current virtual adapters that you don't want to migrate right now. This is illustrated in Figure 5.65. Click Next to continue.

FIGURE 5.65
For each virtual adapter migrating to the dvSwitch, you must assign the virtual adapter to an existing dvPort group.

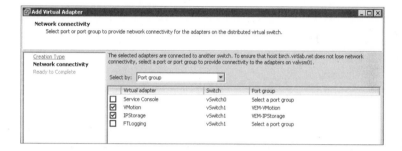

8. Review the changes to the dvSwitch—which are helpfully highlighted for easy identification—and click Finish to commit the changes.

After creating or migrating a virtual adapter, the same dialog box allows for changes to the virtual port, such as modifying the IP address, changing the dvPort group to which the adapter is assigned, or enabling features such as VMotion or fault tolerance logging. You would remove virtual adapters using this dialog box as well.

The Manage Physical Adapters link allows you to add or remove physical adapters connected to ports in the dvUplinks port group on the dvSwitch. Although you can specify physical adapters during the process of adding a host to a dvSwitch, as shown earlier, it might be necessary at times to connect a physical NIC to a port in the dvUplinks port group on the dvSwitch after the host is already participating in the dvSwitch.

Perform the following steps to add a physical network adapter in an ESX/ESXi host to the dvUplinks port group on the dvSwitch:

1. Launch the vSphere Client, and connect to a vCenter Server instance.

2. On the vSphere Client home screen, select the Hosts and Clusters option under Inventory. Alternately, from the View menu, select Inventory ➤ Hosts and Clusters. The Ctrl+Shift+H hotkey will also take you to the correct view.

3. Select an ESX/ESXi host in the inventory list on the left, click the Configuration tab in the pane on the right, and select Networking from the Hardware list.

4. Click to change the view from Virtual Switch to Distributed Virtual Switch.

5. Click the Manage Physical Adapters link. This opens the Manage Physical Adapters dialog box, as shown in Figure 5.66.

FIGURE 5.66
The Manage Physical Adapters dialog box provides information on physical NICs connected to the dvUplinks port group and allows you to add or remove uplinks.

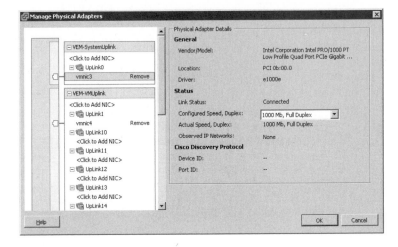

6. To add a physical network adapter to the dvUplinks port group, click the Click To Add NIC link.

7. In the Add Physical Adapter dialog box, select the physical adapter to be added to the dvUplinks port group, and click OK.

8. Click OK again to return to the vSphere Client.

In addition to being able to migrate virtual adapters, you can use vCenter Server to assist in migrating virtual machine networking between vNetwork Standard Switches and vNetwork Distributed Switches, as shown in Figure 5.67.

This tool, accessed using the Migrate Virtual Machine Networking link on the Summary tab of a dvSwitch, will reconfigure all selected virtual machines to use the selected destination network. This is a lot easier than individually reconfiguring a bunch of virtual machines!

Setting Up Private VLANs

Private VLANs are a new feature of vSphere that build upon the functionality of vNetwork Distributed Switches. Private VLANs are possible only when using dvSwitches and are not available to use with vNetwork Standard Switches.

First, I'll provide a quick overview of private VLANs. Private VLANs (PVLANs) are a way to further isolate ports within a VLAN. For example, consider the scenario of hosts within a demilitarized zone (DMZ). Hosts within a DMZ rarely need to communicate with each other, but using a VLAN for each host quickly becomes unwieldy for a number of reasons. Using PVLANs, you can isolate hosts from each other while keeping them on the same IP subnet. Figure 5.68 provides a graphical overview of how PVLANs work.

PVLANs are configured in pairs: the primary VLAN and any secondary VLANs. The primary VLAN is considered the *downstream* VLAN; that is, traffic to the host travels along the primary VLAN. The secondary VLAN is considered the *upstream* VLAN; that is, traffic from the host travels along the secondary VLAN.

To use PVLANs, first configure the PVLANs on the physical switches connecting to the ESX/ESXi hosts, and then add the PVLAN entries to the dvSwitch in vCenter Server.

FIGURE 5.67
The Migrate Virtual Machine Networking tool automates the process of migrating virtual machines from vSwitches to dvSwitches and back again.

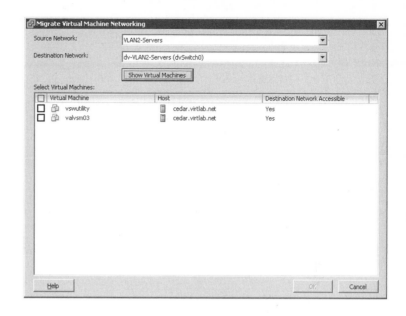

FIGURE 5.68
Private VLANs can help isolate ports on the same IP subnet.

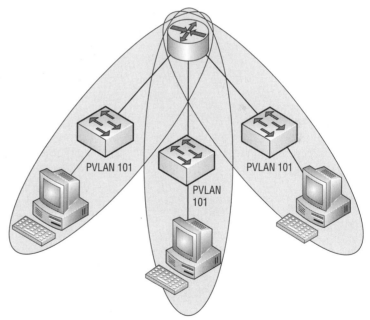

Perform the following steps to define PVLAN entries on a dvSwitch:

1. Launch the vSphere Client, and connect to a vCenter Server instance.

2. On the vSphere Client home screen, select the Networking option under Inventory. Alternately, from the View menu, select Inventory ➢ Networking, or press the Ctrl+Shift+N hotkey.

3. Select an existing dvSwitch in the Inventory pane on the left, select the Summary tab in the pane on the right, and click the Edit Settings option in the Commands section.

4. Select the Private VLAN tab.

5. Add a primary VLAN ID to the list on the left.

6. For each primary VLAN ID in the list on the left, add one or more secondary VLANs to the list on the right, as shown in Figure 5.69.

FIGURE 5.69
Private VLANs entries consist of a primary VLAN and one or more secondary VLAN entries.

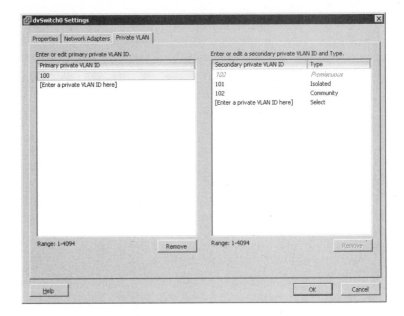

Secondary VLANs are classified as one of the two following types:

◆ Isolated: Ports placed in secondary PVLANs configured as isolated are allowed to communicate only with promiscuous ports in the same secondary VLAN. I'll explain promiscuous ports shortly.

◆ Community: Ports in a secondary PVLAN are allowed to communicate with other ports in the same secondary PVLAN as well as with promiscuous ports.

Only one isolated secondary VLAN is permitted for each primary VLAN. Multiple secondary VLANs configured as community VLANs are allowed.

7. When you finish adding all the PVLAN pairs, click OK to save the changes and return to the vSphere Client.

After the PVLAN IDs have been entered for a dvSwitch, you must create a dvPort group that takes advantage of the PVLAN configuration. The process for creating a dvPort group was described previously. Figure 5.70 shows the Create Distributed Virtual Port Group Wizard for a dvPort group that uses PVLANs.

FIGURE 5.70
When creating a dvPort group with PVLANs, the dvPort group is associated with both the primary VLAN ID and a secondary VLAN ID.

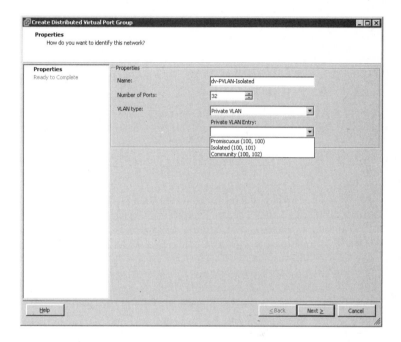

In Figure 5.70 you can see mention of the term *promiscuous* again. In PVLAN parlance, a promiscuous port is allowed to send and receive Layer 2 frames to any other port in the VLAN. This type of port is typically reserved for the default gateway for an IP subnet, for example, a Layer 3 router.

Private VLANs are a powerful configuration tool but also a complex configuration topic and one that can be difficult to understand. For additional information on Private VLANs, I recommend visiting Cisco's website at www.cisco.com and searching for *private VLANs*.

As with vNetwork Standard Switches, vNetwork Distributed Switches provide a tremendous amount of flexibility in designing and configuration a virtual network. But, as with all things, there are limits to the flexibility. Table 5.2 lists some of the configuration maximums for vNetwork Distributed Switches.

As if adding vNetwork Distributed Switches to vSphere and ESX/ESXi 4.0 wasn't a big enough change from earlier versions of VMware Infrastructure, there's something even bigger in store for you: the very first third-party vNetwork Distributed Switch: the Cisco Nexus 1000V.

TABLE 5.2: Configuration Maximums for ESX/ESXi Networking Components (vNetwork Distributed Switches)

CONFIGURATION ITEM	MAXIMUM
Switches per vCenter Server	16
Switches per ESX/ESXi host	16
dvPort groups per switch on vCenter Server	512
dvPort groups per ESX/ESXi host	512
Ports per switch on vCenter Server	8,000
Hosts per switch on vCenter Server	300
Virtual machines per switch on vCenter Server	3,000
VLANs or private VLANs	512, limited by port groups

Installing and Configuring the Cisco Nexus 1000V

The Cisco Nexus 1000V is a third-party vNetwork Distributed Switch, the first of its kind. Built as part of a joint engineering effort between Cisco and VMware, the Nexus 1000V completely changes the dynamics in how the networking and server teams interact in environments using VMware vSphere.

Prior to the arrival of the Cisco Nexus 1000V, the reach of the networking team ended at the uplinks from the ESX/ESXi host to the physical switches. The networking team had no visibility into and no control over the networking inside the ESX/ESXi hosts. The server team, which used the vSphere Client to create and manage vSwitches and port groups, handled that functionality. The Cisco Nexus 1000V changes all that. Now the networking group will create the port groups that will be applied to virtual machines, and the server group will simply attach virtual machines to the appropriate port group—modeling the same behavior in the virtual environment as exists in the physical environment. In addition, organizations gain per-VM network statistics and much greater insight into the type of traffic that's found on the ESX/ESXi hosts.

The Cisco Nexus 1000V has the following two major components:

◆ The Virtual Ethernet Module (VEM), which executes inside the ESX/ESXi hypervisor and replaces the standard vSwitch functionality. The VEM leverages the vNetwork Distributed Switch APIs to bring features like quality of service (QoS), private VLANs, access control lists, NetFlow, and SPAN to virtual machine networking.

◆ The Virtual Supervisor Module (VSM), which is a Cisco NX-OS instance running as a virtual machine. The VSM controls multiple VEMs as one logical modular switch. All configuration is performed through the VSM and propagated to the VEMs automatically.

The Cisco Nexus 1000V marks a new era in virtual networking. Let's take a closer look at installing and configuring the Nexus 1000V.

Installing the Cisco Nexus 1000V

To install the Nexus 1000V, you must first install at least one VSM. After a VSM is up and running, you use the VSM to push out the VEMs to the various ESX/ESXi hosts that use the Nexus 1000V as their dvSwitch. Fortunately, users familiar with setting up a virtual machine have an advantage in setting up the VSM because it operates as a virtual machine.

Installation of the Nexus 1000V is a fairly complex process, with a number of dependencies that must be resolved before installation. For more complete and detailed information on these dependencies, I encourage you to refer to the official Cisco Nexus 1000V documentation. The information provided here describes the installation at a high level.

Perform the following steps to install a Nexus 1000V VSM:

1. Use the vSphere Client to establish a connection to a vCenter Server or an ESX/ESXi host.

2. Create a new virtual machine with the following specifications:

    Guest operating system: Other Linux (64-bit)

    Memory: 2048 MB

    CPUs: 1 vCPU

    Network adapters: 3 e1000 network adapters

    Virtual disk: 3GB

    For more information on creating virtual machines, you can refer to Chapter 7.

3. Configure the network adapters so that the first e1000 adapter connects to a VLAN created for Nexus control traffic, the second e1000 adapter connects to the management VLAN, and the third e1000 network adapter connects to a VLAN created for Nexus packet traffic. *It is very important that the adapters are configured in exactly this order.*

4. Attach the Nexus 1000V VSM ISO image to the virtual machine's CD-ROM drive, and configure the CD-ROM to be connected at startup, as shown in Figure 5.71.

FIGURE 5.71
The ISO image for the Nexus 1000V VSM should be attached to the virtual machine's CD-ROM drive for installation.

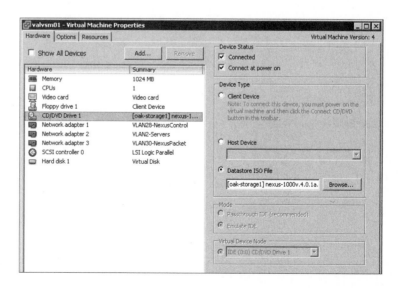

5. Power on the virtual machine.

6. From the boot menu, select Install Nexus 1000V And Bring Up The New Image.

7. After the installation is complete, walk through the setup wizard. During the setup wizard, you are prompted to provide information such as the password for the admin user account; the VLAN IDs for the management, packet, and data VLANs; the IP address to be assigned to the VSM; and the default gateway for the VSM.

After the VSM is up and running and has connectivity to the network, you must connect the VSM to vCenter Server. To connect the VSM to vCenter Server, you must first create a plug-in on the vCenter Server and then configure the VSM with the correct information. This plug-in is specific to the VSM in question, so repeat this process for each VSM deployed in the environment. Perform the following steps to create a VSM-specific plug-in on the vCenter Server:

1. Open an Internet browser such as Internet Explorer or Firefox, and go to the VSM's IP address. For example, if the VSM's management IP address is 10.20.30.40, go to `http://10.20.30.40`.

2. Download the file `cisco_nexus_1000v_extension.xml`, and save it to a location on your local system.

3. Open the vSphere Client, and establish a connection to a vCenter Server instance.

4. Choose Manage Plug-Ins from the Plug-Ins menu.

5. Right-click in a blank area of the Plug-In Manager dialog box, and select New Plug-In from the context menu, as shown in Figure 5.72.

FIGURE 5.72
The Cisco Nexus 1000V VSM-specific plug-in is created from the Plug-in Manager dialog box.

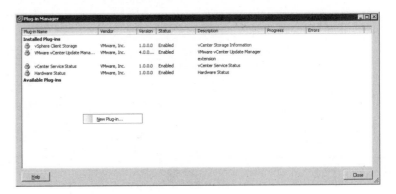

6. Browse to and select the `cisco_nexus_1000v_extension.xml` file you downloaded previously, and then click Register Plug-In.

7. vCenter Server displays a dialog box that indicates that the extension was successfully registered. Click OK.

8. The new extension/plug-in will not be listed in the Plug-In Manager dialog box. Click Close to return to the vSphere Client.

With the extension registered with vCenter Server, you're now ready to configure the VSM to connect to vCenter Server.

Perform the following steps to configure the VSM to connect to vCenter Server:

1. Using PuTTY.exe (Windows) or a terminal window (Linux or Mac OS X), establish an SSH session to the VSM, and log in as the admin user.

2. Enter the following command to enter configuration mode:

   ```
   config t
   ```

3. Type in the following set of commands to configure the connection to the vCenter Server, replacing DatacenterName with the name of your datacenter within vCenter Server and replacing 172.16.1.10 with the IP address of your vCenter Server instance:

   ```
   svs connection vc
   vmware dvs datacenter-name DatacenterName
   protocol vmware-vim
   remote ip address 172.16.1.10
   ```

4. Copy the running configuration to the startup configuration so that it is persistent across reboots:

   ```
   copy run start
   ```

5. While still in the svs-conn context—the VSM prompt will say something like n1000v(config-svs-conn)—enter the connect command to connect to the vCenter Server. The first time the connection is made, it might take up to 10 seconds.

   ```
   connect
   ```

6. The VSM will connect to the vCenter Server and connect a new dvSwitch. This new dvSwitch will be visible under Inventory ➤ Networking.

7. Once again, save the running configuration:

   ```
   copy run start
   ```

At this point, you have the VSM connected to and communicating with vCenter Server. The next step is to configure a system uplink port profile; this is the equivalent of the dvUplinks dvPort group used by native dvSwitches and will contain the physical network adapters that will connect the Nexus 1000V to the rest of the network.

1. Using PuTTY.exe (Windows) or a terminal window (Linux or Mac OS X), establish an SSH session to the VSM, and log in as the admin user.

2. Enter the following command to activate configuration mode:

   ```
   config t
   ```

3. Enter the following commands to create the system uplink port profile:

   ```
   port-profile system-uplink
   switchport mode trunk
   system vlan 100, 200
   switchport trunk allowed vlan 100, 200
   vmware port-group
   ```

```
no shut
capability uplink
state enabled
```

Replace the VLAN IDs on the `system vlan` statement with the VLAN IDs of the control and packet VLANs. Likewise, specify the control and packet VLANs—along with any other VLANs that should be permitted across these uplinks—on the `switchport trunk allowed vlan` command.

If you would like to specify a different name for the dvPort group in vCenter Server than the name given in the `port-profile` statement, append that name to the `vmware-port group` command like this:

```
vmware port-group dv-SystemUplinks
```

4. Copy the running configuration to the startup configuration so that it is persistent across reboots:

```
copy run start
```

Only one step remains, and that is adding ESX/ESXi hosts to the Cisco Nexus 1000V dvSwitch. For this procedure, it is highly recommended to have vCenter Update Manager already installed and configured. More information on vCenter Update Manager was provided in Chapter 4.

If vCenter Update Manager is already installed and configured, then you can add an ESX/ESXi host to the Nexus 1000V dvSwitch using the same procedure outlined earlier in this chapter with a native dvSwitch. See the "Creating vNetwork Distributed Switches."

MULTIPLE UPLINK GROUPS

One key change between a native dvSwitch and the Cisco Nexus 1000V is that the Nexus 1000V supports multiple uplink groups. When adding a host to the Nexus dvSwitch, be sure to place the physical network adapters for that host into the appropriate uplink group(s).

Removing a host from a Nexus dvSwitch is the same as for a native dvSwitch, so refer to those procedures earlier in the "Creating a vNetwork Distributed Switch" section for more information.

Configuring the Cisco Nexus 1000V

All configuration of the Nexus 1000V is handled by the VSM, typically at the CLI via SSH or Telnet. Like other members of the Cisco Nexus family, the Nexus 1000V VSM runs NX-OS, which is similar to Cisco's Internetwork Operating System (IOS). Thanks to the similarity to IOS, I expect that many IT professionals already familiar with IOS will be able to transition into NX-OS without too much difficulty.

The bulk of the configuration of the Nexus 1000V VSM is performed during installation. After installing the VSM and the VEMs are pushed out to the ESX/ESXi hosts, most configuration tasks after that involve creating, modifying, or removing *port profiles*. Port profiles are the Nexus 1000V counterpart to VMware port groups.

Perform the following steps to create a new port profile:

1. Using `PuTTY.exe` (Windows) or a terminal window (Linux or Mac OS X), establish an SSH session to the VSM, and log in as the admin user.

2. If you are not already in privileged EXEC mode, indicated by a hash sign after the prompt, enter privileged EXEC mode with the `enable` command, and supply the password.

3. Enter the following command to enter configuration mode:

```
config t
```

4. Enter the following commands to remove a port profile:

```
port-profile vm-access-ipstorage
switchport mode access
switchport access vlan 31
vmware port-group dv-VLAN31-IPStorage
no shut
state enabled
```

These commands create a port profile and matching dvPort group in vCenter Server. Ports in this dvPort group will be access ports in VLAN 31. Obviously, you can change the VLAN ID on the `switchport access vlan` statement, and you can change the name of the dvPort group using the `vmware port-group` statement.

5. Copy the running configuration to the startup configuration so that it is persistent across reboots:

```
copy run start
```

Upon completion of these steps, a dvPort group, either with the name specified on the `vmware port-group` statement or with the name of the port profile, will be listed in the vSphere Client under Inventory ➤ Networking.

Perform the following steps to delete an existing port profile and the corresponding dvPort group:

1. Using `PuTTY.exe` (Windows) or a terminal window (Linux or Mac OS X), establish an SSH session to the VSM, and log in as the admin user.

2. If you are not already in privileged EXEC mode, indicated by a hash sign after the prompt, enter privileged EXEC mode with the `enable` command, and supply the password.

3. Enter the following command to enter configuration mode:

```
config t
```

4. Enter the following commands to create a new port profile:

```
no port-profile vm-access-ipstorage
```

If there are any virtual machines assigned to the dvPort group, the VSM CLI will respond with an error message indicating that the port profile is currently in use. You must reconfigure the virtual machine(s) in question to use a different dvPort group before this port profile can be removed.

5. The port profile and the matching dvPort group are removed. You will be able to see the dvPort group being removed in the Tasks list at the bottom of the vSphere Client, as shown in Figure 5.73.

FIGURE 5.73
When you remove
a port profile via
the VSM CLI, the
corresponding dvPort
group is also removed
from vCenter Server.

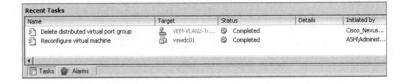

6. Copy the running configuration to the startup configuration so that it is persistent across reboots:

   ```
   copy run start
   ```

Perform the following steps to modify an existing port profile and the corresponding dvPort group:

1. Using PuTTY.exe (Windows) or a terminal window (Linux or Mac OS X), establish an SSH session to the VSM, and log in as the admin user.

2. If you are not already in privileged EXEC mode, indicated by a hash sign after the prompt, enter privileged EXEC mode with the enable command, and supply the password.

3. Enter the following command to enter configuration mode:

   ```
   config t
   ```

4. Enter the following commands to configure a specific port profile:

   ```
   port-profile vm-access-ipstorage
   ```

5. Change the name of the associated dvPort group with this command:

   ```
   vmware port-group VEM-VLAN31-Storage
   ```

   If there are any virtual machines assigned to the dvPort group, the VSM CLI will respond with an error message indicating that the port profile was updated locally but not updated in vCenter Server. You must reconfigure the virtual machine(s) in question to use a different dvPort group and repeat this command in order for the change to take effect.

6. Change the access VLAN of the associated dvPort group with this command:

   ```
   switchport access vlan 100
   ```

7. Remove the associated dvPort group, but leave the port profile intact with this command:

   ```
   no state enabled
   ```

8. Shut down the ports in the dvPort group with this command:

   ```
   shutdown
   ```

Because the VSM runs NX-OS, a wealth of options are available for configuring ports and port profiles. For more complete and detailed information on the Cisco Nexus 1000V, refer to the official Nexus 1000V documentation and the Cisco website at www.cisco.com.

Configuring Virtual Switch Security

Even though vSwitches and dvSwitches are considered to be "dumb switches"—with the exception of the Nexus 1000V—you can configure them with security policies to enhance or ensure Layer 2 security. For vNetwork Standard Switches, you can apply security policies at the vSwitch or at the port group level. For vNetwork Distributed Switches, you apply security policies only at the dvPort group level. The security settings include the following three options:

- ◆ Promiscuous Mode
- ◆ MAC Address Changes
- ◆ Forged Transmits

Applying a security policy to a vSwitch is effective, by default, for all connection types within the switch. However, if a port group on that vSwitch is configured with a competing security policy, it will override the policy set at the vSwitch. For example, if a vSwitch is configured with a security policy that rejects the use of MAC address changes but a port group on the switch is configured to accept MAC address changes, then any virtual machines connected to that port group will be allowed to communicate even though it is using a MAC address that differs from what is configured in its VMX file.

The default security profile for a vSwitch, shown in Figure 5.74, is set to reject Promiscuous Mode and to accept MAC address changes and forged transmits. Similarly, Figure 5.75 shows the default security profile for a dvPort group on a dvSwitch.

FIGURE 5.74
The default security profile for a vSwitch prevents Promiscuous mode but allows MAC address changes and forged transmits.

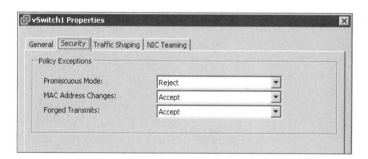

FIGURE 5.75
The default security profile for a dvPort group on a dvSwitch matches that for a standard vSwitch.

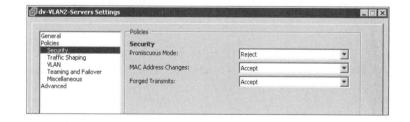

Each of these security options is explored in more detail in the following sections.

Promiscuous Mode

The Promiscuous Mode option is set to Reject by default to prevent virtual network adapters from observing any of the traffic submitted through the vSwitch. For enhanced security, allowing

Promiscuous mode is not recommended because it is an insecure mode of operation that allows a virtual adapter to access traffic other than its own. Despite the security concerns, there are valid reasons for permitting a switch to operate in Promiscuous mode. An intrusion detection system (IDS) requires the ability to identify all traffic to scan for anomalies and malicious patterns of traffic.

Previously in this chapter, recall that I talked about how port groups and VLANs did not have a one-to-one relationship and that there might be occasions when you have multiple port groups on a vSwitch configured with the same VLAN ID. This is exactly one of those situations—you have a need for a system, the IDS, to see traffic intended for other virtual network adapters. Rather than granting that ability to all the systems on a port group, you can create a dedicated port group for just the IDS system. It will have the same VLAN ID and other settings but will allow Promiscuous mode instead of rejecting Promiscuous mode. This allows you, the VMware administrator, to carefully control which systems are allowed to use this powerful and potentially security-threatening feature.

As shown in Figure 5.76, the virtual switch security policy will remain at the default setting of Reject for the Promiscuous Mode option, while the virtual machine port group for the IDS will be set to Accept. This setting will override the virtual switch, allowing the IDS to monitor all traffic for that VLAN.

FIGURE 5.76
Promiscuous mode, though a reduction in security, is required when using an intrusion detection system.

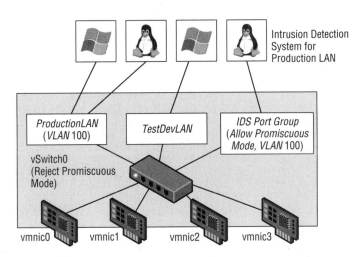

MAC Address Changes and Forged Transmits

When a virtual machine is created with one or more virtual network adapters, a MAC address is generated for each virtual adapter. Just as Intel, Broadcom, and others manufacture network adapters that include unique MAC address strings, VMware is also a network adapter manufacturer that has its own MAC prefix to ensure uniqueness. Of course, VMware doesn't actually manufacture anything because the product exists as a virtual NIC in a virtual machine. You can see the 6-byte, randomly generated MAC addresses for a virtual machine in the configuration file (.vmx) of the virtual machine, as shown in Figure 5.77. A VMware-assigned MAC address begins with the prefix 00:50:56 or 00:0C:29. The value of the fourth set (XX) cannot exceed 3F to prevent conflicts with other VMware products, while the fifth and sixth sets (YY:ZZ) are generated randomly based on the Universally Unique Identifier (UUID) of the virtual machine that is tied to the location of the virtual machine. For this reason, when a virtual machine location is changed, a prompt appears prior to successful boot. The prompt inquires about keeping the UUID or generating a new UUID, which helps prevent MAC address conflicts.

MANUALLY SETTING THE MAC ADDRESS

Manually configuring a MAC address in the configuration file of a virtual machine does not work unless the first three bytes are VMware-provided prefixes and the last three bytes are unique. If a non-VMware MAC prefix is entered in the configuration file, the virtual machine will not power on.

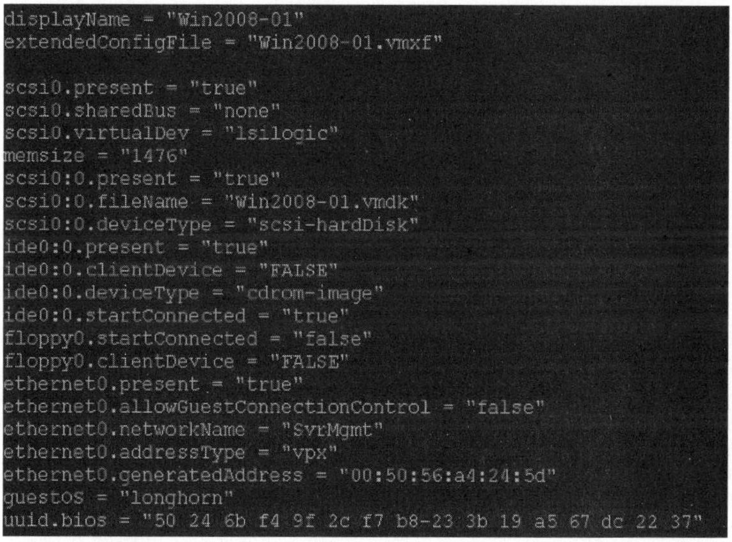

FIGURE 5.77
A virtual machine's initial MAC address is automatically generated and listed in the configuration file for the virtual machine.

```
displayName = "Win2008-01"
extendedConfigFile = "Win2008-01.vmxf"

scsi0.present = "true"
scsi0.sharedBus = "none"
scsi0.virtualDev = "lsilogic"
memsize = "1476"
scsi0:0.present = "true"
scsi0:0.fileName = "Win2008-01.vmdk"
scsi0:0.deviceType = "scsi-hardDisk"
ide0:0.present = "true"
ide0:0.clientDevice = "FALSE"
ide0:0.deviceType = "cdrom-image"
ide0:0.startConnected = "true"
floppy0.startConnected = "false"
floppy0.clientDevice = "FALSE"
ethernet0.present = "true"
ethernet0.allowGuestConnectionControl = "false"
ethernet0.networkName = "SvrMgmt"
ethernet0.addressType = "vpx"
ethernet0.generatedAddress = "00:50:56:a4:24:5d"
guestOS = "longhorn"
uuid.bios = "50 24 6b f4 9f 2c f7 b8-23 3b 19 a5 67 dc 22 37"
```

All virtual machines have two MAC addresses: the initial MAC and the effective MAC. The initial MAC address is the MAC discussed in the previous paragraph that is generated automatically and that resides in the configuration file. The guest operating system has no control over the initial MAC address. The effective MAC address is the MAC address configured by the guest operating system that is used during communication with other systems. The effective MAC address is included in network communication as the source MAC of the virtual machine. By default, these two addresses are identical. To force a non-VMware-assigned MAC address to a guest operating system, change the effective MAC address from within the guest operating system, as shown in Figure 5.78.

The ability to alter the effective MAC address cannot be removed from the guest operating system. However, the ability to let the system function with this altered MAC address is easily addressable through the security policy of a vSwitch. The remaining two settings of a virtual switch security policy are MAC Address Changes and Forged Transmits. Both of these security policies are concerned with allowing or denying differences between the initial MAC address in the configuration file and the effective MAC address in the guest operating system. As noted earlier, the default security policy is to accept the differences and process traffic as needed.

FIGURE 5.78
A virtual machine's source MAC address is the effective MAC address, which by default matches the initial MAC address configured in the VMX file. The guest operating system, however, may change the effective MAC.

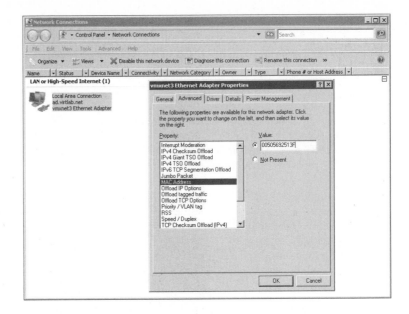

The difference between the MAC Address Changes and Forged Transmits security settings involves the direction of the traffic. MAC Address Changes is concerned with the integrity of incoming traffic, while Forged Transmits oversees the integrity of outgoing traffic. If the MAC Address Changes option is set to Reject, traffic will not be passed through the vSwitch to the virtual machine (incoming) if the initial and the effective MAC addresses do not match. If the Forged Transmits option is set to Reject, traffic will not be passed from the virtual machine to the vSwitch (outgoing) if the initial and the effective MAC addresses do not match. Figure 5.79 highlights the security restrictions implemented when MAC Address Changes and Forged Transmits are set to Reject.

FIGURE 5.79
The MAC Address Changes and Forged Transmits security options deal with incoming and outgoing traffic, respectively.

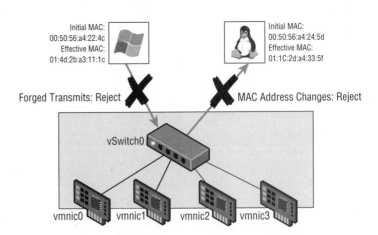

For the highest level of security, VMware recommends setting MAC Address Changes, Forged Transmits, and Promiscuous Mode on each vSwitch to Reject. When warranted or necessary, use port groups to loosen the security for a subset of virtual machines to connect to the port group.

VIRTUAL SWITCH POLICIES FOR MICROSOFT NETWORK LOAD BALANCING

As with anything, there are, of course, exceptions. For virtual machines that will be configured as part of a Microsoft network load-balancing (NLB) cluster set in Unicast mode, the virtual machine port group must allow MAC address changes and forged transmits. Systems that are part of an NLB cluster will share a common IP address and virtual MAC address.

The shared virtual MAC address is generated by using an algorithm that includes a static component based on the NLB cluster's configuration of Unicast or Multicast mode plus a hexadecimal representation of the four octets that make up the IP address. This shared MAC address will certainly differ from the MAC address defined in the VMX file of the virtual machine. If the virtual machine port group does not allow for differences between the MAC addresses in the VMX and guest operating system, NLB will not function as expected. VMware recommends running NLB clusters in Multicast mode because of these issues with NLB clusters in Unicast mode.

Perform the following steps to edit the security profile of a vSwitch:

1. Use the vSphere Client to establish a connection to a vCenter Server or an ESX/ESXi host.

2. Click the hostname in the inventory panel on the left, select the Configuration tab in the details pane on the right, and then select Networking from the Hardware menu list.

3. Click the Properties link for the virtual switch.

4. Click the name of the virtual switch under the Configuration list, and then click the Edit button.

5. Click the Security tab, and make the necessary adjustments.

6. Click OK, and then click Close.

Perform the following steps to edit the security profile of a port group on a vSwitch:

1. Use the vSphere Client to establish a connection to a vCenter Server or an ESX/ESXi host.

2. Click the hostname in the inventory panel on the left, select the Configuration tab in the details pane on the right, and then select Networking from the Hardware menu list.

3. Click the Properties link for the virtual switch.

4. Click the name of the port group under the Configuration list, and then click the Edit button.

5. Click the Security tab, and make the necessary adjustments.

6. Click OK, and then click Close.

Perform the following steps to edit the security profile of a dvPort group on a dvSwitch:

1. Use the vSphere Client to establish a connection to a vCenter Server instance.

2. On the vSphere Client home screen, select the Networking option under Inventory. Alternately, from the View menu, select Inventory ➢ Networking.

3. Select an existing dvPort group in the Inventory pane on the left, select the Summary tab in the pane on the right, and click the Edit Settings option in the Commands section.

4. Select Security from the list of policy options on the left side of the dialog box.

5. Make the necessary adjustments to the security policy.

6. Click OK to save the changes and return to the vSphere Client.

Managing the security of a virtual network architecture is much the same as managing the security for any other portion of your information systems. Security policy should dictate that settings be configured as secure as possible to err on the side of caution. Only with proper authorization, documentation, and change management processes should security be reduced. In addition, the reduction in security should be as controlled as possible to affect the least number of systems if not just the systems requiring the adjustments.

The Bottom Line

Identify the components of virtual networking. Virtual networking is a blend of virtual switches, physical switches, VLANs, physical network adapters, virtual adapters, uplinks, NIC teaming, virtual machines, and port groups.

Master It What factors contribute to the design of a virtual network and the components involved?

Create virtual switches (vSwitches) and distributed virtual switches (dvSwitches). vSphere introduces a new type of virtual switch, the vNetwork Distributed Virtual Switch, as well as continuing to support the host-based vSwitch (now referred to as the vNetwork Standard Switch) from previous versions. vNetwork Distributed Switches bring new functionality to the vSphere networking environment, including private VLANs and a centralized point of management for ESX/ESXi clusters.

Master It You've asked a fellow VMware vSphere administrator to create a vNetwork Distributed Virtual Switch for you, but the administrator is having problems completing the task because he or she can't find the right command-line switches for `esxcfg-vswitch`. What should you tell this administrator?

Install and perform basic configuration of the Cisco Nexus 1000V. The Cisco Nexus 1000V is the first third-party Distributed Virtual Switch for VMware vSphere. Running Cisco's NX-OS, the Nexus 1000V uses a distributed architecture that supports redundant supervisor modules and provides a single point of management. Advanced networking functionality like quality of service (QoS), access control lists (ACLs), and SPAN ports are made possible via the Nexus 1000V.

Master It   A VMware vSphere administrator is trying to use the vSphere Client to make some changes to the VLAN configuration of a dvPort group configured on a Nexus 1000V, but the option to edit the settings for the dvPort group isn't showing up. Why?

Create and manage NIC teaming, VLANs, and private VLANs.   NIC teaming allows for virtual switches to have redundant network connections to the rest of the network. Virtual switches also provide support for VLANs, which provide logical segmentation of the network, and private VLANs, which provide added security to existing VLANs while allowing systems to share the same IP subnet.

Master It   You'd like to use NIC teaming to bond multiple physical uplinks together for greater redundancy and improved throughput. When selecting the NIC teaming policy, you select Route Based On IP Hash, but then the vSwitch seems to lose connectivity. What could be wrong?

Configure virtual switch security policies.   Virtual switches support security policies for allowing or rejecting promiscuous mode, allowing or rejecting MAC address changes, and allowing or rejecting forged transmits. All of the security options can help increase Layer 2 security.

Master It   You have a networking application that needs to see traffic on the virtual network that is intended for other production systems on the same VLAN. The networking application accomplishes this by using promiscuous mode. How can you accommodate the needs of this networking application without sacrificing the security of the entire virtual switch?

Chapter 6

Creating and Managing Storage Devices

The storage infrastructure supporting VMware has always been a critical element of any virtual infrastructure. This chapter will help you with all the elements required for a proper storage subsystem design for vSphere 4, starting with VMware storage fundamentals at the datastore and virtual machine level and extending to best practices for configuring the storage array. Good storage design is critical for anyone building a virtual datacenter.

In this chapter, you will learn to:

◆ Differentiate and understand the fundamentals of shared storage, including SANs and NAS

◆ Understand vSphere storage options

◆ Configure storage at the vSphere ESX 4 layer

◆ Configure storage at the virtual machine layer

◆ Leverage new vSphere storage features

◆ Leverage best practices for SAN and NAS storage with vSphere 4

The Importance of Storage Design

Storage design has always been important, but it becomes more so as vSphere is used for larger workloads, for mission-critical applications, for larger clusters, and as the cloud operating system in a 100 percent virtualized datacenter. You can probably imagine why this is the case:

Advanced capabilities   VMware's advanced features depend on shared storage; VMware High Availability (HA), VMotion, VMware Distributed Resource Scheduler (DRS), VMware Fault Tolerance, and VMware Site Recovery Manager all have a critical dependency on shared storage.

Performance   People understand the benefit that server virtualization brings—consolidation, higher utilization, more flexibility, and higher efficiency. But often, people have initial questions about how vSphere can deliver performance for individual applications when it is inherently consolidated and oversubscribed. Likewise, the overall performance of the virtual machines and the entire vSphere cluster are both dependent on shared storage, which is similarly inherently highly consolidated, and oversubscribed.

Availability The overall availability of the virtual machines and the entire vSphere cluster are both dependent on the shared storage infrastructure. Designing in high availability into this infrastructure element is paramount. If the storage is not available, VMware HA will not be able to recover, and the aggregate community of VMs on the entire cluster can be affected.

Whereas there are design choices at the server layer that can make the vSphere environment relatively more or less optimal, the design choices for shared resources such as networking and storage can make the difference between virtualization success and failure. This is regardless of whether you are using storage area networks (SANs), which present shared storage as disks or logical units (LUNs), or whether you are using network attached storage (NAS), which presents shared storage as remotely accessed file systems or a mix of both. Done correctly, a shared storage design lowers the cost and increases the efficiency, performance, availability, and flexibility of your vSphere environment.

This chapter breaks down these topics into the following four main sections:

◆ "Shared Storage Fundamentals" covers broad topics of shared storage that are critical with vSphere, including hardware architectures, protocol choices, and key terminology. Although these topics will be applicable to any environment that uses shared storage, understanding these core technologies is a prerequisite to understanding how to apply storage technology in the context of vSphere.

◆ "VMware Storage Fundamentals" covers how storage technologies covered in the previous section are applied and used in VMware environments including vSphere.

◆ "New vStorage Features in vSphere 4" covers the key changes and new features in vSphere 4 that are related to storage—at the storage array level, at the vSphere ESX 4 layer, and at the virtual machine layer.

◆ "Leveraging SAN and NAS Best Practices" covers how to pull all the topics discussed together to move forward with a design that will support a broad set of vSphere 4 configurations.

Shared Storage Fundamentals

vSphere 4 significantly extends the storage choices and configuration options relative to VMware Infrastructure 3.x. These choices and configuration options apply at two fundamental levels: the ESX host level and the virtual machine level. The storage requirements for each vSphere cluster and the virtual machines it supports are unique—making broad generalizations impossible. The requirements for any given cluster span use cases, from virtual servers to desktops to templates and CD/DVD images. The virtual server use cases that vary from light utility VMs with few storage performance considerations to the largest database workloads possible with incredibly important storage layout considerations.

Let's start by examining this at a fundamental level. Figure 6.1 shows a simple three-host vSphere 4 cluster attached to shared storage.

It's immediately apparent that the vSphere ESX 4 hosts and the virtual machines will be contending for the shared storage asset. In an analogous way to how vSphere ESX 4 can consolidate many virtual machines onto a single host, the shared storage consolidates all the storage needs of all the virtual machines.

FIGURE 6.1
A vSphere cluster with
three nodes connected
to shared storage

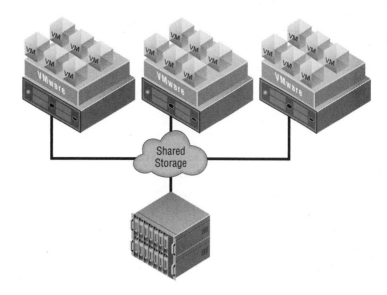

What are the implications of this? The virtual machines will depend on and share the performance characteristics of the underlying storage configuration that supports them. Storage attributes are just as important as CPU cycles (measured in megahertz), memory (measured in megabytes), and vCPU configuration. Storage attributes are measured in capacity (gigabytes) and performance, which is measured in bandwidth (MB per second or MBps), throughput (I/O per second or IOps), and latency (in milliseconds).

DETERMINING PERFORMANCE REQUIREMENTS

How do you determine the storage performance requirements of a host that will be virtualized or, in fact, a single vSphere ESX host or a complete vSphere cluster? There are many "rules of thumb" for key applications, and the best practices for every application could fill a book unto itself. Here are some quick considerations:

◆ Online Transaction Processing (OLTP) databases need low latency (as low as you can get, but a few milliseconds is a good target. They are also sensitive to input/output operations per second (IOps), because their I/O size is small (4KB to 8KB). TPC-C and TPC-E benchmarks generate this kind of I/O pattern.

◆ Decision Support System Business Intelligence databases, and SQL Servers that support Microsoft Office SharePoint Server need high bandwidth, which can be hundreds of megabytes per second because their I/O size is large (64KB to 1MB). They are not particularly sensitive to latency, TPC-H benchmarks generate the kind of I/O pattern used by these use cases.

◆ Copying files, deploying from templates, using Storage VMotion, and backing up VMs (within the guest or from a proxy server via the vStorage backup API) without using array-based approaches generally all need high bandwidth. In fact, the more, the better.

So, what does VMware need? The answer is basic—the needs of the vSphere environment are the aggregate sum of all the use cases across all the VMs of the cluster, which can cover a broad set of requirements. If the virtual machines are *all* small-block workloads and you don't do backups inside guests (which generate large-block workloads), then it's all about IOps. If the virtual machines are *all* large-block workloads, then it's all about MBps. More often than not, a virtual datacenter has a mix, so the storage design should be flexible enough to deliver a broad range of capabilities—but without overbuilding.

How can you best determine what you will need? With small workloads, too much planning can result in overbuilding. You can use simple tools, including VMware Capacity Planner, Windows Perfmon, and top in Linux, to determine the I/O pattern of the hosts that will be virtualized.

Also, if you have many VMs, consider the aggregate performance requirements, and don't just look at capacity requirements. After all, 1,000 VMs with 10 IOps each need an aggregate of 10,000 IOps, which is 50 to 80 fast spindles worth, regardless of the capacity (in gigabytes or terabytes) needed.

Use large pool designs for generic, light workload VMs.

Conversely, focused, larger VM I/O workloads (such as virtualized SQL Servers, SharePoint, Exchange, and other use cases) should be where you spend some time planning and thinking about layout. There is a great deal of VMware published best practices and VMware partner reference architecture documentation that can help with virtualizing Exchange, SQL Server, Oracle, and SAP workloads. We have listed a few resources for you here:

◆ Reference architecture

   http://virtualgeek.typepad.com/virtual_geek/2009/05/integrated-vsphere-enterprise-workloads-all-together-at-scale.html

◆ Exchange

   www.vmware.com/solutions/business-critical-apps/exchange/resources.html

◆ SQL Server

   www.vmware.com/solutions/business-critical-apps/sql/resources.html

◆ Oracle

   www.vmware.com/solutions/business-critical-apps/oracle/

◆ SAP

   www.vmware.com/partners/alliances/technology/sap-resources.htm

The overall availability of the virtual machines and the entire vSphere cluster is dependent on the same shared storage infrastructure so a robust, redundant design is paramount. If the storage is not available, VMware HA will not be able to recover, and the consolidated community of VMs will be affected.

One critical premise of storage design is that more care and focus should be put on the availability of the configuration than on the performance or capacity requirements:

◆ With advanced vSphere options such as Storage VMotion and advanced array techniques that allow you to add, move, or change storage configurations nondisruptively, it is unlikely that you'll create a design where you can't nondisruptively fix performance issues.

◆ Conversely, in virtual configurations, the availability impact of storage issues is more pronounced, so greater care needs to be used in an availability design than in the physical world.

An ESX server can have one or more storage options actively configured, including the following:

◆ Fibre Channel

◆ Fibre Channel over Ethernet

◆ iSCSI using software and hardware initiators

◆ NAS (specifically, NFS)

◆ Local SAS/SATA/SCSI storage

◆ InfiniBand

Shared storage is the basis for most of VMware storage because it supports the virtual machines themselves. Shared storage in both SAN configurations (which encompasses Fibre Channel, iSCSI, FCoE) and NAS is always highly consolidated. This makes it very efficient. In an analogous way that VMware can take many servers with 10 percent utilized CPU and memory and consolidate them to make them 80 percent utilized, SAN/NAS takes the direct attached storage in servers that are 10 percent utilized and consolidates them to 80 percent utilization.

Local storage is used in a limited fashion with VMware in general, and local storage in vSphere serves even less of a function than it did in VMware Infrastructure 3.x because it is easier to build and add hosts using ESX host profiles.

How carefully does one need to design their local storage? The answer is simple—careful planning is not necessary for storage local to the vSphere ESX/ESXi host. vSphere ESX/ESXi 4 stores very little locally, and by using host profiles and distributed virtual switches, it can be easy and fast to replace a failed ESX host. During this time, VMware HA will make sure the virtual machines are running on the other ESX hosts in the cluster. Don't sweat HA design in local storage for ESX. Spend the effort making your shared storage design robust.

Local storage is still used by default in vSphere ESX 4 installations as the ESX userworld swap (think of this as the ESX host swap and temp use), but not for much else. Unlike ESX 3.x, where VMFS mounts on local storage are used by the Service Console, in ESX 4, although there is a Service Console, it is functionally a virtual machine using a virtual disk on the local VMFS storage.

 Real World Scenario

NO LOCAL STORAGE? NO PROBLEM!

What if you don't *have* local storage? (Perhaps you have a diskless blade system, for example.) There are many options for diskless systems, including booting from Fibre Channel/iSCSI SAN, and even (experimental) Preboot Execution Environment (PXE) network-based boot methods. There is also a new interesting option using USB boot. When using ESXi or ESXi installable on a USB-booted system without local storage, one of the first steps is to configure a datastore. What is not immediately obvious is that you must configure a userworld swap location to enable VMware HA. You do this using the ESXi host's advanced settings (as shown here). Configure the ScratchConfig.ConfiguredScratchLocation property, enabling the property and rebooting.

(ScratchConfig.ConfiguredScratchLocation must be a unique location for each ESX host; if need be, create subdirectories for each host.) On reboot, make sure that userworld swap is enabled.

Before going too much further, it's important to cover several basics of shared storage:

◆ Common storage array architectures

◆ RAID technologies

◆ Midrange and enterprise storage design

◆ Protocol choices

The high-level overview in the following sections is neutral on specific storage array vendors, because the internal architectures vary tremendously. However, these sections will serve as an important baseline for the discussion of how to apply these technologies (see the "VMware Storage Fundamentals" section), as well as the analysis of new technologies (see the "New vStorage Features in vSphere 4" section).

Common Storage Array Architectures

This section is remedial for anyone with basic storage experience but is needed for VMware administrators with no preexisting storage knowledge. For people unfamiliar with storage, the topic can be a bit disorienting at first. Servers across vendors tend to be relatively similar, but the same logic can't be applied to the storage layer, because core architectural differences are vast between storage vendor architectures. In spite of that, storage arrays have several core architectural elements that are consistent across vendors, across implementations, and even across protocols.

The elements that make up a shared storage array consist of external connectivity, storage processors, array software, cache memory, disks, and bandwidth:

External connectivity   The external (physical) connectivity between the storage array and the hosts (in this case, the VMware ESX 4 servers) is generally Fibre Channel or Ethernet, though InfiniBand and other rare protocols exist. The characteristics of this connectivity define the maximum bandwidth (given no other constraints, and there usually are other constraints) of the communication between the host and the shared storage array.

Storage processors   Different vendors have different names for storage processors, which are considered the "brains" of the array. They are used to handle the I/O and run the array software. In most modern arrays, the storage processors are not purpose-built ASICs but instead are general-purpose CPUs. Some arrays use PowerPC, some use specific ASICs, and some use custom ASICs for specific purposes. But in general, if you cracked open an array, you would most likely find an Intel or AMD CPU.

Array software   Although hardware specifications are important and can define the scaling limits of the array, just as important are the functional capabilities the array software provides. The array software is at least as important as the array hardware. The capabilities of modern storage arrays are vast—similar in scope to vSphere itself—and vary wildly between vendors. At a high level, the following list includes some examples of these array capabilities; this is not an exhaustive list but does include the key functions:

- Remote storage replication for disaster recovery. These technologies come in many flavors with features that deliver varying capabilities. These include varying recovery point objectives (RPOs)—which is a reflection of how current the remote replica is at any time ranging from synchronous, to asynchronous and continuous. Asynchronous RPOs can range from minutes to hours, and continuous is a constant remote journal which can recover to varying Recovery Point Objectives. Other examples of remote replication technologies are technologies that drive synchronicity across storage objects or "consistency technology," compression, and many other attributes such as integration with VMware Site Recovery Manager.

- Snapshot and clone capabilities for instant point-in-time local copies for test and development and local recovery. These also share some of the ideas of the remote replication technologies like "consistency technology" and some variations of point-in-time protection and replicas also have "TiVo-like" continuous journaling locally and remotely where you can recovery/copy any point in time.

- Capacity reduction techniques such as archiving and deduplication.

- Automated data movement between performance/cost storage tiers at varying levels of granularity.

- LUN/file system expansion and mobility, which means reconfiguring storage properties dynamically and nondisruptively to add capacity or performance as needed.

- Thin provisioning.

- Storage quality of service, which means prioritizing I/O to deliver a given MBps, IOps, or latency.

The array software defines the "persona" of the array, which in turn impacts core concepts and behavior in a variety of ways. Arrays generally have a "file server" persona (sometimes with the ability to do some block storage by presenting a file as a LUN) or a "block" persona (generally with no ability to act as a file server). In some cases, arrays are combinations of file servers and block devices put together.

Cache memory   Every array differs on how this is implemented, but all have some degree of nonvolatile memory used for various caching functions—delivering lower latency and higher IOps throughput by buffering I/O using write caches and storing commonly read data to deliver a faster response time using read caches. Nonvolatility (meaning it survives a power loss) is critical for write cache because the data is not yet committed to disk, but it's not critical for read caches. Cached performance is often used when describing shared storage array performance maximums (in IOps, MBps, or latency) in specification sheets. These results are generally not reflective of real-world scenarios. In most real-world scenarios, performance tends to be dominated by the disk performance (the type and amount of disks) and is helped by write cache in most cases but only marginally by read caches (with the exception of large Relational Database Management Systems, which depend heavily on read-ahead cache algorithms). One VMware use case that is helped by read caches can be cases where many boot images are stored only once (through use of VMware or storage array technology), but this is also a small subset of the overall virtual machine IO pattern.

Disks   Arrays differ on which type of disks (often called *spindles*) they support and how many they can scale to support. Fibre Channel (usually in 15KB RPM and 10KB RPM variants), SATA (usually in 5400 RPM and 7200 RPM variants), and SAS (usually in 15K RPM and 10K RPM variants) are commonplace, and enterprise flash disks are becoming mainstream. The type of disks and the number of disks are very important. Coupled with how they are configured, this is usually the main determinant of how a storage object (either a LUN for a block device or a file system for a NAS device) performs. Shared storage vendors generally use disks from the same disk vendors, so this is an area where there is commonality across shared storage vendors. The following list is a quick reference on what to expect under a random read/write workload from a given disk drive:

- 7200RPM SATA: 80 IOps

- 10KB RPM SATA/SAS/Fibre Channel: 120 IOps

- 15KB RPM SAS/Fibre Channel: 180 IOps

- A commercial solid-state drive (SSD) based on Multi-Layer Cell (MLC) technology: 1000–2000 IOps

- An Enterprise Flash Drive (EFD) based on single-layer cell (SLC) technology and much deeper, very high-speed memory buffers: 6000–30,000 IOps

Bandwidth (megabytes per second)   Performance tends to be more consistent across drive types when large-block, sequential workloads are used (such as single-purpose workloads like archiving or backup to disk), so in these cases, large SATA drives deliver strong performance at a low cost.

RAID Technologies

Redundant Array of Inexpensive (sometimes "independent") Disks (RAID) is a fundamental, but critical, method of storing the same data several times, and in different ways to increase the data availability, and also scale performance beyond that of a single drive. Every array implements various RAID schemes (even if it is largely "invisible" in file server persona arrays where RAID is done below the primary management element which is the filesystem).

Think of it this way: "disks are mechanical spinning rust-colored disc surfaces. The read/write heads are flying microns above the surface. While they are doing this, they read minute magnetic field variations, and using similar magnetic fields, write data by affecting surface areas also only microns in size."

THE "MAGIC" OF DISK DRIVE TECHNOLOGY

It really is a technological miracle that magnetic disks work at all. What a disk does all day long is analogous to a 747 flying 600 miles per hour 6 inches off the ground and reading pages off a book while doing it!

In spite of all that, hard disks have unbelievable reliability statistics, but they do fail, and fail predictably unlike other elements of a system. RAID schemes embrace this by leveraging multiple disks together and using copies of data to support I/O until the drive can be replaced and the RAID protection can be rebuilt. Each RAID configuration tends to have different performance characteristics and different capacity overhead impact.

View RAID choices as one factor among several in your design, not as the most important but not the least important either. Most arrays layer additional constructs on top of the basic RAID protection. (These constructs have many different names, but ones that are common are *metas*, *virtual pools*, *aggregates*, and *volumes*.)

Remember, all the RAID protection in the world won't protect you from an outage if the connectivity to your host is lost, if you don't monitor and replace failed drives and allocate drives as hot spares to automatically replace failed drives, or if the entire array is lost. It's for these reasons that it's important to design the storage network properly, to configure hot spares as advised by the storage vendor, and monitor for and replace failed elements. Always consider a disaster recovery plan and remote replication to protect from complete array failure.

Let's examine the RAID choices:

RAID 0 This RAID level offers no redundancy and no protection against drive failure (see Figure 6.2). In fact, it has a *higher* aggregate risk than a single disk because any single disk failing affects the whole RAID group. Data is spread across all the disks in the RAID group, which is often called a *stripe*. Although it delivers very fast performance, this is the only RAID type that is not appropriate for any production VMware use, because of the availability profile.

RAID 1, 1+0, 0+1 These "mirrored" RAID levels offer high degrees of protection but at the cost of 50 percent loss of usable capacity (see Figure 6.3). This is versus the raw aggregate capacity of the sum of the capacity of the drives. RAID 1 simply writes every I/O to two drives and can balance reads across both drives (since there are two copies). This can be coupled with RAID 0 or with RAID 1+0 (or RAID 10), which mirrors a stripe set, and with RAID 0+1, which stripes data across pairs of mirrors. This has the benefit of being able to withstand multiple drives failing, but only if the drives fail on different elements of a stripe on different mirrors. The other benefit of mirrored RAID configurations is that, in the case of a failed drive, rebuild times can be very rapid, which shortens periods of exposure.

FIGURE 6.2
A RAID 0 configuration. The data is striped across all the disks in the RAID set, providing very good performance but very poor availability.

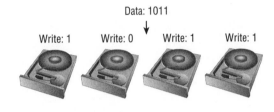

FIGURE 6.3
A RAID 10 2+2 configuration, which provides good performance and good availability but at the cost of 50 percent of the usable capacity

Parity RAID (RAID 5, RAID 6)   These RAID levels use a mathematical calculation (an XOR parity calculation) to represent the data across several drives. This tends to be a good compromise between the availability of RAID 1 and the capacity efficiency of RAID 0. RAID 5 calculates the parity across the drives in the set and writes the parity to another drive. This parity block calculation with RAID 5 is rotated amongst the arrays in the RAID 5 set. (RAID 4 is a variant that uses a dedicated parity disk rather than rotating the parity across drives.)

Parity RAID schemes can deliver very good performance. There is always some degree of "write penalty." For a full-stripe write, the only penalty is the parity calculation and the parity write, but in a partial-stripe write, the old block contents need to be read, a new parity calculation needs to be made, and all the blocks need to be updated. However, generally modern arrays have various methods to minimize this effect.

Conversely, read performance is excellent, because a larger number of drives can be read from than with mirrored RAID schemes. RAID 5 nomenclature refers to the number of drives in the RAID group, so Figure 6.4 would be referred to as a RAID 5 4+1 set. In the figure, the storage efficiency (in terms of usable to raw capacity) is 80 percent, which is much better than RAID 1 or 10.

FIGURE 6.4
A RAID 5 4+1 configuration

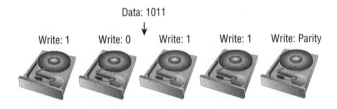

RAID 5 can be coupled with stripes, so RAID 50 is a pair of RAID 5 sets with data striped across them.

When a drive fails in a RAID 5 set, I/Os can be fulfilled using the remaining drives and the parity drive, and when the failed drive is replaced, the data can be reconstructed using the remaining data and parity.

A KEY RAID 5 CONSIDERATION

One downside to RAID 5 is that only one drive can fail in the RAID set. If another drive fails before the failed drive is replaced and rebuilt using the parity data, data loss occurs. The period of exposure to data loss because of the second drive failing should be mitigated.

The period of time that a RAID 5 set is rebuilding should be as short as possible to minimize the risk. The following designs aggravate this situation by creating longer rebuild periods:

◆ Very large RAID groups (think 8+1 and larger), which cause more reads needed to reconstruct the failed drive.

◆ Very large drives (think 1TB SATA and 500GB Fibre Channel drives), which cause there to be more data to be rebuilt.

◆ Slower drives that struggle heavily during the period that they are providing the data to rebuild the replaced drive and simultaneously support production I/O (think SATA drives, which tend to be slower during the random I/O that tends to characterize a RAID rebuild). The period of a RAID rebuild is actually one of the most ''stressful'' parts of a disk's life. Not only must it service the production I/O workload, but it must provide data to support the rebuild, and it is known that drives are statistically more likely to fail during a rebuild than during normal duty cycles.

The following technologies all mitigate the risk of a dual drive failure (and most arrays do various degrees of each of these items):

◆ Using proactive hot sparing, which shortens the period of the rebuild substantially by automatically starting the hot spare *before* the drive fails. The failure of a disk is generally preceded with recoverable read errors (which are recoverable; they are detected and corrected using on-disk parity information) or write errors, both of which are noncatastrophic. When a threshold of these errors occurs *before* the disk itself fails, the failing drive is replaced by a hot spare by the array. This is much faster than the rebuild after the failure, because the bulk of the failing drive can be used for the copy and because only the portions of the drive that are failing need to use parity information from other disks.

◆ Using smaller RAID 5 sets (for faster rebuild) and striping the data across them using a higher-level construct.

◆ Using a second parity calculation and storing this on another disk.

This last type of RAID is called RAID 6 (RAID-DP is a RAID 6 variant that uses two dedicated parity drives, analogous to RAID 4). This is a good choice when very large RAID groups and SATA are used.

Figure 6.5 shows an example of a RAID 6 4+2 configuration. The data is striped across four disks, and a parity calculation is stored on the fifth disk. A second parity calculation is stored on another disk. RAID 6 rotates the parity location with I/O, and RAID-DP uses a pair of dedicated parity disks. This provides good performance and good availability but a loss in capacity efficiency. The purpose of the second parity bit is to withstand a second drive failure during RAID rebuild periods. It is important to use RAID 6 in place of RAID 5 if you meet the conditions noted in the "A Key RAID 5 Consideration" section and are unable to otherwise use the mitigation methods noted.

FIGURE 6.5
A RAID 6 4+2 configu-
ration

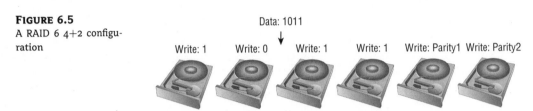

Data: 1011

Write: 1   Write: 0   Write: 1   Write: 1   Write: Parity1   Write: Parity2

Netting out this RAID stuff? Basically, don't worry about it too much. There are generally more important considerations. Just don't use RAID 0. Use hot spare drives, and follow the vendor best practices on hot spare density. EMC, for example, generally recommends one hot spare for every 30 drives in its arrays.

For most VMware use, RAID 5 is a good balance of capacity efficiency, performance, and availability. Use RAID 6 if you have to use very large SATA RAID group or don't have proactive hot spares. RAID 10 schemes still make sense in ultra write performance conditions. Remember that for your VMware cluster it doesn't all have to be one RAID type; in fact, mixing different RAID types can be very useful to deliver different tiers of performance/availability.

For example, you can use most datastores with parity RAID 5 as the default LUN configuration, sparingly use RAID 10 schemes where needed, and use Storage VMotion to nondisruptively make the change for the particular virtual machine that needs it.

Make sure that you have enough spindles in the RAID group to meet the aggregate workload of the LUNs you create in that RAID group. Some storage arrays have the ability to nondisruptively add spindles to a RAID group to add performance as needed.

Midrange and Enterprise Storage Design

There are some major differences in physical array design that can be pertinent in a VMware datacenter design.

Traditional midrange storage arrays are generally arrays with dual-storage processor cache designs where the cache is localized to one storage processor or another, though commonly mirrored between them. (Remember that all vendors call dual-storage processors something slightly different; sometimes they are called *controllers*.) In cases where one of the storage processors fails, the array remains available, but in general, performance is degraded (unless you drive the storage processors to only 50 percent storage processor utilization during normal operation).

Enterprise storage arrays are generally considered to be those that scale to many more controllers and a much larger global cache (memory can be accessed through some common shared model). In these cases, multiple elements can fail while the array is being used at a very high degree of utilization—without any significant performance degradation. Other characteristics of enterprise arrays are support for mainframes and other characteristics that are beyond the scope of this book.

Hybrid designs exist as well, such as scale-out designs where they can scale out to more than two storage processors but without the features otherwise associated with enterprise storage arrays. Often these are iSCSI-only arrays and leverage iSCSI redirection techniques (which are not options of the Fibre Channel or NAS protocol stacks) as a core part of their scale-out design.

Where it can be confusing is that VMware and storage vendors use the same words to express different things. To most storage vendors, an *active/active* storage array is an array that can service I/O on all storage processor units at once, and an *active/passive* design is where one storage process is idle until it takes over for the failed unit. VMware has specific nomenclature for these terms that is focused on the model for a *specific LUN*. Here are its definitions from the "VMware vSphere iSCSI SAN Configuration Guide":

> An active-active storage system, which allows access to the LUNs simultaneously through all the storage ports that are available without significant performance degradation. All the paths are active at all times (unless a path fails).
>
> An active-passive storage system, in which one port or an SP is actively providing access to a given LUN. The other ports or SPs act as backup for the LUN and can be actively providing access to other LUN I/O. I/O can be sent only to an active port. If access through the primary storage port fails, one of the secondary ports or storage processors becomes active, either automatically or through administrator intervention.
>
> A virtual port storage system, which allows access to all available LUNs through a single virtual port. These are active-active storage devices, but hide their multiple connections though a single port. The ESX/ESXi multipathing has no knowledge of the multiple connections to the storage. These storage systems handle port failover and connection balancing transparently. This is often referred to as "transparent failover."

So, what's the scoop here? VMware's definition is based on the multipathing mechanics, not whether you can use both storage processors at once. The active-active and active-passive definitions apply equally to Fiber Channel and iSCSI (and FCoE) arrays, and the virtual port definition applies to only iSCSI (because it uses an iSCSI redirection mechanism that is not possible on Fiber Channel).

SEPARATING THE FINE LINE BETWEEN ACTIVE/ACTIVE AND ACTIVE/PASSIVE

Wondering why VMware specifies the "...without significant performance degradation" in the active/active definition? Hang on to your hat! Most midrange arrays support something called ALUA. What the heck *is* ALUA? ALUA stands for *Asymmetrical Logical Unit Access*.

Midrange arrays usually have an internal interconnect between the two storage processors used for write cache mirroring and other management purposes.

ALUA was an addition to the SCSI standard that enables a LUN to be presented via its primary path and via an asymmetrical (significantly slower) path via the secondary storage processor, transferring the data over the internal interconnect.

The key is that the "nonoptimized path" generally comes at a significant performance degradation. The midrange arrays don't have the internal interconnection bandwidth to deliver the same response on both storage processors, because there is usually a relatively small, or higher latency internal interconnect used for cache mirroring that is used for ALUA vs. enterprise arrays that have a very high bandwidth internal model. VMware ESX/ESXi 4 does support ALUA with arrays that implement ALUA compliant with the SPC-3 standard.

Without ALUA, on an array with an "active/passive" LUN ownership model, paths to a LUN are shown as *"active,"* *"standby"* (designates that the port is reachable, but is on a processor which does not have the LUN), and *"dead."* When the failover mode is set to ALUA, a new state is possible: *"active non-optimized."* This is not shown distinctly in the vSphere client GUI, but looks instead like a normal "active path." The difference is that it is not used for any I/O.

So, should you configure your mid-range array to use ALUA? Follow your storage vendor's best practice. For some arrays this is more important than others. Remember, however, that the "nonoptimized" paths will not be used even if you select the Round-Robin policy. An "active/passive" array using ALUA is not functionally equivalent to an "active/passive" array where all paths are used. This behavior can be different if using a third party Multipathing module—see the "vStorage APIs for Multipathing" section.

By definition, all enterprise arrays are active/active arrays (by VMware's definition), but not all midrange arrays are active/passive. To make things even more confusing, not all active/active arrays (again, by VMware's definition) are enterprise arrays!

So, what do you do? What kind of array architecture is the right one for VMware? The answer is simple: as long as you select one on VMware's Hardware Compatibility List (HCL), they all work; you just need to understand how the one *you* have works.

Most customers' needs are met by midrange arrays, regardless of whether they have an active/active, active/passive, or virtual port (iSCSI only) design or whether they are NAS devices. Generally, only the most mission-critical virtual workloads at the highest scale require the characteristics of enterprise-class storage arrays. In these cases, *scale* refers to: number of virtual machines that number in the thousands, number of datastores that number in the hundreds, local and remote replicas that number in the hundreds, the highest possible workloads—all consistently even after component failures.

The most important considerations are as follows:

◆ If you have a midrange array, recognize that it is possible to oversubscribe the storage processors significantly, such that if a storage processor fails, performance will be degraded. For some customers, that is acceptable because storage processor failure is rare. For others, it is not, in which case you should limit the workload on either storage processor to less than 50 percent or consider an enterprise array.

◆ Understand the failover behavior of your array. Active/active arrays use the fixed-path selection policy by default, and active/passive arrays use the most recently used (MRU) policy by default. (See the "vStorage APIs for Multipathing" section for more information.)

◆ Do you need specific advanced features? For example, if you want to do disaster recovery, make sure your array has integrated support on the VMware Site Recovery Manager HCL. Or, do you need array-integrated VMware snapshots? Do they have integrated management tools? Have they got a vStorage API road map? Push your array vendor to illustrate its VMware integration and the use cases it supports.

Protocol Choices

VMware vSphere 4 offers several shared protocol choices, ranging from Fibre Channel, iSCSI, FCoE, and Network File System (NFS), which is a form of NAS. A little understanding of each goes a long way in designing your VMware vSphere environment.

FIBRE CHANNEL

SANs are most commonly associated with Fibre Channel storage, because Fibre Channel was the first protocol type used with SANs. However, *SAN* refers to a network topology, not a connection protocol. Although often people use the acronym *SAN* to refer to a Fibre Channel SAN, it is completely possible to create a SAN topology using different types of protocols, including iSCSI, FCoE and InfiniBand.

SANs were initially deployed to mimic the characteristics of local or direct attached SCSI devices. A SAN is a network where storage devices (Logical Units—or LUNs—just like on a SCSI or SAS controller) are presented from a storage target (one or more ports on an array) to one or more initiators. An initiator is usually a host bus adapter (HBA), though software-based initiators are also possible for iSCSI and FCoE. See Figure 6.6.

FIGURE 6.6
A Fibre Channel SAN presenting LUNs from a target array (in this case an EMC CLARiiON, indicated by the name DGC) to a series of initiators (in this case QLogic 2432)

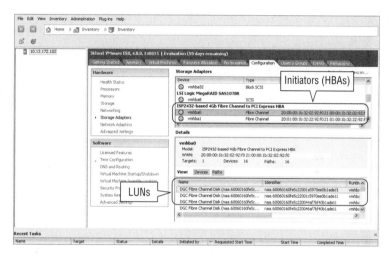

Today, Fibre Channel HBAs have roughly the same cost as high-end multiported Ethernet interfaces or local SAS controllers, and the per-port cost of a Fibre Channel switch is about twice that of a high-end managed Ethernet switch.

Fibre Channel uses an optical interconnect (though there are copper variants), which is used since the Fibre Channel protocol assumes a very high-bandwidth, low-latency, and lossless physical layer. Standard Fibre Channel HBAs today support very high-throughput, 4Gbps and 8Gbps, connectivity in single-, dual-, and even quad-ported options. Older, obsolete HBAs supported only 2Gbps. Some HBAs supported by vSphere ESX 4 are the QLogic QLE2462 and Emulex LP10000. You can find the authoritative list of supported HBAs on the VMware HCL at www.vmware.com/resources/compatibility/search.php. For end-to-end compatibility (in other words, from host to HBA to switch to array), every storage vendor maintains a similar compatibility matrix. For example, EMC e-Lab is generally viewed as the most expansive storage interoperability matrix.

Although in the early days of Fibre Channel there were many different types of cables and there was the interoperability of various Fibre Channel initiators, firmware revisions, switches, and targets (arrays), today interoperability is broad. Still, it is always a best practice to check and maintain your environment to be current with the vendor interoperability matrix. From a connectivity standpoint, almost all cases use a common OM2 (orange-colored cables) multimode duplex LC/LC cable, as shown in Figure 6.7. There is a newer OM3 (aqua-colored cables) standard that is used for longer distances and is generally used for 10Gbps Ethernet and 8Gbps Fibre Channel (which otherwise have shorter distances using OM2). They all plug into standard optical interfaces.

The Fibre Channel protocol can operate in three modes: point-to-point (FC-P2P), arbitrated loop (FC-AL), and switched (FC-SW). Point-to-point and arbitrated loop are rarely used today for host connectivity, and they generally predate the existence of Fibre Channel switches. FC-AL is commonly used by some array architectures to connect their "back-end spindle enclosures" (vendors call these different things, but they're the hardware element that contains and supports the physical disks) to the storage processors, but even in these cases, most modern array designs are moving to switched designs, which have higher bandwidth per disk enclosure.

FIGURE 6.7
A standard Fibre Channel multimode duplex LC/LC fiber-optic cable. Historically viewed as more expensive than Ethernet, they can be roughly the same cost as Cat5e. This 3-meter cable, for example, cost $5 U.S.

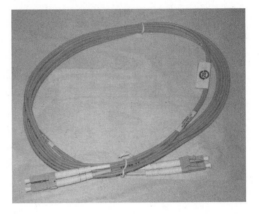

Fibre Channel can be configured in several topologies. On the left in Figure 6.8, point-to-point configurations were used in the early days of Fibre Channel Storage prior to broad adoption of SANs. (However, with modern, extremely high array port densities, point-to-point is making a bit of a comeback.) On the right is an arbitrated loop configuration. This is almost never used in host configuration but is sometimes used in array "back-end" connectivity. Both types have become rare for host connectivity with the prevalence of switched Fibre Channel SAN (FC-SW).

FIGURE 6.8
A comparison of Fibre Channel point-to-point and arbitrated loop topologies

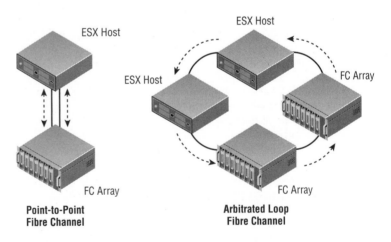

As Figure 6.9 shows, each ESX host has a minimum of two HBA ports, and each is physically connected to two Fibre Channel switches. Each switch has a minimum of two connections to two redundant front-end array ports (across storage processors).

All the objects (initiators, targets, and LUNs) on a Fibre Channel SAN are identified by a unique 64-bit identifier called a *worldwide name* (WWN). WWNs can be worldwide port names (a port on a switch) or node names (a port on an endpoint). For people unfamiliar with Fibre Channel, this concept is simple. It's the same technique as Media Access Control (MAC) addresses on Ethernet. Figure 6.10 shows a vSphere ESX 4 host with 4Gbps Fibre Channel HBAs, where the highlighted HBA has the following worldwide node name: worldwide port name (WWnN: WWpN):

20:00:00:1b:32:02:92:f0 21:00:00:1b:32:02:92:f0

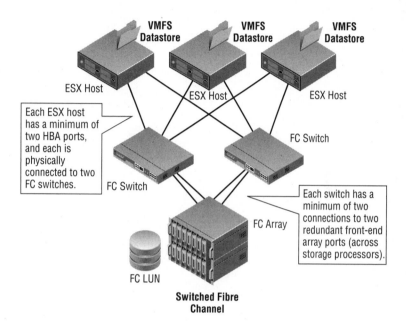

FIGURE 6.9

The most common Fibre Channel configuration: a switched Fibre Channel (FC-SW) SAN. This enables the Fibre Channel LUN to be easily presented to all the hosts in an ESX cluster, while creating a redundant network design.

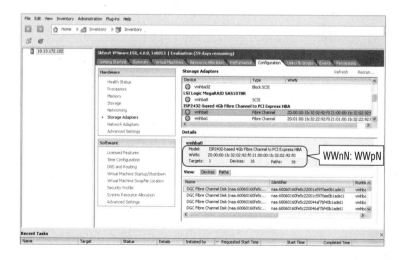

FIGURE 6.10

Fibre Channel WWN examples—note the worldwide node names and the worldwide port names of the QLogic HBAs in the vSphere ESX host

Like Ethernet MAC addresses, WWNs have a structure. The most significant two bytes are used by the vendor (the four hexadecimal characters starting on the left) and are unique to the vendor, so there is a pattern for QLogic or Emulex HBAs or array vendors. In the previous example, these are QLogic HBAs connected to an EMC CLARiiON array.

Fibre Channel and FCoE SANs also have a critical concept of zoning. Zoning is used by Fibre Channel switches to restrict which initiators and targets can see each other as if they were on a common bus. If you have Ethernet networking experience, the idea is somewhat analogous to VLANs with Ethernet.

Zoning is used for the following two purposes:

- To ensure that a LUN that is required to be visible to multiple hosts in a cluster (for example in a VMware vSphere cluster, a Microsoft cluster, or an Oracle RAC cluster) has common visibility to the underlying LUN, while ensuring that hosts that should *not* have visibility to that LUN do not. For example, it's used to ensure that VMFS volumes aren't visible to Windows Servers (with the exception of backup proxy servers using VCB or software that uses the vStorage APIs for Data Protection).

- To create fault and error domains on the SAN fabric, where noise, chatter, errors are not transmitted to all the initiators/targets attached to the switch. Again, it's somewhat analogous to one of the uses of VLANs to partition very dense Ethernet switches into broadcast domains.

Zoning is configured on the Fibre Channel switches via simple GUIs or CLI tools and can be configured by port or by WWN:

- Using port-based zoning, you would zone by configuring your Fibre Channel switch to "put port 5 and port 10 into zone that we'll call zone_5_10." Any WWN you physically plug into port 5 could communicate only to a WWN physically plugged into port 10.

- Using WWN-based zoning, you would zone by configuring your Fibre Channel switch to "put WWN from this HBA and these array ports into a zone we'll call "ESX_4_host1_CX_SPA_0." In this case, if you moved the cables, the zones would move to the ports with the WWNs.

You can see in the vSphere ESX configuration shown in Figure 6.11, the LUN itself is given an unbelievably long name that combines the initiator WWN (ones starting with 20/21), the Fibre Channel switch ports (the ones starting with 50), and the NAA identifier. (You can learn more about NAA identifiers in the "New vStorage Features in vSphere 4" section.) This provides an explicit name that uniquely identifies not only the storage device but the full end-to-end path.

This is also shown in a shorthand runtime name, but the full name is explicit and always globally unique (we'll give you more details on storage object naming later in this chapter).

Zoning should not be confused with LUN masking. *Masking* is the ability for a host or an array to intentionally ignore WWNs that it *can* actively see (in other words, that are zoned to it). This can be used to further limit what LUNs are presented to a host (commonly used with test and development replicas of LUNs).

You can put many initiators and targets into a zone and group zones together (Figure 6.12). Every vSphere ESX/ESXi host in a vSphere cluster must be zoned such that it can see each LUN. Also, every initiator (HBA) needs to be zoned to all the front-end array ports that *could* present the LUN. So, what's the best configuration practice? The answer is single-initiator zoning. This creates smaller zones, creates less cross talk, and makes it more difficult to administratively make an error that removes a LUN from all paths to a host or many hosts at once with a switch configuration error.

FIGURE 6.11
The new explicit storage object names used in vSphere. The runtime name is shorthand.

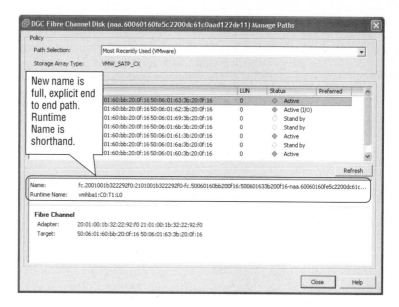

FIGURE 6.12
There are many ways to configure zoning. Left: multi-initiator zoning. Center: two zones. Right: single-initiator zoning.

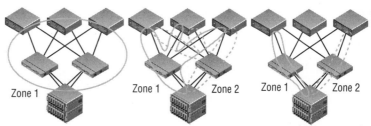

Remember that the goal is to ensure that every LUN is visible to all the nodes in the vSphere cluster. The left side of the figure is how most people who are not familiar with Fibre Channel start—multi-initiator zoning, with all array ports and all the ESX Fibre Channel initiators in one massive zone. The middle is better—with two zones, one for each side of the HA Fibre Channel SAN design, and each zone includes all possible storage processors front-end ports (critically, at least one from each storage processor!). The right one is the best and recommended zoning configuration—single-initiator zoning.

When using single-initiator zoning as shown in the figure, each zone consists of a single initiator and all the potential array ports (critically—at least one from each storage processor!). This reduces the risk of administrative error and eliminates HBA issues affecting adjacent zones, but it takes a little more time to configure. It is always critical to ensure that each HBA is zoned to at least one front-end port on each storage processor

Except for iSCSI-specific concepts and Fibre Channel switch zoning, the configuration of Fibre Channel and iSCSI LUNs in vSphere ESX 4 is the same and follows the tips described in the ''Configuring an iSCSI LUN'' section.

iSCSI

iSCSI brings the idea of a block storage SAN to customers with no Fibre Channel infrastructure. iSCSI is an IETF standard for encapsulating SCSI control and data in TCP/IP packets, which in turn are encapsulated in Ethernet frames. Figure 6.13 shows how iSCSI is encapsulated in TCP/IP and Ethernet frames. TCP retransmission is used to handle dropped Ethernet frames or significant transmission errors. Storage traffic can be intense relative to most LAN traffic. This makes minimizing retransmits, minimizing dropped frames, and ensuring that you have "bet-the-business" Ethernet infrastructure important when using iSCSI.

FIGURE 6.13
How iSCSI is
encapsulated in TCP/IP
and Ethernet frames

Although often Fibre Channel is viewed as higher performance than iSCSI, in many cases iSCSI can more than meet the requirements for many customers, and carefully planned and scaled-up iSCSI infrastructure can, for the most part, match the performance of a moderate Fibre Channel SAN.

Also, the overall complexity of iSCSI and Fibre Channel SANs are roughly comparable and share many of the same core concepts. Arguably, getting the first iSCSI LUN visible to a vSphere ESX host is simpler than getting the first Fibre Channel LUN visible for people with expertise with Ethernet but not Fibre Channel, since understanding worldwide names and zoning is not needed. However, as you saw earlier, these are not complex topics. In practice, designing a scalable, robust iSCSI network requires the same degree of diligence that is applied to Fibre Channel; you should use VLAN (or physical) isolation techniques similarly to Fibre Channel zoning and need to scale up connections to achieve comparable bandwidth. Look at Figure 6.14, and compare it to the switched Fibre Channel network diagram in Figure 6.9.

FIGURE 6.14
Notice how the topology
of an iSCSI SAN is the
same as a switched Fibre
Channel SAN.

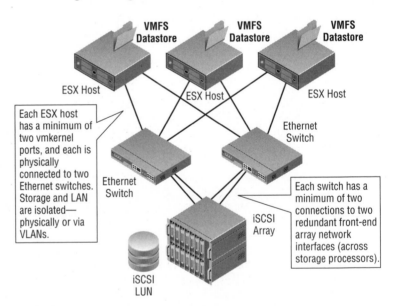

Each ESX host has a minimum of two VMkernel ports, and each is physically connected to two Ethernet switches. Storage and LAN are isolated—physically or via VLANs. Each switch has a minimum of two connections to two redundant front-end array network interfaces (across storage processors).

The one additional concept to focus on with iSCSI is the concept of *fan-in-ratio*. This applies to all shared storage networks, but the effect is often the most pronounced with Gigabit Ethernet (GbE) networks. Across all shared networks, there is almost always a higher amount of bandwidth available across all the host nodes than there is on the egress of the switches and front-end connectivity of the array. It's important to remember that the host bandwidth is gated by congestion wherever it occurs. Don't minimize the array port to switch configuration. If you connect only four GbE interfaces on your array and you have a hundred hosts with two GbE interfaces each, then expect contention.

Also, when examining iSCSI and iSCSI SANs, many core ideas are similar to Fibre Channel and Fibre Channel SANs, but in some cases there are material differences. Let's look at the terminology:

iSCSI initiator   An iSCSI initiator is a logical host-side device that serves the same function as a physical host bus adapter in Fibre Channel or SCSI/SAS. iSCSI initiators can be software initiators (which use host CPU cycles to load/unload SCSI payloads into standard TCP/IP packets and perform error checking). Examples of software initiators that are pertinent to VMware administrators are the native vSphere ESX software initiator and the guest software initiators available in Windows XP and later and in most current Linux distributions. The other form of iSCSI initiators are hardware initiators. These are QLogic QLA 405x and QLE 406x host bus adapters that perform all the iSCSI functions in hardware. An iSCSI initiator is identified by an iSCSI qualified name. An iSCSI initiator uses an iSCSI network portal that consists of one or more IP addresses. An iSCSI initiator "logs in" to an iSCSI target.

iSCSI target   An iSCSI target is a logical target-side device that serves the same function as a target in Fibre Channel SANs. It is the device that hosts iSCSI LUNs and masks to specific iSCSI initiators. Different arrays use iSCSI targets differently—some use hardware, some use software implementations—but largely this is unimportant. More important is that an iSCSI target doesn't necessarily map to a physical port as is the case with Fibre Channel; each array does this differently. Some have one iSCSI target per physical Ethernet port; some have one iSCSI target per iSCSI LUN, which is visible across multiple physical ports; and some have logical iSCSI targets that map to physical ports and LUNs in any relationship the administrator configures within the array. An iSCSI target is identified by an iSCSI Qualified Name. An iSCSI target uses an iSCSI network portal that consists of one or more IP addresses.

iSCSI Logical Unit (LUN)   An iSCSI LUN is a LUN hosted by an iSCSI target. There can be one or more LUNs "behind" a single iSCSI target.

iSCSI network portal   An iSCSI network portal is one or more IP addresses that are used by an iSCSI initiator or iSCSI target.

iSCSI Qualified Name (IQN)   An iSCSI qualified name (IQN) serves the purpose of the WWN in Fibre Channel SANs; it is the unique identifier for an iSCSI initiator, target, or LUN. The format of the IQN is based on the iSCSI IETF standard.

Challenge Authentication Protocol (CHAP)   CHAP is a widely used basic authentication protocol, where a password exchange is used to authenticate the source or target of communication. Unidirectional CHAP is one-way; the source authenticates to the destination, or, in the case of iSCSI, the iSCSI initiator authenticates to the iSCSI target. Bidirectional CHAP is two-way; the iSCSI initiator authenticates to the iSCSI target, and vice versa, before communication is established. Although Fibre Channel SANs are viewed as "intrinsically" secure because they are physically isolated from the Ethernet network and although initiators not zoned to targets cannot communicate, this is not by definition true of iSCSI. With iSCSI, it is possible (but not recommended) to use the same Ethernet segment as general LAN traffic, and there is no intrinsic "zoning" model. Because the storage and general networking traffic could share networking infrastructure, CHAP is an optional mechanism to authenticate the source and destination of iSCSI traffic for some additional security. In practice, Fibre Channel and iSCSI SANs have the same security, and same degree of isolation (logical or physical).

IP Security (IPsec)   IPsec is an IETF standard that uses public-key encryption techniques to secure the iSCSI payloads so that they are not susceptible to man-in-the-middle security attacks. Like CHAP for authentication, this higher level of optional security is part of the iSCSI standards because it is possible (but not recommended) to use a general-purpose IP network for iSCSI transport—and in these cases, not encrypting data exposes a security risk (for example, a man-in-the-middle could determine data on a host they can't authenticate to by simply reconstructing the data from the iSCSI packets). IPsec is relatively rarely used, as it has a heavy CPU impact on the initiator and the target.

Static/dynamic discovery   iSCSI uses a method of discovery where the iSCSI initiator can query an iSCSI target for the available LUNs. Static discovery involves a manual configuration, whereas dynamic discovery issues an iSCSI-standard *SendTargets* command to one of the iSCSI targets on the array. This target then reports all the available targets and LUNs to that particular initiator.

iSCSI Naming Service (iSNS)   The iSCSI Naming Service is analogous to the Domain Name Service (DNS); it's where an iSNS server stores all the available iSCSI targets for a very large iSCSI deployment. iSNS is relatively rarely used.

Figure 6.15 shows the key iSCSI elements in a logical diagram. This diagram shows iSCSI in the broadest sense, and the iSCSI implementation varies significantly between VMware ESX 3.*x* and vSphere ESX 4.

FIGURE 6.15
The elements of the iSCSI IETF standard

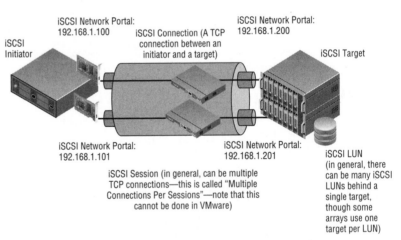

In general, the iSCSI session can be multiple TCP connections, called "Multiple Connections Per Session." Note that this cannot be done in VMware. An iSCSI initiator and iSCSI target can communicate on an iSCSI network portal that can consist of one or more IP addresses. The concept of network portals is done differently on each array—some always having one IP address per target port, some using network portals extensively—there is no wrong or right, but they are different. The iSCSI initiator logs into the iSCSI target, creating an iSCSI session. It is possible to have many iSCSI sessions for a single target, and each session can potentially have multiple

TCP connections (multiple connections per session). There can be varied numbers of iSCSI LUNs behind an iSCSI target—many or just one. Every array does this differently. Note that the particulars of the VMware software iSCSI initiator implementation are covered in detail in the "iSCSI Multipathing and Availability Considerations" section.

What about the furious debate about hardware iSCSI initiators (iSCSI HBAs) versus software iSCSI initiators? Figure 6.16 shows the difference between software iSCSI on generic network interfaces, those that do TCP/IP offload, full iSCSI HBAs. Clearly there are more things the host (the ESX server) needs to process with software iSCSI initiators, but the additional CPU is relatively light. Fully saturating several GbE links will use only roughly one core of a modern CPU, and the cost of iSCSI HBAs is usually less than the cost of slightly more CPU. More and more often—software iSCSI initiators are what the customer chooses.

FIGURE 6.16
Some parts of the stack are handled by the adapter card versus the ESX host CPU in various implementations.

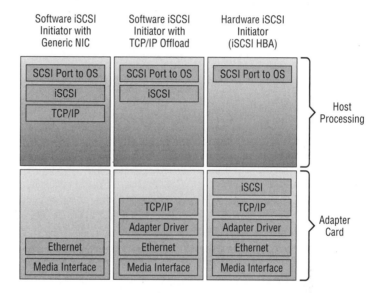

One thing that remains the exclusive domain of the hardware iSCSI initiators (iSCSI HBAs) are boots from iSCSI SAN scenarios, though arguably an ESXi or boot from USB provides a simple alternative.

In prior versions of ESX, the configuration of iSCSI required the configuration of the ESX host firewall to open the iSCSI TCP port (3620), but in vSphere ESX/ESXi, as soon as the iSCSI service is enabled, the firewall port is opened appropriately.

Likewise, in VMware ESX 3.*x* (but not ESXi) the configuration required adding a Service Console port to the same vSwitch used for the iSCSI VMkernel traffic. This is no longer required on either vSphere ESX 4 or ESXi 4 (see the "New vStorage Features in vSphere 4," section, which covers changes in the iSCSI initiator in vSphere ESX 4).

Configuring an iSCSI LUN

In this section, we will show how to configure an iSCSI target and LUN on the storage array and connect the iSCSI LUN to a vSphere ESX 4 server. This will reinforce the architectural topics discussed earlier.

Every array does the array-specific steps differently, but they generally have similar steps. In this example, we have used an EMC Celerra virtual storage array (VSA) that you can download from `http://virtualgeek.typepad.com`. It allows you to complete this procedure even if you don't have a shared storage array.

Perform the following steps to configure an iSCSI LUN and connect it to a vSphere ESX 4 server:

1. Configure the iSCSI target.

   The first step is the configuration on the array side. Every iSCSI array does this differently. In Figure 6.17, using the EMC Celerra VSA, you right-click Wizards, select New iSCSI Target, and then follow the instructions. The EMC Celerra and NetApp FAS arrays are architecturally similar; an iSCSI target is assigned to logical interfaces that can be physical ports, groups of physical ports in link aggregation configurations, or multiple physical ports configured as a multi-interface iSCSI network portal. EMC CLARiiON and others don't require an iSCSI target to be configured (every physical Ethernet port for iSCSI traffic is an iSCSI target). Dell/EqualLogic and HP/Lefthand use an iSCSI target for each LUN, and the iSCSI target is transparent to the user. You will need to know the IP address for your iSCSI target for the next steps.

FIGURE 6.17
Launching the iSCSI target wizard in the EMC Celerra VSA

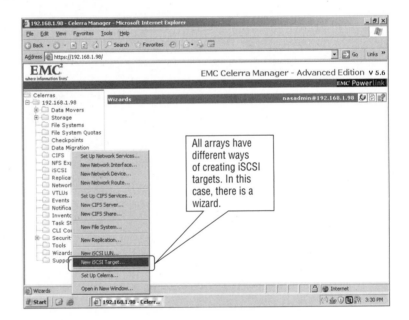

2. Configure the iSCSI LUN.

   Like step 1, every array configures LUNs differently. Using the EMC Celerra VSA, you right-click Wizards (as shown in Figure 6.17), select Create iSCSI LUN, and then follow the instructions. A step-by-step example is available at `http://virtualgeek.typepad.com`.

   Every iSCSI array also does this differently. The EMC Celerra and NetApp FAS arrays are architecturally similar; an iSCSI target is created in a target file system, which in turn is configured in the wizard or manually on a back-end block storage design. In these cases, the file system is the mechanism where array-level thin provisioning is delivered. Most block-only arrays configure their LUNs in a RAID-group, or *pool* (which is a set of RAID groups grouped into a second-order abstraction layer). Often this pool is the vehicle whereby array-level thin provisioning is delivered. All the array mechanisms will require you to specify the target size for the LUN.

3. Make sure that a VMkernel port is configured so that it can be used for iSCSI.

To continue configuring iSCSI, you need to ensure that you have a VMkernel port configured on a vSwitch/dvSwitch and that the vSwitch/dvSwitch is using one or more physical NICs that are on a physical network with connectivity to the iSCSI target. Figure 6.18 shows two vmknics on a vSwitch with two physical Ethernet adapters. (Note that the iSCSI VMkernel ports are on a different subnet than the general LAN and are not on the same physical network as the general LAN. VLANs are a viable alternative to logically isolate iSCSI from the LAN.)

You learned how to create VMkernel port groups in Chapter 5.

FIGURE 6.18
Configuring iSCSI requires a VMkernel port to be reachable from the iSCSI target. In this case, we have two VMkernel ports configured on vSwitch2.

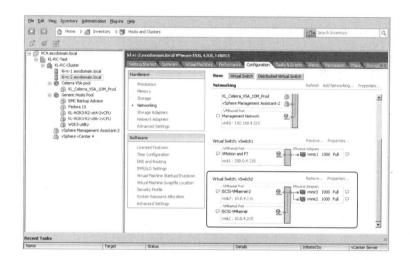

4. Enable the ESX iSCSI software initiator.

The next step is to enable the iSCSI software initiator. By selecting the iSCSI software initiator in the Storage Adapters section of the Configuration tab and then clicking Properties, you are presented with the dialog box shown in Figure 6.19. Select the Enabled radio button. Note that after enabling the iSCSI initiator, the iSCSI name (IQN) for the iSCSI software initiator appears (you can copy the IQN directly from the dialog box).

Before doing the next steps, it's a good idea to ping between the VMkernel IP addresses that will be used for the iSCSI initiator and the iSCSI target. If you can't successfully ping the iSCSI target from the initiator, basic connectivity issues exist. If the ping fails, here's a suggested troubleshooting sequence:

a. Physical cabling: Are the link lights showing a connected state on the physical interfaces on the ESX host, the Ethernet switches, and the iSCSI arrays?

b. VLANs: If you've configured VLANs, have you properly configured the same VLAN on the host, the switch, and the interface(s) that will be used on the array for the iSCSI target?

c. IP routing: Have you properly configured the IP addresses of the vmknic and the interface(s) that will be used on the array for the iSCSI target? Are they on the same subnet? If not, they should be. Although iSCSI can be routed, it's not a good idea generally, because routing adds significant latency and isn't involved in a "bet-the-business" storage Ethernet network. In addition, it's not a good idea in the VMware storage use case.

d. If the ping succeeds but subsequently the iSCSI initiator can't log in to the iSCSI target, check whether TCP port 3620 is being blocked by a firewall somewhere in the path. In ESX 3.x, the ESX host firewall was required to be explicitly opened. This is not a requirement in ESXi 3.x or vSphere 4, where enabling the iSCSI service automatically opens the firewall port.

FIGURE 6.19

After the iSCSI service is enabled, the iSCSI qualified name is shown (and can be copied to the clipboard).

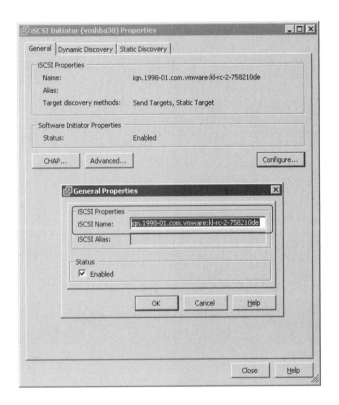

5. Configure dynamic discovery.

On the iSCSI initiator properties page, select the "Dynamic Discovery" tab, then click the "add" button. Input the IP address of the iSCSI target. Configuring discovery tells the iSCSI initiator what iSCSI target it should communicate with to get details about storage that is available to it, and actually has the iSCSI initiator log in to the target—which makes it "known" to the iSCSI target (see Figure 6.20). This also populates all the other known iSCSI targets, and populates the "Static Discovery" entries.

FIGURE 6.20
Adding the iSCSI target
to the list of send
targets will have the
iSCSI initiator attempt
to log in to the iSCSI
target and issue a
SendTargets command
(which returns other
known iSCSI targets).

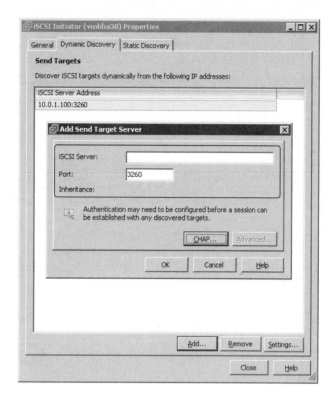

6. Connect the iSCSI LUN to the ESX iSCSI initiator.

   When you configure dynamic discovery, the ESX iSCSI software initiator logs in to the iSCSI target (including an authentication challenge/response if CHAP is configured) and then issues a SendTargets command (if you said yes to the rescan default prompt). Now, since the iSCSI LUN wasn't yet masked, it wasn't discovered. But, the process of the logging in means that the iSCSI initiator IQN is now known by the iSCSI target, which makes connecting the iSCSI LUN to the ESX iSCSI initiator simpler.

   You need to configure the masking on the iSCSI target that will select the LUNs that will be exposed to the iSCSI initiator (and in an ESX cluster, it would be presented to the iSCSI initiator IQNs of *all* the ESX hosts in the cluster).

   Every iSCSI array does the following differently. On the EMC Celerra VSA, navigate to iSCSI and then Targets. Right-click a target, select Properties, and then go to the LUN Mask tab. You will see a screen like the one in Figure 6.21. Note that in the figure the two vSphere ESX 4 hosts have logged in to the array, and each of their iSCSI initiators are logged in to the EMC Celerra VSA. Each has two iSCSI LUNs (LUN 10 and LUN 20) currently masked to it. Without logging in by configuring the dynamic discovery and rescanning for new devices via the previous step, they would not be shown, and would need to be entered manually by typing (or cutting and pasting) the IQN.

   On an EMC CLARiiON, ensure that the ESX hosts are registered with the array (vSphere ESX 4 servers automatically register with EMC CLARiiONs via the VMkernel, where prior versions of VMware ESX required manual registration or installing the Navisphere Agent in the Service Console). Then simply group the hosts in a storage group.

On a NetApp FAS array, configure the iSCSI initiators into an initiator group, and configure the LUN to be masked to the initiator group.

FIGURE 6.21
All arrays have a mechanism to mask LUNs to specific initiators. Ensure that the iSCSI LUNs being used are correctly masked to all the iSCSI initiators in the vSphere cluster.

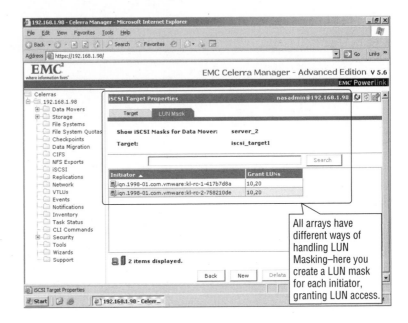

7. Rescan for new devices.

Now that the LUN is being presented to the iSCSI target, a rescan will discover it. Rescanning for new devices can be done at any time in the Storage Adapter screen by selecting "rescan." Scanning for new storage devices issues a ReportLUNs command to the known iSCSI targets with active sessions. If everything is properly configured, the iSCSI LUNs will appear on the ESX server's Storage Configuration tab.

Although we're showing how to rescan at the ESX host level, in vSphere 4 you can rescan at the vSphere cluster level across all the hosts in the cluster (covered in the "New vStorage Features in vSphere 4" section).

8. Check to make sure the LUN is shown in the storage adapter's properties.

At this point, the LUN will be shown underneath the iSCSI adapter in the properties pane (Figure 6.22). The iSCSI LUNs are grouped by the iSCSI targets.

Congratulations, you've just finished configuring an iSCSI LUN and connecting it to a vSphere ESX 4 server!

Fibre Channel and FCoE configurations follow the same sequence (including the masking step) but don't involve setting up the iSCSI initiator and checking for routing. They also require Fibre Channel switch zoning to make sure that the WWNs can reach each other.

FIGURE 6.22

After selecting any adapter (here the iSCSI software initiator), the LUN will be shown underneath the iSCSI adapter in the properties pane.

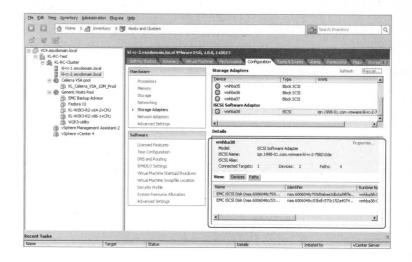

iSCSI Multipathing and Availability Considerations

With iSCSI, though the Ethernet stack can technically be used to perform some multipathing and load balancing, this is not how iSCSI is generally designed. iSCSI uses the same multipath I/O (MPIO) storage framework as Fibre Channel and FCoE SANs.

Regardless of the multipathing configuration, driving iSCSI traffic down more than one Ethernet link for a single iSCSI target was not possible when using the VMware ESX software initiator in VMware versions prior to vSphere ESX/ESXi 4.

Beyond basic configuration, there are several important iSCSI network considerations, all of which can be called "building bet-the-business Ethernet." Remember, you're creating the network here that will support the entire VMware environment. Accordingly, do the following:

◆ Separate your IP storage and LAN network traffic on separate physical switches, or be willing and able to logically isolate them using VLANs.

◆ Enable Flow-Control (which should be set to *receive* on switches and *transmit* on iSCSI targets).

◆ Enable spanning tree protocol only with either RSTP or portfast enabled.

◆ Filter/restrict bridge protocol data units on storage network ports.

◆ Configure jumbo frames (always end-to-end, meaning in every device in all the possible IP storage network paths). Support for jumbo frames for iSCSI (and NFS) was added in VMware ESX 3.5U3 and later.

◆ Strongly consider using Cat6a cables rather than Cat5/5e. Can 1GbE work on Cat 5e cable? Yes. Are you building a bet-the-business Ethernet infrastructure yet you're worried about the cable cost delta? Remember that retransmissions will absolutely recover from errors, but they have a more significant impact in IP storage use cases (that are generally much more active) than in general networking use cases. Using Cat6a also offers a potential upgrade to 10G Base-T, which requires this higher-quality cable plant.

◆ For large-scale IP storage, ensure your Ethernet switches have the proper amount of port buffers and other internals to properly support iSCSI and NFS traffic optimally. This can be important with the very busy IP storage networks, particularly with high peak burst loads. With internal ingress/egress port buffers, for example, there is a significant difference between a Cisco Catalyst 3750 series switch and a Cisco Catalyst 6500 series switch—and this is also true of most Ethernet switches.

Although vSphere adds support for IPv6 for VM networks and VMkernel networks, IPv4 works just fine for IP storage use cases. iSCSI also affords one storage option not generally available via other protocols—the use of in-guest iSCSI initiators. As an example, the Microsoft iSCSI initiator (freely available for Windows Server 2003, 2000, and XP, and embedded in Windows Server 2008, Windows Vista, and Windows 7) or the Linux iSCSI initiator can log in to an iSCSI target from the guest operating system. In this case, the iSCSI traffic uses the virtual machine NICs, not the VMkernel NICs, and all multipathing is governed by MPIO in the guest.

This has roughly a similar CPU overhead as the ESX software initiator, and it is absolutely supported over VMotion operations because the iSCSI stack can easily handle several dropped packets without dropping an iSCSI connection (using TCP retransmission). Note that Storage VMotion is *not* supported in this case. (Because the storage is "invisible" to the ESX/ESXi layer, it looks like general network traffic.) Likewise, VMware snapshots, and any feature dependent on VMware snapshots, are not supported.

So, why use this technique? In ESX 3.*x* it was a way to drive high throughput as a workaround to the limits of the ESX iSCSI software initiator, but this is no longer necessary with the new software initiator in vSphere ESX 4. This is covered in detail in the "Improvements to the Software iSCSI Initiator" section. It was also possible to easily configure Microsoft clusters (both Windows 2003 and Windows 2008 clusters) using the Microsoft iSCSI initiator in the guest. The other reason that remains applicable is that it can enable great flexibility in presenting test/development replicas of databases in virtual machines to other virtual machines directly and programmatically (without needing to manage the ESX-layer presentation steps).

FIBRE CHANNEL OVER ETHERNET (FCOE)

Fibre Channel as a protocol doesn't specify the physical transport it runs over. However, unlike TCP, which has retransmission mechanics to deal with a lossy transport, Fibre Channel has far fewer mechanisms for dealing with loss and retransmission, which is why it requires a lossless, low-jitter, high-bandwidth physical layer connection. It's for this reason that Fibre Channel traditionally is run over relatively short optical cables rather than unshielded twisted-pair (UTP) cables used by Ethernet.

This new standard is called Fibre Channel over Ethernet (FCoE). It's maintained by the same T11 body as Fibre Channel, and the standard is FC-BB-5.

What is the physical cable plant for FCoE? The answer is whatever the 10GbE cable plant uses. Today 10GbE connectivity is generally optical (same cables as Fibre Channel) and Twinax (which is a pair of coaxial copper cables), InfiniBand-like CX cables, and some emerging 10Gb UTP use cases via the new 10G Base-T standard. Each has their specific distance-based use cases and varying interface cost, size, and power consumption.

It is notable at the time of writing this book, while there are several standards for 10GbE connectivity, there is currently no standard for *lossless Ethernet*. This idea of lossless Ethernet is an important element—and there are various pre-standard implementations. The standardization effort is underway via the IEEE and is officially referred to as Datacenter Bridging (DCB), though sometimes it is referred to as *datacenter Ethernet* (DCE) and sometimes as *converged enhanced Ethernet* (CEE). One area of particular focus is "Priority Flow Control" or "Per Priority Pause"—under 802.1Qbb, which is an active project.

Why use FCoE over NFS or iSCSI over 10GbE? The answer is usually driven by the following two factors:

◆ There are existing infrastructure, processes, and tools in large enterprises that are designed for Fibre Channel, and they expect WWN addressing, not IP addresses. This provides an option for a converged network and greater efficiency, without a "rip and replace" model. In fact, the early prestandard FCoE implementations did not include elements required to cross multiple Ethernet switches. These elements, called FIP, are part of the official FC-BB-5 standard and are required in order to comply with the final standard. This means that most FCoE switches in use today function as FCoE/LAN/Fibre Channel bridges. This makes them excellent choices to integrate and extend existing 10GbE/1GbE LANs and Fibre Channel SAN networks. The largest cost savings, power savings, cable and port reduction, and impact on management simplification are on this layer from the vSphere ESX Server to the first switch.

◆ Certain applications require an lossless, extremely low-latency transport network model—something that cannot be achieved using a transport where dropped frames are normal and long-window TCP retransmit mechanism are the protection mechanism. Now, this is a very high-end set of applications, and those historically were not virtualized. However, in the era of vSphere 4, the goal is to virtualize every workload, so I/O models that can deliver those performance envelopes, while still supporting a converged network, become more important.

In practice, the debate of iSCSI vs. FCoE vs. NFS on 10GbE infrastructure is not material. All FCoE adapters are "converged" adapters. They support native 10GbE (and therefore also NFS and iSCSI) as well as FCoE simultaneously, and they appear in the vSphere ESX/ESXi server as multiple 10GbE network adapters and multiple Fibre Channel adapters. If you have FCoE support, in effect you have it all. All protocol options are yours.

A list of FCoE adapters supported by vSphere can be found on the I/O section of the VMware compatibility guide.

NFS

The Network File System (NFS) protocol is a standard originally developed by Sun Microsystems to enable remote systems to be able to access a file system on another host as if it was locally attached. VMware vSphere (and ESX 3.x) implements a client compliant with NFSv3 using TCP.

When NFS datastores are used by VMware, no local file system (i.e., VMFS) is used. The file system is on the remote NFS server. This moves the elements of storage design related to supporting the file system from the ESX host to the NFS server; it also means that you don't need to handle zoning/masking tasks. This makes configuring an NFS datastore one of the easiest storage options to simply get up and running.

Figure 6.23 shows the configuration and topology of an NFS configuration.

Technically, any NFS server that complies with NFSv3 over TCP will work with VMware, but similarly to the considerations for Fibre Channel and iSCSI, the infrastructure needs to support your entire VMware environment. As such, only use NFS servers that are explicitly on the VMware HCL.

Using NFS datastores moves the elements of storage design associated with LUNs from the ESX hosts to the NFS server. The NFS server has an internal block storage configuration, using some RAID levels and similar techniques discussed earlier, and creates file systems on those block storage devices. With most enterprise NAS devices, this configuration is automated, and is done "under the covers." Those file systems are then exported via NFS and mounted on the ESX hosts in the cluster.

FIGURE 6.23
The configuration and topology of an NFS configuration is similar to iSCSI from a connectivity standpoint but very different from a configuration standpoint.

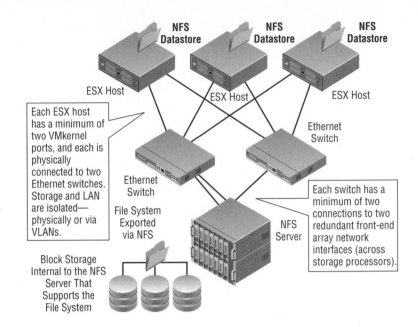

In the early days of using NFS with VMware, NFS was categorized as being a lower performance option for use with ISOs and templates but not for production virtual machines. If production virtual machines were used on NFS datastores, the historical recommendation would be to relocate the virtual machine swap to block storage. NFS datastores can absolutely support a broad range of VMware workloads and does not require you to relocate the virtual machine swap. But in the cases where NFS will be supporting a broad set of production virtual machine use cases, pay attention to the NFS server back-end design and network infrastructure. You need to apply the same degree of care to for "bet-the-business NAS" as you would if you were using block storage. The point is that in the VMware use case, your NFS server isn't being used as a traditional file server where performance and availability requirements are relatively low. Rather, it's being used as an NFS server supporting a mission-critical application—in this case the vSphere cluster and all the VMs on the datastores on that NFS server.

Beyond the IP storage considerations for iSCSI (which are similarly useful on NFS storage configurations), also consider the following:

◆ Consider using switches that support cross-stack EtherChannel. This can be useful in creating high-throughput, highly available configurations.

◆ Multipathing and load balancing for NFS use the networking stack of ESX, not the storage stack—so be prepared for careful configuration of the end-to-end network and NFS server configuration.

◆ Each NFS datastore uses two TCP sessions to the NFS server: one for NFS control traffic and the other for the data traffic. In effect, this means that the vast majority of the NFS traffic for a single datastore will use a single TCP session, which in turn means that link aggregation will use one Ethernet link per datastore. To be able to use the aggregate throughput of multiple Ethernet interfaces, multiple datastores are needed, and the expectation should be that no single datastore will be able to use more than one link's worth of bandwidth. The new approach available to iSCSI (multiple iSCSI sessions per iSCSI target) is not available in the NFS use case. Techniques for designing high-performance NFS datastores are discussed in subsequent sections.

Like in the previous sections covering the common storage array architectures, the protocol choices available to the VMware administrator are broad. You can make most vSphere deployments work well on all protocols, and each has advantages and disadvantages. The key is to understand how to determine what would work best for you. In the following section, I'll summarize how to make these basic storage choices.

Making Basic Storage Choices

As noted in the previous section, most VMware workloads can be met by midrange array architectures (regardless of active/active, active/passive, or virtual port design). Use enterprise array designs when mission-critical and very large-scale virtual datacenter workloads demand uncompromising availability and performance linearity.

As shown in Table 6.1, each storage protocol choice can support most use cases. It's not about one versus the other but rather about understanding and leveraging their differences and applying them to deliver maximum flexibility.

TABLE 6.1:   Storage Choices

FEATURE	FIBRE CHANNEL SAN	iSCSI SAN	NFS
ESX boot	Yes	Hardware initiator only	No
Virtual machine boot	Yes	Yes	Yes
Raw device mapping	Yes	Yes	Yes
Dynamic extension	Yes	Yes	Yes
Availability and scaling model	Storage stack (PSA), ESX LUN queues, array configuration	Storage stack (PSA), ESX LUN queues, array configuration	Network Stage (NIC teaming and routing), network and NFS server configuration
VMware feature support (VM HA, VMotion, Storage VMotion, Fault Tolerance)	Yes	Yes	Yes

Picking a protocol type has historically been focused on the following criteria:

VMware feature support   Although historically major VMware features such as VM HA and VMotion initially required VMFS, they are now supported on all storage types, including raw device mappings (RDMs) and NFS datastores. VMware feature support is generally not a protocol selection criteria, and there are only a few features that lag on RDMs and NFS, such as native ESX snapshots on physical compatibility mode RDMs and Site Recovery Manager on

NFS (which will be supported shortly after vSphere 4 via subsequent Site Recovery Manager releases).

Storage capacity efficiency   Thin provisioning behavior at the vSphere layer universally and properly applied drives a very high efficiency, regardless of protocol choice. Applying thin provisioning at the storage array (both on block and NFS objects) delivers a higher overall efficiency than applying it only at the VMware layer. Emerging additional array capacity efficiency techniques (such as detecting and reducing storage consumed when there is information in common using compression and data deduplication) are currently most efficiently used on NFS datastores but are expanding to include block use cases. One common error is to look at storage capacity (GB) as the sole vector of efficiency—in many cases, the performance envelope requires a fixed number of spindles even with advanced caching techniques. Often in these cases, efficiency is measured in "spindle density" not in "GB." For most vSphere customers, efficiency tends to be a function of operational process, rather than protocol or platform choice.

Performance   Many VMware customers see similar performance regardless of a given protocol choice. Properly designed iSCSI and NFS over Gigabit Ethernet can support very large VMware deployments, particularly with small-block (4KB–64KB) I/O patterns that characterize most general Windows workloads and don't need more than roughly 80MBps of 100 percent read or write I/O bandwidth or 160MBps of mixed I/O bandwidth. This difference in the throughput limit is due to the 1Gbps/2Gbps bidirectional nature of 1GbE—pure read or pure write workloads are unidirectional, mixed workloads are bidirectional.

Fibre Channel generally delivers a better performance envelope with very large-block I/O (virtual machines supporting DSS database workloads or SharePoint), which tend to demand a high degree of throughput. Less important generally but still important for some workloads, Fibre Channel delivers a lower-latency model and also tends to have a faster failover behavior because iSCSI and NFS always depend on some degree of TCP retransmission for loss and, in some iSCSI cases, ARP—all of which drive failover handling into tens of seconds versus seconds with Fibre Channel or FCoE. Load balancing and scale-out with IP storage using multiple Gigabit Ethernet links with IP storage can work for iSCSI to drive up throughput. Link aggregation techniques can help—they work only when you have many TCP sessions. This is possible for the first time in VMware configurations using IP storage when using vSphere ESX/ESXi 4 and iSCSI. In 2009 and 2010, broader availability of 10GbE brings similar potentially higher-throughput options to NFS datastores.

You can make every protocol configuration work in almost all use cases; the key is in the details (covered in this chapter). In practice, the most important thing is what you know and feel comfortable with.

The most flexible vSphere configurations tend to use a combination of both VMFS (which requires block storage) and NFS datastores (which require NAS), as well as RDMs on a selective basis (block storage).

The choice of which block protocol should be used to support the VMFS and RDM use cases depends on the enterprise more than the technologies and tends to follow this pattern:

◆ iSCSI for customers who have never used and have no existing Fibre Channel SAN infrastructure

◆ Fibre Channel for those with existing Fibre Channel SAN infrastructure that meet their needs

◆ FCoE for those upgrading existing Fibre Channel SAN infrastructure

vSphere can be applied to a very broad set of use cases—from the desktop/laptop to the server and on the server workloads—ranging from test and development to heavy workloads and mission-critical applications. A simple "one size fits all" can work, but only for the simplest deployments. The advantage of vSphere is that all protocols and all models are supported. Becoming fixated on one model alone means that not everything is virtualized that can be and the enterprise isn't as flexible and efficient as it can be.

Now that you've learned about the basic principles of shared storage and determined how to make the basic storage choices for your environment, it's time to see how these are applied in the VMware context.

VMware Storage Fundamentals

This section of the chapter examines how the shared storage technologies covered earlier are applied in vSphere. We will cover these elements in a logical sequence. We will start with core VMware storage concepts. Next, we'll cover the storage options in vSphere for datastores to contain groups of virtual machines (VMFS version 3 datastores and NFS datastores). We'll follow with options for presenting disk devices directly into VMs (raw device mappings). Finally, we'll examine VM-level storage configuration details.

Core VMware Storage Concepts

The core concept of virtual machine encapsulation results in virtual machines being represented by a set of files, discussed in "Virtual Machine-Level Storage Configuration." These virtual machine files reside on the shared storage infrastructure (the exception is an RDM, which will be discussed subsequently).

In general, VMware uses a shared-everything storage model. All nodes of a vSphere cluster use commonly accessed storage objects using block storage protocols (Fibre Channel, iSCSI, and FCoE, in which case the storage objects are LUNs) or network attached storage protocols (NFS, in which case the storage objects are NFS exports). Although it is technically possible to have storage objects (LUNs and NFS exports) that are not exposed to all the nodes of a vSphere cluster, this is not a best practice and should be avoided because it increases the likelihood of configuration error and constrains higher-level VMware functions (such as VMware HA, VMotion, and DRS), which expect to operate across the vSphere cluster.

How the storage objects are presented to the VMkernel and managed in vCenter varies on several factors. Let's explore the most common options.

Several times over the next sections, I will refer to parts of the VMware vSphere storage stack, as shown in Figure 6.24.

Let's take a look at the first logical layer, which is configuring shared "containers" for virtual machines such as VMware File System and Network File System datastores.

VMFS version 3 Datastores

The VMware File System (VMFS) is the most common configuration option for most VMware deployments. It's analogous (but different) to NTFS for Windows Server and ext3 for Linux. Like these file systems, it is native; it's included with vSphere and operates on top of block storage objects.

The purpose of VMFS is to simplify the storage environment in the VMware context. It would clearly be difficult to scale a virtual environment if each virtual machine directly accessed its own storage rather than storing the set of files on a shared volume. It creates a shared storage pool that is used for a set of virtual machines.

FIGURE 6.24
The vSphere storage stack

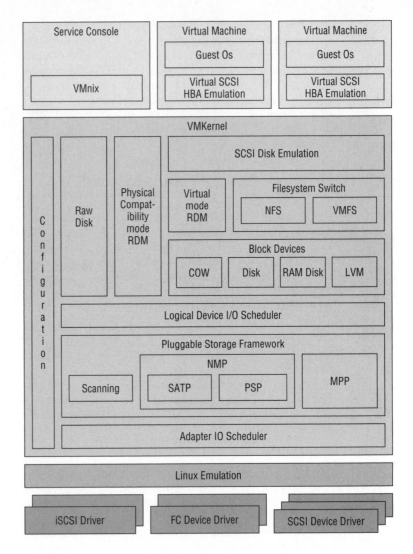

VMFS differs from these common file systems in several important fundamental ways:

◆ It was designed to be a clustered file system from its inception, but unlike most clustered file systems, it is simple and easy to use. Most clustered file systems come with manuals the size of a phone book.

◆ This simplicity is derived from its simple and transparent distributed locking mechanism. This is generally much simpler than traditional clustered file systems with network cluster lock managers (the usual basis for the giant manuals).

◆ It enables simple direct-to-disk, steady-state I/O that results in very high throughput at a very low CPU overhead for the ESX server.

◆ Locking is handled using metadata in a hidden section of the file system. The metadata portion of the file system contains critical information in the form of on-disk lock structures (files) such as which vSphere 4 ESX server is the current owner of a given virtual machine, ensuring that there is no contention or corruption of the virtual machine (Figure 6.25).

FIGURE 6.25
A VMFS version 3 volume and the associated metadata

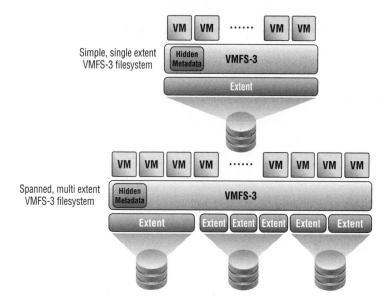

◆ When these on-disk lock structures are updated, the ESX 4 host doing the update, which is the same mechanism that was used in ESX 3.*x*, momentarily locks the LUN using a nonpersistent SCSI lock (SCSI Reserve/Reset commands). This operation is completely transparent to the VMware administrator.

◆ These metadata updates do *not* occur during normal I/O operations and are not a fundamental scaling limit.

◆ During the metadata updates, there is minimal impact to the production I/O (covered in a VMware white paper at www.vmware.com/resources/techresources/1059). This impact is negligible to the other hosts in the ESX cluster, and more pronounced on the host holding the SCSI lock.

◆ These metadata updates occur during the following:

   ◆ The creation of a file in the VMFS datastore (creating/deleting a VM, for example, or taking an ESX snapshot)

   ◆ Actions that change the ESX host that "owns" a virtual machine (VMotion and VMware HA)

   ◆ The final stage of a Storage VMotion operation in ESX 3.5 (but not vSphere)

   ◆ Changes to the VMFS file system itself (extending the file system or adding a file system extent)

VMFS is currently at version 3 and does not get updated as part of the VMware Infrastructure 3.*x* to vSphere 4 upgrade process, one of many reasons why the process of upgrading from VI3.5 to vSphere can be relatively simple.

VSPHERE AND SCSI-3 DEPENDENCY

One major change in vSphere is that in Virtual Infrastructure 3.x, both SCSI-2 and SCSI-3 devices were supported; in vSphere 4, only SCSI-3compliant block storage objects are supported. Most major storage arrays have or can be upgraded via their array software for full SCSI-3 support, but check with your storage vendor before doing so. If your storage array doesn't support SCSI-3, the storage details shown on the Configuration tab for the vSphere host will not display correctly.

In spite of this requirement, vSphere still uses SCSI-2 reservations for general ESX-level SCSI reservations (not to be confused with guest-level reservations). This is important for Asymmetrical Logical Unit (ALUA) support, covered in the "vStorage APIs for Multipathing" section.

Creating a VMFS Datastore

Perform the following steps to configure a VMFS datastore on the iSCSI LUN that was previously configured in the section "Configuring an iSCSI LUN":

1. Rescan for devices. Check to see whether the LUN you will be using for VMFS is shown under the configuration's Storage Adapters list. (LUNs appear in the bottom of the vSphere client properties pane associated with a storage adapter.) If you've provisioned a LUN that doesn't appear, rescan for new devices.

2. Select Shared Storage Type: Moving to the Storage section of the configuration, select *Add Storage* in the upper right hand part of the screen. You will be presented with the *Add Storage* dialog. Select Disk/LUN.

3. Select the LUN. In the next step of the *Add Storage* wizard, you will see the LUN name and identifier information, along with the LUN number and its size (and the VMFS label if it has been used). Select the LUN you want to use, and click Next.

   You'll see a summary screen with the details of the LUN selected and the action that will be taken; if it's a new LUN (no preexisting VMFS partition), the wizard will note that a VMFS partition will be created. If there is an existing VMFS partition, you will be presented with some options; see the "New vStorage Features in vSphere 4" section on resignaturing for more information.

4. Name the datastore. In the next step of the wizard, you name the datastore. Use a descriptive name. For example, you might note that this is a VMFS volume that is used for light VMs. Additional naming information that is useful and worth consideration in a naming scheme includes an array identifier, a LUN identifier, a protection detail (RAID type and whether it is replicated remotely for disaster recovery purposes). Clear datastore naming can help the VMware administrator later in determining virtual machine placement.

5. Pick the VMFS allocation size (Figure 6.26). All file systems have an allocation size. For example, with NTFS, the default is 4KB. This is the smallest size any file can be. Smaller allocation sizes mean that smaller maximum file sizes can be supported, and the reverse is also true. Generally, this VMFS default is *more* than sufficient, but if you know you will need a single VMDK file to be larger than 256GB (which has a corresponding minimum allocation size of 1MB), select a larger allocation size. A little known fact is that VMFS version 3 will actually change its allocation size dynamically, so select a large allocation size only in cases where you are certain you will have large files (usually a virtual disk) in the datastore.

6. You will get a final summary screen in the wizard like the one in Figure 6.27. Double-check all the information, and click Finish. The new datastore will appear in the Storage section of the ESX Configuration tab and also in the datastores at the inventory-level view in the vSphere client. In VMware Infrastructure 3.*x* clusters, rescanning for the new VMFS datastore would have needed to be repeated across the cluster, but in vSphere 4, this step is done automatically.

FIGURE 6.26
Select the maximum file size; this defines the minimum size of any file system allocation but also the maximum size for any individual file.

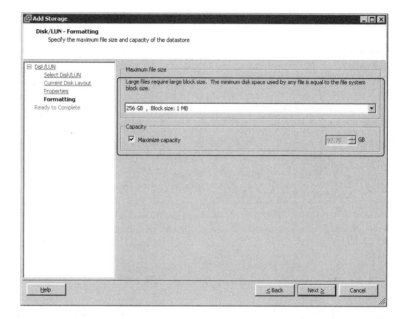

FIGURE 6.27
Check the confirmation details prior to hitting Finish.

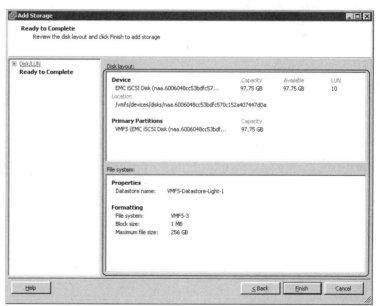

The vSphere volume manager can partition volumes up to 2TB minus 512 bytes in size. This ESX maximum limit is the same as ESX/ESXi 3.5. Commonly believed to be a "32-bit/64-bit" or VMFS version 3 limit, that is not correct. The vSphere VMkernel is fully 64-bit. The approximately 2TB partition limit is because of ESX/ESXi 4's use of cylinder/head/sector (CHS) partition management rather than GUID partition tables (GPT).

WHAT HAPPENS NEAR THE 2TB BOUNDARY

If you use a LUN that is exactly 2TB in vSphere ESX 4, you will get an error when creating the VMFS partition. This is normal. There are 512 bytes per LUN that are used for internal ESX purposes, and using all 2TB can actually result in an unexpected out-of-space condition in ESX 3.x. This new behavior in vSphere eliminates this negative corner case, but it means that the maximum VMFS volume is 2TB-512 bytes, or 2,199,023,255,040 bytes. You can present the LUNs to ESX 3.5 hosts and have VMFS volumes created on a 2TB LUN, though this is *not* recommended because it will result in the potential out-of-space condition being possible once again.

Also, in VMware ESX 3.0.x, if a LUN larger than 2TB is presented to an ESX host, make sure not to use the "maximum size" default during the VMFS creation or extension process. Although it is possible to create a VMFS volume past the 2TB limit, in ESX 3.0 it will make the VMFS volume inaccessible (VMware Knowledge Base article 1004230). Since ESX 3.5.x, this behavior has been corrected. If a LUN is presented that is larger than 2TB, only the space greater than the 2TB limit is shown as available to use. For example, a 2.5TB LUN will show only 500GB as available to partition.

A VMFS file system exists on one or more partitions or extents. It can be extended by dynamically adding more extents; up to 32 extents are supported. There is also a 64TB maximum VMFS version 3 file system size. Note that individual files in the VMFS file system can span extents, but the maximum file size is determined by the VMFS allocation size during the volume creation, and the maximum remains 2TB with the largest allocation size selected. In prior versions of VMware ESX, adding a partition required an additional LUN, but in vSphere, VMFS file systems can be dynamically extended into additional space in an existing LUN (discussed in the "New vStorage Features in vSphere 4" section). Figure 6.28 shows a VMFS volume with two extents.

Selecting the properties for a VMFS version 3 file system with multiple extents shows a screen like in Figure 6.28. In this example, the spanned VMFS includes two extents—the primary partition (in this case a 10GB LUN) and the additional partition (in this case a 100GB LUN). As files are created, they are spread around the extents, so although the volume isn't striped over the extents, the benefits of the increased performance and capacity are used almost immediately.

It is a widely held misconception that having a VMFS file system that spans multiple extents is *always* a bad idea and acts as a simple "concatenation" of the file system. In practice, although adding a VMFS extent adds more space to the file system as a concatenated space, as new objects (VMs) are placed in the file system, VMFS version 3 will randomly distribute those new file objects across the various extents—without waiting for the original extent to be full. VMFS version 3 (since the days of ESX 3.0) allocates the initial blocks for a new file randomly in the file system, and subsequent allocations for that file are sequential. This means that files are distributed across the file system and, in the case of spanned VMFS volumes, across multiple LUNs. This will naturally distribute virtual machines across multiple extents.

LOCKING IN A MULTI-EXTENT VMFS CONFIGURATIONS

Note that the metadata that VMFS uses is always stored in the first extent of a VMFS volume. This means that in VMFS volumes that span extents, the effects of SCSI locking during the short moments of metadata updates apply only to the LUN backing the first extent.

FIGURE 6.28
A VMFS file system with two extents: one 100GB and one 10GB

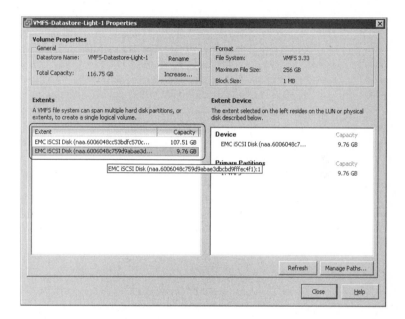

A common question is about VMFS fragmentation. VMFS version 3 does not generally need defragmentation as compared with most file systems. The number of files is very low (low thousands vs. millions for a "traditional" file system of the same corresponding capacity), and it is composed of small numbers of very large files (virtual disks measured in tens or hundreds of gigabytes versus general-purpose files measured in megabytes). It is possible to nondisruptively defragment VMFS version 3 using Storage VMotion to a fresh datastore.

In addition, having a VMFS datastore that is composed of multiple extents across multiple LUNs increases the parallelism of the underlying LUN queues.

There is a downside to these spanned VMFS configurations. You will more rapidly use LUNs and will by definition reach the maximum LUN count. The maximum LUN count is 256, but in practice for an ESX cluster it's 256—1 × the number of ESX hosts in the cluster. (There is always one LUN used for each ESX host—even ESXi.) This means that you will have a lower maximum number of VMFS volumes if you use multiple-extent VMFS configurations. Though, generally, most ESX clusters have far fewer than the maximum number of LUNs and VMFS volumes, even when array LUN snapshots and other items are factored in. Most relatively large VMware clusters have 10 to 20 VMFS datastores.

Also widely unknown is that VMFS version 3 datastores that span extents are more resilient than generally believed. Removing the LUN supporting a VMFS version 3 extent will *not* make the spanned VMFS datastore unavailable. The exception is the first extent in the VMFS file system that contains the metadata section of the VMFS file system; removing this will result in the datastore being unavailable, but this is no better or no worse than a single-extent VMFS volume. Removing an extent affects only that portion of the datastore supported by that extent; reconnecting the LUN restores full use of that portion of the VMFS datastore. VMFS version 3 and virtual machines are relatively resilient to this "crash consistent" behavior which is a common term for filesystem behavior after a hard shutdown or crash. While "crash resilient," note that just like any action that removes a datastore or portion of a datastore while VMs are active, the removal of a VMFS extent *can* result in corrupted VMs and should not be done intentionally.

This desire for very large datastores is rooted in the idea that one massive datastore for all the VMs would be a simple, rather than a formal requirement. It is best practice to have multiple storage objects (of all kinds—both block and NAS), because it increases the degree of parallelism that the VMkernel is able to achieve with multiple LUN queues and multiple storage paths for load balancing. It also decreases the risk of a single administrative error affecting a potentially very large number of virtual machines.

This philosophy also applies in the case of IP storage (both iSCSI and NFS), not only for the same reasons as Fibre Channel or FCoE storage, but also, since for IP storage, having multiple datastores is an important factor in load balancing and aggregate throughput because of an increased number of TCP connections. Furthermore, placing very large amounts of VMs in a single datastore has an impact during various operations (backup and disaster recovery), such as integration with array snapshot technologies; it also can represent a large aggregation of risk into a single object.

One big datastore for all the VMs is a simple way to start, but it's not the right way to build a production vSphere cluster that will scale. One storage object per VM isn't right, but one storage object for *all* VMs isn't right either. In the "Leveraging SAN and NAS Best Practices" section, we provide pragmatic guidance for the number of VMs per datastore.

ALIGNING VMFS VOLUMES

Do you need to align the VMFS volumes? Yes, but no manual effort is required. When you create a VMFS datastore with the vCenter GUI, it always provides the right alignment offset. This aligns the I/O along the underlying RAID stripes of the array, minimizing extra I/O operations and providing a more efficient use of what is usually the most constrained storage resource—IOps.

What about the maximum number of VMs in a given VMFS volume? There is an absurdly high upper maximum of 3,011 VMs in a single VMFS datastore, but in practice, the number is much lower. In general, the limit isn't governed by the SCSI lock mechanism, though that can be a smaller factor; it's governed by the number of virtual machines contending for the underlying LUN queues and the performance of the LUN itself that support the VMFS datastore. Keeping the ESX host LUNs queues below the default maximum of 32 (can be increased to a maximum of 64) is a desired goal. Note that having multiple LUNs supporting a spanned VMFS file system not only increases the array-side queues (if your array uses per-LUN queues) but also increases the ESX-side LUN queues supporting the volume, which in turn increases the number of VMs and the total aggregate I/O handling of the VMFS datastore.

In summary, keep the following tips in mind when working with VMFS file systems that span extents:

◆ Always start simple. Start with single-extent VMFS datastores on a single LUN.

◆ Don't use spanned VMFS just because you want one big datastore for all your VMs.

◆ Do use spanned VMFS if you do need a VMFS datastore that is larger than the volume limits of 2TB-512 bytes.

◆ Do use spanned VMFS if you need an extremely high-performance VMFS datastore. (In this case, a single VMFS datastore is supported by multiple LUN queues and multiple paths.) These configurations can deliver some of the highest vSphere aggregate storage I/O performance.

◆ Use spanned VMFS only if your storage array can manage the group of LUNs that represent as a consistency group, which is a mechanism that some arrays have to actively enforce this idea that a collection of LUNs are all related at the host level. This enforces treating them as a single unit for all array-level provisioning and replication tasks.

Overall, VMFS is simple to use, simplifies virtual machine storage management, is robust at very large cluster scales, and is scalable from a performance standpoint to very high workloads.

THE IMPORTANCE OF LUN QUEUES

Queues are an important construct in block storage use cases (across all protocols, including iSCSI Fibre Channel, and FCoE). Think of a queue as a line at the supermarket checkout. Queues exist on the server (in this case the ESX server), generally at both the HBA and LUN levels. They also exist on the storage array. Every array does this differently, but they all have the same concept. Block-centric storage arrays generally have these queues at the target ports, array-wide, and array LUN levels, and finally at the spindles themselves. File-server centric designs generally have queues at the target ports, and array-wide, but abstract the array LUN queues as the LUNs exist actually as files in the file system. However, fileserver centric designs have internal LUN queues underneath the file systems themselves, and then ultimately at the spindle level—in other words it's "internal" to how the file server accesses its own storage.

The queue depth is a function of how fast things are being loaded into the queue and how fast the queue is being drained. How fast the queue is being drained is a function of the amount of time needed for the array to service the I/O requests. This is called the "Service Time" and in the supermarket checkout is the speed of the person behind the checkout counter (ergo, the array service time, or the speed of the person behind the checkout counter). To determine how many outstanding items are in the queue, use ESXtop, hit U to get to the storage screen, and look at the QUED column.

The array service time itself is a function of many things, predominantly the workload, then the spindle configuration, then the write cache (for writes only), then the storage processors, and finally, with certain rare workloads, the read caches.

Why is this important? Well, for most customers it will never come up, and all queuing will be happening behind the scenes. However, for some customers, LUN queues are one of the predominant things with block storage architectures that determines whether your virtual machines are happy or not from a storage performance.

When a queue overflows (either because the storage configuration is insufficient for the steady-state workload or because the storage configuration is unable to absorb a burst), it causes many upstream effects to "slow down the I/O." For IP-focused people, this effect is very analogous to TCP windowing, which should be avoided for storage just like queue overflow should be avoided.

You can change the default queue depths for your HBAs and for each LUN. (See www.vmware .com for HBA-specific steps.) After changing the queue depths on the HBAs, a second step is needed to at the VMkernel layer. The amount of outstanding disk requests from VMs to the VMFS file system itself must be increased to match the HBA setting. This can be done in the ESX advanced settings, specifically Disk.SchedNumReqOutstanding, as shown in Figure 6.29. In general, the default settings for LUN queues and Disk.SchedNumReqOutstanding are the best.

CHANGING LUN COUNT MAXIMUMS

You can reduce the maximum number of LUNs that an ESX server supports from the maximum of 256 to a lower number using the ESX advanced setting Disk.MaxLUN. Reducing the maximum can speed up the time for bus rescans. In general, changing this setting is not recommended, because it is easy to forget that the setting was changed or easy to forget to change it for all the ESX servers in a cluster—making troubleshooting when LUNs aren't discovered during bus rescans frustrating.

FIGURE 6.29
It is possible to adjust the advanced properties for advanced use cases, increasing the maximum number of outstanding requests allowed to match adjusted queues.

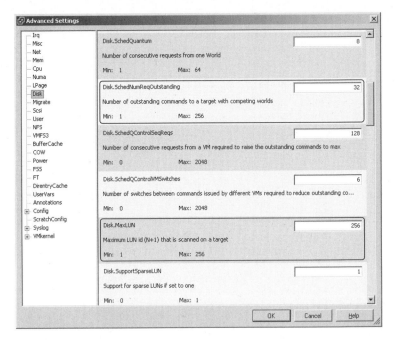

If the queue overflow is not a case of dealing with short bursts but rather that you are underconfigured for the steady state workload, making the queues deeper can have a downside—higher latency. Then it overflows anyway. This is the predominant case, so before increasing your LUN queues, check the array service time. If it's taking more than 10 minutes to service I/O requests, you need to improve the service time, usually by adding more spindles to the LUN or by moving the LUN to a faster-performing tier.

NFS Datastores

NFS datastores are used in an analogous way to VMFS—as a shared pool of storage for virtual machines. Although there are many supported NFS servers and VMware, there are two primary NFS servers used with VMware environments, EMC Celerra and NetApp FAS. Therefore, in this section, we'll make some vendor-specific notes. As with all storage devices, you should follow the best practices from your vendor's documentation, because those will supersede any comments made in this book. You can find the vendor-specific documentation at the following websites:

◆ EMC Celerra: "Introduction to Using EMC Celerra with VMware vSphere 4 - Applied Best Practices": http://www.emc.com/collateral/hardware/white-papers/h6337-introduction-using-celerra-vmware-vsphere-wp.pdf

◆ NetApp: "NetApp and VMware vSphere: Storage Best Practices": http://media.netapp
   .com/documents/tr-3749.pdf

Although VMFS and NFS are both "shared pools of storage for VMs," in other ways, they are
different. The two most important differences between VMFS and NFS datastore options are as
follows:

◆ The file system itself is not on the ESX host at all (in the way that VMFS is "on" the ESX
   host accessing a shared LUN) but is simply accessing a remote file system on an NFS server
   using the NFS protocol via an NFS client.

◆ All the VMware elements of high availability and performance scaling design are not part
   of the storage stack but are part of the networking stack of the ESX server.

NFS datastores need to handle the same access control requirements that VMFS delivers
using the metadata and SCSI locks during the creation and management of file-level locking.
On NFS datastores, the same file-level locking mechanism is used (but unlike VMFS, it is
not hidden) by the VMkernel, and NFS server locks in place of the VMFS SCSI reservation
mechanism to make sure that the file-level locks are not simultaneously changed. A very
common concern with NFS storage and VMware is performance. There is a common misconception that NFS cannot perform as well as block storage protocols—often based on
historical ways NAS and block storage have been used. Although it is true that NAS and block
architectures are different and, likewise, their scaling models and bottlenecks are generally
different, this perception is mostly rooted in how people have used NAS historically. NAS
traditionally is relegated to non-mission-critical application use, while SANs have been used
for mission-critical purposes. For the most part this isn't rooted in core architectural reasons
(there are differences at the extreme use cases), rather, just in how people have used these
technologies in the past. It's absolutely possible to build enterprise-class NAS infrastructure
today.

So, what is a reasonable performance expectation for an NFS datastore? From a bandwidth
standpoint, where 1Gbps Ethernet is used (which has 2Gbps of bandwidth bidirectionally),
the reasonable bandwidth limits are 80MBps (unidirectional 100 percent read or 100 percent
write) to 160MBps (bidirectional mixed read/write workloads) for a single NFS datastore.
Because of how TCP connections are handled by the ESX NFS client, almost all the bandwidth
for a single NFS datastore will always use only one link. From a throughput (IOps) standpoint,
the performance is generally limited by the spindles supporting the file system on the NFS
server.

This amount of bandwidth is sufficient for many use cases, particularly groups of virtual
machines with small block I/O patterns that aren't bandwidth limited. Conversely, when a
high-bandwidth workload is required by a single virtual machine or even a single virtual disk,
this is not possible with NFS, without using 10GbE.

VMware ESX 4 does support jumbo frames for all VMkernel traffic including NFS (and iSCSI)
and should be used. But it is then critical to configure a consistent, larger maximum transfer
unit frame size on *all* devices in all the possible networking paths; otherwise, Ethernet frame
fragmentation will cause communication problems.

VMware ESX 4, like ESX 3.*x*, uses NFS v3 over TCP and does not support NFS over UDP.

The key to understanding why NIC teaming and link aggregation techniques cannot be used to
scale up the bandwidth of a single NFS datastore is how TCP is used in the NFS case. Remember
that the MPIO-based multipathing options used for block storage and in particular iSCSI to exceed
the speed of a link are not an option, as NFS datastores use the networking stack, not the storage

stack. The VMware NFS client uses two TCP sessions per datastore (as shown in Figure 6.30): one for control traffic and one for data flow (which is the vast majority of the bandwidth). With all NIC teaming/link aggregation technologies, Ethernet link choice is based on TCP connection. This happens either as a one-time operation when the connection is established with NIC teaming, or dynamically, with 802.3ad. Regardless, there's always only one active link per TCP connection, and therefore only one active link for all the data flow for a single NFS datastore. This highlights that, like VMFS, the "one big datastore" model is not a good design principle. In the case of VMFS, it's not a good model because of the extremely large number of VMs and the implications on LUN queues (and to a far lesser extent, SCSI locking impact). In the case of NFS, it is not a good model because the bulk of the bandwidth would be on a single TCP session and therefore would use a single Ethernet link (regardless of network interface teaming, link aggregation, or routing).

FIGURE 6.30
Every NFS datastore has two TCP connections to the NFS server.

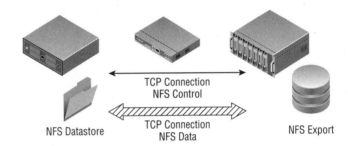

NFS Datastore

TCP Connection
NFS Control

TCP Connection
NFS Data

NFS Export

The default maximum number of NFS datastores per ESX host is eight but can be increased (Figure 6.31). The maximum in VMware Infrastructure 3.5 was 32 datastores, but it has increased to 64 in vSphere ESX 4. Using more NFS datastores drives makes more efficient use of the Ethernet network (more TCP sessions result in better link aggregation/NIC teaming), and also most NFS servers deliver better performance with multiple file systems because of internal multithreading and better scaling of their own back-end block device queues.

One particularity is that the VMware NFS client must have full root access to the NFS export. If the NFS export was exported with `root squash`, the file system will not be able to mount on the ESX host. (Root users are downgraded to unprivileged file system access. On a traditional Linux system, when `root squash` is configured on the export, the remote systems are mapped to the "nobody" account.)

Generally, one of the following two configuration options are used for NFS exports that are going to be used with VMware ESX hosts:

◆ The NFS export uses the `no_root_squash` option, and the ESX hosts are given explicit read/write access.

◆ The ESX host IP addresses are added as root-privileged hosts on the NFS server. Figure 6.32 shows a sample configuration on an EMC Celerra, where the IP addresses of the vSphere ESX hosts are noted as having root access to the exported file system.

CREATING AN NFS DATASTORE

In this procedure, we will create an NFS datastore.

Every array does the array-specific steps differently, but they are similar. In this procedure, we have used an EMC Celerra virtual storage array that you can download from http://virtualgeek.typepad.com; it allows you to complete this procedure even if you don't have a NFS server.

FIGURE 6.31
The maximum number of datastores can be easily increased from the default of 8 up to a maximum of 64.

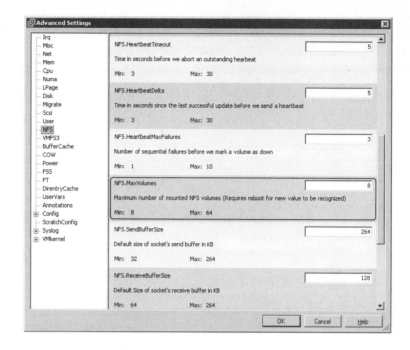

FIGURE 6.32
Each ESX server needs to have root access to the NFS export.

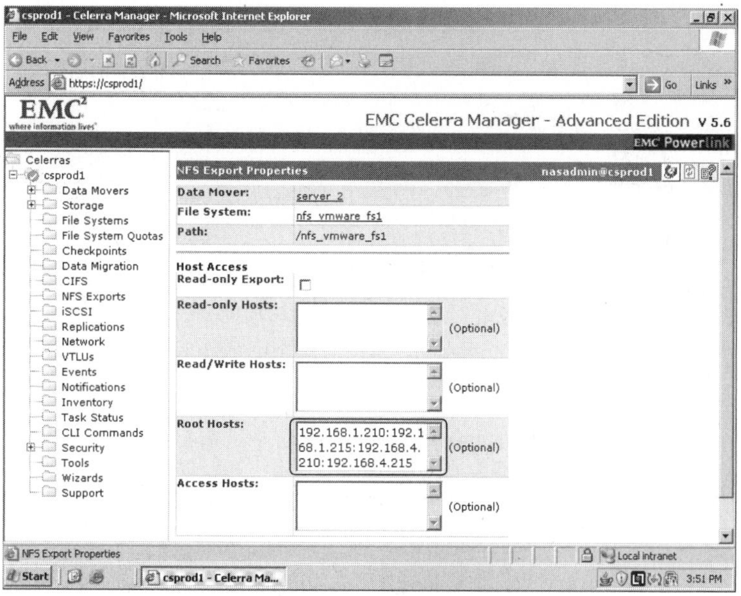

Perform the following steps to configure a file system on the NAS device, export it via NFS, and mount the NFS datastore on a vSphere ESX 4 server:

1. Via the array management framework, create a file system (Figure 6.33). In this case, we've used the Celerra Create Filesystem Wizard. You will need to select the containing structure (Aggregate for NetApp or Automated Volume Manager storage pool for Celerra), which selects the back-end block structure that supports the file system, though the detail of the underlying volume layout on the block objects is automated (unless specific performance goals are required and manual configuration of the block and volume layout supporting the file system is needed).

FIGURE 6.33
Using the wizard to create a file system

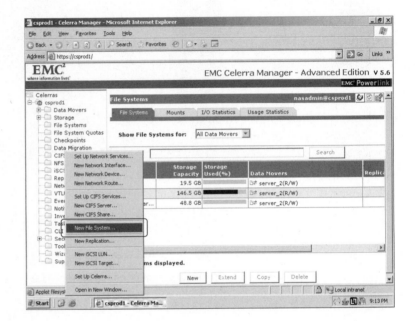

2. Configure a VMkernel port to be used for NFS. To configure NFS datastores, you need a VMkernel port on the network that is attached to the NFS server. In this example, as shown in Figure 6.34, we are not configuring any additional VMkernel ports and are just using the management network. Although quick and simple, this is not a best practice for a production datastore. By definition, the management network is on the LAN, whereas NFS traffic is used for production VMs should be on an isolated physical network or minimally isolated on a separate VLAN. Configuring NFS as is being done in this example would be appropriate only for very light use for items such as ISOs/templates because busy LAN traffic could interfere with the production datastores. This type of configuration, however, makes getting data on and off the ESX cluster very simple because the NFS export can be mounted on any server attached to the LAN, which can route to the NFS server (provided a given security configuration on the NFS server).

FIGURE 6.34

NFS datastores require a VMkernel port that can connect to the NFS server. In this example, the NFS datastore is being mounted via the management interface, but this is not a best practice.

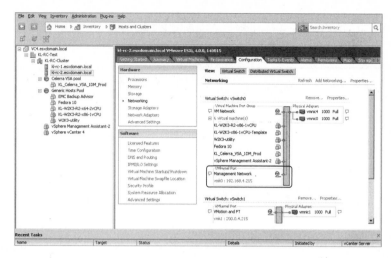

3. Configure the NFS export. Via the array management framework, ensure that NFS is enabled, and then configure the NFS export; ensure that the ESX servers have root access by specifying their IP addresses, as shown in Figure 6.34. Every NFS server does this differently. On the Celerra, you can access the NFS Exports configuration as shown in Figure 6.35.

BASIC NETWORKING HYGIENE

Before doing the next steps, it's a good idea to ping between the VMkernel IP addresses that will be used and the NFS server. This is useful in iSCSI cases as well. If you can't successfully ping the NFS server (or iSCSI target) from the VMkernel port, basic connectivity issues exist. If the ping fails, follow these troubleshooting steps:

1. Check the physical cabling. Are the link lights showing a connected state on the physical interfaces on the ESX host, the Ethernet switches, and the iSCSI arrays?

2. Check VLANs. If you've configured VLANs, have you properly configured the same VLAN on the host, the switch, and the interface(s) that will be used on the array for the iSCSI target?

3. Check IP routing. Have you properly configured the IP addresses of the vmknic and the interface(s) that will be used on the array for the NFS server? Are they on the same subnet? If not, they should be. Although NFS can absolutely be routed (after all, it's running on top of TCP), it's not a good idea, especially in the VMware storage use case. (Routing between subnets adds significant latency and isn't involved in a "bet-the-business" storage Ethernet network.)

---

4. Add the NFS datastore. Navigate to the storage tab on an ESX server, and select Add Storage. The first step of the wizard offers a choice between Disk/LUN and Network File System; select Network File System.

FIGURE 6.35
Configuring NFS exports
for the file system

FIGURE 6.35
Configuring NFS exports
for the file system

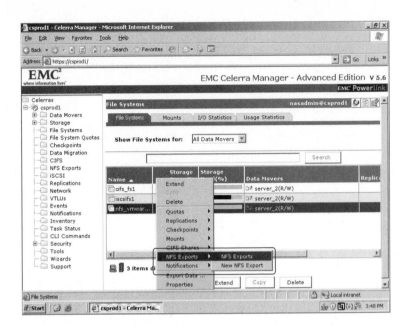

5. Locate the network file system. The next step in the wizard is where you specify the NFS details. In Figure 6.36, the server is the IP address or the domain name of the NFS server, and the folder is the path to the exported file system on the NFS server.

FIGURE 6.36
Specifying the correct
NFS server and mount
point information,
and supplying an NFS
datastore name, will
need to be done on
every ESX server in
the cluster.

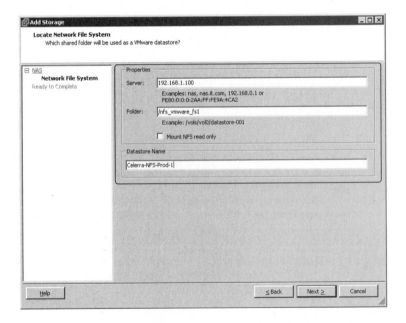

Generally identifying the NFS server by IP addresses is recommended, but it is not recommended to use a domain name because it places an unnecessary dependency on DNS and because generally it is being specified on a relatively small number of hosts. There are, of course, some cases where a domain name may be applicable—for example, where NAS virtualization techniques are used to provide transparent file mobility between NFS servers—but this is relatively rare.

This is also where you name the datastore. Use a descriptive name. For the example here, I've noted that this is an NFS server name that is used for light production VMs. Additional, naming details that are useful and worth consideration in a naming scheme are an array identifier, a file system identifier, and a protection detail (RAID type and replication) identifier.

Clicking Next presents a summary screen. Double-check all the information, and click Finish. The new datastore will appear in the Storage section of the ESX Configuration tab and also in the datastores at the inventory-level view in the vSphere client.

Unlike VMFS datastores in vSphere, you need to complete this configuration on each host in the vSphere cluster. Also, it's important to use consistent NFS properties (for example, a consistent IP/domain name), as well as common datastore names; this is not enforced.

As you can see, using NFS requires a simple series of steps, several fewer than using VMFS. Furthermore, it doesn't involve any specific array-side configuration beyond selecting the AVM storage pool (EMC) or FlexVol (NetApp) and picking a capacity for the file system.

However, a consideration with NFS datastores at significant bandwidth (MBps) or throughput (IOps) involves careful planning and design.

Both NetApp and EMC Celerra (as of this writing) recommend an important series of advanced ESX parameter settings to maximize performance (including increasing memory assigned to the networking stack and changing other characteristics). Please refer to the EMC/NetApp best practices/solution guides for the latest recommendations at the websites given earlier.

SUPPORTING LARGE BANDWIDTH (MBPS) WORKLOADS ON NFS

Bandwidth for large I/O sizes is generally gated by the transport link (in this case the TCP session used by the NFS datastore being 1Gbps or 10Gbps) and overall network design. At larger scales, the same care and design should be applied that would be applied for iSCSI or Fibre Channel networks. In this case, it means carefully planning the physical network/VLAN, implementing end-to-end jumbo frames, and leveraging enterprise-class Ethernet switches with sufficient buffers to handle significant workload. At 10GbE speeds, features such as TCP Segment Offload (TSO) and other offload mechanisms, as well as the processing power and I/O architecture of the NFS server, become important for NFS datastore and ESX performance.

SUPPORTING LARGE THROUGHPUT (IOPS) WORKLOADS ON NFS

High-throughput (IOps) workloads are usually gated by the back-end configuration (as true of NAS devices as it is with block devices) and not the protocol or transport since they are also generally low bandwidth (MBps). By "back-end," I mean the array target. If the workload is cached, then it's determined by the cache response, which is almost always astronomical. However, in the real world, most often the performance is not determined by cache response; the performance is determined by the spindle configuration that supports the storage object. In the case of NFS datastores, the storage object is the file system, so the considerations that apply at the ESX server for VMFS (disk configuration and interface queues) apply within the NFS server. So, on a NetApp filer, the IOps achieved is primarily determined by the FlexVol/aggregate/RAID group configuration. On a Celerra, they are likewise primarily determined by the Automated Volume

Manager/dVol/RAID group configuration. Although there are other considerations (at a certain point, the filer/datamovers scale and the host's ability to generate I/Os become limited), but up to the limits that users commonly encounter, far more often performance is constrained by the back-end disk configuration that supports the file system. Make sure that your file system has sufficient back-end spindles in the container to deliver performance for all the VMs that will be contained in the file system exported via NFS.

NFS HIGH AVAILABILITY DESIGN

High-availability design for NFS datastores is substantially different from with block storage devices. Block storage devices use MPIO, which is an end-to-end path model. For ethernet networking and NAS, the domain of link selection is from one Ethernet MAC to another Ethernet MAC, or one link hop. This is configured from the host to switch, from switch to host, and from NFS server to switch, and switch to NFS server; Figure 6.37 shows the comparison. In the figure, "Link Aggregation" is used more accurately; it can be either static NIC teaming or 802.3ad.

FIGURE 6.37
NFS uses the networking stack, not the storage stack for high availability and load balancing.

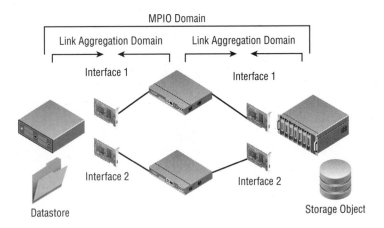

The mechanisms used to select one link or another are fundamentally the following:

♦ A NIC teaming/link aggregation choice, which is set up per TCP connection and is either static (set up once and permanent for the duration of the TCP session) or dynamic (can be renegotiated while maintaining the TCP connection but still always on one link or another)

♦ A TCP/IP routing choice, where an IP address (and the associated link) is selected based on a layer-3 routing choice—note that this doesn't imply traffic crosses subnets via a gateway, only that the ESX server selects the NIC or a given datastore based on the subnet.

Figure 6.38 shows the basic decision tree.

The path on the left has a topology that looks like Figure 6.39. Note that the little arrows mean that link aggregation/static teaming is configured from the ESX host to the switch and on the switch to the ESX host; in addition, note that there is the same setup on both sides for the switch to NFS server relationship.

FIGURE 6.38
The simple choices to configure highly available NFS datastores and how they depend on your network configuration

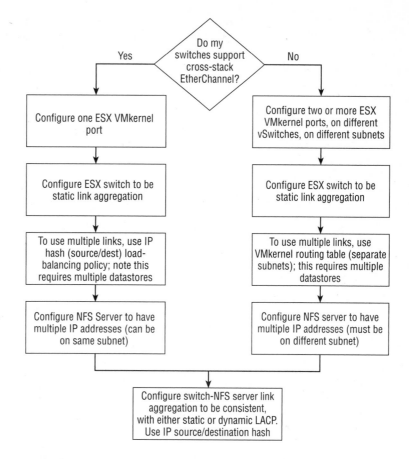

FIGURE 6.39
If you have a network switch that supports cross-stack EtherChannel, you can easily create a network team that spans switches.

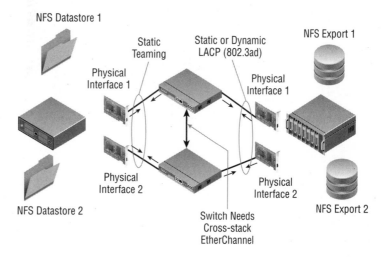

The path on the right has a topology that looks like Figure 6.40. You can also use link aggregation/teaming on the links in addition to the routing mechanism, but this has limited value—remember that it won't help with a single datastore. Routing is the selection mechanism for the outbound NIC for a datastore, and each NFS datastore should be reachable via an alias on both subnets.

FIGURE 6.40
If you have a basic network switch without cross-stack EtherChannel or don't have the experience or control of your network infrastructure, you can use VMkernel routing by placing multiple VMkernel network interfaces on separate vSwitches and different subnets.

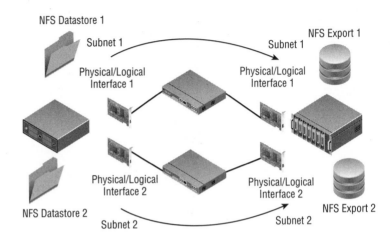

Another consideration of HA design with NFS datastores is that NAS device failover is generally longer than a native block device. A block storage device generally can failover after a "front-end" (or storage processor) failure in seconds (or milliseconds). Conversely, NAS devices tend to failover in tens of seconds (and more importantly can be longer depending on the NAS device and the configuration specifics). There are NFS servers that fail over faster, but these tend to be relatively rare in VMware use cases. This long failover period should not be considered intrinsically negative but rather a configuration question that determines the fit for NFS datastores based on the virtual machine service level agreement (SLA) expectation.

The key questions are, how much time elapses before ESX does something about a datastore being nonreachable, and what is the guest behavior during that time period?

First, the same concept exists with Fibre Channel and iSCSI, though, as noted, generally in shorter time intervals. This time period depends on specifics of the HBA configuration, but in general it is less than 30 seconds for Fibre Channel and 60 seconds for iSCSI. This block failover behavior extends into vSphere, unless using a third-party multipathing plug-in like EMC PowerPath/VE with vSphere, in which case path failure detection can be near instant.

Second, timeouts can be extended to survive reasonable filer (NetApp) and datamover (EMC Celerra) failover intervals.

Both NetApp and Celerra (at the time of this writing) recommend the same ESX failover settings. Please refer to the EMC/NetApp best practices/solution guides for the latest recommendation.

To extend the timeout value for NFS datastores, you change the values in the Advanced Settings dialog box shown in Figure 6.41.

FIGURE 6.41

When configuring NFS datastores, it's important to extend the ESX host and guest storage timeouts to match the vendor best practices because NFS server failover periods can vary.

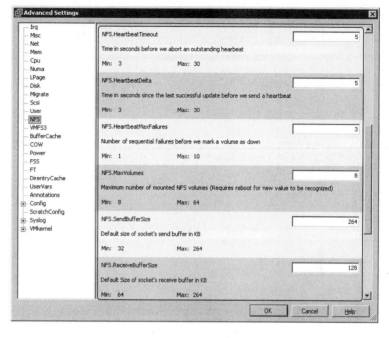

The settings that both EMC and NetApp recommend are as follows. You should configure these settings across all ESX hosts.

NFS.HeartbeatDelta (NFS.HeartbeatFrequency in ESX 3.x)	12
NFS.HeartbeatTimeout	5
NFS.HeartbeatMaxFailures	10

This is how these work:

◆ Every NFS.HeartbeatFrequency (or 12 seconds), the ESX server checks to see that the NFS datastore is reachable.

◆ Those heartbeats expire after NFS.HeartbeatTimeout (or 5 seconds), after which another heartbeat is sent.

◆ If NFS.HeartbeatMaxFailures (or 10) heartbeats fail in a row, the datastore is marked as unavailable, and the VMs crash.

This means that the NFS datastore can be unavailable for a maximum of 125 seconds before being marked unavailable, which covers the large majority of both NetApp and EMC Celerra failover events.

What does a guest see during this period? It sees a nonresponsive SCSI disk on the vSCSI adapter (similar to the failover behavior of a Fibre Channel or iSCSI device, though the interval is generally shorter). The disk timeout is how long the guest OS will wait while the disk is nonresponsive before throwing an I/O error. This error is a "delayed write error," and for a boot volume will result in the guest O/S crashing. Windows, for example, has a disk timeout default of 60 seconds. A recommendation is to increase the guest disk timeout value to match the NFS datastore timeout value. Otherwise, the virtual machines can timeout their boot storage (which will cause a crash) while ESX is still waiting for the NFS datastore within the longer timeout value. Without extending the guest timeout, if guest-level VMware HA is configured, the virtual machines will reboot (when the NFS datastore returned), but obviously extending the timeout is preferable to avoid this extra step and the addition delay and extra IO workload it generates.

Perform the following steps to set operating system timeout for Windows servers to match the 125-second maximum set for the datastore:

1. Back up your Windows registry.

2. Select Start ➤ Run, type **regedit.exe**, and click OK.

3. In the left panel hierarchy view, double-click HKEY_LOCAL_MACHINE, then System, then CurrentControlSet, then Services, and then Disk.

4. Select the TimeOutValue value, and set the data value to 125 (decimal).

What if you need a storage device presented directly to a virtual machine, not a shared "container" as is the case with VMFS and NFS datastores? The next section discusses the most common options.

Raw Device Mapping

Although the concept of shared "pool" mechanisms (VMFS or NFS) for virtual machine storage works well for the many virtual machine storage use cases, there are certain select cases where the storage device must be presented directly to the virtual machine.

This is done via raw device mapping. (You can also use in-guest iSCSI initiators; see the "iSCSI Multipathing and Availability Considerations" section.) RDMs are presented to a vSphere cluster and then via vCenter directly to a virtual machine. Subsequent data I/O bypasses the VMFS and volume manager completely, though management is handled via a mapping file that is stored on a VMFS volume.

RDMs should be viewed as a tactical tool in the VMware administrators' toolkit rather than a common use case. A common misconception is that RDMs perform better than VMFS. In reality, the performance delta between the storage types is within the margin of error of tests. Although it is possible to "oversubscribe" a VMFS or NFS datastore (because they are shared resources) and not an RDM (because it is presented to specific VMs only), this is better handled through design and monitoring rather than through the extensive use of RDMs. In other words, if you are worried about over-subscription of a storage resource, and that's driving a choice of an RDM over a shared datastore model, simply choose to not put multiple VMs in the "pooled" datastore.

RDMs can be configured in two different modes:

Physical compatibility mode (pRDM) In this mode, all I/O passes directly through to the underlying LUN device, and the mapping file is used solely for locking and VMware management tasks. Generally, when a storage vendor says "RDM without specifying further," it means physical compatibility mode RDM.

Virtual mode (vRDM) In this mode, all I/O travels through the VMFS layer. Generally, when VMware says "RDM," without specifying further it means virtual mode RDM.

Contrary to common misconception, both modes support almost all VMware advanced functions such as VM HA, VMotion, and Site Recovery Manager (as of Site Recovery Manager 1.0 update 1), but there is one important difference: virtual mode RDMs can be included in a VMware snapshot, but physical mode RDMs cannot.

This inability to take a native VMware snapshot of a pRDM also means that features that depend on VMware snapshots (the vStorage APIs for Data Protection, VMware Data Recovery, and Storage VMotion) don't work with pRDMs.

Virtual mode RDMs can be a source or destination of Storage VMotion in vSphere, and they can go from virtual mode RDM to virtual disks, but physical mode RDMs cannot.

When a feature specifies RDM as an option, make sure to check the type: physical compatibility mode or virtual mode.

The most common use cases for RDMs are virtual machines configured as Microsoft Windows clusters. In Windows Server 2008, this is called Windows Services for Clusters (WSFC), and in Windows Server 2003, this is called Microsoft Cluster Services (MSCS). Minimally, the quorum disk in these configurations requires an RDM configuration. vSphere added the SCSI 3 virtual machine persistent reservations needed for Windows 2008 WSFC support. Using this feature requires that the pRDM is configured in the guest using the new virtual LSI Logic SAS controller (Figure 6.42). Make sure this virtual SCSI controller is used for all virtual disks for Windows 2008 clusters.

FIGURE 6.42

When configuring Windows 2008 clusters with RDMs, make sure to use the LSI Logic SAS virtual SCSI controller in the guest configuration.

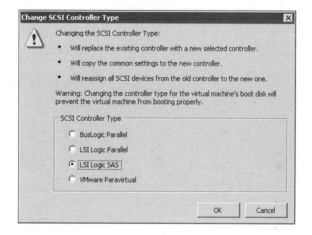

You can find the VMware HCL at the following website:

`www.vmware.com/resources/compatibility/search.php`

You can find the VMware Microsoft cluster requirements at the following website:

`http://kb.vmware.com/selfservice/microsites/search.do?language=en_US&cmd=displayKC&externalId=1004617`

Another important use case of pRDMs is that they have a "unique VMware super ability." They can be presented from a virtual machine to a physical host interchangeably. This means that in cases where an independent software vendor (ISV) hasn't yet embraced virtualization and indicates that virtual configurations are not supported, the RDMs can easily be moved to a physical host to reproduce the issue on a physical machine. As an example, this is useful in Oracle on VMware use cases. (Note that as of this writing, not one of these ISV support stances has been based on an actual technical issue.)

In a small set of use cases, storage vendor features and functions depend on the guest directly accessing the LUN and therefore need pRDMs. For example, certain arrays such as EMC Symmetrix use "in-band" communication for management to isolate management from the IP network. This means the management traffic is communicated via the block protocol (most commonly Fibre Channel). In these cases, EMC gatekeeper LUNs are used for host-array communication and if they are used in a Virtual Machine (commonly where EMC Solutions Enabler is used) require pRDMs.

Another example of storage features that are associated with RDMs are those related to storage array features such as application-integrated snapshot tools. These are applications that integrate with Microsoft Exchange, SQL Server, SharePoint, Oracle and other applications to handle recovery modes and actions. Examples include EMC's Replication Manager, NetApp's SnapManager family, and Dell/EqualLogic's Auto Volume Replicator tools. Earlier generations of these tools required the use of RDMs, but most of the vendors now can manage these without the use of RDMs and integrate with vCenter APIs. Check with your array vendor for the latest details.

Virtual Machine-Level Storage Configuration

Let's move from ESX-level storage configuration to the storage configuration details for individual virtual machines.

WHAT STORAGE OBJECTS MAKE UP A VIRTUAL MACHINE

Virtual machines consist of a set of files, and each file has a distinct purpose. Looking at the datastore browser on two virtual machines, as shown in Figure 6.43, you can see these files.

FIGURE 6.43
The various files that make up a virtual machine

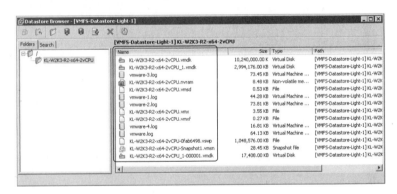

Here is what each of the files is used for:

.vmx the virtual machine configuration file

.vmx.lck the virtual machine lock file created when a virtual machine is in a powered-on state. As an example of VMFS locking, it is locked when this file is created, deleted, or modified, but not for the duration of startup/shutdown. Note that the .lck files are not shown in the datastore browser, as they are hidden in the VMFS case, and obscured in the datastore browser itself in the NFS case. In the NFS case, if you mount the NFS datastore directly on another host, you can see the .lck files. These should not be modified.

.nvram the virtual machine BIOS configuration

.vmdk a virtual machine disk

-000#.vmdk   a virtual machine disk that forms a post-snapshot state when coupled with the base .vmdk

.vmsd   the dictionary file for snapshots that couples the base vmdk with the snapshot vmdk

.vmem   the virtual machine memory mapped to a file when the virtual machine is in a powered-on state

.vmss   the virtual machine suspend file created when a virtual machine is in a suspended state

-Snapshot#.vmsn   the memory state of a virtual machine whose snapshot includes memory state

.vswp   the virtual machine swap

How Much Space Does a Virtual Machine Consume?

The answer to this question—like so many—is "it depends." It depends on whether the machine is thinly provisioned or thick. And if it's thick, it depends on whether it's on a datastore that uses underlying thin provisioning at the array level. But, there are other factors that are often not considered. Virtual machines are more than just their virtual disk files. They also need to store their snapshots, which can consume considerable datastore capacity.

How Much Space Can Snapshots Consume?

Although generally small relative to the virtual disk, each snapshot grows as blocks in the virtual disk are changed, so the rate of change and the time that has elapsed from the snapshot determine the size of the snapshot file.

In the worst case, such as when every block in the virtual disk that has a snapshot is changed, the snapshot files will be the same size as the virtual disk file itself.

Because many snapshots can be taken of any given virtual disk, a great deal of storage capacity can ultimately be used by snapshots.

Snapshots of running machines also optionally snapshot the memory state in addition to the virtual disks.

The storage capacity consumed by snapshots shouldn't be viewed negatively. The ability to easily snapshot the state of a virtual machine is a very powerful benefit of using VMware and is nearly impossible on physical machines. That benefit consumes some storage on the datastores and so, incurs some cost. It is easy in vSphere to track space consumed by snapshots. (See the "Storage Management Improvements" section for more details on how to report on capacity used by snapshots.)

Other elements of virtual machines that can also consume considerable storage are the virtual machine swap and their suspended state. (The virtual memory swap represents the difference between the configured virtual machine memory and the allocated memory via VMware's ballooning mechanism and is stored in the .vswp file.)

Rather than spend a lot of time planning for these additional effects, which are very difficult to plan because they depend on a very large number of variables, estimate based on templates or a small number of representative virtual machines. Very commonly, the additional space for snapshots and virtual machine swap are estimated as 25 percent in addition to the space needed for the virtual disks themselves. Then use thin provisioning if your array doesn't support thin provisioning natively at the VMware layer to be as efficient as possible, and use the storage layer and the new VMware Storage Views reports and alerts to track utilization.

It's much easier to manage (through managed datastore objects and storage views) and react in nondisruptive ways to unanticipated storage consumption in vSphere than it was in prior versions (via VMFS extension, VMFS extents, and improved Storage VMotion). These are covered in the "New vStorage Features in vSphere 4" section.

VIRTUAL DISKS

Virtual disks are how virtual machines encapsulate their disk devices (if not using RDMs) and warrant further understanding. Figure 6.44 shows the properties of a VM. Hard disk 1 is a virtual disk on a VMFS volume, is 12 GB in size, but is thinly provisioned. Hard disk 2, conversely, is an RDM.

FIGURE 6.44
Configuration of virtual disks for a guest

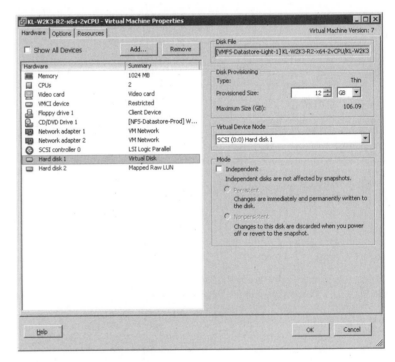

Virtual disks come in the following three formats:

Thin In this format, the size of the VDMK file on the datastore is only however much is used within the VM itself (Figure 6.45). For example, if you create a 500GB virtual disk and place 100GB of data in it, the VMDK file will be 100GB in size. As I/O occurs in the guest, the VMkernel zeroes out the space needed right before the guest I/O is committed and grows the VMDK file similarly. Sometimes, this is referred to as a "sparse file."

FIGURE 6.45
A thin virtual disk
example

Thick (otherwise known as *zeroedthick*)   In this format, the size of the VDMK file on the datastore is the size of the virtual disk that you create, but within the file, it is not "prezeroed" (Figure 6.46). For example, if you create a 500GB virtual disk and place 100GB of data in it, the VMDK will appear to be 500GB at the datastore file system, but it contains only 100GB of data on disk. As I/O occurs in the guest, the VMkernel zeroes out the space needed right before the guest I/O is committed, but the VDMK file size does not grow (since it was already 500GB).

FIGURE 6.46
A thick virtual disk
example. Note that the
400GB isn't zeroed, so if
you are using array-level
thin provisioning, only
100GB is used.

Eagerzeroedthick   Eagerzeroedthick virtual disks are truly thick. In this format, the size of the VDMK file on the datastore is the size of the virtual disk that you create, and within the file, it is prezeroed (Figure 6.47). For example, if you create a 500GB virtual disk and place 100GB of data in it, the VMDK will appear to be 500GB at the datastore file system, and it contains 100GB of data and 400GB of zeros on disk. As I/O occurs in the guest, the VMkernel does not need to zero the blocks prior to the I/O occurring. This results in improved I/O latency and less back-end storage I/O operations during initial I/O operations to "new" allocations in the guest OS, but it results in significantly more back-end storage I/O operation up front during the creation of the VM.

FIGURE 6.47
An eagerzeroedthick
example. Note that the
400GB that isn't actually
in use yet by the virtual
machine is prezeroed,
so the full 500GB is
consumed immediately.

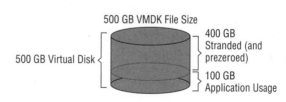

This third virtual disk format is not evident immediately from the vCenter management GUI, but when you create a virtual disk on a VMFS volume, if you select a fault-tolerant VM, it configures an eagerzeroedthick virtual disk. Alternatively, vmkfstools can be used via the CLI/remote CLI to convert to this disk type.

The eagerzeroedthick virtual disk format is required for the VMware Fault Tolerance (FT) feature on VMFS. (If they are thin or thick virtual disks, conversion occurs automatically as the VMware Fault Tolerance feature is enabled.) It is notable that the use of VMware Fault Tolerance on NFS does not enforce this. The use of the eagerzeroedthick virtual disk format continues to also be used in two cases. The first is that it is mandatory for

Microsoft clusters. VMware maintains a Microsoft clustering guide at the following website: www.vmware.com/pdf/vi3_35/esx_3/r35u2/vi3_35_25_u2_mscs.pdf. The second is that eagerzeroedthick is sometimes recommended in the highest I/O workload virtual machines, where the slight latency and additional I/O created by the "zeroing" that occurs as part of virtual machine I/O to new blocks is unacceptable. An important note is that this performance impact is transient and only perceptible for new filesystem allocations within the virtual machine guest operating system, as these require those parts of the virtual disk to contain zeroes. From a performance standpoint, there is no significant difference between thick and prezeroed virtual once a block to portions of the virtual disk have been written to at least once.

In VMware Infrastructure 3.5, the CLI tools such as the Service Console or RCLI could be used to configure the virtual disk format to any type, but when created via the GUI, certain configurations were the default (with no GUI option to change the type):

◆ On VMFS datastores, new virtual disks defaulted to thick (zeroedthick)

◆ On NFS datastores, new virtual disks defaulted to thin.

◆ Deploying a VM from a template defaulted to eagerzeroedthick format.

◆ Cloning a VM defaulted to an eagerzeroedthick format.

This is why creating a new virtual disk has always been very fast, but in VMware Infrastructure 3.x, cloning a VM or deploying a VM from a template, even with virtual disks that are nearly empty, took much longer.

Also, storage array-level thin-provisioning mechanisms work well with thin and thick formats, but not with the eagerzeroedthick format (since all the blocks are zeroed in advance). Therefore, potential storage savings of storage array-level thin provisioning were lost as virtual machines were cloned or deployed from templates.

In vSphere, the default behavior for datastore types, GUI options, and virtual disk format during clone/template operations have all changed substantially, resulting in far more efficient disk usage. This topic is covered in more detail in the "New vStorage Features in vSphere 4."

ALIGNING VIRTUAL DISKS

Do you need to align the virtual disks? The answer is yes. Although not absolutely mandatory, it's recommended that you follow VMware's recommended best practices for aligning the volumes of guest OSs—and do so across all vendor platforms, and all storage types. These are the same as the very mature standard techniques for aligning the partitions in standard physical configurations from most storage vendors.

Why do this? Aligning a partition aligns the I/O along the underlying RAID stripes of the array, which is particularly important in Windows environments (Windows Server 2008 automatically aligns partitions). This alignment step minimizes the extra I/Os by aligning the I/Os with the array RAID stripe boundaries. Extra I/O work is generated when the I/Os cross the stripe boundary with all RAID schemes, as opposed to a "full stripe write." Aligning the partition provides a more efficient use of what is usually the most constrained storage array resource—IOps. If you align a template and then deploy from a template, you maintain the correct alignment.

Why is it important to do across vendors, and across protocols? Changing the alignment of the guest OS partition is a difficult operation once data has been put in the partition—so it is best done up front when creating a VM, or when creating a template. In the future, you may want to use Storage VMotion to move from one configuration to another, and re-aligning your virtual machines would be next to impossible.

VIRTUAL SCSI ADAPTERS

Virtual SCSI adapters are what you configure on your virtual machines and attach virtual disks and RDMs to. You can have a maximum of 4 virtual adapters per virtual machine, and each virtual adapter can have 15 devices (virtual disks or RDMs). In the guest, each virtual SCSI adapter has its own HBA queue, so for very intense storage workloads, there are advantages to configuring many virtual SCSI adapters within a single guest.

There are several types of virtual adapters in vSphere ESX 4, as shown in Figure 6.48.

FIGURE 6.48
The various virtual SCSI adapters that can be used by a virtual machine. You can configure up to four virtual SCSI adapters for each virtual machine.

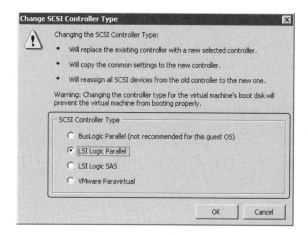

Two of these choices are new and are available only if the virtual machines are upgraded to virtual machine 7 (the virtual machine version determines the configuration options, limits and devices of a virtual machine): the LSI Logic SAS virtual SCSI controller (used for W2K8 cluster support) and the VMware paravirtualized SCSI controller, which delivers higher performance. These will be covered in the "New vStorage Features in vSphere 4" section.

Now we have covered all the fundamentals of storage in VMware environments and can move on to the new and exciting changes to storage in vSphere 4.

New vStorage Features in vSphere 4

In this section, we'll cover all the changes and new features in vSphere 4 that are related to storage. Together, these can result in huge efficiency, availability, and performance improvements for most customers.

Some of these include new features inherent to vSphere:

◆ Thin Provisioning

◆ VMFS Expansion

◆ VMFS Resignature Changes

◆ Hot Virtual Disk Expansion

◆ Storage VMotion Changes

◆ Paravirtualized vSCSI

◆ Improvements to the Software iSCSI Initiator

◆ Storage Management Improvements

And some of these are new features which focus on integration with third party storage-related functionality:

◆ VMDirectPath I/O and SR-IOV

◆ vStorage APIs for Multipathing

◆ vStorage APIs

Let's take a look at what's new!

Thin Provisioning

The virtual disk behavior in vSphere has changed substantially in vSphere 4, resulting in significantly improved storage efficiency. Most customers can reasonably expect up to a 50 percent higher storage efficiency than with ESX/ESXi 3.5, across all storage types. The changes that result in this dramatic efficiency improvement are as follows:

◆ The virtual disk format selection is available in the creation GUI, so you can specify type without reverting to vmkfstools command-line options.

◆ Although vSphere still uses a default format of thick (zeroedthick), for virtual disks created on VMFS datastores (and thin for NFS datastores), in the "Add Hardware" dialog box in the "Create a Disk" step, there's a simple radio button to thin-provision the virtual disk. You should select this if your block storage array doesn't support array-level thin provisioning. If your storage array supports thin provisioning, both thin and thick virtual disk types consume the same amount of actual storage, so you can leave it at the default.

◆ There is a radio button to configure the virtual disk in advance for the VMware Fault Tolerance (FT) feature which employs the eagerzeroedthick virtual disk format on VMFS volumes, or if the disk will be used in a Microsoft Cluster configuration. Figure 6.49 shows the new virtual disk configuration wizard. Note that in vSphere 4 the virtual disk type can be easily selected via the GUI, including thin provisioning across all array and datastore types. Selecting Support Clustering Features Such As Fault Tolerance creates an eagerzeroedthick virtual disk on VMFS datastores.

Perhaps most important, when using the VMware clone or deploy from template operations, vSphere ESX no longer always uses the eagerzeroedthick format. Rather, when you clone a virtual machine or deploy from a template, a dialog box will appear which enables you to select the destination virtual disk type to thin, thick, or the same type as the source (defaults to the same type as the source). In making the use of VMware-level thin provisioning more broadly applicable, improved reporting on space utilization was needed, and if you examine the virtual machine's Resources tab, you'll see it shows the amount of storage used vs. the amount provisioned (Figure 6.50). Here, the VM is configured as having a total of 22.78GB of storage (what appears in the VM as available), but only 3.87GB is actually being used on the physical disk.

FIGURE 6.49
The new virtual disk configuration wizard

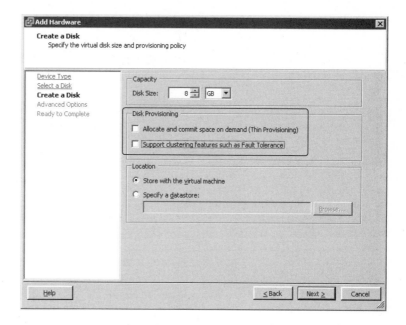

FIGURE 6.50
The Resources tab for a virtual machine now shows more details, including what is used and what is provisioned.

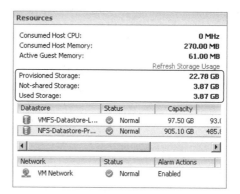

WHY IS THE CHANGE OF BEHAVIOR OF VIRTUAL DISKS DEPLOYED FROM CLONES AND TEMPLATES SO IMPORTANT?

Previously in VMware Infrastructure 3.x, creating a clone of a virtual machine or deploying from a template would always create an eagerzeroedthick virtual disk. This made all storage array-level thin provisioning ineffective in these cases, regardless of your array vendor or protocol type.

Of course this was how customers deployed the majority of their virtual machines!

In vSphere 4, when cloning or deploying from a template, the virtual disk type can be specified in the GUI and is either thin or thick (zeroedthick)—both of which are "storage array thin provisioning friendly" since they don't prezero empty space. This is shown below in Figure 6.51. The new clone and template behavior represents a huge storage savings for customers who upgrade, because most virtual machines are deployed from clones and templates.

FIGURE 6.51
Clone Virtual Machine
Disk Format wizard
screen

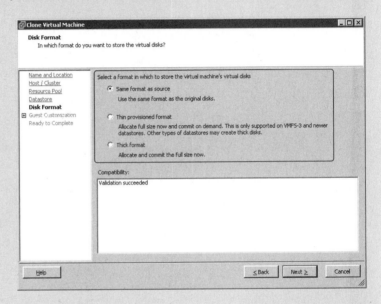

The additional benefit is that this accelerates the actual clone/template operation itself significantly—often completing in a fraction of the time it would in VMware Infrastructure 3.x.

HOW TO CONVERT TO EAGERZEROEDTHICK VIRTUAL DISKS

The virtual disk format can be easily changed from thin to eagerzeroedthick (use cases were noted in the "Virtual Disks" section of this chapter). It can be done via the GUI in two places—but both are somewhat confusing.

The first method is the most straightforward. If you select Perform a Storage VMotion, you can change the virtual disk type. This is simple, but a little confusing as the use of the word "thick" on this dialog box refers to "eagerzeroedthick." This is covered in detail in the section on "Storage VMotion Changes." The other confusing element is that it *requires* that the Storage VMotion go to a different target datastore—in spite of appearing to work if you simply specify the same source and destination datastore.

The second method is a little more convoluted but can be done without actually moving the virtual machine from one datastore to another. It is available in the vSphere Client GUI but not in a "natural" location (which would be on the virtual machine's Settings screen). If you navigate in the datastore browser to a given virtual disk and right-click, you'll see a GUI option for Inflate. If the virtual disk is thin format and is on a VMFS datastore (it is never an option on an NFS datastore), this "inflate" option will be selectable.

The last method is the CLI option—which remains similar to VMware ESX 3.x. At the service console, if using vSphere ESX, the command syntax for this command is as follows:

```
vmkfstools --inflatedisk -a <vSCSI adapter type (buslogic, lsi, etc)
<path to vdmk file>
```

Or if using the remote CLI/vMA (which generally should be preferred regardless of whether using vSphere ESXi where they are mandatory, or vSphere ESX where they are optional), enter the following command:

```
Vmkfstools.pl <conn_options> --inflatedisk -a <vSCSI adapter type
(buslogic, lsi, etc) <path to vdmk file>
```

CAN I SHRINK A VIRTUAL DISK?

You cannot "shrink" a thick or eagerzeroedthick disk to thin format directly through the virtual machine settings in the vSphere client, but you can do this via the new Storage VMotion (discussed later in this section).

THIN PROVISIONING: SHOULD YOU DO IT IN THE ARRAY OR IN VMWARE?

The general answer is that *both* are right.

If your array supports thin provisioning, it's generally more efficient to use array-level thin provisioning in most operational models. If you thick provision at the LUN or file system level, there will always be large amounts of unused space until you start to get it highly utilized, unless you start small and keep extending the datastore, which operationally is heavyweight.

Also, when you use thin provisioning techniques at the array level using NFS or block storage, you always benefit. In vSphere, the common default virtual disk types—both thin and thick (with the exception of eagerzeroedthick, which in vSphere is used far more rarely)—are friendly to storage array-level thin provisioning since they don't prezero the files.

Thin provisioning also tends to be more efficient the larger the scale of the thin pool. On an array, this construct (often called a *pool*) tends to be larger than a single datastore and therefore more efficient, as thin provisioning is more efficient at larger scales of "thinly provisioned objects" in the oversubscribed "pool."

Is there a downside to thin on thin? Not really, if you are able and willing to carefully monitor usage at both the VMware and the storage layer. Use VMware or third-party usage reports in conjunction with array-level reports, and set thresholds with notification and automated action on both the VMware layer and the array level, if your array supports that. (See the "Managed Datastore Objects" section for more information.) Why? Thin provisioning needs to be carefully managed for "out-of-space" conditions, because you are oversubscribing an asset that has no back door. Unlike how VMware oversubscribes guest memory that can use virtual machine swap if needed, if you run out of actual capacity for a datastore, the datastore will be dismounted and cause an outage for the virtual machines. When you use thin on thin, it can be marginally more efficient but can accelerate the transition to oversubscription and an outage.

An example here is instructive. If the total amount of provisioned space at the virtual disk layer in a datastore is 500GB with thick virtual disks, then the datastore needs to be at least 500GB in size, and therefore the LUN or NFS exported file system would need to look as if it were at least 500GB in size. Now, those thick virtual disks are not actually using 500GB; imagine that they are 100GB of used space, and the remainder is empty. If you use thin provisioning at the storage array level, you provisioned a LUN or file system that was 500GB, but only 100GB in the "pool" is used. The space used could not exceed 500GB, so monitoring is needed only at the storage layer.

Conversely, if you used thin virtual disks, technically the datastore would need to be only 100GB in size. The exact same amount of storage is being used (100GB), but clearly there is a possibility of quickly needing more than 100GB, since the virtual disks could grow up to 500GB without any administrative action only the virtual machines are writing more data in their guest operating systems. Therefore, the datastore *and* the underlying storage LUN/file system would need to be monitored closely, and the administrator would need to be ready to respond with more storage on the array and by growing the datastore if needed.

There are only two exceptions to the "always thin provision at the array level if you can" guideline. The first is in the most extreme performance use cases, because the thin-provisioning architectures generally have a performance impact (usually marginal—and this varies from array to array) versus a traditional thick storage configuration. The second are large, high-performance RDBMS storage objects when the amount of array cache is significantly smaller than the database; ergo, the actual back-end spindles are tightly coupled to the host I/O. These database structures have internal logic that generally expect "I/O locality," which is a fancy way of saying that they structure data expecting the on-disk structure to reflect their internal structure. With very large array caches, the host and the back-end spindles with RDBMS-type workloads can be decoupled, and this consideration is irrelevant. These two cases are important but rare. "Always thin provision at the array level if you can" is a good general guiding principle.

VMFS Expansion

The VMFS file system can be easily and dynamically expanded in vSphere without adding extents up to the limit of a single volume (2TB-512 bytes), after which continued expansion requires the addition of volumes and VMFS extents.

VMFS volumes in vSphere can be expanded up to the 2TB-512 byte limit, and further increases can be achieved using spanned extents. In Figure 6.52, which shows a datastore's properties, you can click Increase.

If the LUN has more capacity than has been configured in the VMFS partition, because most modern storage arrays can nondisruptively add capacity by extending a LUN, it will reflect that in the Expandable column (Figure 6.53). After clicking Next twice, Figure 6.54 shows the result: a single VMFS partition that is 110GB in size.

VMFS Resignature Changes

Whenever a LUN is presented to an ESX host to be used as a VMFS datastore, it is signed with a VMFS signature. The ESX hosts and vSphere clusters also track the LUNs with an identifier. This identifier was and the LUN identifier was the LUN ID on older ESX 3.*x* versions and the NAA as of ESX 3.5. Prior to vSphere, when a VMFS volume was presented to an ESX cluster that the cluster had previously or currently accessed (with the same VMFS signature but a different

LUN identifier), how the event was handled was relatively complex. Managing the storage device in that case required changing advanced settings such as DisallowSnapshotLUN=0 and LVM.EnableResignature=1. This had two problems: the first was that it was a general ESX host setting, not a LUN-specific setting, and so applied universally to all the LUN objects on that ESX host; the second was that it was a little confusing.

FIGURE 6.52
Click Increase.

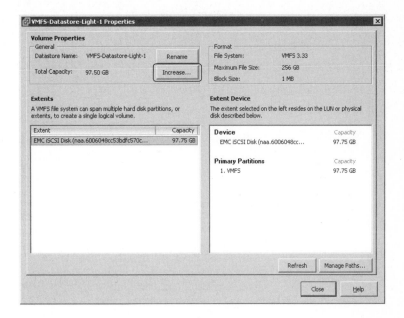

FIGURE 6.53
Yes, it's expandable.

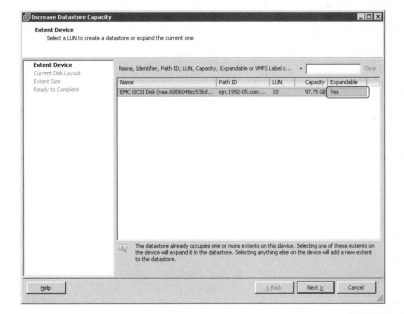

FIGURE 6.54
VMFS file system that
spans extents

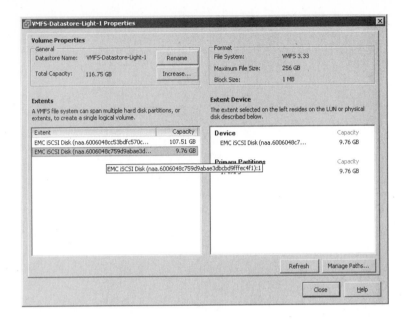

In vSphere 4, when the same condition occurs, a new, simple GUI appears when using the Add Storage option; you have three possibilities:

◆ Keep The Existing Signature is the equivalent of setting DisallowSnapshotLUN = 0 and LVM.EnableResignature = 0.

◆ Assign A New Signature is the equivalent of setting DisallowSnapshotLUN = 0 and LVM.EnableResignature = 1.

◆ Format The Disk.

The benefit is that these options are simple, clear, and transient (unlike the prior advanced settings techniques that required setting the value, completing the action, and then reverting it to the original state). It's also a LUN-specific, not ESX-wide, setting.

Hot Virtual Disk Expansion

Prior to vSphere, extending a virtual disk required that the virtual machine not be running. In vSphere, that ability can be executed while the virtual machine is on (Figure 6.55).

There are a few caveats to extending virtual disks. First, the virtual machine needs to be virtual machine type version 7 (you can upgrade the virtual machine type by right clicking on the virtual machine and selecting "Upgrade Virtual Hardware"). Extending a virtual disk that is in the eagerzeroedthick format cannot be done via the GUI whether the virtual machine is on or off.

Storage VMotion Changes

Storage VMotion was a feature introduced in VMware Infrastructure 3.5, and it became immediately very popular because it eliminated two of the common causes of planned downtime: moving a virtual machine from one datastore to another; and storage array maintenance or upgrades.

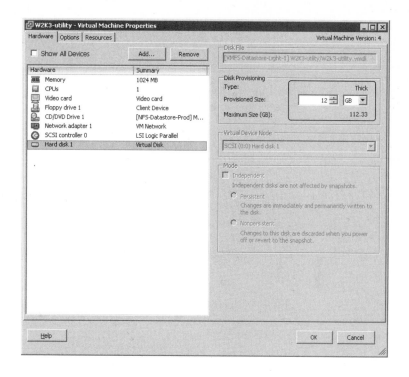

The use cases were broad, and none required that a VM be turned off. Here is a list of key use cases:

◆ Moving a virtual machine for performance optimization (moving from a slow datastore to a fast datastore, and vice versa)

◆ Moving a virtual machine for capacity optimization (from a highly utilized datastore to a less utilized datastore)

◆ For storage tiering (moving noncritical VMs from datastores on Fibre Channel drives to datastores on SATA drives)

◆ Wholesale nondisruptive array migration

Some of these use cases are also possible at the array level on various arrays with virtualized storage features.

The advantage of doing this at the array or fabric level for both block devices (LUNs) and NAS devices (files) is that the capability can be applied to non-VMware ESX hosts, and that, generally, these virtualized storage capabilities can generally move storage at two to ten times the speed of VMware Storage VMotion. Virtualized storage functionality comes in two types.

The first type are cases where the "storage virtualization" is done within the array itself. An example of this type of function is the EMC Virtual LUNs capability.

The second type are cases where the "storage virtualization" can be done across multiple arrays also generally in heterogeneous storage environments. Examples of this second type include EMC Invista, EMC Rainfinity, IBM SVC, HDS USP-V, and NetApp vFilers.

SO . . . WHAT QUALIFIES AS STORAGE VIRTUALIZATION?

This is a case where there are so many ways to define a topic that it tends to result in no consistent definition.

All vendors typically take a self-centered position on this topic. If you look at VMware as the "example" of Server virtualization, it can be instructive in comparison.

On the one hand, "internal to array" storage virtualization helps drive increased consolidation, oversubscription, and non-disruptive change—all attributes of what VMware does for servers.

On the other hand, only "external to array" storage virtualization can drive that consolidation and oversubscription across multiple heterogeneous arrays. They can also help for non-disruptive full-array migrations in heterogeneous environments. VMware does this for heterogeneous servers to be sure, but the analogy is a little more complex, as unlike the server case, which are extreme commodities, today most customers leverage advanced array functions.

All the "external to array" storage virtualization techniques involve the storage arrays themselves presenting storage to something in the middle—between the host. At that point, the characteristics of the storage in *every way* are determined by the "storage virtualization" device in the middle—for better and worse. Every feature, every capability, all the performance and availability characteristics are now those of the "storage virtualization" device and not the storage arrays themselves. Traditionally, these have fewer capabilities and lower availability designs than a storage array—though over time that may change.

In this author's opinion, all storage arrays are "virtualized" by almost any definition because they abstract the physical from the logical and allow the oversubscription of resources for higher efficiencies. This enables flexibility for administrators and the ability to change critical attributes on the fly and non-disruptively should be considered mandatory array capabilities of any modern array.

For large customers with many arrays and a heterogeneous storage environment they should evaluate and consider the trade-off advantages and disadvantages of a heterogeneous storage virtualization strategy using devices external to the storage arrays themselves.

The disadvantage of the array and fabric level of storage virtualization and data mobility is that the operations tend to occur at the datastore level, not at the more granular virtual machine or even virtual disk level. The only exceptions are file virtualization technologies such as EMC Rainfinity that operate on individual files, not LUNs or file systems. Another disadvantage of the array- and fabric-level options is that they depend on specific hardware.

Because Storage VMotion brought similar capabilities to anyone using VMware Infrastructure 3.5 with no dependency on any other hardware or software and had many very important use cases, it immediately became widely used.

In vSphere, Storage VMotion has been dramatically improved, with both immediately apparent superficial changes and also significant "under the hood" changes.

Immediately visible is that Storage VMotion now has a GUI interface: right-click and choose Migrate (Figure 6.56).

It's notable that the GUI provides three options (Change Host, Change Datastore, and Change Both Host And Datastore), but only VMotion *or* Storage VMotion can be selected while the virtual machine is on. The third option (changing both at the same time) is available only when the virtual machine is off, although you can relocate the host where a VM is executing and relocate the datastore where it resides nondisruptively—just do VMotion and Storage VMotion in sequence.

FIGURE 6.56
Storage VMotion in
vSphere has a GUI.

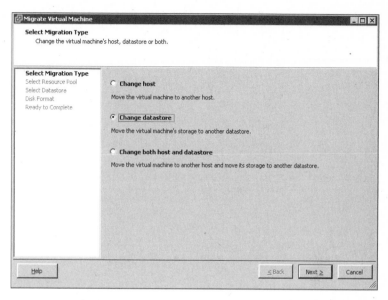

Storage VMotion is now supported on all protocols. VMFS (both iSCSI, Fibre Channel, and FCoE) was supported in ESX 3.5, and NFS is now supported as a source or a destination (Figure 6.57). RDMs are also widely supported. You can use Storage VMotion to migrate from RDM to RDM (both physical compatibility mode and virtual mode), as well as from RDM to virtual disk.

FIGURE 6.57
NFS datastores as source
or target

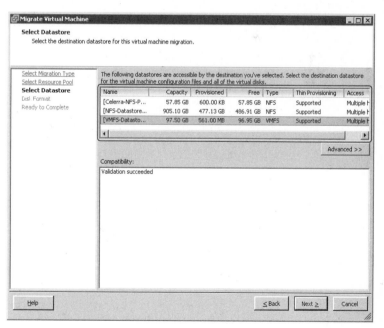

In vSphere, Storage VMotion can have any type of datastore as a source and as a target. It can even be used for virtual RDM to virtual RDM and also from virtual RDM to virtual disk.

The Storage VMotion GUI maintains the extreme flexibility to even move *portions* of a VM—moving some virtual disks to one location and moving others to another location (Figure 6.58).

FIGURE 6.58
Storage VMotion can provide a degree of control and granularity not available in any storage array or fabric virtualization, namely, the ability to move parts of a virtual machine as specified.

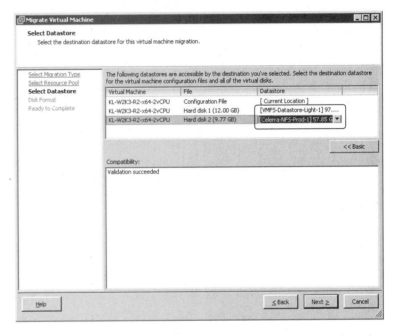

Perhaps more important (but less visible) are the substantial changes under the hood. Understanding these changes requires a short examination on how Storage VMotion worked in VMware Infrastructure 3.5. Figure 6.59 shows the sequence of steps that occur during a Storage VMotion operation in VMware Infrastructure 3.5.

FIGURE 6.59
Storage VMotion internals with VMware Infrastructure 3.5

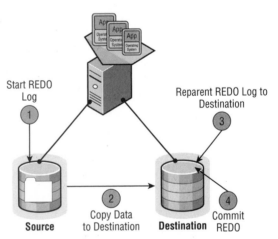

In VMware Infrastructure 3.5, as shown in Figure 6.59, Storage VMotion starts with the process of an ESX snapshot (step 1), after which the closed VMDK files are copied to the destination (step 2). Then the redo file logs are gradually "reparented" until they are in sync with the source (step 3), at which point they are committed (step 4). The speed of this process is heavily dependent on the performance of the source and destination datastores and on the contention from the workloads in those datastores. However, 1GB/minute is achievable, and on large-scale migrations, where Storage VMotion across multiple datastores are used in parallel, +5GB/minute is achievable.

HOW MANY STORAGE VMOTIONS CAN BE DONE AT ONCE?

One Storage VMotion per datastore at once is a recommended limit, and 4 simultaneous Storage VMotion operations per ESX host at once is hard limit. These limits are the same between VMware Infrastructure 3.x and vSphere 4.

In vSphere, Storage VMotion operates in some substantially improved ways as shown in Figure 6.60. One of the major changes is the file snapshot-centric mechanism has been changed to a new mechanism: changed block tracking (CBT). It's much faster in general, and it's significantly faster and more reliable during the final stages of the Storage VMotion operation.

FIGURE 6.60
The new Storage VMotion internal operations in vSphere 4

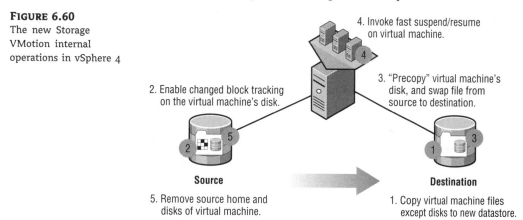

4. Invoke fast suspend/resume on virtual machine.

2. Enable changed block tracking on the virtual machine's disk.

3. "Precopy" virtual machine's disk, and swap file from source to destination.

Source

Destination

5. Remove source home and disks of virtual machine.

1. Copy virtual machine files except disks to new datastore.

During a Storage VMotion operation in vSphere 4, the first step is that all the files except the VMDKs are copied to the new target location. The second step is that Changed Block Tracking is enabled. The third step is that the bulk of the existing VDMK and vswap files are copied to the new location. During this third step, the changed block locations can be stored on disk or in memory; for most operations, usually memory is used. Subsequently, the baseline blocks are synchronized from the source to the destination—much like with VMotion and then changed blocks. First, these occur in large groups, and then they occur in subsequently smaller and smaller iterations. After they are nearly synchronized, the fourth step occurs, which encompasses a fast suspend/resume interval, which is all that is required to complete the final copy operation. At this point, the virtual machine is running with the virtual disks in the new location. The final, fifth step is when source home and source disks are removed.

This new mechanism is considerably faster than the mechanism used in ESX 3.5 and eliminates the need for the 2× memory requirement needed in 3.5. It should be noted that the primary determinant of Storage VMotion operation speed is still the bandwidth of the source and the destination datastores.

STORAGE VMOTION PERFORMANCE IMPACT

Storage VMotion applies a heavy additional I/O workload on the source and destination datastore.

The workload created by Storage VMotion (reading from the source and writing to the target) tends to be large-block, sequential I/O patterns driving a large amount of bandwidth (MBps). Conversely, the general virtual machine workloads on the source and destination datastores are random, smaller-block (as they are a mix of different I/O sizes) I/O patterns.

This results in the Storage VMotion workload's tendency to dominate and "swamp" the normal VM I/O workload on the source and destination datastores, increasing their guest-level latency (ms response time) and decreasing their guest-level bandwidth (MBps) and throughput (IOps).

There is no "throttle" on Storage VMotion (as there is on VMotion), and it is not governed in any way by DRS rules.

In very performance sensitive environments, scheduling Storage VMotion operations is a best practice.

Several important Storage VMotion restrictions remain in vSphere 4, the most important of which is that any preexisting snapshots need to be removed.

It's notable that during a Storage VMotion operation, the virtual disk format can be changed from thin to eagerzeroedthick.

STORAGE VMOTION ISN'T CHANGING THE VIRTUAL DISK TYPE THE WAY I EXPECT - WHAT AM I DOING WRONG?

The GUI for the virtual disk type during a Storage VMotion isn't entirely clear. The destination format options shown are "thin" and "thick." In this dialog box, "thick" refers to "eagerzeroedthick." This is an important difference from the dialogs during the creation of the virtual machine's virtual disk, where if you don't select "thin," the default on VMFS is the "thick" (or zeroedthick) format. This means you can use the Storage VMotion GUI to go from thin to eagerzeroedthick virtual disk formats and back, but not to the "thick" (zeroedthick) format.

Also, while the Storage VMotion GUI suggests that you could have the same source and destination datastore (simply using Storage VMotion as a "non-disruptive virtual disk format change"), the operation will complete successfully in the task list, but no changes will occur. To do this, you need to use the "inflate" option—see the Thin Provisioning section above.

This can happen in both directions, including going from eagerzeroedthick to thin.

Paravirtualized vSCSI

VMware introduced its first paravirtualized I/O driver in VMware Infrastructure 3.5, with the use of the VMXNET network driver installed when you install VMware Tools. (It has been updated to the third generation, VMXNET3, with the vSphere 4 release.) Paravirtualized guest OS drivers communicate more directly with the underlying Virtual Machine Monitor (VMM); they deliver higher throughput and lower latency, and they usually significantly lower the CPU impact of the I/O operations.

In vSphere, VMware has included a paravirtualized virtual SCSI adapter that can be easily selected in the virtual machine's settings (Figure 6.61).

FIGURE 6.61
The new paravirtualized
SCSI controller type

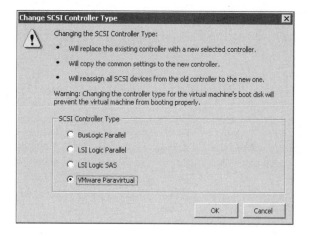

In testing, the paravirtualized SCSI driver has shown 30 percent improvements in performance for virtual disks stored on VMFS datastores supported by iSCSI-connected targets, and it has shown between 10 percent and 50 percent improvement for Fiber Channel–connected targets in terms of throughput (IOps) at a given CPU utilization (or lower CPU utilization at a given IOps). In fact, it often delivered half the latency as observed from the guest.

Improvements to the Software iSCSI Initiator

The iSCSI software initiator has undergone substantial improvements in vSphere ESX 4 in many areas.

As with the Storage VMotion changes in vSphere, the changes to the ESX software iSCSI initiator has both immediately apparent superficial changes and also significant "under the hood" changes.

The immediately apparent changes are as follows:

◆ vSphere ESX 4 no longer needs an iSCSI Service Console port. All iSCSI session control and data communication occurs via the iSCSI VMkernel port.

◆ iSCSI security options have been expanded to include mutual (or bidirectional) CHAP. This has both the initiator authenticating to the array and the array authenticating to the initiator. This is not supported by all iSCSI targets, so check with your array vendor.

◆ It has improved support for advanced hardware offload and error checking.

However, the most important changes are those that are "under the hood." These require a short historical detour to examine the behavior of the iSCSI initiator in ESX 3.x.

The ESX 3.x iSCSI initiator supported only a single iSCSI session to a given iSCSI target, and each session could support only a single TCP/connection (Figure 6.62). This resulted in the practical maximum throughput when using the ESX iSCSI software initiator to connect to any iSCSI target (and all the LUNs behind the iSCSI target) being limited to the bandwidth of a single Ethernet link. Also, in ESX 3.x there were no abilities to distribute I/O workloads down multiple targets to a single LUN. Remember that all iSCSI arrays operate differently—some have a single iSCSI

FIGURE 6.62

In ESX 3.*x*, the software iSCSI initiator could have only one TCP connection per iSCSI session and one iSCSI session per target.

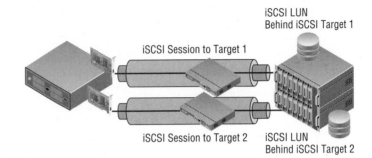

iSCSI LUN
Behind iSCSI Target 1

iSCSI Session to Target 1

iSCSI Session to Target 2

iSCSI LUN
Behind iSCSI Target 2

LUN for every iSCSI target, some have a single iSCSI LUN exposed via multiple iSCSI targets, and some have many iSCSI LUNs exposed behind a single target.

In vSphere ESX 4, the ground-up rewrite of the iSCSI initiator improves CPU efficiency in general and now supports multiple iSCSI sessions per iSCSI target. Although there can still be only a single TCP connection per iSCSI session (ergo no multiple connections per session), the fact that there are multiple iSCSI sessions (each with one TCP connection) means that bandwidth and throughput to a single iSCSI target can be aggregated across multiple links to a single target as shown in Figure 6.63.

FIGURE 6.63

In vSphere ESX 4, the software iSCSI initiator can still have only one TCP connection per iSCSI session but can have multiple iSCSI sessions per target.

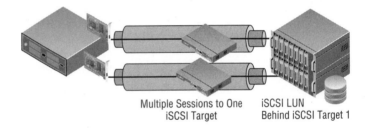

Multiple Sessions to One
iSCSI Target

iSCSI LUN
Behind iSCSI Target 1

Why is this important? Remember, with block storage, the multipathing occurs in the storage stack using MPIO, and the "on-ramp" for MPIO is the iSCSI port, which is the endpoint of an iSCSI session. In vSphere, this multipathing portion of the storage stack has been significantly enhanced and enables the possibility of driving I/O down multiple paths simultaneously (see "Pluggable Storage Architecture"). However, the MPIO stack still needs multiple iSCSI ports and multiple paths to a LUN to have any chance of driving across multiple links.

For iSCSI that present a single LUN across multiple iSCSI targets, and one session per target, the only iSCSI initiator configuration steps are to bind the iSCSI initiator to multiple ESX host interfaces. The LUN is accessible via several targets—which by definition means multiple iSCSI sessions each with one iSCSI port. Driving I/O down multiple paths therefore doesn't depend on reconfiguring the iSCSI initiator to connect to a single target multiple times and simply involves changing the multipathing configuration (see "Pluggable Storage Architecture").

But for iSCSI arrays that present one or multiple LUNs behind a single iSCSI target, configuring the environment to drive multiple Ethernet links end-to-end involves two steps. The first is the same as the paragraph above—binding the iSCSI initiator to multiple vmnic interfaces. The second step is that iSCSI target needs to be configured to have multiple IP addresses and multiple interfaces in its iSCSI Network Portal. At that point, the initiator would need to be able to drive multiple iSCSI ports to a single iSCSI target after the same multipathing configuration.

Check with your vendor for the specific instructions (as this can also be handled using the Pluggable Storage Architecture via third part integration modules).

Let's see how we can bind the vSphere 4 initiator to multiple vmnic interfaces!

Binding the iSCSI Initiator to Multiple Interfaces

The following sequence is not entirely simple. The best practice is to configure this before you start using the iSCSI LUN for various purposes.

First, this is what the GUI will tend to look like before configuring multiple paths. The number of paths shown will be a function of the number of Ethernet ports the LUN is visible on (in this case, there is only one Ethernet port on the target). Even though there may be many targets shown, if physical NICs are simply aggregated on the vSwitch with the iSCSI VMkernel NIC, only one Ethernet link will be used by the ESX host (Figure 6.64).

FIGURE 6.64
An iSCSI LUN with a single path

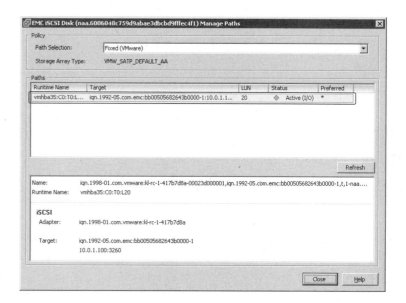

Perform the following steps to add an iSCSI session to an iSCSI target and configure round-robin multipathing to drive I/O down both Ethernet links:

1. In the vSphere client, assign the VMkernel iSCSI NIC to a specific physical NIC by overriding the vSwitch aggregation default policy. On the Networking tab, examine the properties of the vSwitch (Figure 6.65).

   Note how the link aggregation assigns both ports as active (Figure 6.66). This will also need to be changed.

2. Add a second VMkernel NIC for iSCSI (and give it an affinity to another physical NIC), as shown in Figure 6.67.

FIGURE 6.65
The vSwitch properties;
the configuration here
requires some changes.

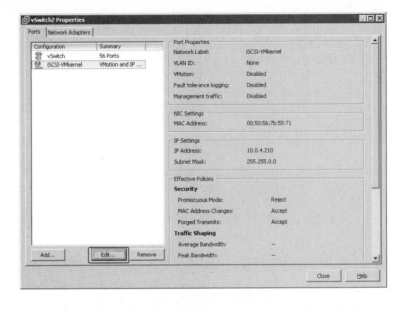

FIGURE 6.66
Multiple VMkernel
ports for iSCSI

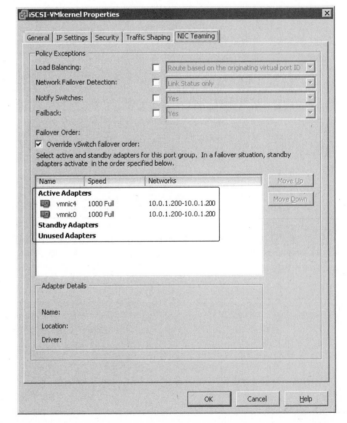

FIGURE 6.67
Add a second iSCSI
VMkernel NIC, and
specify the physical
NIC binding.

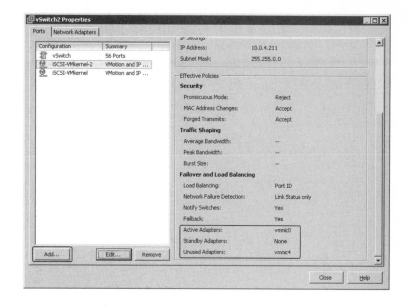

3. Configure the software iSCSI initiator to use both VMkernel NICs. You can do this via the
   CLI (vSphere ESX 4 only) or RCLI or vMA (vSphere ESX 4 and ESXi 4). First, you need to
   find the VMkernel NIC names. Using vSphere vMA, use the following command:

   ```
   vicfg-vmknic -l
   ```

   to see that the two iSCSI VMkernel NICs created in earlier steps are vmk2 and vmk3
   (Figure 6.68).

FIGURE 6.68
Issuing vicfg-vmknic
-l, you can see that
the iSCSI-VMkernel
port is using the vmk2
interface and that
the iSCSI-VMkernel-2
port is using the
vmk3 interface.

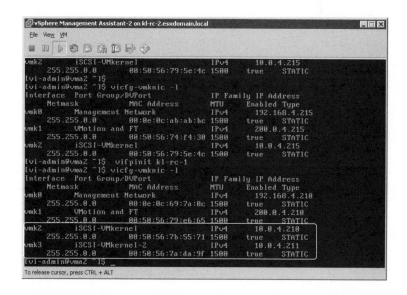

Next check the iSCSI SW initiator vmhba name in the Storage Adapters section, and then force the iSCSI software initiator to use all the vmknics. (In this example, the command is issued twice, once with VMkernelportname as vmk2 and also with vmk3). Issue the following command:

```
`esxcli swiscsi nic add -n VMkernelportname -d vmhba_name`
```

This change might require a reboot to take effect. Returning to the multipathing screen, if all the steps were successfully completed, you will see a larger number of paths for the target LUN (Figure 6.69). If you had two paths to start (two array ports) and added three ESX host software iSCSI VMkernel ports, you will see a total of six paths (two times three). In this example, I started with one path, and now there are two shown. Note that only one path is still being used for all the I/O.

FIGURE 6.69
After those configuration steps, the same iSCSI LUN shows two paths.

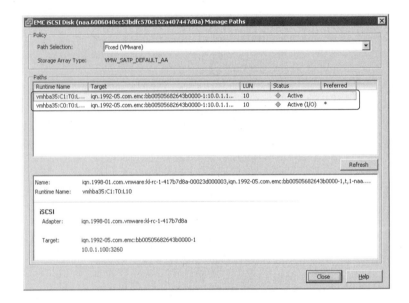

The Pluggable Storage Architecture (see "Storage Management Improvements") now has multiple iSCSI sessions to load balance. The native Storage Array Type plug-in (SATP) detects all arrays against the native SATP list and applies either the fixed or most recently used (MRU) Path Selection plug-in (PSP).

4. Configure the round-robin path selection policy (Figure 6.70). To actually use both paths, either force a change to the Round Robin PSP setting or use a third-party multipathing plug-in (MPP) such as EMC PowerPath/VE.

WHAT'S THE MAXIMUM NUMBER OF LINKS THAT YOU CAN USE FOR ISCSI?

You can use the method shown earlier to drive I/O down eight separate vmnics. Testing has shown that vSphere is able to drive 9Gbps of iSCSI throughput through a single ESX host.

FIGURE 6.70
If you select the Round Robin, you can see that both paths are active.

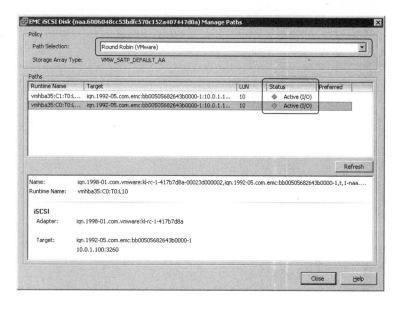

Although this sequence might seem somewhat complex, this is a major leap forward. The ability to drive more than a single Ethernet link for a *single* storage object has been difficult in VMware environments either with iSCSI-based VMFS datastores/RDMs or with NFS datastores. For Fibre Channel and FCoE, there was also no way to drive I/O across multiple Fibre Channel ports for a single LUN prior to vSphere (due to the lack of more sophisticated path selection policies in the MPIO stack that also affected iSCSI), but the higher throughput of a single link tended to minimize that restriction. For cases with Gigabit Ethernet, the only mainstream way was to drive *aggregate* bandwidth by using many iSCSI targets and many NFS datastores. However, no one would use more than one link because link aggregation techniques work only if there are many TCP sessions. Many customers were okay with this, particularly if the VMs were small-block I/O and therefore IOps-centric, not MBps-centric.

Historically, with VMware ESX 3.x there were only four workarounds for iSCSI storage customers needing large bandwidth (MBps) to a single storage object. These are still options in vSphere in cases where multiple Ethernet links need to be used for a single iSCSI target, but for some reason MPIO at the VMkernel layer is not desired. These workarounds are as follows:

◆ Use in-guest iSCSI initiators like the Microsoft iSCSI initiator, which uses the virtual machine networks, not the VMkernel networks.

◆ Use spanned VMFS volumes and multiple separate iSCSI LUNs, each with their own iSCSI target. Remember that in versions prior to ESX 3.5, the limit is one iSCSI session/TCP connection per *target,* and each target can have one or more LUNs behind it.

◆ Use 10GbE, using a larger transport bandwidth to get around the one TCP session per target (and therefore one link only) limit.

◆ Switch to Fibre Channel or FCoE for a given LUN; some arrays can migrate a LUN between iSCSI and Fibre Channel/FCoE transparently.

With this new capability, multiple Ethernet links can be used for high throughput (MBps) to single VMFS datastores or RDMs using iSCSI.

Storage Management Improvements

As VMware environments scale, visualizing the underlying infrastructure becomes more critical for planning and troubleshooting. Also, efficiency starts with having an accurate view of how you're using the assets already deployed. Where is there free capacity? How thin is the thin provisioning? It's not only a question of efficiency but also availability. Being able to plan the capacity utilization of a system is important for predictive planning and avoiding out-of-space conditions.

It's for these reasons that customers use tools, and it's why VMware has a new Storage Views tab with maps and reporting functions in vCenter 4. These native tools represent a small subset of the capabilities, granularity, and visibility provided by enterprise storage resource management tools that integrate with the vCenter APIs under the VMware Ready program, such as EMC Control Center and Storage Scope, Vkernel, Vizoncore, Veeam and others.

Let's examine the new tools available in vSphere 4 to get improved visibility, reporting, and manageability of the storage that vSphere uses.

STORAGE VIEW REPORTS AND MAPS

The Storage Views tab in the vCenter cluster-level view has two views: Reports and Maps.

HAVING TROUBLE GETTING STORAGE VIEW REPORTS AND MAPS WORKING?

The features of the Storage Views tab are dependent on the VMware VirtualCenter Management Webservices service. Check to make sure this service is started by navigating to the Windows Services Microsoft Management Console (MMC) on the vCenter server and manually starting the service if necessary.

The Reports view provides "at-a-glance" reports on the multipathing state, space consumption of the VMs and their snapshots, and other details, as shown in Figure 6.71. The report can be customized and sorted. By navigating to different levels in the vCenter datacenter view, you can get different levels of detail. The reports can be easily exported in Excel, CSV, and XML, and as web pages.

FIGURE 6.71
The new Storage Views tab's views; viewing the virtual machine details

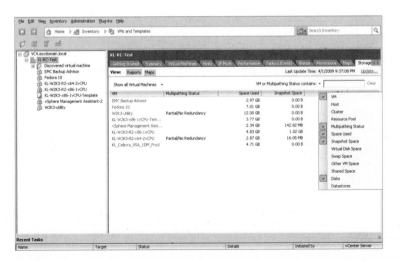

A great example use of the Reports view is to solve the riddle of how much storage space is being consumed by snapshots and which are the greatest unexpected consumers of storage capacity. If those snapshots are not needed, you can collapse the snapshots and reclaim the space.

The other feature of the new Storage View tab is the new Maps view (Figure 6.72). Maps provide a visual representation of the relationships of the storage objects in a way that is simple and easy to understand. The relationships are shown with a little more detail than the reports in vSphere, including multipathing details, the arrays, and the LUNs behind them. The reports now have a simple zoom control and can be exported in most graphics formats and also the Visio-compatible EMF format.

FIGURE 6.72

The new Storage Views tab's Maps view; a simple visual representation of the entire storage configuration

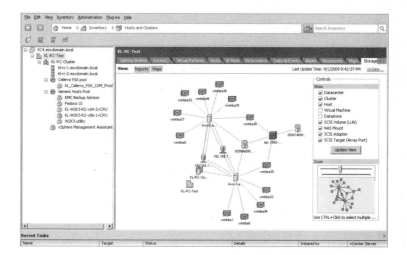

MANAGED DATASTORE OBJECTS

Managed datastore objects are a major improvement in vSphere regarding storage. Now that datastores are managed objects, it is possible to limit access control to specific vCenter users and to assign alerts and actions against the datastores.

Datastores can also be grouped in folders and can have permissions applied (Figure 6.73).

Alerts and actions are particularly useful in environments where users can self-provision VMs or where tools such as VMware Lab Manager are used to create virtual machines rapidly. This sort of self-service or automation makes it more complex to track capacity usage. To set alerts on datastores, navigate to the Datastore inventory view, right-click a datastore, and choose Alarm ➤ Add Alarm.

Alerts can be set on datastores and VMs for many triggers and can be composite triggers. These alerts can be used to check and help manage critical storage events that previously would have been difficult to track and would have passed unheeded (Figure 6.74). Some examples are as follows:

◆ Is the datastore 80 percent full?

◆ Has the datastore been oversubscribed (including thin provisioning) beyond 75 percent?

◆ Has the datastore become unavailable to any ESX host in the cluster?

◆ Is a VM using more than 100GB of storage?

◆ Is a VM using more than 50GB of snapshot space?

FIGURE 6.73
Configuring datastore
folders and datastore
permissions

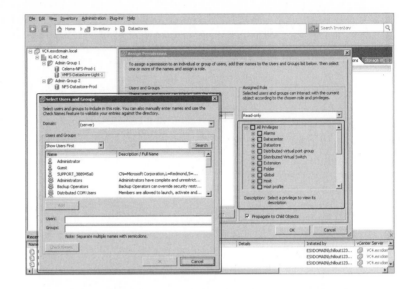

FIGURE 6.74
Configuring datastore
alarm triggers

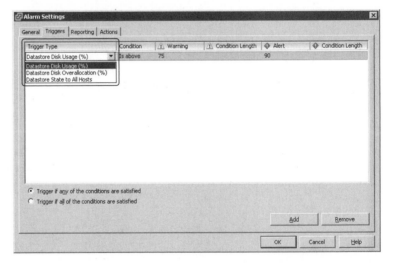

Based on those triggers, if the event occurs, a series of actions can be taken, as shown in
Figure 6.75: sending an email, setting an SNMP trap, or running a command. This gives the flexibility of almost any action based on the event trigger.

CLUSTER-WIDE RESCAN

With vSphere 4, it is much simpler to manage block storage at the level of a cluster, rather than
one individual ESX host at a time. This can be particularly useful for very large clusters. Although
scanning for new devices can still be done at the individual host level, right-clicking an ESX cluster
object gives you the Rescan For Datastores option. Additionally, rescan times have significantly
improved with vSphere 4.

FIGURE 6.75
Configuring datastore
alarm actions

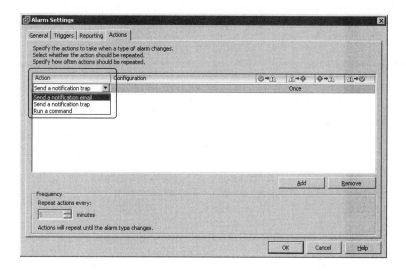

VMDirectPath I/O and SR-IOV

The two technologies discussed in this section, VMDirectPath I/O and SR-IOV are best thought of as "emerging technology areas" rather than mainstream use cases for most vSphere users. They are not required for the vast majority of virtualization use cases.

VMDirectPath I/O is a VMware technology that can be used with I/O hardware to reduce the CPU impact of high-bandwidth throughput workloads by "bypassing" the hypervisor. It is supported for specific networking adapters in vSphere ESX 4, and it is experimental for specific storage adapters in vSphere ESX 4.

When VMDirectPath is enabled, the guest I/O devices are able to bypass the virtualization layer completely. It leverages Intel I/O Acceleration Technology (Intel I/O AT) and Intel Virtualization Technology for Directed I/O (VT-d) for networking, and it leverages Fibre Channel N_Port ID Virtualization (NPIV) for storage devices. These specific hardware dependencies limit the first generation of VMDirectPath in vSphere ESX 4 to specific devices. Supported VMDirectPath I/O configurations for networks are limited to specific interfaces based on the Intel 82598 10 Gigabit Ethernet Controller. Experimental configurations for storage are limited to storage I/O devices with the QLogic QLA25xx 8Gb Fibre Channel and the LSI 3442e-R and 3801e (1068 chip–based) 3Gb SAS adapters.

In vSphere 4, use of the VMDirectPath disables many advanced VMware functions for the virtual machine with any VMDirectPath-enabled device, including the following:

◆ VMotion

◆ Hot add/remove of virtual devices

◆ Suspend and resume

◆ Record and replay

◆ Fault tolerance

◆ High availability

◆ Memory overcommitment and page sharing

The development direction for VMDirectPath is evaluating the ability to move the I/O stream nondisruptively in and out of "pass-through" and "virtual" I/O paths.

The ultimate goal of VMDirectPath is to provide further CPU offload and efficiency with *very* heavy I/O workloads. To be explicit, VMDirectPath is not required for these very high-bandwidth workloads as vSphere has demonstrated it's ability to support them without VMDirectPath I/O, but rather it can support them more efficiently by using less ESX server CPU cycles via hardware offloads.

Enabling VMDirectPath is done in the vSphere client and requires a one-time ESX host reboot.

Likewise, Single Root I/O Virtualization (SR-IOV) is an emerging technology standard that enables a single physical PCI device function (generally network or storage I/O adapters) to be virtualized into multiple virtual functions and can be used for VMware and non-VMware use cases. SR-IOV is noted here, because it can enable a single physical interface to be used by multiple virtual machines even when VMDirectPath is used to communicate directly to the hardware. While SR-IOV can be used generally to make a single PCI device appear to the host (in this case the vSphere ESX server), exposing those multiple devices directly to the guest requires a hypervisor bypass such as NPIV or IOV, and these can benefit from VMDirectPath for CPU offload). In these configurations, the device is represented by physical functions (PF) supported by PF drivers in the VMkernel. A shipping example of SR-IOV is the Cisco Palo Mezzanine card available for the Cisco Unified Computer System (UCS) blades and Cisco rack-mount servers. This allows a single mezzanine card interface to logically appear as up to 128 different interfaces to the ESX layer.

Figure 6.76 shows a logical diagram of how SR-IOV can access a single physical adapter as several logical interfaces and how those can be accessed through the virtualization layer or by bypassing the virtualization layer.

FIGURE 6.76
SR-IOV can access a single physical adapter as several logical interfaces.

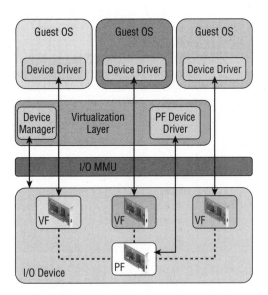

VMDirectPath and SR-IOV represent possible future directions for vSphere and virtualization in general but will be relatively rarely used in the near term.

Conversely, several of the vStorage APIs represent the future direction of vSphere and also are immediately useful for all use cases.

vStorage APIs for Multipathing

In vSphere 4, VMware and VMware technology partners have spent considerable effort overhauling how the elements of the ESX storage stack that deal with multipathing work. The VMware ESX 4 stack has been updated with the vStorage APIs for Multipathing or Pluggable Storage Architecture (PSA), as shown in Figure 6.77.

FIGURE 6.77
The vSphere PSA model

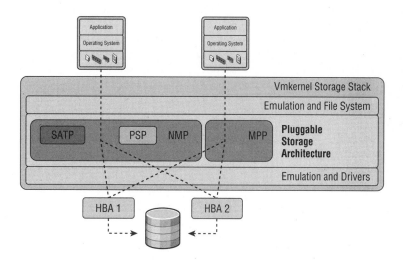

In VMware ESX 3.5, the storage multipathing behavior of VMware Infrastructure was relatively primitive and rigid, and after earlier sections, it should be clear how critical the storage infrastructure can be for a virtualized datacenter. On a host boot or bus rescan, the array ID was presented via SCSI commands, and the multipathing policy was set based on fixed lists of array failover types for a given set of arrays. This architecture was very rigid and was updated only between major VMware releases.

In vSphere ESX 4, the modular Pluggable Storage Architecture makes multipathing behavior in vSphere much more flexible. There are four modules:

◆ Native Multipathing plug-in (NMP)

◆ Storage Array Type plug-in (SATP)

◆ Path Selection plug-in (PSP)

◆ Multipathing plug-in (MPP)

An ESX host can have multiple modules in use at any point and can be connected to multiple arrays, and the combination of which modules are used (a NMP/SATP/PSP combination or a MPP) can be configured on a LUN-by-LUN basis.

Let's see how they work together.

NMP MODULE

The NMP module handles overall MPIO behavior and array identification. The NMP leverages the SATP and PSP modules and isn't generally configured in any way.

SATP MODULES

SATP modules handle path failover for a given storage array and determine the failover type for a LUN.

vSphere ESX/ESXi 4 ships with SATPs for a broad set of arrays and with generic SATPs for nonspecified arrays (and a local SATP for local storage). The SATP modules contain the rules on how to handle array-specific actions or behavior, as well as any specific operations needed to manage array paths. This makes the NMP modular (unlike the NMP in prior versions); it doesn't need to contain the array-specific logic, and additional modules for new arrays can be added without changing the NMP. Using the SCSI Array ID that reported via a SCSI query, the NMP selects the appropriate SATP to use. After that, the SATP monitors, deactivates, and activates paths (and when a manual rescan occurs, detects new paths)—providing information up to the NMP. The SATP also performs array-specific tasks such as activating passive paths on active/passive arrays.

To see what array SATP modules exist, enter the following command:

```
esxcli nmp satp list
```

It returns these results (note that the default PSP for a given SATP is also shown):

```
Name                Default PSP     Description
VMW_SATP_ALUA_CX    VMW_PSP_FIXED   Supports EMC CX that use the ALUA protocol
VMW_SATP_SVC        VMW_PSP_FIXED   Supports IBM SVC
VMW_SATP_MSA        VMW_PSP_MRU     Supports HP MSA
VMW_SATP_EQL        VMW_PSP_FIXED   Supports EqualLogic arrays
VMW_SATP_INV        VMW_PSP_FIXED   Supports EMC Invista
VMW_SATP_SYMM       VMW_PSP_FIXED   Supports EMC Symmetrix
VMW_SATP_LSI        VMW_PSP_MRU     Supports LSI and other arrays
VMW_SATP_EVA        VMW_PSP_FIXED   Supports HP EVA
VMW_SATP_DEFAULT_AP VMW_PSP_MRU     Supports non-specific active/passive arrays
VMW_SATP_CX         VMW_PSP_MRU     Supports EMC CX that do not
                                    use the ALUA protocol
VMW_SATP_ALUA       VMW_PSP_MRU     Supports non-specific arrays that use
                                    the ALUA protocol
VMW_SATP_DEFAULT_AA VMW_PSP_FIXED   Supports non-specific active/active arrays
VMW_SATP_LOCAL      VMW_PSP_FIXED   Supports direct attached devices
```

PSP MODULES

The PSP module handles the actual path used for every given I/O.

The NMP assigns a default PSP, which can be overridden manually for every LUN based on the SATP associated with that device. vSphere supports the following three PSPs "out of the box":

◆ MRU selects the path it used most recently. If this path becomes unavailable, the ESX host switches to an alternative path and continues to use the new path while it is available. This is the default for active/passive array types.

◆ Fixed uses the designated preferred path, if it has be configured. Otherwise, it uses the first working path discovered at system boot time. If the ESX host cannot use the preferred path, it selects a random alternative available path. The ESX host automatically reverts to the preferred path as soon as the path becomes available. This is the default for active/active array types (or active/passive arrays that use ALUA with SCSI 2 reservation mechanisms—in these cases, they appear as active/active).

◆ Round robin rotates the path selection between all available paths and enables basic load balancing across the paths. This is neither a weighted algorithm nor is it responsive to queue depth but is a significant improvement. In prior ESX/ESXi versions, there was no way to load balance a LUN, and customers needed to statically distribute LUNs across paths, which was a poor proxy for true load balancing.

To see what SATP is being used for a given LUN in the vCenter GUI, you can use the datastore inventory or navigate to the storage adapter properties for a given vSphere ESX host. Figure 6.78 shows the screen you will see.

FIGURE 6.78
For a given LUN, the SATP that applies is shown in the LUN properties dialog box, and the PSP can be overridden manually.

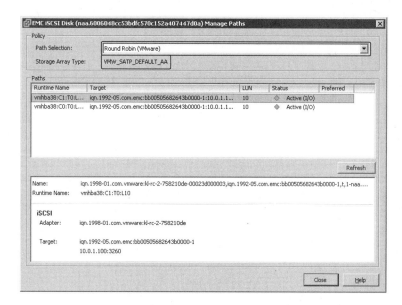

In the previous example, the array is an EMC Celerra (in fact, it's an EMC Celerra Virtual Storage Appliance), so the default SATP reports this as an active/active array, and the generic WWW_SATP_DEFAULT_AA is selected.

The default PSP was Fixed (VMware), which has been manually changed to Round Robin (VMware). A change in the PSP takes place *immediately* when you change it. There is no confirmation. Note that the PSP is configurable on a LUN-by-LUN basis.

WHAT IS ALL THE STUFF SHOWN IN THE LUN PROPERTIES DIALOG BOXES?

In the runtime name, the *C* is the Channel identifier, the *T* is the target identifier, and the *L* is the LUN number.

And that long text string starting with *naa*? This is the Network Address Authority ID, which is a unique identifier for the target and a LUN. This ID is guaranteed to be persistent through reboots and is used throughout vSphere. You can copy the NAA ID to the clipboard of the vSphere client by right-clicking the name in the configuration screen, as shown here.

If the NAA identifier name is now persistent between reboots, does that mean that the runtime name isn't? Yes, that's exactly right. And in ESX 3.5 (even in later updates where the NAA identifier name was starting to be used extensively), for arrays that used the MRU path policy, path selection would revert to the first enumerated device on reboot. This tended to mean that for any system that used the MRU policy, over time all the workload would tend to gravitate to one array port per storage processor and one ESX path—regardless of how carefully paths were manually balanced by the administrator. Figure 6.79 shows an EMC CLARiiON from a customer using ESX 3.5; note that one array port is significantly more utilized than the others.

WHAT PSP IS RIGHT IF YOU'RE USING ALUA

What do you do if your array can be configured to use ALUA—and therefore could use the fixed, MRU, or round-robin policy? See the "Midrange and Enterprise Storage Design" section for information on ALUA.

The fixed and MRU path failover policies deliver failover only and work fine with active/active and active/passive designs, regardless of whether ALUA is used. Of course, they both drive workloads down a single path. (See "vStorage APIs for Multipathing" for more information.) Ensure that you manually select active I/O paths that are the "good" ports, which are the ones where the port is on the storage processor "owning" the LUN. You don't want to select the "bad" ports, which are the higher-latency, lower-throughput ones that transit the internal interconnect to get to the LUN.

The out-of-the-box load-balancing policy in vSphere (round-robin) doesn't use the "non-optimized" paths (though they are noted as "active" in the vSphere GUI). Third-party multipathing plug-ins that are aware of the difference between the asymmetrical path choices can optimize an ALUA configuration.

FIGURE 6.79
An EMC CLARiiON supporting a VMware workload where the front-end ports are not well balanced

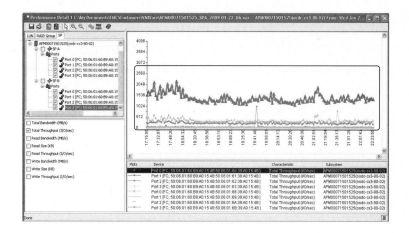

MPP Modules

The MPP module can add significantly enhanced multipathing to vSphere, and for the given LUNs it supports, it replaces the NMP, including the SATP and PSP. The MPP claim policy (the LUNs that it manages) can be on a LUN by LUN and array by array basis, and MPPs can coexist with NMP. The MPP can change:

◆ Path selection: Handled by the PSP normally to provide more sophisticated path selection than basic round robin—including selecting by host queue depth (and in some cases the array target port state)

The vStorage APIs for multipathing were written not only to be more modular but to support third-party extensibility; third-party SATPs, PSPs, and MPPs are technically possible. At the time of this writing, EMC PowerPath/VE was the only generally available MPP, though other vendors are likely to create third party SATPs, PSPs, and potentially full MPPs. Once the MPP is loaded on an ESX host via the vSphere client's host update tools, all multipathing for LUNs managed by that MPP become fully automated.

EMC PowerPath/VE is a third-party multipathing plug-in that supports a broad set of EMC and non-EMC array types. PowerPath/VE dramatically enhances load balancing, performance, and availability using the following techniques:

◆ Better availability through active management of intermittent path behavior

◆ Better availability through more rapid path state detection

◆ Better availability through automated path discovery behavior without manual rescan

◆ Better performance through better path selection using weighted algorithms, which is critical in cases where the paths are unequal (ALUA)

◆ Better performance by monitoring and adjusting to ESX host queue depth to select the path for a given I/O, shifting the workload from heavily used paths to lightly used paths

◆ Better performance with some arrays by predictive optimization based on the array port queues (which are generally the first point of contention and tend to affect all the ESX hosts simultaneously; without predictive advance handling, they tend to cause simultaneous path choice across the ESX cluster)

vStorage APIs for Site Recovery Manager

Although not a new set of APIs, the vSphere vStorage APIs for Site Recovery Manager (SRM) have been grouped in with the vStorage APIs. The SRM APIs are used for integrating array replication with VMware's Site Recovery Manager product. This can automate VMware disaster recovery by integrating VMware-level activities, such as VMFS handling, VM registration, IP addressing, and virtual machine start sequence, with the underlying array replication, such as mapping virtual machines to replicated LUNs and consistency groups, replicating data, changing replication state, and promoting replicas at the remote site.

Storage array vendors need to create a storage replication adapter (SRA) that integrates with the Site Recovery Manager APIs. The SRAs are qualified by VMware and are available on www.vmware.com when Site Recovery Manager is downloaded.

VMware Site Recovery Manager is beyond the scope of this book. It is worth noting that at the time of this writing, Site Recovery Manager does not support vSphere 4, though support is expected later in 2009.

VSTORAGE APIS FOR DATA PROTECTION

vSphere also included updates for how backup vendors can integrate with vSphere via new APIs focused on backup—the vStorage APIs for Data Protection. While not explicitly a primary production storage-related topic, it is part of the vStorage API set. This is an update to the idea of VMware Consolidated Backup introduced in VMware Infrastructure 3.*x*. Unlike VCB, the backup proxy doesn't require VMware software to be able to read the data off the datastore. Instead, the backup software vendor writes to the new vStorage APIs for Data Protection which leverages the new vSphere changed block tracking features and implements APIs to be able to handle various backup and restore tasks. These new backup APIs don't eliminate the concept of the "backup proxy" (in fact, proxies are needed for both Windows and Linux if file-level restores for both guest operating systems are required) and don't change some of the core VCB mechanics (based off ESX snapshots of VMs, and the backup/restore sequencing).

This is one way of doing backup, and an improvement over VMware Consolidated Backup. Other mechanisms are by leveraging array snapshot capabilities, and both traditional guest-based methods and non-traditional (including source based deduplication) methods.

Many backup vendors support multiple methods, and each has advantages and disadvantages. Many customers will have a backup and restore strategy for vSphere that will combine these methods for different recovery scenarios.

VSTORAGE APIS FOR ARRAY INTEGRATION (VAAI)

The vSphere vStorage APIs will likely continue to be expanded in future vSphere releases to include various mechanisms to improve overall efficiency, leverage storage offloads, and provide further virtual machine awareness to the storage arrays that support this API set.

For example, in various forums, several array vendors have demonstrated prototype vStorage API for array integration. By leveraging advanced array features and advanced SCSI commands, the time to clone and provision VMs can be reduced significantly, and ESX snapshots can be accelerated by using array snapshot techniques and using extraneous I/O (such as the same I/O from the same or multiple

ESX hosts, groups of "zero" writes that are associated with I/Os for thin or thick virtual disks, and the creation of prezeroed virtual disks).

These vStorage APIs for array integration technologies are not part of vSphere 4, though they're important to understand, because they represent the longer-term direction for storage and vSphere. What's most important, of course, is how to leverage the technologies available today.

Let's start pulling everything you've learned in the previous sections together!

Leveraging SAN and NAS Best Practices

After all the discussion of configuring and managing storage in VMware vSphere 4 environments, these are the core principles:

◆ Pick a storage architecture for your immediate and midterm scaling goals. Don't design for extreme growth scenarios. You can always use Storage VMotion to migrate up to larger arrays.

◆ Consider using VMFS and NFS together; the combination provides a great deal of flexibility.

◆ When sizing your initial array design for your entire vSphere environment, think about availability, performance (IOps, MBps, latency), and then capacity—always together and generally in that order.

The last point in the previous list cannot be overstated. People who are new to storage tend to think primarily in the dimension of storage capacity (TB) and neglect availability and performance. Capacity is generally not the limit for a proper storage configuration. With modern large-capacity disks (300GB+ per disk is common) and capacity reduction techniques such as thin provisioning, deduplication and compression, you can fit a *lot* on a very small number of disks. Therefore, capacity is not always the driver of efficiency.

To make this clear, an example scenario will help. First, let's work through the capacity-centered planning dynamic:

◆ You determine you will have 150 virtual machines that are 50GB in size each.

◆ This means that at a minimum, if you don't apply any special techniques, you will need 7.5TB (150 × 50GB). Because of extra space for ESX snapshots and virtual machine swap, you assume 25 percent overhead, so you plan 10TB of storage for your vSphere environment.

◆ With 10TB, you could fit that on approximately 13 large 1TB SATA drives (assuming a 10+2 RAID 6 and one hot spare.

◆ Thinking about this further and trying to be more efficient, you determine that while the virtual disks will be configured to be 50GB, on average they will need only 20TB, and the rest will be empty, so you can use thin provisioning at the vSphere or storage array layer. Using this would reduce the requirement to 3TB, and you decide that with good use of vSphere managed datastore objects and alerts, you can cut the extra space down from 25 percent to 20 percent. This reduces the requirement down to 3.6TB.

◆ Also, depending on your array, you may be able to deduplicate the storage itself, which has a high degree of commonality. Assuming a conservative 2:1 deduplication ratio, you would then need only 1.5TB of capacity—and with an additional 20 percent for various things, that's 1.8TB.

◆ With only 1.8TB needed, you could fit that on a very small 3+1 RAID 5 using 750GB drives, which would net 2.25TB.

This would be much cheaper, right? Much more efficient, right? After all, we've gone from thirteen 1TB spindles to four 750GB spindles.

It's not that simple. This will be clear going through this a second time, but this time working through the same design with a performance-centered planning dynamic:

◆ You determine you will have 150 virtual machines (the same as before).

◆ You look at their workloads, and although they spike at 200 IOps, they average at 50 IOps, and the duty cycle across all the VMs doesn't seem to spike at the same time, so you decide to use the average.

◆ You look at the throughput requirements and see that although they spike at 200MBps during a backup, for the most part, they drive only 3MBps. (For perspective, copying a file to a USB 2 memory stick can drive 12MBps—so this is a very small amount of bandwidth for a server.) The I/O size is generally small—in the 4KB size.

◆ Among the 150 virtual purpose machines, while most are general purpose servers, there are 10 that are "big hosts" (for example Exchange servers and some Sharepoint back-end SQL Servers) that require specific planning, so you put them aside to design separately using the reference architecture approach. The remaining 140 VMs can be characterized as needing an average of 7000 IOps (140 × 50 IOps) and 420MBps of average throughput (140 × 3MBps).

◆ Assuming no RAID losses or cache gains, 7000 IOps translates to the following:

    ◆ 39 15K RPM Fibre Channel/SAS drives (7000 IOps/180 IOps per drive)

    ◆ 59 10K RPM Fibre Channel/SAS drives (7000 IOps/120 IOps per drive)

    ◆ 87 5400 RPM SATA drives (7000 IOps/80 IOps per drive)

    ◆ 7 enterprise flash drives (7000 IOps/10K IOps per drive)

◆ Assuming no RAID losses or cache gains, 420MBps translates into 3360Mbps. At the array and the ESX hosts layers, this will require the following:

    ◆ Two 4Gbps Fibre Channel array ports (although it could fit on one, you need two for high availability).

    ◆ Two 10GbE ports (though it could fit on one, you need two for high availability).

    ◆ Four 1GbE ports for iSCSI or NFS. NFS will require careful multidatastore planning to hit the throughput goal. iSCSI will require careful multipathing configuration to hit the throughput goal.

◆ If using block devices, you'll need to distribute VMs across datastores to design the datastores and backing LUNs themselves to ensure that they can support the IOps of the VMs they contain to ensure that the queues don't overflow.

◆ It's immediately apparent that the SATA drives are not ideal in this case (they would require 87 spindles!). At the time of writing this book, the sweet spot in the disk market from a combined price/capacity/performance standpoint are the 300GB 15,000 RPM drives, and that's reflected in this configuration. Using these 300GB 15,000 RPM drives (without using Enterprise Flash Disks) at a minimum you will have 11.7TB of raw capacity, assuming 10 percent RAID 6 capacity loss (10.6TB usable). This is more than enough to store the thickly provisioned virtual machines, not to mention their thinly provisioned and then deduplicated variations.

◆ Will thin provisioning and deduplication techniques save capacity? Yes. Could you use that saved capacity? Maybe, but probably not. Remember, we've sized the configuration to meet the IOps workload—unless the workload is lighter than we measured or the additional workloads you would like to load on those spindles generates no I/O during the periods the virtual machines need it. The spindles will all be busy servicing the existing virtual machines, and additional workloads will increase the I/O service time.

What's the moral of the story? That thin provisioning and data deduplication have no usefulness? That performance is all that matters?

No. The moral of the story is that to be efficient you need to think about efficiency in every dimension: performance, capacity, power, operational simplicity, and flexibility. Here is a simple five-step sequence you can use to guide the process:

1. Look at your workload, and examine the IOps, MBps, and latency requirements.

2. Put the outliers to one side, and plan for the average.

3. Use reference architectures and a focused plan to design a virtualized configuration for the outlier heavy workloads.

4. Plan first on the most efficient way to meet the aggregate performance workloads.

5. Then by using the performance configuration developed in step 4, back into the most efficient capacity configuration to hit that mark. Some workloads are performance bound (ergo step 4 is the constraint), and some are "capacity bound" (ergo step 5 is the constraint).

Let's quantify all this learning into applicable best practices:

When thinking about performance:

◆ Do a little engineering by simple planning or estimation. Measure sample hosts, or use VMware Capacity Planner to profile the IOps and bandwidth workload of each host that will be virtualized onto the infrastructure. If you can't measure, at least estimate. For virtual desktops, estimate between 5 to 20 IOps. For light servers, estimate 50 to 100 IOps. Usually, most configurations are IOps bound, not throughput bound, but if you can, measure the average I/O size of the hosts (or again, use Capacity Planner). Although estimation can work for light server use cases, for heavy servers, don't ever estimate—measure it—it's so easy to measure, it's absolutely a "measure twice, cut once" case, particularly for virtual machines you know will have a heavy workload.

◆ For large applications (Exchange, SQL Server, SharePoint, Oracle, MySQL, and so on), the sizing, layout, and best practices for storage for large databases workloads are not dissimilar to physical deployments and can be a good choice for RDMs or VMFS volumes with no other virtual disks. Also, leverage joint reference architectures available from VMware and the storage vendors.

◆ Remember that the datastore will need to be able to have enough IOps and capacity for the total of all the virtual machines. Just remember 80 to 180 IOps per spindle depending on spindle type (refer to the "Disks" section in "Common Storage Array Architectures") to support the aggregate of all the VMs in it. If you just add up all the aggregate IOps needed by the sum of the VMs that will be in a datastore, you have a good approximation of the total. Additional I/Os are generated by the "zeroing" activity that occurs for thin and thick (but not eagerzeroedthick), but this tends to be negligible. You lose some IOps because of the RAID protection, but you know you're in the ballpark if the number of spindles supporting the datastore (via a file system and NFS or a LUN and VMFS) times the number of IOps per spindle is more than the total number of IOps needed for the aggregate workload. Keep your storage vendor honest, and you'll have a much more successful virtualization project!

◆ Cache benefits are difficult to predict; they vary a great deal. If you can't do a test, assume they will have large effect improving VM boot times with RDBMS environments on VMware, but almost no effect otherwise, so plan your spindle count cautiously.

When thinking about capacity:

◆ Consider not only the virtual machine disks in the datastores but also their ESX snapshots, their swap, and their suspended state and memory. A good rule of thumb is to assume 25 percent more than from the virtual disks alone. If you use thin provisioning at the array level, oversizing the datastore has no downside because only what is necessary is actually used.

◆ There is no exact best practice datastore sizing model. Historically, people have recommended one fixed size or another. A simple model is to select a standard guideline for the number of VMs you feel comfortable with in a datastore, multiply that number by the average size of the virtual disks of each virtual machine, add the overall 25 percent extra space and use that as a standardized building block. Remember, VMFS and NFS datastores don't have an effective limit on the number of virtual machines—with VMFS you need to consider disk queuing and to a lesser extent SCSI reservations, with NFS you need to consider the bandwidth to a single datastore.

◆ Be flexible and efficient. Use thin provisioning, at the array level if possible, and if your array doesn't support it, using it at the VMware layer. It never hurts (so long as you monitor), but don't count on it resulting in needing fewer spindles (because of performance requirements).

◆ If your array doesn't support thin provisioning but does support extending LUNs, use VMware-layer thin provisioning, but start with smaller VMFS volumes to avoid oversizing and being inefficient.

◆ In general, don't oversize. Every modern array can add capacity dynamically, and you can use Storage VMotion to redistribute workloads. Use the new managed datastore function to set thresholds and actions, and then extend LUNs and the VMFS datastores using the new vSphere VMFS extension capability, or grow NFS datastores.

◆ Use the Performance reports, Storage Views and managed datastore objects to monitor utilization and drive to higher degrees of efficiency.

When thinking about availability:

◆ Spend the bulk of your storage planning and configuration time to ensure your design has high availability. Check that array configuration, storage fabric (whether Fibre Channel or Ethernet), and NMP/MPP multipathing configuration (or NIC teaming/link aggregation and routing for NFS) are properly configured. Spend the effort to stay up-to-date with the interop matrixes of your vendors and the firmware update processes.

◆ Remember, you can deal with performance and capacity issues as they come up nondisruptively (VMFS expansion/extends, array tools to add performance, and Storage VMotion). Something that affects the overall storage availability will be an emergency.

When deciding on a virtual machine datastore placement philosophy, there are two common models: the predictive scheme and the adaptive scheme.

Predictive scheme:

◆ Create several datastores (VMFS or NFS) with different storage characteristics, and label each datastore according to its characteristics.

◆ Locate each application in the appropriate RAID for its requirements by measuring the requirements in advance.

◆ Run the applications, and see whether virtual machine performance is acceptable (or monitor the HBA queues as they approach the queue-full threshold).

◆ Use RDMs sparingly as needed.

Adaptive scheme:

◆ Create a standardized datastore "building block" model (VMFS or NFS).

◆ Place virtual disks on the datastore. Remember, regardless of what you hear, there's no practical "datastore maximum" number. The question is the performance scaling of the datastore.

◆ Run the applications and see whether disk performance is acceptable (on a VMFS datastore, monitor the HBA queues as they approach the queue-full threshold).

◆ If performance is acceptable, you can place additional virtual disks on the datastore. If it is not, you create a new datastore and use Storage VMotion to distribute the workload.

◆ Use RDMs sparingly.

Our preference is a hybrid. Specifically, you can use the adaptive scheme coupled with starting with two wildly divergent datastore performance profiles (the idea from the predictive scheme), one for "utility" VMs and one for "priority" VMs.

Always read, follow, and leverage the key documentation:

◆ VMware's Fibre Channel and iSCSI SAN configuration guides

◆ VMware's HCL

◆ Your storage vendor's best practices/solutions guides

Sometimes the documents go out of date. Don't just ignore the guidance if you think it's incorrect; use the online community or reach out to VMware or your storage vendor to get the latest information.

Most important, have no fear!

Physical host and storage configurations have historically been extremely static, and the penalty of error in storage configuration from a performance or capacity standpoint was steep. The errors of misconfiguration would inevitably lead not only to application issues, but complex work and downtime to resolve. This "pain of error" has ingrained in administrators a tendency to overplan when it comes to performance and capacity.

Between the capabilities of modern arrays to modify many storage attributes dynamically and Storage VMotion (the ultimate "get out of jail free card"—including complete array replacement!), the penalty and risk is less about misconfiguration, and now the risk is more about oversizing or overbuying. You cannot be trapped with an underperforming configuration you can't change nondisruptively.

More important than any storage configuration or feature per se is to design a highly available configuration that meets your immediate needs and is as flexible to change as VMware makes the rest of the IT stack.

The Bottom Line

Differentiate and understand the fundamentals of shared storage, including SANs and NAS. VMware vSphere depends on shared storage for advanced functions, cluster-wide availability, and the aggregate performance of all the virtual machines in a cluster. Designing high-performance and highly available shared storage infrastructure is possible on Fibre Channel, FCoE, and iSCSI SANs and is possible using NAS; in addition, it's available for midrange to enterprise storage architectures. Always design the storage architecture to meet the performance requirements first, and then ensure that capacity requirements are met as a corollary.

Master It Identify examples where each of the protocol choices would be ideal for different vSphere 4 deployments.

Master It Identify the three storage performance parameters and the primary determinant of storage performance and how to quickly estimate it for a given storage configuration.

Understand vSphere storage options. vSphere has three fundamental storage presentation models: VMFS on block, NFS, and RDM. The most flexible configurations use all three, predominantly via a "shared container" model and selective use of RDMs.

Master It Characterize use cases for VMFS datastores, NFS datastores, and RDMs.

Master It If you're using VMFS and there's one performance metric to track, what would it be? Configure a monitor for that metric.

Configure storage at the vSphere ESX 4 layer. After a shared storage platform is selected, the VMware vSphere ESX/ESXi 4 cluster needs a storage network configured. The network (whether Fibre Channel or Ethernet based) must be designed to meet availability and throughput requirements, which is influenced by protocol choice and vSphere fundamental storage stack (and in the case of NFS, network stack) architecture. Proper network design involves physical redundancy and physical or logical isolation mechanisms (SAN zoning and network VLANs). With connectivity in place, configure LUNs and VMFS datastores and/or NFS exports/NFS datastores using the predictive or adaptive model (or a hybrid model). Use Storage VMotion to resolve hot spots and other nonoptimal virtual machine placement.

Master It   What would best identify an oversubscribed VMFS datastore from a performance standpoint? How would you identify the issue? What is it most likely to be? What would be two possible corrective actions you could take?

Master It   A VMFS volume is filling up. What are three possible nondisruptive corrective actions you could take?

Master It   What would best identify an oversubscribed NFS volume from a performance standpoint? How would you identify the issue? What is it most likely to be? What are two possible corrective actions you could take?

Configure storage at the virtual machine layer.   With datastores in place, create virtual machines. During the creation of the virtual machines, place VMs in the appropriate datastores, and employ selective use of RDMs, but only where required. Over time, monitor for excessive space consumption due to VMware native snapshots, and consider collapsing snapshots for very significant space consumption cases.

Master It   Without turning the machine off, convert the virtual disks on a VMFS volume from thin to eagerzeroedthick and back to thin.

Master It   Identify where you would use a physical compatibility mode RDM, and configure that use case.

Master It   Take a series of ESX snapshots with and without memory snapshots. Then, without using the storage views and only using the datastore browser, determine from the file structure how much space the snapshots are consuming. Predict the result of deleting snapshots. Delete the snapshots, and match the result with your expectations.

Leverage new vSphere storage features.   Use managed datastore alerts to manage and optimize utilization. Leverage the new thin provisioning options independently or together with array thin provisioning to drive a higher asset utilization of your shared storage infrastructure. Use the storage views and maps to pinpoint a single point of failure and report on the overall asset use. Use Storage VMotion to not only resolve nonoptimal storage configuration but to transform between thin and thick virtual disk configurations. Leverage the paravirtualized SCSI adapter with the new Virtual Machine 7 format to drive higher I/O performance with lower CPU utilization. If you are using ESX 3.5 with iSCSI using the software iSCSI initiator, use the new initiator's multiple sessions per target to drive higher throughput (and configure it this way to start if using vSphere 4 for the first time). Enable the Round-Robin path selection policy on LUNs manually. Consider a third-party multipathing plug-in (MPP) as an option to simplify the vSphere storage configuration while improving performance and availability.

Master It   Configure an iSCSI target, and then configure multiple iSCSI VMkernel connections to a single iSCSI target. (If you don't have an iSCSI array, you can always download the freely available EMC Celerra VSA from http://virtualgeek.typepad.com.)

Leverage best practices for SAN and NAS storage with vSphere 4. Read, follow, and leverage key VMware and storage vendors' best practices/solutions guide documentation. Don't oversize up front, but instead learn to leverage VMware and storage array features to monitor performance, queues, and back-end load—and then nondisruptively adapt. Plan for performance first and capacity second. (Usually capacity is a given for performance requirements to be met.) Spend design time on availability design and on the large heavy I/O VMs, and use flexible pool design for the general-purpose VMFS and NFS datastores.

Master It Quickly estimate the minimum usable capacity needed for 200 virtual machines with an average VM size of 40GB. Make some assumptions about ESX snapshots. What would be the raw capacity needed in the array if you used RAID 10? RAID 5 4+1? RAID 6 10+2? What would you do to nondisruptively cope if you ran out of capacity?

Master It Using the configurations in the previous question, what would the minimum amount of raw capacity need to be if the VMs are actually only 20GB of data in each VM, even though they are provisioning 40GB and you used thick on an array that didn't support thin provisioning? What if the array *did* support thin provisioning? What if you used Storage VMotion to convert from thick to thin (both in the case where the array supports thin provisioning and in the case where it doesn't)?

Master It Estimate the number of spindles needed for 100 virtual machines that drive 200 IOps each and are 40GB in size. Assume no RAID loss or cache gain. How many if you use 500GB SATA 7200 RPM? 300GB 10K Fibre Channel/SAS? 300GB 15K Fibre Channel/SAS? 160GB consumer-grade SSD? 200GB Enterprise Flash?

Chapter 7

Creating and Managing Virtual Machines

The ESX or ESXi hosts are installed, vCenter Server is running, the networks are blinking, the SAN is carved, and the VMFS volumes are formatted ... let the virtualization begin! With the virtual infrastructure in place, you as the administrator must shift your attention to deploying the virtual machines.

In this chapter, you will learn to:

♦ Create a virtual machine

♦ Install a guest operating system

♦ Install VMware Tools

♦ Manage and modify a virtual machine

♦ Create templates and deploy virtual machines

Creating a Virtual Machine

It is common for IT professionals to refer to a Windows or Linux system running on an ESX/ESXi host as a *virtual machine*. Strictly speaking, this phrase is not 100 percent accurate. A virtual machine is really just a set of virtual hardware selected for the purpose of running a guest operating system. Just as a physical machine is a physical machine before the installation of an operating system, a virtual machine is a virtual machine before the installation of a guest operating system. From an everyday usage perspective, though, you can go on calling the Windows or Linux system a virtual machine. You might see references here to "guest operating system instances"; these would be instances of Windows, Linux, or Solaris installed on a virtual machine.

So, what kind of virtual hardware makes up a virtual machine? By default, VMware ESX/ESXi presents the following fairly generic hardware to the virtual machine:

♦ Phoenix BIOS

♦ Intel motherboard

♦ Intel PCI IDE controller

♦ IDE CD-ROM drive

♦ BusLogic or LSI Logic parallel SCSI controller

♦ AMD or Intel CPU, depending upon the physical hardware

◆ Intel e1000 or AMD PCnet NIC

◆ Standard VGA video adapter

This generic hardware was selected to provide the broadest level of compatibility across all the supported guest operating systems. As a result, it's possible to use commercial off-the-shelf drivers within a virtual machine. However, the guest operating systems can also utilize drivers written by VMware. These drivers are not as complex as using manufacturer-released drivers for specific hardware components and are optimized for virtualization. For example, the drivers for the VMware SVGA II are not as heavy or invasive as the drivers for, say, an nVidia GeForce video adapter. Figure 7.1 shows virtual hardware identified by Windows Server 2003's Device Manager while running in a virtual machine. Noticeably, much of the third-party device driver installation is replaced with the virtualized hardware that the ESX/ESXi host is providing.

FIGURE 7.1
VMware ESX/ESXi provides virtualization-optimized hardware and drivers to guest operating systems.

A virtual machine, as shown in Figure 7.2, can consist of the following virtual hardware devices:

◆ Processors: One, two, four, or eight processors with VMware Virtual SMP

◆ Memory: Maximum of 255GB of RAM

◆ SCSI adapter: Maximum of four SCSI adapters with 15 devices per adapter for a total of 60 SCSI devices per VM; it's possible to boot only from one of the first eight

◆ Network adapter: Maximum of 10 network adapters

◆ Parallel port: Maximum of three parallel ports

◆ Serial port: Maximum of four serial ports

◆ CD/DVD: Maximum of four CD/DVD drives (up to four IDE devices per virtual machine, in any combination of CD/DVD drives or IDE hard drives)

◆ Floppy drive: Maximum of two floppy disk drives on a single floppy disk controller

◆ Keyboard, video card, and mouse

FIGURE 7.2
A virtual machine consists of virtual processors, SCSI adapters, network adapter, CD/DVD drives, memory, and more.

Hard drives are not included in the previous list because virtual machine hard drives are generally added as SCSI devices. With up to four SCSI adapters and 15 SCSI devices per adapter, it is possible to attach 60 hard drives to a virtual machine. If you are using IDE hard drives, then the virtual machine is subject to the limit of four IDE devices per virtual machine, as mentioned earlier.

SIZE LIMITS FOR VIRTUAL HARD DRIVES

The maximum size for any virtual hard drive presented to a virtual machine is just shy of 2TB. More precisely, it is 2TB minus 512B. That's a lot of storage for just one virtual machine!

To better understand virtual machines, though, you must not just consider how a virtual machine appears from the perspective of the guest operating system, as I've just done. You must also consider how a virtual machine appears to the ESX/ESXi host.

From the perspective of an ESX/ESXi host, a virtual machine consists of several types of files stored on a supported storage device. The two most common files that comprise a virtual machine are the configuration file and the virtual hard disk file. The configuration file—hereafter referred to as the VMX file—is identified by a .vmx extension and functions as the structural definition of the virtual machine. The VMX file defines the virtual hardware that resides in the virtual machine.

The number of processors, the amount of RAM, the number of network adapters, the associated MAC addresses, the networks to which the network adapters connect, and the number, names, and locations of all virtual hard drives are stored in the configuration file.

The virtual hard disk file, identified by a .vmdk extension and hereafter referred to the VMDK file, holds the actual data stored by a virtual machine. Each VMDK file represents a hard drive. For a virtual machine running Windows, the first VMDK file would typically be the storage location for the C: drive. For a Linux system, it would typically be the storage location for the root, boot, and a few other partitions. Additional VMDK files can be added to provide additional storage locations for the virtual machine, and each VMDK file would appear as a physical hard drive to the virtual machine.

A few other files also make up a virtual machine; you'll take a look at those in a few moments. First, let's create a virtual machine using the vSphere Client.

Perform the following steps to create a virtual machine:

1. If it's not already running, launch the vSphere Client, and connect to a vCenter Server instance or an individual ESX/ESXi host.

2. In the inventory tree, right-click the name of a cluster or an individual ESX/ESXi host, and select the New Virtual Machine option, as shown in Figure 7.3. Alternatively, use the File menu or the Ctrl+N keyboard shortcut to launch the wizard.

FIGURE 7.3
You can launch the Create New Virtual Machine Wizard from the context menu of an ESX/ESXi cluster or an individual ESX/ESXi host.

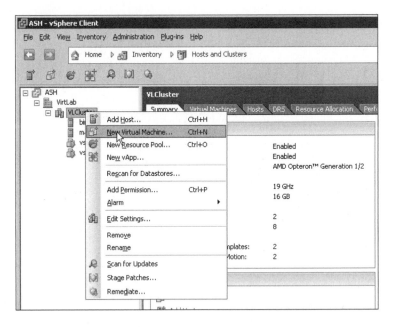

3. When the Create New Virtual Machine Wizard opens, select the Custom radio button, shown in Figure 7.4, and then click Next. The Custom selection exposes a much greater set of options when creating a virtual machine, such as the virtual machine version, RAM, number of virtual CPUs, SCSI controller type, and more virtual machine disk options.

4. Type a name for the virtual machine, select a location in the inventory where the virtual machine should reside, and click Next, as shown in Figure 7.5.

FIGURE 7.4
The Custom option exposes more configuration options to users when creating new virtual machines.

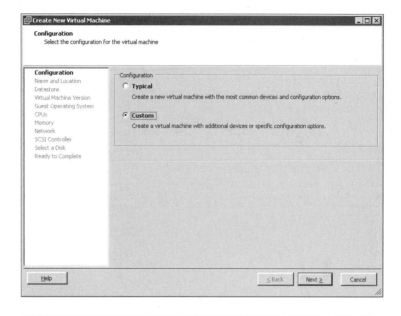

FIGURE 7.5
The display name of the virtual machine is used as the name of the folder in which it will reside on the selected datastore and the prefix for all the corresponding virtual machine files (for example, VMX and VMDK).

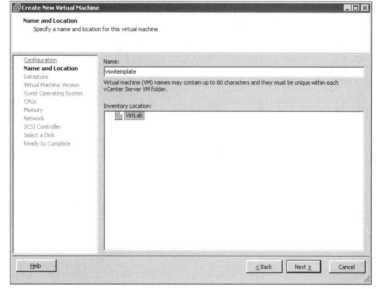

LOGICAL INVENTORY AND PHYSICAL INVENTORY

The inventory location you select when creating a new virtual machine, as shown in Figure 7.5, is a logical location. This inventory location does not correspond to the server on which that virtual machine will run or the datastore on which that virtual machine will be stored. This logical inventory displays in the vSphere Client when you select VMs and Templates as the Inventory view.

5. Select a datastore where the virtual machine files will be located, as shown in Figure 7.6, and then click Next.

FIGURE 7.6
You can store virtual machines in any of the datastores available to an ESX/ESXi host as long as the space requirements meet the needs of the virtual machine.

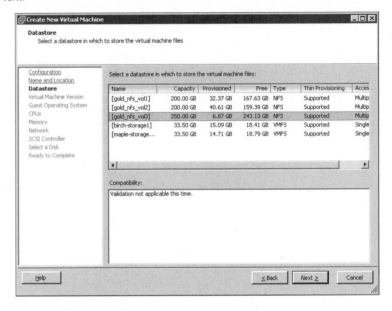

6. Select a VMware virtual machine version, as shown in Figure 7.7. If the virtual machines will be shared with ESX/ESXi hosts running 3.0 or later, then choose version 4. Otherwise, choose version 7. Click Next.

FIGURE 7.7
Choose Virtual Machine Version: 7 unless virtual machines or storage are shared with previous versions of ESX/ESXi.

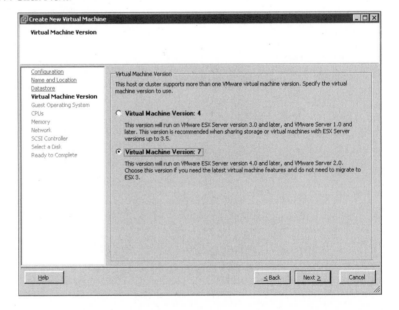

RUNNING VIRTUAL MACHINES FROM PREVIOUS VERSIONS OF ESX/ESXI

Unlike upgrades from previous major versions of ESX, version 4 allows you to run virtual machines created in earlier versions of ESX/ESXi without any sort of upgrade process. Some readers may recall that the upgrade from ESX 2.x to ESX 3.x, for example, required a "DMotion" upgrade process or significant downtime for the VMs.

This is not to say that there won't be any downtime for VMs when upgrading from ESX 3.x, just that the downtime isn't required to occur during the upgrade of the hosts themselves. Instead, the tasks that do require VM downtime—upgrading VMware Tools and upgrading the virtual hardware from version 4 to version 7—can be scheduled and performed at a later date.

---

7. Select the radio button that corresponds to the operating system vendor, select the correct operating system version, and then click Next, as shown in Figure 7.8.

FIGURE 7.8
The vSphere Client makes recommendations on RAM, NICs, and SCSI controllers based on the operating system vendor and version selected here.

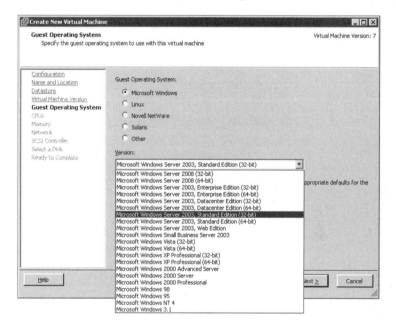

8. Select the number of virtual CPUs to include in the virtual machine, and then click Next, as shown in Figure 7.9.

9. Configure the virtual machine with the determined amount of RAM by clicking the up and down arrows or typing the value, as shown in Figure 7.10, and then click Next. The vSphere Client displays recommendations about the minimum and recommended amounts of RAM based on the earlier selection of operating system and version.

The amount of RAM configured on this page is the amount of RAM the guest operating system reflects in its system properties, and it is the most that a guest operating system will ever be able to use. The setting on this page is not a guarantee that physical memory will be used to achieve the configured value. As discussed in later chapters, memory for a virtual machine might be physical RAM, VMkernel swap file space, or some combination of the two.

FIGURE 7.9
You can configure virtual machines with one, two, four, or eight virtual machines, depending on licensing and the guest OS.

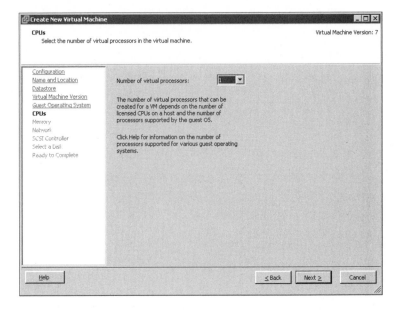

FIGURE 7.10
The RAM configured on the Memory page of the Create New Virtual Machine Wizard is the maximum amount of RAM the guest operating system will be able to use.

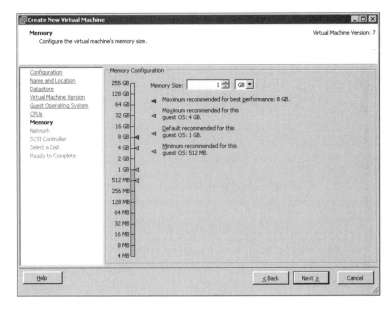

10. Select the number of network adapters, the type of each network adapter, and the network to which each adapter will connect, as shown in Figure 7.11.

FIGURE 7.11
You can configure a virtual machine with up to four network adapters, of the same or different types, that reside on the same or different networks as needed.

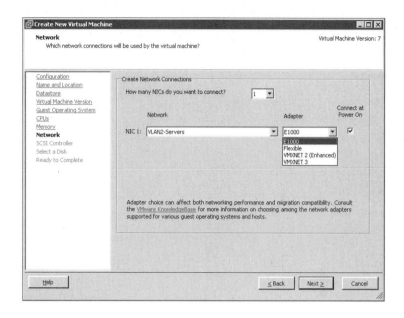

VIRTUAL MACHINE SCSI CONTROLLERS

Windows 2000 has built-in support for the BusLogic parallel SCSI controller, while Windows Server 2003 and later operating systems have built-in support for the LSI Logic parallel SCSI controller. Additionally, Windows Server 2008 has support for the LSI Logic SAS controller. Windows XP doesn't have built-in support for any of these, requiring a driver disc during installation. Choosing the wrong controller will result in an error during the operating system installation. The error states that hard drives cannot be found. Choosing the wrong SCSI controller during a physical to virtual (P2V) operation will result in a "blue screen error" for a Windows guest operating system inside the virtual machine, and the Windows installation will fail to boot after conversion.

11. Select the radio button that corresponds to the appropriate SCSI adapter for the operating system selected on the Guest Operating System page of the Create New Virtual Machine Wizard. The correct default driver should already be selected based on the previously selected operating system. For example, the LSI Logic parallel adapter is selected automatically when Windows Server 2003 is selected as the guest operating system, but LSI Logic SAS adapter is selected when Windows Server 2008 is chosen as the guest operating system.

12. Select the appropriate radio button for the virtual disk to be used, as shown in Figure 7.12. There are three options:

◆ The Create A New Virtual Disk option allows the user to create a new virtual disk (a VMDK file) that will house the guest operating system's files and data.

◆ The Use An Existing Virtual Disk option allows a virtual machine to be created using a virtual disk that is already configured with a guest operating system and that resides in an available datastore.

◆ The Raw Device Mappings option allows a virtual machine to have raw SAN LUN access. I will discuss this in more detail in Chapter 6.

Select the Create A New Virtual Disk option, and click Next.

FIGURE 7.12
You can create a new virtual disk when a new virtual machine is created, or you can use an existing virtual disk.

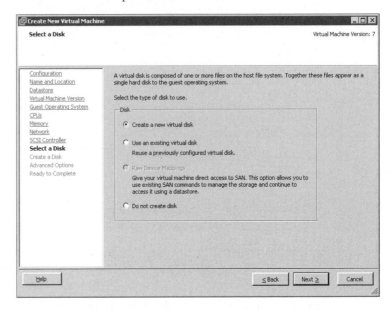

ADDING EXISTING DISKS

The existing virtual disk doesn't have to contain an instance of the guest operating system; it can contain data that perhaps will serve as a secondary drive inside the virtual machine. The ability to add existing disks with data makes virtual hard drives extremely portable, allowing users to move them from virtual machine to virtual machine without repercussions.

---

13. When the Create A New Virtual Disk option is selected, options are available for the creation of the new virtual disk, as shown in Figure 7.13. First, configure the desired disk size for the virtual machine hard drive. The maximum size will be determined by the format of the datastore on which the virtual disk is stored. Next, select the appropriate disk provisioning option:

◆ To thin provision the disk and allocate virtual disk storage on demand instead of up front, select the Allocate And Commit Space On Demand (Thin Provisioning) box.

◆ To enable clustering features, select the Support Clustering Features Such As Fault Tolerance box.

Under the options for the location of the new virtual disk, there are two options from which to select:

◆ The option Store With The Virtual Machine will place the file in the same subdirectory as the configuration file and the rest of the virtual machine files. This is the most commonly selected option and makes managing the virtual machine files easier.

◆ The option Specify A Datastore allows you to store the virtual machine file separately from the rest of the files. You'd typically select this option when adding new virtual hard disks to a virtual machine or when you need to separate the operating system virtual disk from a data virtual disk.

FIGURE 7.13
Virtual disks can be thin provisioned and configured to support clustering features such as fault tolerance.

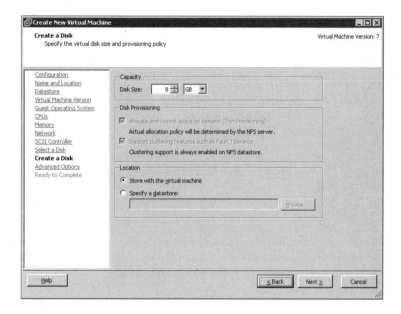

14. The Advanced Options page lets you specify the SCSI node or IDE controller to which the virtual disk is connected and also allows you to configure a virtual disk in Independent mode, as shown in Figure 7.14. As noted in the wizard, this page is normally not altered and can be accepted by clicking Next.

◆ The Node drop-down list reflects the 15 different SCSI nodes available on each of the four SCSI adapters a virtual machine supports. When using an IDE controller, this drop-down shows the four different IDE nodes that are available.

◆ By not selecting the Independent mode option, you ensure that the virtual disk remains in the default state that allows virtual machine snapshots to be created. If you select the Independent check box, you can configure the virtual disk as a persistent disk, in which changes are written immediately and permanently to the disk, or as a nonpersistent disk, which discards all changes when the virtual machine is turned off.

SCSI AND IDE HARD DISKS IN VIRTUAL MACHINES

If the first hard drive attached to the virtual machine when the virtual machine is created is configured as an IDE hard drive, then you will have the ability to configure additional hard drives as IDE hard drives as well (up to four IDE devices per virtual machine). If the first hard drive attached to the virtual machine when the virtual machine is created is configured as a SCSI hard drive, then you will have only SCSI as an option for all subsequent hard drives.

FIGURE 7.14
You can configure the virtual disk on a number of different SCSI adapters and SCSI IDs, and you can configure it as an independent disk.

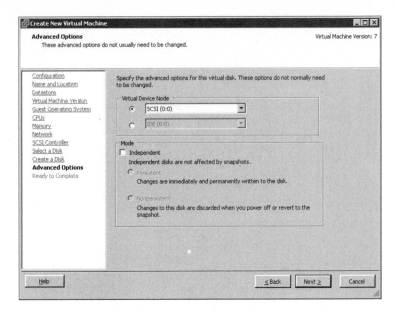

15. Complete a final review of the virtual machine configuration and then click Finish, as shown in Figure 7.15.

FIGURE 7.15
Reviewing the configuration of the Create New Virtual Machine Wizard ensures the correct settings for the virtual machine and prevents mistakes that require deleting and re-creating the virtual machine.

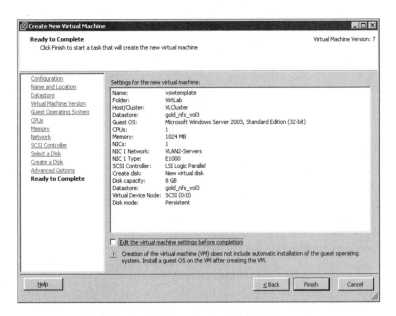

Out of all the options available during the creation of a new virtual machine, there are two areas that consistently generate questions from new and experienced users alike:

◆ How should I handle naming my virtual machines?

◆ How big should I make the virtual disks?

The display name given to a virtual machine might seem like a trivial assignment, but you must ensure an appropriate naming strategy is in place. I recommend making the display names of virtual machines match the hostnames configured in the guest operating system being installed. For example, if the intention is to name the guest operating system host Server1, then the virtual machine display name should match with Server1. If spaces are used in the virtual display name—which is allowed—then using command-line tools to manage virtual machines becomes a bit tricky because the spaces will have to be quoted out on the command line. In addition, since DNS hostnames cannot include spaces, using spaces in the virtual machine name would create a disparity between the virtual machine name and the guest operating system hostname. Ultimately, this means you should avoid using spaces and special characters that are not allowed in standard DNS naming strategies to ensure similar names both inside and outside the virtual machine.

The display name assigned to a virtual machine also becomes the name of the folder in the VMFS volume where the virtual machine files will live. At the file level, the associated configuration (VMX) and virtual hard drive (VMDK) files will assume the name supplied in the display named text box during virtual machine creation. This is shown in Figure 7.16.

FIGURE 7.16
The display name assigned to a virtual machine is used in a variety of places.

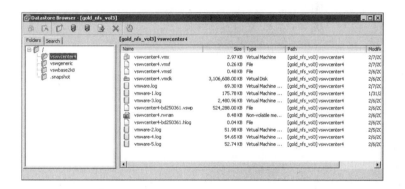

The answer to the second question is a bit more complicated. There are many different approaches, but there are some best practices that facilitate the management, scalability, and backup of virtual machines. First and foremost, virtual machines should be created with multiple virtual disk files as a means of separating the operating system from the custom user data. Separating the system files and the user data will make it easier to increase the number of data drives in the future and will allow for a more practical backup strategy. A system drive of 25GB to 30GB, for example, will provide ample room for the initial installation and continued growth of the operating system. The data drives across different virtual machines will vary in size because of underlying storage system capacity and functionality, the installed applications, the function of the system, and the number of users who connect to the computer. However, because the extra hard drives are not operating system data, it will be easier to make adjustments to those drives when needed.

Keep in mind that additional virtual hard drives will pick up on the same naming scheme as the original virtual hard drive. For example, a virtual machine named Server1 that has an original virtual hard disk file named `Server1.vmdk` will name the new virtual hard disk file `Server1_1.vmdk`. Each additional file will increment the last number, making it administratively easy to identify all virtual disk files related to a particular virtual machine.

Real World Scenario

PROVISIONING VIRTUAL MACHINES IS NOT THE SAME AS PROVISIONING PHYSICAL MACHINES

Provisioning virtual machines needs to be approached differently than how you've provisioned physical machines in the past. After all, isn't it underutilized and over-provisioned servers that have led you to use virtualization to consolidate your workloads?

In the physical world, you provision servers based on the maximum you think that server might ever need throughout its lifetime. Since the intended workload for a server might shift over that lifetime, you probably tend to provision the physical server with more CPU resources and more RAM than it really needs.

In the virtual environment, though, virtual machines should be provisioned only with the resources they really need. Additional resources can be added later should the workload need them, sometimes with no downtime required.

In the event that you don't make this shift in thinking, you'll end up much like a client of mine that had the same problem. During the early phases of the client's consolidation project, they provisioned virtual machines with the same level of resources given to physical machines. It wasn't until they ran out of resources in the virtual environment and had a far lower consolidation ratio than anticipated that I was able to convince them to change their provisioning practices. Once the provisioning practices were changed, the customer was able to improve their consolidation ratio without negatively impacting the level of service they were able to provide. Right-sizing your virtual machines is a good thing!

Later in this chapter in the section titled, "Creating Templates and Deploying Virtual Machines," you'll revisit this concept to see how to use templates to implement and maintain an optimal virtual machine configuration that separates the system data from the user data.

Installing a Guest Operating System

A new virtual machine is analogous to a physical computer with an empty hard drive. All the components are there but without an operating system. After creating the virtual machine, you're ready to install a supported guest operating system. Some of the more commonly installed guest operating systems supported by ESX/ESXi include the following:

◆ Windows Vista (x86 and x64)

◆ Windows Server 2008 Standard/Enterprise/Datacenter (x86 and x64)

◆ Windows Server 2003 Web/Standard/Enterprise/Datacenter (x86 and x64)

◆ Windows Small Business Server 2003

◆ Windows XP (x86 and x64)

◆ Windows 2000

- Windows NT 4

- Red Hat Enterprise Linux 2.1/3.0/4.0/5.0

- SUSE Linux Enterprise Server 8/9/10

- NetWare 5.1/6.0/6.5

- Solaris 10 operating system for x86 platforms (32-bit and 64-bit)

Installing any of these supported guest operating systems follows the same common order of steps for installation on a physical server, but the nuances and information provided during the install of each guest operating system might vary greatly.

One task that is greatly beneficial in a virtual environment but that isn't typically required in a virtual environment concerns guest OS installation media. In the physical world, administrators would typically put the OS installation media in the physical server's optical drive, install the OS, and then be done with it. Well, in a virtual world, the process is similar, but here's the issue—where do you put the CD when the server is virtual? There are a couple of different ways to handle it. One way is quick and easy, and the second way takes a bit longer but pays off later.

Virtual machines have a few different ways to access data stored on optical disks. As shown in Figure 7.17, virtual machines can access optical disks in one of three different ways:

- Client Device: This option allows an optical drive local to the computer running the vSphere Client to be mapped into the virtual machine. For example, if you are using the vSphere Client on your corporate-issued HP laptop, you have the option of simply inserting a CD/DVD into your local optical drive and mapping that into the virtual machine with this option.

- Host Device: This option maps the ESX/ESXi host's optical drive into the virtual machine. VMware administrators would have to insert the CD/DVD into the server's optical drive in order for the virtual machine to have access to the disc.

- Datastore ISO File: This last option maps an ISO image (see the "ISO Image Basics" sidebar) into the virtual machine. Although using an ISO image may require one additional step—creating the ISO image from the physical disk—more and more software is being distributed as an ISO image that can be leveraged directly from within your vSphere environment.

FIGURE 7.17
Virtual machines can access optical disks physically located on the vSphere Client system, located on the ESX/ESXi host, or stored as an ISO image.

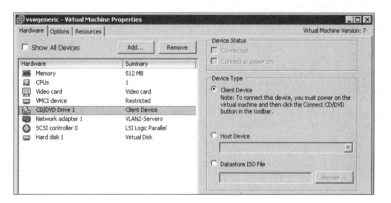

ISO IMAGE BASICS

An ISO image is an archive file of an optical disk. The name is derived from the International Organization for Standardization (ISO) 9660 file system standard used with CD-ROM media, and the ISO format is widely supported by many different software vendors. A variety of software applications can work with ISO images. In fact, most CD-burning software applications for Windows, Linux, and Mac OS X can create ISO images from existing physical disks or burn ISO images to a physical disk.

ISO images are the recommended way to install a guest operating system because they are faster than using an actual optical drive and can be quickly mounted or dismounted with very little effort.

Perform the following steps to install a guest operating system using an ISO file on a shared datastore:

1. Use the vSphere Client to connect to a vCenter Server instance or an individual ESX/ESXi host where a virtual machine has been created.

2. In the inventory tree, right-click the new virtual machine, and select the Edit Settings menu option. The Virtual Machine Properties window opens.

3. Select the CD/DVD Drive 1 hardware option.

4. Select the Datastore ISO File radio button, and select the Connect At Power On check box.

5. Click the Browse button to browse a datastore for the ISO file of the guest operating system.

6. Navigate through the available datastore options to find the ISO file of the guest operating system to be installed. After you select the ISO file, the properties page is configured similar to Figure 7.18.

7. Right-click the virtual machine, and select the Open Console option. Alternatively, you can use the Console in the details pane of the vSphere Client application.

8. Click the green Power On button from the toolbar of the console session. Alternatively, you can use the menu bar and select VM ➢ Power ➢ Power On. The virtual machine boots from the mounted ISO image and begins the installation of the guest operating system, as shown in Figure 7.19.

9. Follow the on-screen instructions to complete the guest operating system installation.

VIRTUAL MACHINE GUEST OPERATING SYSTEMS

For a complete list of guest operating systems and all respective information regarding installation notes and known issues, refer to the PDF available on the VMware website at www.vmware.com/pdf/GuestOS_guide.pdf.

After you install the guest operating system, you should then install VMware Tools. I'll discuss VMware Tools installation and configuration in the next section.

FIGURE 7.18
Virtual machines can treat ISO images as if they were CD/DVD drives, including booting from them for installation.

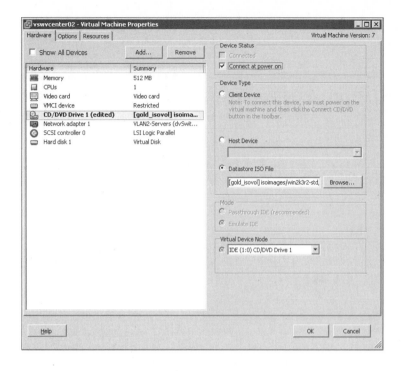

FIGURE 7.19
When the new virtual machine is turned on for the first time, it will boot from the CD/DVD drive to begin the installation of the guest operating system.

 **Real World Scenario**

MICROSOFT LICENSING AND WINDOWS ACTIVATION FOR VIRTUAL MACHINES

As the virtualization market has matured, Microsoft has adjusted its licensing practices to reflect that market. In spite of those adjustments—or perhaps because of them—there is still confusion about the virtualization licensing available for the Windows Server operating system. The following list of licensing data is a culmination of information from both Microsoft and VMware:

◆ Microsoft Windows Server licenses are attached to the physical machine, not to the virtual machine.

◆ A licensed copy of Windows Server 2008 Datacenter Edition entitles a user to install and run an unlimited number of virtual Windows instances on the physical server to which that license is assigned.

◆ Similarly, a licensed copy of Windows Server 2008 Enterprise Edition grants the user the right to install and run up to four Windows instances on the physical server to which the license is assigned.

◆ A license for Windows Server 2008 Standard Edition allows the user to run a single virtual Windows instance on the physical server to which the license is assigned.

◆ Downgrade rights exist so that a physical server licensed with Windows Server 2008 Datacenter Edition can run unlimited virtual machines running Datacenter Edition, Enterprise Edition, Standard Edition, or any mix of the three. This also applies to running previous versions of Windows Server.

◆ VMotion, which moves a running virtual machine to a new host, does not violate a Microsoft licensing agreement as long as the target ESX/ESXi host is licensed for the post-VMotion number of virtual machines. For example, if an ESX/ESXi host named ESX01 has four running instances of Windows in virtual machines, a second ESX host named ESX02 has three running instances of Windows in virtual machines, and each of the physical systems has been assigned a Windows Server 2008 Enterprise Edition license, then it is within the licensing agreement to perform a VMotion move of one virtual machine from ESX01 to ESX02. However, a VMotion move from ESX02 to ESX01 would violate the licensing agreement because ESX01 is licensed to run only up to four instances of Windows at a time.

Because Microsoft requires Windows Server licenses to be attached to physical hardware, many organizations are choosing to license their physical hardware with Windows Server 2008 Datacenter Edition. This gives the organization the ability to run an unlimited number of Windows Server instances on that hardware and downgrade or previous version rights allow the organization to use Standard, Enterprise, or Datacenter Edition of Windows Server 2003 or Windows Server 2008.

Activation is another area requiring a bit of planning. If your licensing structure for a Windows Server guest operating system does not fall under the umbrella of a volume licensing agreement, you will be required to activate the operating system with Microsoft within 60 days of installation. Activation can be done automatically over the Internet or by calling the provided regional phone number. With Windows Server operating systems specifically, the activation algorithm takes into account the hardware specifications of the server. In light of this, when enough hardware changes have been made to significantly change the operating system, Windows requires reactivation. To facilitate the activation process and especially to reduce the possibility of reactivation, make adjustments to memory and processors, and install VMware Tools prior to performing the activation.

Installing VMware Tools

Although VMware Tools is not installed by default, the package is an important part of a virtual machine. VMware Tools offers several great benefits without any detriments. In other words, installing VMware Tools should be standard practice and not a debatable step in the deployment of a virtual machine. The VMware Tools package provides the following:

- Optimized SCSI driver
- Enhanced video and mouse performance
- Virtual machine heartbeat
- Virtual machine quiescing for snapshots and backups
- Enhanced memory management

The VMware Tools package is available for Windows, Linux, NetWare, Solaris, and FreeBSD; however, the installation methods vary because of the differences in the guest operating systems. In all cases, the installation of VMware Tools starts when you select the option to install VMware Tools from the vSphere Client. Recall our discussion earlier about ISO images and how ESX/ESXi uses them to present CDs/DVDs to virtual machines? That's exactly the functionality that is being leveraged in this case. The guest operating system will reflect a mounted CD-ROM that has the installation files for VMware Tools. In the event you're curious, you'll find the VMware Tools ISO images located in the /vmimages/tools-isoimages directory on an ESX server. They are placed there automatically; you do not have to download them or obtain them from the installation CD-ROM, and you do not need to do anything to manage or maintain them.

Perform these steps to install VMware Tools in virtual machines with a Windows Server 2008 guest operating system:

1. Use the vSphere Client to connect to a vCenter Server or an individual ESX/ESXi host.

2. Right-click the virtual machine in the inventory tree, and select Guest ➢ Install/Upgrade VMware Tools.

3. A warning message displays that indicates that VMware Tools cannot be installed until the guest operating system is installed. Click OK.

4. An AutoPlay dialog box appears, prompting the user for action. Select the option Run Setup.exe. If the VMware Tools installation process does not begin automatically, open Windows Explorer, and double-click the CD/DVD drive icon. The VMware Tools installation should then launch.

5. Click Next on the Welcome To The Installation Wizard For VMware Tools page.

6. Select the appropriate setup type for the VMware Tools installation, and click Next. The Typical radio button will suffice for most situations. The Complete installation option

installs more features than are used by the current product, while the Custom installation option allows for the greatest level of feature customization.

7. Click Install.

8. After the installation is complete, click Finish.

9. Click Yes to restart the virtual machine immediately, or click No to manually restart the virtual machine at a later time.

After installing VMware Tools in a Windows guest operating system, configuring graphics hardware acceleration to its maximum setting provides a much smoother console session performance. The VMware Tools installation routine reminds the user to set this value at the end of the installation, but if the user chooses not to set hardware acceleration at that time, it can easily be set later. This is highly recommended to optimize the graphical performance of the virtual machine's console.

Perform the following steps to adjust the hardware acceleration in a virtual machine running Windows Server 2003 or Windows XP:

1. Right-click an empty area of the Windows desktop, and select the Properties option.

2. Select the Settings tab, and click the Advanced button.

3. Select the Troubleshooting tab.

4. Move the Hardware Acceleration slider to the Full setting on the right, as shown in Figure 7.20.

FIGURE 7.20
Adjusting the hardware acceleration feature of a Windows guest operating system is a common and helpful adjustment for improving mouse performance.

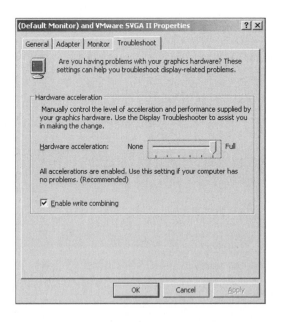

After the VMware Tools installation is complete and the virtual machine is rebooted, the system tray displays an icon of the VMware logo. The logo in the system tray, shown in Figure 7.21, indicates a successful VMware Tools installation.

FIGURE 7.21
After VMware Tools are installed on a Windows-based virtual machine, the VMware logo displays in the system tray.

By double-clicking the VMware logo in the system tray, you open the VMware Tools Properties dialog box, shown in Figure 7.22. Here you can configure time synchronization, hide VMware Tools from the taskbar, and create scripts to suspend, resume, shut down, or turn on a virtual machine.

FIGURE 7.22
Use VMware Tools to configure time synchronization with the Service Console.

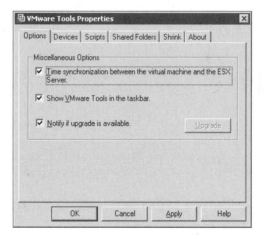

Use caution when enabling time synchronization between the guest operating system and the console operating system host since Windows domain members rely on Kerberos for authentication and Kerberos is sensitive to time differences between computers. A Windows-based guest operating system that belongs to an Active Directory domain is already configured with a native time synchronization process against the domain controller of its domain that functions as the PDC Emulator operations master. If the Service Console time is different from the PDC Emulator operations master domain controller, the guest operating system could end up moving outside the five-minute window that Kerberos allows. After the five-minute window is exceeded, Kerberos begins experiencing errors with authentication and replication.

You can take a few different approaches to managing time synchronizations in a virtual environment. The first approach involves not using VMware Tools time synchronization and relying instead on the W32Time service and a PDC Emulator with a registry edit that configures synchronization with an external time server. Another approach involves disabling the native time synchronization across the Windows domain and then relying on the VMware Tools feature. A third approach might be to synchronize the VMware ESX hosts and the PDC Emulator operations master with the same external time server and then to enable the VMware Tools option for synchronization. In this case, both the native W32Time service and VMware Tools should be adjusting the time to the same value.

CONFIGURING NTP ON ESX

If you do choose to synchronize the guest operating system to the ESX host using VMware Tools, be sure to synchronize the ESX host to an authoritative time source using NTP. Refer to Chapter 2 for more information on exactly how to configure ESX to synchronize with an NTP-based time server.

Perform the following steps to install VMware Tools into a Linux guest operating system:

1. Use the vSphere Client to connect to a vCenter Server instance or an individual ESX/ESXi host.

2. You will need access to the console of the virtual machine onto which you're installing VMware Tools. Right-click the virtual machine, and select Open Console.

3. Log into the Linux guest operating system using an account with appropriate permissions. This will typically be the root account.

4. From the console's VM menu, select Guest ➢ Install/Upgrade VMware Tools. Click OK to the dialog box that pops up.

5. From a Linux terminal prompt, mount the CD/DVD drive with this command:

   ```
   mount /media/cdrom
   ```

6. Change directories to the location of the VMware Tools mount point using the following command:

   ```
   cd /media/cdrom
   ```

7. Extract the compressed tar file (with the .tar.gz extension) to a temporary directory, and then change to that temporary directory using the following commands:

   ```
   tar -zxf VMwareTools-4.0.0-140815.tar.gz -C /tmp
   cd /tmp/vmware-tools-distrib
   ```

8. In the /tmp/vmware-tools-distrib directory, run the vmware-install.pl Perl script using the following command:

   ```
   ./vmware-install.pl
   ```

Figure 7.23 shows the commands for steps 4 through 7.

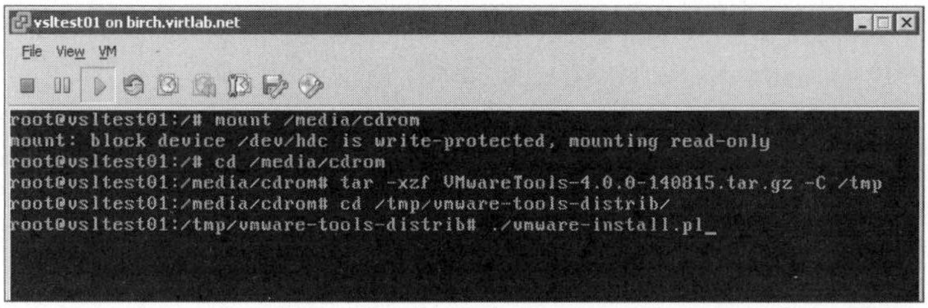

FIGURE 7.23
Installing VMware Tools for Linux from the command line involves extracting the tools and running the install file.

9. The installer will provide a series of prompts for information such as where to place the binary files, where the init scripts are located, and where to place the library files. Default answers are provided in brackets; you can just press Enter unless you need to specify a different value that is appropriate for this Linux system.

10. After the installation is complete, remove the temporary installation directory using these commands:

```
rm -rf /tmp/vmware-tools-distrib
```

11. Unmount the CD/DVD drive with these commands:

```
cd /
umount /media/cdrom
```

The steps described here were performed on a virtual machine running the server distribution of Ubuntu Linux 7.04. Because of variations within different distributions of Linux, the commands you may need to install VMware Tools within another distribution may not match what I've listed here. However, these steps do provide a general guideline of what the procedure looks like.

VMWARE TOOLS FOR LINUX

When installing VMware Tools to a Linux guest operating system, the path to the TAR file and the numbers in the TAR filename will vary. Depending upon your Linux distribution, the VMware Tools installer may also provide instructions on replacing the Ethernet driver with an updated VMXNet driver. Typically, these instructions involve unloading the older drivers, scanning for new devices, loading the new VMXNet driver, and then bringing the network interfaces back up.

You can determine the existence of VMware Tools by checking for the icon displayed on the notification bar inside the guest operating system or by using the vSphere Client. As shown in Figure 7.24, the Summary tab of a virtual machine object identifies the status of VMware Tools as well as other information such as operating system, CPU, memory, DNS (host) name, IP address, and current ESX/ESXi host.

In the event you are upgrading to vSphere from a previous version of VMware Infrastructure, you may have outdated versions of VMware Tools running in your guest operating systems. You'll want to upgrade these in order to get the latest drivers.

For Windows-based guest operating systems, the process of upgrading VMware Tools is as simple as right-clicking a virtual machine and selecting Guest ➢ Install/Upgrade VMware Tools. Select the option labeled Automatic Tools Upgrade, and click OK. vCenter Server will install the updated VMware Tools and automatically reboot the virtual machine, if necessary.

FIGURE 7.24
You can view details about VMware Tools, DNS name, IP address, and so forth, from the Summary tab of a virtual machine object.

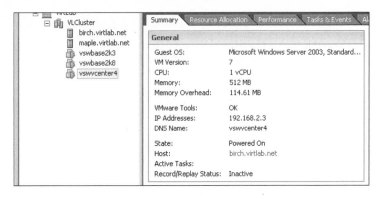

For other guest operating systems, upgrading VMware Tools typically means running through the install process again. You can refer to the instructions for installing VMware Tools on Ubuntu Linux earlier in this chapter, for example, for information on upgrading VMware Tools in a Linux virtual machine.

Managing and Modifying Virtual Machines

Just as physical machines require hardware upgrades, a virtual machine might require hardware upgrades to meet changing performance demands. Perhaps a new memory-intensive client-server application requires an increase in memory, or a new data-mining application requires a second processor or additional network adapters for bandwidth-heavy FTP traffic. In each of these cases, the virtual machine requires a modification of the virtual hardware configured for the guest operating system to use.

In most cases, modifying a virtual machine requires that the virtual machine is powered off. There are exceptions to this rule, as shown in Figure 7.25. You can hot-add a USB controller, an Ethernet adapter, a hard disk, or a SCSI device.

When adding new virtual hardware to a virtual machine using the vSphere Client, the screens are very similar to the screens used while creating a virtual machine. For example, to add a new virtual hard drive to an existing virtual machine, you would use the Add button at the top of the Virtual Machine Properties dialog box. This was displayed earlier in this chapter in Figure 7.17. From there, the vSphere Client uses the same steps shown in Figures 7.12, 7.13, and 7.14 earlier in this chapter. The only difference is that now you're adding a new virtual hard drive to an existing virtual machine.

Perform the following steps to add an Ethernet adapter to a virtual machine:

1. Launch the vSphere Client, and connect to a vCenter Server instance or an individual ESX/ESXi host.

2. Right-click the virtual machine, and select Edit Settings.

3. Click the Add button at the top of the Virtual Machine Properties dialog box.

4. Select Ethernet Adapter, and click Next.

5. Select the network adapter type, the network to which it should be connected, and whether the network adapter should be connected at power on, as shown in Figure 7.26. Click Next to continue.

6. Review the settings, and click Finish.

FIGURE 7.25
Users can add some types of hardware while the virtual machine is powered on.

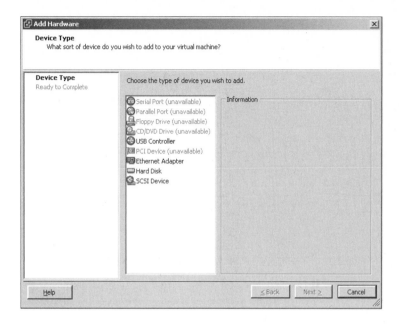

FIGURE 7.26
To add a new network adapter, you must select the adapter type, the network, and whether it should be connected at power on.

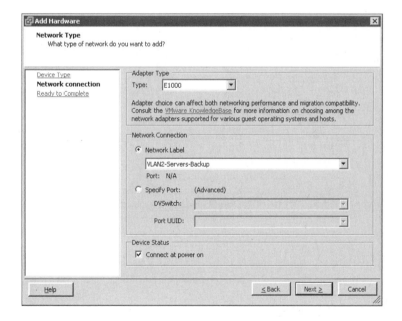

Besides adding new virtual hardware, users can make other changes while a virtual machine is powered on. For example, you can mount and unmount CD/DVD drives and floppy disk images while a virtual machine is turned on. You can also assign and reassign adapters to virtual networks while a virtual machine is running.

POWERING OFF VS. SHUTTING DOWN THE GUEST

You might notice that the right-click context menu of a virtual machine contains two items that appear to do the same the function. One of them is Power ➢ Power Off, and the other is Guest ➢ Shut Down Guest. What's the difference between these two?

The Power ➢ Power Off command does exactly that: it powers off the virtual machine. It's like pulling the power cord out unexpectedly. The guest operating system has no time to prepare for a shutdown.

The Guest ➢ Shut Down Guest command issues a shutdown command to the guest operating system so that the guest operating system can shut down in an orderly fashion. This command requires that VMware Tools is already installed, and it ensures that the guest operating system won't be corrupted or damaged by an unexpected shutdown.

In day-to-day operation, use the Shut Down Guest option. The Power Off option should be used only when it is absolutely necessary.

Otherwise, changes to the configuration of a virtual machine can take place only when the virtual machine is in a powered-off state. When a virtual machine is powered off, all the various configuration options are available to change: RAM, virtual CPUs, or adding or removing other hardware components such as CD/DVD drives or floppy drives.

DOES ANYONE STILL USE FLOPPY DRIVES?

New virtual machines created in a vSphere environment automatically come with a floppy drive, although in my experience it is rarely used. In fact, about the only time that it does get used is when a custom storage driver needs to be added during installation of a Windows-based guest operating system. Unless you know you will need to use a floppy drive, it's generally safe to remove the floppy drive from the hardware list.

As administrators, we perform the majority of our work on virtual machines from the vSphere Client. There are those infrequent occasions when we have to work directly with the files that make up the virtual machine. In Figure 7.16 earlier in this chapter, you saw how there are many files that relate to a working virtual machine. Now let's take a closer look at the two main files involved: the configuration (VMX) file and the virtual hard disk (VMDK) file.

The VMX file identifies the configuration of the virtual machine with respect to the virtual hardware allocated to the virtual machine. Listing 7.1 shows a sample VMX file for a virtual machine named vswvcenter4.

LISTING 7.1:   Example Virtual Machine Configuration (VMX) File

```
#!/usr/bin/vmware
.encoding = "UTF-8"
config.version = "8"
virtualHW.version = "7"
svga.autodetect = "TRUE"
mks.enable3d = "TRUE"
pciBridge0.present = "TRUE"
```

```
pciBridge4.present = "TRUE"
pciBridge4.virtualDev = "pcieRootPort"
pciBridge4.functions = "8"
pciBridge5.present = "TRUE"
pciBridge5.virtualDev = "pcieRootPort"
pciBridge5.functions = "8"
pciBridge6.present = "TRUE"
pciBridge6.virtualDev = "pcieRootPort"
pciBridge6.functions = "8"
pciBridge7.present = "TRUE"
pciBridge7.virtualDev = "pcieRootPort"
pciBridge7.functions = "8"
vmci0.present = "TRUE"
nvram = "vswvcenter4.nvram"
deploymentPlatform = "windows"
virtualHW.productCompatibility = "hosted"
unity.customColor = "|23C0C0C0"
tools.upgrade.policy = "useGlobal"
powerType.powerOff = "soft"
powerType.powerOn = "default"
powerType.suspend = "hard"
powerType.reset = "soft"

displayName = "vswvcenter4"
extendedConfigFile = "vswvcenter4.vmxf"

scsi0.present = "TRUE"
scsi0.sharedBus = "none"
scsi0.virtualDev = "lsilogic"
memsize = "512"
scsi0:0.present = "TRUE"
scsi0:0.fileName = "vswvcenter4.vmdk"
scsi0:0.deviceType = "scsi-hardDisk"
ide1:0.present = "TRUE"
ide1:0.clientDevice = "TRUE"
ide1:0.deviceType = "atapi-cdrom"
ide1:0.startConnected = "FALSE"
ethernet0.present = "TRUE"
ethernet0.networkName = "VLAN2-Servers"
ethernet0.addressType = "generated"
guestOSAltName = "Microsoft Windows Server 2003, Standard Edition (32-bit)"
guestOS = "winnetstandard"
uuid.location = "56 4d 1b c2 dc 77 31 53-ea 20 44 37 1a c1 86 ea"
uuid.bios = "56 4d f5 be f1 4b 53 1d-00 0b cc 8d fa ca 7b 25"
vc.uuid = "52 b0 d0 c2 4d 7e 5f 8f-75 99 a5 4f ec 4e f1 18"

ide1:0.fileName = ""

ethernet0.generatedAddress = "00:0c:29:ca:7b:25"
```

```
tools.syncTime = "FALSE"
cleanShutdown = "FALSE"
replay.supported = "FALSE"
sched.swap.derivedName =
"/vmfs/volumes/c83d6653-20abe8b7/vswvcenter4/vswvcenter4-bd250361.vswp"
scsi0:0.redo = ""
vmotion.checkpointFBSize = "16777216"
pciBridge0.pciSlotNumber = "17"
pciBridge4.pciSlotNumber = "21"
pciBridge5.pciSlotNumber = "22"
pciBridge6.pciSlotNumber = "23"
pciBridge7.pciSlotNumber = "24"
scsi0.pciSlotNumber = "16"
ethernet0.pciSlotNumber = "32"
vmci0.pciSlotNumber = "33"
ethernet0.generatedAddressOffset = "0"
vmci0.id = "-87393499"
hostCPUID.0 = "0000000168747541444d416369746e65"
guestCPUID.0 = "0000000168747541444d416369746e65"
userCPUID.0 = "0000000168747541444d416369746e65"
hostCPUID.1 = "00040f120002080000002001178bfbff"
guestCPUID.1 = "00020f100000080080000001078bbbff"
userCPUID.1 = "00040f120002080000000001078bbbff"
hostCPUID.80000001 = "00040f12000002d10000001febd3fbff"
guestCPUID.80000001 = "00020f10000002d100000000e3d3bbff"
userCPUID.80000001 = "00040f12000002d100000000e3d3bbff"
evcCompatibilityMode = "TRUE"

migrate.hostlog = "./vswvcenter4-bd250361.hlog"

sched.cpu.min = "0"
sched.cpu.units = "mhz"
sched.cpu.shares = "normal"
sched.mem.minsize = "0"
sched.mem.max = "512"
sched.mem.shares = "normal"
guest.commands.allowSharedSecretLogin = ""
guest.commands.sharedSecretLogin.com.vmware.vcIntegrity = ""

floppy0.present = "FALSE"

scsi0:1.fileName = "vswvcenter4_1.vmdk"
scsi0:1.mode = "persistent"
scsi0:1.ctkEnabled = "FALSE"
scsi0:1.deviceType = "scsi-hardDisk"
scsi0:1.present = "FALSE"
scsi0:1.redo = ""
```

Reading through the vswvcenter4.vmx file, you will notice the following facts about this virtual machine:

◆ The virtual machine is configured for the 32-bit version of Windows Server 2003 Standard Edition.

◆ The virtual machine is configured for 512MB of RAM.

◆ The VM's hard drive is located in the file vswvcenter4.vmdk.

◆ The VM has a single CD-ROM that does not start connected.

◆ The floppy drive is not configured.

◆ The virtual machine has a single network adapter configured to the VLAN2-Servers port group.

◆ The VM's single network adapter has an automatically generated MAC address of 00:0c:29:ca:7b:25.

◆ There used to be a second SCSI hard disk attached to this VM, which was stored in the file vswvcenter4_1.vmdk, but this disk is no longer present.

Although the VMDK file is not human-readable, it is arguably the most important file for a virtual machine. You can rebuild a VMX configuration file quite easily, but a VMDK is the data behind the virtual hard drive and is not as easy to rebuild. Referring to Figure 7.16, you'll see only a single VMDK file listed. In actuality, though, there are two files. These files are presented as a single file from the vSphere Client, so to see them you must go to the Service Console. From there, as shown in Figure 7.27, you'll see that there are two VMDK files. Of particular interest is the file that ends with -flat.vmdk. The -flat.vmdk file for a virtual machine is where the actual virtual machine data is stored; the smaller of the two VMDK files is actually a header file. This header file, shown in Listing 7.2, just provides information about the -flat.vmdk file.

FIGURE 7.27
There are actually two different VMDK files for every virtual hard disk in a virtual machine, even though the vSphere Client shows only a single file.

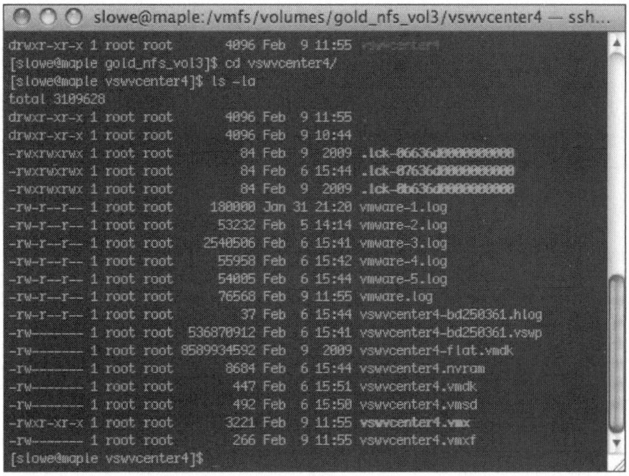

LISTING 7.2:   Example VMDK Header File

```
# Disk DescriptorFile
version=1
encoding="UTF-8"
CID=6837ce5f
parentCID=ffffffff
createType="vmfs"

# Extent description
RW 16777216 VMFS "vswvcenter4-flat.vmdk"

# The Disk Data Base
#DDB

ddb.virtualHWVersion = "7"
ddb.uuid = "60 00 C2 93 d6 4b 69 30-d4 2b 4c 2a d7 ec ce 3c"
ddb.geometry.cylinders = "1044"
ddb.geometry.heads = "255"
ddb.geometry.sectors = "63"
ddb.adapterType = "lsilogic"
ddb.thinProvisioned = "1"
ddb.toolsVersion = "8192"
```

When browsing a datastore using the vSphere Client, as shown earlier in Figure 7.16, both VMDK files are combined into a single file entry, the size of which reflects the current size of the −flat.vmdk file. In a thin provisioned scenario, this size reflects only the size that is currently allocated by the guest operating system; otherwise, it reflects the maximum size of the virtual hard disk.

ALIGNING VIRTUAL MACHINE FILE SYSTEMS

In Chapter 6 I introduced the concept of aligning the VMFS file system, and I also suggested that the virtual machine's file system should be aligned. If you construct virtual machines with separate virtual hard drives for the operating system and data, then you are most concerned with the alignment of the file system for the data drive because the greatest amount of I/O occurs on that drive. For example, a virtual machine with Disk 0 (that holds the operating system) and a blank disk called Disk 1 (that holds data that will incur significant I/O) should have Disk 1 aligned.

Perform the following steps to align Disk 1 of the virtual machine:

1. Log in to the virtual machine using an account with administrative credentials.

2. Open a command prompt, and type **Diskpart**.

3. Type **list disk**, and press Enter.

4. Type **select disk 1**, and press Enter.

5. Type **create partition primary align = 64**, and press Enter.

6. Type **assign letter = X**, where *X* is an open letter that can be assigned.

7. Type **list part** to verify the 64KB offset for the new partition.

8. Format the partition.

Perhaps you are thinking that this seems like a tedious task to perform for all your virtual machines. It *is* a tedious task; however, the benefit of doing this is realized most when there is a significant I/O requirement. Keep in mind that you could also perform this task in the template that is used to provision new virtual machines.

Just like previous versions of vCenter Server (then called VirtualCenter), vCenter Server 4 supports virtual machine snapshots. Snapshots provide administrators with the ability to create point-in-time snapshots of a virtual machine. VMware administrators can then revert to their pre-snapshot state in the event the changes made since the snapshot should be discarded. Or, if the changes should be preserved, the administrator can commit the changes and delete the snapshot. Snapshots are leveraged by vCenter Update Manager and are also used by the VMware Consolidated Backup framework.

Perform the following steps to create a snapshot of a virtual machine:

1. Use the vSphere Client to connect to a vCenter Server instance or an individual ESX/ESXi host.

2. Right-click the virtual machine name in the inventory tree, select Snapshot, and then select Take Snapshot.

3. Provide a name and description for the snapshot, and then click OK, as shown in Figure 7.28.

FIGURE 7.28
Providing names and descriptions for snapshots is an easy way to manage multiple historical snapshots.

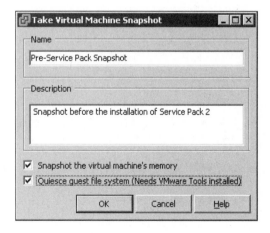

As shown in Figure 7.28, there are two options when taking snapshots:

◆ The option labeled Snapshot The Virtual Machine's Memory specifies whether the RAM of the virtual machine should also be included in the snapshot. When this option is selected, the current contents of the virtual machine's RAM are written to a file ending in a `.vmsn` extension.

◆ The option labeled Quiesce Guest File System (Needs VMware Tools Installed) controls whether the guest file system will be quiesced—or quieted—so that the guest file system is considered consistent. This can help ensure that the data within the guest file system is intact in the snapshot.

When a snapshot is taken, depending upon the previous options, some additional files are created on the datastore, as shown in Figure 7.29.

FIGURE 7.29
When a snapshot is taken, some additional files are created on the virtual machine's datastore.

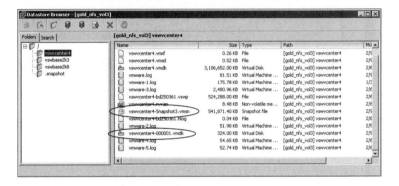

It is a common misconception for administrators to think of snapshots as full copies of virtual machine files. As can be clearly seen in Figure 7.29, a snapshot is not a full copy of a virtual machine. VMware's snapshot technology allows for minimal space consumption while still reverting to a previous snapshot by only allocating enough space to store the changes, rather than making a full copy.

To demonstrate snapshot technology and illustrate its behavior, I performed the following steps:

1. I created the virtual machine with a default installation of Windows Server 2003 with a single hard drive (recognized by the guest operating system as drive C:).

2. I took a snapshot named testsnap1.

3. I added approximately 500MB of data to drive C:, represented as vswvcenter4.vmdk.

4. I took a second snapshot named testsnap2.

5. I once again added approximately 500MB of data to drive C:, represented as vswvcenter4.vmdk.

Review Table 7.1 for the results I recorded after each step.

As you can see from Table 7.1, the virtual machine is unaware of the presence of the snapshot and the extra VMDK files that are created. ESX/ESXi, however, knows to write changes to the virtual machine's virtual disk to the snapshot VMDK, properly known as a *delta disk*. These delta disks start out very small and over time grow to accommodate the changes stored within them.

Despite the storage efficiency that snapshots attempt to maintain, over time they can eat up a considerable amount of disk space. Therefore, use them as needed, but be sure to remove older snapshots on a regular basis. Also be aware there are performance ramifications to using snapshots. Because disk space must be allocated to the delta disks on demand, ESX/ESXi hosts must update the metadata files (.sf files) every time the differencing disk grows. To update the metadata files, LUNs must be locked, and this adversely affects the performance of other virtual machines and hosts using the same LUN. Finally, note that snapshots can't be used in conjunction with certain other vSphere features. For example, VMs that have a snapshot present cannot have VMware Fault Tolerance (FT) enabled. Despite these concerns, you'll find snapshots helpful when making risky changes to production servers (such as renaming the domain or installing service packs).

TABLE 7.1: Snapshot Demonstration Results

	VMDK SIZE	NTFS SIZE	NTFS FREE SPACE
Start (pre-first snapshot)			
vswvcenter4.vmdk (C:)	3.1GB	7.9GB	4.9GB
First snapshot (pre-data copy)			
vswvcenter4.vmdk (C:)	3.1GB	7.9GB	4.9GB
vswcenter4-000001.vmdk	140KB		
First snapshot (post-data copy)			
vswvcenter4.vmdk (C:)	3.1GB	7.9GB	4.4GB
vswcenter4-000001.vmdk	566MB		
Second snapshot (pre-data copy)			
vswvcenter4.vmdk (C:)	3.1GB	7.9GB	4.4GB
vswcenter4-000001.vmdk	566MB		
vswcenter4-000002.vmdk	116KB		
Second snapshot (post-data copy)			
vswvcenter4.vmdk (C:)	3.1GB	7.9GB	3.8GB
vswcenter4-000001.vmdk	566MB		
vswcenter4-000002.vmdk	564MB		

To delete a snapshot or revert to a snapshot, you use the Snapshot Manager to view and delete snapshots or revert to an earlier snapshot.

Perform the following steps to access the Snapshot Manager:

1. Use the vSphere Client to connect to a vCenter Server instance or an individual ESX/ESXi host.

2. In the inventory tree, right-click the name of the virtual machine, and from the context menu select Snapshot ➢ Snapshot Manager. Alternately, you can also click the Snapshot Manager button on the vSphere Client toolbar.

3. Select the appropriate snapshot to fall back to, and then click the Go To button, as shown in Figure 7.30.

FIGURE 7.30
The Snapshot Manager can revert to previous snapshots, but all data written since that snapshot that hasn't been backed up elsewhere will be lost.

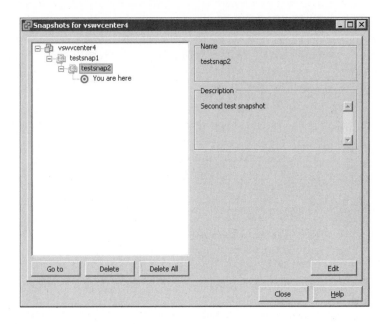

To further illustrate the nature of snapshots, see Figure 7.31 and Figure 7.32. Figure 7.31 shows the file system of a virtual machine running Windows Server 2003 after data has been written into two new folders named temp1 and temp2. Figure 7.32 shows the same virtual machine, but after reverting to a snapshot taken before that data was written. As you can see, it's as if the new folders never even existed.

FIGURE 7.31
This virtual machine running Windows Server 2003 has had some data placed into two temporary folders.

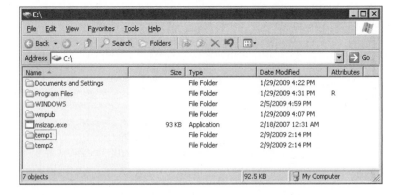

FIGURE 7.32
The same virtual machine, after reverting to a snapshot taken before the temporary folders were created, no longer has any record of the data.

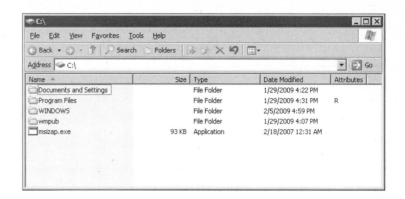

REVERTING TO A SNAPSHOT

Reverting to a snapshot incurs a loss of data. Any data that was written since the snapshot has occurred will no longer be available, along with any applications that were installed since the snapshot was taken. Therefore, revert to snapshots only if you have determined that the loss of data is acceptable or if the data is backed up elsewhere.

Creating Templates and Deploying Virtual Machines

If you've ever wished there were a faster way to provision a new server into your environment, then VMware fulfills that wish in a big way. In a vSphere environment, what would traditionally take several hours to do is now reduced to a matter of minutes. With the templates feature of vCenter Server, you can roll out new virtual machines quickly and easily with limited administrative effort.

vCenter Server offers two different options for creating templates: Clone To Template and Convert To Template. As the name suggests, the Clone To Template feature copies a virtual machine to a template format, leaving the original virtual machine intact. Similarly, the Convert To Template feature involves a virtual machine that is changed to a template format, thereby removing the ability to turn on the virtual machine without converting back to a virtual machine format.

When considering which virtual machines should become templates, remember that the idea behind a template is to have a pristine system configuration that can be customized as needed for deployment to the target environment. Any information stored on a virtual machine that becomes a template will become part of the new system that is deployed from that template. If you have virtual machines that are critical servers for production environments that have applications installed, those are not good candidates to become templates.

In fact, I recommend creating a new virtual machine specifically for use as a template or creating the template from a virtual machine as soon after creation as possible. This ensures that the template is as pristine as possible and that all virtual machines cloned from that template will start out the same way.

You can convert a virtual machine to a template using the right-click menu of the virtual machine or the Convert To Template link in the Commands list. Figure 7.33 shows two ways an existing virtual machine can be converted into a template format. To make updates to a template, you must first convert the template back to a virtual machine, then update it, and finally convert it back to a template.

FIGURE 7.33
Users can either convert a virtual machine to a template or clone the virtual machine to a template.

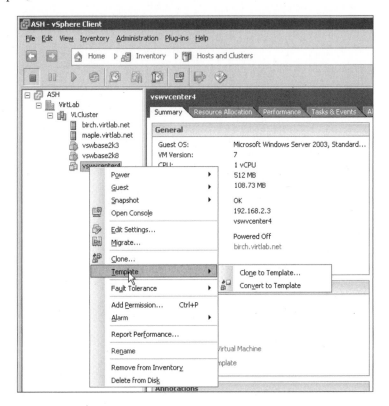

The Clone To Template feature provides the same end result as the conversion method in creating a template that can be deployed as a new virtual machine, but it differs from the conversion method in that the virtual machine remains intact. By leaving the virtual machine in a format that can be turned on, the Clone To Template feature facilitates making updates to the template. This means you don't have to store the template object definition in the same datastore from which the virtual machine was built.

Perform these steps to clone a virtual machine into a template format:

1. Use the vSphere Client to connect to a vCenter Server instance. Cloning and templates are not supported when using the vSphere Client to connect directly to an ESX/ESXi host.

2. Right-click the virtual machine to be used as a template, and select Template ➤ Clone To Template.

3. Type a name for the new template in the Template Name text box, select a location in the inventory to store the template, and then click Next, as shown in Figure 7.34.

4. Select the host or cluster where the template should be hosted, and click Next.

FIGURE 7.34
Templates should have meaningful names that describe the pristine environment provided by the template.

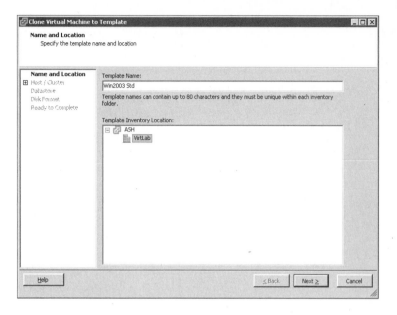

5. Select the datastore where the template should be stored, and click Next.

6. Select the disk format for the template, shown in Figure 7.35, and click Next. Three options are available for the template's disk format:

FIGURE 7.35
vCenter Server offers three options for storing a template's virtual disks.

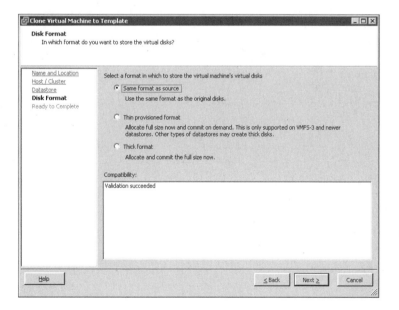

- ◆ The Same Format As Source option keeps the template's virtual disks in the same format as the virtual machine that is being cloned.

◆ Thin Provisioned Format commits space on demand, meaning that it will occupy only as much space as is currently used by the guest operating system.

◆ Thick Format allocates and commits the full size of the virtual disks upon creation.

7. Review the template configuration information, and click Finish.

Templates have a different icon than the one used to identify a virtual machine in the vCenter Server inventory. The template objects are available by clicking a datacenter object and then selecting the Virtual Machines tab, or by adjusting the inventory view to the VMs and Templates view.

After you have created a library of templates, provisioning a new virtual machine is as simple as right-clicking the template you'd like to use as the base system image. For virtual machines running Windows as the guest operating system, VMware has included a component within the template processes that eliminates the need for administrators to perform tasks that force uniqueness on the virtual machine created from the template. The catch is that an administrator must extract Sysprep and its associated files to a directory created during the installation of vCenter Server. If these files are not extracted before you deploy a virtual machine, the guest customization page of the Deploy Template Wizard will be unavailable. Figure 7.36 shows the Guest Customization page of the Deploy Template Wizard on a vCenter Server that has not had the Sysprep files extracted.

FIGURE 7.36
If the Sysprep files are not extracted and stored on the vCenter Server system, you won't be able to customize the guest operating system when you deploy from a template.

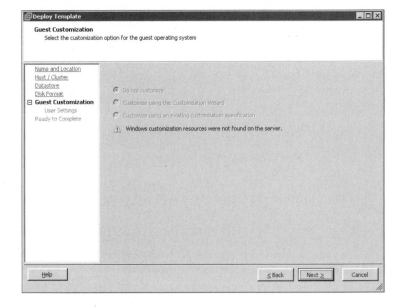

Perform these steps to allow guest operating system customization of Windows Server 2003 x86 guest operating system templates:

1. Insert the Windows Server 2003 x86 CD into the disk drive of the vCenter Server.

2. Navigate to the /support/tools/deploy.cab directory on the Windows Server 2003 CD.

3. As shown in Figure 7.37, copy the sysprep.exe and setupcl.exe files to this directory:

```
C:\Documents and Settings\All Users\Application Data\VMware\VMware
VirtualCenter\sysprep\svr2003
```

FIGURE 7.37
Customizing the Windows guest operating system requires the extraction of the `sysprep.exe` and `setupcl.exe` files to a specific directory on the vCenter Server.

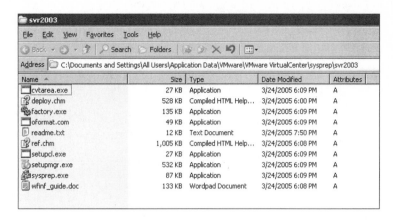

Perform these steps to deploy a virtual machine from a template:

1. Use the vSphere Client to connect to a vCenter Server instance. Cloning and templates are not supported when using the vSphere Client to connect directly to an ESX/ESXi host.

2. Locate the template object to be used as the virtual machine baseline.

3. Right-click the template object, and select Deploy Virtual Machine From This Template.

4. Type a name for the new virtual machine in the virtual machine's Name text box, select a location in the inventory to store the virtual machine, and then click Next, as shown in Figure 7.38.

FIGURE 7.38
The virtual machine's display name is the friendly name reflected in the vCenter Server inventory and should match the guest operating system's hostname.

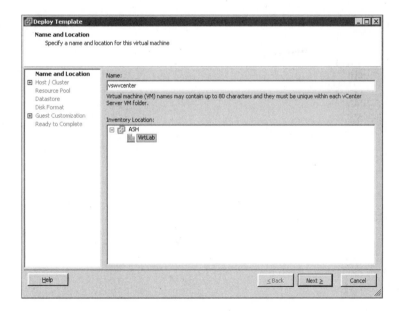

5. Select a host on which the virtual machine should run, and then click Next.

6. Select a datastore location for the virtual machine files, as shown in Figure 7.39. Click the Advanced button if you want to specify an alternate storage location for virtual machine disk files.

FIGURE 7.39
Select a datastore for a new virtual machine based on the VMotion, DRS, and HA constraints of your organization.

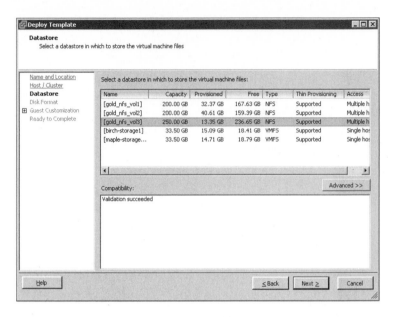

7. Select the disk format for the virtual machine to be created from the template.

8. For first-time template deployments, as shown in Figure 7.40, select the Customize Using The Customization Wizard option to create a new XML-based answer file, and then click Next.

FIGURE 7.40
The vSphere Client Windows Guest Customization Wizard allows you to create an answer file that provides unattended installations of a guest operating system. The answer file data is stored in the vCenter Server database.

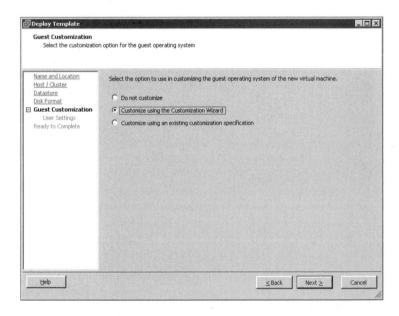

9. At this point, the vSphere Client Windows Guest Customization Wizard starts. Provide a name and organization to be used for virtual machines built from the customization file.

10. For simplicity and consistency, as shown in Figure 7.41, select the Use The Virtual Machine Name option to specify that the guest operating system hostname be the same as the display name, and then click Next.

FIGURE 7.41
vCenter Server's customization functionality can ensure that the virtual machine name is the same as the guest operating system's hostname.

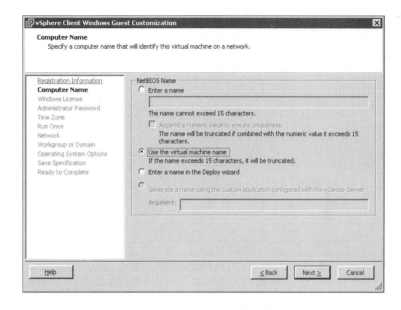

11. Enter a valid Windows product key, configure the licensing mode, and click Next.

12. Enter an administrator password, and click Next.

13. Enter the appropriate time zone for the new virtual machine, and click Next.

14. Enter any commands that should run one time at the end of the setup, and click Next.

15. Configure the network adapter to use DHCP and standard settings with the Typical option; to manually configure each network interface, select Custom, and then click Next. If you select Custom, then you must configure the settings for each of the network adapters in the virtual machine accordingly.

16. Specify the workgroup or domain membership of the new guest operating system, and click Next.

17. In almost all instances, you'll want to ensure that the Generate New Security ID (SID) check box is selected. Click Next.

18. As shown in Figure 7.42, ensure the Save This Customization Specification For Later Use check box is selected, provide a name for the customization file, enter a description as needed, and then click Next.

19. Review the customization information, and then click Finish.

20. Review the template deployment information, select the Power On The New Virtual Machine After Creation option as needed, and then click Finish.

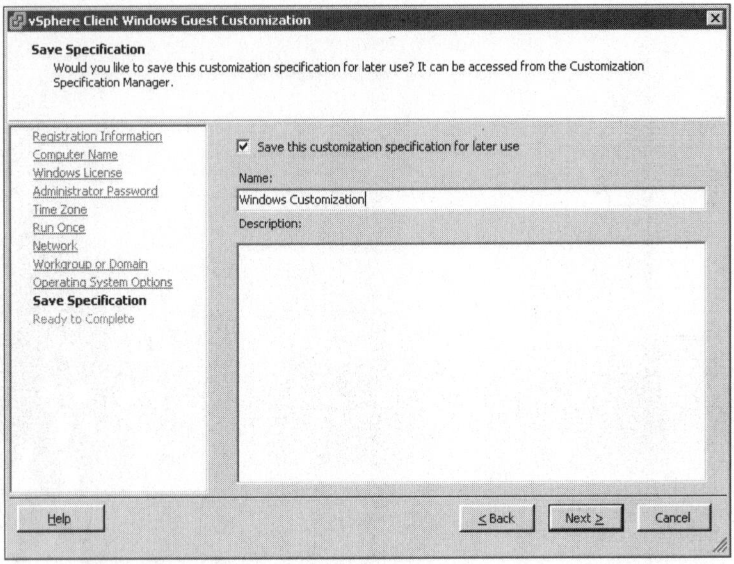

FIGURE 7.42
You can save and reuse customization specifications for future virtual machine deployments.

VIRTUAL MACHINE CLONING

Although templates might be the most common means of deploying a new virtual machine, it is possible to clone any virtual machine, even powered-on virtual machines! The right-click menu of a virtual machine provides a Clone option that allows you to make a copy without first converting to a template. The Clone To New Virtual Machine option from the Commands list on a virtual machine summary page accomplishes the same task. The wizard that initiates this will provide similar options to the wizard you use when cloning from a template. Keep in mind that unless you customize the guest operating system, an exact copy of the original virtual machine will be made. This could be especially useful when you're looking to create a test environment that mirrors a live production environment.

The Bottom Line

Create a virtual machine. A virtual machine is a collection of virtual hardware pieces, like a physical system—one or more virtual CPUs, RAM, video card, SCSI devices, IDE devices, floppy drives, parallel and serial ports, and network adapters. This virtual hardware is virtualized and abstracted from the underlying physical hardware, providing portability for the virtual machine.

Master It Create two virtual machines, one intended to run Windows Server 2003 and a second intended to run Windows Server 2008. Make a list of the differences in the configuration that are suggested by the Create New Virtual Machine Wizard.

Install a guest operating system. Just as a physical machine needs an operating system, a virtual machine also needs an operating system. VMware ESX and ESXi support a broad range of 32-bit and 64-bit operating systems, including all major versions of Windows Server, Windows

Vista, Windows XP, and Windows 2000, as well as various flavors of Linux, FreeBSD, Novell NetWare, and Solaris.

Master It   What are the three ways in which a guest operating system can access data on a CD/DVD, and what are the advantages of each approach?

Install VMware Tools.   For maximum performance of the guest operating system, it needs to have virtualization-optimized drivers that are specially written for and designed to work with the VMware ESX/ESXi hypervisor. VMware Tools provides these optimized drivers as well as other utilities focused on better operation in virtual environments.

Master It   A fellow administrator contacts you and is having a problem installing VMware Tools. This administrator has selected the Install/Upgrade VMware Tools command, but nothing seems to be happening inside the virtual machine. What could be the cause of the problem?

Manage and modify a virtual machine.   Once a virtual machine has been created, the vSphere Client makes it easy to manage and modify the virtual machine. Virtual hardware can be added to or removed from the virtual machine, network adapters can be modified, and CD/DVD drives can be mounted or unmounted as necessary. Some types of virtual hardware can be "hot-added" while the virtual machine is turned on, while other types require that the virtual machine is powered off.

Master It   Which method is preferred for modifying the configuration of a virtual machine—editing the VMX file or using the vSphere Client?

Create templates and deploy virtual machines.   vCenter Server's templates feature provides an excellent way to quickly and easily deploy consistent virtual machines. With options to clone or convert an existing virtual machine to a template, vCenter Server makes it easy to create templates. Then, once a template has been created, vCenter Server can clone virtual machines from that template, customizing them in the process to ensure that each one is unique. The customization specifications that vCenter Server uses to customize the cloned virtual machines can be saved and reused numerous times.

Master It   Of the following tasks, which are appropriate to be performed on a virtual machine running Windows Server 2008 that will eventually be turned into a template?

   a. Align the guest operating system's file system to a 64KB boundary?
   b. Join the virtual machine to Active Directory?
   c. Perform some application-specific configurations and tweaks?
   d. Install all patches from the operating system vendor?

Chapter 8

Migrating and Importing Virtual Machines

Converting existing systems into virtual machines is the essence of building a virtual infrastructure. Consolidating physical systems provides significant intrinsic savings in the areas of physical space, power consumption, and hardware costs. In this chapter, I'll cover the native tools available for performing a server consolidation by migrating physical computers into virtual machines.

In this chapter, you will learn to:

- ◆ Use vCenter Server Guided Consolidation

- ◆ Perform physical-to-virtual migrations of running computers

- ◆ Perform physical-to-virtual migrations of computers that are powered off

- ◆ Import virtual appliances

Setting Up the Conversion Tools

Two key conversion tools are involved in physical-to-virtual (P2V) operations. The first of these tools is VMware vCenter Converter. vCenter Converter is the tool that is responsible for actually performing the P2V conversion. The second tool is called Guided Consolidation, and its purpose is to gather information about physical computers in your environment and then make recommendations about which computers can or should be moved into the virtual environment via a P2V operation. As you can see, these tools are complementary in many respects.

Each of these tools requires a separate installation after you've installed vCenter Server. We'll start with the installation of vCenter Converter and then move on to the installation of Guided Consolidation.

Installing VMware vCenter Converter

Like so many other vCenter-related components, the installation files for VMware vCenter Converter are found on the VMware vCenter media and are installed using the vCenter Installer. Figure 8.1 shows the VMware vCenter Installer with the option for installing vCenter Converter.

Installing vCenter Converter is a two-step process. The first step involves using the installer to get the application installed. The second step is installing the vSphere Client plug-in, which makes the functionality of vCenter Converter actually accessible from within the vSphere Client. After you have performed both of these steps, you will be able to initiate a P2V (or even a virtual-to-virtual, a V2V) operation from within the vSphere Client.

FIGURE 8.1
VMware vCenter Converter is installed from the vCenter installation media.

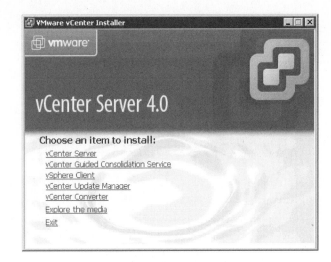

Perform the following steps to install VMware vCenter Converter:

1. Log in to the vCenter Server computer as a user with administrative privileges.

2. Run the VMware vCenter Installer by inserting the installation media into the optical drive or by double-clicking the optical drive in My Computer to invoke AutoPlay.

3. From the VMware vCenter Installer, click the option to install vCenter Converter.

4. When prompted for language, select English (United States) or the appropriate language for your installation. Click OK to proceed.

5. Click Next at the Welcome screen to start the installation process.

6. Select the check box to indicate that you accept the terms of the license agreement, and then click Next.

7. Select an installation location, and click Next.

8. Click Typical or Custom, and then click Next. If you choose Custom, you will see all the installation options, which is helpful even if you accept the default values for those options.

9. If you selected Custom, you now have the opportunity to customize which portions of the application will be installed. Unless you have a specific reason to change the values, accept the defaults. Click Next to continue.

10. The next screen, shown in Figure 8.2, requests information on the vCenter Server instance with which vCenter Converter should connect.

11. Click Next to continue without changing the default TCP ports for vCenter Converter. There is generally no need to change the default port assignments.

12. Click Next to accept the default way of identifying the vCenter Converter system on the network. There is generally no reason to change the default setting.

FIGURE 8.2

You'll need to supply connection information for vCenter Converter to connect to vCenter Server.

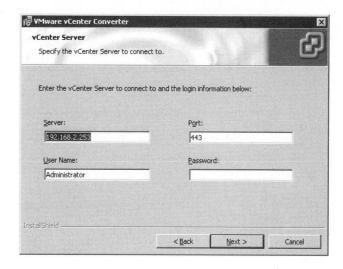

13. Click Install to actually install vCenter Converter.

14. Click Finish to complete the installation.

VMware vCenter Converter is now installed, but you now need to install and enable the vSphere Client plug-in in order to actually be able to use it. This is very similar to what you've already seen with vCenter Update Manager and its corresponding plug-in.

Perform the following steps to install the vCenter Converter plug-in:

1. Launch the vSphere Client if it is not already running, and connect to a vCenter Server instance.

2. From the Plug-Ins menu, select Manage Plug-Ins. The Plug-in Manager dialog box displays, as shown in Figure 8.3.

FIGURE 8.3

After you've installed vCenter Converter, the vCenter Converter plug-in is available in the vSphere Client.

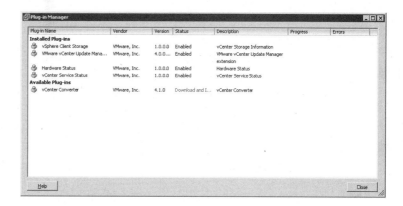

3. Click the link to download and install the vCenter Converter plug-in.

4. When prompted for a language, select English (United States), and click OK.

5. On the Welcome screen, click Next to start the installation.

6. Click Install to install the plug-in.

7. Click Finish to complete the installation.

The vCenter Converter plug-in will now be listed in the Manage Plug-Ins dialog box as installed and enabled.

After you've installed both vCenter Converter and the vSphere Client plug-in, a new option appears on the right-click context menu for an ESX/ESXi host: Import Machine. This new menu option, shown in Figure 8.4, is what calls vCenter Converter and initiates a conversion operation.

FIGURE 8.4
Use the Import Machine menu command to launch vCenter Converter from within the vSphere Client.

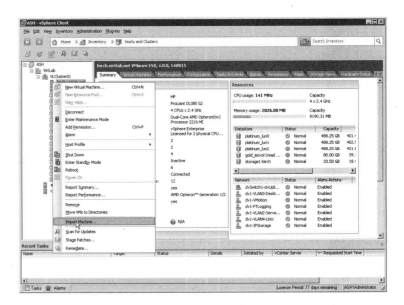

I'll discuss the details of using vCenter Converter later in this chapter. First I'll show how to install Guided Consolidation.

Installing the Guided Consolidation Service

The vCenter Guided Consolidation Service (referred to hereafter as just Guided Consolidation) is also installed from the vCenter Installer, just like vCenter Converter.

Perform the following steps to install Guided Consolidation:

1. Log in to a computer running vCenter Server using an account with administrative privileges.

2. Run the VMware vCenter Installer by inserting the installation media into the optical drive or by double-clicking the optical drive in My Computer to invoke AutoPlay.

3. From the VMware vCenter Installer (shown earlier in Figure 8.1), click the option to install the vCenter Guided Consolidation Service.

4. When prompted for language, select English (United States) or the appropriate language for your installation. Click OK to proceed.

5. On the Welcome screen for the installation of VMware vCenter Guided Consolidation, click Next.

6. Select the box to accept the terms of the license agreement, and click Next.

7. Select the location where you would like Guided Consolidation installed, and then click Next.

8. Guided Consolidation relies upon a Windows service, VMware vCenter Collector Service, that runs in the background. The VMware vCenter Collector service runs in the context of a specific user account, and this user account is the account used to connect to remote systems. In order for Guided Consolidation to work properly, the user account you specify here needs to have administrative privileges both locally on the server where you are installing Guided Consolidation as well as on any remote Windows servers that may be analyzed by Guided Consolidation. This user account also needs sufficient privileges to query the Active Directory database, if you are using Active Directory. Specify the username and password of the account under which the VMware vCenter Collector service will run, and then click Next.

 Real World Scenario

PERMISSIONS AND PRIVILEGES FOR GUIDED CONSOLIDATION

Although the vCenter Guided Consolidation Service and VMware Capacity Planner are two very different products, they both attempt to solve the same problem: gathering information from remote systems and making recommendations for consolidation based on that information. After having used both in numerous real-world situations, it's clear that Guided Consolidation shares many of the same requirements as Capacity Planner with regard to the permissions and privileges required in order to work.

For example, as mentioned earlier, Guided Consolidation requires administrative permissions on all remote Windows systems selected for analysis and data collection. Without administrative permissions, Guided Consolidation is unable to perform the necessary queries to gather configuration and performance data from the remote systems. To simplify this process in real-world deployments of Guided Consolidation, I recommend using Active Directory whenever possible. Run Guided Consolidation on a server that is a member of the domain, and select domain member servers for analysis. You can then create a dedicated account, used only by Guided Consolidation, to which you can grant administrative permissions to all systems within the domain. With one step, you've now ensured that all remote systems selected for analysis, assuming they are domain members, will have the correct configuration to allow Guided Consolidation to gather the information it needs. After you have completed your analysis with Guided Consolidation, you can disable this account so that it does not represent a security risk.

Additionally, like Capacity Planner, Guided Consolidation requires that the Remote Registry service is running on both the vCenter Server as well as all remote Windows Systems selected for analysis and data collection. If the Remote Registry service is not running, then Guided Consolidation, like Capacity Planner, will fail to gather information and will fail to provide recommendations for consolidation. Again, leveraging Active Directory is helpful in resolving this issue. I recommend creating a Group Policy Object (GPO) that sets the Remote Registry service to run automatically. This helps ensure that the remote systems are ready to work with Guided Consolidation.

With a little bit of preparation, you can ensure that your remote Windows servers are ready for analysis by Guided Consolidation and ensure that Guided Consolidation is able to provide complete and accurate recommendations for consolidating your physical servers onto your VMware vSphere environment.

USE A DEDICATED USER ACCOUNT FOR GUIDED CONSOLIDATION

Best practices recommend using a dedicated user account, often referred to as a *service account*, for Guided Consolidation. In addition, best practices also recommend avoiding the use of the built-in Administrator account. This is for a number of reasons, but the primary reason is that using a dedicated service account prevents problems when the password to the built-in Administrator account changes. In addition, when the password on this dedicated service account changes, the effect of that change will be limited to only Guided Consolidation.

9. Click Next to use the default network ports.

10. Specify the IP address or fully qualified domain name of the vCenter Server instance to which Guided Consolidation should connect. You will also need to supply a username and password with administrative credentials on the vCenter Server computer, as shown in Figure 8.5.

FIGURE 8.5
The Guided Consolidation installer will need administrative credentials to extend the vCenter Server installation.

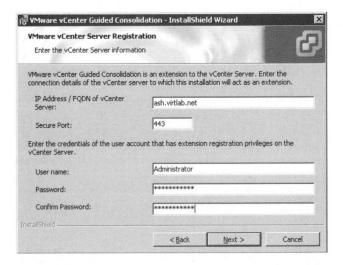

11. Click Next to accept the default identity of the computer running Guided Consolidation.

12. Click Install to start the installation of Guided Consolidation.

13. Click Finish to complete the installation.

After installation is complete, Guided Consolation is available in the vSphere Client using either the navigation bar or the menu. Figure 8.6 shows using the navigation bar to access Guided Consolidation.

FIGURE 8.6
Guided Consolidation is fully integrated into the vSphere Client.

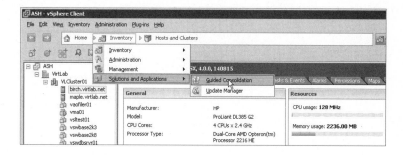

Navigate over to Guided Consolidation (note that you can also use the menu by selecting View ➤ Solutions And Applications ➤ Guided Consolidation) because that's what I'm discussing next.

Using Guided Consolidation

You've installed Guided Consolidation, but what is it exactly? Guided Consolidation is a simple-to-use tool for gathering performance and utilization data from physical computers in order to determine their eligibility as potential virtualization candidates. As the monitoring period goes on and more information is gathered, Guided Consolidation becomes increasingly confident about its recommendations for virtualization. Although VMware has a more robust product in the VMware Capacity Planner, this light version is a perfect fit for small and medium-sized businesses.

Before consolidation can begin, there must be a datacenter object and a host added to the vCenter Server inventory. As you saw previously, Guided Consolidation is accessible from the menu of vCenter Server. Within this area of the vSphere Client, you'll select the systems that Guided Consolidation will scan in order to determine virtualization candidacy. Recall from earlier, however, that Guided Consolidation has certain authentication and permission requirements in order to successfully scan systems. So, before you add any systems to Guided Consolidation, you should first specify authentication information.

Guided Consolidation can scan systems that exist as members of a workgroup or part of a domain. A set of default credentials can be configured when scanning systems with similar administrator account settings, while at the same time custom credentials can be set for the nondomain systems or those with nonstandard administrator account settings.

USING A DOMAIN MIGHT BE EASIER

You will probably find using Guided Consolidation much easier if the computer on which you install Guided Consolidation is a member of the same domain as the computers you want to assess. Because Guided Consolidation needs administrative access to the remote computers that are being monitored, membership in an Active Directory domain means you can leverage groups and group memberships in the domain to extend permissions to all computers in the domain.

Perform the following steps to configure the Service and Default credentials for Guided Consolidation:

1. Use the vSphere Client to connect to a vCenter Server instance.

2. From the menu, select View ➢ Solutions And Applications ➢ Guided Consolidation. You can also use the navigation bar.

3. Click the Configuration tab.

4. Click the Change button in the Default System Credentials section.

5. In the Default Credentials dialog box, shown in Figure 8.7, enter the username and password for a user account with membership in the local administrators group and the Log On as a Service user right. Preface the user account with the appropriate domain name for a domain account or the server name for a nondomain account.

6. Click OK.

FIGURE 8.7
Preface the service account credentials with the domain or server name where the account is stored.

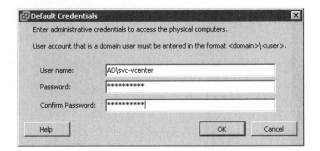

Also on the Configuration tab, you can see the status of the various services upon which Guided Consolidation relies. This information is on the Configuration tab in the Health Status area.

After you set the default credentials, you can initiate an analysis of systems from the Analysis tab. As noted earlier, the analysis of target systems becomes more confident as time passes and the amount of data collected increases. Typically, it takes at least 24 hours for the analysis algorithms to become confident in the consolidation plan.

Perform the following steps to begin an analysis with Guided Consolidation:

1. Use the vSphere Client to connect to a vCenter Server instance.

2. From the navigation bar, go to Guided Consolidation. You can also use the menu and select View ➢ Solutions And Applications ➢ Guided Consolidation.

3. Click the Start Analysis button.

4. In the Add To Analysis dialog box, there are several options for discovering computers to add to the analysis. You can specify a comma-separated list of computer names and IP addresses, you can specify an IP address range, and you can import a file with a list of computer names or IP addresses. For the purposes of this step, I'm going to use a workgroup, as shown in Figure 8.8.

Select the check box to browse computers by domains, and then select the domain or workgroup you want to use from the drop-down list. Recall that if you are using an Active Directory domain, the account you selected during the installation of Guided Consolidation needs to have permission to query Active Directory.

FIGURE 8.8
Guided Consolidation discovers domains and workgroups of potential target computers.

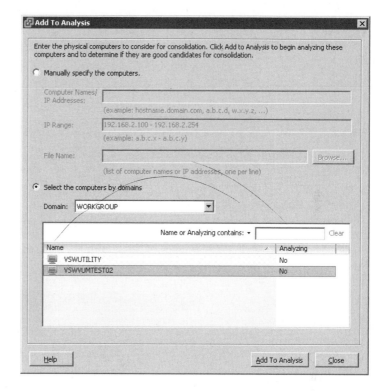

5. Guided Consolidation lists the computers in that domain or workgroup. From that list, select the computer or computers that you want to add to the analysis, and select Add To Analysis.

6. If the credentials defined as the default system credentials are not appropriate for the system to be monitored, enter the appropriate username and password in the Set Authentication dialog box. If three systems require three different sets of credentials, then you must select each system individually from the list of computer names. Otherwise, just use the default credentials.

As shown in Figure 8.9, select Use The Configured Default Credentials option.

7. Click OK.

After you complete these steps, the analysis begins and runs until the confidence level is sufficient for making a recommendation about virtualizing the physical target system.

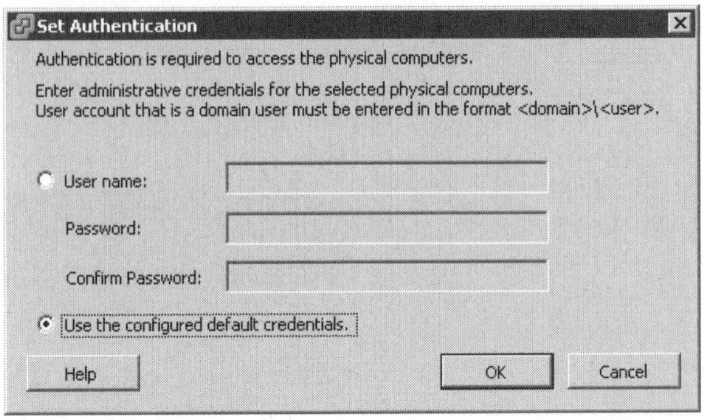

FIGURE 8.9
Authentication credentials can be customized for nondomain systems, or the default credentials can be passed through to the target systems.

ANALYZING PHYSICAL COMPUTERS

Analyzing a physical computer requires the appropriate administrative rights and IP connectivity to the computer. Be sure to disable any software firewalls that might be preventing communication with the physical computer.

After 24 to 48 hours, Guided Consolidation gains enough confidence with the consolidation plan, and the status value of the analyzed systems changes, as shown in Figure 8.10.

FIGURE 8.10
After the confidence of Guided Consolidation reaches a high level, the analyzed systems will be noted as ready for consolidation.

You can observe a consolidation plan for one or more of the analyzed systems by selecting the system or systems and then clicking the Plan Consolidation button. As shown in Figure 8.11, the Consolidation Plan dialog box details the computer name, the recommended destination, and a star rating to identify how likely a candidate the system is for virtualization. The rating system ranges from one to five, with five stars indicating that the system is an excellent virtualization candidate for the given host.

From the Consolidation Plan dialog box, you can select one or more of the analyzed systems and then click the Consolidate button. Clicking the Consolidate button causes the VMware Converter to import the system as a virtual machine into the existing vCenter Server inventory, as shown in Figure 8.12.

Guided Consolidation can provide many small and medium businesses with a simplified P2V migration strategy through its simple and intuitive interface. Although it might not be as robust as the full VMware Capacity Planner utility, it is free and does not require any outside experience or assistance. In truth, the best migration plans come from the intimate knowledge administrators have about the physical systems that have been deployed over their tenure. Guided Consolidation and VMware Capacity Planner are excellent ways to provide validated and documented proof of the benefits and capabilities of constructing a private cloud infrastructure with VMware vSphere.

FIGURE 8.11
A consolidation plan is generated for each of the analyzed systems. The plan includes a recommended destination host and rating.

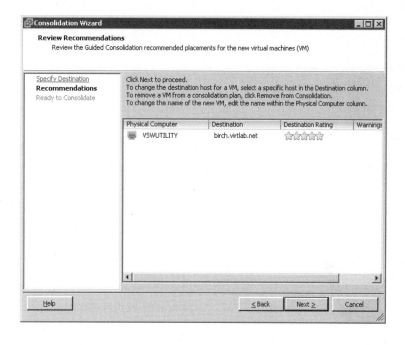

FIGURE 8.12
Multiple systems can be converted to virtual machines with a single click as part of the consolidation plan generated by vCenter Server.

Now that you have a consolidation plan, you're ready to start the consolidation process by starting some P2V migrations.

Using vCenter Converter to Perform P2V Migrations

Guided Consolidation provides the information you need as an end user to know how many of your physical systems you can convert and which systems are good candidates for conversion. But how do you actually perform the conversion? That's where vCenter Converter comes into play.

vCenter Converter, which you installed earlier in this chapter, is the tool you'll use to actually perform migrations. This tool can perform both P2V migrations as well as virtual-to-virtual migrations. VMware used to have two separate tools for P2V and V2V operations: P2V Assistant and VMware Importer. vCenter Converter combines the functionality of both tools into a single tool.

So, what can you do with vCenter Converter? Well, you can migrate physical machines into virtual machines by performing one of the following:

◆ A *hot* (or live) migration, which is the conversion of a running physical computer

◆ A *cold* migration, which is the conversion of a physical computer that is powered off

To perform a hot migration, vCenter Converter has an agent that is installed within the operating system on the physical source computer. vCenter Converter and the vCenter Converter agent can be run on any of the following operating systems:

- Windows Vista 32-bit (experimental on 64-bit)
- Windows Server 2003 32-bit and 64-bit
- Windows XP Professional 32-bit and 64-bit
- Windows 2000
- Windows NT with Service Pack 6 and Internet Explorer 5 and newer

WINDOWS ACTIVATION

Servers running Windows Server 2003 that are installed using retail media and keys that require activation will require a reactivation after the P2V migration. The Windows Activation algorithm tracks changes to hardware specifications in a system, and when the amount of hardware change is deemed significant, the Windows Activation is once again required.

The migration of a physical system to a virtual machine incurs drastic changes to the hardware specifications of the system. Everything from the CPU to network card to video adapter to disk controllers is altered as part of the migration process. It is these changes that force the Windows Activation algorithm to require a reactivation. In addition, do not be surprised if the Internet-based activation procedure is not successful. You might find that you are forced into calling the toll-free Windows Activation phone line to explain that the old system is being decommissioned in favor of the new virtual machine and that you are not in breach of your licensing agreement with Microsoft.

You can also use vCenter Converter to import virtual machines into VMware vSphere. vCenter Converter supports importing all of the following virtual machine types:

- VMware Workstation 4.x, 5.x, and 6.x
- VMware ACE 2.x
- VMware Fusion 1.x and 2.x
- VMware Player 1.x and 2.x
- ESX Server 3.x
- ESX Server 2.5 if managed by VirtualCenter 2.x
- GSX Server 3.x
- VMware Server 1.x and 2.x
- VirtualCenter 2.x
- Microsoft Virtual PC 7 and newer
- Microsoft Virtual Server

In addition to these virtual machine formats, vCenter Converter also imports third-party system images created with the following products:

◆ Symantec Backup Exec System Recovery 7 (formerly LiveState Recovery)

◆ Norton Ghost

◆ Acronis True Image 9

Let's look at one of each of the two types of P2V migrations.

Performing Hot Migrations

Hot migration, or the migration of a running physical computer, is ideal for those systems that cannot afford to be taken offline and do not perform consistent changes to local data. Systems like web servers or print servers are excellent candidates for hot migrations because they generally have a static set of data. Hot migration allows administrators to convert the physical system to a virtual machine and then to cut over to the virtual machine and decommission the physical machine without losing data.

NO HOT MIGRATIONS FOR DOMAIN CONTROLLERS

Microsoft does not recommend or support hot migrations of Active Directory domain controllers. When migrating domain controllers into virtual machines on VMware vSphere, use a cold migration instead.

Perform the following steps to conduct a hot migration of a running computer:

1. Use the vSphere Client to connect to a vCenter Server instance.

2. Right-click a cluster or ESX/ESXi host object in the vCenter Server inventory, and select the Import Machine option.

3. Click the Next button on the Source page of the Import Wizard.

4. Select Physical Computer from the drop-down list, and click Next, as shown in Figure 8.13.

5. Enter the target computer information, including the name or IP address and the appropriate user account information, as shown in Figure 8.14, and then click the Next button. The user account must have administrative privileges on the target computer being converted to a virtual machine.

SOURCE MACHINE NAME RESOLUTION IS NEEDED

For the P2V process to work successfully, the physical source machine must be able to resolve the network name of the vCenter Server. Otherwise, the P2V Wizard will report an error at this stage in the wizard.

---

6. Select to uninstall the vCenter Converter Agent automatically or manually in the Remote Installation Required warning dialog box, and then click the Yes button to continue.

FIGURE 8.13
vCenter Converter converts physical computers into virtual machines.

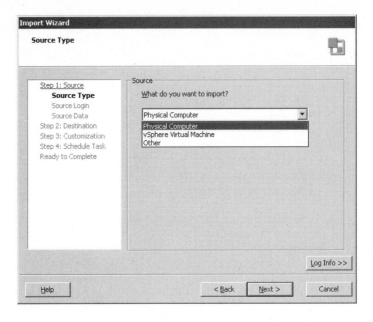

FIGURE 8.14
In addition to identifying the target computer by name or IP address, you must supply administrative credentials to perform a hot migration.

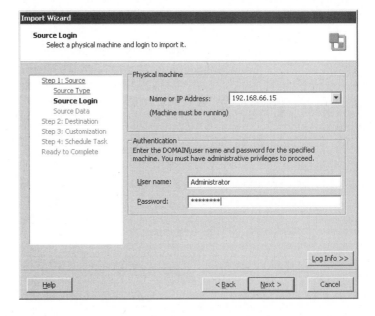

7. On the Source Data page, shown in Figure 8.15, select the volumes that should be converted as part of the P2V migration process. Figure 8.16 shows that you can resize source volumes during the P2V process; this helps with "right sizing" your virtual machines to make better use of resources in a virtual environment.

FIGURE 8.15
vCenter Converter can migrate all, some, or only one of the volumes that exist on the physical computer.

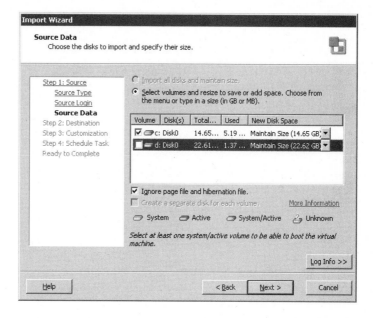

FIGURE 8.16
vCenter Converter allows volumes to be resized (increased or decreased) as part of the migration process.

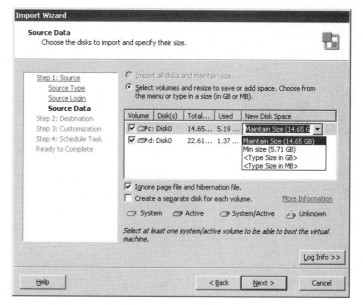

You can tell vCenter Converter to ignore volumes by deselecting the respective check box. Also note that when you migrate multiple volumes, there is a check box for placing these volumes in separate virtual disks.

8. Click Next after you've configured the Source Data page appropriately for the migration.

9. Click Next to begin configuring the destination details of the migration process.

10. Provide a virtual machine name and the location in the vCenter Server inventory where the virtual machine will reside, and then click Next.

11. Select a datastore with sufficient storage for the new virtual machine disk files, and click Next. By default, the virtual machine configuration (VMX) file and the virtual machine disk (VMDK) files are stored in the same datastore. The Advanced button exposes an option that allows you to place the VMX file separately from the VMDK files.

12. On the Networks page, select the number of network adapters for the new virtual machine, and select the port group or dvPort group to which each network adapter should be connected. Then click Next.

13. On the Customization page, select the check boxes labeled Install VMware Tools and Remove All System Restore Checkpoints (Recommended); then click Next.

    You will generally select the option to customize the virtual machine only when both the physical machine and the virtual machine will remain up and running and part of the production network. Leave the box deselected to maintain all existing settings of the physical computer. If you select the option to customize the virtual machine, a series of prompts asks you for the following information:

    ◆ Computer information

    ◆ Windows license

    ◆ Time zone

    ◆ Network settings

    ◆ Workgroup/domain

14. On the Schedule Task page, select to perform the migration immediately, or schedule it to take place at a later time; then click Next.

15. To power on the virtual machine after the migration is complete, select the Power check box on the new virtual machine after creation.

    If you want to wait until the physical box is powered off before using the virtual machine (recommended to avoid IP address conflicts), then leave this check box deselected. Click the Finish button to begin the conversion.

16. The Recent Tasks pane of vCenter Server will detail the progress of the conversion process, as shown in Figure 8.17.

FIGURE 8.17
vCenter Server's Recent Tasks pane will monitor the progress of the P2V migration.

ELIMINATING EXCESS IN A P2V

Oftentimes physical servers are purchased with more hardware than is required simply because the budget is there to support it. For example, it is not uncommon to find simple domain controllers or print servers with hundreds of gigabytes of empty space. Although this is not a huge administrative concern in a physical server environment, it is a red flag in the P2V migration process. The process of converting a physical machine to a virtual machine should involve an inspection of the resources assigned to the physical server as it is migrated. In this case, when converting a domain controller or print server with hundreds of gigabytes of free storage, it is best to adjust the disk size as part of the conversion process. This ensures that expensive SAN storage is not aimlessly consumed by virtual machines that will never utilize the resource to its full capacity.

The same can be said for memory and CPU resource allocation. As part of the migration, RAM and CPU allocations should be revisited and adjusted to better suit the demands of the virtual machine. For example, a domain controller with two dual-core processors and 4GB of RAM is severely overal-located. Although the conversion process does not directly allow these two resources to be adjusted as part of the conversion wizard, they can easily be adjusted after the virtual machine has been created, prior to the first power-on.

After the P2V conversion is complete, you still need to coordinate the actual switchover from the physical system to the virtual system. Generally, this involves a few different steps:

1. Shut down the physical server (or change the name and IP address of the physical server, if it needs to continue running).

2. Turn on the virtual server. Because the IP address and network name are identical to the physical server, users should be able to resume using the server without any modification on their part.

3. Permanently decommission or repurpose the physical server.

After the cutover is complete, there is one more task I recommend you complete. I recommend performing some cleanup tasks on the new virtual machine. Because it was converted from a physical system, there might be legacy device drivers installed that are no longer necessary. Removing these systems can improve the performance and stability of the new virtual machine.

For a Windows-based virtual machine, perform the following steps to view and remove unnecessary drivers:

1. Log in to the new Windows-based virtual machine using an account with administrative credentials.

2. Open a command prompt, and enter **set devmgr_show_nonpresent_devices=1**.

3. From that same command prompt, enter **start %systemroot%\system32\devmgmt.msc**. This will open Device Manager. It's important that you do this from the same command prompt; otherwise, Device Manager won't show you all the devices you need to see.

4. From the View menu, select Show Hidden Devices.

5. Remove devices that are clearly specific to the physical hardware upon which this operating system instance used to run. For example, if Windows had previously been running on HP hardware, you would remove the HP RAID array driver since it is no longer necessary. The same goes for old network card drivers and old video drivers.

If you've already installed the VMware Tools—which I highly recommend—you can also improve the guest operating system performance by changing the virtual disk controller to LSI Logic Parallel. You can change the virtual disk controller by editing the settings for the virtual machine, as I described in Chapter 7.

At this point, the new virtual machine should be ready for action!

Now that I've shown you what a hot migration looks like, I'll talk about cold migrations. Cold migrations are similar, but they're different enough that you'll learn about that process in a bit more detail.

Performing Cold Migrations

The process referred to as a *cold migration* involves converting a physical machine to a virtual machine while the physical machine is not in a running state. This type of conversion is best for servers that have constantly changing data sets. For example, computers that run SQL Server or Exchange Server are good candidates for cold migrations. The downside is that the server must be taken offline as part of a planned outage. Cold migrations are preferable for database and mail servers because the hot migration does not continuously update as the conversion is in progress. Therefore, if a hot migration begins at 9 p.m., the virtual machine would be consistent as of that time. Any updates since the 9 p.m. start time would not be captured in the virtual machine.

Naturally, a computer cannot be migrated while powered off completely, so the cold migration is not about migrating a physical computer that is powered off. Rather, it is the migration of a physical computer not booted into the standard default operating system. The cold clone process begins by booting the computer from the CD/DVD-ROM drive with the VMware Converter boot CD installed. You can download the VMware Converter boot CD from VMware's website at www.vmware.com/download and then burn it to CD or DVD media.

MINIMUM RAM REQUIRED FOR COLD MIGRATION

The target physical computer must be configured with more than 264MB of RAM to perform a cold migration, or vCenter Converter will display an error and refuse to continue.

Perform the following steps to cold migrate a physical computer into a virtual machine:

1. Boot the target computer from the VMware vCenter Converter boot CD.

2. Click the I Accept the Terms In The License Agreement radio button, and then click OK.

3. After accepting the license agreement, you are prompted to update the network parameters. If you are not using DHCP or if you need to manually adjust the network configuration, click the Yes button to adjust the network properties.

4. Click OK after you have adjusted the network properties as needed.

5. The VMware vCenter Converter window opens. Click the Import Machine button to launch the VMware Converter Import Wizard.

6. Click Next.

7. On the Source Data page of the wizard, select either the Import All Disks And Maintain Size option or the Select Volumes And Resize To Save Or Add Space option.

8. After the volumes are resized as needed, click Next to continue.

9. On the Destination Type page, select the destination for the import. For enterprise P2V migrations, select the vSphere Virtual Machine option, and click Next.

10. On the Destination Login page, provide the name or IP address of the vCenter Server and the appropriate credentials to authenticate. Click Next.

11. On the Virtual Machine Name And Folder page, type a display name for the virtual machine, and select the desired location in the vCenter Server inventory. Click Next.

12. On the Host Or Cluster page, select the host, cluster, or resource pool under which the virtual machine will run, and then click Next.

13. On the Datastore page, select the datastore where the virtual machine disk files will be stored. Use the Advanced button to supply unique datastores for the different virtual machine disk files. Click Next.

14. On the Networks page, select the number of network adapters to include in the new virtual machine, and then select the virtual machine network that each network adapter should be connected to. Click Next.

15. On the Customization page, select the check boxes marked Install VMware Tools and Remove All System Restore Checkpoints (Recommended).

    If you want to change the identity of the virtual machine to be different from the target system, select the check box Customize The Identity Of The Virtual Machine.

    Selecting this option adds the following pages to the VMware Converter Import Wizard:

    ◆ Computer Info

    ◆ Windows License

    ◆ Time Zone

    ◆ Network Settings

    ◆ Workgroup/Domain

16. Click Next to continue.

17. On the Ready To Complete page, select the check box Power On The Virtual Machine After Creation, and then click the Finish button. The progress of the cold migration process will be monitored in the VMware vCenter Converter utility.

After this process finishes, the P2V conversion is complete, and the physical system is already powered down. You can complete the migration by simply powering on the new virtual machine. However, remember that you must disconnect the physical system from the network if you ever want to boot it up; otherwise, you will create an IP address conflict and could possibly disrupt service to your users.

P2V OR V2V ARE ONE AND THE SAME

Although this section discusses using the VMware vCenter Converter to perform P2V migrations, you can use the tool to perform V2V migrations as well. When you perform a V2V migration, you follow the same wizard-based interface you saw while performing a P2V migration.

Aside from the obvious purpose of moving virtual machines between ESX/ESXi and VMware's hosted products like VMware Workstation or VMware Fusion, performing V2V migrations is a powerful method for solving problems regarding the over- or underallocation of disk space in a virtual machine. By using VMware vCenter Converter, as you have seen in this chapter, you can increase or decrease the amount of space allocated to a volume as needed. This allows administrators to use a nondestructive process to easily manage volume sizes in Windows virtual machines. Typically, doing this requires costly third-party tools and can incur damage to the system if not done properly.

Importing Virtual Appliances

A very useful feature of vCenter Server is the ability to import virtual appliances. A virtual appliance is a specialized virtual machine with a dedicated purpose. vCenter Server can browse virtual appliances that exist as files on your local disk or local network, or vCenter Server can import virtual appliances from the VMware Virtual Appliance Marketplace. If you browse the Virtual Appliance Marketplace at www.vmware.com/appliances, you will find that appliances exist across a multitude of categories, including the following:

◆ Administration

◆ App/Web Server

◆ Communications

◆ Database

◆ Networking

◆ Security

There are a couple of different ways to deploy a virtual appliance. vCenter Server supports the Open Virtualization Format OVF (formerly known as the Open Virtual Machine Format) for deploying virtual appliances.

The first way is to deploy a virtual appliance from an OVF file by simply selecting File ➢ Deploy OVF Template. This initiates a wizard that walks you through importing the OVF-based virtual appliance. Figure 8.18 shows that vCenter Server can deploy OVF templates stored locally as well as OVF templates that are stored remotely and are accessible via a uniform resource locator (URL).

The second way to import virtual appliances is to deploy a virtual appliance directly across the Internet via the VMware Virtual Appliance Marketplace. This option, too, is found on the File menu of the vSphere Client.

Aside from selecting the source location of the virtual appliance, the process of importing a virtual appliance is the same regardless of whether you are importing from a local set of files or downloading it across the Internet.

Perform the following steps to import a virtual appliance:

1. From within the vSphere Client, go to the File menu, and select Deploy From OVF Template.

2. Select the source location of the virtual appliance—which must be provided in OVF format—and click Next.

3. The OVF Template Details screen summarizes the information about the virtual appliance. Click Next to continue.

4. Click the Accept button to accept the end user license agreement, and click Next.

5. Supply a name for the virtual appliance, and select a location within the vCenter Server inventory.

6. Select a cluster, an ESX/ESXi host or a resource pool where the virtual appliance will run, and then click Next.

7. Choose the datastore where you want to store the virtual appliance. If you are unsure of how much space the virtual appliance requires, the OVF Template Details screen, described in step 3 of this process, shows how much space the virtual appliance requires. Click Next after you've selected the datastore you want to use.

8. For each source network defined in the OVF template, map that source network to a destination network in vCenter Server. The destination networks are port groups or dvPort groups, as you can see in Figure 8.19.

9. The Ready To Complete screen summarizes the actions to be taken during the virtual appliance import. If everything is correct, click Finish; if anything is incorrect, use the Back button to go back and make the correct selection.

FIGURE 8.18
vCenter Server uses a wizard to deploy templates from OVF.

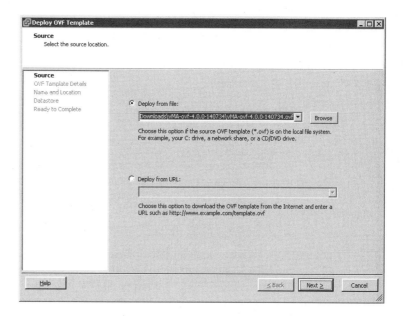

After the virtual appliance is imported into vCenter Server, it is treated like any other virtual machine in the inventory. While some of the available appliances are production ready and free for use, others are operated under trial conditions and must be purchased for extended production utilization.

FIGURE 8.19
Source networks defined in the OVF template are mapped to port groups and dvPort groups in vCenter Server.

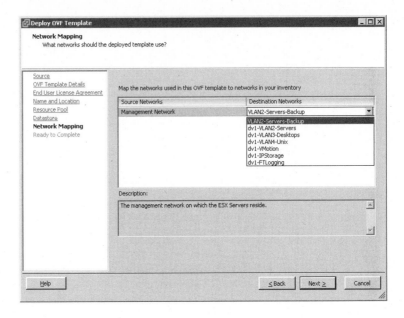

The Bottom Line

Use vCenter Server Guided Consolidation. vCenter Guided Consolidation is integrated into vCenter Server. Guided Consolidation analyzes physical computers, gathers performance statistics and configuration information, and makes recommendations around how those physical computers should be consolidated as virtual machines. This functionality helps organizations figure out how to convert their infrastructure and take advantage of VMware vSphere.

Master It What requirement is there for user accounts with vCenter Guided Consolidation?

Perform physical-to-virtual migrations of running computers. VMware vCenter Converter has the ability to perform P2V conversions on running physical computers. This allows organizations to convert systems with a minimum of downtime. This type of P2V conversion process is best suited for physical computers with relatively static data sets.

Master It During the process of performing a P2V conversion on a physical system running Windows Server 2003, the wizard fails about halfway through with an error regarding name resolution. How can you resolve this issue?

Perform physical-to-virtual migrations of computers that are powered off. In addition to conversions of running physical systems, vCenter Converter can use a boot CD to perform cold migrations, for example, conversions of physical systems when the installed operating system is not running. This type of conversion involves greater downtime but is best suited for applications with very dynamic data sets, such as email systems or database servers.

Master It   List two advantages and two disadvantages of using vCenter Converter's cold migration functionality.

Import virtual appliances.   Virtual appliances are virtual machines that have been packaged with a pre-installed guest operating system and tuned for a specific purpose. Often, the guest operating system is stripped down to only those components necessary to support its intended function; this helps improve performance and reduce the footprint. Virtual appliances are typically distributed in Open Virtualization Format (OVF, formerly referred to as Open Virtual Machine Format). VMware also provides an online marketplace where virtual appliances can be distributed.

Master It   A vendor has given you a ZIP file containing a virtual machine they are calling a virtual *appliance*. Upon looking inside the ZIP file, you see several VMDK files and a VMX file. Will you be able to use vCenter Server's import functionality to import this as a virtual appliance? If not, how can you get this virtual machine into your infrastructure?

Chapter 9

Configuring and Managing VMware vSphere Access Controls

Centralizing the management of virtual machines and their ESX/ESXi hosts has become an issue in most growing datacenters. Delegating control to the appropriate users so they can assist in managing the virtual infrastructure is also a large part of the centralized management model. For instance, how do you assign permissions to a group of users responsible for setting up virtual machines to test a new application? They might need to create the virtual machine and manage its access to resources, but they might need to be restricted in what they can do in other areas of the virtual infrastructure.

You can manage the permissions to a virtual infrastructure through vCenter Server or directly through an ESX/ESXi host.

In this chapter, you will learn to:

◆ Manage and maintain ESX/ESXi permissions

◆ Manage and maintain vCenter Server permissions

◆ Manage virtual machines using the web console

Managing and Maintaining ESX/ESXi Host Permissions

Both vCenter Server and ESX/ESXi hosts use the same structured security model to grant users the ability to manage portions of the virtual infrastructure. This model consists of users, groups, roles, privileges, and permissions, as shown in Figure 9.1.

The items that differ between the non–vCenter Server environment and the vCenter Server environment are predominantly in the following two areas:

◆ The location of the user and group objects created

◆ The level of granularity of the roles and privileges available in each environment

For environments that don't have vCenter Server, or where the administrator chooses to have users authenticate directly to the ESX/ESXi hosts to perform management tasks, it is important to start with a discussion of the security model.

Permissions to an ESX/ESXi host are assigned to users and groups that exist locally on that specific host.

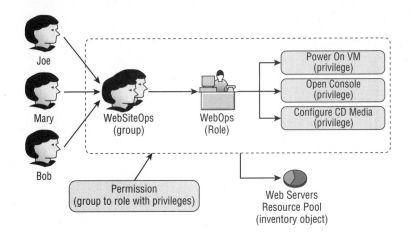

FIGURE 9.1
vCenter Server and ESX/ESXi share a common security model for assigning access control.

Perform the following steps to view the ESX/ESXi users and groups:

1. Launch the vSphere Client if it is not already running, and connect to an ESX/ESXi host.

2. Navigate to the Hosts And Clusters inventory view by selecting View ≻ Inventory ≻ Hosts And Clusters from the menu. You can also use the navigation bar or the Ctrl+Shift+H keyboard shortcut.

3. Select an ESX/ESXi host in the inventory tree on the left, and then click the Users & Groups tab in the content pane on the right.

When you construct a virtual infrastructure, it is important from a security standpoint to identify who in your organization needs access to your ESX/ESXi host to perform any level of management, using either an SSH connection (such as PuTTY, WinSCP, FastSCP, and so forth), the vSphere Client, or the web interface that we will discuss later in this chapter (in the ''Managing Virtual Machines Using the Web Console'' section). You should distribute the root username and password with caution. If you determine that multiple users should be allowed direct access to an ESX/ESXi host, provide each user with their own user account.

SOME TOOLS ARE NOT AVAILABLE FOR USE WITH ESXI

Although both VMware ESX and VMware ESXi manage and store users and groups locally, the lack of a user-accessible console operating system in ESXi means that tools such as PuTTY, WinSCP, FastSCP, and so forth, are not usable with ESXi. For all intents and purposes, you can fully manage ESXi only by using the vSphere Client.

As mentioned at the beginning of the chapter, the vCenter Server and ESX/ESXi security model are made up of users or groups, roles, privileges, and permissions. In the security model's most basic format, users or groups are assigned to a role that has privileges. The user-role-privilege combination is then associated with an object in the inventory as a permission.

You'll see two buttons on the Users & Groups tab: the Users button and the Groups button. Users and groups—or at least the groups—are created in order to assign the group to the appropriate role. So, what exactly is a *role*?

ESX/ESXi host permissions are set up to help simplify assignment. Rather than choose the individual privilege to be assigned each time you need to delegate, you assign a user or group to a role. Then, the role is granted a privilege or group of privileges. An ESX/ESXi host has three default roles: No Access, Read-Only, and Administrator.

Although these roles are fairly straightforward, let's take a closer look at each of them:

No Access   The No Access role works as the name suggests. This role prevents access to an object or objects in the inventory. The No Access role can be used if a user was granted access higher up in the inventory. The No Access role can also be used at lower-level objects to prevent object access. For example, if a user is granted permissions at the ESX/ESXi host but should be prevented access to a specific virtual machine, you could use the No Access role on that specific virtual machine.

Read-Only   Read-Only allows a user to see the objects within the vSphere Client inventory. It does not allow the user to interact with any of the visible objects in any way. For example, a user with the Read-Only permission would be able to see a list of virtual machines in the inventory but could not act on any of them.

Administrator   The Administrator role has the utmost authority, but it is only a role, and it needs to be assigned using a combination of a user or group object and an inventory object such as a virtual machine.

With only three built-in roles on ESX/ESXi hosts, the defaults don't leave room for much flexibility. However, don't let that slow you down. The limits of the default roles are easily overcome by creating custom roles. You can create custom roles that will better suit your needs, or you can clone existing roles to make additional roles to modify for your own purposes.

You should not modify the default roles. If a role does not suit the management needs, create a custom role. If you alter a default role, it might present a scenario where other administrators unknowingly grant too few or too many permissions by assigning membership in a default role.

I've spoken a couple of times so far about creating custom roles, so let's take a closer look at how to do that.

DEFAULT ESX/ESXI PERMISSION ASSIGNMENTS

By default, when ESX/ESXi is installed, the only user that exists is the root user, and root has full administrative permissions to the entire server. This default set of permissions changes when an ESX/ESXi host is managed by vCenter Server. The process of adding a host to vCenter Server adds an agent (the vCenter Server Agent) and an additional Service Console account called vpxuser. The vpxuser account has a 32-character, complex, randomly generated password that is also granted membership in the Administrator role on an ESX/ESXi host. This assignment enables the vCenter Server service to carry out tasks on the ESX/ESXi hosts in the inventory.

Creating Custom Roles

If you find that the default roles provided with ESX/ESXi don't suit your organization's needs with regard to permissions and management, then you should create custom roles to better map to your business needs. For example, assume that a set of users needs to interact with the console of a virtual machine and also needs to change the CD and floppy media of those virtual machines. These needs aren't properly reflected in any of the default roles, so a custom role is necessary.

Perform the following steps to create a custom role named Operator:

1. Launch the vSphere Client if it is not already running, and connect to an ESX/ESXi host.

2. Navigate to the Administration area by using the navigation bar or by selecting View ➢ Administration ➢ Roles. You can also press the Ctrl+Shift+R keyboard shortcut.

3. Click the Add Role button.

4. Type the name of the new role in the Name text box (in this example, **Operator**), and then select the privileges that will be required by members of the role, as shown in Figure 9.2.

   The privileges shown in Figure 9.2 allow users or groups assigned to the Operator role to interact with the console of a virtual machine, change the CD and floppy media, and change the power state of a virtual machine.

FIGURE 9.2
Custom roles strengthen management capabilities and add flexibility to permission delegations.

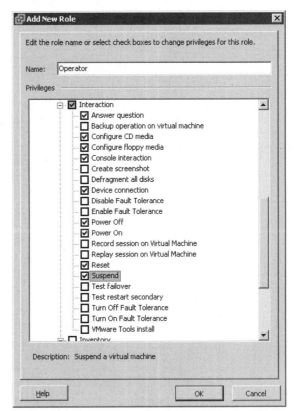

PERMISSIONS FOR CHANGING VIRTUAL MEDIA

To change floppy and CD media using floppy disk images (files with an .flp extension) and CD/DVD disk images (files with an .iso extension) that are stored on a SAN volume, you will also need to grant that group Browse Datastore privileges at the root of the hierarchy—in this case, at the ESX/ESXi host itself.

5. Click OK to complete the custom role creation.

The new Operator role is now defined, but it's not operational yet. You must still assign users or groups to the role and apply the role to the ESX/ESXi host or virtual machine(s).

Granting Permissions

As simple and useful as roles are, they are not functional until a user or group is assigned to the role and then the role is assigned to an inventory object. Assume that a group of users exists that needs to interact with all virtual machines that are web servers. If access control is managed through the ESX/ESXi host, then you have to create a user account on that host together with a new group—for example, WebSiteOps. After you've created these local users and groups, you can execute the security model.

Perform the following steps to grant virtual machine access control to a local user or group:

1. Launch the vSphere Client if it is not already running, and connect to an ESX/ESXi host.

2. Right-click the object in the inventory tree on the left to which permission should be assigned, and click the Add Permission option. In this case, right-click the ESX/ESXi host.

3. Click the Add button in the Assign Permissions dialog box.

4. In the Select Users And Groups dialog box, select the appropriate user or group (in this case, WebSiteOps), click the Add button, and then click OK. This returns you to the Assign Permissions dialog box, where the user or group is listed on the left side of the dialog box.

5. From the Assigned Role drop-down list, choose the role to which the selected users or groups should be assigned. In this case, select Operator—the role you defined earlier—from the drop-down list to assign that role to the WebSiteOps group.

What if you have an ESX/ESXi host that will host 30 virtual machines and 10 of those are the web server virtual machines? As previously demonstrated, this approach then requires that you assign permissions on each of the 10 web server virtual machines. Clearly, this is not an efficient process. Further growth resulting in more web server virtual machines would require additional administrative effort to ensure access control. When you create a role, you'll notice an option, Propagate To Child Objects, that you can use to facilitate access control implementation.

This option works like the inheritance settings in a Windows file system. It allows the privileges assigned in this role to be applied to objects beneath the selected object. For example, if the Operator role is applied as a permission on the ESX/ESXi host in the inventory panel and the Propagate To Child Objects option is enabled, all members of the Operator role will be able to interact with *all* the virtual machines hosted on the ESX/ESXi host. Although this certainly simplifies access control implementation, it adds another problem: the permissions of the Operator role have been overextended and now apply to all virtual machines and not just the web servers. With access control granted at the host level, members of the Operator role will be able to change floppy and CD media and use the console of the web server virtual machines, but they will also be able to do that on any other virtual machine in the inventory.

This issue presents one of the drawbacks of managing access control on an individual ESX/ESXi host. Keep in mind as well that all of the steps we have discussed so far would have to be performed on each ESX/ESXi host in the virtual infrastructure. What if there were some way to organize the inventory of virtual machines? In other words, what if you could create a "container object" for the web server virtual machines and put all of the web server virtual machines within that object? Then you could assign the group to the role at the parent object level and let inheritance take over. As shown in Figure 9.3, the problem is that folder objects are not possible on a single ESX/ESXi host. That means your only option is a resource pool.

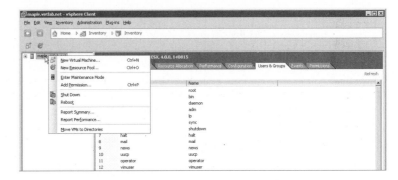

Using Resource Pools to Assign Permissions

A *resource pool* is actually a special object. Think of it like a folder of sorts. I'll discuss resource pools in much greater detail in the next chapter, but the good news here is that they can help you organize your virtual machines. One byproduct of resource pools is the ability to manipulate and manage many virtual machines as objects within the logical resource pool object.

Perform the following steps to create a resource pool:

1. Launch the vSphere Client if it is not already running, and connect to an ESX/ESXi host.

2. Navigate to the Inventory view by using the navigation bar, by using the Ctrl+Shift+H keyboard shortcut, or by selecting View ➢ Inventory ➢ Inventory from the menu.

3. Right-click the ESX/ESXi host, and select New Resource Pool, as shown previously in Figure 9.3.

4. Type a resource pool name in the Name text box, in this case **WebServers**.

5. Configure the resource allocations, if desired, to establish limits and reservations for the resource pool. The limit establishes a hard cap on the resource usage, while the reservations establish a resource guarantee.

    I'll discuss resource allocations in detail in Chapter 10, "Managing Resource Allocation."

6. Click OK.

So now that you've created a WebServers resource pool, you can place virtual machines into the resource pool, as shown in Figure 9.4.

Additionally, resource pools become inventory objects to which permissions can be assigned. The same process you followed earlier, described in the section "Granting Permissions," applies here as well. Simply assign permission to the resource pool, and ensure that the Propagate To Child Objects check box is selected. Those permissions will also apply to all the virtual machines in the resource pool.

Using resource pools helps you accomplish a couple of key goals: better organization for your virtual machines and better control over permissions assigned to those virtual machines.

I've shown you how to assign permissions, but what about when permissions need to be removed? Let's look at that next.

FIGURE 9.4
As an object in the inventory, resource pools are potential levels of infrastructure management.

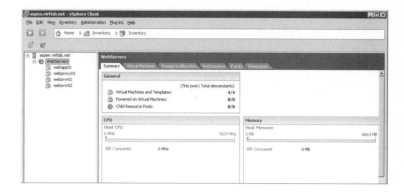

Removing Permissions

When management needs change or when improper assignments have been made, you can remove permissions. In the section "Granting Permissions," you walked through the process of assigning the Operators role permission on the ESX/ESXi host. Now that you have a resource group in place to give you more granular control over permissions, you should remove the permissions you previously applied to the host.

Perform the following steps to remove permissions on an object in the inventory:

1. Launch the vSphere Client if it is not already running, and connect to an ESX/ESXi host.

2. Navigate to Inventory view using the navigation bar, the menu, or the keyboard shortcut.

3. Select the object in the inventory, and then select the Permissions tab. In this case, you need to remove the permissions from the ESX/ESXi host, so select the host from the inventory.

4. Right-click the permissions entry to be deleted from the list of existing permissions, and then click the Delete option.

You should see a warning indicating that users may retain their permissions because of an assignment higher in the hierarchy; however, in this case, that is what you are trying to accomplish. You want the users to have access to the virtual machines as a result of permissions applied at the resource pool, not the ESX/ESXi host.

After permissions are assigned throughout the inventory, it is easy to lose track of what has been previously done. Of course, if your company mandates documentation, there might already be a solid audit trail. However, it is easy to see existing role usage from within the vSphere Client.

Identifying Permission Usage

As the inventory of virtual machines and resource pools grows larger and more complex, it's very likely that the permissions granted to these various objects will also become very complex. In addition, as company needs and management strategies change over time, these permissions need to change as well. Combined, these factors can create an environment where the permissions usage is quite complex and hard to decipher.

To help combat this issue, the vSphere Client's Roles view helps administrators identify where roles have been assigned and what permissions have been granted in the inventory.

Perform the following steps to identify where a role has been assigned as a permission:

1. Launch the vSphere Client if it is not already running, and connect to an ESX/ESXi host.

2. Navigate to the Roles view using the navigation bar, the Ctrl+Shift+R keyboard shortcut, or the View ➤ Administration ➤ Roles menu item.

3. Click the role whose usage you want to identify.

The details pane identifies where in the inventory hierarchy the role is used.

Using the vSphere Client's Roles view allows you, the administrator, to track down where permissions have been assigned so that you can edit or remove permissions when necessary. But it's not only permissions that need to be removed—sometimes roles need to be removed, too.

Editing and Removing Roles

Over time, it is almost inevitable that management needs will change. At times, you might have to create new roles, edit an existing role, or even delete a role. If the privileges assigned to a role are no longer applicable in your environment, you should edit the role to add or remove the necessary privileges.

Perform the following steps to edit a role:

1. Launch the vSphere Client if it is not already running, and connect to an ESX/ESXi host.

2. Navigate to the Roles view using the navigation bar, the menu, or the keyboard shortcut.

3. Right-click the role you want to edit, and select Edit Role.

4. Make the desired changes by adding or removing privileges in the Edit Role dialog box. Click OK when you finish.

Note that ESX/ESXi won't allow you to edit the default roles.

If a role is no longer used, it should be removed to minimize the number of objects to be viewed and managed.

Perform the following steps to delete a role:

1. Launch the vSphere Client if it is not already running, and connect to an ESX/ESXi host.

2. Navigate to the Roles view using the navigation bar, the Ctrl+Shift+R keyboard shortcut, or the View ➤ Administration ➤ Roles menu item.

3. Right-click the role to be deleted, and select Remove.

When a role is in use and is selected for removal, the ESX/ESXi host offers the opportunity to transfer the existing role members to a new role or to simply drop all members from the role. This eliminates the opportunity for accidentally deleting roles that are being used in the inventory.

Now that you understand how to work with local users, groups, roles, and permissions on an ESX/ESXi host, be aware that you more than likely will not be doing much of this. Managing local user accounts is administratively more cumbersome because of the lack of centralized management and authentication. This is, of course, because the bulk, if not all, of your access control strategies should revolve around Windows-based user accounts accessing the vCenter Server environment. This offers the advantage of having centralized permissions management and storage, integration with your existing Active Directory authentication infrastructure, and support for passthrough authentication with the vSphere Client.

Managing and Maintaining vCenter Server Permissions

The security model for vCenter Server is identical to that explained in the previous section for an ESX/ESXi host: take a user or group, and assign them to a role for a specific inventory object. The difference in the vCenter Server security model is the origin of the user or group objects. In the vCenter Server environment, the users and groups are actually Windows users and groups, but exactly which users will depend on whether your vCenter Server computer is a part of a domain. If the vCenter Server computer belongs to a workgroup, then the users and groups are stored in the local Security Accounts Manager (SAM) database on that server and are managed through the Local Users And Groups node of the Computer Management snap-in. If the vCenter Server computer belongs to an Active Directory domain, then the users and groups available for assignment to roles are pulled from the Active Directory database and are managed through the Active Directory Users And Groups snap-in. This is fairly typical for a Windows Server-based application and also helps you continue to manage all the users in your network in one place: Active Directory. If you don't have the ability to create users and/or groups in Active Directory, you need to make arrangements with your Active Directory administration team to assist you in that area. After the users and/or groups are created, they will be available for you to assign roles to them through vCenter Server.

I will assume that the vCenter Server environment is based on a server that is part of an Active Directory domain for the purposes of this discussion, although the procedure for assigning permissions remains essentially the same if you have a workgroup-based installation. The key is to remember where to create the users and groups that you need to use.

VCENTER SERVER IN A WORKGROUP VS. VCENTER SERVER IN A DOMAIN

You can install vCenter Server on a Windows Server 2003 system that belongs to a workgroup or a domain. In most cases, you'll install vCenter Server on a computer that belongs to a Windows Active Directory domain. As a result, you will sign into vCenter Server under the context of a domain user account. This centralizes account management but does present a possible security risk by extending virtual infrastructure permissions to users who were not necessarily intended to have these permissions. Here's how.

The default permissions in a vCenter Server installation provide the local Administrators group of the vCenter Server computer with membership in the Administrator role at the root of the inventory. Because the Domain Admins group is a member of the local Administrators group, all Domain Admins have complete rights in the vCenter Server infrastructure. In most cases, this configuration violates the principle of least privilege.

To mitigate the risk involved with the default configuration, create a new, dedicated Active Directory group that contains only virtual infrastructure administrators. This group can then replace the local Administrators group in the vCenter Server root permissions list. After you've created the new group and granted it rights in vCenter Server, you can remove the local Administrators permissions entry from the root of the vCenter Server inventory, which will remove the original security concern.

---

vCenter Server has a more structured hierarchy with greater depth than an ESX/ESXi host. As mentioned previously, the only way to organize virtual machines on an individual ESX/ESXi host is to build a resource pool and then move the appropriate virtual machines into that resource pool. The vCenter Server hierarchy opens opportunities to create folder structures for organizing objects such as datacenters and virtual machines. First, though, you'll want to deepen your understanding of vCenter Server's hierarchy.

Understanding vCenter Server's Hierarchy

As a centralized management server for all of your ESX/ESXi hosts, virtual machines, templates, datastores, and networks, vCenter Server supports a rich hierarchy of objects. To fully leverage this hierarchy to your advantage, you must first have a complete understanding of the hierarchy. Some of this information I covered in Chapter 3, "Installing and Configuring vCenter Server," but I want to expand upon that information here. I'll start by discussing the datacenter object.

WORKING WITH DATACENTER OBJECTS

In the vCenter Server environment, you start by creating, at a minimum, a datacenter (also referred to as a *datacenter object*). The datacenter object is the building block of a vCenter Server hierarchy, much like organizational units are the building blocks of an Active Directory structure. You must have a datacenter object in vCenter Server before you can even add the first ESX/ESXi host. You're not limited to a single datacenter object; in fact, you may even want multiple datacenter objects, depending upon your organization.

Perform the following steps to create a datacenter object:

1. Launch the vSphere Client if it is not already running, and connect to a vCenter Server instance.

2. Navigate to the Hosts And Clusters view.

3. Right-click the vCenter Server object in the inventory, and select New Datacenter.

4. Type a name for the new datacenter object.

So, what exactly is a datacenter object used for? In addition to providing an organizational container in which you store ESX/ESXi hosts, clusters, folders, virtual machines, resource pools, networks, and datastores, the datacenter also serves as a boundary. The datacenter is a boundary for the configuration of VMotion, VMware High Availability (HA), and VMware Distributed Resource Scheduler (DRS). In other words, you can migrate a virtual machine with VMotion to another host only in the same datacenter where it is currently running, in the same way that VMware HA can fail over to another host only in the same datacenter. VMotion and VMware DRS are discussed in Chapter 10; VMware HA is covered in more detail in Chapter 11, "Ensuring High Availability and Business Continuity."

Although the datacenter object is important—and every vCenter Server hierarchy will have at least one datacenter object—there are other objects that you will use as you build out the vCenter Server hierarchy to meet your needs. The next object I'll cover is the folder.

WORKING WITH FOLDERS

What happens if there are 30 datacenters in your organization—some located in Europe, some in North America, and some in South America—all with different teams of administrators managing them? The simple answer is to create folders under the root object in vCenter Server and then create (or move) your datacenter objects under those folders. Creating folders under the root and placing datacenter objects beneath them allows for broader access control management. Think about why you create folders on network drives: to organize files and other folders and to simplify the assignment of permissions to many objects. Designing a vCenter Server inventory employs the same logic.

In the same way you can use folders to organize datacenters, you can also create folders *inside* the datacenter to organize virtual machines according to your needs. For more detailed micromanaging scenarios, you can create folders within folders. Figure 9.5 details an inventory structure where datacenters are organized by geography and servers are managed by the rack in which they exist.

FIGURE 9.5
Creating folders beneath a datacenter provides more granular access control and management strategies.

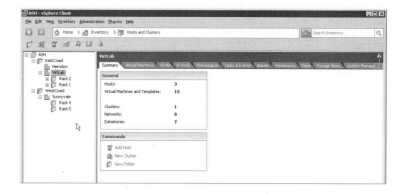

So far, I've discussed folders only within the context of using them to organize datacenters or objects inside datacenters. Recall that vCenter Server offers two main views of the objects within the inventory: Hosts And Clusters and VMs And Templates. For the most part, I have discussed using folders in the default view of Hosts And Clusters, but the VMs And Templates view is extremely valuable for organizing virtual machines with respect to the management and access control needs of the traditional Windows administrators. In addition, each of these inventory views—Hosts And Clusters and VMs And Templates—maintains its own independent folder hierarchy. For example, changes to objects in the Hosts And Clusters view does not necessarily result in changes to the objects in the VMs And Templates view. Figure 9.6 shows details of a VMs And Templates view constructed to support access control implementation based on the types of virtual machines in the infrastructure. The inventory view consists of several custom folders called Finance VMs, Medical System VMs, and Infrastructure VMs. These folders, like those in the Hosts And Clusters view, provide a boundary for assigning permissions.

FIGURE 9.6
The VMs And Templates view maintains its own hierarchical structure to enhance access control possibilities.

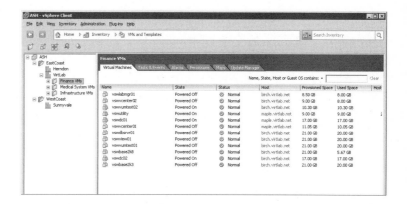

By maintaining separate and independent hierarchies using folders, in each of these two views vSphere administrators gain a tremendous amount of flexibility. For example, the VMs And Templates view could be organized based on department or business unit, while the Hosts And

Clusters view could be organized based on a geographical basis. In both views, vSphere administrators use folders to build the structure and hierarchy needed to properly support the needs of the organization.

Folders aren't the only tool you can use to structure your hierarchy, but they are the only two that span both the Hosts And Clusters view and the VMs And Templates view. The next tool I'll discuss in building your vCenter Server hierarchy, the resource pool, is valid only in Hosts And Clusters view.

ORGANIZING WITH RESOURCE POOLS

As I explained previously, resource pools are used to organize virtual machines. The key difference between a "regular" folder and a resource pool is that a resource pool allows vSphere administrators to manipulate the allocation of CPU and memory resources to virtual machines within the pool. Folders don't provide that functionality. In addition, you can use resource pools only in the Hosts And Clusters inventory view of vCenter Server; you can use folders in both the Hosts And Clusters view and the VMs And Templates view. I won't go into more detail on resource pools here, because I've already discussed how you would use them to organize virtual machines and apply permissions in the section "Using Resource Pools to Assign Permissions."

The resource allocation aspect of resource pools is discussed in detail in Chapter 10.

Now that I've shown you all the various pieces that are used in the vCenter Server hierarchy—datacenters, folders, resource pools, ESX/ESXi hosts, and clusters—I'd like to tie it all together with a look at how you combine all these objects to create the hierarchy that you and your business needs.

PUTTING TOGETHER A VCENTER SERVER HIERARCHY

I've already stated that vCenter Server is designed as an enterprise management application for all of the ESX/ESXi hosts in your worldwide organization. To be an effective enterprise management application for your virtual infrastructure, though, vCenter Server needs to be structured and modeled to fit how your organization manages resources. So, the question remains: how do you manage resources? Is your management strategy based on geography, departments, or projects? Or do you prefer an arbitrary management style? Whatever the approach you use, vCenter Server supports that approach by flexibly combining the building blocks I've already discussed: datacenters, folders, and resource pools. Perhaps a comparison might help.

Think about what would happen if you were to place every document in your computer at the root of your hard drive. Finding documents would be difficult to say the very least, and assigning permissions to objects would be similarly difficult. Thus would be the case if your virtual infrastructure objects (hosts, resource pools, virtual machines, templates) were all located in a flat structure under the root.

Take, for example, an organization with offices in St. Petersburg, Florida, and Los Angeles, California, where each office has several ESX/ESXi hosts and dozens of virtual machines and template objects. The infrastructure is constructed so that the hosts in Los Angeles are attached to a shared storage device in Los Angeles, and the St. Petersburg ESX/ESXi hosts are attached to a second shared storage device local to their site. Keep in mind that these servers can talk to each other via a WAN connection, but they can access storage only in their specific region. In addition, the company has IT staff in each location. How would you structure vCenter Server's hierarchy to best suit this organization?

The simplest vCenter Server hierarchy would have two datacenters, one for St. Petersburg and one for Los Angeles. Within each of these datacenter objects, the local IT staff for that location could use folders and/or resource pools to organize virtual machines, templates, and ESX/ESXi hosts as needed.

This example could just as easily have been detailed as a departmental-specific configuration in which the finance, marketing, and sales departments have their own respective ESX/ESXi hosts. In this case, the datacenter objects would be labeled by department rather than physical location.

In any case, you should now have a pretty good idea of how to use the various building blocks of the vCenter Server hierarchy to construct a model that is appropriate for your organization. Now let's examine vCenter Server's roles.

Understanding vCenter Server's Roles

Where the ESX/ESXi host is quite limited in its default roles, vCenter Server provides more default roles, thereby offering a much greater degree of flexibility in constructing access control. Although both security models offer the flexibility of creating custom roles, ESX/ESXi includes three default roles, while vCenter Server provides nine default roles, including the same three offered in ESX/ESXi. Figure 9.7 details the default vCenter Server roles. These roles are visible from within the vSphere Client by selecting View ➤ Administration ➤ Roles.

FIGURE 9.7
The vCenter Server default roles offer much more flexibility than an individual ESX/ESXi host.

As you can see, VMware provides a large number of roles in a default vCenter Server installation. Remember, just like the default ESX/ESXi roles, it is considered a best practice to *not* modify the default roles provided by VMware. Editing the defaults could result in over- or under-assigning permissions. If the default roles are edited and other administrators are unaware of the alteration, the use of the default role results in unexpected privileges or a lack of any privileges. If you need a similar role to one that is a default, then clone that role, and change the permissions assignment for the cloned role. In fact, vCenter Server will prevent you from modifying the No Access, Read-Only, and Administrator roles—you must clone them in order to customize them.

The key to using these roles effectively is to understand the functions of each of the roles that VMware provides:

No Access This role is just what it sounds like—it permits a user or group no access. But why do you need it? The idea behind this role is to prevent a user or group that has permissions at some point higher in the hierarchy from having permissions on the object to which this role is assigned. For instance, you may have granted Bob the Virtual Machine User role at the datacenter level, which would permit him to administer all of the virtual machines in the datacenter, but there is a security concern about him having access to one of the accounting virtual machines in that datacenter. You could assign Bob to the No Access role on the Accounting virtual machine, which would effectively supersede his Virtual Machine User privileges.

Read-Only Read-Only allows users to see the vCenter Server inventory. It does not allow them to interact with any of the virtual machines in any way through the vSphere Client or the web client except to see the power status of each virtual machine in the inventory where they have the Read-Only role applied.

Administrator A user assigned to an object with the Administrator role will have full administrative capabilities over that object in vCenter Server. Note that this does *not* grant *any* privileges within the guest operating systems installed inside the virtual machines. For instance, a user assigned the Administrator role for a virtual machine may be able to change the RAM assigned to the virtual machine and alter its performance parameters (Shares, Reservations, and Limits) but may not even have the permissions to log into that virtual machine unless that user has been granted that right from within the guest operating system.

The Administrator role can be granted at any object level in the hierarchy, and the user or group that is assigned the role at that level will have vCenter Server administrative privileges over that object and (if the inheritance box is selected) any child objects in the hierarchy.

Aside from the No Access, Read-Only, and Administrator roles, the rest of the roles are sample roles. These are intended to provide vSphere users with an idea of how to structure roles and permissions to model the appropriate administrative structure.

Virtual Machine Power User The Virtual Machine Power User sample role assigns permissions to allow a user to perform most functions on virtual machines. This includes tasks such as configuring CD and floppy media, changing the power state, taking and deleting snapshots, and modifying the configuration. These permissions apply only to virtual machines. The idea here is, as an example, if users are granted this role at a datacenter level, they would only be able to manage virtual machines in that datacenter and would not be able to change settings on objects such as resource pools in that datacenter.

Virtual Machine User The Virtual Machine User sample role grants the user the ability to interact with a virtual machine, but not the ability to change its configuration. Users can operate the virtual machine's power controls and change the media in the virtual CD-ROM drive or floppy drive as long as they also have access to the media they want to change. For instance, a user who is assigned this role for a virtual machine will be able to change the CD media from an ISO image on a shared storage volume to their own client system's physical CD-ROM drive. If you want them to have the ability to change from one ISO file to another (both stored on a Virtual Machine File System [VMFS] volume or Network File System [NFS] volume), they will also need to be granted the Browse Datastore permission at the parent of the Datastore object in the vCenter Server hierarchy—usually the datacenter that the ESX/ESXi host is located in.

Resource Pool Administrator The Resource Pool Administrator sample role grants the user the ability to manage and configure resources with a resource pool including virtual machines, child pools, scheduled tasks, and alarms.

VMware Consolidated Backup User As the role name suggests, the VMware Consolidated Backup sample role grants the user the privileges required for performing a backup of a virtual machine using VCB.

Datacenter Consumer The Datastore Consumer sample role is targeted at users who need only a single permission: the permission to allocate space from a datastore. Clearly, this role is very limited.

Network Consumer Similar to the Datastore Consumer role, the Network Consumer sample role has only a single permission, and that is the permission to assign networks.

These default roles provide a good starting point, but they won't meet every company's needs. If you need something more than what is provided by default, you'll need to create a custom role. I describe this process in the next section.

Working with vCenter Server Roles

What if the default roles supplied with vCenter Server don't provide you with the necessary functionality for a particular grouping of users? Well, it depends on what the problem is. Let's take the most basic problem. You've chosen a best fit role to assign a user privileges, but the role you've selected lacks a key permission, or perhaps the role you've selected grants a few permissions that you don't want included. To get the exact fit you need, you can simply clone the role and then customize the cloned role.

Perform the following steps to clone a role in vCenter Server:

1. Launch the vSphere Client if it is not already running, and connect to a vCenter Server instance.

2. Navigate to the Roles area using the menu, the navigation bar, or the keyboard shortcut.

3. Right-click the role that you want to clone, and select Clone from the context menu.

After you've cloned the role, you can add or remove privileges as needed. I described the process of editing a role earlier in this chapter in the section "Editing and Removing Roles."

Understanding vCenter Server Privileges

Roles are very useful, but now that you've started to peek into the properties of the roles and how to edit roles, you also need to understand each of the privileges and what they do for you in terms of customizing roles. Remember that privileges are individual tasks that are assigned to roles. Without privileges assigned, roles are useless, so it's important to understand the privileges available within vCenter Server.

This is a rather long list of privileges, but it's broken down into some general categories, so you'll begin by looking at what each of the categories means in general terms:

Alarms Controls the ability to create, modify, delete, disable, and acknowledge vCenter Server alarms.

Datacenter Controls the ability to create, delete, move, and rename datacenters inside vCenter Server.

Datastore Controls who can access files stored on an ESX/ESXi attached volume. This permission needs to be assigned at the parent object of the ESX/ESXi host itself—for instance, a datacenter, an ESX/ESXi cluster, or a folder that contains ESX/ESXi hosts.

Distributed Virtual Port Group Controls who can create, delete, or modify distributed virtual port groups on distributed virtual switches.

Distributed Virtual Switch   Controls the right to create, delete, modify, or move vNetwork Distributed Switches; add or remove ESX/ESXi hosts; and configure ports on a distributed virtual switch.

Extension   Controls the ability to register, update, or unregister extensions in vCenter Server. The two existing extensions include VMware Update Manager and VMware Converter.

Folder   Controls the creation, deletion, and general manipulation of folders in the vCenter Server hierarchy.

Global   Includes the ability to manage vCenter Server license settings and server settings such as SNMP and SMTP.

Host   Controls what users can do with the ESX/ESXi host in the inventory. This includes tasks such as adding and removing ESX/ESXi hosts from the inventory, changing the host's memory configuration, or changing the Service Console firewall setting's network configuration.

Host Profile   Controls creating, editing, deleting, or viewing host profiles.

Network   Controls the configuration or removal of networks from the vCenter Server inventory.

Performance   Controls the ability of users to modify the intervals at which the performance chart information is displayed on the Performance tab of an object.

Permissions   Controls who has the ability to modify the permissions assigned to a role and who can manipulate a role/user combination for a particular object.

Resource   Controls resource pool manipulation, including creating, deleting, or renaming the pool; also controls migration by using VMotion and applying DRS recommendations.

Scheduled Task   Controls the configuration of tasks and the ability to run a task that is scheduled inside vCenter Server.

Sessions   Controls the ability to view and disconnect vSphere Client sessions connected to vCenter Server and to send a global message to connected vSphere Client users. As shown in Figure 9.8, a user without Sessions privileges cannot terminate vSphere Client sessions.

FIGURE 9.8
Session control in vCenter Server allows a user to disconnect vSphere Client sessions.

Storage Views   Controls changing the server configuration and looking at storage views.

Tasks   Controls the ability to create or update tasks.

vApp   Controls the configuration and management of vApps, such as the ability to add virtual machines to a vApp; clone, create, delete, export, or import a vApp; power on or power off the vApp; or view the Open Virtualization Format (OVF) environment.

Virtual Machine   Controls the manipulation of virtual machines in the vCenter Server inventory, including the ability to create, delete, or connect to the remote console of a virtual machine; to control the power state of a virtual machine; to change floppy and CD media; and to manipulate templates among other privileges.

VMware vCenter Update Manager   Controls who has the ability to manage system baselines and updates as well as configure the vCenter Update Manager service.

How these various privileges are assigned to roles is what really matters. As you saw earlier, vCenter Server ships with some default roles already defined. Some of these—namely, the No Access, Read-Only, and Administrator roles—are fairly well understood and cannot be modified. The other predefined roles are listed in Table 9.1 along with the privileges that are assigned to each role by default.

As you can see, vCenter Server is very specific about the privileges you can assign to roles. Because these privileges are specific, this can sometimes complicate the process of granting users the ability to perform seemingly simple tasks within vCenter Server. Let's review a couple of examples so you can get a better grasp on how privileges, roles, and permissions combine in vCenter Server.

DELEGATING THE ABILITY TO CREATE VIRTUAL MACHINES AND INSTALL A GUEST OPERATING SYSTEM

One common access control delegation in a virtual infrastructure is to give a group of users the rights to create virtual machines. After just browsing through the list of available privileges, it might seem simple to accomplish this. It is, however, more complex than meets the eye. Providing a user with the ability to create a virtual machine involves assigning a combination of privileges at multiple levels throughout the vCenter Server inventory.

Combining Privileges, Roles, and Permissions in vCenter Server

So far, I've shown you all the pieces you need to know in order to structure vCenter Server so as to support your company's management and operational requirements. How these pieces fit together, though, can sometimes be more complex than you might expect. In the next few paragraphs, I will walk you through an example of how these pieces fit together.

Here's the scenario. Within your IT department, one group handles building all Windows servers. Once the servers are built, operational control of the servers is handed off to a separate group. Now that you have virtualized your datacenter, this same separation of duties needs to be re-created within vCenter Server. Sounds simple, right? You just need to configure vCenter Server so that this group has the ability to create virtual machines. This group is represented within Active Directory with a group object (this Active Directory group is named IT-Provisioning), and you'd like to leverage the Active Directory group membership to control who is granted these permissions within vCenter Server.

In the following steps, I've deliberately kept some of the steps at a high level. For example, I don't go into how to create a role or how to assign that role to an inventory object as a permission because those tasks are covered elsewhere in this chapter.

Perform the following steps to allow a Windows-based group to create virtual machines:

1. Use the vSphere Client to connect to a vCenter Server instance. Log in with a user account that has been assigned the Administrator role within vCenter Server.

TABLE 9.1:   Table of Privileges for Default Roles

PREDEFINED ROLE	ASSIGNED PRIVILEGES
Virtual Machine Power User	Datastore ➢ Browse Datastore Global ➢ Cancel Task Scheduled Task ➢ Create Task, Delete Task, Remove Task, Run Task Virtual Machine ➢ Configuration ➢ Add Existing Disk, Add New Disk, Add or Remove Device, Advanced, Change CPU Count, Change Resource, Disk Lease, Memory, Modify Device Settings, Remove Disk, Rename, Reset Guest Information, Settings, Upgrade Virtual Hardware Virtual Machine ➢ Interaction ➢ Answer Question, Configure CD Media, Configure Floppy Media, Console Interaction, Device Connection, Power On, Power Off, Reset, Suspend, VMware Tools Install Virtual Machine ➢ State ➢ Create Snapshot, Remove Snapshot, Rename Snapshot, Revert To Snapshot
Virtual machine User	Global ➢ Cancel Task Scheduled Task ➢ Create Task, Delete Task, Remove Task, Run Task Virtual Machine ➢ Interaction ➢ Answer Question, Configure CD Media, Configure Floppy Media, Console Interaction, Device Connection, Power On, Power Off, Reset, Suspend, VMware Tools Install
Resource pool Administrator	Alarms ➢ Create Alarm, Modify Alarm, Remove Alarm Datastore ➢ Browse Datastore Folder ➢ Create Folder, Delete Folder, Move Folder, Rename Folder Global ➢ Cancel Task, Log Event, Set Custom Attribute Permissions ➢ Modify Permissions Resource ➢ Assign Virtual Machine To Resource Pool, Create Resource Pool, Migrate, Modify Resource Pool, Move Resource Pool, Query VMotion, Relocate, Remove Resource Pool, Rename Resource Pool Scheduled Task ➢ Create Task, Delete Task, Remove Task, Run Task Virtual Machine ➢ Configuration ➢ Add Existing Disk, Add New Disk, Add Or Remove Device, Advanced, Change CPU Count, Change Resource, Disk Lease, Memory, Modify Device Settings, Raw Device, Remove Disk, Rename, Reset Guest Information, Settings, Upgrade Virtual Hardware Virtual Machine ➢ Interaction ➢ Answer Question, Configure CD Media, Configure Floppy Media, Console Interaction, Device Connection, Power On, Power Off, Reset, Suspend, VMware Tools Install Virtual Machine ➢ Inventory ➢ Create, Move, Remove Virtual Machine ➢ Provisioning ➢ Allow Disk Access, Allow Read-Only Disk Access, Allow Virtual Machine Download, All Virtual Machine Files Upload, Clone Template, Clone Virtual Machine, Create Template From Virtual Machine, Customize, Deploy Template, Mark As Template, Mark As Virtual Machine, Modify Customization Specification, Read Customization Specifications Virtual Machine ➢ State ➢ Create Snapshot, Remove Snapshot, Rename Snapshot, Revert To Snapshot

TABLE 9.2:   Table of Privileges for Default Roles

PREDEFINED ROLE	ASSIGNED PRIVILEGES
VMware Consolidated Backup User	Virtual Machine ➢ Configuration ➢ Disk Lease Virtual Machine ➢ Provisioning ➢ Allow Read-Only Disk Access, Allow Virtual Machine Download Virtual Machine ➢ State ➢ Create Snapshot, Remove Snapshot
Datastore Consumer	Datastore ➢ Allocate Space
Network Consumer	Network ➢ Assign Network

2. Create a new role called VMCreators.

3. Assign the following privileges to the VMCreators role:

> Virtual Machine ➢ Inventory ➢ Create
>
> Virtual Machine ➢ Configuration ➢ Add New Disk
>
> Virtual Machine ➢ Configuration ➢ Add Existing Disk
>
> Virtual Machine ➢ Configuration ➢ Raw Device

4. Create a new role called VMAssigners.

5. Assign the following privileges to the VMAssigners role:

> Resource ➢ Assign Virtual Machine To Resource Pool

6. Assign the Windows-based group IT-Provisioning the VMCreators role on a folder or datacenter object.

7. Assign the same Windows-based group the VMAssigners role on a resource pool, host, or cluster.

8. Assign the same Windows-based group the Read-Only role on a datacenter object or a folder containing a datacenter object. Disable the propagation if the role is assigned directly to the datacenter. Leave the propagation enabled if the role is assigned to a folder that contains the datacenter object.

At this point, the privileges for creating a virtual machine are complete; however, the IT-Provisioning group from steps 6 through 8 does not have the rights to mount a CD/DVD image and therefore cannot install a guest operating system. Therefore, more permissions are required in order to allow the IT-Provisioning group to not only create the virtual machines and place them in the right place within vCenter Server but also to install the guest operating system within those virtual machines.

Perform the following steps to allow the Windows-based IT-Provisioning group to install a guest operating system from a CD/DVD image file:

1. Use the vSphere Client to connect to a vCenter Server instance. Log in with a user account that has been assigned the Administrator role within vCenter Server.

2. Create a new role named GOS-Installers.

3. Assign the following privileges to the GOS-Installers role:

    Datastore ➤ Browse Datastore

    Virtual Machine ➤ Configuration

    Virtual Machine ➤ Interaction

4. Assign the Windows-based IT-Provisioning group the GOS-Installers role on the datacenter object.

As you can see, the seemingly simple task of creating a virtual machine actually involves three different roles and three different sets of permissions.

Real World Scenario

vCenter Server Permissions Interaction

In organizations, both large and small, users often belong to multiple groups, and those groups are assigned different levels of permissions on different objects. In this sidebar, I'll talk about the effects of multiple group memberships and multiple permission assignments in the virtual infrastructure.

In one scenario, let's look at the effective permissions when a user belongs to multiple groups that have different permissions on objects at different levels in the inventory. In the example, a user named Rick Avsom is a member of the Res_Pool_Admins and VM_Auditors Windows groups. The Res_Pool_Admins group is assigned membership in the Resource Pool Admins vCenter Server role, and the permission is set at the Production resource pool. The VM_Auditors group is assigned membership in the Read-Only vCenter Server role, and the permission is set at the Win2008-02 virtual machine. The Win2008-02 virtual machine resides within the Production resource pool.

When logged on to the vCenter Server computer as Rick Avsom, the inventory reflects only the objects available to him through his permissions. Based on the permission assignment described, Rick Avsom will be able to manage the Production resource pool and will have full privileges over the Win2008-01 virtual machine to which the Resource Pool Admin privileges are propagating. However, Rick Avsom will not be able to manage the Win2008-02 virtual machine to which he is limited to Read-Only privileges. The conclusion to this example is that users in multiple groups with conflicting permissions on objects lower in the inventory are granted only the permissions configured directly on the object.

Another common scenario to understand is the effective permissions when a user belongs to multiple groups that have different permissions on the same objects. In this example, a user named Sue Rindlee is a member of the VM_Admins and VM_Auditors Windows groups. The VM_Admins group has been assigned membership in the Virtual Machine Power User vCenter Server role, and the VM_Auditors group is assigned membership in the Read-Only vCenter Server role. Both of these roles have been assigned permissions on the Production resource pool.

When logged on to the vCenter Server computer as Sue Rindlee, the inventory reflects only the objects available to her through her permissions. Based on the permission assignment described, Sue Rindlee will be able to modify all of the virtual machines in the Production resource pool. This validates that Sue's Virtual Machine Power User status through membership in the VM_Admin group prevails over the Read-Only status obtained through her membership in the VM_Auditors group.

The conclusion to this scenario is that the effective permission is a cumulative permission when a user belongs to multiple groups with different permissions on the same object. Even if Sue Rindlee belonged to a group that had been assigned to the No Access vCenter Server role, her Virtual Machine Power User role would prevail. However, if Sue Rindlee's user account was added directly to a vCenter Server object and assigned the No Access role, then she would not have access to any of the objects to which that permission has propagated.

Even with a good understanding of permission propagation, you should always proceed with caution and always maintain the principle of least privilege to ensure that no user has been extended privileges beyond those that are needed as part of a job role.

When delegating authority, it is always better to err on the side of caution. Do not provide more permissions than are necessary for the job at hand. Just as in any other information systems environment, your access control implementation is a living object that will consistently require consideration and revision. Manage your permissions carefully, be flexible, and expect that users and administrators alike are going to be curious and will push their access levels to the limits. Stay a step ahead, and always remember the principle of least privilege.

Now that you've looked at how to assign permissions, roles, and privileges within vCenter Server, there's one more area that I need to discuss with you. What do you do when you can't get to the vSphere Client? What functionality does VMware vSphere provide, if any? And how does this solution tie into vCenter Server's access controls? All these questions are answered in the next section.

Managing Virtual Machines Using the Web Console

Imagine a situation where you are away from your desk at the office and you get a call or a page indicating that there is a problem with a virtual machine in one of your datacenters. This type of situation has been known to happen. Your desk isn't close at hand, and you don't have your laptop with you. How can you quickly take a look at the virtual machine in order to diagnose the issue? Even though you do have access to a computer where you are, this computer doesn't have the vSphere Client installed, and without the vSphere Client, you have no way of managing your VMware vSphere environment. Is there a workaround that will allow you to quickly help resolve this issue?

Fortunately, VMware has included an optional web-based management console that you can install on your vCenter Server computer and that is installed by default on all of your ESX/ESXi hosts. All it requires is a web browser and IP connectivity. This would allow you to access to the VMware vSphere environment even when the vSphere Client is not available.

vCENTER SERVER WEB ACCESS BROWSER REQUIREMENTS

Connecting to the vCenter Server web-based management console from a Windows or Linux client requires any of the following browsers:

◆ Internet Explorer 6.0 or later (Windows only)

◆ Netscape Navigator 7.0

◆ Mozilla 1.*x*

◆ Firefox 1.0.7 or later

This web-based console can give you access to the virtual machines running in your infrastructure, and it is based on the Apache Tomcat web service. The Apache Tomcat web service is part of the vCenter Server installation, as you learned in Chapter 3. Tomcat is most commonly known for its use as a web server running on Linux operating systems. However, the Windows version of Tomcat is used for the web access component of vCenter Server instead of building on top of the Internet Information Services (IIS) web server available natively in Windows. This web access component, like the vSphere Client, maintains the level of security as defined by the permissions established in vCenter Server.

Perform the following steps to use the web console to access and manage virtual machines on a vCenter Server computer:

1. Open a web browser, and type in the IP address or fully qualified domain name of the vCenter Server computer.

2. At the default vCenter Server web page, click the Log In To Web Access link.

3. Type a valid username and password at the vSphere Web Access login page.

After you enter a valid Windows username and password for a user who has permissions in vCenter Server, you'll see an inventory of the virtual machines, as shown in Figure 9.9.

WEB-BASED VIRTUAL MACHINE MANAGEMENT

The vCenter Server web console is used solely for the purpose of accessing and managing virtual machines. There will not be any ESX/ESXi hosts listed in the inventory; you must perform all host management tasks through the vSphere Client or from a command line.

Selecting an individual virtual machine alters the layout of the web console by offering additional tabs and links for managing the virtual machine. Figure 9.10 shows the default view after a virtual machine has been selected in the inventory. In addition to the five management tabs, the toolbar at the top of the page contains buttons for managing the virtual machine power states.

The Events tab details the most recent events that have occurred for the selected virtual machine. Events in this view include information on changes in power state as well as resource utilization.

The Alarms tab allows you to examine the recent alerts that this virtual machine has triggered according to the alarms that are configured for the virtual machine. Alarm creation and management is discussed in detail in Chapter 12, "Monitoring VMware vSphere Performance."

FIGURE 9.9
vCenter Server Web Access lets you access and manage the virtual machines that are available to you.

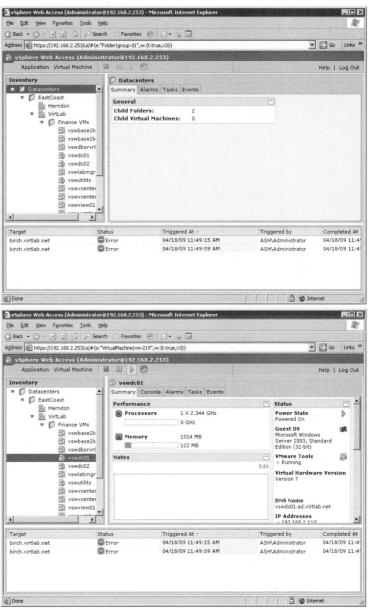

FIGURE 9.10
You can view details on console access, hardware management, and power management.

The Tasks tab lists any tasks that have recently taken place upon the virtual machine along with any tasks that might still be in progress.

As shown in Figure 9.11, the Console tab provides access to a console session for the virtual machine that grants access similar to using a keyboard and mouse connected directly to a physical server. Note that the first time you access the Console tab in a web browser, you will be prompted to install a plug-in to enable the functionality of the Console tab.

FIGURE 9.11
The Console tab opens
a separate window and
provides desktop access
to a virtual machine
when traditional in-band
management tools are
inoperable.

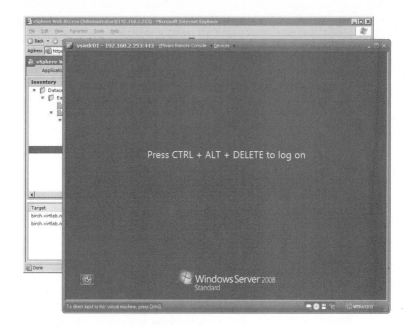

WEB SERVICE CONNECTIONS

The web console is not meant to be a replacement for Terminal Services, Remote Desktop, VNC, Citrix, or any other remote management tool. The greatest value to the web console is during the situation where the aforementioned in-band management tools are unable to connect to a server. The web console will provide access for the purposes of troubleshooting and restoring common remote management tools. However, the web console also poses problems when multiple users establish connections. Because the connection is considered a console session, multiple users would be forced to share mouse and keyboard control unlike a typical Remote Desktop or Terminal Services connection, where users would be unaware of each other's presence without some investigation.

You can log in to a virtual machine desktop through the web console by pressing Ctrl+Alt+Insert or by clicking the Virtual Machine menu in the toolbar and then selecting the Troubleshoot ➢ Send Ctrl+Alt+Delete option.

When a virtual machine is selected, the Commands section on the right side of the page contains a Generate Virtual Machine Shortcut link, which generates a URL that provides direct access to a virtual machine's console. Figure 9.12 shows the details of the remote URL generation page. By default, the Limit View To The Remote Console and Limit View To A Single Virtual Machine options are selected, thereby confining the remote console URL to only the target virtual machine. The URL begins with the IP address or fully qualified domain name of the vCenter Server depending on how the connection has been established in the web browser.

The URL is rather long and therefore not one to be committed to memory. For the user who needs occasional access to a virtual machine, the remote console URL can be pasted into an e-mail message or instant messaging session. After the user clicks the link, an authentication page will open. The ID that the user authenticates with must have at least the Virtual Machine User role assigned to it for the link to function as expected.

FIGURE 9.12

A URL generated for a virtual machine provides direct access to a console session; however, successful access still requires authentication and privileges.

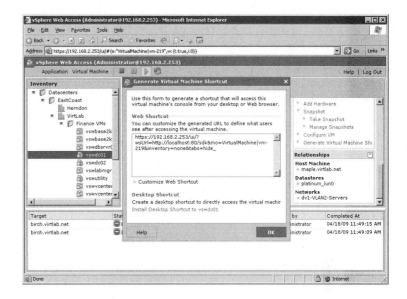

REMOTE CONSOLE URLs

The web access component of an individual ESX/ESXi host is identical in nature to the one shown here for vCenter Server. However, you can view only the virtual machines on that specific host. In addition, if a remote console URL is created by connecting to an individual ESX/ESXi host, the URL will begin with the IP address or fully qualified domain name of that host instead of the vCenter Server computer's information. The problem with this arises when the virtual machine is relocated to a new host as a result of VMotion or VMware HA. The relocation of the virtual machine in this case invalidates the URL. Because of these limitations, you should always create remote console URLs by connecting to a Virtual Center server and not an ESX/ESXi host.

The Bottom Line

Manage and maintain ESX/ESXi permissions. VMware ESX and VMware ESXi provide a structured approach to permissions based on users, groups, roles, and privileges. This approach provides granular access to virtual machines and related resources.

Master It You've granted permission to one of your administrators on an ESX host by adding this administrator's account to the Administrator role. Now this administrator is trying to manage a couple of virtual machines on another host but can't. You've verified this administrator does have an account on the other host. What could be the problem?

Manage and maintain vCenter Server permissions. vCenter Server centralizes the management of users and groups for permissions by integrating with Active Directory. In addition, vCenter Server extends the structured approach using users, groups, roles, and privileges not only to ESX/ESXi hosts and virtual machines but also to datastores, networks, resource pools, vCenter Update Manager, vApps, and host profiles, to name a few.

Master It A group of administrators needs full access to a specific subset of virtual machines. All these virtual machines have been placed within a resource pool. This resource pool also contains some other virtual machines to which this group of administrators should *not* have access. Without having to move the extra VMs out of the resource pool, what is the best way to grant permissions to this subset of virtual machines?

Manage virtual machines using the web console. In addition to using the vSphere Client, vCenter Server also provides web-based access to perform basic management tasks, such as changing power states, managing snapshots, or viewing the virtual machine console.

Master It With vCenter Server Web Access, is it possible to provide a URL to view the console of a specific virtual machine? If so, how?

Chapter 10

Managing Resource Allocation

The idea that we can take a single physical server and host many virtual machines has a great deal of value in today's dynamic datacenter environments, but let's face it—there are limits to how many virtual machines that can be hosted on a VMware ESX/ESXi platform. The key to making the most of your virtualization platform is understanding how key resources—memory, processors, disks, and networks—are consumed by the virtual machines running on the host and how the host itself consumes resources. The method the ESX/ESXi host uses to arbitrate access to each resource is a bit different. This chapter discusses how the ESX/ESXi host allocates these resources, how you can change the way these resources are allocated, and how you can monitor the consumption of these resources over time.

In this chapter, you will learn to:

◆ Manage virtual machine memory and CPU allocation

◆ Create and manage resource pools

◆ Configure and execute VMotion

◆ Create and manage clusters

◆ Configure and manage VMware Distributed Resource Scheduler

Allocating Virtual Machine Resources

One of the most significant advantages of server virtualization is the ability to allocate resources to a virtual machine based on the machine's actual performance needs. In the traditional physical server environment, a server is often provided with more resources than it really needs because it was purchased with a specific budget in mind and the server specifications were maximized for the budget provided. For example, does a Dynamic Host Configuration Protocol (DHCP) server really need dual processors, 4GB of RAM, and 146GB mirrored hard drives? In most situations, the DHCP server will most certainly underutilize those resources. In the virtual world, you can create a virtual machine better suited for the DHCP services provided by the virtual machine. For this DHCP server, then, you would assemble a virtual machine with a more suitable 1GB of RAM, access to a single CPU, and 20GB of disk space, all of which are provided by the ESX/ESXi host on which the virtual machine is running. Then, you can create additional virtual machines with the resources they need to operate effectively without wasting valuable memory, CPU cycles, and disk storage. As you add more virtual machines, each machine places additional demand on the ESX/ESXi host, and the host's resources are consumed to support the virtual machines. At a certain point, either the host will run out of resources or you will need to find an alternate way to share access to a limited resource.

As the vSphere administrator, you need to understand how to allocate resources effectively, how ESX/ESXi manages allocated resources, and what happens when ESX/ESXi runs out of a resource. In this chapter, I'll examine resource allocation across two major resources, memory and CPU. In addition, I'll look at VMotion and VMware Distributed Resource Scheduler (DRS), two features that are helpful in managing resource allocation in a vSphere environment.

THE GAME PLAN FOR GROWTH

One of the most challenging aspects of managing a virtual infrastructure is managing growth without jeopardizing performance and without overestimating. For organizations of any size, it is critical to establish a plan for managing virtual machine and ESX/ESXi host growth.

The easiest approach is to construct a resource consumption document that details the following:

◆ What is the standard configuration for a new virtual machine to be added to the inventory? Be sure to specify critical configuration points such as the size of the operating system drive, the size of any data drives, and how much RAM is allocated.

◆ What are the decision points for creating a virtual machine with specifications beyond the standard configuration?

◆ How much of a server's resources can be consumed before availability and performance levels are jeopardized?

◆ At the point where the resources for an ESX/ESXi host (or an entire cluster) are consumed, do we add a single host or multiple hosts at one time?

◆ What is the maximum size of a cluster for our environment? When does adding another host (or set of hosts) constitute building a new cluster?

The first virtual machine resource I'll examine is memory. In many instances, memory is the first resource to come under constraints, so taking a look at memory first is warranted.

Allocating Virtual Machine Memory

Let's start with a discussion of how memory is allocated to a virtual machine. Later in this section I'll discuss the mechanisms ESX/ESXi uses to arbitrate access to the memory under contention and what you as an administrator can do to change how virtual machines use the memory assigned to them.

When you create a new virtual machine through the vSphere Client, the wizard asks you how much memory the virtual machine should have, as shown in Figure 10.1. The vSphere Client suggests a default value based on the selected guest operating system.

The amount of memory you allocate on this screen is the amount the guest operating system will see—in this example, it is 1024MB. This is the same as when you build a system and put two 512MB memory sticks into the system board. If you install Windows 2003 in this virtual machine, Windows will report 1024MB of RAM installed. Ultimately, this is the amount of memory the virtual machine "thinks" it has. Like a physical system with two 512MB memory sticks installed, this virtual machine will never be able to use more than 1024MB of RAM.

Let's assume you have an ESX/ESXi host with 4GB of physical RAM available to run virtual machines (in other words, the Service Console and VMkernel are using some RAM, and there's

4GB left over for the virtual machines). In the case of our new virtual machine, it will comfortably run, leaving approximately 3GB for other virtual machines (there is some additional overhead that I discuss later, but for now let's assume that the 3GB is available to other virtual machines).

FIGURE 10.1
The memory configuration settings for a virtual machine indicate the amount of RAM the virtual machine "thinks" it has.

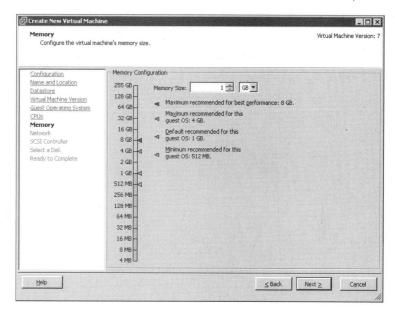

What happens when you run three more virtual machines each configured with 1GB of RAM? Each of the additional virtual machines will request 1GB of RAM from the ESX/ESXi host. At this point, four virtual machines will be accessing the physical memory.

What happens when you launch a fifth virtual machine? Will it run? The short answer is yes, and some of the key technologies that enable administrators to overcommit memory—that is, to allocate more memory to virtual machines than is actually installed in the VMware ESX/ESXi host—are quite advanced and unique to VMware ESX and ESXi.

Understanding ESX/ESXi Advanced Memory Technologies

VMware ESX and ESXi are unique among hypervisors on the market today in that they support a number of different technologies for advanced memory management. As a result of these advanced memory management technologies, VMware ESX/ESXi is the only commercially available hypervisor on the market capable of performing memory overcommitment.

The first of these technologies is *idle page reclamation*. Using idle page reclamation, ESX/ESXi will reclaim memory pages that are not being actively used by the virtual machine, clear out the reclaimed pages, and reallocate those memory pages to other virtual machines. A second memory management technology is *transparent page sharing*, in which identical memory pages are shared among virtual machines to reduce the total number of memory pages needed. Finally, VMware ESX/ESXi can use a *balloon driver*, installed with the VMware Tools, to force a VM to use less memory than its configured maximum. The balloon driver requests memory from the guest operating system within the virtual machine—a process calling *inflating*—and then passes that memory back to the hypervisor for use by other virtual machines.

Although these advanced memory management technologies allow ESX/ESXi to allocate more memory to virtual machines than there is actual RAM in the physical server, at some point it becomes necessary to exercise some control over how the virtual machines access and use the memory allocated to them.

HOW DOES THE BALLOON DRIVER WORK?

The balloon driver is part of the VMware Tools, which I described in detail in Chapter 7. As such, it is a guest operating system-specific driver, meaning that Linux VMs would have a Linux-based balloon driver, Windows VMs would have a Windows-based balloon driver, and so forth.

Regardless of the guest operating system, the balloon driver works in the same fashion. When the ESX/ESXi host is running low on physical memory, the hypervisor will signal the balloon driver to grow. To do this, the balloon driver will request memory from the guest operating system. This causes the balloon driver's memory footprint to grow, or to *inflate*. The memory that is granted to the balloon driver is then passed back to the hypervisor. The hypervisor can use these memory pages to supply memory for other virtual machines, reducing the need to swap and minimizing the performance impact of the memory constraints. When the memory pressure on the host passes, the balloon driver will *deflate*, or return memory to the guest operating system.

Controlling Memory Allocation

Like all physical resources, memory is a finite resource. At some point, if you continue creating virtual machines and assigning memory to these virtual machines, you will run out of memory. The advanced memory management technologies in ESX/ESXi help with the efficient use of this finite resource, but even so, at some point it will become necessary to enforce stronger controls over how virtual machines use the memory assigned to them. ESX/ESXi provides some additional settings in the virtual machines' configuration that affect memory allocation and memory management. On the Resources tab of a virtual machine's properties dialog box, you will see three options for controlling how a virtual machine uses the memory assigned to it: Reservation, Limit, and Shares. In this discussion, I will examine the Limit and Reservation settings and then return later to deal with the Shares setting. These controls are available not only for memory but also for CPU. I'll touch on using these controls for CPU allocation later in this chapter in the section "Allocating Virtual Machine CPU Capacity."

The steps for editing a Reservation, Limit, or Shares value for either memory or CPU are the same.

Perform the following steps to edit the reservation, limit, or shares of a virtual machine:

1. Use the vSphere Client to connect to a vCenter Server instance or directly to an ESX/ESXi host.

2. Drill down through the inventory to find the virtual machine to be edited.

3. Right-click the virtual machine, and select the Edit Settings option.

4. Click the Resources tab.

5. On the Resources tab, select the CPU or Memory options from the Settings list on the left.

6. Adjust the Shares, Reservation, and Limit values as desired.

The following sections detail the ramifications of setting custom memory reservations, memory limits, and memory shares.

Setting a Custom Memory Reservation

The memory reservation is an optional setting for each virtual machine. The memory reservation amount specified on the Resources tab of the virtual machine settings is the amount of actual, real physical memory that the ESX/ESXi host *must* provide to this virtual machine for the virtual machine to power on. The default is 0MB, or no reservation. A virtual machine with a reservation is guaranteed the amount of RAM configured in its Reservation setting. In the previous example, the virtual machine configured with 1GB of RAM and the default reservation of 0MB means the ESX/ESXi host does not have to provide the virtual machine with any physical memory. If the ESX/ESXi host is not required to provide actual RAM to the virtual machine, then where will the virtual machine get its memory? The answer is that it provides swap, or more specifically something called *VMkernel swap*.

VMkernel swap is a file created when a virtual machine is powered on with a `.vswp` extension. The per-virtual machine swap files created by the VMkernel reside by default in the same datastore location as the virtual machine's configuration file and virtual disk files. By default, this file will be equal to the size of the RAM that you configured the virtual machine with, and you will find the file in the same folder where the rest of the virtual machine's files are stored.

In theory, this means a virtual machine can get its memory allocation entirely from VMkernel swap—or disk—resulting in virtual machine performance degradation. If the virtual machine is configured with a reservation or a limit, the VMkernel swap file could differ.

THE SPEED OF RAM

How slow is VMkernel swap when compared to RAM? If you make some basic assumptions regarding RAM access times and disk seek times, you can see that both appear fairly fast in terms of a human but that in relation to each other, RAM is much faster:

$$\text{RAM access time} = 10 \text{ nanoseconds (for example)}$$

$$\text{Disk seek time} = 8 \text{ milliseconds (for example)}$$

The difference between these is calculated as follows:

$$0.008 \div 0.000000010 = 800,000$$

RAM is accessed 800,000 times faster than disk. Or to put it another way, if RAM takes 1 second to access, then disk would take 800,000 seconds to access—or nine and a quarter days:

$$((800,000 \div 60 \text{ seconds}) \div 60 \text{ minutes}) \div 24 \text{ hours}$$

As you can see, if virtual machine performance is your goal, it is prudent to spend your money on enough RAM to support the virtual machines you plan to run. There are other factors, but this is a significant one.

Does this mean that a virtual machine will get all of its memory from swap when ESX/ESXi host RAM is available? No. ESX/ESXi will attempt to provide each virtual machine with all the memory it requests, up to the maximum amount configured for that virtual machine. Obviously, a virtual machine configured with only 1024MB of RAM cannot request more than 1024MB of RAM. However, when an ESX/ESXi host doesn't have enough RAM available to satisfy the memory needs of the virtual machines it is hosting and when technologies such as transparent page sharing, idle page reclamation, and the balloon driver aren't enough, the VMkernel is forced to page some of each virtual machine's memory out to the individual virtual machine's VMkernel swap file.

Is there a way you can control how much of an individual virtual machine's memory allocation can be provided by swap and how much must be provided by real physical RAM? Yes. This is where a memory reservation comes into play. By default, a virtual machine has a memory reservation of 0MB, which means that potentially all of the virtual machine's memory could be paged out to the VMkernel swap file if necessary.

Let's look at what happens if you decide to set a memory reservation of 512MB for this virtual machine, shown in Figure 10.2. How does this change the way this virtual machine gets memory?

FIGURE 10.2
This virtual machine has a memory reservation of 512MB.

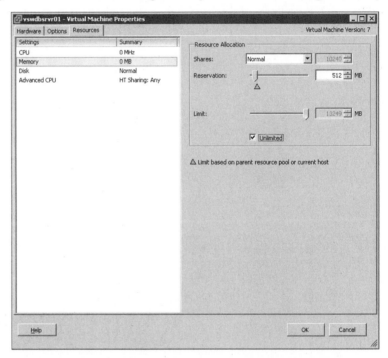

In this example, when this virtual machine is started, the host must provide at least 512MB of real RAM to support this virtual machine's memory allocation. In fact, 512MB of RAM is *guaranteed* for that VM. The host can provide the remaining 512MB of RAM from either physical RAM or VMkernel swap, as shown in Figure 10.3. In this case, because some of the virtual machine's RAM is guaranteed to come from physical RAM, ESX/ESXi reduces the size of the VMkernel swap file by the amount of the reservation. Therefore, the VMkernel swap file is reduced in size to 512MB. This behavior is consistent with what I've shown you so far: with a reservation of 0MB, the VMkernel swap file is the same size as the amount of configured memory. As the reservation increases, the size of the VMkernel swap file decreases in size correspondingly.

This behavior ensures that a virtual machine has at least some high-speed memory available to it if the ESX/ESXi host is running more virtual machines than it has actual RAM to support, but there's also a downside. If you assume that each of the virtual machines you start on this host have a 512MB reservation and you have 4GB of available RAM in the host to run virtual machines, then you will be able to launch only eight virtual machines concurrently ($8 \times 512MB = 4096MB$). On a more positive note, if each virtual machine is configured with an initial RAM allocation of 1024MB, then you're now running virtual machines that would need 8GB of RAM on a host with only 4GB. ESX/ESXi uses the technologies described earlier—idle page reclamation, transparent page sharing, and the balloon driver—to manage the fact that you, as the administrator, have allocated more RAM than is physically installed in the server.

FIGURE 10.3
Memory allocation for a virtual machine with 1024MB of memory configured and a 512MB reservation

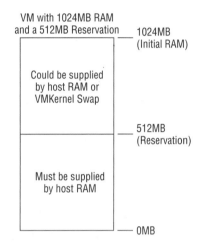

VM with 1024MB RAM and a 512MB Reservation

1024MB (Initial RAM)

Could be supplied by host RAM or VMKernel Swap

512MB (Reservation)

Must be supplied by host RAM

0MB

Real World Scenario

USE MEMORY OVERCOMMITMENT WISELY

Although you can overcommit memory with VMware ESX/ESXi, be careful doing so. You must carefully weigh the performance considerations. Although VMware ESX/ESXi has advanced memory management technologies such as transparent page sharing and idle page reclamation that help conserve memory, any workload that actually needs its memory may take a performance hit if that memory isn't available. In my experience, many workloads running in Windows-based virtual machines utilize only a portion of their configured memory.

In these sorts of environments, it's generally safe to overcommit memory by as much as 50 percent of the physical RAM installed in the server without seeing noticeable performance degradation. This means a server with 32GB of RAM could potentially host virtual machines configured to use 48GB of RAM. Larger overcommitment ratios are certainly very possible, and I've seen larger ratios in certain environments. However, the key to wisely using memory overcommitment to maximize the value of your vSphere deployment is knowing the needs of the virtual machines and how they consume resources.

Setting a Custom Memory Limit

If you look back at Figure 10.2, you will also see a setting for a memory limit. By default, all new virtual machines are created without a limit, which means that the initial RAM you assigned to it during creation is its effective limit. So, what exactly is the purpose of the Limit setting? The limit sets the actual limit on how much physical RAM may be utilized by that virtual machine.

To see this behavior in action, let's now change the limit on this virtual machine from the Unlimited default setting to 768MB.

So, what is the effective result of this configuration? Here's how it breaks down:

◆ The virtual machine is configured with 1024MB of RAM, so the guest operating system running inside that virtual machine believes that it has 1024MB of RAM available to use.

◆ The virtual machine has a reservation of 512MB of RAM, which means that the ESX/ESXi host *must* allocate 512MB of physical RAM to the virtual machine. This RAM is guaranteed to this virtual machine.

◆ Assuming the ESX/ESXi host has enough physical RAM installed and available, the hypervisor will allocate memory to the virtual machine as needed up to 768MB (the limit). Upon reaching 768MB, the balloon driver kicks in to prevent the guest operating system from using any more memory. When the guest operating system's memory demands drop below 768MB, the balloon driver deflates and returns memory to the guest. The effective result of this behavior is that the memory that the guest operating system uses remains below 768MB (the limit).

◆ The 256MB "gap" between the reservation and the limit may be supplied by either physical RAM or VMkernel swap space. ESX/ESXi will allocate physical RAM if it is available.

With this in mind, think about the server administrator who wants a new virtual machine with 16GB of RAM. You know his application doesn't need it, but you can't talk him out of his request—and worse than that, your supervisor has decided you need to build a virtual machine that actually has 16GB of RAM. Consider creating the virtual machine with an initial allocation of 16GB, and set a reservation of 1GB and a limit of 2GB. The operating system installed in the virtual machine will report 16GB of RAM (making that person happy and keeping your supervisor happy, too). The virtual machine will always consume 1GB of host memory. If your host has available RAM, then the virtual machine might consume up to 2GB of real physical memory. However, the 2GB limit means that the virtual machine won't consume more than 2GB of physical RAM at any time.

WHY USE LIMITS?

You might be asking yourself, "Why should I even use limits? Why not just set the configured limit to whatever you want the virtual machine to use?" That's a good question! Going back to the example in the text, consider the virtual machine configured with 16GB of RAM and a 2GB limit. If the applications running in that virtual machine needed more than 2GB of RAM, the limit can be changed dynamically while the virtual machine is running—no reboot or downtime is required. This would allow you to "add" memory to the virtual machine without having to reboot the guest operating system. Although vSphere does support the hot-add of memory for some guest operating systems, this technique effectively means you can hot-add memory to any guest operating system.

Had the virtual machine been configured with 2GB of RAM and no limit, increasing the amount of memory available to the guest operating system would, in the vast majority of cases, require downtime to shut down the virtual machine, increase the configured RAM, and then restart the virtual machine.

Working together, an initial allocation of memory, a memory reservation, and a memory limit can be powerful tools in efficiently managing the memory available on an ESX/ESXi host. But there is still one more tool to examine, and that's the memory shares. I'll discuss that next.

Setting a Custom Memory Shares Value

In Figure 10.2, there was a third setting called Shares that I have not discussed. The share system in VMware is a proportional share system that provides administrators with a means of assigning resource priority to virtual machines. For example, with memory settings, shares are a way of establishing a priority setting for a virtual machine requesting memory that is greater than the virtual machine's reservation but less than its limit. In other words, if two virtual machines want more memory than their reservation limit and the ESX/ESXi host can't satisfy both of them using RAM, then you can set share values on each virtual machine so that one gets higher-priority access to the RAM in the ESX/ESXi host than the other. Some would say that you should just increase the reservation for that virtual machine. Although that might be a valid technique, it may limit the total number of virtual machines that a host can run as indicated earlier in this chapter. Increasing the configured amount also requires a reboot of the virtual machine to become effective, but shares can be dynamically adjusted while the virtual machine remains powered on.

For the sake of this discussion, let's assume you have two virtual machines (VM1 and VM2) each with a 512MB reservation and a 1024MB limit, and both are running on an ESX/ESXi host with less than 2GB of RAM available to the virtual machines. If the two virtual machines in question have an equal number of shares (let's assume it's 1,000 each), then as each virtual machine requests memory above its reservation value, each virtual machine will receive an equal quantity of RAM from the ESX/ESXi host. Furthermore, because the host cannot supply all of the RAM to both virtual machines, each virtual machine will swap equally to disk (VMkernel swap file). This is assuming, of course, that ESX/ESXi cannot reclaim memory from other running virtual machines using the balloon driver or other memory management technologies described previously.

If you change VM1's Shares setting to 2000, then VM1 now has twice the shares VM2 has assigned to it. This also means that when VM1 and VM2 are requesting the RAM above their respective Reservation values, VM1 gets two RAM pages for every one RAM page that VM2 gets. If VM1 has more shares, VM1 has a higher-priority access to available memory in the host. Because VM1 has 2,000 out of 3,000 shares allocated, it will get 67 percent; VM2 has 1,000 out of 3,000 shares allocated and therefore gets only 33 percent. This creates the two-to-one behavior I described earlier. Each VM is allocated RAM pages based on the proportion of the total number of shares allocated across all virtual machines.

It gets more difficult to predict the actual memory utilization and the amount of access each virtual machine gets as more virtual machines run on the same ESX/ESXi host. Later in this chapter I'll discuss more sophisticated methods of assigning memory limits, reservations, and shares to a group of virtual machines using resource pools.

I've talked about how VMware ESX/ESXi use some advanced memory management technologies, but there is another aspect of virtualization that you must also consider: overhead. In the next section, I'll provide some information on the memory overhead figures when using ESX/ESXi.

Addressing Memory Overhead

As they say, nothing in this world is free, and in the case of memory on an ESX/ESXi host, there is a cost. That cost is memory overhead. There are several basic processes on an ESX/ESXi host that will consume host memory. The VMkernel itself, the Service Console (only on ESX; 272MB by default, 800MB maximum), and each virtual machine that is running will cause the VMkernel to allocate some memory to host the virtual machine above the initial amount that you assign to it. The amount of RAM allocated to host each virtual machine depends on the configuration of each virtual machine, as shown in Table 10.1.

As you go about planning the allocation of memory to your virtual machines, be sure to keep these memory overhead figures in mind. You will want to include these overhead values in your calculations of how memory will be assigned and used, especially if you plan on using virtual machines with large amounts of memory and a large number of virtual CPUs. As you can see in Table 10.1, the memory overhead in those situations is fairly substantial.

TABLE 10.1: Virtual Machine Memory Overhead

MEMORY ASSIGNED (MB)	1 vCPU	2 vCPUs	3 vCPUs	4 vCPUs	5 vCPUs	6 vCPUs	7 vCPUs	8 vCPUs
256	113	159	201	241	293	334	375	416
512	117	165	206	247	303	344	385	426
1024	124	176	217	258	322	363	404	446
2048	138	198	239	281	360	401	443	484
4096	166	242	284	325	437	479	520	561
8192	222	331	373	414	591	633	675	716
16384	335	508	550	592	900	943	986	1028
32768	560	863	906	949	1516	1559	1603	1647
65536	1011	1572	1616	1660	2746	2792	2838	2884
131072	1912	2990	3036	3083	5220	5273	5326	5379
262144	3714	5830	5885	5938	10142	10205	10267	10329

Source: "vSphere Resource Management Guide" from VMware's website at www.vmware.com

Allocating and managing CPU resources is equally as important as allocating and managing memory, so in the next section I'll discuss how to allocate and manage CPU capacity.

Allocating Virtual Machine CPU Capacity

When you create a new virtual machine using the vSphere Client, the only question you are asked related to the CPU is, "Number of virtual processors?" This CPU setting effectively lets the guest operating system utilize one, two, four, or eight virtual CPUs on the host system, depending upon the guest operating system and the vSphere license.

When the VMware engineers designed the virtualization platform, they started with a real system board and modeled the virtual machine after it—in this case, it was based on the Intel 440BX chipset. The PCI bus was something the virtual machine could emulate and could be mapped to input/output devices through a standard interface, but how could a virtual machine emulate a CPU? The answer was "no emulation." Think about a virtual system board that has a "hole" where the CPU socket goes—and the guest operating system simply looks through the hole and sees one of the cores in the host server. This allowed the VMware engineers to avoid writing CPU emulation software that would need to change each time the CPU vendors introduced new instruction sets. If there was an emulation layer, it would also add a significant quantity of overhead, which would limit the performance of the virtualization platform by adding more computational overhead.

So, how many CPUs should a virtual machine have? Creating a virtual machine to replace a physical DHCP server that runs at less than 10 percent CPU utilization at its busiest point in the day surely does not need more than one virtual CPU. As a matter of fact, if you give this virtual machine two virtual CPUs (vCPUs), then you would effectively limit the scalability of the entire host. Here's why . . .

The VMkernel simultaneously schedules CPU cycles for multi-vCPU virtual machines. This means that when a dual-vCPU virtual machine places a request for CPU cycles, the request goes into a queue for the host to process, and the host has to wait until there are at least two cores or hyperthreads (if hyperthreading is enabled) with concurrent idle cycles to schedule that virtual machine. A *relaxed coscheduling* algorithm provides a bit of flexibility in allowing the cores to be scheduled on a slightly skewed basis, but even so, it can be more difficult for the hypervisor to find open time slots on at least two cores. This occurs even if the virtual machine needs only a few clock cycles to do some menial task that could be done with a single processor. Think about it this way: you need to cash a check at the bank, but because of the type of account you have, you need to wait in line until two bank tellers are available *at the same time*. Normally, one teller could handle your request, and you would be on your way—but now you have to wait. What about the folks behind you in the queue as you wait for two tellers? They are also waiting longer because of you.

On the other hand, if a virtual machine needs two vCPUs because of the load it will be processing on a constant basis, then it makes sense to assign two vCPUs to that virtual machine—but only if the host has four or more CPU cores total. If your ESX host is an older-generation dual-processor single-core system, then assigning a virtual machine two vCPUs will mean that the virtual machine owns all of the CPU processing power on that host every time it gets CPU cycles. You will find that the overall performance of the host and any other virtual machines will be less than stellar.

ONE (CPU) FOR ALL . . . AT LEAST TO BEGIN WITH

Every virtual machine should be created with only a single virtual CPU so as not to create unnecessary contention for physical processor time. Only when a virtual machine's performance level dictates the need for an additional CPU should one be allocated. Remember that multi-CPU virtual machines should be created only on ESX/ESXi hosts that have more cores than the number of virtual CPUs being assigned to the virtual machine. A dual-vCPU virtual machine should be created only on a host with two or more cores, a quad-vCPU virtual machine should be created only on a host with four or more cores, and an eight-vCPU virtual machine should be created only on a host with eight or more cores.

Default CPU Allocation

Like the memory settings I discussed earlier, the Shares, Reservation, and Limit settings can be configured for CPU capacity as well.

When a new virtual machine is created with a single vCPU, the total maximum CPU cycles for that virtual machine equals the clock speed of the host system's core. In other words, if you create a new virtual machine, it can see through the "hole in the system board," and it sees whatever the core is in terms of clock cycles per second—an ESX/ESXi host with 3GHz CPUs in it will allow the virtual machine to see one 3GHz core.

Setting a Custom CPU Reservation

The default CPU reservation for a new virtual machine starts at 0MHz. Therefore, by default, a virtual machine is not guaranteed any CPU activity by the VMkernel. This means that when the virtual machine has work to be done, it places its CPU request into the CPU queue so that the VMkernel can handle the request in sequence along with all of the other virtual machines' requests. On a lightly loaded ESX/ESXi host, it's unlikely the virtual machine will wait long for CPU time; however, on a heavily loaded host, the time this virtual machine may have to wait could be significant.

If you were to set a 500MHz reservation, as shown in Figure 10.4, this would effectively make that amount of CPU available instantly to this virtual machine if there is a need for CPU cycles.

FIGURE 10.4
A virtual machine configured with a 300MHz reservation for CPU activity is guaranteed that amount of CPU capacity.

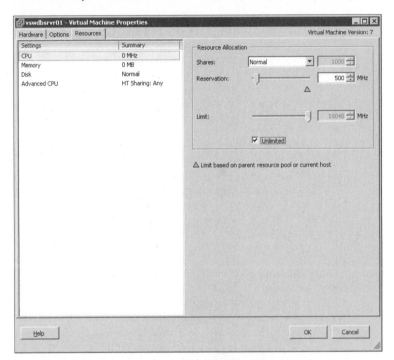

This option also has another effect similar to that of setting a memory reservation. If each virtual machine you create has a 500MHz reservation and your host has 6000MHz of CPU capacity, you can deploy no more than 12 virtual machines (500MHz × 12 = 6000MHz) even if all of them are idle. The host system must be able to satisfy all of the Reservation values concurrently. Now, does that mean each virtual machine is limited to its 500MHz? Absolutely not—that's the good news. If VM1 is idle and VM2 needs more than its CPU reservation, the ESX/ESXi host will schedule more clock cycles to VM2. If VM1 suddenly needs cycles, VM2 doesn't get them anymore, and they are assigned to VM1.

Setting a Custom CPU Limit

In addition to a CPU reservation, every virtual machine also has an option that you can set to place a limit on the amount of CPU allocated. This effectively limits the virtual machine's ability to see a maximum number of clock cycles per second, regardless of what the host has available. Keep in mind that a single virtual CPU virtual machine hosted on a 3GHz, quad-processor ESX/ESXi host will see only a single 3GHz core as its maximum, but as administrator you could alter the limit to hide the actual maximum core speed from the virtual machine. For instance, you could set a 500MHz limit on that DHCP server so that when it re-indexes the DHCP database, it won't try to take all of the 3GHz on the processor that it can see. The CPU limit provides you with the ability to throttle the virtual machine with less processing power than is available on a core on the physical host. Not every virtual machine needs to have access to the entire processing capability of the physical processor core.

INCREASING CONTENTION IN THE FACE OF GROWTH

One of the most common problems administrators can encounter occurs when several virtual machines without limits are deployed on a new virtualized environment. The users get accustomed to stellar performance levels early in the environment life cycle, but as more virtual machines are deployed and start to compete for CPU cycles, the relative performance of the first virtual machines deployed will degrade.

One approach to this issue is to set a reservation of approximately 10 to 20 percent of a single core's clock rate and add approximately 20 percent to that value for a limit on the virtual machine. For example, with 3GHz CPUs in the host, each virtual machine would start with a 300MHz reservation and a 350MHz limit. This would ensure that the virtual machine performs similarly on both a lightly loaded ESX/ESXi host and on a more heavily loaded ESX/ESXi host. Consider setting these values on the virtual machine that you use to create a template because these values will pass to any new virtual machines that were deployed from that template. Note that this is only a starting point. It is possible to limit a virtual machine that really does need more CPU capabilities, and you should always actively monitor the virtual machines to determine whether they are using all of the CPU you are providing them with.

If the numbers seem low, feel free to increase them as needed. The important concept is setting appropriate expectations for virtual machine performance.

Assigning a Custom CPU Shares Value

In a manner similar to memory allocation, you can assign CPU share values to a virtual machine. The shares for CPU will determine how much CPU is provided to a virtual machine in the face of contention with other virtual machines needing CPU activity. All virtual machines, by default, start with an equal number of shares, which means that if there is competition for CPU cycles on an ESX/ESXi host, each virtual machine gets serviced with equal priority. Keep in mind that this share value affects only those CPU cycles that are greater than the reservation set for the virtual machine. In other words, the virtual machine is granted access to its reservation cycles regardless of what else is happening on the host, but if the virtual machine needs more—and there's competition—then the share values come into play.

Several conditions have to be met for shares to even be considered for allocating CPU cycles. The best way to determine this is to consider several scenarios. For the scenarios I'll cover, assume the following details about the environment:

- The ESX/ESXi host includes dual, single-core, 3GHz CPUs.

- The ESX/ESXi host has one or more virtual machines.

Scenario 1 The ESX host has a single virtual machine running. The shares are set at the defaults for the running virtual machines. Will the Shares value have any effect in this scenario? No. There's no competition between virtual machines for CPU time.

Scenario 2 The ESX host has two idle virtual machines running. The shares are set at the defaults for the running virtual machines. Will the Shares values have any effect in this scenario? No. There's no competition between virtual machines for CPU time because both are idle.

Scenario 3 The ESX host has two equally busy virtual machines running (both requesting maximum CPU capacity). The shares are set at the defaults for the running virtual machines. Will the Shares values have any effect in this scenario? No. Again, there's no competition between virtual machines for CPU time, this time because each virtual machine is serviced by a different core in the host.

CPU AFFINITY NOT AVAILABLE WITH CLUSTERS

If you are using a VMware Distributed Resource Scheduler-enabled cluster configured in fully automated mode, CPU affinity cannot be set for virtual machines in that cluster. You must configure the cluster for manual or partially automated mode in order to use CPU affinity.

Scenario 4 To force contention, both virtual machines are configured to use the same CPU by setting the CPU affinity. The ESX/ESXi host has two equally busy virtual machines running (both requesting maximum CPU capacity). This ensures contention between the virtual machines. The shares are set at the defaults for the running virtual machines. Will the Shares values have any effect in this scenario? Yes! But in this case, because all virtual machines have equal Shares values, each virtual machine has equal access to the host's CPU queue, so you don't see any effects from the Shares values.

Scenario 5 The ESX/ESXi host has two equally busy virtual machines running (both requesting maximum CPU capacity with CPU affinity set to the same core). The shares are set as follows: VM1 is set to 2,000 CPU shares, and VM2 is set to the default 1,000 CPU shares. Will the Shares values have any effect in this scenario? Yes. In this case, VM1 has double the number of shares that VM2 has. This means that for every clock cycle that VM2 is assigned by the host, VM1 is assigned two clock cycles. Stated another way, out of every three clock cycles assigned to virtual machines by the ESX/ESXi host, two are assigned to VM1, and one is assigned to VM2.

Scenario 6 The ESX/ESXi host has three equally busy virtual machines running (each requesting maximum CPU capabilities with CPU affinity set to the same core). The shares are set as follows: VM1 is set to 2,000 CPU shares, and VM2 and VM3 are set to the default 1,000 CPU shares. Will the Shares values have any effect in this scenario? Yes. In this case, VM1 has double the number of shares that VM2 and VM3 have assigned. This means that for every two clock cycles that VM1 is assigned by the host, VM2 and VM3 are each assigned a single clock cycle. Stated another way, out of every four clock cycles assigned to virtual machines by the ESX/ESXi host, two cycles are assigned to VM1, one is assigned to VM2, and one is assigned to VM3. You can see that this has effectively watered down VM1's CPU capabilities.

Scenario 7 The ESX/ESXi host has three virtual machines running. VM1 is idle while VM2 and VM3 are equally busy (each requesting maximum CPU capabilities, and all three virtual machines are set with the same CPU affinity). The shares are set as follows: VM1 is set to 2,000 CPU shares, and VM2 and VM3 are set to the default 1,000 CPU shares. Will the Shares values have any effect in this scenario? Yes. But in this case VM1 is idle, which means it isn't requesting any CPU cycles. This means that VM1's shares value is not considered when apportioning the host CPU to the active virtual machines. In this case, VM2 and VM3 would equally share the host CPU cycles because their shares are set to an equal value.

AVOID CPU AFFINITY SETTINGS

You should avoid the CPU affinity setting at all costs. Even if a virtual machine is configured to use a single CPU (for example, CPU1), it does not guarantee that it will be the only virtual machine accessing that CPU, unless every other virtual machine is configured not to use that CPU. At this point, VMotion capability will be unavailable for every virtual machine. In short, don't do it. It's not worth losing VMotion. Use shares, limits, and reservations as an alternative.

Given these scenarios, if you were to extrapolate to an eight-core host with 30 or so virtual machines, it would be difficult to set Shares values on a VM-by-VM basis and to predict how the system will respond. Additionally, if the scenarios were played out on a DRS cluster, where virtual machines can dynamically move from host to host based on available host resources, it would be even more difficult to predict how an individual virtual machine would get CPU resources based strictly on the share mechanisms. The question then becomes, "Are shares a useful tool?" The answer is yes, but in large enterprise environments, you need to examine resource pools and the ability to set share parameters along with reservations and limits on collections of virtual machines. And with that, I'll introduce resource pools.

Using Resource Pools

The previously discussed settings for virtual machine resource allocation (memory and CPU reservations, limits, and shares) are methods used to designate the priority of an individual virtual machine compared to other individual virtual machines also seeking access to resources. In much the same way as you assign users to groups and then assign permissions to the groups, you can leverage resource pools to make the allocation of resources to collections of virtual machines a less tedious and more effective process.

A resource pool is a special type of container object, much like a folder, in the Hosts And Clusters inventory view. You can create a resource pool on a stand-alone host, as you saw in Chapter 9, or as a management object in a DRS cluster (discussed later in this chapter). Figure 10.5 shows the creation of a resource pool.

If you examine the properties of the resource pool, you'll see there are two sections: one for CPU settings (Reservation, Limit, and Shares) and another section with similar settings for memory. When you apply resource settings to a resource pool, those settings affect all the virtual machines found within that resource pool. This provides a scalable way to adjust the resource settings for groups of virtual machines. Setting CPU and memory shares, reservations, and limits on a resource pool is very much like setting these values on individual virtual machines. The behavior of these values, however, can be quite different on a resource pool than on an individual virtual machine.

To illustrate how to set shares, reservations, and limits on a resource pool, as well as to explain how these values work when applied to a resource pool, I'll use an example to frame the discussion. In this example, there is an ESX/ESXi host with two resource pools. The resource pools are named ProductionVMs and DevelopmentVMs. Figure 10.6 and Figure 10.7 show the values that have been configured for the ProductionVMs and DevelopmentVMs resource pools, respectively.

FIGURE 10.5
You can create resource pools on individual hosts and within clusters. A resource pool provides a management and performance configuration layer in the vCenter Server inventory.

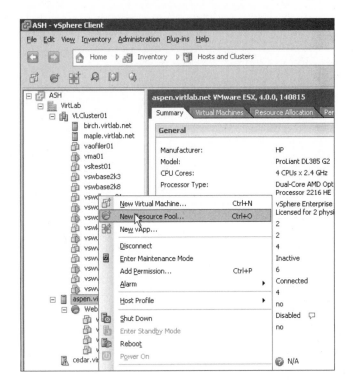

In the next couple of sections, refer to the resource pools in Figures 10.6 and 10.7 as I explain how to configure resource pools and how resource pools handle resource allocation. First, I'll show you how to configure resource pools.

Configuring Resource Pools

Before I can show you how resource pools behave with regard to resource allocation, you must first create and configure the resource pools. Use the resource pools shown in Figures 10.6 and 10.7 as examples for creating and configuring resource pools.

To create a resource pool, simply right-click either an individual ESX/ESXi host or a cluster of ESX/ESXi hosts, and select New Resource Pool. In the Create Resource Pool dialog box, you'll need to supply a name for the new resource pool and set the CPU Resources and Memory Resources values as desired.

After you create the resource pools, you must move the virtual machines into the appropriate resource pool by clicking the virtual machine in the inventory panel and dragging it onto the appropriate resource pool. The result is similar to that shown in Figure 10.8.

In this particular example, you have two classifications of servers: production and development. You've created a resource pool for each classification: ProductionVMs for the virtual servers classified as production and DevelopmentVMs for those virtual servers classified as development. The goal in this example is to ensure that if there's competition for a particular resource, the virtual machines in production should be assigned higher-priority access to that resource. In addition to that goal, you need to ensure that the virtual machines in development cannot consume more than 4GB of physical memory with their running virtual machines. You don't care how many virtual machines run concurrently as part of the development group as long as they don't collectively consume more than 4GB of RAM. Finally, you need to ensure that a minimum amount of resources are guaranteed for both groups of virtual machines.

FIGURE 10.6
The ProductionVMs resource pool is guaranteed CPU and memory resources, and higher-priority access to resources in the face of contention.

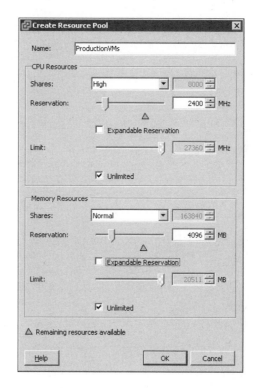

To achieve your goal of guaranteeing resources for the production virtual machines, you will set the ProductionVMs resource pool to use the following settings (refer to Figure 10.6):

- CPU Resources area: Shares value of High

- CPU Resources area: Reservation value of 2400MHz

- CPU Resources area: Expandable Reservation check box for CPU Reservation is deselected

- CPU Resources area: no CPU limit (Unlimited check box is selected)

- Memory Resources area: Reservation of 4096MB

- Memory Resources area: Expandable Reservation check box under Reservation is deselected

- Memory Resources area: No memory limit (Unlimited check box is selected)

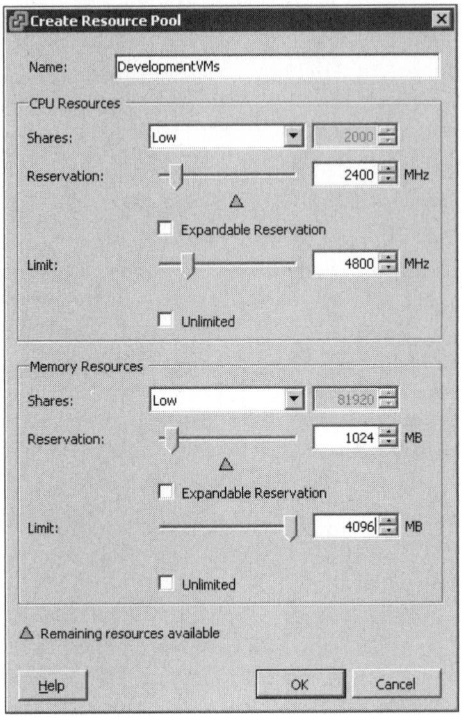

FIGURE 10.7
The DevelopmentVMs resource pool is configured for lower-priority access to CPU and memory in the event of resource contention.

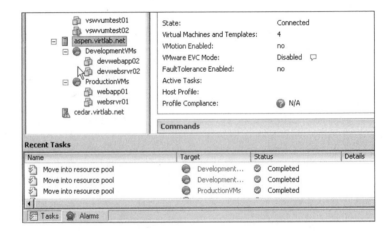

FIGURE 10.8
Virtual machines assigned to a resource pool consume resources allocated to the resource pool.

Similarly, you will apply the following settings to the DevelopmentVMs resource pool (see Figure 10.7):

◆ CPU Resources area: Reservation value of 2400MHz

◆ CPU Resources area: Expandable Reservation check box for Reservation is deselected

◆ CPU Resources area: Limit value of 4800MHz

- Memory Resources area: Reservation value of 1024MB

- Memory Resources area: Expandable Reservation check box under Reservation is deselected

- Memory Resources area: Limit value of 4096MB

Again, setting the values on the DevelopmentVMs resource pool involves right-clicking the resource pool, selecting Edit Settings, and then setting the values you need.

Now that you have an example to work with, I'll explain what these settings will do to the virtual machines contained in each of the resource pools.

Understanding Resource Allocation with Resource Pools

In the previous section I walked you through creating a couple of resource pools called ProductionVMs and DevelopmentVMs. The values for these resource pools are illustrated in Figures 10.6 and 10.7. The goal behind creating these resource pools and setting the values on them was to ensure that a certain level of resources would always be available to production virtual machines (those found in the ProductionVMs resource pool) and limit the resources used by the development virtual machines (VMs found in the DevelopmentVMs resource pool). In this example, you used all three values—Shares, Reservation, and Limit—in an effort to accomplish your goal. Let's look at the behavior of each of these values when used on a resource pool.

First I'll examine the Shares value assigned to the resource pools. As you can see in Figure 10.6, the ProductionVMs resource pool's CPU shares are set to High (8000). Figure 10.7 shows the DevelopmentVMs CPU shares set to Low (2000). The effect of these two settings is similar to that of comparing two virtual machines' Shares values for CPU—except in this case, if there is any competition for CPU resources between virtual machines in the ProductionVMs and DevelopmentVMs resource pools, the entire ProductionVMs resource pool and all the VMs in it would have higher priority. Figure 10.9 shows how this would break down with two virtual machines in each resource pool.

FIGURE 10.9
Two resource pools with different Shares values will be allocated resources proportional to their percentage of share ownership.

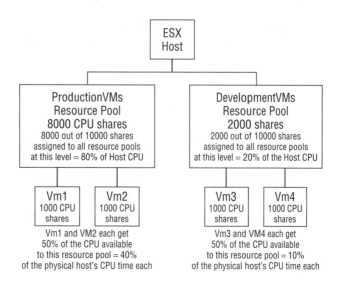

SHARES APPLY ONLY DURING ACTUAL RESOURCE CONTENTION

Remember that share allocations come into play only when virtual machines are fighting one another for a resource, in other words, when an ESX/ESXi host is actually unable to satisfy all the requests for a particular resource. If an ESX/ESXi host is running only four virtual machines on top of two dual-core processors, there won't be much contention to manage and Shares values won't apply. Be sure to keep this in mind when reviewing the results of Shares allocations like those displayed in Figure 10.9.

The next setting in the resource pool properties to evaluate is CPU Reservation for the CPU. Continuing on with the examples shown in Figures 10.6 and 10.7, you can see a CPU Reservation value of 2400MHz has been set on both resource pools. (The ESX/ESXi hosts in the cluster hosting these resource pools have dual-core 2.4GHz AMD Opteron CPUs, so this essentially reserves a single core for each resource pool.) This setting ensures that at least 2400MHz of CPU time is available for all the virtual machines located in each resource pool. Assuming that the ESX/ESXi host has a total of 9600MHz CPU (4 × 2400MHz = 9600MHz), this means 4800MHz of CPU time is available to other resource pools. If two more resource pools are created with a Reservation value of 2400MHz each, then the cumulative reservations on the system have reserved all available host CPU capacity (2400MHz × 4 = 9600MHz). This configuration means the administrator will not be able to create any additional resource pools or any individual virtual machines with Reservation values set.

Part of the CPU Reservation setting is the option to make the reservation expandable. An expandable reservation (noted as such by selecting the Exandable Reservation check box) allows a resource pool to "borrow" resources from its parent host or parent resource pool in order to satisfy reservations set on individual virtual machines within the resource pool. Note that a resource pool with an expandable reservation would only "borrow" from the parent in order to satisfy reservations, not in order to satisfy requests for resources in excess of the reservations. Neither of the resource pools has expandable reservations, so you will be able to assign only 2400MHz of CPU capacity as reservations to individual virtual machines within each resource pool. Any attempt to reserve more than that amount will result in an error message explaining that you've exceeded the allowed limit.

Deselecting the Expandable Reservation check box does not limit the total amount of CPU capacity available to the resource pool; it limits only the total amount of CPU capacity that can be reserved within the resource pool. To set an upper limit on actual CPU usage, you'll need to use a CPU Limit setting.

CPU Limit is the third setting on each resource pool. The behavior of the CPU Limit on a resource pool is similar to its behavior on individual virtual machines, except in this case the limit applies to all virtual machines in the resource pool. All virtual machines combined are allowed to consume up to this value. In the example, the ProductionVMs resource pool does not have a CPU limit assigned. In this case, the virtual machines in the ProductionVMs resource pool are allowed to consume as many CPU cycles as the ESX/ESXi hosts in the cluster are able to provide. The DevelopmentVMs resource pool, on the other hand, has a CPU Limit setting of 4800MHz, meaning that all the virtual machines in the DevelopmentVMs resource pool are allowed to consume a maximum of 4800MHz of CPU capacity.

For the most part, CPU shares, reservations, and limits behave similarly on resource pools as they do on individual virtual machines. The same is also true for memory shares, reservations, and limits.

In the memory portion of the resource pool settings, the first setting is the Shares value. This setting works in much the same way as memory shares worked on individual virtual machines. It determines which group of virtual machines will be the first to give up memory via the balloon driver—or if memory pressure is severe enough, page out to disk—in the face of contention. However, this setting is used to set a priority value for all virtual machines in the resource pool when competing for resources with virtual machines in other resource pools. Looking at the memory share settings in our example (ProductionVMs = Normal and DevelopmentVMs = Low), this means that if host memory is limited, virtual machines in the DevelopmentVMs resource pool that need more memory than their reservation would have a lower priority than an equivalent virtual machine in the ProductionVMs resource pool. Figure 10.9, which I used earlier to help explain CPU shares on resource pool, applies here as well.

The second setting is the resource pool's memory Reservation. The memory Reservation value will reserve this amount of host RAM for virtual machines in this resource pool, which effectively ensures that there is some actual RAM that is guaranteed to the virtual machines in this resource pool. As I explained in the discussion on CPU reservations, the Expandable Reservation check box does not limit how much memory the resource pool can use but rather how much memory you can reserve within the resource pool.

The memory Limit value is how you would set a limit on how much host RAM a particular group of virtual machines can consume. If administrators have been given the Create Virtual Machines permission in the DevelopmentVMs resource pool, then the memory Limit value would prevent those administrators from running virtual machines that will consume more than that amount of actual host RAM. In our example, the memory Limit value on the DevelopmentVMs resource pool is set to be 4096MB. How many virtual machines can administrators in development create? They can create as many as they want.

Although this setting does nothing to limit creating virtual machines, it will place a limit on running virtual machines. So, how many can they run? The cap placed on memory use is not a per virtual machine setting but a cumulative setting. They might be able to run only one virtual machine with all the memory, or multiple virtual machines with lower memory configurations. Assuming that each virtual machine is created without an individual memory Reservation value, the administrator can run as many virtual machines concurrently as she wants! The problem will be that once the virtual machines consume 4096MB of host RAM, anything above that amount will need to be provided by VMkernel swap. If she builds four virtual machines with 1024MB as the initial memory amount, then all four virtual machines will consume 4096MB (assuming no overhead) and will run in real RAM. If an administrator tried to run 20 virtual machines configured for 512MB of RAM, then all 20 virtual machines will share the 4096MB of RAM, even though their requirement is for 10240MB ($20 \times 256MB$)—the remaining amount of RAM would be provided by VMkernel swap. At this point, performance would be noticeably slow.

If you want to clear a limit, select the Unlimited check box. This is true for both CPU limits as well as memory limits. By now you should have a pretty fair idea of how ESX/ESXi allocates resources to virtual machines, as well as how you can tweak those settings to meet your specific demands and workloads.

Sometimes, though, tweaking or fine-tuning resource allocation isn't quite enough. What happens when the virtual machines on one ESX/ESXi host are fully utilizing that host's CPU capacity but another ESX/ESXi host is underutilized? That's where VMotion comes into play.

Exploring VMotion

I've defined the VMware VMotion feature as the ability to perform a live migration of a virtual machine from one ESX/ESXi host to another without service interruption. This is a no-downtime operation; the end users do not know and are not aware that the virtual machine has been migrated between physical ESX/ESXi hosts. This is an extremely effective tool for load-balancing virtual machines across ESX/ESXi hosts. Additionally, if an ESX/ESXi host needs to be powered off for hardware maintenance or some other function that would take it out of production, VMotion can be used to migrate all active virtual machines from the host going offline to another host without waiting for a hardware maintenance window because the virtual machines will remain available to the users who need them.

VMotion works by copying the contents of virtual machine memory from one ESX/ESXi host to another and then transferring control of the virtual machines' disk files to the target host.

VMotion operates in the following sequence:

1. An administrator initiates a migration of a running virtual machine (VM1) from one ESX/ESXi host (esxi-01) to another (esxi-02), shown in Figure 10.10.

FIGURE 10.10
Step 1 in a VMotion migration is invoking a migration while the virtual machine is powered on.

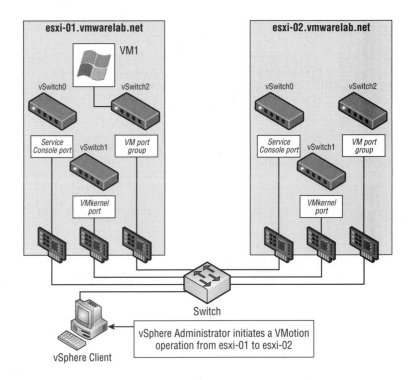

2. The source host (esxi-01) begins copying the active memory pages VM1 has in host memory to the destination host (esxi-02). During this time, the virtual machine still services clients on the source (esxi-01). As the memory is copied from the source host to the target, pages in memory could be changed. ESX/ESXi handles this by keeping a log of changes that occur in the memory of the virtual machine on the source host after that memory address has been copied to the target host. This log is called a *memory bitmap*. See Figure 10.11.

FIGURE 10.11
Step 2 in a VMotion migration is starting the memory copy and adding a memory bitmap.

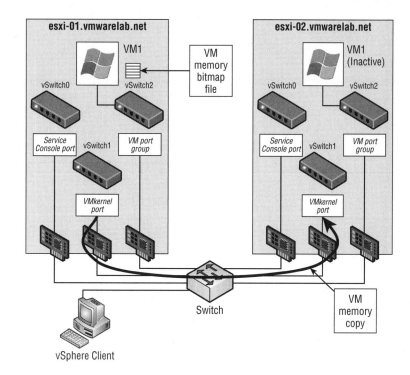

3. After the entire contents of RAM for the virtual machine being migrated have been transferred to the target host (esxi-02), then VM1 on the source ESX/ESXi host (esxi-01) is *quiesced*. This means that it is still in memory but is no longer servicing client requests for data. The memory bitmap file is then transferred to the target (esxi-02). See Figure 10.12.

THE MEMORY BITMAP

The memory bitmap does not include the contents of the memory address that has changed; it simply includes the addresses of the memory that has changed—often referred to as the *dirty memory*.

---

4. The target host (esxi-02) reads the addresses in the memory bitmap file and requests the contents of those addresses from the source (esxi-01). See Figure 10.13.

5. After the contents of the memory referred to in the memory bitmap file have been transferred to the target host, the virtual machine starts on that host. Note that this is not a reboot—the virtual machine's state is in RAM, so the host simply enables it. At this point a Reverse Address Resolution Protocol (RARP) is sent by the host to register its MAC address against the physical switch port to which the target ESX/ESXi host is connected. This process enables the switch infrastructure to send network packets to the appropriate ESX/ESXi host from the clients that are attached to the virtual machine that just moved.

FIGURE 10.12
Step 3 in a VMotion migration involves quiescing VM1 and transferring the memory bitmap file from the source ESX/ESXi host to the destination ESX/ESXi host.

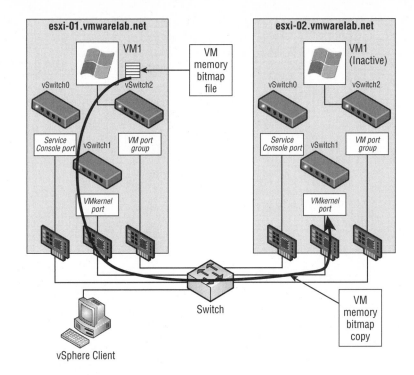

FIGURE 10.13
In step 4 in a VMotion migration, the actual memory listed in the bitmap file is fetched from the source to the destination (dirty memory).

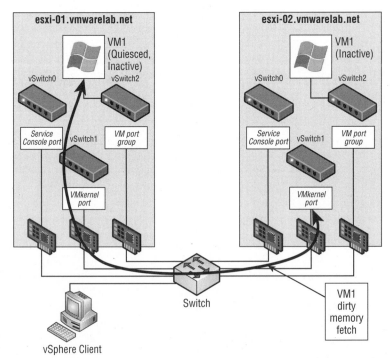

6. After the virtual machine is successfully operating on the target host, the memory the virtual machine was using on the source host is deleted. This memory becomes available to the VMkernel to use as appropriate, as shown in Figure 10.14.

TRY IT WITH PING-T

Following the previous procedure carefully, you'll note there will be a time when the virtual machine being moved is not running on either the source host *or* the target host. This is typically a very short period of time. Testing has shown that a continuous ping (ping -t) of the virtual machine being moved might, on a bad day, result in the loss of one ping packet. Most client-server applications are built to withstand the loss of more than a packet or two before the client is notified of a problem.

FIGURE 10.14
In step 6 in a VMotion migration, vCenter Server deletes the virtual machine from the source ESX/ESXi host.

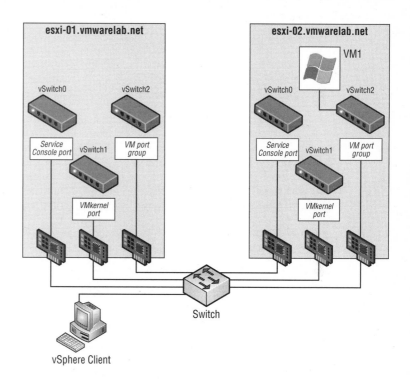

Examining VMotion Requirements

The VMotion migration is pretty amazing, and when users see it work for the first time in a live environment, they are extremely impressed. However, detailed planning is necessary for this procedure to function properly. The hosts involved in the VMotion process have to meet certain requirements, along with the virtual machines being migrated.

Each of the ESX/ESXi hosts that are involved in VMotion must meet the following requirements:

◆ Shared storage for the virtual machine files (VMFS or NFS datastore)

◆ A Gigabit Ethernet network interface card (NIC) with a VMkernel port defined and enabled for VMotion on each host.

This VMkernel port can be on a vNetwork Standard Switch, on a vNetwork Distributed Switch, or on a third-party distributed virtual switch like the Cisco Nexus 1000V, but it must be enabled for VMotion. The Gigabit Ethernet NIC should preferably be dedicated to VMotion traffic, although it is acceptable to share this NIC with other traffic types if necessary.

In Chapter 5, I provided the steps for creating a VMkernel port on a vSwitch. I included instructions for creating a VMkernel port on either a vNetwork Standard Switch or a vNetwork Distributed Switch. I'll review the steps for creating a VMkernel port on a vNetwork Distributed Switch again just for clarity.

Perform the following steps to create a VMkernel port on an existing vNetwork Distributed Switch:

1. Launch the vSphere Client if it is not already running, and connect to an instance of vCenter Server.

2. Navigate to the Hosts And Clusters inventory view.

3. From the inventory list on the left, select an ESX/ESXi host that is already participating in the vNetwork Distributed Switch.

4. Select the Configuration tab from the contents pane on the right.

5. Switch the view to Distributed Virtual Switch using the buttons just below the tab bar.

6. Click the Manage Virtual Adapters link.

7. In the Manage Virtual Adapters dialog box, click the link to add a new virtual adapter.

8. In the Add Virtual Adapter dialog box, select New Virtual Adapter, and click Next.

9. Select VMkernel, and click Next.

10. Choose the correct port group from the drop-down list, and then be sure to select the box Use This Virtual Adapter For VMotion. Click Next.

11. Specify an IP address and network mask for this VMkernel interface. If the VMotion network is nonroutable, leave the default gateway blank, or simply use the default gateway assigned for the Service Console. Click Next.

12. Review the graphical diagram that shows the pending changes to the distributed switch. If everything is correct, click Finish to complete adding the VMkernel interface. Otherwise, use the Back button to change the settings accordingly.

In addition to the configuration requirements I just outlined (shared storage and a VMotion-enabled VMkernel port), a successful VMotion migration between two hosts also relies on all of the following conditions being met:

◆ Both the source and destination hosts must be configured with identical virtual switches that have correctly configured, VMotion-enabled VMkernel ports. If you are using vNetwork Distributed Switches, both hosts must be participating in the same vNetwork Distributed Switch.

◆ All port groups to which the virtual machine being migrated is attached must exist on both of the ESX/ESXi hosts. Port group naming is case sensitive, so create identical port groups on each host, and make sure they plug into the same physical subnets or VLANs.

A virtual switch named Production is not the same as a virtual switch named PRODUC-TION. Remember that to prevent downtime the virtual machine is not going to change its network address as it is moved. The virtual machine will retain its MAC address and IP address so clients connected to it don't have to resolve any new information to reconnect.

◆ Processors in both hosts must be compatible. When a virtual machine is transferred between hosts, the virtual machine has already detected the type of processor it is running on when it booted. Since the virtual machine is not rebooted during a VMotion, the guest assumes the CPU instruction set on the target host is the same as on the source host. You can get away with slightly dissimilar processors, but in general the processors in two hosts that perform VMotion must meet the following requirements:

   ◆ CPUs must be from the same vendor (Intel or AMD).

   ◆ CPUs must be from the same CPU family (PIII, P4, Opteron).

   ◆ CPUs must support the same features, such as the presence of SSE2, SSE3, and SSE4, and NX or XD (see the sidebar "Processor Instruction").

   ◆ For 64-bit virtual machines, CPUs must have virtualization technology enabled (Intel VT or AMD-v).

I'll talk more about processor compatibility later in this chapter in the section "Enhanced VMotion Compatibility."

PROCESSOR INSTRUCTION

Streaming SIMD Extensions 2 (SSE2) was an enhancement to the original Multimedia Extension (MMX) instruction set found in the PIII processor. The enhancement was targeted at the floating-point calculation capabilities of the processor by providing 144 new instructions. SSE3 instruction sets are an enhancement to the SSE2 standard targeted at multimedia and graphics applications. The new SSE4 extensions target both the graphics and the application server.

AMD's eXecute Disable (XD) and Intel's NoExecute (NX) are features of processors that mark memory pages as data only, which prevents a virus from running executable code at that address. The operating system needs to be written to take advantage of this feature, and in general, versions of Windows starting with Windows 2003 SP1 and Windows XP SP2 support this CPU feature.

The latest processors from Intel and AMD have specialized support for virtualization. The AMD-V and Intel Virtualization Technology (VT) must be enabled in the BIOS in order to create 64-bit virtual machines.

In addition to the VMotion requirements for the hosts involved, these are the requirements that must be met by the virtual machine to be migrated:

◆ The virtual machine must not be connected to any device physically available to only one ESX/ESXi host. This includes disk storage, CD/DVD drives, floppy drives, serial ports, or parallel ports. If the virtual machine to be migrated has one of these mappings, simply deselect the Connected check box beside the offending device. For example, you won't be able to migrate a virtual machine with a CD/DVD drive connected; to disconnect the drive and allow VMotion, simply deselect the Connected box.

- The virtual machine must not be connected to an internal-only virtual switch.

- The virtual machine must not have its CPU affinity set to a specific CPU.

- The virtual machine must not have a physical mode raw device mapping (RDM).

- The virtual machine must have all disk, configuration, log, and nonvolatile random access memory (NVRAM) files stored on a volume visible to both the source and the destination ESX/ESXi host.

If you start a VMotion migration and vCenter Server finds an issue that is considered a violation of the VMotion compatibility rules, you will see an error message. In some cases, a warning, not an error, will be issued. In the case of a warning, the VMotion migration will still succeed. For instance, if you have cleared the check box on the host-attached floppy drive, vCenter Server will tell you there is a mapping to a host-only device that is not active. You'll see a prompt asking whether the migration should take place anyway.

VMware states that you need a Gigabit Ethernet NIC for VMotion; however, it does not have to be dedicated to VMotion. When you're designing the ESX/ESXi host, dedicate a NIC to VMotion if possible. You thus reduce the contention on the VMotion network, and the VMotion process can happen in a fast and efficient manner.

Now that I've reviewed all the various prerequisites, both for ESX/ESXi hosts and virtual machines, let's actually perform a VMotion migration.

Performing a VMotion Migration

After you've verified the ESX/ESXi host requirements as well as the virtual machine requirements, then you are ready to perform a VMotion migration.

Perform the following steps to conduct a VMotion migration of a running virtual machine:

1. Launch the vSphere Client if it is not already running, and connect to a vCenter Server instance. VMotion requires vCenter Server.

2. Navigate to either the Hosts And Clusters or VMs And Templates inventory view.

3. Select a powered-on virtual machine in your inventory, right-click the virtual machine, and select Migrate.

4. Select Change Host, and then click Next.

5. Choose the target host. Figure 10.15 shows a target host that produces validation errors; that is, vCenter Server has found errors that would prevent a successful VMotion operation. Figure 10.16 shows a compatible and properly configured host selected.

   After you've selected the correct target host, click Next.

6. If you have any resource pools defined on the target host or target cluster, you'll need to select the target resource pool (or cluster).

   Most of the time the same resource pool (or cluster) that the virtual machine currently resides in will suffice. Choosing a different resource pool might change that virtual machine's priority access to resources. If no resource pool is defined on the target host, then vCenter Server skips this step entirely.

FIGURE 10.15
vCenter Server will show you errors found during validation of the selected target host in a VMotion operation.

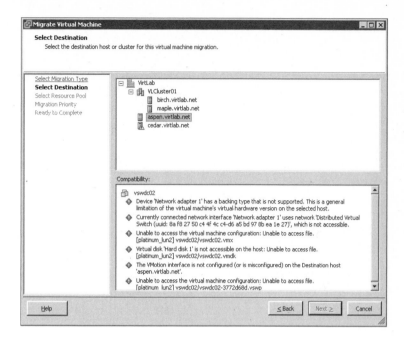

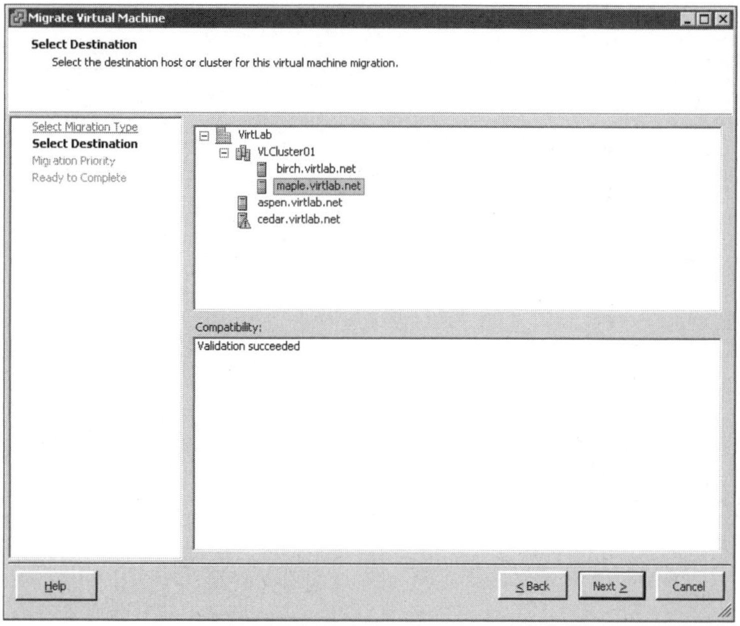

FIGURE 10.16
If vCenter Server does not show any validation errors, then the VMotion operation is allowed to proceed.

7. Select the priority that the VMotion migration needs to proceed with. High priority simply reserves the resources on the target host in advance of the VMotion operation, thus ensuring that the virtual machine will have enough resources to run after the migration is complete. Click Next to continue.

8. Review the settings, and click Finish if all the information is correct. If there are any errors, use the Back button to correct the errors.

9. The virtual machine should start to migrate. Often, the process will pause at about 10 percent in the progress dialog box and then again at 90 percent. The 10 percent pause occurs while the hosts in question establish communications and gather the information for the pages in memory to be migrated; the 90 percent pause occurs when the source virtual machine is quiesced and the dirty memory pages are fetched from the source host, as shown in Figure 10.17.

FIGURE 10.17
The Tasks pane of the vSphere Client shows the progress of the VMotion operation.

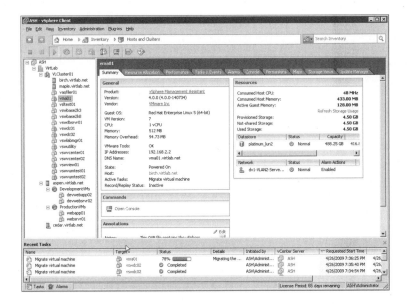

VMOTION IS NOT A HIGH-AVAILABILITY FEATURE

VMotion is a great feature, but it is not a high-availability feature. Yes, it can be used to improve uptime by preventing downtime because of planned outages, but VMotion will not provide any protection in the event of an unplanned host failure. For that functionality, you'll need VMware High Availability (HA) and VMware Fault Tolerance (FT), two features that are discussed in Chapter 11.

VMotion is an invaluable tool for virtual administrators and certainly is the feature that put ESX/ESXi on the map. VMotion is a *reactive* tool, though; an administrator has to manually initiate VMotion. How much more powerful would VMotion be if VMware vSphere used VMotion *proactively*? That is the basis for VMware Distributed Resource Scheduler, a feature that you can enable on ESX/ESXi clusters. Before we get to the details of DRS, you need to understand clusters.

Investigating Clusters

As virtual environments grow, organizations can and will add multiple ESX/ESXi hosts to handle the workload of the ever-increasing, sometimes exponentially increasing, number of virtual machines. Some of the concerns with adding a number of stand-alone ESX/ESXi hosts, even those managed by vCenter Server, include the following issues:

◆ What happens when a host fails?

◆ How can I effectively balance the load across more than one ESX/ESXi host?

VMware vSphere 4 handles both of these issues by creating a cluster of ESX/ESXi hosts.

What is a cluster? A cluster is 2 to 32 ESX/ESXi hosts that work cooperatively to provide features such as VMware HA and VMware DRS. Clusters themselves are implicitly resource pools; however, resource pools can be built under a cluster. This gives the administrator a larger collection of resources to carve up, and the virtual machine can run on any node in the cluster and still be affected by its membership in the resource pool.

Cluster setup is fairly straightforward. There are no special hardware requirements beyond what an ESX/ESXi host should already have. Each host has to be able to talk to the other hosts on the Service Console network (or the Management network in ESXi), and all nodes of the cluster must be managed by the same vCenter Server instance. Additionally, all hosts in the cluster must belong to the same datacenter in vCenter Server because the cluster is a child of a datacenter object.

To create a cluster, right-click a datacenter object in the vCenter Server Hosts And Clusters inventory view, and select the New Cluster option. This launches the New Cluster Wizard.

Perform the following steps to create a new cluster using the New Cluster Wizard:

1. In the first screen of the New Cluster Wizard, supply a name for the cluster. You can also optionally enable VMware DRS or VMware HA. I'll explain VMware DRS in the next section of this chapter; I cover VMware HA in Chapter 11. Click Next.

2. Enable or disable Enhanced VMotion Compatibility (EVC) for the cluster you are creating. I explain EVC later in this chapter in the section titled "Ensuring VMotion Compatibility." Click Next.

3. Choose where you would like to store VM swap files. The recommended choice is to store them with the virtual machines; you should select this option unless you have a specific reason otherwise. Click Next.

4. Click Finish to create the cluster.

After the cluster is created, you can move ESX/ESXi hosts into the cluster by dragging and dropping them onto the cluster object.

CLUSTER LIMITS

There is a functional limit to the number of hosts in a cluster, but it depends on which features are enabled on the cluster itself. For ESX/ESXi 4 with vCenter Server 4, the absolute limit is 32 ESX hosts per cluster. However, VMware's *recommended* maximum number of hosts is 16 in each circumstance. If you have more hosts in the datacenter than will (or can) be used in one cluster, consider building multiple clusters, which can be a benefit based on processor matching for VMotion and different cluster settings.

If an ESX/ESXi host contains resource pools and is added to a non-DRS cluster, a warning message appears stating that existing resource pools will be removed. To preserve resource pools and the settings on the ESX/ESXi host added to the cluster, select the No option. This will cancel moving the ESX/ESXi host into the cluster.

To prevent this warning message, you can enable DRS on the cluster. I'll explain DRS in more detail in the next section, but for now if you need to enable DRS, right-click the cluster object, and select Edit Settings from the context menu. Then select the Turn On VMware DRS check box.

If an ESX/ESXi host contains resource pools and is added to a DRS-enabled cluster, a wizard is initiated that allows existing resource pools to be deleted or maintained. The options provided by the wizard for handling the existing resource pools are as follows:

◆ You can put all the ESX/ESXi host's virtual machines into the cluster's root resource pool and delete the resource pools currently defined on the ESX/ESXi host.

◆ You can create a new resource pool in the cluster and place the existing resource pools on the ESX/ESXi host under this new resource pool. This preserves the existing resource pools and resource pool hierarchy. By default the name for the new resource pool is "Grafted from" followed by the hostname of the ESX/ESXi host being added.

Selecting the second option—to preserve the existing resource pools and hierarchy—results in a new resource pool that contains the child resource pools from the ESX/ESXi host. Figure 10.18 illustrates how this looks in vCenter Server's Hosts And Clusters inventory view.

FIGURE 10.18
Resource pools kept when a host is added to a cluster will, by default, fall under a parent pool that begins with the name "Grafted from" followed by the hostname.

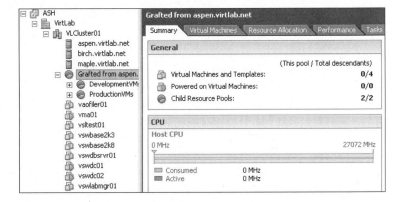

After the resource pools have been migrated, eliminate the additional resource pool (Grafted from . . .) created using one of the two following methods:

◆ Drag the child resource pools from the newly created resource pool, and drop them onto the cluster itself.

◆ Move the virtual machines from the imported resource pools into other existing resource pools in the cluster (after adjusting the resource pools to reflect the new reservations and/or limits required to support the newly added virtual machines).

After using either of these methods, simply delete the resource pool after all the virtual machines in it have been moved elsewhere within the vCenter Server inventory.

Because Chapter 11 deals extensively with VMware HA, next I'll focus on VMware DRS and how it affects resource management.

Exploring VMware DRS

VMware DRS is a feature of vCenter Server on the properties of a cluster that balances load across multiple ESX/ESXi hosts. It has the following two main functions:

◆ To decide which node of a cluster should run a virtual machine when it's powered on, a function often referred to as *intelligent placement*

◆ To evaluate the load on the cluster over time and either make recommendations for migrations or use VMotion to automatically move virtual machines to create a more balanced cluster workload

Fortunately, if you like to retain control, you can set how aggressively DRS will automatically move virtual machines around the cluster.

If you start by looking at the DRS properties—you can view these properties by right-clicking a DRS-enabled cluster, selecting Edit Settings, and then clicking the VMware DRS heading on the left—you will see there are three selections regarding the automation level of the DRS cluster: Manual, Partially Automated, and Fully Automated. The slider bar affects only the actions of the Fully Automated setting on the cluster. These settings control the initial placement of a virtual machine and the automatic movement of virtual machines between hosts. I'll examine the behavior of these automation levels in the next few sections.

Manual Automation Behavior

When a DRS cluster is set to Manual, every time you power on a virtual machine, the cluster prompts you to select the ESX/ESXi host upon which that virtual machine should be hosted. The dialog box rates the available hosts according to suitability at that moment in time: the higher the priority, the better the choice, as shown in Figure 10.19.

FIGURE 10.19
A DRS cluster set to Manual requires you to specify where the virtual machine should be powered on.

The Manual setting also suggests VMotion migrations when DRS detects an imbalance between ESX/ESXi hosts in the cluster. This is an averaging process that works over longer periods of time than many of us are used to in the information technology field. It is unusual to see DRS make any recommendations unless an imbalance has existed for longer than five minutes. The recommended list of migrations is available by selecting the cluster in the inventory and then selecting the DRS tab.

From the DRS tab, the Apply Recommendations button allows you to agree with any pending DRS recommendations and initiate a migration. VMotion handles the migration automatically.

Partially Automated Behavior

If you select the Partially Automated setting on the DRS properties, DRS will make an automatic decision about which host a virtual machine should run on when it is initially powered on (without prompting the user who is performing the power-on task) but will still prompt for all migrations on the DRS tab. Thus, initial placement is automated, but migrations are still manual.

Fully Automated Behavior

The third setting for DRS is Fully Automated. This setting makes decisions for initial placement without prompting and also makes automatic VMotion decisions based on the selected automation level (the slider bar).

There are five positions for the slider bar on the Fully Automated setting of the DRS cluster. The values of the slider bar range from Conservative to Aggressive. Conservative automatically moves migrations evaluated with five stars. Any other migrations are listed on the DRS tab and require administrator approval. If you move the slider bar from the most conservative setting one stop to the right, then all four- and five-star migrations are automatically approved; three stars and less will wait for administrator approval. With the slider all the way over to the Aggressive setting, any imbalance in the cluster that causes a recommendation is automatically approved. Be aware that this can cause additional stress in your ESX/ESXi host environment, because even a slight imbalance will trigger a migration.

Calculations for migrations can change regularly. Assume that during a period of high activity DRS makes a recommendation with three stars, and the automation level is set so three-star migrations need manual approval but the recommendation is not noticed (or an administrator is not even in the office). An hour later, the virtual machines that caused the three-star migration in the first place have settled down and are now operating normally. At this point, the DRS tab no longer reflects the migration recommendation. The recommendation has since been withdrawn. This behavior occurs because if the migration was still listed, an administrator might approve it and cause an imbalance where one did not exist.

In many cases, five-star migrations have little to do with load on the cluster. Instead, five-star migrations are generally the result of one of two conditions. The first condition that causes a five-star migration recommendation is when you put a host into Maintenance Mode, as shown in Figure 10.20.

Maintenance Mode is a setting on a host that allows virtual machines currently hosted on it to continue to run but does not permit new virtual machines to be launched on that host either manually or via a VMotion or DRS migration. Additionally, when a host belonging to an automated DRS cluster is placed into Maintenance Mode, all of the virtual machines currently running on that host receive a five-star migration recommendation, which causes all virtual machines on that host to be migrated to other hosts (assuming they meet the requirements for VMotion).

The second condition that will cause a five-star migration recommendation is when two virtual machines defined in an anti-affinity rule are run on the same host or when two virtual machines defined in an affinity rule are run on different hosts. This leads us to a discussion of DRS rules.

A QUICK REVIEW OF DRS CLUSTER PERFORMANCE

Monitoring the detailed performance of a cluster is an important task for any virtual infrastructure administrator, particularly monitoring the CPU and memory activity of the whole cluster as well as the respective resource utilization of the virtual machines within the cluster. The Summary tab of the details pane for a cluster object includes information on the configuration of the cluster as well as statistics regarding the current load distribution. Additionally, the View Resource Distribution Chart link allows you to open a graphical chart that shows the current resource distribution of the ESX/ESXi hosts in the cluster.

FIGURE 10.20
An ESX/ESXi host put into Maintenance Mode cannot power on new virtual machines or be a target for VMotion.

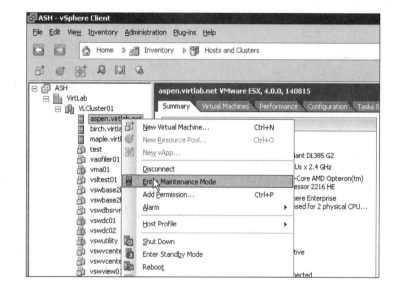

DRS Rules

An administrator creates DRS rules to control how DRS decides which virtual machines should be combined with which other virtual machines, as well as which virtual machines should be kept separate by the DRS process. Consider the rules page shown in Figure 10.21.

Consider an environment with two mail server virtual machines. In all likelihood, administrators would not want both mail servers to reside on the same ESX/ESXi host. At the same time, administrators would want a web application server and the back-end database server to reside on the same hosts. That might be a combination that should always be together to ensure rapid response times between them. These two scenarios could be serviced very well with DRS rules.

Perform the following steps to create a DRS anti-affinity rule:

1. Launch the vSphere Client if it is not already running, and connect to a vCenter Server instance. DRS and DRS rules cannot be managed when connected to a specific ESX/ESXi host; you must connect to a vCenter Server instance.

2. Navigate to the Hosts And Clusters inventory view.

3. Right-click the DRS cluster where the rules need to exist, and select the Edit Settings option.

4. Click the Rules option.

5. Click the Add button near the bottom of the dialog box.

6. Type a name for the rule, and select the type of rule to create:

    ◆ For anti-affinity rules, select the Separate Virtual Machines option.

    ◆ For affinity rules, select the Keep Virtual Machines Together option.

7. Click the Add button to include the necessary virtual machines in the rule. Simply select the check box for the virtual machines you want to include in the DRS rule.

8. Click OK.

9. Review the new rule configuration to ensure it is correct.

10. Click OK.

FIGURE 10.21
DRS supports both affinity (Keep Virtual Machines Together) and anti-affinity rules (Separate Virtual Machines).

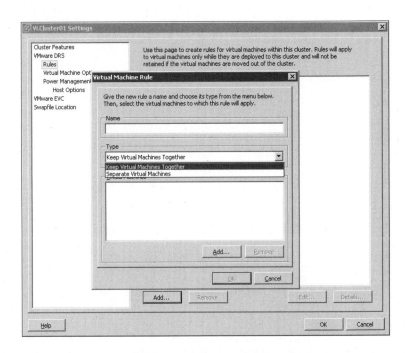

With DRS rules, it is possible to create fallible rules, such as building a "Separate virtual machines" rule that has three virtual machines in it on a DRS cluster that has only two hosts. In this situation, vCenter Server will generate report warnings because DRS cannot satisfy the requirements of the rule.

If you need to, you can temporarily disable DRS rules by deselecting the check box next to the rule.

Although most virtual machines should be allowed to take advantage of the DRS balancing act, there will likely be enterprise-critical virtual machines that administrators are adamant about not being VMotion candidates. However, the virtual machines should remain in the cluster to take advantage of the high availability HA feature. In other words, virtual machines will take part in HA but not DRS despite both features being enabled on the cluster. As shown in Figure 10.22, virtual machines in a cluster can be configured with individual DRS compatibility levels.

Figure 10.22 also shows that the ability to set automation levels on specific virtual machines can be disabled by deselecting the Enable Individual Virtual Machine Automation Levels check box.

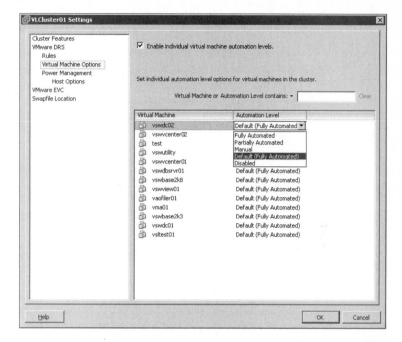

This dialog box lists the virtual machines that are part of the cluster and their default automation levels. In this case, all virtual machines are set at Fully Automated because that's how the automation level of the cluster was set. The administrator can then selectively choose virtual machines that are not going to be acted upon by DRS in the same way as the rest in the cluster. The automation levels available include the following:

- Fully Automated

- Manual

- Partially Automated

- Disabled

- Default (inherited from the cluster setting)

The first three options work as discussed previously in this chapter. The Disabled option turns off DRS, including the automatic host selection at startup and the migration recommendations. The Default option configures the virtual machine to accept the automation level set at the cluster.

AT LEAST BE OPEN TO CHANGE

Even if a virtual machine or several virtual machines have been chosen not to participate in the automation of DRS, it is best not to set virtual machines to the Disabled option because recommendations will not be provided. It is possible that a four- or five-star recommendation could be provided that suggests moving a virtual machine an administrator thought was best on a specific host. Yet the migration might suggest a different host. For this reason, the Manual option is better. At least be open to the possibility that a virtual machine might perform better on a different host.

VMware vSphere provides a number of tools for administrators to make their lives easier as long as the tools are understood and set up properly. It might also be prudent to monitor the activities of these tools to see whether a change to the configuration might be warranted over time as your environment grows. Monitoring and alarms are discussed in detail in Chapter 12.

DRS is a valuable and useful part of VMware vSphere, and it builds upon VMotion to enable vSphere administrators to be more proactive about managing their environments. The fact that DRS relies upon and uses VMotion to work, though, also means that VMotion compatibility becomes more important. In the next section, I'll discuss a couple of ways to help ensure VMotion compatibility.

Ensuring VMotion Compatibility

In the section "Examining VMotion Requirements," I discussed some of the prerequisites that are required in order to perform a VMotion operation. In particular, I mentioned that VMotion has some fairly strict CPU requirements. Specifically, the CPUs must be from the same vendor, must be in the same family, and must share a common set of CPU instruction sets and features.

In a situation where two physical hosts exist in a cluster and there are CPU differences between the two hosts, VMotion will fail. Because VMotion will fail, DRS will also fail to function in any sort of automated fashion. (It would still make recommendations regarding intelligent placement and migrations, but of course those migrations would not be successful.) I often refer to this issue as a *VMotion boundary*. Until recent versions of ESX/ESXi 3.x and appropriate support from Intel and AMD in their processors, there was no fix for this issue.

However, in recent versions of ESX/ESXi 3.x and continuing into ESX/ESXi 4.0, VMware supports hardware extension from Intel and AMD to help mitigate these CPU differences. In fact, ESX/ESXi provides a couple of ways to address this issue, either in part or in whole. Let's take a look at some of these ways.

Per-Virtual Machine CPU Masking

vCenter Server offers the ability to create custom CPU masks on a per-virtual machine basis. Although this can offer a tremendous amount of flexibility in enabling VMotion compatibility, it's also important to note that, with one exception, this is *completely unsupported by VMware*.

What is the one exception? On a per-virtual machine basis, you'll find a setting that tells the virtual machine to show or mask the No Execute/Execute Disable (NX/XD) bit in the host CPU, and this specific instance of CPU masking is fully supported by VMware. Masking the NX/XD bit from the virtual machine tells the virtual machine that there's no NX/XD bit present. This is useful if you have two otherwise compatible hosts with an NX/XD bit mismatch. If the virtual machine doesn't know there's an NX or XD bit on one of the hosts, it won't care if the target host has or doesn't have that bit if you migrate that virtual machine using VMotion. The greatest VMotion compatibility is achieved by masking the NX/XD bit. If the NX/XD bit is exposed to the virtual machine, as shown in Figure 10.23, the BIOS setting for NX/XD must match on both the source and destination ESX/ESXi hosts.

FIGURE 10.23
The option for masking the NX/XD bit is controlled on a per-virtual machine basis.

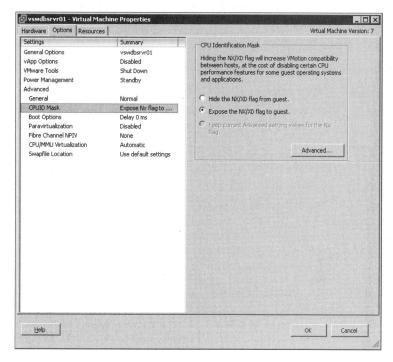

For features other than the NX/XD bit, you would have to delve into custom CPU masks. This is where you will step outside the bounds of VMware support. Looking at the dialog box in Figure 10.23, you'll note the Advanced button. Clicking the Advanced button opens the CPU Identification Mask dialog box, shown in Figure 10.24.

Within this dialog box, you can create custom CPU masks to mark off specific bits within the CPU ID value. I won't go into great detail here because all of this is unsupported by VMware. However, refer to the sidebar "More Information on CPU Masking" for a couple of URLs that provide additional information if you are interested.

 **Real World Scenario**

MORE INFORMATION ON CPU MASKING

Creating custom CPU masks is one way to ease potential VMotion incompatibilities. Remember, though, that this is completely unsupported by VMware, so it's useful only in test and development environments where you are not running production workloads and don't need the full support of VMware behind you.

If your test lab is anything like my test lab, it's full of older hardware that's been cycled out of production. This often creates the exact kind of environment where VMotion does not work as expected because of differences in the underlying CPUs. As a result, I had to create some custom CPU masks to allow VMotion between some old Pentium III servers (OK, so they were really old servers) and some newer Pentium 4 servers. At that time, VMware did not have anything like EVC, and the hardware vendors didn't have anything like the current hardware virtualization extensions. I had to use an ISO image that VMware included on the ESX 3.0.x installation disc. This bootable ISO image, which does not appear to be included on the vSphere 4 ESX installation media, provided output on the CPUID response from the CPUs. The hexadecimal output from that disc had to be converted to binary and compared in order to find which bits had to be masked in a custom CPU mask.

I documented all the steps and the techniques involved in creating these custom CPU masks on my website. If you are interested in getting more information on custom CPU masks, you can review the following web pages:

http://blog.scottlowe.org/2006/09/25/sneaking-around-vmotion-limitations/

http://blog.scottlowe.org/2007/06/19/more-on-cpu-masking/

Both of these web pages provide in-depth details from the real-life work that I did creating custom CPU masks in my own test lab.

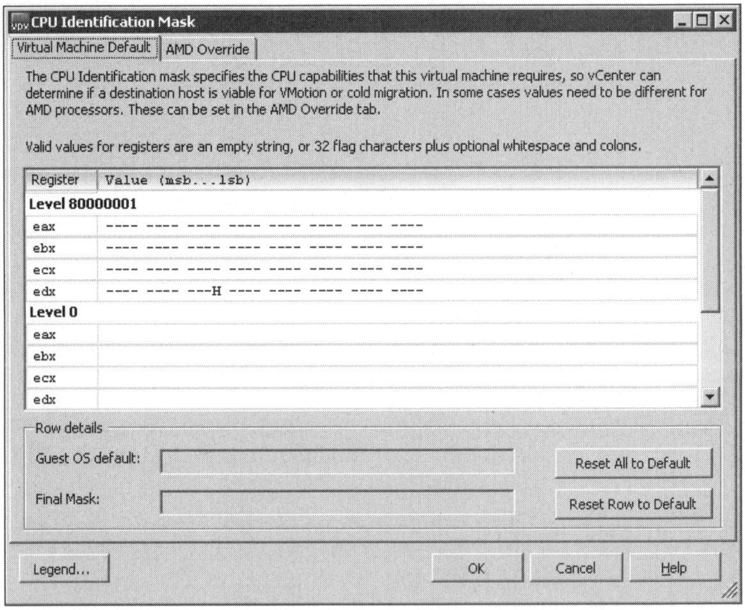

FIGURE 10.24
The CPU Identification Mask dialog box allows you to create custom CPU masks.

Fortunately, there's an easier—and fully supported—way of handling this issue, and it's called Enhanced VMotion Compatibility.

Enhanced VMotion Compatibility

Recognizing that potential compatibility issues with VMotion could be a significant problem, VMware worked closely with both Intel and AMD to craft functionality that would address this issue. On the hardware side, Intel and AMD put functions in their CPUs that would allow them to modify the CPU ID value returned by the CPUs. Intel calls this functionality FlexMigration;

AMD simply embedded this functionality into their existing AMD-V virtualization extensions. On the software side, VMware created software features that would take advantage of this hardware functionality to create a common CPU ID baseline for all the servers within a cluster. This functionality, originally introduced in VMware ESX/ESXi 3.5 Update 2, is called Enhanced VMotion Compatibility (EVC).

EVC is enabled at the cluster level. Figure 10.25 shows the EVC controls for a cluster.

FIGURE 10.25
EVC is enabled and disabled at the cluster level.

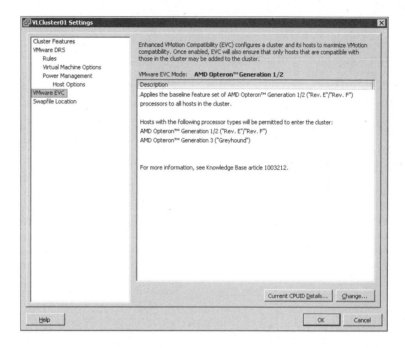

As you can see in Figure 10.25, EVC is currently enabled on this cluster. This cluster contains servers with AMD Opteron processors, so EVC is using a Gen 1/Gen 2 AMD Opteron baseline. To change the baseline that EVC is using, click the Change button. This opens a dialog box that allows you to disable EVC or to change the EVC baseline, as illustrated in Figure 10.26.

When you enable EVC and set the processor baseline, vCenter Server then calculates the correct CPU masks that are required and communicates that information to the ESX/ESXi hosts. The ESX/ESXi hypervisor then works with the underlying Intel or AMD processors to create the correct CPU ID values that would match the correct CPU mask. When vCenter Server validates VMotion compatibility by checking CPU compatibility, the underlying CPUs will return compatible CPU masks and CPU ID values.

Keep in mind that some CPU-specific features—such as newer multimedia extensions, for example—may be disabled when vCenter Server and ESX/ESXi disable them via EVC. Virtual machines that rely upon these advanced extensions may be affected by EVC.

In the next chapter, I'll move from resource allocation to an in-depth discussion of how to provide higher levels of availability to your virtual machines.

FIGURE 10.26
You can enable or disable EVC, as well as change the processor baseline EVC uses.

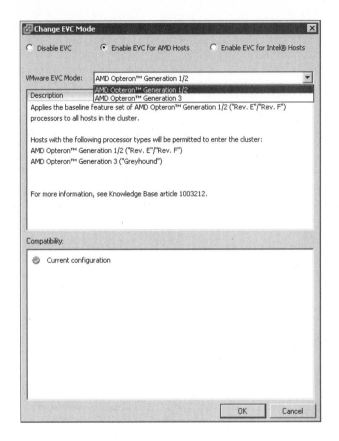

The Bottom Line

Manage virtual machine memory and CPU allocation. In a VMware vSphere environment, the ESX/ESXi hosts control virtual machine access to physical resources like RAM and CPU. To effectively manage and scale VMware vSphere, administrators must understand how to allocate memory and CPU resources to virtual machines, including how to use reservations, limits, and shares. Reservations provide guarantees to resources, limits provide a cap on resource usage, and shares help adjust the allocation of resources in a constrained environment.

Master It To guarantee certain levels of performance, your IT director believes that all virtual machines must be configured with at least 2GB of RAM. However, you know that many of your applications rarely use this much memory. What might be an acceptable compromise to help ensure performance?

Create and manage resource pools. Managing resource allocation and usage for large numbers of virtual machines creates too much administrative overhead. Resource pools provide a mechanism for administrators to apply resource allocation policies to groups of virtual machines all at the same time. Resource pools use reservations, limits, and shares to control and modify resource allocation behavior.

Master It   Your company runs both test/development workloads and production workloads on the same hardware. How can you help ensure that test/development workloads do not consume too many resources and impact the performance of production workloads?

Configure and execute VMotion.   VMotion is a feature that allows running virtual machines to be migrated from one physical ESX/ESXi host to another physical ESX/ESXi host with no downtime to end users. To execute VMotion, both the ESX/ESXi hosts and the virtual machines must meet specific configuration requirements. In addition, vCenter Server performs validation checks to ensure that VMotion compatibility rules are observed.

Master It   A certain vendor has just released a series of patches for some of the guest operating systems in your virtualized infrastructure. You request an outage window from your supervisor, but your supervisor says to just use VMotion to prevent downtime. Is your supervisor correct? Why or why not?

Create and manage clusters.   Clusters provide the basic building block for a number of advanced VMware vSphere features, including VMware Distributed Resource Scheduler, VMware High Availability, and Enhanced VMotion Compatibility. Clusters are collections of ESX/ESXi hosts and can contain resource pools for more efficient allocation of resources within the cluster.

Master It   What features discussed thus far are dependent upon clusters? What features discussed so far are not dependent upon clusters?

Configure and manage VMware Distributed Resource Scheduler.   VMware Distributed Resource Scheduler enables vCenter Server to automate the process of conducting VMotion migrations to help balance the load across ESX/ESXi hosts within a cluster. DRS can be as automated as desired, and vCenter Server has flexible controls for affecting the behavior of DRS as well as the behavior of specific virtual machines within a DRS-enabled cluster.

Master It   You want to take advantage of VMware DRS to provide some load balancing of virtual workloads within your environment. However, because of business constraints, you have a few workloads that should not be automatically moved to other hosts using VMotion. Can you use DRS? If so, how can you prevent these specific workloads from being affected by DRS?

Chapter 11

Ensuring High Availability and Business Continuity

After all your servers are installed, all storage is provisioned, all virtual networking is pinging, and all virtual machines are running, it is time to define the strategies or the methods to put into place in a virtual infrastructure that will provide high availability and business continuity. The deployment of a virtual infrastructure opens many new doors for disaster-recovery planning. The virtual infrastructure administrator will lead the charge into a new era of ideologies and methodologies for ensuring that business continues as efficiently as possible in the face of corrupted data, failed servers, or even lost datacenters.

With the release of VMware vSphere, we have been given more tools at our disposal to reach our goal of increased uptime and recoverability of the infrastructure. You'll learn about the methods and new features available to reach this goal.

In this chapter, you will learn to:

◆ Understand Windows clustering and the types of clusters

◆ Understand built-in high availability options

◆ Understand the differences between VCB and VCDR

◆ Understand data replication options

Clustering Virtual Machines

Let's start with the most well-known technique for helping administrators achieve high availability: Microsoft Clustering Service (MSCS), or *failover clustering* as it is called in Windows 2008. Failover clustering in Windows 2008 is used when critical services and applications call for the highest levels of availability. Microsoft Windows Server 2003 and 2008 both support network load balancing (NLB) clusters as well as server clusters depending on the version of the Windows Server operating system that is installed on the server. Moving forward, I'll just use the term Microsoft Clustering Service or MSCS to describe any forms or versions of Windows clustering.

Microsoft Clustering

The NLB configuration involves an aggregation of servers that balances the requests for applications or services. In a typical NLB cluster, all nodes are active participants in the cluster and are consistently responding to requests for services. NLB clusters are most commonly deployed as a means of providing enhanced performance and availability. NLB clusters are best suited for scenarios involving Internet Information Services (IIS), virtual private networking (VPN), and Internet Security and Acceleration (ISA) server, to name a few. Figure 11.1 details the architecture of an NLB cluster.

FIGURE 11.1
An NLB cluster can contain up to 32 active nodes that distribute traffic equally across each node. The NLB software allows the nodes to share a common name and IP address that is referenced by clients.

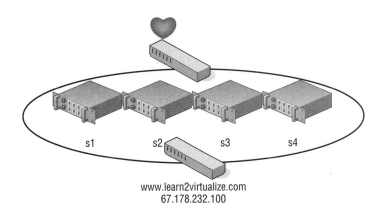

www.learn2virtualize.com
67.178.232.100

NLB SUPPORT FROM VMWARE

As of this writing, VMware supports NLB, but you will need to run NLB in multicast mode to support VMotion and virtual machines on different physical hosts. You will also need to configure static Address Resolution Protocol (ARP) entries on the physical switch to achieve this. If NLB is running in unicast mode, then the virtual machines will all need to be running on the same host. Another option to consider would be the use of third-party load balancers to achieve the same results.

Unlike NLB clusters, server clusters are used solely for the sake of availability. Server clusters do not provide performance enhancements outside of high availability. In a typical server cluster, multiple nodes are configured to be able to own a service or application resource, but only one node owns the resource at a given time. Server clusters are most often used for applications like Microsoft Exchange, Microsoft SQL Server, and DHCP services, which each share a need for a common datastore. The common datastore houses the information accessible by the node that is online and currently owns the resource, as well as the other possible owners that could assume ownership in the event of failure. Each node requires at least two network connections: one for the production network and one for the cluster service heartbeat between nodes. Figure 11.2 details the structure of a server cluster.

The different versions of Windows Server 2003 and 2008 offer various levels of support for NLB and server clusters. Table 11.1 outlines the cluster support available in each version of Windows Server 2003. The only difference in Windows 2008 is that a server cluster can have up to 16 nodes.

TABLE 11.1: Windows Server 2003 Clustering Support

OPERATING SYSTEM	NETWORK LOAD BALANCING	SERVER CLUSTER
Windows Server 2003/2008 Web Edition	Yes (up to 32 nodes)	No
Windows Server 2003/2008 Standard Edition	Yes (up to 32 nodes)	No
Windows Server 2003/2008 Enterprise Edition	Yes (up to 32 nodes)	Yes (up to 8 nodes in 2003 and 16 nodes in 2008)
Windows Server 2003/2008 Datacenter Edition	Yes (up to 32 nodes)	Yes (up to 8 nodes in 2003 and 16 nodes in 2008)

WINDOWS CLUSTERING STORAGE ARCHITECTURES

Server clusters built on Windows Server 2003 can support only up to eight nodes, and Windows 2008 can support up to 16 nodes when using a Fibre Channel–switched fabric. Storage architectures that use SCSI disks as direct attached storage or that use a Fibre Channel–arbitrated loop result in a maximum of only two nodes in a server cluster. Clustering virtual machines in an ESX/ESXi host utilizes a simulated SCSI shared storage connection and is therefore limited to only two-node clustering. In addition, in ESX 3.x, the clustered virtual machine solution uses only SCSI 2 reservations, not SCSI 3 reservations, and supports only the SCSI miniport drivers, not the Storport drivers. This has been changed in VMware vSphere, which now allows SCSI 3 reservations and the use of the Storport drivers.

FIGURE 11.2
Server clusters are best suited for applications and services like SQL Server, Exchange Server, DHCP, and so on, that use a common data set.

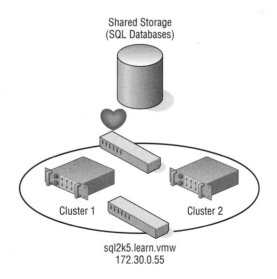

Shared Storage
(SQL Databases)

Cluster 1   Cluster 2

sql2k5.learn.vmw
172.30.0.55

MSCS, when constructed properly, provides automatic failover of services and applications hosted across multiple cluster nodes. When multiple nodes are configured as a cluster for a service or application resource, as I said previously, only one node owns the resource at any given time. When the current resource owner experiences failure, causing a loss in the heartbeat between the cluster nodes, another node assumes ownership of the resource to allow continued access with minimal data loss. To configure multiple Windows Server nodes into a Microsoft cluster, the following requirements must be met:

◆ Nodes must be running either Windows Server Enterprise Edition or Datacenter Edition

◆ All nodes should have access to the same storage device(s)

◆ All nodes should have two similarly connected and configured network adapters: one for the production network and one for the heartbeat network

◆ All nodes should have Microsoft Cluster Services for the version of Windows that you are using

Virtual Machine Clustering Scenarios

The clustering of Windows Server virtual machines using Microsoft Cluster Services can be done in one of three different configurations. The following gives you a quick peek now, and I will get into more details in a minute:

Cluster in a box   The clustering of two virtual machines on the same ESX/ESXi host is also known as a *cluster in a box*. This is the easiest of the three configurations to set up. No special configuration needs to be applied to make this configuration work.

Cluster across boxes   The clustering of two virtual machines that are running on different ESX/ESXi hosts is known as a *cluster across boxes*. VMware had restrictions in place for this configuration in earlier versions: the cluster node's C: drive must be stored on the host's local storage or local VMFS datastore, the cluster shared storage must be stored on Fibre Channel external disks, and you must use raw device mappings on the storage. This has been changed and updated to allow .vmdk files on the SAN and to allow the cluster VM boot drive or C: drive on the SAN, but VMotion and Distributed Resource Scheduling (DRS) are not supported using Microsoft-clustered virtual machines. The exact warning from VMware is "Clustered virtual machines cannot be part of VMware clusters (DRS or HA)."

Physical to virtual clustering   The clustering of a physical server and a virtual machine together is often referred as a *physical to virtual cluster*. This configuration of using both physical and virtual servers together gives you the best of both worlds, and the only other added restriction is that you cannot use virtual compatibility mode with the RDMs. I'll cover these options in more detail and show how to set them up in a virtual environment later in this chapter.

Clustering has long been considered an advanced technology implemented only by those with high technical skills in implementing and managing high-availability environments. Although this might be more rumor than truth, it is certainly a more complex solution to set up and maintain.

Although you might achieve results setting up clustered virtual machines, you may not receive support for your clustered solution if you violate any of the clustering restrictions put forth by VMware. The following list summarizes and reviews the do's and don'ts of clustering virtual machines as published by VMware:

◆ 32-bit and 64-bit virtual machines can be configured as nodes in a server cluster.

◆ Majority Node Set clusters with application-level replication (for example, Microsoft Exchange 2007 Cluster Continuous Replication) is now supported.

- Only two-node clustering is allowed.

- Clustering is not supported on iSCSI or NFS disks.

- Clustering does not support NIC teaming in the virtual machines.

- Virtual machines configured as cluster nodes must use the LSI Logic SCSI adapter and the vmxnet network adapter.

- Virtual machines in a clustered configuration are not valid candidates for VMotion, and they can't be part of a DRS or HA cluster.

- ESX/ESXi hosts that run virtual machines that are part of a server cluster can now be configured to perform a boot from SAN.

- ESX/ESXi hosts that run virtual machines that are part of a server cluster cannot have both QLogic and Emulex HBAs.

There is something else that you need to do. You must set the I/O timeout to 60 seconds or more by modifying HKLM\System\CurrentControlSet\Services\Disk\TimeOutValue, and if you re-create a cluster, you need to reset the value again.

So, let's get into some more details on clustering and look at the specific clustering options available in the virtual environment. I will start with the most basic design configuration, the cluster in a box.

Examining Cluster-in-a-Box Scenarios

The cluster-in-a-box scenario involves configuring two virtual machines hosted by the same ESX/ESXi host as nodes in a server cluster. The shared disks of the server cluster can exist as .vmdk files stored on local VMFS volumes or on a shared VMFS volume. Figure 11.3 details the configuration of a cluster in a box.

FIGURE 11.3
A cluster-in-a-box configuration does not provide protection against a single point of failure. Therefore, it is not a common or suggested form of deploying Microsoft server clusters in virtual machines.

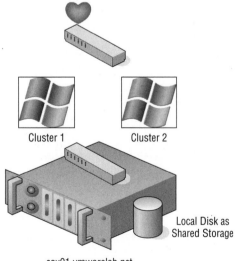

Cluster 1   Cluster 2

Local Disk as
Shared Storage

esx01.vmwarelab.net

After reviewing the diagram of a cluster-in-a-box configuration, you might wonder why you would want to deploy such a thing. The truth is, you wouldn't want to deploy cluster-in-a-box configuration because it still maintains a single point of failure. With both virtual machines running on the same host, if that host fails, both virtual machines fail. This architecture contradicts the very reason for creating failover clusters. A cluster-in-a-box configuration still contains a single point of failure that can result in downtime of the clustered application. If the ESX/ESXi host hosting the two-node cluster-in-a-box configuration fails, then both nodes are lost, and a failover does not occur. This setup might, and I use *might* loosely, be used only to "play" with clustering services or to test clustering services and configurations. But ultimately, even for testing, it is best to use the cluster-across-box configurations to get a better understanding of how this might be deployed in a production scenario.

CONFIGURATION OPTIONS FOR VIRTUAL CLUSTERING

As suggested in the first part of this chapter, server clusters are deployed for high availability. High availability is not achieved by using a cluster-in-a-box configuration, and therefore this configuration should be avoided for any type of critical production applications and services.

Examining Cluster-Across-Boxes Configurations

Although the cluster-in-a-box scenario is more of an experimental or education tool for clustering, the cluster-across-boxes configuration provides a solid solution for critical virtual machines with stringent uptime requirements—for example, the enterprise-level servers and services like SQL Server and Exchange Server that are heavily relied on by the bulk of end users. The cluster-across-boxes scenario, as the name applies, draws its high availability from the fact that the two nodes in the cluster are managed on different ESX/ESXi hosts. In the event that one of the hosts fails, the second node of the cluster will assume ownership of the cluster group, and its resources and the service or application will continue responding to client requests.

The cluster-across-boxes configuration requires that virtual machines have access to the same shared storage, which must reside on a Fibre Channel storage device external to the ESX/ESXi hosts where the virtual machines run. The virtual hard drives that make up the operating system volume of the cluster nodes can be a standard VMDK implementation; however, the drives used as the shared storage must be set up as a special kind of drive called a *raw device mapping* (RDM). An RDM is a feature that allows a virtual machine to establish direct access to a LUN on a SAN device.

USING RAW DEVICE MAPPINGS IN YOUR VIRTUAL CLUSTERS

An RDM is not a direct access to a LUN, and it is not a normal virtual hard disk file. An RDM is a blend between the two. When adding a new disk to a virtual machine, as you will soon see, the Add Hardware Wizard presents the RDMs as an option on the Select a Disk page. This page defines the RDM as having the ability to give a virtual machine direct access to the SAN, thereby allowing SAN management. I know this seems like a contradiction to the opening statement of this sidebar; however, I'm getting to the part that, oddly enough, makes both statements true.

By selecting an RDM for a new disk, you're forced to select a compatibility mode for the RDM. An RDM can be configured in either Physical Compatibility mode or Virtual Compatibility mode. The Physical Compatibility mode option allows the virtual machine to have direct raw LUN access. The

Virtual Compatibility mode, however, is the hybrid configuration that allows raw LUN access but only through a VMDK file acting as a proxy. The following image details the architecture of using an RDM in Virtual Compatibility mode.

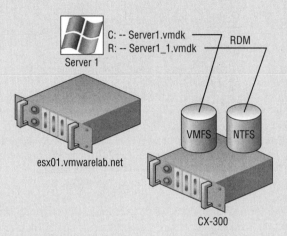

So, why choose one over the other if both are ultimately providing raw LUN access? Because the RDM in Virtual Compatibility mode uses a VMDK proxy file, it offers the advantage of allowing snapshots to be taken. By using the Virtual Compatibility mode, you will gain the ability to use snapshots on top of the raw LUN access in addition to any SAN-level snapshot or mirroring software. Or, of course, in the absence of SAN-level software, the VMware snapshot feature can certainly be a valuable tool. The decision to use Physical Compatibility or Virtual Compatibility is predicated solely on the opportunity and/or need to use VMware snapshot technology or when using physical to virtual clustering.

A cluster-across-box configuration requires a more complex setup than a cluster-in-a-box configuration. When clustering across boxes, all proper communication between virtual machines and all proper communication from virtual machines and storage devices must be configured properly. Figure 11.4 provides details on the setup of a two-node virtual machine cluster-across-box configurations using Windows Server guest operating systems.

Make sure you document things well when you start using RDMs. Any storage that is presented to ESX and is not formatted with VMFS will show up as available storage. If all the administrators are not on the same page, it is easy to take a LUN that was used for an RDM and reprovision that LUN as a VMFS datastore, effectively blowing away the RDM data in the process. I have seen this mistake happen firsthand, and let me tell you, the process is very quick to erase any data that is there. I have gone so far as to create a separate column in vCenter Server to list any RDM LUNs that are configured to make sure everyone has a reference point to refer to.

Let's keep moving and perform the following steps to configure Microsoft Cluster Services on Windows 2003 across virtual machines on separate ESX/ESXi hosts.

FIGURE 11.4
A Microsoft cluster built on virtual machines residing on separate ESX hosts requires shared storage access from each virtual machine using an RDM.

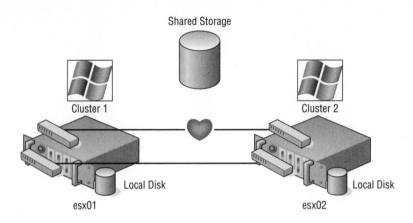

CREATING THE FIRST CLUSTER NODE IN WINDOWS 2003

Perform the following steps to create the first cluster node:

1. Inside the vSphere client, create a virtual machine that is a member of a Windows Active Directory domain.

2. Right-click the new virtual machine, and select the Edit Settings option.

3. Click the Add button, and select the Hard Disk option.

4. Select the Raw Device Mappings radio button, and then click the Next button.

5. Select the appropriate target LUN from the list of available targets.

6. Select the datastore location where the VMDK proxy file should be stored, and then click Next.

7. Select the Virtual radio button to allow VMware snapshot functionality for the RDM, and then click Next.

8. Select the virtual device node to which the RDM should be connected, as shown in Figure 11.5, and then click Next.

9. Click the Finish button.

10. Right-click the virtual machine, and select the Edit Settings option.

11. Select the new SCSI controller that was added as a result of adding the RDMs on a separate SCSI controller.

12. Select the Virtual radio button under the SCSI Bus Sharing options, as shown in Figure 11.6.

13. Repeat steps 2 through 9 to configure additional RDMs for shared storage locations needed by nodes of a Microsoft server cluster.

FIGURE 11.5
The virtual device node for the additional RDMs in a cluster node must be on a different SCSI node.

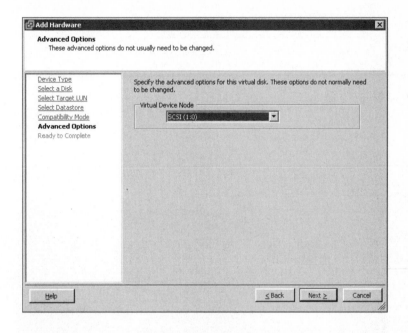

FIGURE 11.6
The SCSI bus sharing for the new SCSI adapter must be set to Virtual to support running a virtual machine as a node in a Microsoft server cluster.

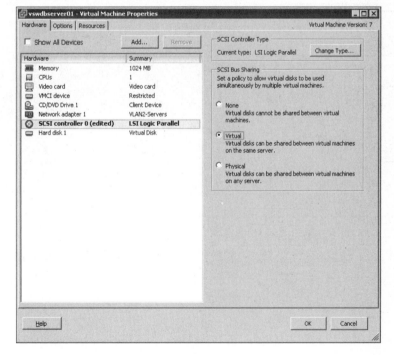

14. Configure the virtual machine with two network adapters. Connect one network adapter to the production network, and connect the other network adapter to the network used for heartbeat communications between nodes. Figure 11.7 shows a cluster node with two network adapters configured.

FIGURE 11.7
A node in a Microsoft server cluster requires at least two network adapters. One adapter must be able to communicate on the production network, and the second adapter is configured for internal cluster heartbeat communication.

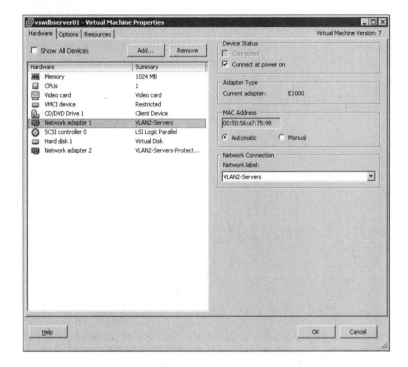

15. Power on the first node of the cluster, and assign valid IP addresses to the network adapters configured for the production and heartbeat networks. Then format the additional drives, and assign drive letters, as shown in Figure 11.8.

16. Shut down the first cluster node.

17. In the VCenter Server inventory, select the ESX/ESXi host where the first cluster node is configured, and then select the Configuration tab.

18. Select Advanced Settings from the Software menu.

19. In the Advanced Settings dialog box, configure the following options:

   ◆ Set the Disk.ResetOnFailure option to 1.

   ◆ Set the Disk.UseLunReset option to 1.

   ◆ Set the Disk.UseDeviceReset option to 0.

FIGURE 11.8
The RDMs presented to the first cluster node are formatted and assigned drive letters.

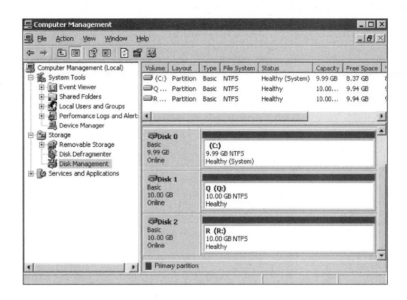

20. Proceed to the next section to configure the second cluster node and the respective ESX/ESXi host.

SCSI NODES FOR RDMs

RDMs used for shared storage in a Microsoft server cluster must be configured on a SCSI node that is different from the SCSI to which the hard disk is connected that holds the operating system. For example, if the operating system's virtual hard drive is configured to use the SCSI0 node, then the RDM should use the SCSI1 node. This rule applies to both virtual and physical clustering.

Because of PCI addressing issues, all RDMs should be added prior to configuring the additional network adapters. If the NICs are configured first, you may be required to revisit the network adapter configuration after the RDMs are added to the cluster node.

CREATING THE SECOND CLUSTER NODE IN WINDOWS 2003

Perform the following steps to create the second cluster node:

1. Starting from inside the vSphere client, create a second virtual machine that is a member of the same Active Directory domain as the first cluster node.

2. Add the same RDMs to the second cluster node using the same SCSI node values.

For example, if the first node used SCSI 1:0 for the first RDM and SCSI 1:1 for the second RDM, then configure the second node to use the same configuration. As in the first cluster node configuration, add all RDMs to the virtual machine before moving on to step 3 to configure the network adapters. Don't forget to edit the SCSI bus sharing configuration for the new SCSI adapter.

3. Configure the second node with an identical network adapter configuration.

4. Verify that the hard drives corresponding to the RDMs can be seen in Disk Manager. At this point, the drives will show as a status of "Healthy," but drive letters will not be assigned.

5. Power off the second node.

6. Edit the advanced disk settings for the ESX/ESXi host with the second cluster node.

CREATING THE MANAGEMENT CLUSTER IN WINDOWS 2003

Perform the following steps to create the management cluster:

1. Starting from Active Directory Users and Computers, if you have the authority, create a new user account that belongs to the same Windows Active Directory domain as the two cluster nodes. The account does not need to be granted any special group memberships at this time.

2. Power on the first node of the cluster, and log in as a user with administrative credentials.

3. Click Start ➢ Programs ➢ Administrative Tools, and select the Cluster Administrator console.

4. Select the Create New Cluster option from the Open Connection To Cluster dialog box. Then click OK.

5. Provide a unique name for the name of the cluster. Ensure that it does not match the name of any existing computers on the network.

6. The next step is to execute the cluster feasibility analysis to check for all cluster-capable resources, as shown in Figure 11.9. Then click Next.

FIGURE 11.9
The cluster analysis portion of the cluster configuration wizard identifies that all cluster-capable resources are available.

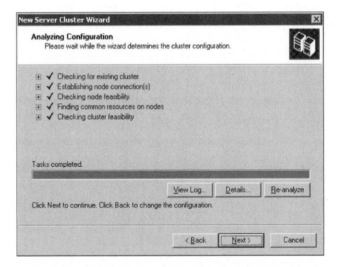

7. Provide an IP address for cluster management. The IP address configured for cluster management should be an IP address that is accessible from the network adapters configured on the production network. Click Next.

8. Provide the account information for the cluster service user account created in step 1. The Cluster Service Account page of the New Server Cluster Wizard acknowledges that the account specified will be granted membership in the local administrators group on each cluster node. Therefore, do not share the cluster service password with users who should not have administrative capabilities. Click Next.

9. At the completion of creating the cluster timeline, shown in Figure 11.10, click Next.

FIGURE 11.10
The cluster installation timeline provides a running report of the items configured as part of the installation process.

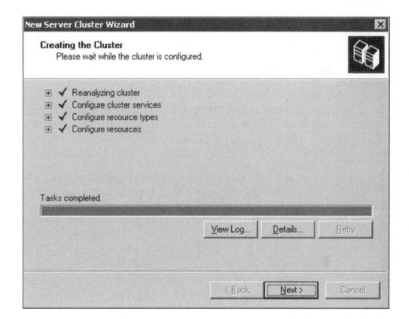

10. Continue to review the Cluster Administrator snap-in, and review the new management cluster that was created, shown in Figure 11.11.

CLUSTER MANAGEMENT

To access and manage a Microsoft cluster, create a Host (A) record in the zone that corresponds to the domain to which the cluster nodes belong.

FIGURE 11.11
The completion of the initial cluster management creation wizard results in a cluster group and all associated cluster resources.

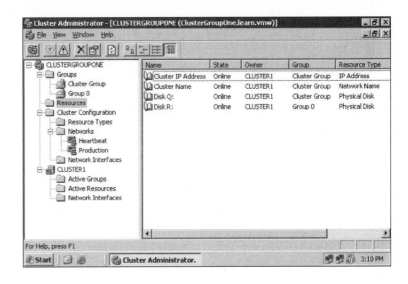

ADDING THE SECOND NODE TO THE MANAGEMENT CLUSTER IN WINDOWS 2003

Perform the following steps to add the second node to the management cluster:

1. Leave the first node powered on, and power on the second node.

2. Starting from the Cluster Administrator, right-click the name of the cluster, select the New option, and then click the Node option, as shown in Figure 11.12.

FIGURE 11.12
After the management cluster is complete, you can add a node.

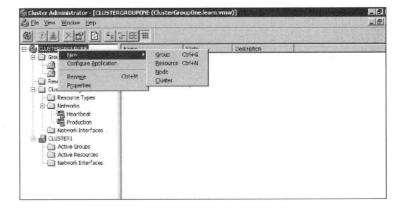

3. Specify the name of the node to be added to the cluster, and then click Next.

4. After the cluster feasibility check has completed (see Figure 11.13), click the Next button.

FIGURE 11.13
A feasibility check is executed against each potential node to validate the hardware configuration that supports the appropriate shared resources and network configuration parameters.

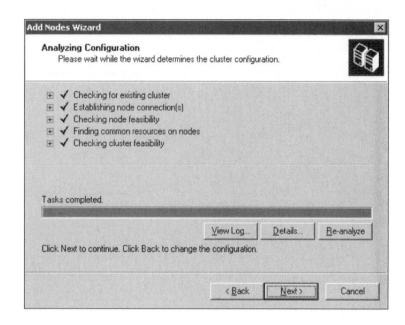

5. Proceed to review the Cluster Administrator, identifying that two nodes now exist within the new cluster.

FEASIBILITY STALL

If the feasibility check stalls and reports a 0x00138f error stating that a cluster resource cannot be found, the installation will continue to run. This is a known issue with the Windows Server 2003 cluster configuration. If you allow the installation to continue, it will eventually complete and function as expected. For more information, visit http://support.microsoft.com/kb/909968.

At this point, the management cluster is complete; from here, application and service clusters can be configured. Some applications, such as Microsoft SQL Server 2005 and Microsoft Exchange Server 2007, are not only cluster-aware applications but also allow for the creation of a server cluster as part of the standard installation wizard. Other cluster-aware applications and services can be configured into a cluster using the cluster administrator.

Examining Physical to Virtual Clustering

The last type of clustering scenario to discuss is physical to virtual clustering. As you might have guessed, this involves building a cluster with two nodes where one node is a physical machine and the other node is a virtual machine. Figure 11.14 details the setup of a two-node physical to virtual cluster.

FIGURE 11.14
Clustering physical machines with virtual machine counterparts can be a cost-effective way of providing high availability.

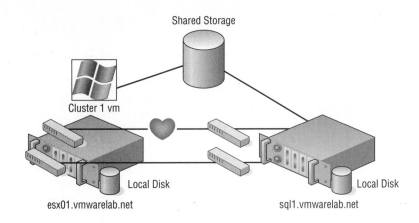

The constraints surrounding the construction of a physical to virtual cluster are identical to those noted in the previous configuration. Likewise, the steps to configure the virtual machine acting as a node in the physical to virtual cluster are identical to the steps outlined in the previous section, with one addition: you must set the RDMs up in Physical Compatibility mode. The virtual machine must have access to all the same storage locations as the physical machine. The virtual machine must also have access to the same pair of networks used by the physical machine for production and heartbeat communication, respectively.

The advantage to implementing a physical to virtual cluster is the resulting high availability with reduced financial outlay. Physical to virtual clustering, because of the two-node limitation of virtual machine clustering, ends up as an N+1 clustered solution, where N is the number of physical servers in the environment plus one additional physical server to host the virtual machines. In each case, each physical virtual machine cluster creates a failover pair. With the scope of the cluster design limited to a failover pair, the most important design aspect in a physical to virtual cluster is the scale of the host running ESX/ESXi host. As you may have figured, the more powerful the ESX/ESXi host, the more failover incidents it can handle. A more powerful ESX/ESXi host will scale better to handle multiple physical host failures, whereas a less powerful ESX/ESXi host might handle only a single physical host failure before performance levels experience a noticeable decline.

Now that I've covered clustering, let's take a look at VMware's version of high availability. VMware has a built-in option called VMware High Availability that is just what the name implies.

Implementing VMware High Availability

High availability has been an industry buzzword that has stood the test of time. The need and/or desire for high availability is often a significant component to any infrastructure design. Within the scope of an ESX/ESXi host, VMware High Availability (HA) is a component of the vSphere 4 product that provides for the automatic failover of virtual machines. But—and it's a big *but* at this point in time—HA does not provide high availability in the traditional sense of the term. Commonly, HA means the automatic failover of a service or application to another server.

Understanding HA

The VMware HA feature provides an automatic restart of the virtual machines that were running on an ESX/ESXi host at the time it became unavailable, shown in Figure 11.15.

FIGURE 11.15
VMware HA provides an automatic restart of virtual machines that were running on an ESX/ESXi host when it failed.

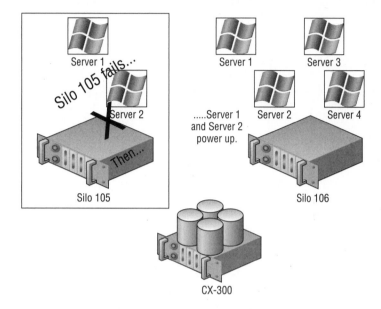

CX-300

In the case of VMware HA, there is still a period of downtime when a server fails. Unfortunately, the duration of the downtime is not a value that can be calculated because it is unknown ahead of time how long it will take to boot a series of virtual machines. From this you can gather that, at this point in time, VMware HA does not provide the same level of high availability as found in a Microsoft server cluster solution. When a failover occurs between ESX/ESXi hosts as a result of the HA feature, there is potential for data loss as a result of the virtual machine that was immediately powered off when the server failed and then brought back up minutes later on another server.

 Real World Scenario

HA EXPERIENCE IN THE FIELD

With that said, I want to mention my own personal experience with HA and the results I encountered. Your mileage might vary but should give you a reasonable expectation of what to expect. I had a VMware ESX/ESXi host that was a member of a five-node cluster. This node crashed sometime during the night, and when the host went down, it took anywhere from 15 to 20 virtual machines with it. HA kicked in and restarted all the virtual machines as expected.

What made this an interesting experience is that the crash must have happened right after the polling of the monitoring and alerting server. All the virtual machines that were on the general alerting schedule were restarted without triggering any alerts. We did have some of those virtual machines with a more aggressive monitoring that did trip off alerts that were recovered before anyone was able to log on to the system and investigate. I tried to argue the point that if an alert never fired, did the downtime really happen? I did not get too far with that argument but was pleased with the results.

In another case, during testing I had a virtual machine running on a two-node cluster. I pulled the power cords on the host that the virtual machine was running to create the failure. My time to recovery from pull to ping was between five and six minutes. That's not too bad for general use but not good enough for everything. VMware Fault Tolerance can now fill that gap for even the most important and critical servers in your environment. I'll talk more about FT in a bit.

In the VMware HA scenario, two or more ESX/ESXi hosts are configured in a cluster. Remember, a VMware cluster represents a logical aggregation of CPU and memory resources, as shown in Figure 11.16. By editing the cluster settings, you can enable the VMware HA feature for a cluster. The HA cluster then determines the number of hosts failures it must support.

FIGURE 11.16
A VMware ESX/ESXi host cluster logically aggregates the CPU and memory resources from all nodes in the cluster.

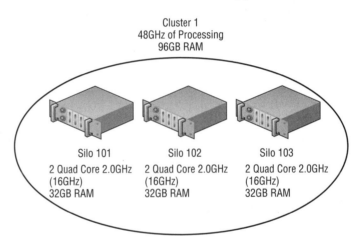

HA: WITHIN, BUT NOT BETWEEN, SITES

A requisite of HA is that each node in the HA cluster must have access to the same SAN LUNs. This requirement prevents HA from being able to failover between ESX/ESXi hosts in different locations unless both locations have been configured to have access to the *same* storage devices. It is not acceptable just to have the data in LUNs the same because of SAN replication software. Mirroring data from a LUN on a SAN in one location to a LUN on a SAN in a hot site is not conducive to allowing HA (VMotion or DRS).

When ESX/ESXi hosts are configured into a VMware HA cluster, they receive all the cluster information. vCenter Server informs each node in the HA cluster about the cluster configuration.

HA AND vCENTER SERVER

Although vCenter Server is most certainly required to enable and manage VMware HA, it is not required to execute HA. vCenter Server is a tool that notifies each VMware HA cluster node about the HA configuration. After the nodes have been updated with the information about the cluster, vCenter Server no longer maintains a persistent connection with each node. Each node continues to function as a member of the HA cluster independent of its communication status with vCenter Server.

When an ESX/ESXi host is added to a VMware HA cluster, a set of HA-specific components are installed on the ESX/ESXi host. These components, shown in Figure 11.17, include the following:

◆ Automatic Availability Manager (AAM)

◆ Vmap

◆ vpxa

FIGURE 11.17
Adding an ESX/ESXi host to an HA cluster automatically installs the AAM, Vmap, and possibly the vpxa components on the host.

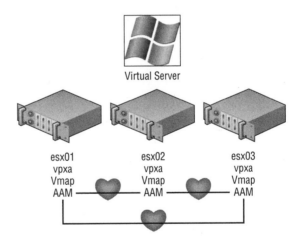

The AAM, effectively the engine or service for HA, is a Legato-based component that keeps an internal database of the other nodes in the cluster. The AAM is responsible for the intracluster heartbeat used to identify available and unavailable nodes. Each node in the cluster establishes a heartbeat with each of the other nodes over the Service Console network, or you can use or define another VMkernel port group for the HA heartbeat. As a best practice, you should provide redundancy to the AAM heartbeat by establishing the Service Console port group on a virtual switch with an underlying NIC team. Though the Service Console could be multihomed and have an AAM heartbeat over two different networks, this configuration is not as reliable as the NIC team. The AAM is extremely sensitive to hostname resolution; the inability to resolve names will most certainly result in an inability to execute HA. When problems arise with HA functionality, look first at hostname resolution. Having said that, during HA troubleshooting, you should identify the answers to questions such as these:

◆ Is the DNS server configuration correct?

◆ Is the DNS server available?

◆ If DNS is on a remote subnet, is the default gateway correct and functional?

◆ Does the /etc/hosts file have bad entries in it?

◆ Does the /etc/resolv.conf have the right search suffix?

◆ Does the /etc/resolv.conf have the right DNS server?

ADDING A HOST TO VCENTER SERVER

When a new host is added into the vCenter Server inventory, the host must be added by its hostname, or the HA will not function properly. As just noted, HA is heavily reliant on successful name resolution. ESX/ESXi hosts should not be added to the vCenter Server inventory using IP addresses.

The AAM on each ESX/ESXi host keeps an internal database of the other hosts belonging to the cluster. All hosts in a cluster are considered either a primary host or a secondary host. However, only one ESX/ESXi host in the cluster is considered the primary host at a given time, with all others considered secondary hosts. The primary host functions as the source of information for all new hosts and defaults to the first host added to the cluster. If the primary host experiences failure, the HA cluster will continue to function. In fact, in the event of primary host failure, one of the secondary hosts will move up to the status of primary host. The process of promoting secondary hosts to primary host is limited to four other hosts. Only five hosts could assume the role of primary host in an HA cluster.

While AAM is busy managing the intranode communications, the vpxa service (or vCenter Server agent) manages the HA components. The vpxa service communicates to the AAM through a third component called the Vmap.

NAME RESOLUTION TIP

If DNS is set up and configured correctly, then you should not need anything else for name resolution. However, as a method of redundancy, consider adding the other VMware ESX and vCenter Server information to the local host file (/etc/hosts). If there is a failure and the ESX/ESXi host is unable to talk to DNS, this setup will ensure that HA would still work as designed.

Configuring HA

Before I detail how to set up and configure the HA feature, let's review the requirements of HA. To implement HA, all of the following requirements should be met:

◆ All hosts in an HA cluster must have access to the same shared storage locations used by all virtual machines on the cluster. This includes any Fibre Channel, iSCSI, and NFS datastores used by virtual machines.

◆ All hosts in an HA cluster should have an identical virtual networking configuration. If a new switch is added to one host, the same new switch should be added to all hosts in the cluster.

◆ All hosts in an HA cluster must resolve the other hosts using DNS names.

A TEST FOR HA

An easy and simple test for identifying HA capability for a virtual machine is to perform a VMotion. The requirements of VMotion are actually more stringent than those for performing an HA failover, though some of the requirements are identical. In short, if a virtual machine can successfully perform a VMotion across the hosts in a cluster, then it is safe to assume that HA will be able to power on that virtual machine from any of the hosts. To perform a full test of a virtual machine on a cluster with four nodes, perform a VMotion from node 1 to node 2, node 2 to node 3, node 3 to node 4, and finally, node 4 back to node 1. If it works, then you have passed the test!

First and foremost, to configure HA, you must create a cluster. After you create the cluster, you can enable and configure HA. Figure 11.18 shows a cluster enabled for HA.

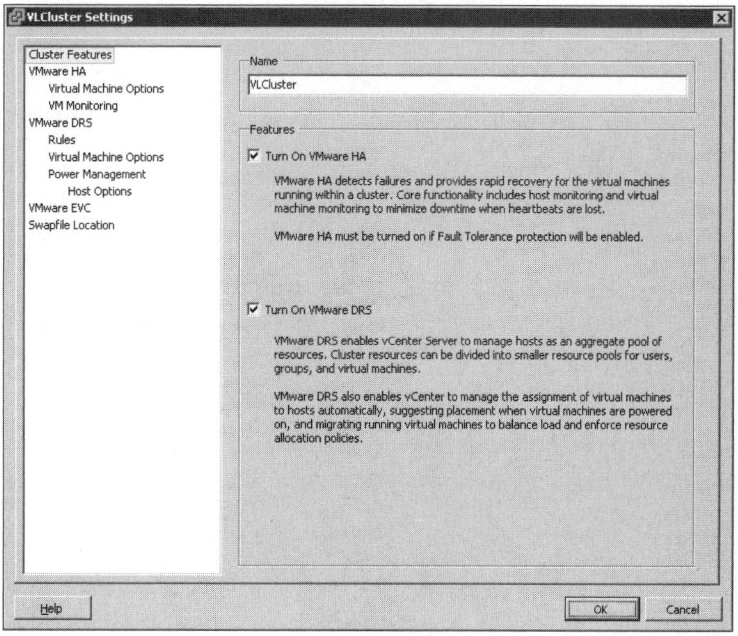

FIGURE 11.18
A cluster of ESX/ESXi hosts can be configured with HA and DRS. The features are not mutually exclusive and can work together to provide availability and performance optimization.

Configuring an HA cluster revolves around three different settings:

◆ Host failures allowed

◆ Admission control

◆ Virtual machine options

The configuration option for the number of host failures to allow, shown in Figure 11.19, is a critical setting. It directly influences the number of virtual machines that can run in the cluster before the cluster is in jeopardy of being unable to support an unexpected host failure. vSphere now gives up the capability to set a percentage for the failover spare capacity or specify a specific node for failover.

FIGURE 11.19
The number of host failures allowed dictates the amount of spare capacity that must be retained for use in recovering virtual machines after failure.

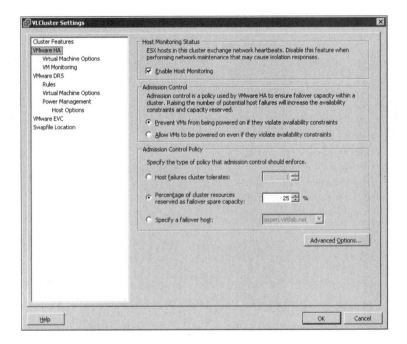

HA CONFIGURATION FAILURE

It is not uncommon for a host in a cluster to fail during the configuration of HA. Remember the stress we put on DNS, or name resolution in general, earlier in this chapter? Well, if DNS is not set correctly, you will find that the host cannot be configured for HA. Take, for example, a cluster with three nodes being configured as an HA cluster to support two-node failure. Enabling HA forces a configuration of each node in the cluster. The image here shows an HA cluster where one of the nodes, Silo 104, has thrown an error related to the HA agent and is unable to complete the HA configuration.

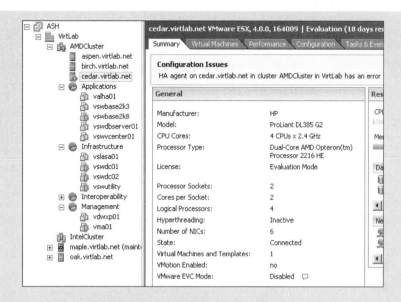

In this example, because the cluster was attempting to allow for two-node failure and there are only two nodes successfully configured, this would be impossible. The cluster in this case is now warning that there are insufficient resources to satisfy the HA failover level. Naturally, with only two nodes, we cannot cover a two-node failure. The following image shows an error on the cluster because of the failure in Silo 104.

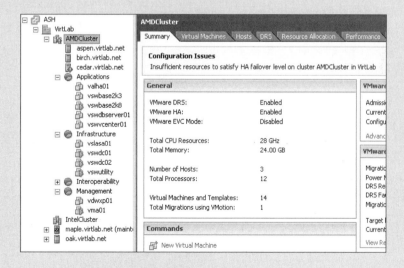

In the Tasks pane of the graphic, you might have noticed that Silo 105 and Silo 106 both completed the HA configuration successfully. This provides evidence that the problem is probably isolated to Silo 104. Reviewing the Tasks & Events tab to get more detail on the error reveals exactly that. The following image shows that the error was caused by an inability to resolve a name. This confirms the suspicion that the error is with DNS.

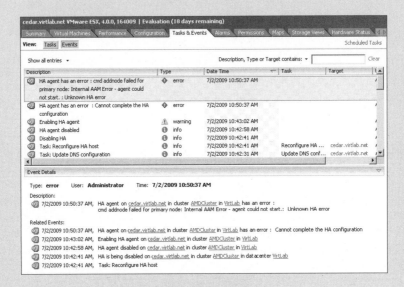

Perform the following steps to review or edit the DNS server for an ESX/ESXi host:

1. Use the vSphere Client to connect to a vCenter Server.

2. Click the Hosts And Clusters button on the Home page.

3. Click the name of the host in the inventory tree on the left.

4. Click the Configuration tab in the details pane on the right.

5. Select DNS And Routing in the Advanced menu.

6. If needed, edit the DNS server, as shown in the following image, to a server that can resolve the other nodes in the HA cluster.

Although they should not be edited on a regular basis, you can also check the /etc/hosts and /etc/resolv.conf files, which should contain static lists of hostnames to IP addresses or the DNS search domain and name servers, respectively. The following image offers a quick look at the information inside the /etc/hosts and /etc/resolv.conf files. These tools can be valuable for troubleshooting name resolution.

After the DNS server, `/etc/hosts`, or `/etc/resolv.conf` has been corrected, the host with the failure can be reconfigured for HA. It's not necessary to remove the HA configuration from the cluster and then reenable it. The following image shows the right-click context menu of Silo 104, where it can be reconfigured for HA now that the name resolution problem has been fixed.

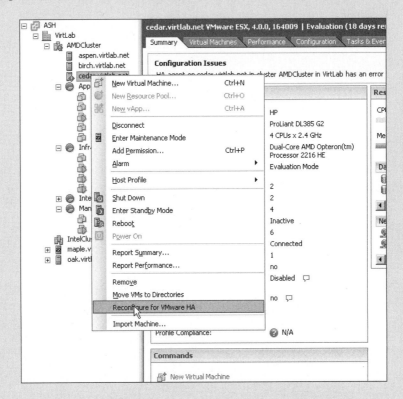

Upon completion of the configuration of the final node, the errors at the host and cluster levels will be removed, the cluster will be configured as desired, and the error regarding the inability to satisfy the failover level will disappear.

To explain the workings of HA and the differences in the configuration settings, let's look at some implementation scenarios. For example, consider five ESX/ESXi hosts named Silo 101 through Silo 105. All five hosts belong to an HA cluster configured to support single-host failure. Each node in the cluster is equally configured with 12GB of RAM. If each node runs eight virtual machines with 1GB of memory allocated to each virtual machine, then 8GB of unused memory across four hosts is needed to support a single-host failure. The 12GB of memory on each host minus 8GB for virtual machines leaves 4GB of memory per host. Figure 11.20 shows our five-node cluster in normal operating mode.

FIGURE 11.20

A five-node cluster configured to allow single-host failure

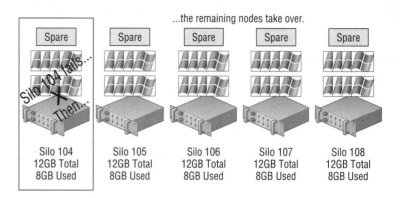

FIGURE 11.21

A five-node cluster configured to allow single-host failure is deficient in resources to support a second failed node.

Let's assume that Service Console and virtual machine overhead consume 1GB of memory, leaving 3GB of memory per host. If Silo 101 fails, the remaining four hosts will each have 3GB of memory to contribute to running the virtual machines orphaned by the failure. The 8GB of virtual machines will then be powered on across the remaining four hosts that collectively have 12GB of memory to spare. In this case, the configuration supported the failover. Figure 11.21 shows our five-node cluster down to four after the failure of Silo 101. Assume in this same scenario that Silo 101 and Silo 102 both experience failure. That leaves 16GB of virtual machines to cover across only three hosts with 3GB of memory to spare. In this case, the cluster is deficient, and not all of the orphaned virtual machines will be restarted.

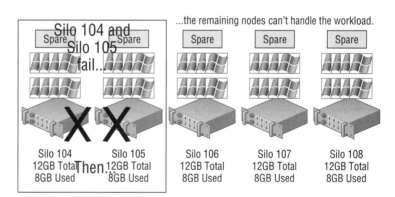

PRIMARY HOST LIMIT

In the previous section introducing the HA feature, I mentioned that the AAM caps the number of primary hosts at five. This limitation translates into a maximum of four host failures allowed in a cluster.

The admission control setting goes hand in hand with the Number Of Host Failures Allowed setting. There are two possible settings for admission control:

◆ Do not power on virtual machines if they violate availability constraints (known as *strict admission control*).

◆ Allow virtual machines to be powered on even if they violate availability constraints (known as *guaranteed admission control*).

In the previous example, virtual machines would not power on when Silo 102 experienced failure because by default an HA cluster is configured to use strict admission control. Figure 11.22 shows an HA cluster configured to use the default setting of strict admission control.

FIGURE 11.22
Strict admission control for an HA cluster prioritizes resource balance and fairness over resource availability.

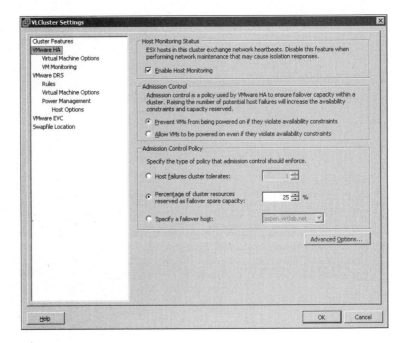

With strict admission control, the cluster will reach a point at which it will no longer start virtual machines. Figure 11.23 shows a cluster configured for two-node failover. A virtual machine with more than 3GB of memory reserved is powering on, and the resulting error is posted, stating that insufficient resources are available to satisfy the configured HA level.

If the admission control setting of the cluster is changed from strict admission control to guaranteed admission control, then virtual machines will power on even in the event that the HA failover level is jeopardized.

Figure 11.24 shows a cluster reconfigured to use guaranteed admission control.

FIGURE 11.23
Strict admission control imposes a limit at which no more virtual machines can be powered on because the HA level would be jeopardized.

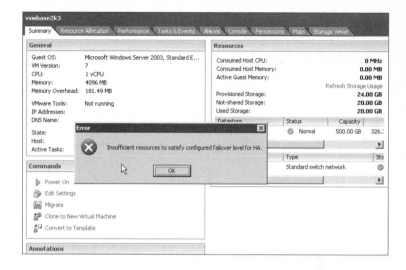

FIGURE 11.24
Guaranteed admission control reflects the idea that when failure occurs, availability is more important than resource fairness and balance.

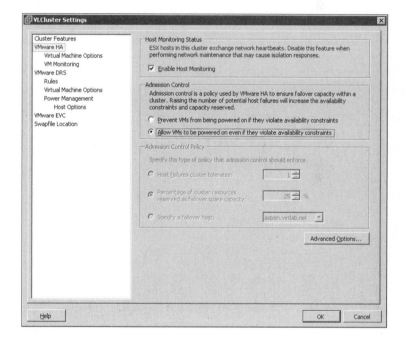

With that same cluster now configured with guaranteed admission control, the virtual machine with more than 3GB of memory can now successfully power on.

OVERCOMMITMENT IN AN HA CLUSTER

When the admission control setting is set to allow virtual machines to be powered on even if they violate availability constraints, you could find yourself in a position where there is more physical memory allocated to virtual machines than actually exists.

This situation, called *overcommitment*, can lead to poor performance on virtual machines that become forced to page information from fast RAM out to the slower disk-based swap file. Yes, your virtual machines will start, but after the host gets maxed out, the whole system and all virtual machines will slow down dramatically. This will increase the amount of time that HA will need to recover the virtual machines. What should have been a 20- to 30-minute recovery could end up being an hour or even more.

HA RESTART PRIORITY

Not all virtual machines are equal. There are some that are more important or more critical and that require higher priority when ensuring availability. When an ESX/ESXi host experiences failure and the remaining cluster nodes are tasked with bringing virtual machines back online, they have a finite amount of resources to fill before there are no more resources to allocate to virtual machines that need to be powered on. Rather than leave the important virtual machines to chance, an HA cluster allows for the prioritization of virtual machines. The restart priority options for virtual machines in an HA cluster include Low, Medium, High, and Disabled. For those virtual machines that should be brought up first, the restart priority should be set to High. For those virtual machines that should be brought up if resources are available, the restart priority can be set to Medium and/or Low. For those virtual machines that will not be missed for a period of time and should not be brought online during the period of reduced resource availability, the restart priority should be set to Disabled. Figure 11.25 shows virtual machines with various restart priorities configured to reflect their importance. Figure 11.25 details a configuration where virtual machines such as domain controllers, database servers, and cluster nodes are assigned higher restart priority.

The restart priority is put into place only for the virtual machines running on the ESX/ESXi hosts that experience an unexpected failure. Virtual machines running on hosts that have not failed are not affected by the restart priority. It is possible then that virtual machines configured with a restart priority of High might not be powered on by the HA feature because of limited resources, which are in part because of lower-priority virtual machines that continue to run. For example, as shown in Figure 11.26, Silo 101 hosts five virtual machines with a priority of High and five other virtual machines with priority values of Medium and Low. Meanwhile, Silo 102 and Silo 103 each hold 10 virtual machines, but of the 20 virtual machines between them, only four are considered of high priority. When Silo 101 fails, Silo 102 and Silo 103 will begin powering the virtual machines with a high priority. However, assume there were only enough resources to power on four of the five virtual machines with high priority. That leaves a high-priority virtual machine powered off while all other virtual machines of medium and low priorities continue to run on Silo 102 and Silo 103.

FIGURE 11.25

Restart priorities help minimize the down-time for more important virtual machines.

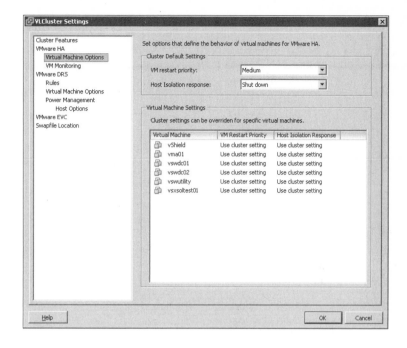

FIGURE 11.26

High-priority virtual machines from a failed ESX/ESXi host might not be powered on because of a lack of resources—resources consumed by virtual machines with a lower priority that are running on the other hosts in an HA cluster.

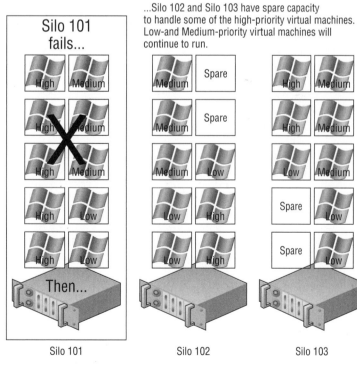

At this point in the vSphere product suite, you can still manually remedy this imbalance. Any disaster recovery plan in a virtual environment built on vSphere should include a contingency plan that identifies virtual machines to be powered off to make resources available for those virtual machines with higher priority as a result of the network services they provide. If the budget allows, construct the HA cluster to ensure that there are ample resources to cover the needs of the critical virtual machines, even in times of reduced computing capacity.

HA ISOLATION RESPONSE

Previously, we introduced the AAM and its role in conducting the heartbeat that occurs among all the nodes in the HA cluster. The heartbeat among the nodes in the cluster identifies the presence of each node to the other nodes in the cluster. When a heartbeat is no longer presented from a node in the HA cluster, the other cluster nodes spring into action to power on all the virtual machines that the missing node was running.

But what if the node with the missing heartbeat was not really missing? What if the heartbeat was missing, but the node was still running? And what if the node with the missing heartbeat is still locking the virtual machine files on a SAN LUN, thereby preventing the other nodes from powering on the virtual machines?

Let's look at two particular examples of a situation VMware refers to as a *split-brained* HA cluster. Let's assume there are three nodes in an HA cluster: Silo 101, Silo 102, and Silo 103. Each node is configured with a single virtual switch for VMotion and with a second virtual switch consisting of a Service Console port and a virtual machines port group, as shown in Figure 11.27.

FIGURE 11.27
ESX/ESXi hosts in an HA cluster using a single virtual switch for Service Console and virtual machine communication

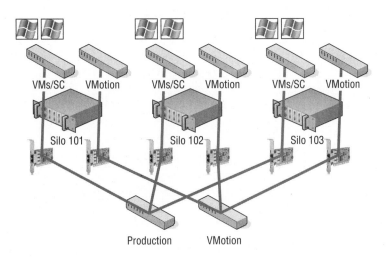

To continue with the example, suppose that an administrator mistakenly unplugs the Silo 101 Service Console network cable. When each of the nodes identifies a missing heartbeat from another node, the discovery process begins. After 15 seconds of missing heartbeats, each node then pings an address called the *isolation response address*. By default this address is the default gateway IP address configured for the Service Console. If the ping attempt receives a reply, the node considers itself valid and continues as normal. If a host does not receive a response, as Silo 101 wouldn't, it considers itself in isolation mode. At this point, the node will identify the cluster's isolation response configuration, which will guide the host to either power off the existing virtual machines it is hosting or leave them powered on. This isolation response value, shown in Figure 11.28, is set on a per-virtual machine basis. So, what should you do? Power off the existing virtual machine? Or leave it powered on?

FIGURE 11.28
The isolation response identifies the action to occur when an ESX/ESXi host determines it is offline but powered on.

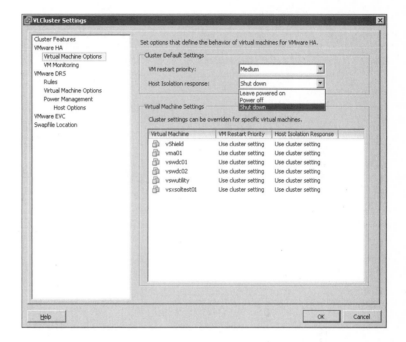

The answer to this question is highly dependent on the virtual and physical network infrastructures in place. In our example, the Service Console and virtual machines are connected to the same virtual switch bound to a single network adapter. In this case, when the cable for the Service Console was unplugged, communication to the Service Console and every virtual machine on that computer was lost. The solution, then, should be to power off the virtual machines. By doing so, the other nodes in the cluster will identify the releases on the locks and begin to power on the virtual machines that were not otherwise included.

In the next example, we have the same scenario but a different infrastructure, so we don't need to worry about powering off virtual machines in a split-brain situation. Figure 11.29 diagrams a virtual networking architecture in which the Service Console, VMotion, and virtual machines all communicate through individual virtual switches bound to different physical network adapters. In this case, if the network cable connecting the Service Console is removed, the heartbeat will once again be missing; however, the virtual machines will be unaffected because they reside on a different network that is still passing communications between the virtual and physical networks.

Figure 11.30 shows the isolation response setting of Leave Powered On that would accompany an infrastructure built with redundancy at the virtual and physical network levels.

FIGURE 11.29
Redundancy in the physical infrastructure with isolation of virtual machines from the Service Console in the virtual infrastructure provides greater flexibility for isolation response.

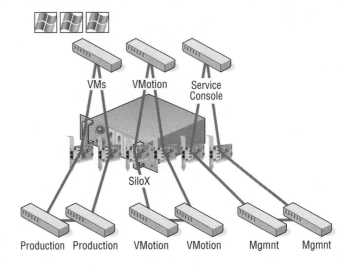

FIGURE 11.30
The option to leave virtual machines running when a host is isolated should be set only when the virtual and the physical networking infrastructures support high availability.

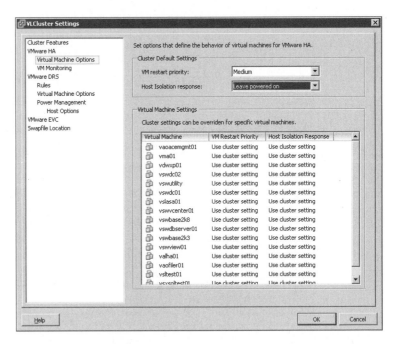

CONFIGURING THE ISOLATION RESPONSE ADDRESS

In some highly secure virtual environments, Service Console access is limited to a single, nonrouted management network. In some cases, the security plan calls for the elimination of a default gateway on the Service Console port configuration. The idea is to lock the Service Console onto the local subnet, thus preventing any type of remote network access. The disadvantage, as you might have guessed, is that without a default gateway IP address configured for the Service Console, there is no isolation address to ping as a determination of isolation status.

It is possible, however, to customize the isolation response address for scenarios just like this. The IP address can be any IP address but should be an IP address that is not going to be unavailable or taken from the network at any time.

Perform the following steps to define a custom isolation response address:

1. Use the vSphere Client to connect to a vCenter server.

2. Open the Hosts And Clusters View, right-click an existing cluster, and select the Edit Settings option.

3. Click the VMware HA node.

4. Click the Advanced Options button.

5. Enter **das.isolationaddress** in the Option column in the Advanced Options (HA) dialog box.

6. Enter the IP address to be used as the isolation response address for ESX/ESXi hosts that miss the AAM heartbeat. The following image shows a sample configuration in which the servers will ping the IP address 172.30.0.2.

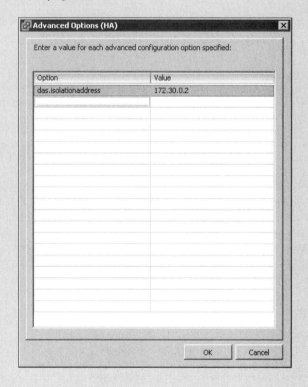

7. Click the OK button twice.

This interface can also be configured with the following options:

◆ das.isolationaddress1: To specify the first address to try

◆ das.isolationaddress2: To specify the second address to try

◆ das.defaultfailoverhost: To identify the preferred host to failover to

◆ das.failuredetectiontime: To change the amount of time required for failover detection

◆ das.AllowNetwork: To specify a different port group to use for HA heartbeat

To support a redundant HA architecture, it is best to ensure that the Service Console port is sitting atop a NIC team where each physical NIC bound to the virtual switch is connected to a different physical switch.

Clustering is configured to give you, the administrator of an environment, a form of fault tolerance, and VMware has taken this concept to a whole other level. Although VMware does not call FT clustering, it functions the same in that FT will failover the primary virtual machine to a secondary virtual machine. VMware Fault Tolerance (FT) is based on vLockstep technology and provides zero downtime, zero data loss, and continuous availability for your applications.

That sounds pretty impressive, doesn't it? But how does it work?

Implementing VMware Fault Tolerance

VMware FT is the evolution of "continuous availability" that works by utilizing VMware vLock-step technology to keep a primary machine and a secondary machine in a virtual lockstep. This virtual lockstep is actually the record/playback technology that VMware introduced in VMware Workstation in 2006. VMware FT will stream data that will be recorded, only nondeterministic events are recorded, and the replay will occur deterministically. By doing it this way, VMware has created a process that matches instruction-for-instruction and memory-for-memory to get identical results.

Deterministic means that the computer processor will execute the same instruction stream on the secondary virtual machine as to end up in the same state as the primary virtual machine. On the other hand, nondeterministic events are functions, such as network/disk/keyboard I/O as well as hardware interrupts. So, the record process will take the data stream, and the playback will perform all the keyboards and mouse clicks. It is pretty slick to move the mouse on the primary virtual machine and see it also move on the secondary virtual machine.

Perform the following steps to enable FT:

1. Starting in the vSphere client, right-click a running virtual machine, and then select Turn Fault Tolerance On, as shown in Figure 11.31.

2. A pop-up message appears to warn you that any thin disks will be converted to eagerthick, and DRS will be disabled for this virtual machine, as shown in Figure 11.32.

FIGURE 11.31
Turning on fault tolerance

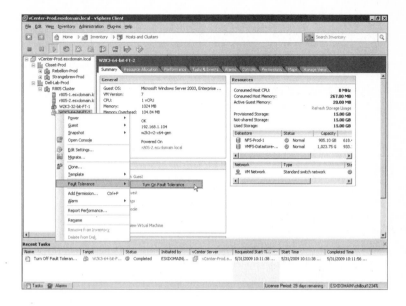

FIGURE 11.32
Warning about disks being converted to eagerthick and that DRS will be disabled on that virtual machine

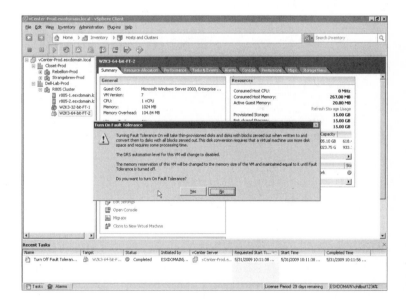

3. After you have selected to enable FT, the creation task begins, as shown in Figure 11.33.

FIGURE 11.33
FT task in progress

It is literally that simple. After VMware FT is turned on, vCenter Server will then initiate the creation of the secondary virtual machine, as shown in Figure 11.34, by using a special type of VMotion. Both the primary and secondary virtual machines will share a common disk between them, and using record/replay, VMware FT will then be able to keep the virtual machines in sync. Only the primary virtual machine will respond across the network, which leaves the secondary virtual machine a silent partner. You can almost compare this to active/passive cluster configuration in that only one node owns the shared network at a time. When the primary VM fails, the secondary VM takes over immediately with no break in network connection. A reverse ARP is sent to the physical switch to notify the network of the new location of the VM. Does that sound familiar? It is exactly what VMotion does when the VM switches to a new host. Once the secondary VM then becomes the primary, the creation of the new secondary VM is repeated until the sync is locked. After the sync is locked, as shown in Figure 11.35, you'll see green icons.

FIGURE 11.34
The vCenter client showing the start FT process on secondary virtual machine

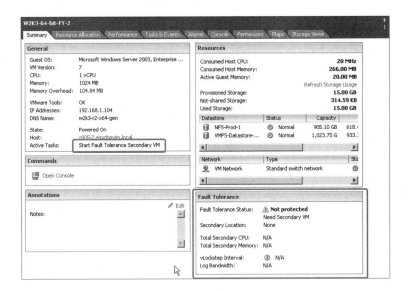

For VMware FT to work, the virtual machines must be a member of an HA-enabled cluster. In this scenario, you will have VMotion, DRS, and HA as available services to use with VMware FT. You will need another VMkernel port group to use for FT logging, so you will need to plan your design to take that addition into account. Just like all the other physical NICs used in your host, the FT logging NIC requires Gigabit Ethernet. VMware recommends using a "dedicated" or "separate" NIC for FT logging, but in my lab I was able to set this up without a dedicated NIC.

I mention this so you know it can work, but I repeat the recommendation is for FT logging to use its own NIC.

FIGURE 11.35
The vCenter client showing the FT process is in sync

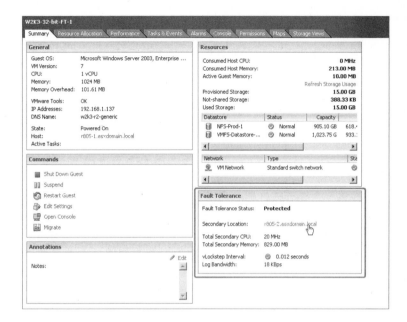

In the event of multiple host failure, VMware HA will do the following:

1. Restart the primary VM.

2. VMware FT will re-create the secondary process again until the sync is locked.

In the case of a guest operating system failure, VMware FT will take no action because, as far as FT is concerned, the VMs are in sync. Both VMs will fail at the same time and place. VMware HA's guest failure monitor can restart the primary, and the secondary creation process will start again. Have you noticed a pattern about the secondary VMs? After the sync has failed, the secondary machine is always re-created.

There is no special hardware as such, but there are some requirements or restrictions for running FT. Let's take a look at some of these requirements/restrictions. You can also call this your checklist for VMware FT success.

◆ Starting with the hardware, you will need to make sure that the processors are supported. At the time of this writing, VMware FT requires Intel 31xx, 33xx, 52xx, 54xx, or 74xx or AMD 13xx, 23xx, or 83xx series processors.

◆ The processors listed in the previous bulleted item all support hardware virtualization (AMD-V, Intel VT), but this setting is usually disabled by default; therefore, you will need to enable this setting in the BIOS of the VMware ESX/ESXi host.

◆ For better performance, it is recommended that hyperthreading and power management (also known as *power-capping*) is turned off in the BIOS.

◆ VMware FT–protected VMs are required to be on shared storage (Fibre Channel, iSCSI, or NFS).

◆ You cannot use physical RDM, but virtual RDM is a supported configuration.

◆ You can use VMotion with an FT-protected VM, but you cannot use Storage VMotion.

◆ N_Port ID Virtualization (NPIV) is not supported with VMware FT.

◆ A virtual disk used with VMware FT must be eagerthick, but during the creation process a thin or sparsely allocated disk will be automatically converted to eagerthick.

◆ Gigabit Ethernet is required, and 10 Gigabit Ethernet is supported with jumbo frames enabled.

◆ All the hosts used for VMware FT must be in an HA-enabled cluster.

◆ DRS cannot be used with VMware FT–enabled virtual machines, but manual VMotion is allowed and supported on one at a time.

◆ The ESX hosts must be running the same version and build of VMware ESX or VMware ESXi.

◆ VMware FT currently supports only those VMs with one vCPU. SMP and multiprocessor VMs are not supported.

◆ Nested page tables/extended page tables (NPT/EPT) are not supported. VMware FT will disable NPT/EPT on the VMware ESX host.

◆ Hot-plugging devices are not supported, so no hardware changes when the VMs are powered on.

◆ USB (must be disabled) and sound devices (cannot be configured) are not supported with VMware FT–enabled VMs.

◆ Snapshots are not supported for VMware FT. Make sure any snapshots are applied or deleted from the VM before protecting the VM with FT.

◆ Virtual machines must be running at a hardware level of 7. Make sure your virtual hardware is upgraded before you begin.

◆ VMware FT–protected guests cannot be running a paravirtualized operating system.

◆ Because VMware FT is, in my opinion, the next generation of clustering, you cannot protect MSCS clusters. Remove MSCS first, or build another VM.

I also make it a habit to store any ISOs on a shared LUN that all ESX/ESXi hosts can see. This way, VMotion will still happen if an ISO gets left connected to a VM. VMware FT should be done the same way, or you will get an error message that will get reported that there is no media on the secondary VM.

You need another VMkernel port group for FT logging, and VMware recommends that you have a pair of NICs for VMotion and a pair of NICs for FT logging. That is a total of four NICs for the VMkernel.

VMware FT is not designed or meant to be run on all your virtual machines. You should use this service sparingly and take this form of fault tolerance only for your most important virtual machines. Suggested general guidelines recommend that there be no more than four to eight VMware FT–protected virtual machines—primary or secondary—on any single ESX/ESXi host. Your mileage will vary, so be cautious in your own environment. Remember, once you have primary and secondary virtual machines locked and in sync, you will be using double the resources for a protected virtual machine.

Now that you have taken a look a couple of different high availability options, let's move on to the next important thing to plan and design for. No configuration or design is complete without considering disaster recovery.

Recovering from Disasters

High availability is only one half of the ability to keep your application/systems up in day-to-day operation. The other half is disaster recovery, which is the ability to recover from a catastrophic failure. Hurricane Andrew and Hurricane Katrina demonstrated the importance of having a well-thought-out and well-designed plan in place. They also showed the importance of being able to execute that plan. Datacenters disappeared from the power of these storms, and the datacenters that remained standing and functioning did not stay functioning long when the generators ran out of gas. I believe when Hurricane Katrina came to visit New Orleans, the aftermath drove the point home that businesses need to be prepared.

I can remember what life was like before virtualization. The disaster recovery (DR) team would show up, and the remote recovery site was slated with the task of recovering the enterprise in a timely manner. A timely manner back then was at least a few days to build and install the recovery servers and then restore the enterprise from the backup media.

Sounds simple, right? Well, in theory, it was supposed to be, but there are always problems that occur during the process. First, during the recovery process, you almost never get to restore your environment at the remote datacenter location to the same make and model that you have running in your current environment. After you restore your data from your backup media, one of the joys is the pretty blue screen that you get because the drivers are different. For the most part, after the restore is finished, you can rerun the installation of the drivers for the recovery servers, but Murphy tends to show up and lay down his law.

Second, the restore process itself is another form of literal contention. If your backup strategy is not designed to consider which servers you want to recover first, then during a disaster, when you try to restore and bring up systems based on importance, you will have a lot a time wasted waiting for tape machines to become available. This contention becomes even worse if your backups span more than one tape. Speaking of tapes, it was not uncommon for tapes to become corrupt and not have the ability to be read. It was common for backups to be done and the tapes to be sent off-site, but the tapes were hardly tested until they were needed. If all goes well, in a few days you might be done, but to be honest, success was sometimes a hard thing to find.

That old-school methodology has advanced and has changed the future with it. Now, a majority of data is kept on the SAN, and the data is replicated to another SAN at your remote disaster recovery co-location site. So, your data is waiting for you when it becomes time to recover, which really speeds up the recovery process in general. At first this was an expensive undertaking because only the high-dollar enterprise SANs had this capability. Over the years, though, this is becoming more the standard and is now a must-have in any SAN environment you work with. I'll cover SAN to SAN replication options a little later.

Now let's take some time and look at the different methods and tools available to use for recovering your environments by using backups.

With the release of VMware vSphere, VMware has also enhanced the ability to work within the storage layer and has set the groundwork for third-party vendors to use the new vStorage APIs for data protection. The vStorage APIs are a framework, not a backup application, and will enable backup vendors to run backups of the virtual machines without having the VMware ESX servers perform any of the processing of these backup tasks. At the time of this writing, most third-party backup vendors are still anywhere from six months to a year from releasing or updating their own backup software to take advantage of this new programming interface. So, in the meantime, we have VMware Consolidated Backup (VCB) for backups to tape and VMware Data Recovery (VCDR) for backups to disk. I will give you more information about VCDR a little later in the chapter. VMware VCB takes the most configuration by the administrators in the field, so it is worth taking a good look at this technology, even with the understanding that VCB is no longer on the VMware road map and will be phased out as the third-party backup vendors move forward using the vStorage APIs.

Backing Up with VMware Consolidated Backup

Virtual machines are no less likely to lose data, become corrupted, or fail than their physical counterparts. And though some might argue against that point, it is most certainly the best way for you to look at virtual machines. With the opposite school of thought, you might be jeopardizing the infrastructure with overconfidence in virtual machine stability. It's better to be safe than sorry. When it comes to virtual machine backup planning, VMware suggests three different methods you can use to support your disaster recovery plan:

◆ Using backup agents inside the virtual machine

◆ Using VCB to perform virtual machine backups

◆ Using VCB to perform file-level backups (Windows guests only)

VCB is VMware's first entry into the backup space. (For those of you who have worked with ESX 2, I am not counting vmsnap.pl and vmres.pl as attempts to provide a backup product). VCB is a framework for backing up that integrates easily into a handful of third-party products. Although VCB can be used on its own, it lacks some of the nice features that third-party backup products bring to the table. These include features such as cataloging backups, scheduling capability, and media management backups. For this reason, I recommend that you use the VCB framework in conjunction with third-party products that have been tested.

More than likely, none of the three methods listed will suffice if used alone. As this chapter provides more details about each of the methods, you'll see how a solid backup strategy is based on using several of these methods in a complementary fashion.

Using Backup Agents in a Virtual Machine

Oh so many years ago when virtualization was not even a spot on your IT road map, you were backing up your physical servers according to some kind of business need. For most organizations, the solution involved the purchase, installation, configuration, and execution of third-party backup agents on the operating systems running on physical hardware. Now that you have jumped onto the cutting edge of technology by leading the server consolidation charge into a virtual IT infrastructure, you can still back up using the same traditional methods. Virtual machines like physical machines are targets for third-party backup tools. The downside to this time-tested model is the need to continue paying for the licenses needed to perform backups across all servers. As shown in Figure 11.36, you'll need a license for every virtual machine you want to back up:

100 virtual machines = 100 licenses. Some vendors allow for a single ESX/ESXi host license that permits an unlimited number of agent licenses to be installed on virtual machines on that host.

FIGURE 11.36
Using third-party backup agents inside a virtual machine does not take advantage of virtualization. Virtual machines are treated just like their physical counterparts for the sake of a disaster recovery plan.

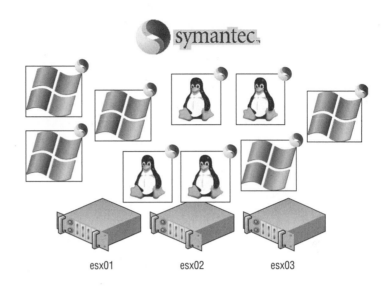

In this case, virtualization has not lowered total ownership costs, and the return on investment has not changed with regard to the fiscal accountability to the third-party backup company. So, perhaps this is not the best avenue that you should travel down. With that being said, let's look at other options that rely heavily on the virtualized aspect of the guest operating system. These options include the following:

- ◆ Using VCB for full virtual machine backups

- ◆ Using VCB for single VMDK backups

- ◆ Using VCB for file-level backups

Let's take a look at each of these, starting with using VCB to capture full backups of the virtual machines.

Using VCB for Full Virtual Machine Backups

As we mentioned briefly in the opening section, VCB is a framework for backup that integrates with third-party backup software. It is a series of scripts that perform online, LAN-free backups of virtual machines or virtual machine files.

VCB FOR FIBRE CHANNEL...AND iSCSI TOO!

When first released, VCB was offered as a Fibre Channel—only solution; VMware did not support VCB used over an iSCSI storage network. The latest release of VCB offers support for use with iSCSI storage.

The requirements for VCB 1.5 include the following:

◆ A physical or virtual server running Windows Server 2003. (Windows 2008 is now supported as a VCB proxy. If using Windows Server Standard Edition, the VCB server must be configured not to automatically assign drive letters using Diskpart to execute automount disable and automount scrub.)

◆ Network connectivity for access to vCenter Server.

◆ Fibre Channel HBA with access to all SAN LUNs where virtual machine files are stored.

◆ Installation of the third-party software prior to installing and configuring VCB.

VCB ON FIBRE CHANNEL WITHOUT MULTIPATHING

The VCB proxy requires a Fibre Channel HBA to communicate with Fibre Channel SAN LUNs regarding backup processes. VCB does not, however, support multiple HBAs or multipathing software like EMC PowerPath. Insert only one Fibre Channel HBA into a VCB proxy.

Figure 11.37 looks at the VCB components and architecture.

If you do not have a SAN in your environment, you still have the ability to run VCB in your environment. Without a SAN, consolidated backup can run in what is called *LAN mode*. This mode will allow you to run VCB on a physical or virtual machine connected to your ESX/ESXi host system over the regular TCP/IP network.

FIGURE 11.37
A VCB deployment relies on several communication mediums, including network access to vCenter Server and Fibre Channel access to all necessary SAN LUNs.

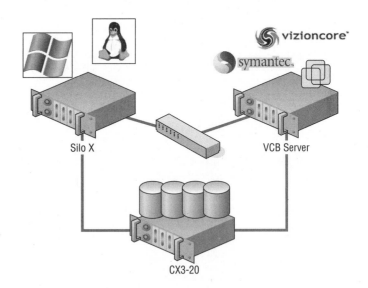

Although considered a framework for backup, VCB can actually be used as a backup product. However, it lacks the nice scheduling and graphical interface features of third-party products like Vizioncore vRanger Pro. Two of the more common VCB commands are the following:

◆ vcbVmName: This command enumerates the various ways a virtual machine can be referenced in the vcbMounter command. Here's an example:

```
vcbVmName -h 172.30.0.120 -u administrator -p Sybex!!
-s ipaddr:172.30.0.24
```

The following are the options:

- ◆ -h <vCenter Server name or IP address>

- ◆ -u <vCenter Server username>

- ◆ -p <vCenter Server user password>

- ◆ -s ipaddr: <IP address of virtual machine to backup>

◆ vcbMounter:

- ◆ -h <vCenter Server name or IP address>

- ◆ -u <vCenter Server username>

- ◆ -p <vCenter Server user password>

- ◆ -a <name | ipaddr | moref | uuid>: <attribute value>

- ◆ -t [fullvm | file]

- ◆ -r <Backup directory on VCB proxy>

VCB PROXY BACKUP DIRECTORY

When specifying the VCB backup directory using the -r parameter, do not specify an existing folder.
For example, if the backup directory E:\VCBBackups already exists and a new backup should be
stored in a subdirectory named Server1, then specify the subdirectory *without* creating it first. In
this case, the -r parameter might read as follows:

```
-r E:\VCBBackups\Server1
```

The vcbMounter command will create the new directory as needed. If the directory is created first,
an error will be thrown at the beginning of the backup process. The error will state that the directory
already exists.

When VCB performs a full backup of a virtual machine, it engages the VMware snapshot
functionality to quiesce the file system and perform the backup. Remember that snapshots are not
complete copies of data. Instead, a snapshot is the creation of a differencing file (or redo log) to
which all changes are written. When the vcbMounter command is used, a snapshot is taken of the
virtual machine, as shown in Figure 11.38.

Any writes that occur during the backup are done to the differencing file. Meanwhile, VCB is
busy making a copy of the VMDK, which is now read-only for the duration of the backup job.
Figure 11.39 details the full virtual machine backup process. After the backup job is completed,
the snapshot is deleted, forcing all writes that occurred to the differencing file to be written to the
virtual machine disk file.

FIGURE 11.38
You can view the snapshots that VCB created in the snapshot manager of a virtual machine.

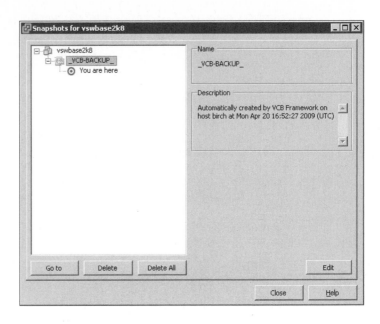

FIGURE 11.39
Performing a full virtual machine backup utilizes the VMware snapshot functionality, which ensures that an online backup is correct as of that point in time.

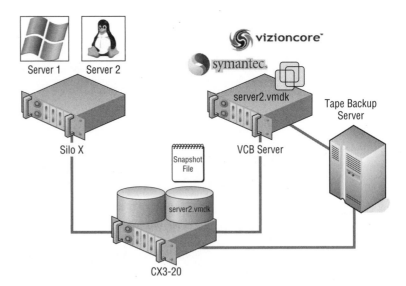

SNAPSHOTS AND VMFS LOCKING

Snapshots grow by default in 16MB increments, and for the duration of time it takes to grow a snapshot, a lock is held on the VMFS volume so the respective metadata can be updated to reflect the change in the snapshot. For this reason, do not instantiate a snapshot for many virtual machines at once. Although the lock is held only for the update to the metadata, the more virtual machines trying at the same time, the greater the chance of contention on the VMFS metadata. From an IT standpoint, this factor should drive your backup strategy to perform backups of many virtual machines only if the virtual machine files have been located on separate VMFS volumes.

Perform the following steps to perform a full virtual machine backup using VCB:

1. Log in to the backup proxy where VCB is installed.

2. Open a command prompt, and change directories to the C:\Program Files\VMware\VMware Consolidated Backup Framework directory.

3. Use the vcbVmName tool to enumerate virtual machine identifiers. At the command prompt, enter the following:

```
vcbVmName <IP or name of VCenter Server> -u <username>
    -p <password> -s ipaddr:<IP address of virtual
    machine to backup>
```

4. From the results of running the vcbVmName tool, select which identifier to use (moref, name, uuid, or ipaddr) in the vcbMounter command.

5. At the command prompt, enter the following:

```
vcbMounter -h <IP or name of VCenter Server> -u
    <username> -p <password> -a ipaddr:<IP address of
    virtual machine to backup> -t fullvm -r <VCB proxy
    backup directory>
```

After the backup is complete, you can review a list of the files in the directory provided in the backup script. Figure 11.40 shows the files created as part of the completed full backup of a virtual machine named Server 1.

REDUNDANT PATHS

Let's look at an example of a VCB backup proxy with a single QLogic Fibre Channel HBA that is connected to a single Fibre Channel switch connected to two storage processors on the storage device. This configuration results in two different paths being available to the VCB server. The following image shows that a VCB server with a single HBA will find LUNs twice because of the redundancy at the storage-processor level.

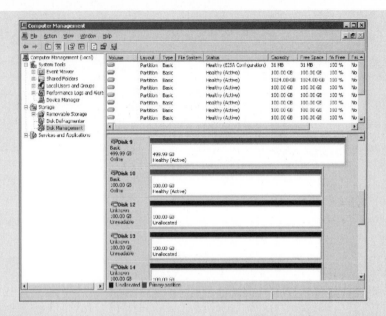

When Disk Management shows this configuration for the older versions of VCB, it presents a problem that causes every backup attempt to fail. For the pre-VCB 1.0.3 versions, the LUNs identified as Unknown and Unreadable must be disabled in Disk Management. The option to disable is located on the properties of a LUN. The following image displays the General tab of LUN properties from Disk Management where a path to a LUN can be disabled. To remove the redundant unused paths from Computer Management, the Device Usage drop-down list should be set to Do Not Use This Device (Disable).

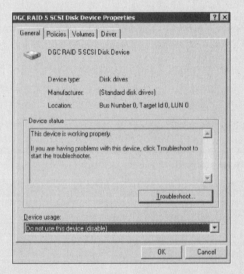

With redundant paths disabled, this will, of course, present a problem when a LUN trespasses to another storage processor. This requires a path to the LUN that is likely disabled.

FIGURE 11.40
A full virtual machine backup that uses VCB creates a directory of files that include a configuration file (VMX), log files, and virtual machine hard drives (VMDK).

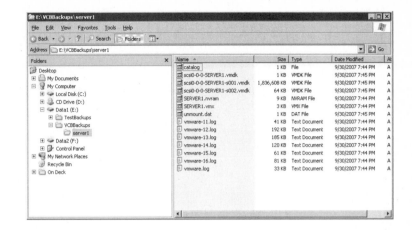

Using VCB for Single VMDK Backups

Sometimes a full backup is just too much: too much data that hasn't changed or too much data that is backed up more regularly and isn't needed again. For example, what if just the operating system drive needs to be backed up and not all the user data stored on other virtual machine disk files? A full backup would back up everything. For those situations, VCB provides a means of performing single virtual machine disk backups.

Perform the following steps for a single VMDK backup:

1. Log in to the backup proxy where VCB is installed.

2. Open a command prompt, and change directories to the C:\Program Files\VMware\VMware Consolidated Backup Framework directory.

3. Use the vcbVmName tool to enumerate virtual machine identifiers. At the command prompt, enter the following:

```
vcbVmName <IP or name of VCenter Server> -u <username>
    -p <password> -s ipaddr:<IP address of virtual
    machine to backup>
```

4. From the results of running the vcbVmName command, note the moref value of the virtual machine.

5. Use the following command to create a snapshot of the virtual machine:

```
vcbSnapshot -h <IP or name of VCenter Server> -u
    <username> -p <password> -c <moref value of
    virtual machine> <name of snapshot>
```

6. Note the snapshot ID (SSID) from the results of step 5.

7. Enumerate the disks within the snapshot using the vcbSnapshot command:

```
vcbSnapshot -h <IP or name of VCenter Server> -u
    <username> -p <password> -l <moref value of
    virtual machine> <snapshot ID>
```

8. Change to the backup directory of the virtual machine, and export the desired VMDK using the vcbExport command:

```
vcbExport -d <name of new VMDK copy> -s <name of
    existing VMDK>
```

9. Remove the snapshot by once again using the vcbSnapshot command:

```
vcbSnapshot -h <IP or name of VCenter Server> -u
    <username> -p <password> -d <moref value of
    virtual machine> <snapshot ID>
```

Using VCB for File-Level Backups

For Windows virtual machines and *only* for Windows virtual machines, VCB offers file-level backups. A file-level backup is an excellent complement to the full virtual machine or the single VMDK backup discussed in the previous sections. For example, suppose you built a virtual machine using two virtual disks: one for the operating system and one for the custom user data. The operating system's virtual disk will not change often with the exception of the second Tuesday of each month when new patches are released. So, that virtual disk does not need consistent and regular backups. On the other hand, the virtual disk that stores user data might be updated quite frequently. To get the best of both worlds and implement an efficient backup strategy, you need to do a single VMDK backup (for the OS) and file-level backup (for the data).

Perform the following steps to conduct a file-level backup using VCB:

1. Log in to the backup proxy where VCB is installed.

2. Open a command prompt, and change directories to C:\Program Files\VMware\VMware Consolidated Backup Framework.

3. Use the vcbVmName tool to enumerate virtual machine identifiers. At the command prompt, enter the following:

```
vcbVmName <IP or name of VCenter Server> -u <username>
    -p <password> -s ipaddr:<IP address of virtual
    machine to backup>
```

4. From the results of running the vcbVmName tool, select which identifier to use (moref, name, uuid, or ipaddr) in the vcbMounter command.

5. As shown in Figure 11.41, enter the following at the command prompt:

```
vcbMounter -h <IP or name of VCenter Server> -u
    <username> -p <password> -s ipaddr:<IP address of
    virtual machine to backup> -t file -r <VCB proxy
    backup directory>
```

6. Browse to the mounted directory to back up the required files and folders.

7. After the file- or folder-level backup is complete, use the following command, shown in Figure 11.42, to remove the mount point:

```
mountvm -u <path to mount point>
```

8. Exit the command prompt.

FIGURE 11.41
A file- or folder-level backup begins with mounting the virtual machine drives as directories under a mount point on the VCB server.

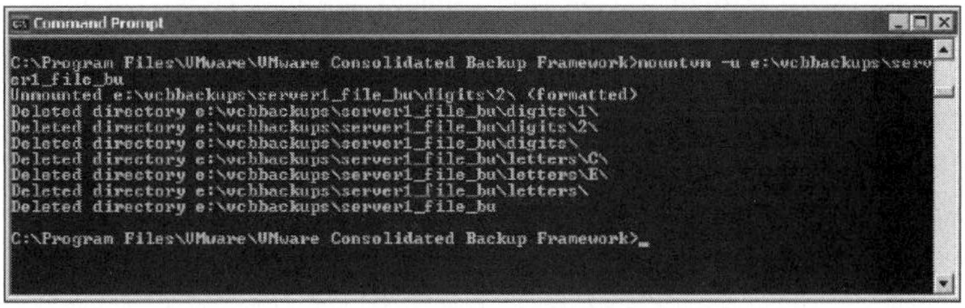

FIGURE 11.42
After performing a file- or folder-level backup using the vcbMounter command, the mount point must be removed using the mountvm command.

If you come across a situation where a snapshot refuses to delete when you issue the mountvm -u command, you can always delete it from the snapshot manager user interface, which is accessible through the VI client.

VCB WITH THIRD-PARTY PRODUCTS

After you master VCB framework by understanding the VCB mounter commands and the way that VCB works, then working with VCB and third-party products is an easy transition. The third-party products simply call upon the VCB framework to perform the vcbMounter command. All the while, the process is wrapped up nicely inside the GUI of the third-party product. This allows for scheduling the backups through backup jobs.

Let's look at an example with Symantec Backup Exec 11d. After the 11d product is installed, followed by the installation of VCB, a set of integration scripts can be extracted from VCB to support the Backup Exec installation. When a backup job is created in Backup Exec 11d, a pre-backup script runs (which calls vcbMounter to create the snapshot and mount the VMDKs), and after the backup job completes, a post-backup script runs to unmount the VMDKs. During the period of time that the VMDKs are mounted into the file system, the Backup Exec product has access to the mounted VMDKs in order to back them up to disk or tape, as specified in the backup job. See the following sample scripts, which perform a full virtual machine backup of a virtual machine with the IP address 192.168.4.1.

First, here's the pre-backup script example:

```
"C:\Program Files\VMware\VMware Consolidated Backup
    Framework\backupexec\pre-backup.bat" Server1_FullVM 192.168.4.1-fullvm
```

Now, here's the post-backup script example:

```
"C:\Program Files\VMware\VMware Consolidated Backup
    Framework\backupexec\post-backup.bat" Server1_FullVM 192.168.1.10-fullVM
```

There is no reference to vcbMounter or the parameters required to run the command. Behind the scenes, the pre-backup.bat and post-backup.bat files are reading a configuration file named config.js to pull defaults for some of the parameters for vcbMounter and then using the information given in the lines shown previously. When vcbMounter extracts the virtual machine files to the file system of the VCB proxy, the files will be found in a folder named 192.168.4.1-fullvm in a directory specified in the configuration file. A portion of the configuration file is shown here. The file identifies the directory to mount the backups to (F:\\mnt), as well as the vCenter server to connect to (vc01.vlearn.vmw) and the credentials to be used (administrator/Password1).

```
/*
 * Generic configuration file for VMware Consolidated Backup (VCB).
 */
/*
 * Directory where all the VM backup jobs are supposed to reside in.
 * For each backup job, a directory with a unique name derived from the
 * backup type and the VM name will be created here.
 * If omitted, BACKUPROOT defaults to c:\\mnt.
 *  * Make sure this directory exists before attempting any VM backups.
 */ BACKUPROOT="F:\\mnt";/*
 * URL that is used by "mountvm" to obtain the block list for a
```

```
* disk image that is to be mounted on the backup proxy.
*
* Specifying this option is mandatory. There is no default
* value.   */ HOST="vc01.learn.vmw"; /*
* Port for communicating with all the VC SDK services.
* Defaults to 902
*/ // PORT="902";
/*
* Username/password used for authentication against the mountvm server.
* Specifying these options is mandatory.
*/ USERNAME="administrator"; PASSWORD="Password1";
```

It is this combination of the configuration file with the parameters passed at the time of execution that results in a successful mount and copy of the virtual machine disk files followed by an unmount.

Depending on the size of the virtual machines to be backed up, it might be more feasible to back up to disk and then create a second backup job to take the virtual machine backups to a tape device.

Now that you have looked at the backup process, the next logical step is to take a look at the restoration or restore process of the virtual machines.

Restoring with VMware Consolidated Backup

Restoring data in a virtual environment can take many forms. If you are using VCB in combination with an approved third-party backup application, there are three specific types of restores:

◆ Centralized restore: One backup agent on the VCB proxy.

◆ Decentralized restore: Several backup agents installed around the network, but not every system has one.

◆ Self-service restore: Each virtual machine contains a backup agent.

Why am I discussing backup agents in the restore section? Remember, the number of backup agents purchased directly influences the virtual machines that can also be restored directly. No matter how you implant the whole backup/restore process, you must understand that it's "either pay me now or pay me later." Something that is easier to back up is often more difficult to restore. On the flip side, something that is the most difficult to back up is often easier to restore. Figure 11.43 shows the difference between the centralized restore and the self-service restore.

SELF-SERVICE RESTORE IS ALWAYS QUICKER

If you are looking for a restore solution focused solely on the speed of the restore and administrative effort, then the self-service restore method is ideal. Of course, the price is a bit heftier than its counterparts because an agent is required in the virtual machine. A centralized restore methodology would require two touches on the data to be restored. The first touch gets the data from the backup media to the VCB proxy server, and the second touch gets the data from the VCB proxy server back into the virtual machine. The latter happens via standard Server Message Block (SMB) or Common Internet File System (CIFS) traffic in a Windows environment. This is a literal *servername**sharename* copy of the data back to the virtual machine where the data exists.

Perhaps the best solution is to find a happy, solid relationship between the self-service restore and the centralized restore methods. This way you can reduce (not necessarily minimize) the number of backup agents while still allowing critical virtual machines to have data restored immediately.

FIGURE 11.43
Backup agents are not just for backup. They also allow restore capability. The number of backup agents purchased and installed directly affects the recovery plan.

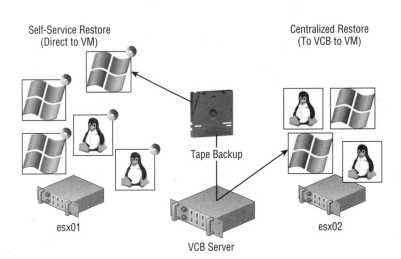

To demonstrate a restore of a full virtual machine backup, let's continue with the earlier examples. Server 1 at this point has a full backup created. Figure 11.44 shows that Server 1 has now been deleted and is gone.

Restoring a Full Virtual Machine Backup

When bad things happen, such as the deletion or corruption of a virtual machine, a restore from a full virtual machine backup will return the environment to the point in time when the backup was taken.

Perform the following steps on a virtual machine from a full virtual machine backup:

1. Connect to the VCB proxy, and use FastSCP or WinSCP to establish a secure copy protocol session with the remote host. Shown in Figure 11.45, the data from the E:\VCBBackups\Server1 folder can be copied into a temporary directory in the Service Console. The temporary directory houses all the virtual machine files from the backup of the original virtual machine.

FIGURE 11.44
A server from the inventory is missing, and a search through the datastores does not locate the virtual machine disk files.

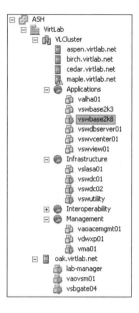

FIGURE 11.45
The FastSCP utility, as the name proclaims, offers a fast, secure copy protocol application to move files back and forth between Windows and ESX.

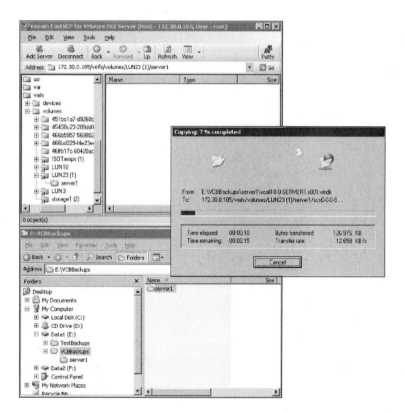

2. Upon completion of the restore to a temporary location process, verify the existence of the files by navigating to the shared site, as shown in Figure 11.46. Use `Putty.exe` to connect to the Service Console, and navigate to the temporary directory where the backup files are stored. Then use the `ls` command to list all the files in the temporary directory.

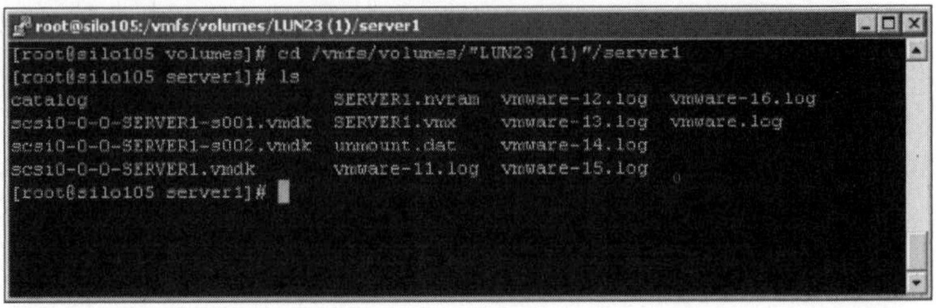

FIGURE 11.46
Virtual machine files needed for the restore are located in the temporary directory specified in the command.

```
root@silo105:/vmfs/volumes/LUN23 (1)/server1
[root@silo105 volumes]# cd /vmfs/volumes/"LUN23 (1)"/server1
[root@silo105 server1]# ls
catalog                         SERVER1.nvram   vmware-12.log   vmware-16.log
scsi0-0-0-SERVER1-s001.vmdk     SERVER1.vmx     vmware-13.log   vmware.log
scsi0-0-0-SERVER1-s002.vmdk     unmount.dat     vmware-14.log
scsi0-0-0-SERVER1.vmdk          vmware-11.log   vmware-15.log
[root@silo105 server1]#
```

3. From a command prompt, enter the following, all on one line:

```
vcbRestore -h 172.30.0.120 -u administrator -p
Sybex123 -s <path to temp directory>
```

4. Upon completion of the restore from the temporary location process, verify the existence of the files by navigating to datastore or by quickly glancing at the tree view of vCenter Server.

Restoring a Single File from a Full Virtual Machine Backup

Problems in the datacenter are not always as catastrophic as losing an entire virtual machine because of corruption or deletion. In fact, it is probably more common to experience minor issues like corrupted or deleted files. A full virtual machine backup does not have to be restored as a full virtual machine. Using the `mountvm` tool, it is possible to mount a virtual machine hard drive into the file system of the backup proxy (VCB) server. After the hard drive is mounted, it can be browsed the same as any other directory on the server.

PUTTING FILES INTO A VMDK

Files cannot be put directly into a VMDK. Restoring files directly to a virtual machine requires a backup agent installed on the virtual machine.

Let's say that a virtual machine named Server 1 has a full backup that has been completed. An administrator deletes a file named FILE TO RECOVER.txt that was on the desktop of his or her profile on Server 1 and now needs to recover the file. (No, it's not in the Recycle Bin anymore.) Using the `mountvm` command, the VMDK backup of Server 1 can be mounted into the file system of the VCB proxy server, and the file can be recovered. Figure 11.42 shows the `mountvm` command used to mount a backup VMDK named `scsi0-0-0-server1.vmdk` into a mount point named `server1_restore_dir` off the root of the E: drive. Figure 11.47 also shows the Windows Explorer application drilled into the mounted VMDK.

FIGURE 11.47

The mountvm command allows a VMDK backup file to be mounted into the VCB proxy server file system, where it can be browsed in search of files or folders to be recovered.

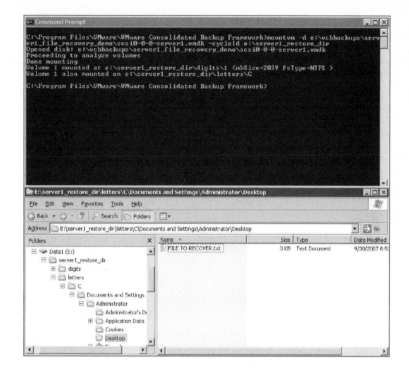

Perform the following steps to conduct a single file restore from a full virtual machine backup:

1. Log in to the VCB proxy, and navigate to the directory holding the backup files for the virtual machine that includes the missing file.

2. Browse the backup directory, and note the name of the VMDK to mount to the VCB file system.

3. Open a command prompt, and change to the C:\Program Files\VMware\VMware Consolidated Backup Framework directory.

4. Enter the following command:

    mountvm -d <name of VMDK to mount> -cycleId <name of   mount point>

5. Browse the file system of the VCB proxy server to find the new mount point. The new mount point will contain a subdirectory named Letters followed by a directory for the drive letter of the VMDK that has been mounted. These directories can now be browsed and manipulated as needed to recover the missing file.

6. After the file or folder recovery is complete, enter the following command:

    mountvm -u <mount point name>

7. Close the command prompt window.

USER DATA BACKUPS IN WINDOWS

Although VCB offers the functionality to mount the virtual machine hard drives for file- or folder-level recovery, I recommend that you back up your custom user data drives and directories on a more regular basis than a full virtual machine backup. In addition to the methods discussed here like the file- and folder-level backups with VCB or third-party backup software like Vizioncore vRanger Pro, there are also tools like Shadow Copies of Shared Folders that are native to the Windows operating system.

Shadow Copies of Shared Folders builds off the Volume Shadow Services available in Windows Server 2003 and newer. It offers scheduled online backups to changes in files that reside in shared folders. The frequency of the schedule determines the number of previous versions that will exist up to the maximum of 63. The value in complementing a VCB and Vizioncore backup strategy with shadow copies is in the restore ease. Ideally, with shadow copies enabled, users can be trained on how to recover deletions and corruptions without involving the IT staff. Only when the previous version is no longer in the list of available restores will the IT staff need to get involved with a single file restore. And for the enterprise-level shadow copy deployment, Microsoft has recently released the System Center Data Protection Manager (SCDPM). SCDPM is a shadow copy on steroids, which is used to provide online frequent backups of files and folders across the entire network.

For more information on Shadow Copies of Shared Folders, visit Microsoft's website at `http://www.microsoft.com/windowsserver2003/techinfo/overview/scr.mspx`.

For more information on System Center Data Protection Manager, visit Microsoft's website at `http://www.microsoft.com/systemcenter/dpm/default.mspx`.

There is another option to use for the restore process, and that is the VMware Converter tools that VMware has built in to the vSphere Server.

Restoring VCB Backups with VMware Converter Enterprise

Perhaps one of the best new features of vCenter Server is the integration of the VMware Converter Enterprise. But to add to its benefit, VMware extended the functionality of the VMware Converter to allow it to perform restores of backups that were made using VMware Consolidated Backup.

During the import process, shown in Figure 11.48, you will need to provide the UNC path to the VMX file for the virtual machine to be restored.

The examples in the previous two figures show the configuration for a backup server named DR1 with a folder that has been shared as MNT. Therefore, the appropriate path for the VMX file of the virtual machine to be restored would be `\\DR1\MNT\192.168.168.8-fullVM\VAC-DC3.vmx`. The remaining steps of the Import Wizard are identical to those outlined in Chapter 7.

This particular feature alone makes vCenter an invaluable tool for building a responsive disaster recovery plan.

With the release of VMware vSphere and specifically the release of the vStorage APIs, VMware has come out with vCenter Disaster Recovery (VCDR).

FIGURE 11.48
The VCB backup files include a VMX file with all the data about the virtual machine.

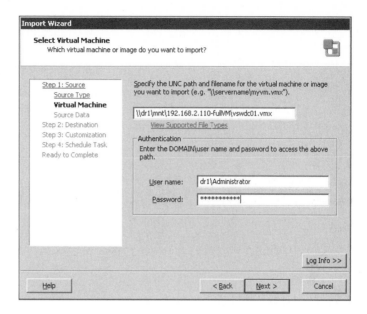

Implementing VMware Data Recovery

VCDR is a disk-based backup and recovery solution. This solution fully integrates with VMware vCenter Server to enable centralized and efficient management backup jobs, and it also includes data deduplication. It is my understanding, at the time of this writing, that VMware Data Recovery will not be a replacement for VCB but rather an enhancement and add-on to vSphere's vCenter Server.

So, how does VCDR work? VMware Data Recovery is composed of three main components. The first component is the VCDR virtual appliance that will manage the backup and recovery process. The second component is the user interface plug-in for VMware vCenter Server. The third and last component is the deduplicated destination storage.

Using the VMware vCenter Server interface, you can pick the virtual machines that you want to protect. You can then schedule the backup job, configure the data retention policy, and select the destination disk that the backup will go to. VMware vCenter Server will then send the job information to the VMware Data Recovery virtual appliance to start the backup process by initiating the point-in-time snapshots of the protected virtual machine. Like its predecessor, VMware Data Recovery frees up network traffic on the LAN by mounting the snapshot directly to the VMware Data Recovery virtual appliance. After the snapshot is mounted, the virtual appliance begins streaming the block-level data directly to the destination storage. It is during this streaming process before the data gets to the destination disks that the VMware Data Recovery appliance will deduplicate the data to ensure the redundant data is eliminated. After all the data has been written to the destination disk, the VMware Data Recovery appliance will then dismount the snapshot and then apply the snapshot to the virtual machine.

The recovery process is a point-in-time file-level or complete system restoration. The VMware Date Recovery virtual appliance will retrieve and stream the specific blocks of data that are needed for the restore. The virtual appliance will efficiently transfer only that data that has changed. This speeds up and streamlines the process. When restoring a single file, or file-level restore, the process is initiated from inside the virtual machine console.

This process in itself is a great improvement from the processes that were needed using VCB. One of my biggest complaints about VCB was the lack of central management, and VCDR really addresses those needs and brings ease of use to the table.

What makes VCDR so much different from VCB is that VCDR plugs into the vStorage APIs to accomplish its tasks. Currently, VCDR is a backup-to-disk product for VMs only, and the appliance does not have an interface to allow for backing up to tape. When using VCB, you can have the backup provider you use with your physical boxes send your backup data to tape, but there is no ability to do the same with the VCDR virtual appliance. Until this restriction has been addressed, VCB will be around for the given future.

VCB allows the use of the same backup software product that you have been running to back up the rest of your physical environment. VCB's life cycle is limited, and VMware has actually taken VCB off its road map for future development. Moving forward, third-party backup software vendors will be updating their solutions to use the new vStorage framework APIs for data protection. These APIs are the framework of the future and not a specific application.

Sometimes when you need to find a solution to a specific problem, you might find the ability to reuse a solution that was designed for something else. Let's take a look at what I call the *office in a box*.

Implementing an Office in a Box

Administrators working in the IT field are expected to find and deploy solutions for problems that they encounter in the field. I do not think we come up with answers to problems but rather solution to problems. These solutions can sometimes be applied to a completely different problem, and the office in a box was one of those solutions.

I have worked in companies that made it a habit to buy or open new offices around the country and the world. After the acquisition was made, the race was on to order equipment, get it shipped to the location, and then get the systems up and running. The typical order cycle would sometime fall way short of what was wanted for the ones leading the charge. This leaves a simple question to ask. What is the quickest way to design, order, and build this new environment? Most of the time, it was an office that was acquired, and the final end result was to fully migrate the original systems to the new environment quickly.

A solution that I designed for this was to create what I call the *office in a box*. I would take a stand-alone server that was fully configured with a VMware ESX/ESXi host and have all the virtual machines that would be needed in an office up and going. There was a domain controller, Microsoft Exchange Server, Microsoft SQL Server, and so on. The idea was to have this confirmation running as a remote site that would be receiving updates from the domain. When the time came that the system was needed, then it would be shipped overnight to the location where it was needed and brought online. Now we have an office that would be fully working in a day. We could start moving data into this site right away, and after the new permanent equipment arrived, it was a very easy process to migrate the virtual machines over and not lose a beat as far as the migration process.

So, how does this fit into disaster recovery? If you do not have a permanent remote datacenter in place, then after a location has been found, you can use this process to help speed up the recovery process. If it takes at least a little time to get your backup tapes delivered, then you can have the infrastructure in place about the same time and will have Active Directory functionality right off the bat. This should give you the appearance of being up and running much quicker.

Now let's take this design and change this just a little. We just got done talking about VCB and VCDR, so what if you took this stand-alone system and used it to receive the virtual machines that were just backed up with VCB and/or VCDR? You would then be able to store a copy of the backups on your systems. When disaster happens, then you could ship this stand-alone system and dramatically decrease your recovery time objectives. Sometimes a solution for one task can open doors as a solution for another task. It is the creativity of the administrator to build on what he already has done to give innovation for something entirely different. Remember, we create solutions, so sometimes you can use what you have and spend time thinking out of the box.

Replicating SANs

The next form of continuity is replication at the SAN level. What used to be a very expensive solution to deploy has become a much more mainstream configuration. The technology to do block-level replication at a SAN level at first was just for the high-end and most expensive SAN solutions but now is a standard configuration in just about all SAN solutions.

To set up this solution, a company would purchase two SANs that would be set up at different locations, and the data would be replicated between the two sites. The replication could occur via the SAN Fibre Channel network or over an IP connection. A snapshot of the LUN would be taken by the SAN, and then the data would be replicated at a block level. The greater the distance between the two sites would also increase the latency or the time the data takes to travel.

The two SANs were communicating with each other via Symmetrix Remote Data Facility (SRDF). SRDF logically pairs a LUN or a group of LUNs from each array and replicates data from one to the other either synchronously or asynchronously. An established pair of LUNs can be split so that separate hosts can access the same data independently and then be resynchronized. This might also be good for backups. Data can be replicated in synchronous or asynchronous mode.

In synchronous mode (SRDF/S), the primary array waits until the secondary array has acknowledged each write before the next write is accepted, ensuring that the replicated copy of the data is always as current as the primary. This is where the resultant latency comes into play and increases significantly with the distance.

Asynchronous SRDF (SRDF/A) transfers to the secondary array in what is known as *contained delta sets*. These contained delta sets are then transferred at defined intervals. Using this method, the remote copy of the data will never be as current as the primary copy, but this method can replicate data over very long distances and with reduced bandwidth requirements.

SRDF is proprietary EMC technology, but the fundamentals will be the same and apply to any SAN or storage vendor. All the vendors will use synchronous or asynchronous replication to move the data between sites. You now also have the ability to sync to more than one remote site at a time, which can give you even greater flexibility when creating your solutions and designs.

Earlier in this chapter I told you that you could not perform HA failover to another site, and as a general rule, this is true, but with SAN replication happening in synchronous mode, you will now be able to do this as long as the distance between the two sites is not too great. If you have two datacenters in different buildings on the same campus, you should be able to use HA to failover to the other building. Your mileage will vary from each of the different storage vendors, but the technology keeps getting better, and the distances keep getting farther.

If you had a real budget for your design and could afford a big enough and private network connection between datacenters, then you have another option. I have seen a WAN accelerator used between two different datacenters across the country and was able to watch a VMotion happen between two different VMware vSphere servers that were 1,000 miles apart. The purpose of mentioning this is that technology keeps changing at such a fast pace. What is not possible this very moment might be just around the corner.

The next big thing to come along in the SAN infrastructure is the ability to do point-in-time restores. The way this works is you have a dedicated disk to be used as the cache that will need to be big enough to hold information for a predetermined amount of time. This time frame could be hours, days, weeks, or months depending on the amount of disk you have provided for this. You know when something major changed in your environment at a specific time. Let's say a virtual machine was deleted by accident. With point-in-time restore, you can dial back in time to right before the virtual machine was deleted. Mount the LUN from that specific moment in time, and restore your virtual machine. This is only one example, and the sky is the limit as far as the practical application of this technology goes.

In this chapter, I discussed that high availability is for increasing uptime, and disaster recovery is for recovery from a problem. The bottom line, to be blunt, is that you better have both in place in your environment. High availability is an important part of any IT shop, and proper thought should be used when creating or designing a solution. You cannot stop there and absolutely must test, test, and test again any solution to make sure that it is working as designed and, most importantly, that it will work when you need it.

The Bottom Line

Understand Windows clustering and the types of clusters. Windows clustering plays a central role in the design of any high availability solution for both virtual and physical servers. Microsoft Windows clustering gives us the ability to have application failover to the secondary server when the primary server fails.

Master It Specifically with regard to Windows clustering in a virtual environment, what are three different types of cluster configurations that you can have?

Understand built-in high-availability options. VMware Virtual Infrastructure has high-availability options built in and available to you out of the box. These options help you provide better uptime for our critical applications.

Master It What are the two types of high-availability options that VMware provides in vSphere?

Understand the differences between VCB and VCDR. VMware has provided some disaster recovery options via backup and restore capability. First there was VMware Consolidated Backup (VCB), and now VMware has introduced VMware Data Center Recovery (VCDR), giving you different options for backing up and restoring your virtual machines.

Master It What are the main differences between VCB and VCDR?

Understand data replication options.   There are other methods to keep continuity in your businesses. Replication of your data to a secondary location is a must to address a company's needs during a real disaster.

> **Master It**   What are three methods to replicate your data to a secondary location as well as the golden rule for any continuity plan?

Chapter 12

Monitoring VMware vSphere Performance

The monitoring of VMware vSphere should be a combination of proactive benchmarking and reactive alarm-based actions. vCenter Server provides both methods to help the administrator keep tabs on each of the virtual machines and hosts as well as the hierarchical objects in the inventory. Using both methods ensures that the administrator is not caught unaware of performance issues or lack of capacity.

vCenter Server provides some exciting new features for monitoring your virtual machines and hosts, such as expanded performance views and charts, and it greatly expands the number and types of alarms available by default. Together, these features make it much easier to manage and monitor VMware vSphere performance.

In this chapter, you will learn to:

◆ Use alarms for proactive monitoring

◆ Work with performance graphs

◆ Gather performance information using command-line tools

◆ Monitor CPU, memory, network, and disk usage by both ESX/ESXi hosts and virtual machines

Overview of Performance Monitoring

Monitoring performance is a key part of every vSphere administrator's job. Fortunately, vCenter Server provides a number of ways to get insight into the behavior of the vSphere environment and the virtual machines running within that environment.

The first tool vCenter Server provides is its alarms mechanism. Alarms can be attached to just about any object within vCenter Server and provide an ideal way to proactively alert the vSphere administrator about potential performance concerns or resource usage. I'll discuss alarms in greater detail later in this chapter in the section "Using Alarms."

Another tool that vCenter Server provides is the Resources pane on the Summary tab of both ESX/ESXi hosts and virtual machines. This Resources pane provides quick "at-a-glance" information on resource usage. This information can be useful as a quick barometer of performance, but for more detailed performance information you will have to search elsewhere—either elsewhere within vCenter Server, as I'll describe later in this chapter, or within the guest operating system itself. Because this tool provides only limited information, I won't discuss it further in this chapter.

Another tool that provides "at-a-glance" performance summary is the Virtual Machines tab, found on vCenter Server objects, datacenter objects, cluster objects, and ESX/ESXi hosts. Figure 12.1 shows the Virtual Machines tab of a cluster object. This tab provides an overview of general performance and resource usage. This information includes CPU utilization, memory usage, and storage space utilized. As with the Resources pane, this information can be useful, but it is quite limited, so I won't discuss it any further in this chapter. However, keep in mind that a quick trip here might help you quickly isolate the one virtual machine that could be causing performance issues for the ESX/ESXi host on which it is running.

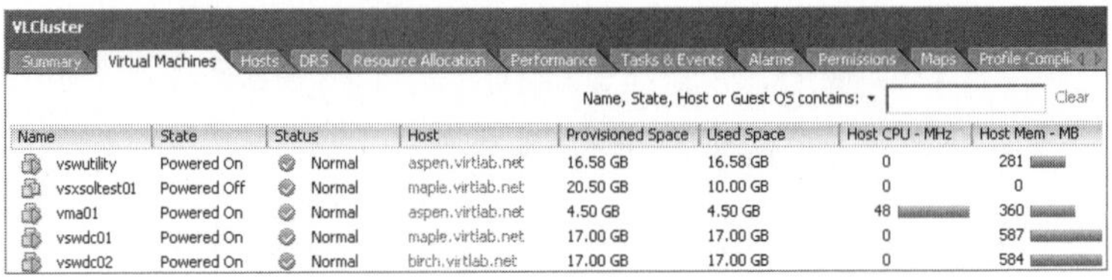

FIGURE 12.1
The Virtual Machines tab of a cluster object offers a quick look at virtual machine CPU and memory usage.

For ESX/ESXi clusters and resource pools, another tool you can use is the Resource Allocation tab. The Resource Allocation tab provides a picture of how CPU and memory resources are being used for the entire pool. This high-level method of looking at resource usage is useful for analyzing overall infrastructure utilization. This tab also provides an easy way of adjusting individual virtual machine or resource pool reservations, limits, and/or shares without editing each object independently.

vCenter Server also offers a very powerful, in-depth tool found on the Performance tab. The Performance tab provides a robust mechanism for creating graphs depicting the actual resource consumption over time for a given ESX/ESXi host or virtual machine. The graphs provide historical information and can be used for trend analysis. vCenter Server provides many objects and counters to analyze the performance of a single virtual machine or host for a selected interval. The Performance tab and the graphs are powerful tools for isolating performance considerations, and I discuss them in greater detail in the section "Working with Performance Graphs."

VMware also provides tools to run at the host level to help isolate and identify problems there. Because these tools require the presence of a Service Console, they work only with VMware ESX and not VMware ESXi. I'll take a look at these tools later in this chapter in the section "Working with Command-Line Tools."

Finally, I'll take the various tools that I've discussed and show how to use them to monitor the four major resources in a VMware vSphere environment: CPU, memory, network, and storage.

Let's get started with a discussion of alarms.

Using Alarms

In addition to the graphs and high-level information tabs, the administrator can create alarms for virtual machines, hosts, networks, and datastores based on predefined triggers provided with vCenter Server. Depending upon the object, these alarms can monitor resource consumption or the state of the object and alert the administrator when certain conditions have been met, such as high resource usage or even low resource usage. These alarms can then provide an action that informs the administrator of the condition by email or SNMP trap. An action can also automatically run a script or provide other means to correct the problem the virtual machine or host might be experiencing.

The creation of alarms to alert the administrator of a specific condition is not new in this version of vCenter Server. But the addition of new triggers, conditions, and actions gives the alarms more usefulness than in previous editions. As you can see in Figure 12.2, the alarms that come with vCenter Server are defined at the topmost object, the vCenter Server object. You'll also note that there are far more predefined alarms in vCenter Server 4 than in previous versions of vCenter Server or VirtualCenter.

FIGURE 12.2

The default alarms for objects in vCenter Server are defined on the vCenter Server object itself.

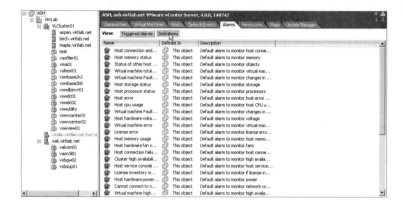

These default alarms are usually generic in nature. Some of the predefined alarms include alarms to alert the administrator if any of the following happen:

◆ A host's storage status, CPU status, voltage, temperature, or power status changes

◆ A cluster experiences a VMware High Availability (HA) error

◆ A datastore runs low on free disk space

◆ A virtual machine's CPU usage, memory usage, disk latency, or even fault tolerance status changes

In addition to the small sampling of predefined alarms I've just described, there are many more, and VMware has enabled users to create alarms on just about any object within vCenter Server. This greatly increases the ability of vCenter Server to proactively alert administrators to changes within the virtual environment before a problem develops.

Because the default alarms are likely too generic for your administrative needs, creating your own alarms is often necessary. Before showing you how to create an alarm, though, I need to first discuss the concept of alarm scope. Once I've discussed alarm scope, I'll walk you through creating a few alarms. Then, in later sections of this chapter, I'll examine the use of those alarms along with other tools to monitor specific types of resource usage.

Understanding Alarm Scopes

When creating alarms, one thing to keep in mind is the *scope* of the alarm. In Figure 12.2, you saw the default set of alarms that are available in vCenter Server. These alarms are defined at the vCenter Server object and thus have the greatest scope—they apply to all objects managed by that vCenter Server instance. It's also possible to create alarms at the datacenter level, the cluster level, the host level, or even the virtual machine level. This allows you, the vSphere administrator, to create specific alarms that are limited in scope and are intended to meet specific monitoring needs.

When you define an alarm on an object, that alarm applies to all objects beneath that object in the vCenter Server hierarchy. The default set of alarms that VMware provides with vCenter Server are defined at the vCenter Server object and therefore apply to all objects—datacenters, hosts, clusters, datastores, networks, and virtual machines—managed by that instance of vCenter

Server. If you were to create an alarm on a resource pool, then the alarm would apply only to virtual machines found in that resource pool. Similarly, if you were to create an alarm on a specific virtual machine, that alarm would apply only to that specific virtual machine.

As you'll see later in this chapter, alarms are also associated with specific types of objects. For example, some alarms apply only to virtual machines, while other alarms apply only to ESX/ESXi hosts. You'll want to use this filtering mechanism to your advantage when creating alarms. For example, if you needed to monitor a particular condition on all ESX/ESXi hosts, you could define a host alarm on the datacenter or vCenter Server object, and it would apply to all ESX/ESXi hosts but not to any virtual machines.

It's important that you keep these scoping effects in mind when defining alarms so that your new alarms work as expected. You don't want to inadvertently exclude some portion of your VMware vSphere environment by creating an alarm at the wrong point in your hierarchy or by creating the wrong type of alarm.

Now you're ready to look at actually creating alarms.

Creating Alarms

As you've already learned, there are many different types of alarms that administrators might want to create. These alarms could be alarms that monitor resource consumption—such as how much CPU time a virtual machine is consuming or how much RAM an ESX/ESXi host has allocated—or these alarms can monitor for specific events, such as whenever a specific distributed virtual port group is modified. In addition, you've already learned that alarms can be created on a variety of different objects within vCenter Server. Regardless of the type of alarm or the type of object to which that alarm is attached, the basic steps for creating an alarm are the same. In the following sections, I'll walk you through creating a couple different alarms so that you have the opportunity to see the options available to you.

CREATING A RESOURCE CONSUMPTION ALARM

First, let's create an alarm that monitors resource consumption. As I discussed in Chapter 7, vCenter Server supports virtual machine snapshots. These snapshots capture a virtual machine at a specific point in time, allowing you to roll back (or revert) to that point-in-time state later. However, snapshots require additional space on disk, and monitoring disk space usage by snapshots was a difficult task in earlier versions of VMware Infrastructure. In vSphere, vCenter Server offers the ability to create an alarm that monitors VM snapshot space.

Before you create a custom alarm, though, you should ask yourself a couple of questions. First, is there an existing alarm that already handles this task for you? Browsing the list of predefined alarms available in vCenter Server shows that although some storage-related alarms are present, there is no alarm that monitors snapshot disk usage. Second, if you're going to create a new alarm, where is the appropriate place within vCenter Server to create that alarm? This refers to the earlier discussion of scope: on what object should you create this alarm so that it is properly scoped and will alert you only under the desired conditions? In this particular case, you'd want to be alerted to any snapshot space usage that exceeds your desired threshold, so a higher-level object such as the datacenter object or even the vCenter Server object would be the best place to create the alarm.

Perform the following steps to create an alarm that monitors VM snapshot disk space usage for all VMs in a datacenter:

1. Launch the vSphere Client if it is not already running, and connect to a vCenter Server instance.

> **YOU MUST USE vCENTER SERVER FOR ALARMS**
>
> You can't create alarms by connecting directly to an ESX/ESXi host; vCenter Server provides the alarm functionality. You must connect to a vCenter Server instance in order to work with alarms.

2. Navigate to an inventory view, such as Hosts And Clusters or VMs And Templates. You can use the menu bar, the navigation bar, or the appropriate keyboard shortcut.

3. Right-click the datacenter object, and select Alarm ➢ Add Alarm.

4. On the General tab in the Alarm Settings dialog box, enter an alarm name and alarm description.

5. Select Virtual Machine from the Monitor drop-down list.

6. Be sure that the radio button marked Monitor For Specific Conditions Or State, For Example, CPU Usage, Power State is selected.

7. On the Triggers tab, click the Add button to add a new trigger.

8. Set Trigger Type to VM Snapshot Size (GB). For this alarm, you're interested in snapshot size only, but other triggers are available:

   ◆ VM Memory Usage (%)

   ◆ VM Network Usage (kbps)

   ◆ VM State

   ◆ VM Heartbeat

   ◆ VM Snapshot Size (GB)

   ◆ VM CPU Ready Time (ms)

9. Ensure that the Condition column is set to Is Above.

10. Set the value in the Warning column to 1.

11. Set the value in the Alert column to 2. Figure 12.3 shows the Triggers tab after changing the Warning and Alert values.

12. On the Reporting tab, leave both the Range value at 0 and the Frequency value at 0. This ensures that the alarm is triggered at the threshold values you've specified and instructs vCenter Server to alert every time the thresholds are exceeded.

> **CAUTION: COUNTER VALUES WILL VARY!**
>
> The Is Above condition is selected most often for identifying a virtual machine, host, or datastore that exceeds a certain threshold. The administrator decides what that threshold should be and what is considered abnormal behavior (or at least interesting enough behavior to be monitored). For the most part, monitoring across ESX/ESXi hosts and datastores will be consistent. For example, administrators will define a threshold that is worthy of being notified about—such as CPU, memory, or

network utilization—and configure an alarm across all hosts for monitoring that counter. Similarly, administrators may define a threshold for datastores, such as the amount of free space available, and configure an alarm across all datastores to monitor that metric.

However, when looking at virtual machine monitoring, it might be more difficult to come up with a single baseline that works for all virtual machines. Specifically, think about enterprise applications that must perform well for extended periods of time. For these types of scenarios, administrators will want custom alarms for earlier notifications of performance problems. This way, instead of reacting to a problem, administrators can proactively try to prevent problems from occurring.

For virtual machines with similar functions like domain controllers and DNS servers, it might be possible to establish baselines and thresholds covering all such infrastructure servers. In the end, the beauty of vCenter Server's alarms is in the flexibility to be as customized and as granular as each individual organization needs.

FIGURE 12.3
On the Triggers tab, define the conditions that cause the alarm to activate.

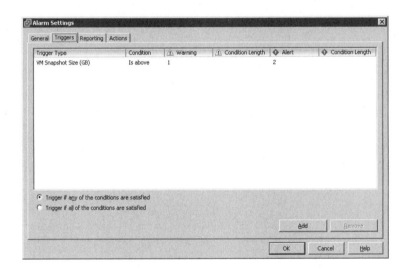

13. On the Actions tab, specify any additional actions that should be taken when the alarm is triggered. Some of the actions that can be taken include the following:

 ◆ Send a notification email.

 ◆ Send a notification trap via SNMP.

 ◆ Change the power state on a VM.

 ◆ Migrate a VM.

 ◆ If you leave the Actions tab empty, then the alarm will alert administrators only within the vSphere Client. For now, leave the Actions tab empty.

CONFIGURING VCENTER SERVER FOR EMAIL AND SNMP NOTIFICATIONS

To have vCenter Server send an email for a triggered alarm, you must configure vCenter Server with an SMTP server. To configure the SMTP server, from the vSphere Client choose the Administration menu, and then select vCenter Server Settings. Click Mail in the list on the left, and then supply the SMTP server and the sender account. I recommend using a recognizable sender account so that when you receive an email, you know it came from the vCenter Server computer. You might use something like vcenter-alerts@vmwarelab.net.

Similarly, to have vCenter Server send an SNMP trap, you must configure the SNMP receivers in the same vCenter Server Settings dialog box under SNMP. You may specify from one to four management receivers to monitor for traps.

---

14. Click OK to create the alarm

The alarm is now created. To view the alarm you just created, select the datacenter object from the inventory tree on the left, and then click the Alarms tab on the right. Select Definitions instead of Triggered Alarms, and you'll see your new alarm listed, like in Figure 12.4.

FIGURE 12.4
The Defined In column shows where an alarm was defined.

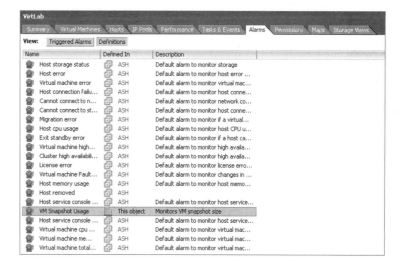

USING RANGE AND FREQUENCY WITH ALARMS

Let's create another alarm. This time you'll create an alarm that takes advantage of the Range and Frequency parameters on the Reporting tab. With the VM snapshot alarm, these parameters didn't really make any sense; all you really needed was just to be alerted when the snapshot size exceeded a certain size. With other types of alarms, it may make sense to take advantage of these parameters.

The Range parameter specifies a tolerance percentage above or below the configured threshold. For example, the built-in alarm for virtual machine CPU usage specifies a warning threshold of 75 percent but specifies a range of 0. This means that the trigger will activate the alarm at exactly 75 percent. However, if the Range parameter were set to 5 percent, then the trigger would not activate the alarm until 80 percent (75 percent threshold + 5 percent tolerance range). This helps prevent alarm states from transitioning because of false changes in a condition by providing a range of tolerance.

The Frequency parameter controls the period of time during which a triggered alarm is not reported again. Using the built-in VM CPU usage alarm as our example, the Frequency parameter is set, by default, to five minutes. This means that a virtual machine whose CPU usage triggers the activation of the alarm won't get reported again—assuming the condition or state is still true—for five minutes.

With that information in mind, let's walk through another example of creating an alarm. This time you'll create an alarm that alerts based on VM network usage.

Perform the following steps to create an alarm that is triggered based on VM network usage:

1. Launch the vSphere Client if it is not already running, and connect to a vCenter Server instance.

2. Navigate to an inventory view, such as Hosts And Clusters or VMs And Templates.

3. Select the datacenter object from the inventory tree on the left.

4. Select the Alarms tab from the content pane on the right.

5. Select the Definitions button just below the tab bar to show alarm definitions instead of triggered alarms.

6. Right-click in a blank area of the content pane on the right, and select New Alarm.

7. Supply an alarm name and description.

8. Set the Monitor drop-down list to Virtual Machines.

9. Select the radio button marked Monitor For Specific Conditions Or State, For Example, CPU Usage, Power State.

10. On the Triggers tab, click Add to add a new trigger.

11. Set the Trigger Type column to VM Network Usage (kbps).

12. Set Condition to Is Above.

13. Set the value of the Warning column to 500, and leave the Condition Length setting at five minutes.

14. Set the value of the Alert column to 1000, and leave the Condition Length setting at five minutes.

15. On the Reporting tab, set Range to 10 percent, and set the Frequency parameter to five minutes.

16. Don't add anything on the Actions tab. Click OK to create the alarm.

Alarms can have more than just one trigger condition. The alarms you've created so far had only a single trigger condition. For an example of an alarm that has more than one trigger condition, look at the built-in alarm for monitoring host connection state. Figure 12.5 shows the two trigger conditions for this alarm. Note that the radio button marked Trigger If All Of The Conditions Are Satisfied is selected, ensuring that only powered-on hosts that are not responding will trigger the alarm.

FIGURE 12.5
You can combine multiple triggers to create more complex alarms.

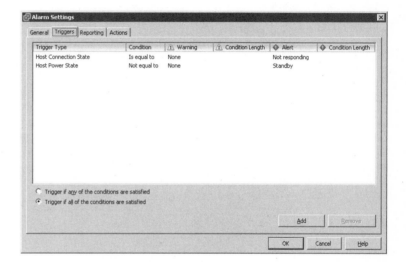

It might seem obvious, but it's important to note that you can have more than one alarm for an object.

As with any new alarm, testing its functionality is crucial to make sure you get the desired results. You might find that the thresholds you configured are not optimized for your environment and either aren't activating the alarm when they should or are activating the alarm when they shouldn't. In these cases, edit the alarm to set the thresholds and conditions appropriately. Or, if the alarm is no longer needed, right-click the alarm, and choose Remove to delete the alarm.

You'll be able to edit or delete alarms only if two conditions are met. First, the user account with which you've connected to vCenter Server must have the appropriate permissions granted in order to edit or delete alarms. Second, you must be attempting to edit or delete the alarm from the object on which it was defined. Think back to my discussion on alarm scope, and this makes sense. You can't delete an alarm from the datacenter object when that alarm was defined on the vCenter Server object. You must go to the object where the alarm is defined in order to edit or delete the alarm.

Now that you've seen some examples of creating alarms—and keep in mind that creating alarms for other objects within vCenter Server follows the same basic steps—let's take a look at managing alarms.

Managing Alarms

Several times so far in this chapter I've directed you to the Alarms tab within the vSphere Client. Up until now, you've been working with the Definitions view of the Alarms tab, looking at defined alarms. There is, however, another view to the Alarms tab, and that's the Triggered Alarms view. Figure 12.6 shows the Triggered Alarms view, which is accessed using the Triggered Alarms button just below the tab bar.

FIGURE 12.6
The Triggered Alarms view shows the alarms that vCenter Server has activated.

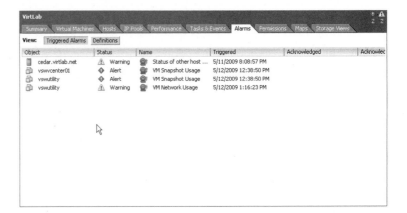

GETTING TO THE TRIGGERED ALARMS VIEW QUICKLY

The vSphere Client provides a handy shortcut to get to the Triggered Alarms view for a particular object quickly. When an object has at least one triggered alarm, small icons appear in the upper-right corner of the content pane for that object. You can see these icons in Figure 12.6. Clicking these icons takes you to the Triggered Alarms view for that object.

The Triggered Alarms view shows all the activated alarms for the selected object and all child objects. In Figure 12.6, the datacenter object was selected, so the Triggered Alarms view shows all activated alarms for all the objects under the datacenter. In this instance, the Triggered Alarms view shows four alarms: one host alarm and three virtual machine alarms.

However, if only the virtual machine had been selected, the Triggered Alarms view on the Alarms tab for that virtual machine would show only the two activated alarms for that particular virtual machine. This makes it easy to isolate the specific alarms you need to address.

After you are in Triggered Alarms view for a particular object, a couple of actions are available to you for each of the activated alarms. For alarms that monitor resource consumption (that is, the alarm definition uses the Monitor For Specific Conditions Or State, For Example, CPU Usage, Power State setting selected under Alarm Type on the General tab), you have the option to acknowledge the alarm. To acknowledge the alarm, right-click the alarm, and select Acknowledge Alarm.

When an alarm is acknowledged, vCenter Server records the time the alarm was acknowledged and the user account that acknowledged the alarm. As long as the alarm condition persists, the alarm will remain in the Triggered Alarms view but is grayed out. When the alarm condition is resolved, the activated alarm disappears.

For an alarm that monitors events (this would be an alarm that has the Monitor For Specific Events Occurring On This Object, For Example, VM Powered On option selected under Alarm Type on the General tab), you can either acknowledge the alarm, as described previously, or reset the alarm status to green. Figure 12.7 illustrates this option.

FIGURE 12.7
For event-based alarms, you also have the option to reset the alarm status to green.

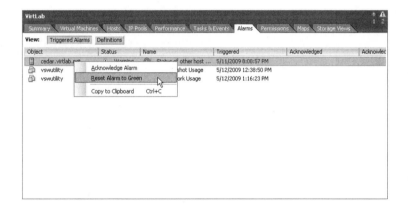

Resetting an alarm to green removes the activated alarm from the Triggered Alarms view, even if the underlying event that activated the alarm hasn't actually been resolved. This behavior makes sense if you think about it. Alarms that monitor events are merely responding to an event being logged by vCenter Server; whether the underlying condition has been resolved is unknown. So, resetting the alarm to green just tells vCenter Server to act as if the condition has been resolved. Of course, if the event occurs again, the alarm will be triggered again.

Now that you've looked at alarms for proactive performance monitoring, let's move on to using vCenter Server's performance graphs to view even more information about the behavior of virtual machines and ESX/ESXi hosts in your VMware vSphere environment.

Working with Performance Graphs

Alarms are a great tool for alerting administrators of specific conditions or events, but alarms don't provide the detailed information that administrators sometimes need to have. This is where vCenter Server's performance graphs come in. vCenter Server has many new and updated features for creating and analyzing graphs. Without these graphs, analyzing the performance of a virtual machine would be nearly impossible. Installing agents inside a virtual machine will not provide accurate details about the server's behavior or resource consumption. The reason for this is elementary: a virtual machine is configured only with virtual devices. Only the VMkernel knows the exact amount of resource consumption for any of those devices because it acts as the arbitrator between the virtual hardware and the physical hardware. In most virtual environments, the virtual machines' virtual devices can outnumber the actual physical hardware devices, necessitating the complex sharing and scheduling abilities in the VMkernel.

By clicking the Performance tab for a datacenter, cluster, host, or virtual machine, you can learn a wealth of information. Before you use these graphs to help analyze resource consumption, I need to help you get to know the performance graphs and legends. I'll start with covering the two different layouts available in performance graphs: the overview layout and the advanced layout. First up is the overview layout.

Overview Layout

The Overview layout is the default view when you access the Performance tab. Figure 12.8 shows you the Overview layout of the Performance tab for an ESX host. Note the horizontal and vertical scrollbars; there's a lot more information here than the vSphere Client can fit in a single screen.

FIGURE 12.8
The Overview layout provides information on a range of performance counters.

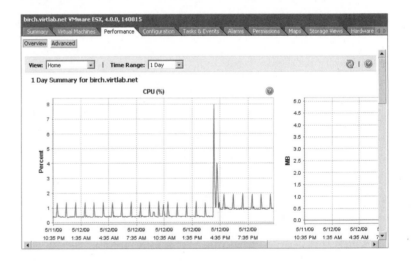

At the top of the Overview layout are options to change the view or to change the date range. The contents of the View drop-down list change depending upon the object you select in the vSphere Client. Table 12.1 lists the different options available, depending upon what type of object you select in the vSphere Client.

Next to the View drop-down list is an option to change the date range for the data currently displayed in the various performance graphs. This allows you to set the time range to a day, a week, a month, or a custom value.

In the upper-right corner of the Overview layout, you'll see a button for refreshing the display and a button for getting help.

Below the gray title bar (where you'll find the View and Time Range drop-down lists, the Refresh button, and the Help button) are the actual performance graphs. The layout and the graphs that are included vary based on the object selected and the option chosen in the View drop-down list. I don't have the room here to list all of them, but a couple of them are shown in Figure 12.9 and Figure 12.10. I encourage you to explore a bit and find the layouts that work best for you.

TABLE 12.1:   View Options on the Performance Tab

IF YOU ARE VIEWING THE PERFORMANCE TAB FOR THIS KIND OF OBJECT . . .	THE VIEW DROP-DOWN LIST CONTAINS THESE OPTIONS:
Datacenter	Clusters Storage
Cluster	Home Resource Pools & Virtual Machines Hosts
Resource pool	Home Resource Pools & Virtual Machines
Host	Home Virtual Machines
Virtual machine	Home Fault Tolerance Storage

FIGURE 12.9

The Performance tab for an ESX/ESXi host in Overview layout includes eight charts, many of which are shown off-screen.

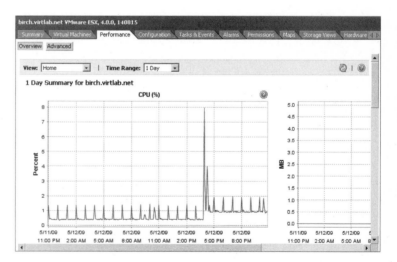

The Overview layout works well if you need a broad overview of the performance data for a datacenter, cluster, resource pool, host, or virtual machine. But what if you need more specific data in a more customizable format? The Advanced layout is the answer, as you'll see in the next section.

Advanced Layout

Figure 12.11 shows the Advanced layout of the Performance tab for a cluster of ESX/ESXi hosts. Here, in the Advanced layout, is where the real power of vCenter Server's performance graphs is made available to you.

FIGURE 12.10
The Storage view of the Performance tab for a virtual machine in Overview layout displays a breakdown of storage utilization.

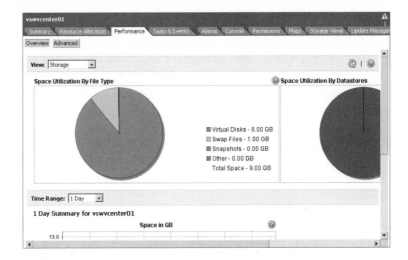

FIGURE 12.11
The Advanced layout of the Performance tab provides much more extensive controls for viewing performance data.

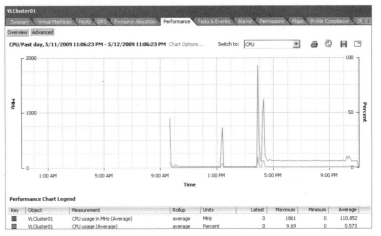

Starting from the top left, you'll see the name of the object being monitored. Just below that is the type of the chart and the time range. The Chart Options link provides access to customize settings for the chart. To the right, you'll find a drop-down list to quickly switch graph settings, followed by buttons to print the chart, refresh the chart, save the chart, or view the chart as a pop-up chart. The Print button allows you to print the chart; the Save button allows you to export the chart as a JPEG graphic. I'll discuss this functionality in the section "Saving Performance Graphs." The Refresh button refreshes the data. The pop-up button opens the chart in a new window. This allows you to navigate elsewhere in the vSphere Client while still keeping a performance graph open in a separate window. Pop-up charts also make it easy to compare one ESX/ESXi host or virtual machine with another host or virtual machine. On each side of the graph are units of measure. In Figure 12.13, the counters selected are measured in percentages and megahertz. Depending on the counters chosen, there may be only one unit of measurement, but no more than two. Next, on the horizontal axis, is the time interval. Below that, the Performance Chart Legend provides color-coded keys to help the user find a specific object or item of interest. This area also breaks down the graph into the object being measured; the measurement being used; the units of measure; and the Latest, Maximum, Minimum, and Average measurements recorded for that object.

Hovering the mouse pointer over the graph at a particular recorded interval of interest displays the data points at that specific moment in time.

Another nice feature of the graphs is the ability to emphasize a specific object so that it is easier to pick out this object from the other objects. By clicking the specific key at the bottom, the key and its color representing a specific object will be emphasized, while the other keys and their respective colors become lighter and less visible. For simple charts such as the one shown previously in Figure 12.11, this might not be very helpful. For busier charts with many performance counters, this feature is very useful.

Now that you have a feel for the Advanced layout, take a closer look at the Chart Options link. This link exposes vCenter Server's functionality in creating highly customized performance graphs. Figure 12.12 shows the Customize Performance Chart dialog box. This dialog box is the central place where you will come to customize vCenter Server's performance graphs. From here, you select the counters to view, the time ranges, and the kind of graph (line graph or stacked graph) to display.

FIGURE 12.12
The Customize Performance Chart dialog box offers tremendous flexibility to create exactly the performance graph you need.

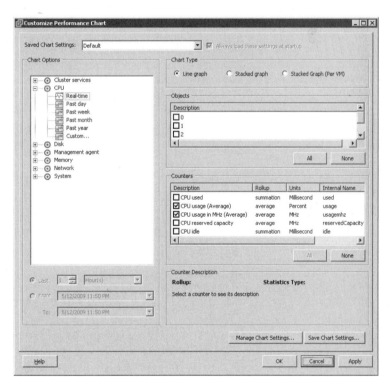

Because there is so much information available in the Customize Performance Chart dialog box, I've grouped the various options and types of information into the sections that follow.

CHOOSING A RESOURCE TYPE

On the left side of the Customize Performance Chart dialog box, you can choose which resource (Cluster Services, CPU, Disk, Management agent, Memory, Network, or System) to monitor or analyze. The actual selections available in this area change depending upon the type of object that you have selected in vCenter Server. That is, the options available when viewing the Performance tab for an ESX/ESXi host are different from the options available when viewing the Performance tab of a virtual machine, a cluster, or a datacenter.

Within each of these resources, different objects and counters are available. Be aware that other factors affect what objects and counters are available to view; for example, in some cases the real-time interval shows more objects and counters than other intervals. The next few sections list the various counters that are available for the different resource types in the Customize Performance Chart dialog box.

If a particular counter is new to you, click it to highlight the counter. At the bottom of the dialog box, in a section called Counter Description, you'll see a description of the counter. This can help you determine which counters are most applicable in any given situation.

SETTING A CUSTOM INTERVAL

Within each of the resource types, you have a choice of intervals to view. Some objects offer a Real-Time option; this option shows what is happening with that resource right now. The others are self-explanatory. The Custom option allows you to specify exactly what you'd like to see on the performance graph. For example, you could specify that you'd like to see performance data for the last eight hours. Having all of these interval options allows you to choose exactly the right interval necessary to view the precise data you're seeking.

VIEWING CPU PERFORMANCE INFORMATION

If you select the CPU resource type in the Chart Options section of the Customize Performance Chart dialog box, you can choose what specific objects and counters you'd like to see in the performance graph. Note that the CPU resource type is not available when viewing the Performance tab of a datacenter object. It is available for clusters, ESX/ESXi hosts, resource pools, and individual virtual machines.

Table 12.2 lists the objects and counters available for CPU performance information. Because CPU performance counters are not available at the datacenter object, the DC column is shaded. Not all these counters are available with all display intervals.

Quite a bit of CPU performance information is available. In the section "Monitoring CPU Usage," I'll discuss how to use these CPU performance objects and counters to monitor CPU usage.

VIEWING MEMORY PERFORMANCE INFORMATION

If you select the memory resource type in the Chart Options section of the Customize Performance Chart dialog box, different objects and counters are available for display in the performance graph. The memory resource type is not available when viewing the Performance tab of a datacenter object. It is available for clusters, ESX/ESXi hosts, resource pools, and individual virtual machines.

In Table 12.3 you'll find the objects and counters available for memory performance information, depending upon the inventory object and display interval selected. As in Table 12.2, the DC column is shaded because memory counters are not available at the datacenter object. Not all these objects are available with all display intervals.

Later, in the section "Monitoring Memory Usage," you'll get the opportunity to use these different objects and counters to monitor how ESX/ESXi and virtual machines are using memory.

TABLE 12.2:   Available CPU Performance Counters

COUNTER	DC	CL	ESX	RP	VM
CPU used		✓	✓	✓	✓
CPU usage (Average)			✓		✓
CPU usage in MHz (Average)		✓	✓	✓	✓
CPU reserved capacity			✓		
CPU idle			✓		✓
CPU ready					✓
CPU system					✓
CPU wait					✓
Cluster total				✓	
CPU entitlement				✓	✓

VIEWING DISK PERFORMANCE INFORMATION

Disk performance is another key area that vSphere administrators need to monitor. Table 12.4 shows you the performance counters that are available for disk performance. Note that these counters aren't supported for datacenters, clusters, and resource pools, but they are supported for ESX/ESXi hosts and virtual machines. I've shaded the DC, CL, and RP columns in Table 12.4 because these counters are not available for datacenter, cluster, or resource pool objects. Not all counters are visible in all display intervals.

You'll use these counters in the section "Monitoring Disk Usage" later in this chapter.

VIEWING NETWORK PERFORMANCE INFORMATION

To monitor network performance, the vCenter Server performance graphs cover a wide collection of performance counters. Network performance counters are available only for ESX/ESXi hosts and virtual machines; they are not available for datacenter objects, clusters, or resource pools.

Table 12.5 shows the different network performance counters that are available. The DC, CL, and RP columns are shaded because network performance counters are not available for datacenter, cluster, and resource pool objects.

You'll use these network performance counters in the "Monitoring Network Usage" section later in this chapter.

VIEWING SYSTEM PERFORMANCE INFORMATION

ESX/ESXi hosts and virtual machines also offer some performance counters in the System resource type. Datacenters, clusters, and resource pools do not support any system performance counters.

TABLE 12.3:   Available Memory Performance Counters

COUNTER	DC	CL	ESX	RP	VM
Memory usage (Average)		✓	✓		✓
Memory overhead (Average)		✓	✓	✓	✓
Memory consumed (Average)		✓	✓	✓	✓
Memory total		✓			
Memory shared common (Average)			✓		
Memory granted (Average)			✓		✓
Memory balloon (Average)			✓		✓
Memory shared (Average)			✓		✓
Memory swap in (Average)			✓		✓
Memory active (Average)			✓		✓
Memory zero (Average)			✓		✓
Memory heap (Average)			✓		
Swap out rate			✓		✓
Memory state			✓		
Memory unreserved (Average)			✓		
Memory reserved capacity			✓		
Memory used by VMkernel			✓		
Swap in rate			✓		✓
Memory swap out (Average)			✓		✓
Available heap memory			✓		
Memory swap used (Average)			✓		
Memory entitlement				✓	
Memory balloon target (Average)					✓
Memory swap target (Average)					✓
Memory swapped (Average)					✓

More information on the system performance counters is available in Table 12.6. Because system performance counters are not available for datacenter, cluster, and resource pool objects, these columns are shaded in Table 12.6.

TABLE 12.4:   Available Disk Performance Counters

COUNTER	DC	CL	ESX	RP	VM
Kernel disk command latency			✓		
Disk read rate			✓		✓
Physical device command latency			✓		
Queue write latency			✓		
Disk commands issued			✓		✓
Physical device read latency			✓		
Disk write requests			✓		✓
Kernel disk read latency			✓		
Disk write latency			✓		
Stop disk command			✓		✓
Disk write rate			✓		✓
Queue command latency			✓		
Disk bus resets			✓		✓
Disk command latency			✓		
Disk read latency			✓		
Disk read requests			✓		✓
Queue read latency			✓		
Kernel disk write latency			✓		
Physical device write latency			✓		
Disk usage (Average)			✓		✓
Highest disk latency			✓		

TABLE 12.5: Available Network Performance Counters

COUNTER	DC	CL	ESX	RP	VM
Network data receive rate			✓		✓
Network packets received			✓		✓
droppedRx			✓		
Network usage (Average)			✓		✓
Network packets transmitted			✓		✓
droppedTx			✓		
Network data transmit rate			✓		✓

The majority of these counters are valid only for ESX/ESXi hosts, and they all center around how resources are allocated or how the ESX/ESXi host itself is consuming CPU resources or memory. As such, I won't be discussing them in any greater detail later in this chapter. I've included them here for the sake of completeness.

VIEWING OTHER PERFORMANCE COUNTERS

These are the other available performance counter types:

◆ ESX/ESXi hosts also offer a resource type (found in the Customize Performance Chart dialog box in the Chart Options section) marked as Management Agent. This resource type has only two performance counters associated with it: Memory used (Average) and Memory swap used (Average). These counters monitor how much memory the vCenter Server agent is using on the ESX/ESXi host.

◆ ESX/ESXi hosts participating in a cluster also have a resource type of Cluster Services, with two performance counters: CPU fairness and Memory fairness. Both of these counters show the distribution of resources within a cluster.

◆ The datacenter object contains a resource type marked as Virtual Machine Operations. This resource type contains performance counters that simply monitor the number of times a particular VM operation has occurred. This includes VM power-on events, VM power-off events, VM resets, VMotion operations, and Storage VMotion operations.

I've included this brief description of these counters for the sake of completeness, but I won't be discussing them any further.

MANAGING CHART SETTINGS

There's one more area of the Customize Performance Chart dialog box that I'll discuss, and that's the Manage Chart Settings and Save Chart Settings buttons in the lower-right corner.

TABLE 12.6:   Available System Performance Counters

COUNTER	DC	CL	ESX	RP	VM
Resource CPU usage (Average)			✓		
Resource memory allocation maximum (in KB)			✓		
Resource CPU running (1 min. average)			✓		
Resource memory overhead			✓		
Resource memory mapped			✓		
Resource memory shared			✓		
Resource memory swapped			✓		
Resource memory zero			✓		
Resource memory share saved			✓		
Resource memory touched			✓		
Resource allocation minimum (in KB)			✓		
Resource CPU maximum limited (1 min.)			✓		
Resource CPU allocation (in MHz)			✓		
Resource CPU active (5 min. average)			✓		
Resource CPU allocation maximum (in MHz)			✓		
Resource CPU running (5 min. average)			✓		
Resource CPU active (1 min. average)			✓		
Resource CPU maximum limited (5 min.)			✓		
Resource CPU allocation shares			✓		
Resource memory allocation shares			✓		
Uptime			✓		✓
cosDiskUsage			✓		
Heartbeat					✓

After you've gone through and selected the resource type, display interval, objects, and performance counters that you'd like to see in the performance graph, you can save that collection of chart settings using the Save Chart Settings button. vCenter Server prompts you to enter a name for the saved chart settings. After a chart setting is saved, you can easily access it again from the drop-down list at the top of the performance graph advanced layout. Figure 12.13 shows the Switch To drop-down list, where two custom chart settings—VM Activity and Cluster Resources—are shown. By selecting either of these from the Switch To drop-down list, you can quickly switch to those settings. This allows you to define the performance charts that you need to see and then quickly switch between them.

FIGURE 12.13

You can access saved chart settings from the Switch To drop-down list.

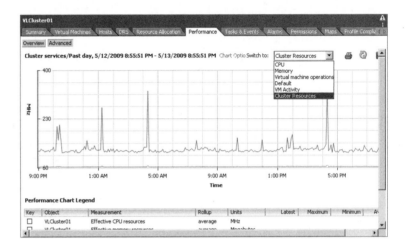

The Manage Chart Settings button allows you to delete chart settings you've saved but no longer need.

In addition to offering you the option of saving the chart settings, vCenter Server also allows you to save the graph.

SAVING PERFORMANCE GRAPHS

When I first introduced you to the Advanced layout view of the Performance tab, I briefly mentioned the Save button. This button, found in the upper-right corner of the Advanced layout, allows you to save the results of the performance graph to an external file for long-term archiving, analysis, or reporting.

When you click the Save button, a standard Windows Save dialog box appears. You have the option of choosing where to save the resulting file as well as the option of saving the chart either as a graphic file or as a Microsoft Excel spreadsheet. If you are going to perform any additional analysis, the option to save the chart data as an Excel spreadsheet is quite useful. The graphics options are useful when you need to put the performance data into a report of some sort.

There's a lot of information exposed via vCenter Server's performance graphs. I'll revisit the performance graphs again in the sections on monitoring specific types of resources later in this chapter, but first I'll introduce you to a few command-line tools you might also find useful in gathering performance information.

Working with Command-Line Tools

In addition to alarms and performance graphs, VMware also provides a couple command-line utilities to help with monitoring performance and resource usage. Unless stated otherwise, these tools work only with VMware ESX and not VMware ESXi, because they rely upon the presence of the Linux-based Service Console present only with VMware ESX.

Using esxtop

You can also monitor virtual machine performance using a command-line tool named esxtop. A great reason to use esxtop is the immediate feedback it gives you after you adjust a virtual machine. Using esxtop, you can monitor all four major resource types (CPU, disk, memory, and network) on a particular ESX host. Figure 12.14 shows some sample output from esxtop.

FIGURE 12.14
esxtop shows real-time information on CPU, disk, memory, and network utilization.

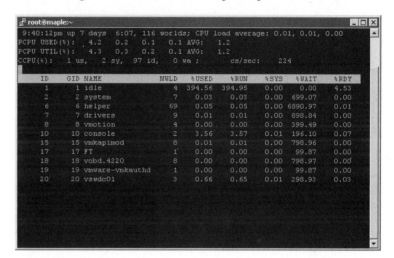

---

esxtop Is ONLY FOR VMware ESX

Because esxtop runs in the Linux-based Service Console, it works only on VMware ESX and not VMware ESXi. VMware supplies a separate tool called resxtop that supports VMware ESXi. I discuss that tool later in this section.

Upon launch, esxtop defaults to showing CPU utilization, as illustrated in Figure 12.14. At the top of the screen are summary statistics; below that are statistics for specific virtual machines and VMkernel processes. To show only virtual machines, press V. Be aware that esxtop, like many Linux commands you'll find in the ESX Service Console, is case sensitive, so you'll need to be sure to use an uppercase V in order to toggle the display of VMs only.

Two CPU counters of interest to view with esxtop are the CPU Used (%USED) and Ready Time (%RDY). You can also see these counters in the virtual machine graphs, but with esxtop they are calculated as percentages. The %WAIT counter is also helpful in determining whether you have overallocated CPU resources to the VM. This might be the case if, for example, you've allocated two vCPUs to a virtual machine that really needs a single vCPU only. While in CPU mode, you can also press lowercase e to expand a virtual machine's CPU statistics so that you can see the different components that are using CPU time on behalf of a virtual machine. This is quite useful in determining what components of a virtual machine may be taking up CPU capacity.

If you switch away to another resource, press C (uppercase or lowercase) to come back to the CPU counters display. At any time when you are finished with esxtop, you can simply press q (lowercase only) to exit the utility and return to the Service Console shell prompt.

---

esxtop SHOWS SINGLE HOSTS ONLY

Remember, esxtop shows only a single ESX host. In an environment where VMotion, VMware Distributed Resource Scheduler (DRS), and VMware High Availability (HA) have been deployed, virtual machines may move around often. Making reservation or share changes while the virtual machine is currently on one ESX host may not have the desired consequences if the virtual machine is moved to another server and the mix of virtual machines on that server represents different performance loads.

To monitor memory usage with esxtop, press m (lowercase only). This gives you real-time statistics about the ESX host's memory usage in the top portion and the virtual machines' memory usage in the lower section. As with CPU statistics, you can press V (uppercase only) to show only virtual machines. This helps you weed out VMkernel resources when you are trying to isolate a problem with a virtual machine. The %ACTV counter, which shows current active guest physical memory, is a useful counter, as are the %ACTVS (slow moving average for long-term estimates), %ACTVF (fast moving average for short-term estimates), %ACTVN (prediction of %ACTV at next sampling), and SWCUR (current swap usage) counters.

To monitor network statistics about the vmnics, individual virtual machines, or VMkernel ports used for iSCSI, VMotion, and NFS, press n (lowercase only). The columns showing network usage include packets transmitted and received and megabytes transmitted and received for each vmnic or port. Also shown in the DNAME column are the vSwitches or dvSwitches and, to the left, what is plugged into them, including virtual machines, VMkernel, and Service Console ports. If a particular virtual machine is monopolizing the vSwitch, you can look at the amount of network traffic on a specific switch and the individual ports to see which virtual machine is the culprit. Unlike other esxtop views, you can't use V (uppercase only) here to show only virtual machines.

To monitor disk I/O statistics about each of the SCSI controllers, press d (lowercase only). Like some other views, you can press V (uppercase only) to show only virtual machines. The columns labeled READS/s, WRITES/s, MBREAD/s, and MBWRTN/s are most often used to determine disk loads. Those columns show loads based on reads and writes per second and megabytes read and written per second.

The esxtop command also lets you view CPU interrupts by pressing i. This command will show you the device(s) using the interrupt and is a great way to identify VMkernel devices, such as a vmnic, that might be sharing an interrupt with the Service Console. This sort of interrupt sharing can impede performance.

Another great feature of esxtop is the ability to capture performance data for a short period of time and then play back that data. Using the command vm-support, you can set an interval and duration for the capture.

Perform the following steps to capture data to be played back on esxtop:

1. Using PuTTY (Windows) or a terminal window (Mac OS X or Linux), open an SSH session to an ESX host.

2. Enter the su – command to assume root privileges.

3. While logged in as root or after switching to the root user, change your working directory to /tmp by issuing the command cd /tmp.

4. Enter the command vm-support -S -i 10 -d 180. This creates an esxtop snapshot, capturing data every 10 seconds, for the duration of 180 seconds.

5. The resulting file is a tarball and is gzipped. It must be extracted with the command tar -xzf esx*.tgz. This creates a vm-support directory that is called in the next command.

6. Run esxtop -R /vm-support* to replay the data for analysis.

For command-line junkies, esxtop is a great tool. Unfortunately, it's limited to VMware ESX because it relies upon the Linux-based Service Console. However, VMware does have a tool for performing some of the same tasks with ESXi. It's a tool called resxtop.

Using resxtop

Because VMware ESXi lacks a user-accessible Service Console where you can execute scripts, you can't use "traditional" esxtop with VMware ESXi. Instead, you have to use "remote" esxtop, or resxtop. The resxtop command is included with the vSphere Management Assistant (vMA), a special virtual appliance available from VMware that provides a command-line interface for managing both VMware ESX and VMware ESXi hosts.

Using resxtop is much the same as using esxtop. Before you can actually view real-time performance data, though, you first have to tell resxtop which remote server you want to use. To launch resxtop and connect to a remote server, enter this command:

```
resxtop --server esx1.vmwarelab.net
```

You'll want to replace esx1.vmwarelab.net with the appropriate hostname or IP address of the ESX/ESXi host to which you want to connect. When prompted, supply a username and password, and then resxtop will launch. Once resxtop is running, you can use the same command to switch between the various views.

Now that I've shown you the various tools that you will use to monitor performance in a VMware vSphere environment, let's go through the four major resources—CPU, RAM, network, and disk—and see how to monitor the usage of these resources.

Monitoring CPU Usage

When monitoring a virtual machine, it's always a good starting point to keep an eye on CPU consumption. Many virtual machines started out in life as underperforming physical servers. One of VMware's most successful sales pitches is being able to take all those lackluster physical boxes that are not busy and convert them to virtual machines. Once converted, virtual infrastructure managers tend to think of these virtual machines as simple, lackluster, and low-utilization servers with nothing to worry over or monitor. The truth, though, is quite the opposite.

When the server was physical, it had an entire box to itself. Now it must share its resources with many other workloads. In aggregate, they represent quite a load, and if some or many of them become somewhat busy, they contend with each other for the finite capabilities of the ESX/ESXi host on which they run. Of course, they don't know they are contending for resources, but the VMkernel hypervisor tries to placate them. Virtual CPUs need to be scheduled, and ESX/ESXi does a remarkable job given that there are more virtual machines than physical processors most of the time. Still, the hypervisor can do only so much with the resources it has, and invariably there comes a time when the applications running in that virtual machine need more CPU time than the host can give.

When this happens, it's usually the application owner who notices first and raises the alarm with the system administrators. Now the vSphere administrators have the task of determining why this virtual machine is underperforming. Fortunately, vCenter Server provides a number of tools that make monitoring and analysis easier. These are the tools you've already seen: alarms, performance graphs, and command-line utilities.

Let's begin with a hypothetical scenario. A help desk ticket has been submitted indicating that an application owner isn't getting the expected level of performance on a particular server, which in this case is a virtual machine. As the vSphere administrator, you need to first delve deeper into the problem and ask as many questions as necessary to discover what the application owner needs to be satisfied with performance. Some performance issues are subjective, meaning some users might complain about the slowness of their applications, but they have no objective benchmark for such a claim. Other times, this is reflected in a specific benchmark, such as the number of transactions by a database server or throughput for a web server. In this case, our issue revolves around benchmarking CPU usage, so our application is CPU intensive when it does its job.

ASSESSMENTS, EXPECTATIONS, AND ADJUSTMENTS

If an assessment was done prior to virtualizing a server, there might be hard numbers to look at to give some details as to what was expected with regard to minimum performance or a service-level agreement (SLA). If not, the vSphere administrator needs to work with the application's owner to make more CPU resources available to the virtual machine when needed.

---

vCenter Server's graphs, which you have explored in great detail, are the best way to analyze usage, both short- and long-term. In this case, let's assume the help desk ticket describes a slowness issue in the last hour. As you've already seen, you can easily create a custom performance graph to show CPU usage over the last hour for a particular virtual machine or ESX/ESXi host.

Perform the following steps to create a CPU graph that shows data for a virtual machine from the last hour:

1. Connect to a vCenter Server instance with the vSphere Client.

2. Navigate to the Hosts And Clusters or VMs And Templates inventory view.

3. In the inventory tree, select a virtual machine.

4. Select the Performance tab from the content pane on the right, and then change the view to Advanced.

5. Click the Chart Options link.

6. In the Customize Performance Chart dialog box, select CPU from the resource type list. Select the Custom interval.

7. Near the bottom of the Chart Options section, change the interval to Last 1 Hours.

8. Set the chart type to Line graph.

9. Select the virtual machine itself from the list of objects.

10. From the list of counters, select CPU Usage In MHz (Average) and CPU Ready. This shows you how much processor is actually being used and how long it's taking to schedule the VM on a physical processor.

11. Click OK to apply the chart settings.

CPU READY

CPU Ready shows how long a virtual machine is waiting to be scheduled on a physical processor. A virtual machine waiting many thousands of milliseconds to be scheduled on a processor might indicate that the ESX/ESXi host is overloaded, a resource pool has too tight a limit, or the virtual machine has too few CPU shares (or, if no one is complaining, nothing at all). Be sure to work with the server or application owner to determine an acceptable amount of CPU Ready for any CPU-intensive virtual machine.

This graph shows CPU utilization for the selected virtual machine, but it won't necessarily help you get to the bottom of why this particular virtual machine isn't performing as well as expected. In this scenario, I would fully expect the CPU Usage in MHz (Average) counter to be high; this simply tells you that the virtual machine is using all the CPU cycles it can get. Unless the CPU Ready counters are also high, indicating that the virtual machine is waiting on the host to schedule it onto a physical processor, you still haven't uncovered the cause of the slowness that triggered the help desk ticket. Instead, you'll need to move to monitoring host CPU usage.

Monitoring a host's overall CPU usage is fairly straightforward. Keep in mind that other factors usually come into play when looking at spare CPU capacity. Add-ons such as VMotion, VMware DRS, and VMware HA directly impact whether there is enough spare capacity on a server or a cluster of servers. Compared to earlier versions of ESX, the Service Console will usually not be as competitive for processor 0 because there are fewer processes to consume CPU time. Agents installed on the Service Console will have some impact, again on processor 0.

SERVICE CONSOLE STUCK ON 0

The Service Console, as noted, uses processor 0, but it will use processor 0 only. The Service Console does not get migrated to other processors even in the face of heavy contention.

Perform the following steps to create a real-time graph for a host's CPU usage:

1. Launch the vSphere Client if it is not already running, and connect to a vCenter Server instance.

2. Navigate to the Hosts And Clusters or VMs And Templates inventory view.

3. In the inventory tree, select a host. This shows you the Summary tab.

4. Click the Performance tab, and switch to Advanced view.

5. Click the Chart Options link.

6. In the Customize Performance Chart dialog box, select the CPU resource type and the Real-Time display interval.

7. Set Chart Type to Stacked Graph (Per VM).

8. Select all objects. You should see a separate object for each VM hosted on the selected ESX/ESXi host.

9. Select the CPU Usage (Average) performance counter.

10. Click OK to apply the chart settings and return to the Performance tab.

This chart shows the usage of all the virtual machines on the selected ESX/ESXi host in a stacked fashion. From this view, you should be able to determine whether there is a specific virtual machine or group of virtual machines that are consuming abnormal amounts of CPU capacity.

VMKERNEL BALANCING ACT

Always remember that on an oversubscribed ESX/ESXi host the VMkernel will load balance the virtual machines based on current loads, reservations, and shares represented on individual virtual machines and/or resource pools.

In this artificial scenario, I identified the application within the virtual machine as CPU-bound, so these two performance charts should clearly identify why the virtual machine isn't performing well. In all likelihood, the ESX/ESXi host on which the virtual machine is running doesn't have enough CPU capacity to satisfy the requests of all the virtual machines. Your solution, in this case, would be to use the resource allocation tools described in Chapter 10 to ensure that this specific application receives the resources it needs to perform at acceptable levels.

Monitoring Memory Usage

Monitoring memory usage, whether on a host or a virtual machine, can be challenging. The monitoring itself is not difficult; it's the availability of the physical resource that can be a challenge. Of the four resources, memory can be oversubscribed without much effort. Depending on the physical form factor chosen to host VMware ESX/ESXi, running out of physical RAM is easy to do. Although the blade form factor creates a very dense consolidation effort, the blades are sometimes constrained by the amount of physical memory and network adapters that can be installed. But even with other regular form factors, having enough memory installed comes down to how much the physical server can accommodate and your budget.

If you suspect that memory usage is a performance issue, the first step is to isolate whether this is a memory shortage affecting the host (you've oversubscribed physical memory and need to add more memory) or whether this is a memory limit affecting only that virtual machine (meaning you need to allocate more memory to this virtual machine or change resource allocation policies). Normally, if the ESX/ESXi host is suffering from high memory utilization, the predefined vCenter

Server alarm will trigger and alert the vSphere administrator. However, the alarm doesn't allow you to delve deeper into the specifics of how the host is using memory. For that, you'll need a performance graph.

Perform the following steps to create a real-time graph for a host's memory usage:

1. Connect to a vCenter Server instance with the vSphere Client.

2. Navigate to the Hosts And Clusters inventory view.

3. In the inventory tree, click an ESX/ESXi host. This shows you the Summary tab.

4. Click the Performance tab, and switch to Advanced view.

5. Click the Chart Options link.

6. In the Customize Performance Chart dialog box, select the Memory resource type and the Real-Time display interval.

7. Select Line Graph as the chart type. The host will be selected as the only available object.

8. In the Counters area, select the Memory Usage (Average), Memory Overhead (Average), Memory Active (Average), Memory Consumed (Average), Memory Used by VMkernel, and Memory Swap Used (Average). This should give you a fairly clear picture of how memory is being used by the ESX/ESXi host.

COUNTERS, COUNTERS, AND MORE COUNTERS

As with virtual machines, a plethora of counters can be utilized with a host for monitoring memory usage. Which ones you select will depend on what you're looking for. Straight memory usage monitoring is common, but don't forget that there are other counters that could be helpful, such as Ballooning, Unreserved, VMkernel Swap, and Shared, just to name a few. The ability to assemble the appropriate counters for finding the right information comes with experience and depends on what is being monitored.

---

9. Click OK to apply the chart options and return to the Performance tab.

These counters, in particular the Memory Swap Used (Average) counter, will give you an idea of whether the ESX/ESXi host is under memory pressure. If the ESX/ESXi host is not suffering from memory pressure and you still suspect a memory problem, then the issue likely lies with the virtual machine.

Perform the following steps to create a real-time graph for a virtual machine's memory usage:

1. Use the vSphere client to connect to a vCenter Server instance.

2. Navigate to either the Hosts And Clusters or the VMs And Templates inventory view.

3. In the inventory tree, click a virtual machine. This shows you the Summary tab.

4. Click the Performance tab, and switch to the Advanced view.

5. Click the Chart Options link.

6. In the Customize Performance Chart dialog box, select the Memory resource type and the Real-Time display interval.

7. Select Line Graph as the chart type.

8. In the list of counters, select to show the Memory Usage (Average), Memory Overhead (Average), Memory Consumed (Average), and Memory Granted (Average) counters. This shows memory usage, including usage relative to the amount of memory configured for the virtual machine.

9. Click OK to apply the chart options and return to the Performance tab.

From this performance graph, you will be able to tell how much of the memory configured for the virtual machine is actually being used. This might reveal to you that the applications running inside that virtual machine need more memory than the virtual machine has been assigned and that adding more memory to the virtual machine—assuming that there is sufficient memory at the host level—might improve performance.

Memory, like CPU, is just one of several different factors that can impact virtual machine performance. Network usage is another area that can impact performance, especially perceived performance.

Monitoring Network Usage

vCenter Server's graphs provide a wonderful tool for measuring a virtual machine's or a host's network usage.

Monitoring network usage requires a slightly different approach than monitoring CPU or memory. With either CPU or memory, reservations, limits, and shares can dictate how much of these two resources can be consumed by any one virtual machine. Network usage cannot be constrained by these mechanisms. Since virtual machines plug into a virtual machine port group, which is part of a vSwitch on a single host, how the virtual machine interacts with the vSwitch can be manipulated by the virtual switch's or port group's policy. For instance, if you need to restrict a virtual machine's overall network output, you would configure traffic shaping on the port group to restrict the virtual machine to a specific amount of outbound bandwidth. Unless you are using vNetwork Distributed Switches or the Nexus 1000V third-party distributed virtual switch, there is no way to restrict virtual machine inbound bandwidth on ESX/ESXi hosts.

VIRTUAL MACHINE ISOLATION

Certain virtual machines may indeed need to be limited to a specific amount of outbound bandwidth. Servers such as FTP, file and print, or web and proxy servers, or any server whose main function is to act as a file repository or connection broker, may need to be limited or traffic shaped to an amount of bandwidth that allows it to meet its service target but not monopolize the host it runs on. Isolating any of these virtual machines to a vSwitch of its own is more likely a better solution, but it requires the appropriate hardware configuration.

To get an idea of how much network traffic is actually being generated, you can measure a virtual machine's or a host's output or reception of network traffic using the graphs in vCenter Server. The graphs can provide accurate information on the actual usage or ample information that a particular virtual machine is monopolizing a virtual switch, especially using the Stacked Graph chart type.

Perform the following steps to create a real-time graph for a stacked graph of transmitted network usage by each virtual machine on an ESX/ESXi host:

1. Launch the vSphere Client if it is not already running, and connect to a vCenter Server instance.

2. Navigate to either the Hosts And Clusters inventory view or the VMs And Templates inventory view.

3. In the inventory tree, click an ESX/ESXi host. This shows you the Summary tab.

4. Click the Performance tab, and switch to Advanced view.

5. Click the Chart Options link.

6. From the Customize Performance Chart dialog box, select the Network resource type and the Real-Time display interval in the Chart Options area.

7. Select a chart type of Stacked Graph (Per VM).

8. In the objects list, be sure all the virtual machines are selected.

9. In the list of counters, select the Network Data Transmit Rate counter. This gives you an idea of how much network bandwidth each virtual machine is consuming outbound on this ESX/ESXi host.

10. Click OK to apply the changes and return to the Performance tab.

What if you wanted a breakdown of traffic on each of the network interface cards (NICs) in the ESX/ESXi host, instead of by virtual machine? That's fairly easily accomplished by another trip back to the Customize Performance Chart dialog box.

Perform the following steps to create a real-time graph for a host's transmitted network usage by NIC:

1. Connect to a vCenter Server instance with the vSphere Client.

2. Navigate to the Hosts And Clusters inventory view.

3. In the inventory tree, select an ESX host. This will show you the Summary tab in the Details section on the right.

4. Select the Performance tab, and switch to Advanced view.

5. Click the Chart Options link.

6. Under Chart Options in the Customize Performance Chart dialog box, select the Network resource type and the Real-Time display interval.

7. Set the chart type to Line Graph.

8. In the objects list, select the ESX/ESXi host as well as all the specific NICs.

9. Select the Network Data Transmit Rate and Network Packets Transmitted counters.

10. Click OK to apply the changes and return to the Performance tab.

Very much like the earlier example for a virtual machine, these two counters will give you a window into how much network activity is occurring on this particular host in the outbound direction for each physical NIC. This is especially relevant if you want to see different rates of usage for each physical network interface, which, by definition, represents different virtual switches.

Now that you've examined how to monitor CPU, memory, and network usage, there's only one major area left: monitoring disk usage.

Monitoring Disk Usage

Monitoring a host's controller or virtual machine's virtual disk usage is similar in scope to monitoring network usage. This resource, which represents a controller or the storing of a virtual machine's virtual disk on a type of supported storage, isn't restricted by CPU or memory mechanisms like reservations, limits, or shares. The only way to restrict a virtual machine's disk activity is to assign shares on the individual virtual machine, which in turn may have to compete with other virtual machines running from the same storage volume. vCenter Server's graphs come to our aid again in showing actual usage for both ESX/ESXi hosts and virtual machines.

Perform the following steps to create a host graph showing disk controller utilization:

1. Use the vSphere Client to connect to a vCenter Server instance.

2. Navigate to the Hosts And Clusters inventory view.

3. In the inventory tree, select an ESX/ESXi host. This shows you the Summary tab in the Details section on the right.

4. Select the Performance tab, and switch to the Advanced view.

5. Click the Chart Options link. This opens the Customize Performance Chart dialog box.

6. Under Chart Options, choose the Real-Time display interval for the Disk resource type.

7. Set the chart type to Line Graph.

8. Selecting an object or objects—in this case a controller—and a counter or counters lets you monitor for activity that is interesting or necessary to meet service levels. Select the objects that represent the ESX/ESXi host and one of the disk controllers.

9. In the counters list, select Disk Read Rate, Disk Write Rate, and Disk Usage (Average/Rate) to get an overall view of the activity for the selected controller.

10. Click OK to return to the Performance tab.

This performance graph will give you an idea of the activity on the selected disk controller. But what if you want to see disk activity for the entire host by each VM? In this case, a Stacked Graph view can show you what you need.

STACKED VIEWS

A stacked view is very helpful in identifying whether one particular virtual machine is monopolizing a volume. Whichever virtual machine has the tallest stack in the comparison may be degrading the performance of other virtual machines' virtual disks.

Now let's switch to the virtual machine view. Looking at individual virtual machines for insight into their disk utilization can lead to some useful conclusions. File and print virtual machines, or any server that provides print queues or database services, will generate some disk-related I/O that needs to be monitored. In some cases, if the virtual machine is generating too much I/O, it may degrade the performance of other virtual machines running out of the same volume. Let's take a look at a virtual machine's graph.

Perform the following steps to create a virtual machine graph showing real-time disk controller utilization:

1. Launch the vSphere Client if it is not already running, and connect to a vCenter Server instance.

2. Navigate to either the Hosts And Clusters view or the VMs And Templates inventory view.

3. In the inventory tree, click a virtual machine. This shows you the Summary tab in the Details section on the right.

4. Select the Performance tab, and switch to Advanced view.

5. Click the Chart Options link to open the Customize Performance Chart dialog box.

6. Under Chart Options, select the Disk resource type and the Real-Time display interval.

7. Set the chart type to Line Graph.

8. Set both objects listed in the list of objects.

9. In the list of counters, select Disk Read, Disk Write, and Disk Usage (Average/Rate).

10. Click OK to apply these changes and return to the Performance tab.

With this graph, you should have an informative picture of this virtual machine's disk I/O behavior. This virtual machine is busy at work generating reads and writes for its application. Does the graph show enough I/O to meet a service-level agreement, or does this virtual machine need some help? The graphs allow administrators to make informed decisions, usually working with the application owners, so that any adjustments to improve I/O will lead to satisfied virtual machine owners.

In addition, by looking at longer intervals of time to gain a historical perspective, you may find that a virtual machine has become busier or fallen off its regular output. If the amount of I/O is just slightly impaired, then adjusting the virtual machine's shares may be a way to prioritize its disk I/O ahead of other virtual machines sharing the volume. The administrator may be forced to move the virtual machine's virtual disk(s) to another volume or LUN if share adjustments don't achieve the required results. You can use Storage VMotion, described in Chapter 6, to perform this sort of LUN-based load balancing without any disruption to the end users.

When evaluating disk utilization for NFS-based datastores, you won't see any statistics or performance information in the Disk counters. To see information on NFS datastores, you'll have to look at the Network counters; specifically, you'll need to look at vmknic usage.

Real World Scenario

PERFORMANCE MONITORING FROM THE INSIDE AND THE OUTSIDE

It's important to remember that the very nature of how virtualization operates means that it is impossible to use performance metrics from within a guest operating system as an indicator of overall resource utilization. Here's why.

In a virtualized environment, each guest operating system "sees" only its slice of the hardware as presented by the VMkernel. A guest operating system that reports 100 percent CPU utilization isn't reporting that it's using 100 percent of the physical server's CPU, but rather that it's using 100 percent of the *CPU capacity given to it by the hypervisor*. A guest operating system that is reporting 90 percent RAM utilization is really only using 90 percent of the *RAM made available to it by the hypervisor*.

Does this mean that performance metrics gathered from within a guest operating system are useless? No, but these metrics cannot be used to establish overall resource usage—only relative resource usage. You must combine any performance metrics gathered from within a guest operating system with matching metrics gathered outside the guest operating system. By combining the metrics from within the guest operating system with metrics outside the guest operating system, you can create a more complete view of how a guest operating system is using a particular type of resource and therefore get a better idea of what steps should be taken to resolve any resource constraints.

For example, if a guest operating system is reporting high memory utilization but the vCenter Server resource management tools are showing that the physical system has plenty of memory available, this tells you that the guest operating system is using everything available to it and might perform better with more memory allocated to it.

Monitoring resources can be tricky, and it requires a good knowledge of the applications running in the virtual machines in your environment. If you are a new vSphere administrator, it's worth it to spend some time using vCenter Server's performance graphs to establish some baseline behaviors. This helps you become much more familiar with the "normal" operation of the virtual machines so that when something unusual or out of the ordinary does occur, you'll be more likely to spot it.

The Bottom Line

Use alarms for proactive monitoring.   vCenter Server offers extensive alarms for alerting vSphere administrators to excessive resource consumption or potentially negative events. You can create alarms on virtually any type of object found within vCenter Server, including datacenters, clusters, ESX/ESXi hosts, and virtual machines. Alarms can monitor for resource consumption or for the occurrence of specific events. Alarms can also trigger actions, such as running a script, migrating a virtual machine, or sending a notification email.

Master It   What are the questions a vSphere administrator should ask before creating a custom alarm?

Work with performance graphs.   vCenter Server's detailed performance graphs are the key to unlocking the information necessary to determine why an ESX/ESXi host or virtual machine is performing poorly. The performance graphs expose a large number of performance counters across a variety of resource types, and vCenter Server offers functionality to save customized chart settings, export performance graphs as graphic figures or Excel workbooks, or view performance graphs in a separate window.

> **Master It**   You find yourself using the Chart Options link in the Advanced view of the Performance tab to frequently set up the same graph over and over again. Is there a way to save yourself some time and effort so that you don't have to keep re-creating the custom graph?

Gather performance information using command-line tools.   VMware supplies a few command-line tools that are useful in gathering performance information. For VMware ESX hosts, `esxtop` provides real-time information about CPU, memory, network, or disk utilization. For both VMware ESX as well as VMware ESXi, `resxtop` can display the same information. Finally, the `vm-support` tool can gather performance information that can be played back later using `esxtop`.

> **Master It**   Compare and contrast the `esxtop` and `resxtop` utilities.

Monitor CPU, memory, network, and disk usage by both ESX/ESXi hosts and virtual machines.   Monitoring usage of the four key resources—CPU, memory, network, and disk—can be difficult at times. Fortunately, the various tools supplied by VMware within vCenter Server can lead the vSphere administrator to the right solution. In particular, using customized performance graphs can expose the right information that will help a vSphere administrator uncover the source of performance problems.

> **Master It**   A junior vSphere administrator is trying to resolve a performance problem with a virtual machine. You've asked this administrator to see whether it is a CPU problem, and the junior administrator keeps telling you that the virtual machine needs more CPU capacity because the CPU utilization is high within the virtual machine. Is the junior administrator correct, based on the information available to you?

Chapter 13

Securing VMware vSphere

On a scale of 1 to 10 in importance, security always rates close to a 10 in setting up and managing a VMware vSphere environment. Well, maybe not—but it should. As VMware has increased the capabilities and features that come with its products, these same products and features must fit within the security policies applied to other servers. Most of the time, VMware ESX/ESXi and vCenter Server fit easily and nicely within those security policies, but sometimes the process is a bit of a challenge. This chapter examines the tools and techniques that will help you ensure your VMware vSphere environment appropriately follows the security policies of your organization.

In this chapter, you will learn to:

◆ Manage local users on ESX/ESXi hosts

◆ Configure authentication on ESX hosts

◆ Control network access to services on ESX hosts

◆ Provide secure network zones

Overview of vSphere Security

Like most other areas of security within information technology, securing a vSphere environment means securing all the different components of VMware vSphere. Specifically, securing VMware vSphere means securing the following:

◆ The ESX/ESXi hosts

◆ vCenter Server

◆ The virtual machines (specifically, the guest operating systems running inside the virtual machines)

◆ The applications running in the virtual machines

I won't be addressing how to secure the applications within your virtual machines because that task falls well outside the scope of this book. I do encourage you, however, to be sure to keep application-level security in mind as you work toward securing your VMware vSphere environment. I discuss each of the other components listed in this chapter. Each of these components has its own unique set of security challenges, and each of these components has different ways of addressing those security challenges. For example, because VMware ESX has a Linux-based Service Console, it has a different set of security challenges than the Windows-based vCenter Server.

As you work your way through this chapter, keep in mind that some of the recommendations I make here have absolutely nothing to do with virtualization. Because virtualizing with VMware vSphere affects many different areas of the datacenter, you also have to consider all those areas when you look at security. Further, some of the recommendations I make are ones that I've also made elsewhere in the book, so you might see some duplicate information. Security should be woven into every aspect of your VMware vSphere design and implementation, so it's completely natural that you'll see some of the same tips during this focused discussion on security.

The first components I discuss securing are the ESX/ESXi hosts.

Securing ESX/ESXi Hosts

Although VMware ESX and VMware ESXi have a lot of components in common, there is one key component that differs between the two of them, especially with regard to security. The presence of the Linux-based Service Console in VMware ESX introduces a number of security challenges not present in VMware ESXi. Because of this key difference with regard to security, most of the information in this section applies only to VMware ESX. The "Securing ESXi Hosts" section later in this chapter specifically discusses VMware ESXi.

ESXi's Hidden Service Console

One common misconception about ESXi is that it does not have a Service Console at all. That is actually not true. ESXi uses an open source software package called BusyBox to create a minimal service console. However, access to this service console is restricted and completely unsupported by VMware.

I'll start my discussion of securing VMware ESX hosts with a look at how VMware ESX handles authentication.

Working with ESX Authentication

The majority of what you need to do as a VMware vSphere administrator involves working with vCenter Server. Still, sometimes it is necessary to connect directly to an ESX host. Although using vCenter Server eliminates the largest part of the need for the local users and groups, the need does not go away entirely. There are instances when a task cannot be accomplished through vCenter Server. Some examples include the following:

◆ vCenter Server is not available or is down.

◆ You are troubleshooting VMware ESX boot and configuration problems.

◆ You are auditing the VMware ESX host configuration and remote access by comparing archived files with live versions of the same files.

Because the need to authenticate directly to ESX still exists, you need to understand what options exist for managing users and groups on ESX hosts. There are two basic options: managing users and groups locally on each host or integrating with Active Directory via Kerberos authentication. I'll cover each of these options in the following sections.

Managing Users and Groups Locally

In most cases, the number and the frequency of use of local user accounts on an ESX host have both diminished considerably. Usually, two or three accounts are all that are needed for access to the Service Console. Why two or three, and not just one? The best reason to have at least two accounts is in case one of the user accounts is unavailable during situations such as user vacations, sickness, or accidents. As you already know, users and groups on ESX hosts are, by default, managed independently per ESX host. Because the need for local accounts is so greatly diminished, many organizations find that the administrative overhead of managing only a couple of accounts across multiple ESX hosts is an acceptable burden.

If this is the case in your environment, you have two ways of managing users and groups locally. You can use command-line tools in the Service Console, or you can use the vSphere Client. Which method is right for you will largely depend upon your experience and preferences. For example, I feel very comfortable using the command line, so using the Service Console command-line interface (CLI) would be my first choice. However, if you are more comfortable with a Windows-based application, then the vSphere Client is the best option for you. I'll describe both methods in this section so you can choose the method that works best for you.

Perform the following steps to create a local user account from the Service Console command-line interface:

1. Using PuTTY.exe (Windows), a terminal window (Linux or Mac OS X), or the physical console, log in to an ESX host, and enter the **su** – command to establish root privileges.

2. Enter the following command to create a new user account, substituting the desired username in the command:

   useradd *username*

3. Enter the following command to set the initial password for this user account:

   passwd *username*

4. Type the new password twice, as indicated by the prompts.

SERVICE CONSOLE USERNAMES AND PASSWORDS

Avoid using any kind of special characters for Service Console usernames or passwords. These characters can cause problems when managing a server from the command line.

After you create the account, I strongly recommend testing the account to be sure that you can log in using the username and password you expect. If, for some reason, you can't log in, you can use the passwd command again to set the password. Don't forget that you must create the user account separately on every ESX host to which that user needs access!

Perform the following steps to delete a user account from an ESX host:

1. Using PuTTY.exe (Windows), a terminal window (Linux or Mac OS X), or the physical console, log in to an ESX host, and enter the **su** – command to establish root privileges.

2. Enter the following command to delete a user account:

   `userdel` *username*

3. Deleting a user account does not, by default, delete the user's home directory. Enter this command to delete the user's home directory:

   `rm -rf /home/`*username*

After you complete this process, the specified user will no longer be able to log into that ESX host using that account.

To reset a user's password, use the `passwd` command as I described previously.

To manage local groups, the process is similar. You would use the `groupadd` command to create a new group, and you would use the `groupdel` command to delete a group. To change a user's membership in a group, use the following command, substituting the correct list of groups and the correct username where appropriate:

`usermod -G` *group1,group2 username*

As I mentioned previously, you can also use the vSphere Client to manage local users and groups. This process also works with VMware ESXi as well as VMware ESX.

Perform the following steps to manage local users and groups with the vSphere Client:

1. Launch the vSphere Client if it is not already running, and connect to an ESX/ESXi host. You cannot manage local users and groups in the vSphere Client while connected to a vCenter Server instance.

2. Select an ESX/ESXi host from the inventory list on the left.

3. Click the Users & Groups tab in the content pane on the right.

On the Users & Groups tab, you can create new users or groups, edit existing users or groups including changing the password, and delete users and groups. If you want to grant that user shell access, select the Grant Shell Access To This User box when creating or editing the user account.

TO VC OR NOT TO VC

The best way to administer your VMware vSphere environment is to connect the vSphere Client to a vCenter Server instance. Although you can connect the vSphere Client to an ESX/ESXi host directly, you lose a great deal of functionality. If you didn't purchase vCenter Server, you may have no other choice than to connect to the ESX/ESXi hosts. In such instances, you'd have to create user accounts locally on the ESX/ESXi hosts for virtual machine administration.

Now that you have an idea of the specific steps used to manage users and groups locally on each ESX host, what are the security challenges involved in managing users and groups locally? And how can those security challenges be addressed? Here are just a couple of examples:

◆ You must manually manage users and groups separately on each and every ESX host. If you forget to delete a user account for a departing employee on a specific ESX host, you've just created a potential security problem.

♦ There is no way to centrally enforce password policies. Although you can set password policies on each ESX host, you have to do this separately on every ESX host in your environment. If you ever need to change the password policy, you must do so on each ESX host individually.

You can address both of these particular security challenges by leveraging functionality provided by VMware with ESX to integrate Service Console authentication into Active Directory, as you'll see in the next section.

ENABLING ACTIVE DIRECTORY INTEGRATION

You've already seen how, by default, VMware ESX uses local users and groups to assign permissions to directories and files. The presence of these local users and groups is the key to the ESX security model, as I showed you in Chapter 9. Although these local users and groups form the foundation of the ESX security model, managing these users and groups locally on every ESX host in the enterprise can create a great deal of administrative overhead and has some security challenges, as I described in the previous section.

What if you were able to continue to accommodate the need for logging into the Service Console of an ESX host but in a way that avoided some of the security challenges of managing users and groups locally?

With a few changes to the underlying authentication modules, you can configure ESX to authenticate user accounts against Microsoft Active Directory (AD) using a protocol called Kerberos. This allows for a consistent way to apply security polices as they relate to user management by allowing AD administrators to centrally control policies on password complexity, expiration, and user account changes at an AD level, bypassing—for the most part—local ESX host setup.

SERVICE CONSOLE USER ACCOUNTS

Even with AD integration, you must still create user accounts locally on the ESX host. When creating those accounts, make sure the names for those accounts match the names in Active Directory. By default, there is no mechanism for reconciling local ESX accounts with AD users. If a user is deleted in AD, you must manually delete the user on the ESX host.

If you are interested in a deeper level of integration with AD that doesn't require you to create local accounts on the ESX host, refer to my website at http://blog.scottlowe.org.

The fastest and easiest way to implement AD authentication is to use the esxcfg-auth tool. You can use this valuable tool to set local user security policies, such as password complexity, reuse, and length. In this case, esxcfg-auth hands over the authentication process to AD by modifying the krb5.conf file, creating the kdc.conf file, and modifying the pam.d file so that connections from the vSphere Client, Secure Shell (SSH), and local console connections all use Kerberos authentication.

Perform the following steps to set up Active Directory authentication:

1. From the ESX host's local console or via a remote hardware console such as HP iLO, log into the VMware ESX host as root. Because you are changing the authentication mechanisms, I don't recommend using a remote connection such as SSH for this process.

2. From the root prompt, use the following command:

```
esxcfg-auth --enablead --addomain <domain_name> --addc <domain_name>
```

You'll want to substitute the correct values for your Active Directory domain name.

ACCESSING LOCAL AND REMOTE DOMAIN CONTROLLERS

In this example, the assumption is that a local domain controller will handle the authentication. In some cases, if there is a firewall between the ESX hosts and the domain controller, the ports listed in /etc/krb5.conf may need to be opened. Also, Active Directory DNS should return the local domain controller for this operation. Although you can specify a domain controller in the previous command, it's better to just name the domain and let DNS sort out the local DC.

---

3. Check the /etc/krb5.conf file to see whether the necessary changes have been made. Listing 13.1 shows the contents of the /etc/krb5.conf file after you've used the esxcfg-auth command.

LISTING 13.1: The Kerberos Configuration File Set for AD Integration

```
# Autogenerated by esxcfg-auth

[domain_realm]
.vmwarelab.net = VMWARELAB.NET
vmwarelab.net = VMWARELAB.NET

[libdefaults]
default_realm = VMWARELAB.NET

[realms]
VMWARELAB.NET = {
    admin_server = vmwarelab.net:464
    default_domain = vmwarelab.net
    kdc = vmwarelab.net:88
```

4. On the ESX host, create only the necessary administrative user accounts, and be sure that the ESX usernames match existing Active Directory usernames. Do not set the passwords for the ESX accounts.

5. While remaining logged in as root, check the process by attempting to log in via SSH as one of the accounts you just created in step 4. When prompted for the password, supply the password for the account in Active Directory.

6. If the process is working, you should be able to log in without any problems. If there are problems, refer to the ESX log files for more information. In particular, the /var/log/secure file provides information on authentication failures.

With Active Directory integration configured, password policies are managed centrally via Active Directory, and user management is—for the most part—also centralized via Active

Directory. Although user accounts must still be managed locally, if a local user account doesn't have a password and doesn't have a matching user account in Active Directory, login attempts will fail.

Although managing how users authenticate is important, it's also important to control how users access the VMware ESX hosts across the network. In the next section, I'll examine how you can control SSH access to your VMware ESX hosts.

Controlling Secure Shell Access

Secure Shell, often referred to just as SSH, is a widely known and widely used encrypted remote console protocol. SSH was originally developed in 1995 to replace other protocols, such as `telnet`, `rsh`, and `rlogin`, that did not provide strong authentication and did not protect against password-sniffing attacks on the network. SSH gained rapid adoption, and the SSH-2 protocol is now a proposed Internet standard with the Internet Engineering Task Force (IETF).

Because VMware ESX leverages a Linux-based Service Console, VMware includes SSH with VMware ESX as a method of remote console access. As a result, vSphere administrators can use an SSH client, such as `PuTTY.exe` on Windows or OpenSSH on Linux or Mac OS X, to remotely access the command-line interface of a VMware ESX host in order to perform management tasks.

Although SSH is considered a secure remote console protocol, starting with VMware Infrastructure 3 and continuing with VMware vSphere 4, the root account is not permitted to log into an ESX host via SSH. This provides better security for the root account, which should be protected at all costs. In previous versions of ESX, the root account could log into the Service Console via SSH, and this provided an avenue to brute-force the root password. By denying SSH access to the root account, VMware closed this potential avenue of attack. Now a malicious user who wants to try to access the root account must have physical access to the server's console or already have an account on the ESX host.

DON'T ENABLE ROOT SSH ACCESS

Enabling root access via SSH violates security best practices. Unless it is absolutely necessary, don't enable root access via SSH. In those cases where it is absolutely necessary, leave it enabled only as long as it remains necessary, and then disable SSH root access again.

The file that defines this policy is `sshd_config`, located in the `/etc/ssh` directory, and the attribute that allows or disallows remote root logins is PermitRootLogin. Keeping this attribute set to No is a security best practice.

Aside from enabling or disabling root access via SSH, you may also want to limit SSH access to only certain users or groups of users. Because the vSphere Client provides the bulk of the functionality necessary to manage ESX hosts, the number of accounts that need direct SSH access to an ESX host is fairly low.

To add another level of protection to your ESX hosts and limit access via SSH to only those users who are authorized, SSH provides some configuration directives that allow you to control exactly who is or isn't allowed to connect via SSH. These restrictions allow easier compliance with security access policies and can be audited to prove such compliance. Of course, one argument against this technique is that there should be only administrative accounts on the server, so all of them would probably need SSH access. Allowing all of them SSH access thus defeats the purpose of controlling SSH access on a per-user basis.

Still, for those times when logging into ESX hosts directly via SSH is required, limiting access to only certain individuals is another piece of a good "defense-in-depth" strategy.

Perform the following steps to limit access to SSH to only certain individuals:

1. From the ESX host's local console or via a remote hardware console such as HP iLO, log into the VMware ESX host as root.

   Because you are changing SSH parameters, I don't recommend using SSH for this process.

2. If the user accounts have not been created, create them using `useradd`. This step is necessary regardless of whether you are using Active Directory integration.

3. Change the working directory to `/etc/ssh`.

4. Enter the following command to make a backup copy of the `sshd_config` file:

   ```
   cp sshd_config sshd_config.backup
   ```

5. Edit the `sshd_config` file with `vi` or `nano`. You should add the AllowUsers attribute, followed on the same line by the usernames in a space-delimited list, like this:

   ```
   AllowUsers slowe rscherer csakac
   ```

6. Save the `sshd_config` file.

7. Enter the following command to restart the SSH daemon (service):

   ```
   service sshd restart
   ```

8. Test the new `sshd_config` file by trying to log on with an account that is valid on the ESX host but is not included on the AllowUsers directive. All attempts to login should fail.

NO IMPLICIT PERMISSIONS WITH ALLOWUSERS

When using the AllowUser attribute with the `sshd_config` file and after creating only the necessary user accounts for administrative purposes, you do not have to specify the DenyUsers attribute. By implicit denial, any other accounts created but not listed in the AllowUsers section are unable to log in remotely with SSH. That is, there are no implicit permissions to log in via SSH when using AllowUsers—you must explicitly include any user you want to have the ability to log in via SSH.

The `sshd_config` file has a few other directives that are related to the AllowUsers directive:

◆ DenyUsers is the opposite of AllowUsers; any user listed with the DenyUsers directive will be denied access to the ESX host via SSH.

◆ AllowGroups is similar to AllowUsers but operates off group names instead of usernames.

◆ DenyGroups works like DenyUsers, but users are denied based on group names and group membership.

You can use Active Directory integration in conjunction with these directives in the `sshd_config` file.

This technique is good for providing another level of security to SSH, but this method is SSH-specific. The next function I'll review, TCP Wrappers, can be used to provide an additional layer of security for multiple types of network connections to an ESX host.

Using TCP Wrappers

For more fine-grained control over network services other than just SSH, you'll want to use TCP Wrappers. TCP Wrappers can restrict specific hosts from connecting to the ESX host. Additionally, TCP Wrappers is transparent to the underlying services, and there's no need to restart those services when changes have been made to the underlying configuration files. This means that you can use TCP Wrappers not only to control access to SSH but also to control access via the vSphere Client.

TCP Wrappers uses two files, /etc/hosts.allow and /etc/hosts.deny, to allow or deny host connections. These files use a flexible syntax for defining the hosts allowed to connect and the hosts not allowed to connect. When evaluating whether a connection should be allowed or denied, TCP Wrappers first looks at the /etc/hosts.allow file and applies the first rule specified for that service. If it finds a matching rule, it allows the connection. If no matching rule is found, TCP Wrappers proceeds to check /etc/hosts.deny for a matching rule. If a matching rule is found in /etc/hosts.deny, the connection is denied.

If no matching rule is found in either /etc/hosts.allow or /etc/hosts.deny, then the connection is allowed.

WATCH THE ORDER OF YOUR RULES

Be careful when you arrange the order of your rules in the /etc/hosts.allow and /etc/hosts.deny files; the first rule matched to a host becomes the policy, even if there is another rule further down that also matches the policy.

As I mentioned earlier, /etc/hosts.allow and /etc/hosts.deny use a flexible syntax for defining the rules. The general syntax for an entry in either file is defined as follows:

```
daemon : client [:option1:option2:...]
```

In this syntax, daemon is the name of the service to which you are allowing or denying access. For SSH, the daemon would be sshd. For access via the vSphere Client, it would be vmware-authd.

Following daemon is client. In this syntax, client is a comma-separated list of hostnames, IP addresses, network addresses, or other special patterns or wildcards.

After client is a series of optional actions. If there are multiple actions, the actions are separated by colons.

Let's look at a few examples to help explain this syntax. Here are some examples of the syntax for entries in /etc/hosts.allow to allow a specific host or group of hosts to connect:

sshd:192.168.31.42:allow This entry controls access to the SSH daemon and allows the computer with the IP address 192.168.31.42 access to the SSH daemon.

sshd:host1.abc.com:allow This entry uses a fully qualified domain name (FQDN) instead of an IP address, but otherwise it is identical to the previous example.

sshd:192.168.31.0/24:allow This time, instead of an IP address or an FQDN, this example uses a network address. All hosts on the 192.168.31.0/24 network are allowed to connect.

But what about /etc/hosts.deny? After the administrator has defined which hosts are allowed to connect, the follow-up is to deny all other hosts. To deny all other hosts, you add this line to the /etc/hosts.deny file:

```
sshd:ALL
```

This denies all access to the SSH daemon. When combined with the rules in /etc/hosts.allow, you have effectively specified that only certain computers and networks will be allowed access to the SSH daemon and all others will be denied.

If you want specific rules to deny traffic, here are some more examples:

```
sshd:192.168.40.33:deny
sshd:host2.abc.com:deny
sshd:ALL:deny
```

As you can see, TCP Wrappers is very flexible and offers you a great deal of control over what systems are allowed to connect to your ESX hosts.

Perform the following steps to limit host connections to a network service such as SSH:

1. From the ESX host's local console or via a remote hardware console such as HP iLO, log into the VMware ESX host as root.

   Because you are changing a configuration that may block your network access if configured incorrectly, I don't recommend performing this procedure remotely.

2. Change the working directory to /etc.

3. Enter the following command to make a backup copy of the hosts.allow file:

   ```
   cp /etc/hosts.allow /etc/hosts.allow.backup
   ```

4. Edit hosts.allow with vi or nano to include only those hosts or networks that should have access and to restrict all others. Remember to be careful of the order of the rules.

5. Save the file.

6. Test the host connections to make sure only those hosts specified have access and all others do not.

Using TCP Wrappers in conjunction with the AllowUsers directive in sshd_config is perfectly acceptable and recommended—TCP Wrappers works on a per-client basis based on IP address, hostname, or network address, while AllowUsers in sshd_config works on a per-username basis. They are complementary.

Another complementary way of adding security to a VMware ESX host is using the Service Console firewall.

Configuring the Service Console Firewall

VMware ESX ships with a firewall that controls traffic into or out of the Service Console. This firewall is based on the Linux iptables firewall, a firewall technology that is readily available on most Linux distributions and is fairly well documented. Although iptables is well documented, working with iptables is not for the uninitiated. However, with the esxcfg-firewall command VMware provides, creating only the necessary firewall rules for proper VMware ESX functionality is much easier.

The default setup for the Service Console firewall is very secure. For both incoming and outgoing connections, only those ports necessary for managing the virtual machines and the ESX host are open. This default mode of operation is High security. The other two modes of operation are Medium security, which doesn't block outgoing ports, and Low security, which doesn't block ingoing or outgoing ports. Some default ports open when using High security are as follows:

◆   902: vSphere Client connections

◆   903: Virtual machine console connection

◆   80/443: Web browser connections

◆   22: SSH client connections

There are several other ports, having mostly to do with Common Information Model (CIM). CIM allows monitoring of many aspects of the hardware and storage of an ESX host.

There are two ways to see what ports are open on an ESX host. One method involves using the vSphere Client connected directly to an ESX host, as illustrated in Figure 13.1.

FIGURE 13.1
The Security Profile area of the Configuration tab in vCenter Server shows the current Service Console configuration.

The second way of determining what ports are currently open is using the `esxcfg-firewall` command at the Service Console. Enter this command to see the current firewall configuration:

```
esxcfg-firewall --query
```

When you consider opening a new port, you can use the vSphere Client connected to vCenter Server or the `esxcfg-firewall` command. Most of the time it is easier to open predefined ports with the vSphere Client, but in some cases, you might need to open a port for a lesser-known service or process, such as monitoring agents.

SERVICE CONSOLE FIREWALL SERVICES

VMware ESX has an XML file named `services.xml`, normally found in `/etc/vmware/firewall`, that defines those services used most often on an ESX host and that are shown in the vSphere Client in the Security Profile area. VMware does not support editing this file to add your own services.

Monitoring the firewall's configuration is an important step in auditing access to an ESX host. As you've already seen in Figure 13.1, using the vSphere Client is one way to monitor currently open ports on the firewall. In some cases, though, newly opened ports will not show up using the vSphere Client. The best way to audit currently open ports and the services using them is to use `esxcfg-firewall -q` from the VMware ESX Service Console.

After auditing the current firewall configuration, you can then use the `esxcfg-firewall` command to open ports defined in the `services.xml` file or those not listed in the profile.

Perform the following steps to enable the firewall for locally defined services:

1. Using `PuTTY.exe` (Windows), a terminal window (Linux or Mac OS X), or the physical console, log in to an ESX host, and enter the **su** – command to establish root privileges.

2. Enter this command to show the list of predefined services:

   ```
   esxcfg-firewall -s
   ```

3. After you've located the service name you need, enter this command to check the current status of that service:

   ```
   esxcfg-firewall -q service_name
   ```

4. Enter this command to enable the predefined service (allow it through the firewall):

   ```
   esxcfg-firewall -e service_name
   ```

5. Verify the status of the service through the firewall by querying the firewall with this command:

   ```
   esxcfg-firewall --query
   ```

If you need to open a port for an agent or another third-party application not listed in `services.xml`, the `esxcfg-firewall` command still does the job, but the administrator has to know exactly what protocols and ports the agent or application uses. For example, the HP Insight Management Agent uses a specific port open to allow users to verify the status of the physical server hardware via a web browser. In this case, the following command would open the necessary port:

```
esxcfg-firewall -o 2381,tcp,in,InsightWebConsole
```

Here's a breakdown of the various parts of that command:

◆ -o opens the port (-c would close the port).

◆ 2381 is the port to be opened.

◆ tcp is the protocol to be used (udp is the other protocol you can use).

◆ in specifies incoming traffic (out is used for outgoing traffic).

◆ InsightWebConsole is the name of the agent or service.

Perform the following steps to open a port for an agent or application not included in the default firewall services list:

1. Using PuTTY.exe (Windows), a terminal window (Linux or Mac OS X), or the physical console, log in to an ESX host, and enter the **su** − command to establish root privileges.

2. Enter this command to open an inbound TCP-based port:

   ```
   esxcfg-firewall -o <port number>,tcp,in,<service name>
   ```

   If the application, agent, or service needed an outbound UDP port, the command would look like this:

   ```
   esxcfg-firewall -o <port number>,udp,out,<service name>
   ```

3. Enter this command to verify that the port is open:

   ```
   esxcfg-firewall --query
   ```

After you made the firewall changes, you still have to install the agent or application and test your connectivity. If at some point you want to close a port that is no longer needed, esxcfg-firewall again can handle that task.

Perform the following steps to close a port in the Service Console firewall:

1. Using PuTTY.exe (Windows), a terminal window (Linux or Mac OS X), or the physical console, log in to an ESX host, and enter the **su** − command to establish root privileges.

2. Query the firewall with this command to check the current status of the port:

   ```
   esxcfg-firewall --query
   ```

3. Enter this command to close an inbound TCP-based port:

   ```
   esxcfg-firewall -c <port number>,<tcp or udp>,<in or out>,<service name>
   ```

4. Enter this command to verify that the port is open:

   ```
   esxcfg-firewall --query
   ```

For more information on the esxcfg-firewall command, use man esxcg-firewall or esxcfg-firewall --help at the Service Console prompt.

With the various methods I've shown you so far—controlling user access to SSH via sshd_config, controlling network access to specific services via TCP Wrappers, and using the Service Console firewall—you should have a pretty good handle on network-based security for the ESX hosts. I'd like to shift the focus now to another way of monitoring ESX host security: auditing files and file changes in the Service Console.

Auditing Service Console Files

Several files on an ESX host tell a lot about the server and how it was configured. Thankfully, the job of tracking your ESX host's configuration is reasonably easy with the vSphere Client. In many instances, though, auditing and monitoring several files directly from the Service Console is warranted because they are stored on the ESX host.

Why do you need to audit these files on a regular basis? For starters, good security on any server begins with knowing how the server is configured. If the configuration has changed, unbeknownst to the administrator, then any security-related decisions could be flawed. Worse, if the change is significant, your virtual machines could suffer, or someone who doesn't have your best interests in mind could sabotage your ESX host. That person won't take down one server—they'll take down many servers.

The files that I'll cover in this section deal with how the server is configured to provide certain services. VMware provides a tool to make the collection of these files easy. As a matter of fact, you can use either the vSphere Client or the Service Console command vm-support. The vm-support command is usually used to troubleshoot problems with your ESX host, but you can also use this command to audit and monitor the same server.

USING vm-support AS DOCUMENTATION

One way to document any changes to the ESX host's configuration is to run vm-support any time a change has been made. In this way, all changes can be tracked over time and compared with specific setups. In a security audit, using the output from this command is vital to complying with regulatory guidelines for server documentation. By running vm-support at least once a month, you also capture log files and other critical files for archive purposes.

Let's look at what you can collect using the Service Console. You'll need to log in as root to run vm-support. As a good practice, use the /tmp directory as the temporary location for the support files.

After vm-support runs and creates the .tgz file, you can copy the file to an archive location, preferably on another server, or extract the file in the current directory to examine the contents.

Perform the following steps to run the vm-support command and extract the files into a temporary directory:

1. Using PuTTY.exe (Windows), a terminal window (Linux or Mac OS X), or the physical console, log in to an ESX host, and enter the **su** – command to establish root privileges.

2. Switch to the /tmp directory.

3. Run the vm-support command.

4. Enter this command to extract the resulting .tgz file into the current directory:

   ```
   tar -xzf <vm-support filename>
   ```

This method captures many files, but one of great importance for auditing is /etc/vmware/esx.conf. This is an important file, because any changes to the overall configuration of the ESX host are documented in this file.

After you have captured the files using vm-support and then extracted those files into a directory, you can compare the timestamps on the "live" file against the archived file captured by vm-support. If there hasn't been a configuration change on the server, the timestamp on the live file should match the timestamp on the archived file. This will indicate to you that the configuration of the ESX host has not been modified. Although this method is not a comprehensive indication of whether the ESX host has been modified, this is a pretty good indicator.

If the timestamps between the "live" file in /etc/vmware and the archived version do not match, how can you compare the captured file, using vm-support, with the current version?

Using a Linux command known as diff, you can compare two files to see exactly what changes were made to the /etc/vmware/esx.conf file and, thus, know what configuration changes were made to the ESX host. Figure 13.2 shows some sample output from the diff command.

FIGURE 13.2
The output of the diff command will show you what changes exist between two versions of a file.

In the sample output shown in Figure 13.2, someone has changed the firewall to allow a VNC server to run on the ESX host's Service Console. Many times, though, you will discover changes to the network configuration, storage, or even services that have been implemented because of changes on the firewall to allow the traffic in or out. The techniques I've shown you here give you one way to monitor and to audit changes to files on the ESX host. Scripting these steps is not difficult and would make the process even faster, especially if you have dozens of ESX hosts to audit.

Most of the items I've discussed here are specific to VMware ESX because they address security concerns resulting from the presence of the Linux-based Service Console. Because it has a different architecture, VMware ESXi has a different set of security concerns.

Securing ESXi Hosts

VMware ESXi lacks the Linux-based Service Console present in VMware ESX and, as a result, also lacks many of the security controls that are available with the Linux-based service console. VMware ESXi lacks the following:

◆ A firewall to protect the Management interfaces

◆ The ability to control network access to services via TCP Wrappers

◆ The ability to audit the configuration of the ESXi host by monitoring configuration files

Because of the limited tools available to you, you can perform only the following actions to help secure your VMware ESXi hosts:

◆ Place the Management interface(s) of the ESXi hosts behind a network-based firewall. This allows you to control the traffic that is allowed to and from the ESXi hosts. If necessary, you may need to add a network interface on your vCenter Server computer and attach that network interface to the same network segment as the ESXi Management interfaces.

◆ Set a root password for the ESXi host. You can set the root password, if it has not already been set, via the server's console by pressing F2. More information on working with the ESXi console is available in Chapter 2.

◆ Use host profiles in vCenter Server. Host profiles can help ensure that the configuration of the VMware ESXi hosts does not drift or change from the settings specified in the host profile.

◆ Keep your ESXi hosts patched and up-to-date. Your best bet for keeping ESXi hosts fully patched is to use vCenter Update Manager, as described in more detail in Chapter 4.

◆ Enable Lockdown Mode for your ESXi hosts. Enabling Lockdown Mode disables console-based user access and direct access via the vSphere Client. Root access via the vSphere Management Assistant (vMA) is also restricted.

Keeping hosts patched isn't just for ESXi hosts, though; it's also for VMware ESX hosts, as I mention in the next section.

Keeping ESX/ESXi Hosts Patched

A final key component in maintaining the security of your vSphere environment is keeping your VMware ESX/ESXi hosts fully patched and up-to-date. On an as-needed basis, VMware releases security patches for VMware ESX and ESXi. Failing to apply these security patches could expose your VMware vSphere environment to potential security risks.

VMware vCenter Update Manager is the tool VMware supplies with vSphere to address this need. I discussed VMware vCenter Update Manager extensively in Chapter 4.

Now that you've looked at the various ways to secure your ESX/ESXi hosts, it's time to move on to securing vCenter Server, the second major component in your VMware vSphere environment.

Securing vCenter Server

For the most part, discussing how to secure vCenter Server entails discussing how to secure Windows Server. As a Windows-based application, vCenter Server relies upon the underlying security features of Windows Server. As a result, a couple of the security recommendations I'll make are common to any Windows Server installation:

◆ Stay current on all Windows Server and vCenter Server patches and updates. This helps protect you against potential security exploits.

◆ Harden the Windows Server installation using published best practices and guidelines from Microsoft. This is true not only for the vCenter Server computer but also for the computer running the separate database server in support of vCenter Server.

A few security recommendations are specific to vCenter Server:

◆ Place the vCenter Server back-end database on a separate physical server, if possible.

◆ If you are using Windows authentication with SQL Server, use a dedicated service account for vCenter Server—don't allow vCenter Server to share a Windows account with other services or applications.

◆ Be sure to secure the separate database server and back-end database using published security practices from the appropriate vendor.

◆ Replace the default vCenter Server self-signed SSL certificate with a valid SSL certificate from a trusted root authority.

In addition to these recommendations, there are also some other steps you should take to ensure that vCenter Server—and the infrastructure being managed by vCenter Server—is appropriately secured and protected. In Chapter 9 I discussed the use of vCenter Server's roles and permissions. When vCenter Server is a member of an Active Directory domain, there are some changes you'll want to make to better leverage Active Directory and vCenter Server's roles and privileges. I discuss those changes in the next section.

Leveraging Active Directory

vCenter Server provides a role-based administration model that gives you, the vSphere administrator, a great deal of flexibility with regard to which users can perform which actions on which objects. When vCenter Server is installed as a member server in an Active Directory domain, however, the default settings in vCenter Server extend permissions to users within Active Directory that aren't necessarily involved in the administration of the vSphere environment.

In Chapter 9, I discussed the relationship between the local Administrators group, the Domain Admins Domain Local group, and the vCenter Server Administrator role. By default, the local Administrators group—this is the Windows group defined locally on that specific Windows server—is given the Administrator role in vCenter Server. This permission assignment happens at the vCenter Server object and propagates down to all child objects. Because the Domain Admins Domain Local group is a member of the local Administrators group, this means that the Domain Admins group is also given the Administrator role in vCenter Server. It has been my experience that in many organizations there are members of the Domain Admins group that don't have anything to do with the virtualization infrastructure. Granting those users privileges inside vCenter Server is a violation of security best practices; removing the default permissions for Domain Admins in vCenter Server is, therefore, a good idea.

Perform the following steps to remove the default permissions for Domain Admins in vCenter Server:

1. In Active Directory, create a Domain Local group named vSphere Administrators (or similar). Make the appropriate Active Directory domain user accounts members of this group. At the very least, be sure to place your own account in this group.

2. Log on to the vCenter Server computer as Administrator.

3. Create a local group, using the Local Users and Groups management console, named vSphere Admins (or similar).

4. Add the Active Directory Domain Local group created in step 1 to this new local group. Also add the local Administrator account to this group.

5. Launch the vSphere Client, if it is not already running, and connect to the appropriate vCenter Server instance.

6. In the inventory tree on the left, select the vCenter Server object at the top of the tree.

7. Click the Permissions tab.

8. Right-click a blank area of the Permissions tab, and select Add Permission.

9. Add the local group you created in step 3, and assign that group the Administrator role. Be sure that the Propagate To Child Objects check box is selected.

10. Click OK to return to the Permissions tab. The new permission should be listed there.

11. Right-click the permission for Administrators, and select Remove. Click Yes in the dialog box prompting for confirmation.

This removes the local Administrators group—and by extension the Domain Admins group—from the Administrator role on the vCenter Server object. Moving forward, only members of the Domain Local group you created will have permission within vCenter Server. You can add or remove users to that Domain Local group to control access to vCenter Server.

Of course, you will also want to create Active Directory groups to match up to other roles—custom or predefined—that you're using within vCenter Server to grant privileges to specific objects.

Before I move on to the topic of securing virtual machines, there is one quick item I'd like to discuss pertaining to how vCenter Server interacts with ESX/ESXi hosts. I think it's important to understand how vCenter Server uses a special user account as a proxy account for managing hosts.

Understanding the vpxuser Account

You are aware by now that ESX/ESXi relies on a local user and group accounts model. When vCenter Server is present, however, most activities are funneled through vCenter Server using Windows accounts that have been assigned a role, which have then been assigned to one or more inventory objects. This combination of Windows account, role, and inventory object creates a permission that allows (or disallows) the user to perform certain functions. Because the user doesn't log into the ESX/ESXi host directly, this minimizes the need for many local user accounts on the ESX/ESXi host and thus provides better security. Alas, there still is a need, however small or infrequent, for local accounts on an ESX/ESXi host used primarily for administration, which is why I talked earlier about managing local users and groups and integrating ESX authentication into Active Directory.

When you are using vCenter Server to manage your virtual infrastructure, you are really only creating a task and not directly interfacing with the ESX/ESXi hosts or the virtual machines. This is true for any user using vCenter Server to manage hosts or virtual machines. For instance, Shane, an administrator, wants to create a new virtual machine. Shane first needs the proper role—perhaps a custom role you created specifically for the purpose of creating new virtual machines—assigned to the proper inventory object.

Assuming the correct role has been assigned to the correct inventory objects—let's say it's a resource pool—Shane has what he needs to create, modify, and monitor virtual machines. But, does Shane's user account have direct access to the ESX/ESXi hosts when he's logged into vCenter Server? No, it does not. In fact, a proxy account is used to communicate Shane's tasks to the appropriate ESX/ESXi host or virtual machine. This account, vpxuser, is the only account that vCenter Server stores and tracks in its back-end database.

VPXUSER SECURITY

The vpxuser account and password are stored in the vCenter Server database and on the ESX/ESXi hosts. It is used to communicate from a vCenter Server computer to an ESX/ESXi host. The vpxuser password consists of 32 (randomly selected) characters, is encrypted using SHA1 on an ESX/ESXi host, and is obfuscated on vCenter Server. Each vpxuser password is unique to the ESX/ESXi host being managed by vCenter Server.

No direct administrator intervention is warranted or advised for this account because that would break vCenter Server functions needing this account. The account and password are never used by humans, and they do not have shell access on any ESX/ESXi hosts. Thus, it isn't necessary to manage this account or include it with normal administrative and regular user account security policies.

Any time vCenter Server polls an ESX/ESXi host or an administrator creates a task that needs to be communicated to an ESX/ESXi host, the vpxuser account is used. All tasks and commands are funneled through vCenter Server so that vCenter Server can apply the appropriate restrictions based on roles, privileges, and permissions.

You're now ready to move on to securing the next major component in your VMware vSphere environment, the virtual machines.

Securing Virtual Machines

As with vCenter Server, any discussion of how to secure a virtual machine is really a discussion of how to secure the guest operating system within that virtual machine. Entire books have been and are being written about how to secure Windows, Linux, Solaris, and the other guest operating systems VMware vSphere supports, so I won't attempt to cover that sort of material here. I will provide two recommendations around securing virtual machines. One of these is specific to the vSphere virtualized environment, whereas the other is much more broad and general.

First, I want to call your attention to the VMware vSphere network security policies.

Configuring Network Security Policies

VMware vSphere provides some outstanding virtual networking functionality, particularly with the addition of the vNetwork Distributed Switch and the Cisco Nexus 1000V third-party distributed virtual switch. These virtual switches provide several different security-related policies you can set to help ensure that the security of your virtual machines is maintained. I discussed all these settings in Chapter 5.

The key security-related network security policies you can set in the vSphere virtual networking environment are as follows:

◆ Promiscuous mode

◆ MAC address changes

◆ Forged transmits

VMware recommends keeping all of these policies set to Reject. If there is a valid business need for one of these features to be allowed, you can use per-port group settings to enable the appropriate feature only for the specific virtual machine or machines that require such functionality. One example I've used before is a network-based intrusion detection/intrusion prevent system (IDS/IPS). Rather than allowing promiscuous mode—required for most IDS/IPS to work—on the entire vSwitch, create a separate port group just for that virtual machine and allow promiscuous mode on that port group only.

When considering the security of your virtual machines, be sure to keep these network security policies in mind, and be sure that they are configured for the correct balance of functionality vs. security.

My next recommendation with regard to securing virtual machines is much more general but still a valid recommendation nevertheless.

Keeping Virtual Machines Patched

As with your ESX/ESXi hosts and your vCenter Server computer, it's imperative to keep the guest operating systems in your virtual machines properly patched. You can use vCenter Update Manager, covered in Chapter 4, to help with this task, but regardless of the system that you use, be sure to use it. My experience has shown me that many security problems could have been avoided with a proactive patching strategy for the guest operating systems in virtual machines.

Although these recommendations are useful, even following these recommendations sometimes may not be enough, especially when your organizations needs tighter access controls on network traffic. For this sort of environment, a new product from VMware called vShield Zones can help.

Providing Virtual Network Security with vShield Zones

vShield Zones is a new product from VMware shipping with VMware vSphere 4. vShield Zones is designed to address one key security problem with virtualized environments: a lack of visibility and control over network traffic at the access layer. Because VMware vSphere virtualizes the access layer via vSwitches and vNetwork Distributed Switches, there is no way for security administrators to even see, much less control, the traffic that flows to virtual machines, from virtual machines, or among virtual machines on an ESX/ESXi host. vShield Zones squarely addresses that problem by providing visibility into the types of traffic that are flowing on the virtual switches in your vSphere environment, as well as providing a level of control over that traffic.

Installing vShield Zones

vShield Zones has two major components, vShield Manager and one or more vShield virtual appliances. vShield Manager is the management station, controlling one or more vShield virtual appliances. You'll use vShield Manager to select ESX/ESXi hosts to protect, for example. The vShield virtual appliances are small virtual machines that perform the actual traffic inspection and control as directed by vShield Manager.

You install vShield Zones using the following three-step process:

1. Deploy the vShield Manager virtual appliance.

2. Configure vShield Manager for integration with vCenter Server.

3. Deploy one or more vShield virtual appliances into your VMware vSphere environment.

DEPLOYING vSHIELD MANAGER

Deploying vShield Manager is the first step in installing vShield Zones. For ease of deployment, vShield Manager is distributed as a virtual appliance using an Open Virtualization Format (OVF) package. To deploy the vShield Manager, you can simply use vCenter Server's Deploy OVF Template command, as I described in Chapter 8.

Perform the following steps to deploy the vShield Manager OVF template:

1. Launch the vSphere Client if it is not already running, and connect to a vCenter Server instance.

2. From File menu, select Deploy OVF Template. The Deploy OVF Template Wizard starts.

3. Assuming you have downloaded the vShield Manager and have it stored locally or on the local area network (LAN), select the Deploy From File option, and use the Browse button to find and select the .ovf file for the vShield Manager. Click Next to continue.

4. Click Next to proceed past the OVF template details display.

5. Specify a name for the vShield Manager and an inventory location in vCenter Server, and then click Next.

6. Select a datastore where you want to store the vShield Manager's configuration (VMX) and virtual machine disk (VMDK) files. Click Next.

7. Select the correct network where you want to map the OVF template's VSMgmt network. Click Next after you've selected the desired destination network.

8. Review the deployment task details, and click Finish if everything is correct. If there are any errors, use the Back button to make the necessary changes.

After the OVF template deployment is complete, you can power on the new virtual machine and proceed with configuring vShield Manager.

CONFIGURING vSHIELD MANAGER

After vShield Manager has been deployed from the OVF template, the first thing you will need to do is configure vShield Manager with a static IP address. After network connectivity is established, you can continue with configuring vShield Manager through the web-based interface. To help with assigning a static IP address to vShield Manager, VMware provides a setup command you can use in vShield Manager's virtual machine console.

Perform the following steps to establish network connectivity to vShield Manager for configuration:

1. Power on the vShield Manager virtual machine, if it is not already powered on.

2. Right-click the vShield Manager virtual machine, and select Open Console.

3. After the vShield Manager VM finishes booting, log in at the `manager login:` prompt with the username *admin* and the password *default*.

4. Type the command **setup**, and press Enter.

5. Follow the prompts to provide the IP address, subnet mask (in number of bits instead of dotted decimal format), and default gateway.

6. When the `setup` command is finished, follow the instructions, and then log out of the vShield Manager console.

At this point, you should verify that you have connectivity to vShield Manager before proceeding. You can use the `ping` command to make sure that you can successfully send to and receive from vShield Manager across the network. If you are not able to communicate with vShield Manager across the network, double-check the configuration of the virtual machine to be sure it is attached to the correct virtual machine port group.

The rest of the configuration for vShield Manager is performed via a web-based interface. From this web-based interface, you will configure a connection to vCenter Server, supply additional network configuration parameters, and register a vSphere Client plug-in.

Perform the following steps to complete the initial configuration of vShield Manager:

1. Open a web browser, and connect to the IP address of vShield Manager. Be sure to use HTTP over Secure Sockets Layer (SSL), also known as HTTPS. If you forget to use HTTPS, the web browser will redirect automatically to an HTTPS connection.

2. Select the Configuration tab.

3. Click the vCenter link.

4. Enter the IP address of the vCenter Server, as well as a username and password used to access vCenter Server.

CONFIGURE DNS FIRST IF USING A HOSTNAME

If you want to use a hostname for the vCenter Server in the configuration for vShield Manager, you'll need to first click the DNS link and set the addresses for the DNS servers in your environment.

---

5. Click Commit after entering the vCenter Server connection information. If the connection is successful, the screen will refresh to include a listing of the vCenter Server inventory on the left side of the web browser window.

6. To register the vSphere Client plug-in, click the vSphere Plug-In link, and then click the Register button.

7. A security warning dialog box appears warning you about the self-signed SSL certificate used by vShield Manager; click Ignore to continue and register the plug-in. After the plug-in is registered, you will be able to access the vShield Manager web interface from the vSphere Client home screen.

vShield Manager is now up and running and configured to communicate with vCenter Server. The next step in setting up vShield Zones is deploying the vShield virtual machines, which I'll discuss in the next section.

DEPLOYING THE VSHIELD VIRTUAL APPLIANCES

Like vShield Manager, the vShield virtual machines are distributed as virtual appliances using an OVF template. To deploy the vShield virtual appliance, you will use the same process as described earlier when deploying vShield Manager.

When you deploy the vShield virtual appliance into your vCenter Server environment, you'll need to map the source networks in the virtual appliance onto actual port groups that you created in vCenter Server. As shown in Figure 13.3, you must configure the following three source networks:

◆ VSMgmt: This is the management network for the vShield appliance. The vShield virtual appliance communicates with vShield Manager over this network interface.

◆ Protected: This port group is where virtual machines protected by the vShield virtual appliance will connect. All traffic to or from this port group must go through the vShield virtual appliance so that it can apply network security policies to the traffic.

◆ Unprotected: This port group is where virtual machines that are not protected by the vShield virtual appliance will connect. As the name implies, the vShield virtual appliance will not control the traffic traveling to or from this port group to the rest of the network.

FIGURE 13.3
You must map the vShield virtual appliance's three source networks to the appropriate port groups in your environment.

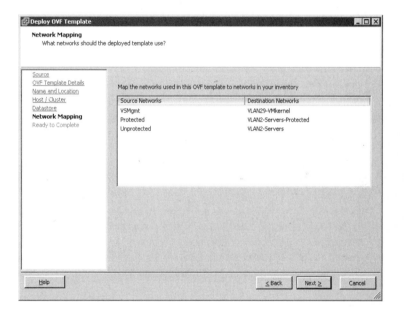

Because of the way the vShield virtual appliances operate, you will need to deploy at least one vShield virtual appliance onto every ESX/ESXi host that has virtual machines you want to protect. If the virtual machines on any particular host use more than one vSwitch, you will need a vShield appliance for each vSwitch on that ESX/ESXi host that has virtual machines attached to it.

To simplify the deployment of multiple instances of the vShield virtual appliance, you should convert the vShield virtual appliance to a vCenter Server template. I described the process for converting a virtual machine to a template in Chapter 7.

With a vShield virtual appliance converted to a template, you're now ready to actually deploy a working instance of the vShield virtual appliance onto a host to protect virtual machines.

> **vNETWORK DISTRIBUTED SWITCHES REQUIRE MANUAL DEPLOYMENT**
>
> vShield Zones currently cannot perform an automated deployment of a vShield virtual appliance to hosts participating in a vNetwork Distributed Switch. To use vShield Zones with a vNetwork Distributed Switch, use the Manual Install link in vShield Manager, and follow the instructions found in the "vShield Zones Administrator's Guide," available from VMware at `www.vmware.com/downloads`.

Perform the following steps to protect an ESX/ESXi host's virtual machines with a vShield virtual appliance:

1. Launch a web browser, and connect to vShield Manager's web interface.

2. Log in as the user *admin* with the password *default*.

3. Select an ESX/ESXi host from the inventory tree on the left side of the web browser window.

4. Click the Install vShield tab on the right side of the web browser window. vShield Manager will collect some information.

5. Click the Configure Install Parameters link.

6. In the Select Template To Clone drop-down list, choose the vShield template you just created.

7. In the Select A Datastore To Place Clone drop-down list, select a datastore in which to store the cloned vShield virtual appliance.

8. Provide a name for the cloned vShield appliance in the Enter A Name For The Clone text box.

9. In the text boxes under the Specify vShield Configuration heading, supply an IP address, subnet mask, default gateway, and (optionally) a secure key. The optional secure key is used to secure communications between the vShield virtual appliance and vShield Manager.

10. Click the Continue button at the top of the web form. vShield Manager will calculate how the new vSwitch and port group layout will look.

11. Review the changes vShield Manager will make to the network configuration on the selected host, and then click the Install button to proceed.

vShield Manager will communicate with vCenter Server to perform the necessary tasks to clone the template, configure the cloned virtual machine, and change the ESX/ESXi host networking configuration. You will see the tasks in the Tasks pane of the vSphere Client, and vShield Manager will show the current task highlighted in blue. It may take several minutes for the series of tasks to complete.

Figure 13.4 shows an example of how an ESX/ESXi host's network configuration will look after vShield Manager has finished deploying a vShield virtual appliance to that host.

FIGURE 13.4
vShield Manager creates an internal-only vSwitch and forces all traffic to flow through the vShield virtual appliance.

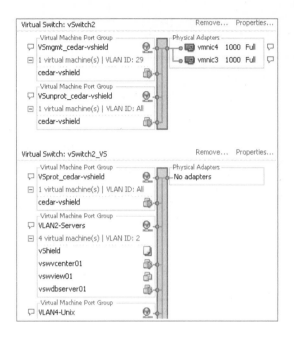

ENABLING VMOTION ON AN INTERNAL-ONLY VSWITCH

VMware Knowledge Base article 1006701 describes how you can edit vCenter Server's vpxd.cfg file to enable VMotion operations for virtual machines attached to an internal-only vSwitch. Without making the change to this file and restarting the vCenter Server service, virtual machines protected by vShield Zones can't be migrated between ESX/ESXi hosts using VMotion. As of the writing of this book, this Knowledge Base article had not been updated for ESX/ESXi 4.0 and vCenter Server 4.0, but I suspect it should work as documented.

As you can see in Figure 13.4, vShield protects virtual machines by placing them on an internal-only vSwitch. The vShield virtual appliance becomes the only way that virtual machines can communicate with the rest of the network. The vShield virtual appliance uses a couple of little-known settings to help make this possible. First, the vShield virtual appliance uses the VLAN ID 4095 on its port groups; this allows the port group to receive all VLAN IDs with the VLAN tags preserved. In addition, the vShield port groups have promiscuous mode, MAC address changes, and forged transmits all set to Accept. Together, these settings allow the vShield virtual appliance to act as an invisible Layer 2 bridge that controls traffic flowing to or from the protected virtual machines without requiring the virtual machines to be reconfigured in any way.

Now that both vShield Manager and at least one vShield virtual appliance have been deployed, you are ready to start protecting virtual machine network traffic with vShield Zones.

Using vShield Zones to Protect Virtual Machines

The configuration of vShield Zones to protect virtual machines is all handled via vShield Manager's web-based interface. vShield Manager uses the concept of the *VM wall*, a VM-specific firewall, to control traffic to or from virtual machines.

VM wall rules can be defined at the datacenter level or the cluster level. VM wall rules operate sort of like vCenter Server permissions: a VM wall rule defined at the datacenter level is inherited by all vShield instances in that datacenter. Similarly, VM wall rules defined at the cluster level are inherited by all vShield instances in that cluster.

VM wall rules can be Layer 2/3 or Layer 4 rules. This means that VM wall rules can operate not only on source destination IP addresses but also on a specific TCP or UDP port. vShield Manager allows you to create VM wall rules manually or to create VM wall rules from reports of existing traffic patterns. These reports are generated automatically by vShield Manager as it observes the traffic moving through the vShield virtual appliances.

Perform the following steps to view the VM wall rules:

1. Launch a web browser, and log into vShield Manager's web interface using the user *admin* and the password *default*.

2. From the inventory tree on the left, select the datacenter object.

3. Click the VM wall tab on the right. vShield Manager displays the VM wall rules defined at the datacenter level.

When you view the VM wall rules at the datacenter level, you will notice two types of datacenter rules. First, *Data Center High Precedence rules* are listed in the first group of rows in the list of VM wall rules, just below the row labeled Data Center High Precedence Rules. These rules are processed first and therefore will override rules defined at the cluster level.

Second, *Data Center Low Precedence rules* are listed just below the row labeled Rules Below This Level Have Lower Precedence Than The Cluster-Level Rules. These are processed after cluster-level rules and therefore will be overridden by cluster-level rules.

The rules listed under Default Rules are processed last and therefore could be overridden by any previous rule.

When creating VM wall rules, then, it's important for you to understand the proper placement of the rule. If you create the rule as a Data Center High Precedence rule, then it will override any rules you may have defined at the cluster level. Likewise, if you create the rule as a Data Center Low Precedence rule, then cluster-level rules may override your rule, creating unexpected behavior.

With this information in mind, you'll now learn how to create a Data Center High Precedence rule to block Internet Relay Chat (IRC) traffic to or from protected servers.

Perform the following steps to create a VM wall rule manually:

1. Launch a web browser, and log in to vShield Manager's web interface using the user *admin* and the password *default*.

2. In the inventory tree on the left, select the datacenter object.

3. Click the VM wall tab on the right. vShield Manager will display the VM wall rules defined at the datacenter level.

4. Click the Add button. A new VM wall will be created as a Data Center Low Precedence rule.

5. For each of the fields (Source Port, Destination, Destination Application, Destination Port, Protocol, Action, Log), double-click the field, and set the desired value. For IRC, set the destination port to 6667 and the protocol to TCP.

6. Set the Action field to DENY.

7. Select the check box to log traffic matching this rule. A dialog box appears warning you that logging can generate a performance impact for rules that match large amounts of traffic. Click OK to continue.

8. Use the Up button to move the new rule into the Data Center High Precedence rules area.

9. Click the Commit button to apply the changes. In the dialog box that appears informing you the changes are going to be applied to vShield, click OK to continue.

The VM wall rule is committed to vShield Manager and then synchronized out to the vShield virtual appliances running on the various ESX/ESXi hosts. The vShield virtual appliances now enforce this traffic rule on the traffic moving to or from the virtual machines they protect.

In the event you are unsure about the ports or protocols you need to specify when creating a rule, you can also create rules from traffic observed by the vShield appliances and reported back to vShield Manager. The VM Flow tab shows information on observed traffic types. The ability to create VM wall rules from a VM flow report is available only for datacenter and cluster objects.

Perform the following steps to create a VM wall rule from the VM flow report:

1. Launch a web browser, and log in to vShield Manager's web interface using the user *admin* and the password *default*.

2. In the inventory tree on the left, select the datacenter object.

3. Click the VM Flow tab.

4. Click the Update Report button to generate a VM flow report. You can adjust the start and end dates of the report, if necessary.

5. Navigate through the tree of allowed or denied traffic types to find the specific type of traffic for which you'd like to create a VM wall rule. Figure 13.5 shows that I've selected outbound NetBIOS broadcasts via UDP.

6. Click the VM wall radio button.

7. A dialog box will appear, confirming that you want to navigate to the VM wall page to add the new rule. Click OK to continue.

8. Modify the fields of the rule to create the desired behavior.

9. Click the Commit button, and when prompted, click OK to proceed with committing the changes to vShield.

FIGURE 13.5
Navigate through the VM flow report to find the specific type of traffic for which you'd like to create a VM wall rule.

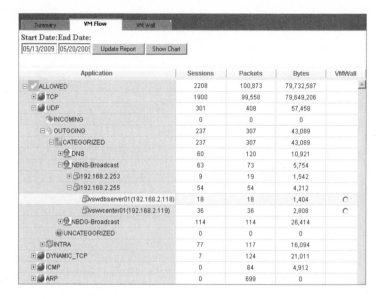

Application	Sessions	Packets	Bytes	VMWall
ALLOWED	2208	100,873	79,732,587	
TCP	1900	99,558	79,649,206	
UDP	301	408	57,458	
INCOMING	0	0	0	
OUTGOING	237	307	43,089	
CATEGORIZED	237	307	43,089	
DNS	60	120	10,921	
NBNS-Broadcast	63	73	5,754	
192.168.2.253	9	19	1,542	
192.168.2.255	54	54	4,212	
vswdbserver01(192.168.2.118)	18	18	1,404	○
vswvcenter01(192.168.2.119)	36	36	2,808	○
NBDG-Broadcast	114	114	26,414	
UNCATEGORIZED	0	0	0	
INTRA	77	117	16,094	
DYNAMIC_TCP	7	124	21,011	
ICMP	0	84	4,912	
ARP	0	699	0	

In the event that you've created a VM wall rule that you no longer need, you can easily delete the VM wall rule using the Delete button on the VM Wall tab. As I mentioned earlier, you can also easily change the order of the VM wall rules using the Up and Down buttons. Although my discussion here has focused on VM wall rules at the datacenter level, the same basic operations apply at the cluster level as well.

---

vSHIELD ZONES FEATURES SNAPSHOTS, TOO

If you've totally messed up your VM wall rules and just need to revert to the previous configuration, you're in luck—vShield Manager takes a snapshot of the current VM wall configuration every time you commit a new set of rules. You can use the Revert To Snapshot drop-down list to select a previous snapshot of VM wall rules and then apply that set of rules using the Commit button.

---

vShield Zones offers a good solution to the lack of visibility and control at the access layer of the network created by the use of virtualization. It is therefore an important part of an overall defense-in-depth strategy. Another part of that strategy is the various security applications that you use in your environment, such as antivirus software. A key feature of VMware vSphere, the VMsafe APIs, offers the ability to drastically change how you use these types of applications in your environment, as you'll see in the next section.

 **Real World Scenario**

DOES VIRTUALIZATION MAKE YOU MORE OR LESS SECURE?

There is a significant debate over whether virtualization makes your environment more or less secure. Although countless arguments are tossed back and forth in this debate, the truth of the matter is not really all that clear.

As some of my colleagues and friends who specialize in security like to say, "Security is a pursuit, not a goal." This means that security needs to be incorporated into every aspect of your infrastructure. If you keep security in mind during the design and implementation of your VMware vSphere environment, I believe that you can improve your security posture. If, on the other hand, you don't observe security-related best practices, then you will almost certainly damage your security posture and make your organization more vulnerable.

These are some of the security-related best practices that you should be sure to follow:

◆ Use virtual network security policies correctly. Disable promiscuous mode, forged transmits, and MAC address changes unless you have a valid business reason for allowing them. When they do need to be allowed, use a separate port group created specifically for that purpose.

◆ Use the access controls and role-based administration model that vCenter Server provides to follow the concept of least privilege—give users only the minimum permissions required to do their jobs.

◆ Properly secure your ESX and ESXi hosts, as described in this chapter.

◆ Don't forget to harden the guest operating systems in your virtual machines. Just because you've virtualized Windows Server 2003 doesn't automatically make it more secure. Follow vendor-provided best practices and guidelines, and bake these into the templates that you use for VM deployment so that every new VM gets the right settings by default.

◆ Implement a strategy for managing your virtual machines, and establish a process for managing the life cycle of your virtual machines; or use a product like VMware vCenter Lifecycle Manager. Just because you *can* create lots of virtual machines doesn't mean you *should*.

◆ Take advantage of VMware vShield Zones to provide VM-level firewalls without needing to rearchitect your network or IP addressing schemes.

VMware vSphere offers some great functionality, and I think that when vSphere's functionality is combined with a purposeful focus on security throughout the design, implementation, and operation of a virtualized environment, you can improve your organization's security profile in the datacenter.

Understanding VMsafe

As an end user of VMware vSphere, the VMsafe application programming interfaces (APIs) are not something you can actually see, configure, enable, disable, or otherwise manipulate. However, understanding what the VMsafe APIs are is, I think, an important part to understanding how security in virtualized environments is evolving and changing.

First introduced in early 2008 at VMware's VMworld Europe user conference, the VMsafe APIs provide a set of published interfaces that third-party application developers can use to build security solutions for virtualized environments. One such solution that is commonly described is an antivirus solution. Without the VMsafe APIs, users are required to run antivirus software inside every guest operating system. If an ESX/ESXi host has 10 virtual machines running on it, then there will be 10 independent copies of antivirus software running. This creates additional load on the virtualization infrastructure.

With a VMsafe-compatible antivirus solution, though, there would be only a single antivirus instance running, and this instance would be running separate from the guest operating systems that it protects. Typically, a VMsafe-compatible solution would be delivered as a virtual appliance. Using the VMsafe APIs, this antivirus virtual appliance would have the ability to perform antivirus functions—such as scanning memory, watching processes, or investigating network traffic—for all the virtual machines and guest operating systems running on that host. By running only a single instance of antivirus and by running that instance outside of the guest operating systems it protects, VMsafe increases both the security of the solution and the efficiency of the solution. No longer will rogue processes within a guest operating system be able to shut down the antivirus protection also running in that same guest operating system, because this single, VMsafe-compatible instance runs outside all of the virtual machines, yet is able to protect all of the virtual machines.

The antivirus solution I describe is only an example. The VMsafe APIs also enable a number of other security solutions, such as intrusion detection and prevention systems and firewalls. For more complete details on the VMsafe APIs, refer to the VMware website at www.vmware.com/technology/security/vmsafe.html.

You should now have a good understanding of some of the steps involved in securing your VMware vSphere environment. In the next chapter, I'll show you some ways to bring automation to your environment.

The Bottom Line

Manage local users on ESX/ESXi hosts. Despite that vCenter Server eliminates most of the uses for local accounts created and managed on each ESX/ESXi host, there is still a small but critical need for local accounts. You can use Linux-based tools like useradd, userdel, groupadd, and groupdel to create and delete local users and groups on ESX hosts. For both ESX and ESXi hosts, the vSphere Client also offers the ability to manage local users and groups.

Master It You've asked an administrator on your team to create some accounts on an ESX host. The administrator is uncomfortable with the Linux command line and is having a problem figuring out how to create the users. Is there another way for this administrator to perform this task?

Configure authentication on ESX hosts. vCenter Server centralizes the authentication of users through integration with Active Directory, but that authentication support does not extend to user accounts that exist directly on ESX hosts. To provide more centralized authentication for ESX hosts you can use the esxcfg-auth command to enable integration with Active Directory. This provides a single point of administration for accounts accessing both vCenter Server as well as ESX hosts directly.

Master It You've just installed a new ESX host into your VMware vSphere environment and used the esxcfg-auth command to enable integration with your Active Directory environment. For some reason, though, you can't authenticate to this new host. You've compared the configuration of this new host to the configuration of other working hosts but can't pinpoint any differences. What could be the problem?

Control network access to services on ESX hosts. VMware ESX allows you to leverage the Linux-based Service Console to control access to network services, like SSH, through a couple of different means. First, VMware supplies an iptables-based firewall configured using the esxcfg-firewall command. Second, you can use TCP Wrappers to control access to a variety of network services. Third, and finally, you can leverage functionality native to SSH to control what user accounts are allowed to log in via SSH. All of these tools are complementary to one another.

Master It   Describe how the Service Console firewall and TCP Wrappers are complementary to each other and where their functionality overlaps.

Provide secure network zones.   VMware vShield Zones provides a network-based security solution designed to eliminate a key problem with virtualized environments: the lack of visibility and control over the network access layer. Using a modular approach consisting of vShield Manager for configuration and management and multiple vShield virtual appliances for policy enforcement, vShield Zones enables administrators to both see and control the traffic flowing through their virtual switches. This makes vShield Zones a key component in a defense-in-depth strategy that also includes traditional physical network security appliances.

Master It   Your CIO believes that it is not safe to use VMware vSphere in environments with multiple trust zones. How can the functionality provided by vShield Zones help you convince her otherwise?

Chapter 14

Automating VMware vSphere

As a VMware vSphere administrator, there are lots of repetitive tasks you'll need to perform. Examples include creating five new virtual machines from a template, changing the network configuration on eighteen virtual machines, or creating a new port group on seven different VMware ESX/ESXi hosts. All these examples are tasks where automation would help you complete the task more quickly, provide greater consistency, save you time, and ultimately save your organization money. Clearly, automation is an area that can benefit every VMware vSphere administrator and every organization that adopts VMware vSphere in their environment.

In this chapter, you will learn to:

◆ Identify some of the tools available for automating VMware vSphere

◆ Configure vCenter Orchestrator

◆ Use a vCenter Orchestrator workflow

◆ Create a PowerCLI script for automation

◆ Leverage shell scripts on VMware ESX

Why Use Automation?

The real question isn't why use automation, but why not use automation? As a former system administrator, I was frequently looking for ways to automate tasks that I had to perform on a regular basis. Whether it was creating user accounts, rebuilding computers, deploying new applications, or querying the status of a remote server in another location, anything that saved me time and prevented me from having to repeat the same steps over and over again was a good thing. The same applies here: anything that can save you time and prevent you from performing the same steps repeatedly in your VMware vSphere environment is a good thing.

You can provide automation in your VMware vSphere environment in a number of ways. Depending upon your programming skill level and your experience, there is likely a toolkit or automation tool that fits you and your needs:

◆ Systems administrators with knowledge of Perl can use the vSphere Software Development Kit (SDK) for Perl, which provides Perl interfaces to the vSphere application programming interface (API).

◆ Administrators with experience in traditional UNIX or Linux shell scripting can create shell scripts to automate some tasks from the VMware ESX Service Console. These tools would not work on VMware ESXi because ESXi does not have a user-accessible service console.

◆ vSphere administrators with knowledge or experience in Microsoft PowerShell can use PowerShell and PowerCLI to create PowerShell scripts that automate tasks within the vSphere environment.

◆ VMware administrators with a background in more serious programming languages such as C# or Java can use the vSphere Web Services SDK to build applications that leverage the web services APIs provided with vSphere.

◆ System administrators with some prior experience in JavaScript could use vCenter Orchestrator, an automation platform installed automatically with vCenter Server, to build workflows.

As you can see, you have lots of options for bringing automation into your vSphere environment—and that's without taking into account any of the numerous third-party solutions available!

In this chapter, I'll focus on three potential solutions for automation in your VMware vSphere environment:

◆ vCenter Orchestrator

◆ PowerShell with PowerCLI

◆ ESX shell scripts

These three solutions address the majority of the needs of most VMware vSphere administrators. I'll start with vCenter Orchestrator.

Using Workflows with vCenter Orchestrator

VMware vCenter Orchestrator is a workflow automation product that allows you to build custom workflows that automate entire sequences of events. vCenter Orchestrator provides access to the vCenter Server API and the more than 800 actions that are available within vCenter Server, allowing you to build workflows that address just about every conceivable need. To give you an idea of the versatility of the vCenter Orchestrator product, keep in mind that the vCenter Orchestrator engine runs underneath VMware vCenter Lifecycle Manager. vCenter Lifecycle Manager is a separate product from VMware that provides automation around the entire virtual machine life cycle, from provisioning all the way to decommissioning, and it is built entirely upon vCenter Orchestrator.

To help users harness the power of vCenter Orchestrator in their environments, vCenter Orchestrator is silently installed when vCenter Server is installed. You might recall that I briefly mentioned vCenter Orchestrator in Chapter 3 during my discussion of the vCenter Server installation process. Now I'd like to delve much deeper into vCenter Orchestrator and show you how you can use it to help provide some automation in your environment.

Although vCenter Orchestrator is installed with vCenter Server, you must configure vCenter Orchestrator separately after the installation is complete. In the next section, I'll walk you through configuring vCenter Orchestrator so that it is ready for you to use.

Configuring vCenter Orchestrator

After you complete the installation of vCenter Server and, with it, vCenter Orchestrator, you can proceed with the configuration of vCenter Orchestrator so that it is ready to use. The process of configuring vCenter Orchestrator involves a number of steps, each of which I will describe in detail in the following sections.

The vCenter Orchestrator configuration process involves, at the very least, the following steps:

1. Start the vCenter Orchestrator Configuration service.

2. Configure the vCenter Orchestrator network connection.

3. Create and test a connection to a working Lightweight Directory Access Protocol (LDAP) server.

4. Set up the back-end database.

5. Import or create a Secure Sockets Layer (SSL) certificate for vCenter Orchestrator.

6. Import the vCenter Server license.

7. Configure the default plug-ins.

I'll walk through each of these steps later in this section, but first you need to ensure your environment meets all of the vCenter Orchestrator prerequisites.

UNDERSTANDING VCENTER ORCHESTRATOR PREREQUISITES

Because vCenter Orchestrator is installed silently with vCenter Server, many of the prerequisites for vCenter Orchestrator are the same as for vCenter Server. Like vCenter Server, vCenter Orchestrator runs on either Windows Server 2003 or Windows Server 2008, and it supports both the 32-bit and 64-bit versions of those operating systems. Also like vCenter Server, vCenter Orchestrator requires a separate back-end database. This back-end database must be separate from the vCenter Server back-end database.

These are the database servers that vCenter Orchestrator supports for this back-end database:

◆ Microsoft SQL Server 2005 SP1 or SP2 (Standard or Enterprise), 32-bit or 64-bit (64-bit support is limited to Enterprise Edition with SP2)

◆ Microsoft SQL Server 2000 SP4 (Standard or Enterprise)

◆ Oracle 10*g* Enterprise Release 2 (10.2.0.3.0), 32-bit or 64-bit

MySQL and PostgreSQL are also supported, but only for testing and evaluation purposes.

USE A SEPARATE PHYSICAL SERVER FOR THE ORCHESTRATOR DATABASE

Because of CPU and memory usage, VMware recommends placing the vCenter Orchestrator database on a separate machine from the vCenter Orchestrator server. These machines should reside in the same data center for high-speed local area network (LAN) connectivity.

If you are planning on using an Oracle database, you must download the Oracle drivers and copy them to the appropriate locations; the vCenter Orchestrator installer does not do this for you. For more complete information on exactly how this is accomplished, refer to the "vCenter Orchestrator Installation and Configuration Guide" available from VMware's website at www.vmware.com/support/pubs/orchestrator_pubs.html.

Additionally, vCenter Orchestrator also requires a working LDAP server in your environment. Supported LDAP servers include OpenLDAP, Novell eDirectory, Sun Java Directory Server, and Microsoft Active Directory.

After you verify that you meet all these prerequisites, then you are ready to get started configuring vCenter Orchestrator.

STARTING THE VCENTER ORCHESTRATOR CONFIGURATION SERVICE

The first step in configuring vCenter Orchestrator is starting the vCenter Orchestrator Configuration service. By default, the vCenter Orchestrator Configuration service is set for Manual startup. In order to be able to access the web-based configuration interface, you must first start this service.

Perform the following steps to start the vCenter Orchestrator Configuration service:

1. Log into the computer running vCenter Server, where vCenter Orchestrator was also installed automatically, as an administrative user.

2. From the Start menu, choose Run.

3. In the Run dialog box, type **services.msc**, and click OK.

4. When the Services window opens, scroll through the list of services in the pane on the right until you see the VMware vCenter Orchestrator Configuration service.

5. Right-click the VMware vCenter Orchestrator Configuration service, and select Start.

6. Verify that the service started correctly by ensuring that the Status column for the VMware vCenter Orchestrator Configuration service lists Started.

After the service starts, you can access the vCenter Orchestrator Web Configuration interface. There are two ways that you can access the vCenter Orchestrator Web Configuration interface:

◆ From the Start menu, select All Programs ➢ VMware ➢ vCenter Orchestrator Web Configuration.

◆ Open a web browser, and go to `http://<computer IP address or DNS name>:8282`.

VCENTER ORCHESTRATOR START MENU ICONS MIGHT BE MISSING

If you installed vCenter Server to run in the context of a dedicated user account—perhaps in order to support Windows authentication to a back-end database running on Microsoft SQL Server—the vCenter Orchestrator Start menu icons are visible only to that user account. To make them visible to other user accounts, you must move them to the All Users portion of the Start menu.

You will log into the vCenter Orchestrator Web Configuration interface using the username *vmware* and the password *vmware*. Although you cannot change the default username, I highly recommend that you change the default password. There is an option for changing the default password in the vCenter Orchestrator Web Configuration interface.

You are now ready to proceed with configuring vCenter Orchestrator. Your first task is configuring the vCenter Orchestrator network connection.

CONFIGURING THE NETWORK CONNECTION

When you first log into the vCenter Orchestrator Configuration interface, you'll see a series of options along the left with red triangles, as shown in Figure 14.1. These red triangles, or status indicators, indicate that this option has not yet been configured. You need to ensure that all these status indicators are green circles before the vCenter Orchestrator Server will start and operate.

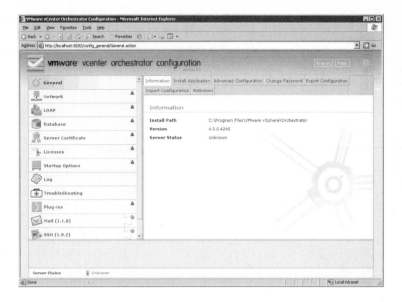

Starting at the top of this list of status indicators, your first task is to configure the network connection.

Perform the following steps to configure the network connection:

1. In the vCenter Orchestrator Configuration interface, click the Network tab on the left side of the window.

2. In the IP Address drop-down list, select the IP address upon which you want the vCenter Orchestrator Server to listen.

3. Click Apply Changes. It is generally not necessary to change any of the default ports for vCenter Orchestrator.

The status indicator for Network should now change from a red triangle to a green circle. Next you need to configure the LDAP connection.

CREATING AND TESTING THE LDAP CONNECTION

vCenter Orchestrator requires a supported LDAP server. In many cases, you will use Active Directory as your supported LDAP server because vCenter Server also integrates with Active Directory. As I mentioned earlier, other LDAP servers are supported. Here I'll explain how to configure vCenter Orchestrator to use Active Directory.

Perform the following steps to use an Active Directory domain controller as your LDAP server:

1. In the vCenter Orchestrator Configuration interface, click the LDAP tab on the left side of the web browser.

2. In the LDAP Client drop-down list, select Active Directory.

3. In the Primary LDAP Host text box, supply the fully qualified domain name (FQDN) of an Active Directory domain controller.

4. In the Secondary LDAP Host text box, supply the FQDN for a secondary Active Directory domain controller.

5. In the Root text box, supply the root DN for your Active Directory domain. For example, if your Active Directory domain name was `vmwarelab.net`, the root DN would be `dc=vmwarelab,dc=net`.

6. In the Username and Password text boxes, supply the username and password that vCenter Orchestrator will use to authenticate against Active Directory. Specify the username in DN format (`cn=username,cn=Users,dc=domain,dc=com`) or universal principal name (UPN) format (`username@domain.com`).

7. In the User Lookup Base text box, supply the base DN that vCenter Orchestrator should use when searching for user accounts. If you are unsure of what to use, specify the same value as the root DN.

8. In the Group Lookup Base text box, supply the base DN that vCenter Orchestrator should use when searching for groups. If you are unsure of what to use, specify the same value as the root DN.

9. In the vCO Admin Group text box, specify the DN of an Active Directory group that should receive vCenter Orchestrator administration rights. This should look something like `cn=Administrators,cn=Builtin,dc=domain,dc=com`.

10. Click the Apply Changes button.

The red triangle status indicator should change to a green circle. If it does not, double-check the LDAP configuration, and try again.

Next you are ready to set up the back-end database.

SETTING UP THE BACK-END DATABASE

Like vCenter Server and vCenter Update Manager, vCenter Orchestrator also requires a back-end database in order to operate. You must configure the back-end database and the vCenter Orchestrator database connection in order for vCenter Orchestrator to work. In this section, I'll walk through setting up a database on Microsoft SQL Server and configuring vCenter Orchestrator to use that database.

Creating and configuring the back-end database on Microsoft SQL Server is straightforward. Create the database, and specify the owner of the database to be either a Windows account or a SQL login. Be sure to note the owner of the database and the password for that owner, because both pieces of information will be necessary when you configure vCenter Orchestrator.

Perform the following steps to configure vCenter Orchestrator to use this back-end database:

1. In the vCenter Orchestrator Configuration interface, select the Database tab from the left side of the web browser window.

2. In the Select/Change Database Type drop-down list, select SQLServer.

3. Supply the username, password, hostname, port, database name, instance name (if using named instances), and domain name in the applicable text boxes. If you are using SQL authentication, leave the domain name text box blank.

4. Click the Install Database link to install the database tables that vCenter Orchestrator needs.

5. Click the Apply Changes button.

The red triangle should change to a green circle to show that database connectivity has been successfully verified.

Next you need to configure the server certificate.

Configuring the Server Certificate

vCenter Orchestrator requires that a valid SSL certificate is installed on the vCenter Orchestrator computer. The Server Certificate section of the vCenter Orchestrator Configuration interface allows you either to create your own self-signed certificate or to import an SSL certificate from an existing certificate authority. If you already have an existing public key infrastructure (PKI) set up within your environment, then I recommend leveraging that PKI and importing a valid SSL certificate from your PKI. Otherwise, you can create a self-signed SSL certificate using the Create A New Certificate Database And Server Certificate link.

Perform the following steps to create a new self-signed certificate for vCenter Orchestrator:

1. In the vCenter Orchestrator Configuration interface, click the Server Certificate tab on the left side of the interface.

2. Click the Create A New Certificate Database And Server Certificate link.

3. For Common Name, supply the FQDN of the vCenter Server computer.

4. For Organization and Organizational Unit, provide appropriate values for your environment.

5. Select the correct country in the Country drop-down list.

6. Click the Create button.

The vCenter Orchestrator Configuration service will generate a new SSL certificate and install it for use by vCenter Orchestrator. The red triangle will also change to a green circle, letting you know that this task has been completed. Next you will import the vCenter Server license.

Importing the vCenter Server License

Although it is installed with vCenter Server, vCenter Orchestrator does not automatically share the vCenter Server licensing information. To let vCenter Orchestrator know what sort of vCenter Server license you have, you will need to import that license into the vCenter Orchestrator Configuration interface.

Perform the following steps to import the vCenter Server license into vCenter Orchestrator:

1. In the vCenter Orchestrator Configuration interface, select the Licenses tab on the left side of the interface.

2. Supply the 25-digit serial number of your vCenter Server license and the license owner.

3. Click the Apply Changes button.

Depending on the vCenter Server license that you own, vCenter Orchestrator will operate in different modes:

◆ For a vCenter Server Standard license, vCenter Orchestrator operates in Server mode. This provides full access to all Orchestrator elements and the ability to run and edit workflows.

◆ For a vCenter Server Foundation or vCenter Server Essentials license, vCenter Orchestrator runs in Player mode. You are granted read-only permission on Orchestrator elements, and you can run workflows, but you cannot edit them.

You're almost done with the vCenter Orchestrator configuration. At this point, all of the status indicators except Startup Options and Plug-Ins should be green. As long as the Startup Options status indicator is still red, you won't be able to start vCenter Orchestrator Server. The last task for you is to configure the plug-ins.

CONFIGURING THE PLUG-INS

vCenter Orchestrator uses a plug-in architecture to add functionality and connectivity to the base workflow engine. By default, vCenter Orchestrator comes with a default set of plug-ins, but you'll need to provide a username and password of an account with administrative permissions in vCenter Orchestrator to install them.

Perform the following steps to install the default set of plug-ins:

1. In the vCenter Orchestrator Configuration interface, click the Plug-Ins tab.

2. Specify the username and password of an account that is a member of the vCO Administration group. This is the group you specified earlier when configuring the LDAP server.

3. Click Apply Changes.

The Plug-Ins status indicator will change to a green circle and, assuming all the other status indicators are also green circles, so will the Startup Options status indicator. However, there is one more essential task you need to complete first, and that is adding a vCenter Server host with which vCenter Orchestrator will communicate.

ADDING A VCENTER SERVER HOST

If you scroll down to the bottom of the list of configuration tabs in the vCenter Orchestrator Configuration interface, you will see a plug-in named vCenter 4.0 (4.0.0). That is the area where you will need to add a vCenter Server host with which vCenter Orchestrator will communicate. Without performing this task, vCenter Orchestrator will work, but it will not be able to automate tasks within vCenter Server—which kind of defeats its purpose.

Perform the following steps to add a vCenter Server host to vCenter Orchestrator:

1. At the bottom of the list of configuration tasks in the vCenter Orchestrator Configuration interface, select the tab labeled vCenter 4.0 (4.0.0).

2. Click the New VirtualCenter Host tab.

3. From the Available drop-down list, select Enabled.

4. In the Host text box, supply the FQDN of the vCenter Server computer you are adding.

5. Under the heading Specify The User Credential For The Administrator Session, specify an administrative username and password for this vCenter Server instance.

6. Under the heading Specify Which Strategy Will Be Used For Managing The Users Logins, select Share A Unique Session, and then supply a username and password to be passed to vCenter Server.

7. Click Apply Changes.

You will note that after you click the Apply Changes button, the vCenter 4.0 status indicator and the Startup Options status indicator changes to red. In order for vCenter Orchestrator to work with vCenter Server over an SSL connection, you must also import the vCenter Server SSL certificate.

Perform the following steps to import the vCenter Server SSL certificate:

1. Click the vCenter 4.0 (4.0.0) tab on the left side of the vCenter Orchestrator Configuration interface.

2. Click the Hosts tab.

3. Click the SSL Certificates link.

4. Because vCenter Orchestrator is installed by default on the same server as vCenter Server, you can import the SSL certificate from a local file. Click the Browse button.

5. Navigate to `C:\Documents and Settings\All Users\Application Data\VMware\VMware VirtualCenter\SSL`, and select the `rui.crt` file.

6. Click the Open button in the Choose File dialog box.

7. Click the Import button to import the selected certificate.

8. Click the vCenter 4.0 (4.0.0) tab again on the left side of the vCenter Orchestrator Configuration interface.

9. Click the Restart The vCO Configuration Server link. This will log you out of the vCenter Orchestrator Configuration interface.

10. Log back into the vCenter Orchestrator Configuration interface.

Now, you are finally ready to install and start the vCenter Orchestrator Server service.

INSTALLING AND STARTING THE VCENTER ORCHESTRATOR SERVER SERVICE

After you complete all the configuration steps, you can install and start the vCenter Orchestrator Server. Before you continue, ensure that all the status indicators in the Configuration Web Interface show a green circle. If any of the status indicators do not have a green circle, you won't be able to start the vCenter Orchestrator Server.

Perform the following steps to install and start the vCenter Orchestrator Server:

1. In the vCenter Orchestrator Configuration interface, click the Startup Options tab.

2. Click the Install vCO Server As A Service link. The interface will change to show a spinning progress meter while the configuration service installs the server service.

3. When the interface returns and indicates success with a green message at the top of the Startup Options screen, click the Start Service link.

4. The vCenter Orchestrator Server service will attempt to start. It might take a few minutes for the service to start, so be patient. You can use the Services management console (select Start ➢ Run, and enter **services.msc**) to verify the status of the vCenter Orchestrator Server service.

After the vCenter Orchestrator Server service is running, you're ready to start using vCenter Orchestrator workflows.

Using an Orchestrator Workflow

So far, you've only seen how to configure the vCenter Orchestrator Server, but now that the server is up and running, you are ready to launch the client and actually run a workflow. The vCenter

Orchestrator Client is the application you will use to actually launch a workflow. You can launch the vCenter Orchestrator Client from the Start menu and then log in with the Active Directory credentials of an account in the vCO Administrators group (this is the group configured earlier when you set up the LDAP server connection for vCenter Orchestrator).

vCenter Orchestrator comes with a library of pre-installed workflows. To view these workflows in the vCenter Orchestrator Client, simply click the Workflows tab on the left side of the window, and then browse through the tree folder structure to see what workflows are already available for you to use. Figure 14.2 shows some of the pre-installed workflows in the vCenter Orchestrator Client.

FIGURE 14.2
The vCenter folder contains all the workflows that automate actions in vCenter Server.

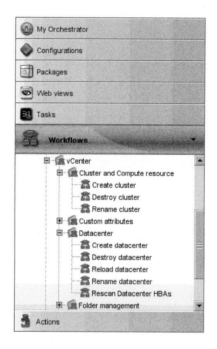

To run any of the workflows in the vCenter Orchestrator Client, you just right-click the workflow and select Execute Workflow. Depending upon the workflow, the vCenter Orchestrator Client prompts you for the information it needs to complete the workflow, such as the name of a virtual machine or the name of an ESX/ESXi host. The information that the vCenter Orchestrator Client prompts you to supply will vary based on the workflow you have selected to run.

Some sample workflows that are available for you in the vCenter Orchestrator Client include the following:

◆ The Rescan Datacenter HBAs workflow, which is used to scan the hosts in a vCenter Server datacenter object and have them initiate a re-scan of their storage controllers to discover new storage

◆ The Shutdown and Destroy VM workflow, which shuts down a virtual machine and then deletes it

◆ The Remove All Snapshots workflow, which deletes all snapshots from the selected virtual machine

CREATING WORKFLOWS IS MOSTLY A DEVELOPER'S TASK

Unfortunately, creating custom workflows is probably beyond the reach of most average vSphere administrators. Creating workflows and actions requires expertise and experience with web development languages like JavaScript. If this is something with which you have some knowledge, then I advise you to download the "vCenter Orchestrator Developer's Guide" from VMware's website at www.vmware.com/support/pubs/orchestrator_pubs.html. This developer guide provides more detailed information on how to create Orchestrator workflows.

vCenter Orchestrator is a powerful tool that is capable of creating some complex and highly interactive workflows. However, vCenter Orchestrator doesn't give up its secrets easily, and creating workflows may be beyond the skills of many vSphere administrators. One automation tool that is much easier to learn and is rapidly gaining popularity in the VMware community, though, is Microsoft PowerShell. PowerShell and PowerCLI can be great tools for automating your VMware vSphere environment, as you'll see in the next section.

Automating with PowerShell and PowerCLI

In late 2006, Microsoft released the release candidate version of a product code-named Monad, the product that would later become PowerShell. PowerShell is an object-oriented scripting language that seeks to combine the simplicity of the UNIX command line with the ability to deal with complex objects—not just text but any kind of object. Since its release, PowerShell has become an important part of many of Microsoft's server-based products, and VMware has provided support for using PowerShell to manage VMware Infrastructure environments in the VI Toolkit for Windows. With the release of vSphere, the VI Toolkit for Windows became PowerCLI.

PowerCLI extends PowerShell so that you can manipulate objects such as virtual machines, ESX/ESXi hosts, or the properties of these objects. Without PowerCLI, PowerShell lacks the information it needs to know how to work with these sorts of objects. By using PowerCLI with PowerShell, you can use PowerShell to create scripts that perform all sorts of tasks within your VMware vSphere environment.

The first step you'll need to take in order to use PowerCLI is to install PowerCLI, as I'll show you in the next section.

Installing PowerCLI

Installing PowerCLI actually means installing a few different components:

◆ Microsoft PowerShell V2 CTP3 (the latest version available as of this writing); available for download from Microsoft's website at www.microsoft.com/download

◆ PowerCLI, available for download from VMware's website at www.vmware.com/download

You might also want to install the VI Toolkit Community Extensions, a set of additional cmdlets (pronounced "command-lets"; these are essentially new commands that manipulate objects or perform tasks within vSphere) for PowerCLI. The VI Toolkit Community Extensions are available for download from http://vitoolkitextensions.codeplex.com on the Source Code tab.

Perform the following steps to install PowerCLI:

1. Install PowerShell V2 CTP3 by launching the installer and proceeding through the wizard. Accept the defaults for each step. On Windows Server 2003 R2 SP2, the PowerShell V2 CTP3 installation was three steps.

2. Next, launch the PowerCLI installer that you downloaded from VMware's website.

3. If the installer displays a dialog box informing you that VMware VIX will be installed at the end of setup, click OK to continue.

4. A warning message displays warning you that the PowerShell execution policy is currently set to Restricted. You will change this later; for now, click Continue to proceed with the installation.

5. On the first screen of the VMware vSphere PowerCLI installation wizard, click Next to start the installation.

6. Select the radio button marked I Accept The Terms In The License Agreement, and click Next.

7. Change the location where PowerCLI will be installed, or click Next to accept the default location.

8. Click Install.

9. After the installation is complete, deselect the box to launch PowerCLI, and click Finish.

Remember the warning about the PowerShell execution policy? Before you can use PowerCLI, you'll need to set the PowerShell execution policy to allow some of the PowerCLI components to execute.

Perform the following steps to set the PowerShell execution policy:

1. In the Start menu, select All Programs ➢ PowerShell V2 (CTP3) ➢ PowerShell V2 (CTP3).

2. At the PowerShell prompt, enter the following command:

```
Set-ExecutionPolicy RemoteSigned
```

3. To verify the setting, enter the following command:

```
Get-ExecutionPolicy
```

The results of the Get-ExecutionPolicy command should be RemoteSigned.

WHAT HAPPENS IF YOU DON'T SET THE EXECUTION POLICY?

Because PowerCLI runs a few PowerShell scripts during startup to load the appropriate snap-ins, failing to set the execution policy to RemoteSigned means these scripts will not run properly. Errors will be returned when these scripts execute, and PowerCLI will not be correctly initialized.

Now you are ready to launch PowerCLI. When you launch PowerCLI, you are greeted with a few quick tips and the PowerShell prompt, as shown in Figure 14.3.

If you are seeing this screen when you launch PowerCLI, then you're ready to start using PowerCLI to manage your VMware vSphere environment. First, though, I'll review the idea of objects and introduce you to a few useful objects in PowerCLI.

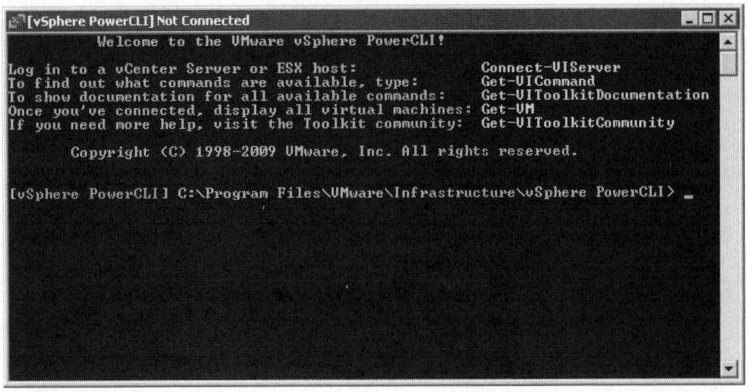

FIGURE 14.3
The PowerCLI startup screen provides quick tips on a few useful commands.

Working with Objects

Everything in PowerShell (and hence PowerCLI) is built upon the idea of objects. For example, an ESX/ESXi host exists as an object in PowerCLI. A virtual machine exists as an object in PowerCLI. A snapshot exists as an object. You will work with these objects in PowerCLI by modifying their properties, creating them, or deleting them.

With PowerCLI specifically, you must first connect to the vSphere environment, either to a vCenter Server instance or to an ESX/ESXi host, before you can work with any of the objects available to you. You can connect to the vSphere environment using the `Connect-VIServer` command, like this:

```
Connect-VIServer -Server <vCenter Server hostname> -User <Username>
-Password <password>
```

GET-HELP IS YOUR FRIEND

The `Get-Help` cmdlet is invaluable as you explore PowerCLI. Any time you are unsure of a command or its syntax, simply use `Get-Help` followed by the command or a portion of the command. If you are unsure how to use `Get-Help`, simply use `Get-Help Get-Help`.

After you connect, you are ready to work with some vSphere objects. Let's say you wanted to list all the ESX/ESXi hosts connected to your vCenter Server instance. You could do that with the following command, which would list all the ESX/ESXi hosts connected to the vCenter Server instances to which you connected with the `Connect-VIServer` command:

```
Get-VMHost
```

This command returns an object or set of objects, each of which represents an ESX/ESXi host.

Next, let's say that you wanted to list all the virtual machines currently running on one of those ESX/ESXi hosts. To do this, you would combine the `Get-VMHost` command in a pipeline (noted by the | symbol) with the `Get-VM` command, like this:

```
Get-VMHost <Hostname> | Get-VM
```

This command would return a list of objects. Each object returned represents a virtual machine running on the specified ESX/ESXi host. You could now take this list of virtual machine objects and combine the objects with another command to list all the virtual network interface cards (NICs) within each virtual machine on the specified ESX/ESXi host:

```
Get-VMHost <Hostname> | Get-VM | Get-NetworkAdapter
```

This command would provide a list of objects, each of which represents a virtual network adapter within a virtual machine. Because the output of this command is objects, you could then use the Select command to selectively filter the output like this:

```
Get-VMHost <Hostname> | Get-VM | Get-NetworkAdapter | Select NetworkName, Type
```

This would produce the output shown in Figure 14.4.

FIGURE 14.4
The Select statement filters the output from commands in PowerCLI.

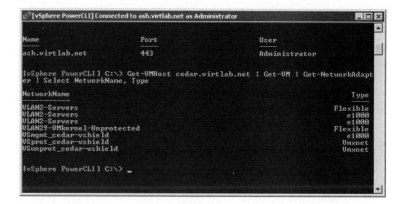

These examples show you how PowerShell and PowerCLI all work with objects and how commands can be combined in a pipeline to create more complex instructions. Table 14.1 describes some of the most commonly used commands and the objects upon which each of these commands operate.

These commands and the objects they retrieve are only half the picture, though. After you have an object, what can you do with it? Table 14.2 describes some commonly used commands to actually manipulate an object.

These two tables are far from a complete reference, but they should give you some idea of the types of things you can automate using PowerCLI.

 Real World Scenario

POWERSHELL RESOURCES

Out of the automation tools I describe in this chapter, I personally am most excited about PowerCLI. Although I am by no means a PowerShell expert—I'll leave that title to others within the virtualization community—I find that PowerShell and PowerCLI offer the right mix of command-line hacking and ease of use for me.

To use PowerCLI, however, you'll have to first learn some basics of PowerShell, much like I did when I first started experimenting with the VI Toolkit for Windows (as PowerCLI used to be known). During my process of learning PowerShell, I found a number of resources to be very helpful. Perhaps most helpful was the VMware PowerCLI Community site at `http://communities.vmware.com /community/developer/windows_toolkit`. This website provides a lot of sample scripts and documentation that can help you learn PowerShell and PowerCLI. In addition, many of the contributors to the VMware PowerCLI Community site also maintain their own blogs and websites with even more information. I highly suggest reviewing as many of these sites as possible during the process of learning PowerShell; they certainly made the process easier for me.

TABLE 14.1:   Commonly Used PowerCLI Commands to Retrieve Objects

POWERCLI CMDLET	OBJECT TYPE RETRIEVED
Get-Datacenter	Datacenter
Get-Datastore	Datastore
Get-Folder	Folder
Get-HardDisk	Virtual hard disk
Get-NetworkAdapter	Virtual network adapter
Get-ResourcePool	Resource pool
Get-Snapshot	Virtual machine snapshot
Get-Template	Virtual machine template
Get-VirtualPortGroup	Port group
Get-VirtualSwitch	Virtual switch
Get-VM	Virtual machine
Get-VMGuest	Virtual machine guest operating system
Get-VMHost	ESX/ESXi host

Now I'll show you how to use the information you've seen so far to automate some processes within VMware vSphere for you.

Running Some Simple PowerCLI Scripts

To get a better idea of how to use PowerCLI to automate your VMware vSphere environment, I'll walk you through a few examples. These should start to give you an idea of how to combine the various pieces of PowerShell and PowerCLI to automate tasks.

TABLE 14.2:   Commonly Used PowerCLI Commands to Manipulate Objects

POWERCLI CMDLET	DESCRIPTION
Move-VM	Moves a VM to a new host, cluster, or datastore
Move-ResourcePool	Moves a resource pool
New-Cluster	Creates a new cluster of ESX/ESXi hosts
New-HardDisk	Creates a new hard disk on a VM
New-NetworkAdapter	Creates a new network adapter on a VM
New-ResourcePool	Creates a new resource pool
New-Snapshot	Creates a new snapshot on a VM
New-VM	Creates a new VM
Remove-Snapshot	Removes a VM snapshot or snapshots
Restart-VMGuest	Restarts a VM guest operating system
Set-CDDrive	Changes VM's virtual CD configuration
Set-Datacenter	Changes the name of the datacenter
Set-Datastore	Changes the name of the datastore
Set-FloppyDrive	Updates a VM's virtual floppy configuration
Set-HardDisk	Changes VM's hard disk configuration
Set-NetworkAdapter	Modifies VM's network adapter configuration
Set-ResourcePool	Updates resource pool configuration
Set-VirtualPortGroup	Updates virtual port group configuration
Set-VirtualSwitch	Changes virtual switch configuration
Set-VM	Changes virtual machine configuration
Set-VMHost	Updates ESX/ESXi host configuration
Set-VMResourceConfiguration	Changes resource allocation for a VM
Shutdown-VMGuest	Shuts down a VM guest operating system
Suspend-VMGuest	Suspends a VM guest operating system

MIGRATING ALL VIRTUAL MACHINES ON A HOST

In the first example, you'll build a simple pipeline using multiple PowerCLI cmdlets. By combining cmdlets in a pipeline, you can build more complex commands, such as the following:

```
Get-VMHost <FirstHost> | Get-VM | Move-VM -destination
(Get-VMHost <SecondHost>)
```

This command relocates all virtual machines on the ESX/ESXi host specified by `FirstHost` to the ESX/ESXi host represented by `SecondHost`. This includes both running virtual machines, which are moved with VMotion, as well as powered-off virtual machines.

MANIPULATING VIRTUAL MACHINE SNAPSHOTS

Let's look at a second example of how to use PowerCLI in your VMware vSphere environment. In this example, you'll use PowerCLI to work with virtual machine snapshots.

Let's say that you need to create a snapshot for all the virtual machines on a particular ESX/ESXi host. This command would accomplish that for you:

```
Get-VMHost <Hostname> | Get-VM | New-Snapshot -Name "Target-Snapsht"
```

If you later needed to remove the snapshot you created, you could use the `Remove-Snapshot` cmdlet to delete those snapshots:

```
Get-VMHost <Hostname> | Get-VM | Get-Snapshot
-Name "Target-Snapsht" | Remove-Snapshot
```

Finally, you could use the `Get-Snapshot` cmdlet to list all snapshots so that you could be sure you had actually created or deleted the snapshots:

```
Get-VMHost <Hostname> | Get-VM | Get-Snapshot
```

This command would return a list of snapshot objects for all the virtual machines on the specified ESX/ESXi host.

RECONFIGURING VIRTUAL MACHINE NETWORKING

In this third example, let's say that you want to move all the virtual machines currently connected to one port group to an entirely different port group. This is actually possible with a one-line command in PowerCLI:

```
Get-VM | Get-NetworkAdapter | Where-Object { $_.NetworkName
-like "OldPortGroupName" } | Set-NetworkAdapter -NetworkName
"NewPortGroupName" -Confirm:$false
```

There are a few new ideas introduced here, so let me break it down a little bit:

◆ The `Get-VM` cmdlet retrieves virtual machine objects.

◆ These virtual machine objects are passed to the `Get-NetworkAdapter` cmdlet, which returns virtual NIC objects.

♦ These virtual NIC objects are parsed using the `Where-Object` cmdlet to include only those virtual NICs whose NetworkName property is like the "OldPortGroupName" string.

♦ The parsed list of virtual NICs is passed to the `Set-NetworkAdapter` cmdlet, which sets the NetworkName property to the "NewPortGroupName" value.

♦ The `Confirm` parameter instructs PowerShell not to ask the user for confirmation of each operation.

MOVING VIRTUAL MACHINES BETWEEN RESOURCE POOLS

In this last example, you'll use PowerCLI to move a group of virtual machines from one resource pool to another resource pool. However, you want to move only a subset of the VMs in this resource pool—only the VMs that are running a Microsoft Windows guest operating system should be moved to the new resource pool.

I'll build this example up in steps. First, you've probably guessed that you can use the `Get-ResourcePool`, `Get-VM`, and `Get-VMGuest` cmdlets to create a list of virtual machine guest operating system objects in the resource pool:

```
Get-ResourcePool <ResourcePoolName> | Get-VM | Get-VMGuest
```

Next you would need to filter the output to return only those objects identified as Microsoft Windows guest operating systems. As you saw in an earlier example, you can use the `Where-Object` cmdlet to filter the output list in a pipeline:

```
Get-ResourcePool <ResourcePoolName> | Get-VM | Get-VMGuest |
Where-Object { $_.OSFullName -match "^Microsoft Windows.*" }
```

This should do it, right? To finish the command out, you should be able to add the `Move-VM` cmdlet and move the VMs to the destination resource pool. Unfortunately, that won't work. You're working with *objects* here, and a virtual machine guest operating system object—which is what is being returned by the `Get-VMGuest` cmdlet—isn't the kind of object that the `Move-VM` cmdlet will accept as input.

Instead, you'll have to use a multiline script for this, as shown in Listing 14.1.

LISTING 14.1: A PowerCLI Script to Selectively Move VMs to a New Resource Pool

```
$VMs = Get-VM -Location (Get-ResourcePool Infrastructure)
foreach ($vm in $VMs) {
$vmguest = Get-VMGuest -VM $vm
if ($vmguest.OSFullName -match "^Microsoft Windows.*") {
Move-VM -VM $vm -Destination (Get-ResourcePool "Windows VMs") } }
```

Again, I'll break down the script so that it is easier to understand:

♦ The first line uses the `Get-VM` and `Get-ResourcePool` cmdlets to retrieve a list of VM objects in the specified resource pool. That list of VM objects is stored in the $VMs variable.

♦ The second line creates a loop that operates for each of the objects in the $VMs variable. Each individual virtual machine object is stored as $vm.

- The third line uses the `Get-VMGuest` cmdlet with the `$vm` variable to retrieve the guest operating system object for that virtual machine object and store the result in the `$vmguest` variable.

- The fourth line tests to see whether the `OSFullName` property of the `$vmguest` object matches a string starting with "Microsoft Windows."

- The fifth line executes only if the test on the fourth line was successful; if it executes, it uses the `Move-VM` and `Get-ResourcePool` cmdlets to move the virtual machine object represented by the `$vm` variable to the resource pool named Windows VMs.

If you were to save the script in Listing 14.1 as `MoveWindowsVMs.ps1`, then you could run it in PowerCLI like this:

```
<Path to Script>\MoveWindowsVMs.ps1
```

There is so much more that you can do with PowerShell and PowerCLI; these simple examples barely scratch the surface. I encourage you to use the numerous PowerCLI resources available online to learn more about PowerCLI and PowerShell.

PowerShell and PowerCLI aren't the only scripting environments around, though; you can also use the Linux-based Service Console in VMware ESX to run standard shell scripts. I'll show how to use shell scripts in the next section.

Using Shell Scripts with VMware ESX

VMware ESX leverages a 64-bit Linux-based Service Console. This Service Console has the ability to run user-created shell scripts to automate tasks that are host-specific. The fact that ESX shell scripts are host-specific is, in my opinion, the biggest weakness of shell scripts. Many of the tasks that you need to perform as a vSphere administrator are not host-specific. With the introduction of the vNetwork Distributed Switch, VMware has removed one key task—configuring vSwitches and port groups—that was host-specific. Similarly, the introduction of host profiles allows for ESX host configuration to be automated via host profiles instead of shell scripts. As a result of these changes within vSphere compared to earlier versions of VMware Infrastructure, the importance of shell scripts has waned. Nevertheless, I'll discuss shell scripts briefly here in the event that you find a need for them in your data center.

Some host-specific tasks within a VMware vSphere environment that you can still automate via an ESX shell script include the following:

- Creating VMkernel interfaces with jumbo frames enabled

- Mounting NFS datastores via the `esxcfg-nas` command

- Enabling a VMkernel interface for VMotion

To help you get a feel for automating tasks such as this using an ESX shell script, I'll work through example scripts for each of these tasks in the following sections.

USING SHELL SCRIPTS WITH ESXI

Although VMware ESXi does not have a Linux-based Service Console that you can access, you might be able to use some of these shell scripts with ESXi by porting them to run within the vSphere Management Assistant (vMA). The vMA is a Linux-based virtual appliance that provides remote command-line interface (CLI) access to VMware ESXi and VMware ESX hosts.

The scripts won't work unmodified; you have to switch the esxcfg-* commands to the matching vicfg-* commands and possibly switch around or add some parameters. For example, you have to add the --vihost <servername> parameter in order to specify which remote ESX/ESXi host you want to modify. More information on the vicfg-* commands is available in Appendix B, "Frequently Used Commands."

Creating VMkernel Interfaces with Jumbo Frames Enabled

VMkernel interfaces are the network interfaces used by the ESX/ESXi hypervisor for tasks like VMotion, VMware Fault Tolerance (FT), and IP-based storage using Network File System (NFS) exports or iSCSI LUNs. As of vSphere 4, VMware provides full support for using jumbo frames for IP-based storage, but vCenter Server does not provide a mechanism whereby you can configure a VMkernel interface to support jumbo frames. Therefore, in order to use jumbo frames, you'll have to revert to the CLI. Because you have to do this on each and every ESX host and because you must use the CLI, this is a natural candidate for using a shell script.

The following two commands are involved in this process:

- You must use esxcfg-vswitch to create or modify the vSwitches and/or port groups involved.

- You must use esxcfg-vmknic to create the VMkernel interface(s).

Before I show you a shell script that will perform this task, I'll walk through the process at a high level:

1. Modify the vSwitch to support a maximum transmission unit (MTU) of 9000. Setting the MTU to 9000 enables jumbo frames.

2. If necessary, create the port group to which you will attach the VMkernel interface.

3. Create a VMkernel NIC, and set the MTU to 9000.

Listing 14.2 shows you a shell script that would accomplish this task.

LISTING 14.2:   A Shell Script That Enables Jumbo Frames Support on a VMkernel Interface

```
#!/bin/sh
#
# Set the MTU for vSwitch1 to 9000
esxcfg-vswitch -m 9000 vSwitch1

# Create a portgroup for new VMkernel interface
esxcfg-vswitch -A JumboVMK vSwitch1
esxcfg-vswitch -v 31 -p JumboVMK vSwitch1

# Create a new VMkernel interface with jumbo frames enabled
esxcfg-vmknic -a -i 172.16.31.204 -n 255.255.255.0 -m 9000 -p JumboVMK
```

You'll note that the shell script in Listing 14.2 starts with the line #!/bin/sh. This is a widely accepted convention that specifies the location of the shell that will process this script. Most every shell script starts with this line. In this case, you are specifying that /bin/sh—which is actually a symbolic link to /bin/bash—is the shell that will process the script. If you wanted to write a Perl script, you would specify !#/usr/bin/perl on the first line so that the script would be processed by Perl, and not by the bash shell.

This shell script assumes the presence of a vSwitch named vSwitch1 and then proceeds to set the MTU for vSwitch1 to 9000. The script then creates a port group called JumboVMK and configures the VLAN ID for that port group. Finally, the script creates a new VMkernel interface and sets the MTU for the interface to 9000.

To use this in your own environment, you would need to supply the correct vSwitch, port group, and IP address information. Then you'd be ready to distribute this to your ESX farm and execute it on each host. You would also need to ensure that your physical switching infrastructure has been properly configured to support jumbo frames as well.

If your environment is not using the vNetwork Distributed Switch, then you could easily extend this shell script to automate the rest of the network configuration for you as well.

Mounting NFS Datastores via the esxcfg-nas Command

Another task that you can perform via the vSphere Client that may be a good candidate for a shell script would be mounting one or more NFS datastores on each ESX host. Going through the process of creating a script for this task would be worth the effort only if you had a number of different NFS datastores that needed to be mounted on each ESX host.

Listing 14.3 shows a simple shell script that mounts five different NFS datastores using the esxcfg-nas command.

LISTING 14.3:   Mounting NFS Datastores with esxcfg-nas

```
#!/bin/sh
#
# Mount the NFS datastores
esxcfg-nas -a -o 172.16.31.100 -s /vol/isoimages -y isoimages
esxcfg-nas -a -o 172.16.31.101 -s /vol/nfsvol1 nfsvol1
esxcfg-nas -a -o 172.16.31.102 -s /vol/nfsvol2 nfsvol2
esxcfg-nas -a -o 172.16.31.103 -s /vol/nfsvol3 third_nfs_volume
esxcfg-nas -a -o 172.16.31.104 -s /vol/nfsvol4 nfs_volume_four
```

You could easily combine the script in Listing 14.3 with the script in Listing 14.2 to automate the creation of a jumbo frames–enabled VMkernel interface and then mount NFS datastores across that new interface.

Enabling a VMkernel Interface for VMotion

There is one other task that is still handled on a per-host basis, and that's enabling a VMkernel interface for VMotion. To do this, you'll use a less common ESX command called vmware-vim-cmd.

This command offers access to a great many different aspects of host configuration, only one of which is enabling a VMkernel interface for VMotion.

In this example, I'll add a few more advanced features, just to give you an idea of what a more complex shell script is capable of doing. Here you will see the shell script equivalent of the PowerCLI pipeline; indeed, PowerCLI took the idea of the pipeline from UNIX shell scripts.

Listing 14.4 shows you the command to enable VMotion on a VMkernel interface. The script takes a command-line argument—that is, input from the user on the command line—that specifies the name of the port group containing the VMkernel interface for which VMotion should be enabled.

LISTING 14.4: Using vmware-vim-cmd and esxcfg-vmknic to Enable VMotion on a VMkernel Interface

```
#!/bin/sh
#
# Determine which vmk to use
vmk='/usr/sbin/esxcfg-vmknic -l | grep $1 | awk '{print $1}''

# Use vmware-vim-cmd to enable VMotion on selected vmk
/usr/bin/vmware-vim-cmd /hostsvc/vmotion/vnic_set $vmk
```

There are a couple of new concepts here, so I'll explain exactly what's happening in this script:

◆ The first command assigns a variable, vmk, to the results of the commands located in backticks. In this case, I've combined esxcfg-vmknic, grep, and awk into a pipeline. The result of the pipeline is something like vmk0 or vmk1—whichever is the VMkernel interface assigned to the port group name the user supplies on the command line.

◆ The contents of the variable $vmk are then used with the vmware-vim-cmd command to enable VMotion on that particular VMkernel interface.

There are lots of ways this script could be improved; for example, there's no error checking to ensure that a matching port group and VMkernel interface are actually found by the first command.

Shell scripting is a fine art, and there is much, much more to writing shell scripts than the tiny snippets I've shown you here. Between shell scripts, vCenter Orchestrator workflows, and PowerCLI scripts, you should have all the tools you need at your disposal for automating your VMware vSphere environment.

The Bottom Line

Identify some of the tools available for automating VMware vSphere. VMware offers a number of different solutions for automating your VMware vSphere environment, including vCenter Orchestrator, PowerCLI, an SDK for Perl, an SDK for web service developers, and shell scripts in VMware ESX. Each of these tools has its own set of advantages and disadvantages.

Master It VMware offers a number of different automation tools. What are some guidelines in helping to choose what automation tool to use?

Configure vCenter Orchestrator. vCenter Orchestrator is installed silently with vCenter Server, but before you can use vCenter Orchestrator, you must configure it properly. The vCenter Orchestrator Configuration interface provides a web-based interface to configuring the various portions of vCenter Orchestrator.

Master It   How can you tell whether some portion of the vCenter Orchestrator configuration is incomplete or incorrect?

Use a vCenter Orchestrator workflow.   After vCenter Orchestrator is configured and is running, you can use the vCenter Orchestrator Client to run a vCenter Orchestrator workflow. vCenter Orchestrators comes with a number of pre-installed workflows to help automate tasks.

Master It   A separate administrator in your environment configured vCenter Orchestrator and has now asked you to run a couple of workflows. However, when you log into the vCenter Server where vCenter Orchestrator is also installed, you don't see the icons for vCenter Orchestrator. Why?

Create a PowerCLI script for automation.   VMware vSphere PowerCLI builds upon the object-oriented PowerShell scripting language to provide administrators with a simple yet powerful way to automate tasks within the vSphere environment.

Master It   If you are familiar with other scripting languages, what would be the biggest hurdle in becoming familiar with PowerShell and PowerCLI, other than syntax?

Leverage shell scripts on VMware ESX.   For tasks that are host-centric, shell scripts on VMware ESX hosts can help provide automation. Some of these shell scripts may also work with slight modifications on the vSphere Management Assistant, which provides a CLI that you can use for managing ESXi hosts.

Master It   What is the biggest drawback of using shell scripts with VMware vSphere?

Appendix A

The Bottom Line

Each of The Bottom Line sections in the chapters suggest exercises to deepen skills and understanding. Sometimes there is only one possible solution, but often you are encouraged to use your skills and creativity to create something that builds on what you know and lets you explore one of many possible solutions.

Chapter 1: Introducing VMware vSphere 4

Identify the role of each product in the vSphere product suite. The VMware vSphere product suite contains ESX and ESXi and vCenter Server. ESX and ESXi provide the base virtualization functionality and enable features like Virtual SMP. vCenter Server provides management for ESX/ESXi and enables functionality like VMotion, Storage VMotion, VMware Distributed Resource Scheduler (DRS), VMware High Availability (HA), and VMware Fault Tolerance (FT). VMware Consolidated Backup is a backup framework that allows for the integration of third-party backup solutions into a vSphere implementation.

Master It Which products are licensed features within the VMware vSphere suite?

Solution Licensed features in the VMware vSphere suite are Virtual SMP, VMotion, Storage VMotion, VMware DRS, VMware HA, and VMware FT.

Recognize the interaction and dependencies between the products in the vSphere suite. VMware ESX and ESXi form the foundation of the vSphere product suite, but some features require the presence of vCenter Server. Features like VMotion, Storage VMotion, VMware DRS, VMware HA, and VMware FT require both ESX/ESXi as well as vCenter Server.

Master It Name three features that are supported only when using vCenter Server along with ESX/ESXi.

Solution All of the following features are available only with vCenter Server: VMware VMotion, Storage VMotion, VMware DRS, VMware HA, and VMware FT.

Understand how vSphere differs from other virtualization products. VMware vSphere's hypervisor, ESX/ESXi, uses a type 1 bare-metal hypervisor that handles I/O directly within the hypervisor. This means that a host operating system, like Windows or Linux, is not required in order for ESX/ESXi to function. Although other virtualization solutions are listed as "type 1 bare-metal hypervisors," most other type 1 hypervisors on the market today require the presence of a "parent partition" or "dom0," through which all virtual machine I/O must travel.

Master It   One of the administrators on your team asked whether he should install Windows Server on the new servers you purchased for ESX. What should you tell him, and why?

Solution   VMware ESX is a bare-metal hypervisor that does not require the installation of a general-purpose host operating system. Therefore, it's unnecessary to install Windows Server on the equipment that was purchased for ESX.

Chapter 2: Planning and Installing VMware ESX and VMware ESXi

Understand the differences among VMware ESX, VMware ESXi Installable, and VMware ESXi Embedded.   Although ESX, ESXi Installable, and ESXi Embedded share the same core hypervisor technology, there are significant differences among the products that may lead organizations to choose one over the other. ESX uses a Linux-based Service Console, for example, while ESXi does not have a Service Console and therefore doesn't have a command-line interface.

Master It   You're evaluating ESX and ESXi as part of a vSphere deployment within your company. What are some of the factors that might lead you to choose ESX over ESXi, or vice versa?

Solution   Hardware support would be one factor to consider. Another key consideration would be third-party tools, scripts, or applications that require the presence of the Service Console in order to operate. Because ESXi does not have a Service Console, that would preclude the use of ESXi in these sorts of situations.

Understand VMware ESX/ESXi compatibility requirements.   Unlike traditional operating systems like Windows or Linux, both ESX and ESXi have much stricter hardware compatibility requirements. This helps ensure a stable, well-tested product line that is able to support even the most mission-critical applications.

Master It   You'd like to run ESXi Embedded, but your hardware vendor doesn't have a model that includes ESXi Embedded. Should you go ahead and buy the servers anyway, even though the hardware vendor doesn't have a model with ESXi Embedded?

Solution   No. ESXi Embedded, in particular, is intended to be deployed on a persistent storage device within a server, like firmware. For ESX and ESXi, only servers found on the Hardware Compatibility List should be used.

Plan a VMware ESX/ESXi deployment.   Deploying ESX or ESXi will affect many different areas of your organization—not only the server team but also the networking team, the storage team, and the security team. There are many decisions that must be considered, including server hardware, storage hardware, storage protocols or connection types, network topology, and network connections. Failing to plan properly could result in an unstable and unsupported implementation.

Master It   Name three areas of networking that must be considered in a vSphere design.

Solution   Among other things, some of the networking areas that must be considered include VLAN support, link aggregation, load-balancing algorithms, and the number of NICs and network ports required.

Install VMware ESX and VMware ESXi Installable.   ESX and ESXi Installable can be installed onto any supported and compatible hardware platform. Because of the architectural differences between ESX and ESXi, the installation routines are quite different.

Master It   Your manager asks you to provide him with a copy of the unattended installation script that you will be using when you roll out ESXi Installable. Is this something you can give him?

Solution   No, ESXi doesn't use an installation script. Installation scripts, also known as kickstart scripts, are used with ESX.

Perform post-installation configuration of VMware ESX and VMware ESXi.   Following the installation of ESX/ESXi, there may be some additional configuration steps that are required. If the wrong NIC is assigned to the Service Console/management network, then the server won't be accessible across the network.

Master It   You've installed ESX on your server, but the Web Access page is inaccessible, and the server doesn't respond to ping. What could be the problem?

Solution   More than likely, the wrong NIC was selected for use with the Service Console. Use the `esxcfg-nics` and `esxcfg-vswitch` commands from the Service Console to unlink the incorrect NIC and link the correct NIC to the virtual switch.

Install the vSphere Client.   ESX, ESXi Installable, and ESXi Embedded are all managed using the vSphere Client, a Windows-only application that provides the functionality to manage the virtualization platform. The easiest way to install the vSphere Client is to download it directly from the Web Access page on one of the installed ESX/ESXi hosts.

Master It   List three ways by which you can install the vSphere Client.

Solution   The three ways are by downloading it from the Web Access page of an ESX/ESXi or vCenter Server host, by installing it from the vCenter Server installation media, or by installing it along with vCenter Server.

Chapter 3: Installing and Configuring vCenter Server

Understand the features and role of vCenter Server.   vCenter Server plays a central role in the management of ESX/ESXi hosts and virtual machines. Key features such as VMotion, Storage VMotion, VMware DRS, VMware HA, and VMware FT are all enabled and made possible by vCenter Server. vCenter Server provides scalable authentication and role-based administration based on integration with Active Directory.

Master It   Specifically with regard to authentication, what are three key advantages of using vCenter Server?

Solution   First, vCenter Server centralizes the authentication so that user accounts don't have to be managed on a per-host basis. Second, vCenter Server eliminates the need to share the root password for hosts or to use complex configurations to allow administrators to perform tasks on the hosts. Third, vCenter Server brings role-based administration for the granular management of hosts and virtual machines.

Plan a vCenter Server deployment.   Planning a vCenter Server deployment includes selecting a back-end database engine, choosing an authentication method, sizing the hardware appropriately, and providing a sufficient level of high availability and business continuity. You must also decide whether you will run vCenter Server as a virtual machine or on a physical system.

Master It   What are some of the advantages and disadvantages of running vCenter Server as a virtual machine?

Solution   Some of the advantages include the ability to easily clone the virtual machine for backup or disaster recovery purposes, the ability to take snapshots to protect against data loss or data corruption, and the ability to leverage features such as VMotion, Storage VMotion, and VMware HA for increased availability.

Some of the disadvantages include the inability to cold clone the vCenter Server virtual machine, cold migrate the vCenter Server virtual machine, or edit the virtual hardware of the vCenter Server virtual machine.

Install and configure a vCenter Server database.   vCenter Server supports several enterprise-grade database engines, including Oracle and Microsoft SQL Server. IBM DB2 is also experimentally supported. Depending upon the database in use, there are specific configuration steps and specific permissions that must be applied in order for vCenter Server to work properly.

Master It   Why is it important to protect the database engine used to support vCenter Server?

Solution   Although vCenter Server uses Microsoft Active Directory for authentication and Microsoft Active Directory Application Mode to store some replicated configuration data, the majority of the information managed by vCenter Server is stored in the back-end database. The loss of the back-end database would mean the loss of significant amounts of data that are crucial to the operation of vCenter Server. Organizations should be sure to take adequate steps to protect the back-end database accordingly.

Install and configure vCenter Server.   vCenter Server is installed using the VMware vCenter Installer. You can install vCenter Server as a stand-alone instance or join a Linked Mode group for greater scalability. vCenter Server will use a predefined ODBC DSN to communicate with the separate database server.

Master It   When preparing to install vCenter Server, are there any concerns about which Windows account should be used during the installation?

Solution   Yes. If you will be using Microsoft SQL Server with Windows authentication, you should log on to the computer that will run vCenter Server using the account that was previously configured with the appropriate permissions on the SQL Server and SQL database. The vCenter Server installer does not provide the ability to choose which account to use; it uses the currently logged-on account.

Use vCenter Server's management features.   vCenter Server provides a wide range of management features for ESX/ESXi hosts and virtual machines. These features include scheduled tasks, topology maps, host profiles for consistent configurations, and event logging.

Master It   Your manager has asked you to prepare an overview of the virtualized environment. What tools in vCenter Server will help you in this task?

Solution   vCenter Server can export topology maps in a variety of graphics formats. The topology maps, coupled with the data found on the Storage Views, Hardware Status, and Summary tabs should provide enough information for your manager.

Chapter 4: Installing and Configuring vCenter Update Manager

Install VUM and integrate it with the vSphere Client.   vCenter Update Manager is installed from the VMware vCenter installation media and requires that vCenter Server has already been installed. Like vCenter Server, vCenter Update Manager requires the use of a back-end database server. Finally, you must install a plug-in into the vSphere Client in order to access, manage, or configure vCenter Update Manager.

Master It   You have vCenter Update Manager installed, and you've configured it from the vSphere Client on your laptop. One of the other administrators on your team is saying that she can't access or configure vCenter Update Manager and that there must be something wrong with the installation. What is the most likely cause of the problem?

Solution   The most likely cause is that the vCenter Update Manager plug-in hasn't been installed in the other administrator's vSphere Client. The plug-in must be installed on each instance of the vSphere Client in order to be able to manage vCenter Update Manager from that instance.

Determine which ESX/ESXi hosts or virtual machines need to be patched or upgraded.
Baselines are the "measuring sticks" whereby vCenter Update Manager knows whether an ESX/ESXi host or guest operating system instance is up-to-date. vCenter Update Manager compares the ESX/ESXi hosts or guest operating systems to the baselines to determine whether they need to be patched and, if so, what patches need to be applied. vCenter Update Manager also uses baselines to determine which ESX/ESXi hosts need to be upgraded to the latest version or which virtual machines need to have their virtual machine hardware upgraded. vCenter Update Manager comes with some predefined baselines and allows administrators to create additional baselines specific to their environments. Baselines can be fixed—the contents remain constant—or they can be dynamic, where the contents of the baseline change over time. Baseline groups allow administrators to combine baselines together and apply them together.

Master It In addition to ensuring that all your ESX/ESXi hosts have the latest critical and security patches installed, you also need to ensure that all your ESX/ESXi hosts have another specific patch installed. This additional patch is noncritical and therefore doesn't get included in the critical patch dynamic baseline. How do you work around this problem?

Solution Create a baseline group that combines the critical patch dynamic baseline with a fixed baseline that contains the additional patch you want installed on all ESX/ESXi hosts. Attach the baseline group to all your ESX/ESXi hosts. When you perform remediation, vCenter Update Manager will ensure that all the critical patches in the dynamic baseline plus the additional patch in the fixed baseline are applied to the hosts.

Use VUM to upgrade virtual machine hardware or VMware Tools. vCenter Update Manager can detect virtual machines with outdated virtual machine hardware versions and guest operating systems that have outdated versions of the VMware Tools installed. vCenter Update Manager comes with predefined baselines that enable this functionality. In addition, vCenter Update Manager has the ability to upgrade virtual machine hardware versions and upgrade the VMware Tools inside guest operating systems to ensure that everything is kept up-to-date. This functionality is especially helpful after upgrading your ESX/ESXi hosts to version 4.0 from a previous version.

Master It You've just finished upgrading your virtual infrastructure to VMware vSphere. What two additional tasks would be beneficial to complete?

Solution Upgrade virtual machine hardware version from version 4 to version 7 and upgrade the VMware Tools installations in the guest operating systems.

Apply patches to ESX/ESXi hosts. Like other complex software products, VMware ESX and VMware ESXi need software patches applied from time to time. These patches might be bug fixes or security fixes. To keep your ESX/ESXi hosts up-to-date with the latest patches, vCenter Update Manager can apply patches to your hosts on a schedule of your choosing. In addition, to reduce downtime during the patching process or perhaps to simplify the deployment of patches to remote offices, vCenter Update Manager can also stage patches to ESX/ESXi hosts before the patches are applied.

Master It How can you avoid virtual machine downtime when applying patches (for example, remediating) your ESX/ESXi hosts?

Solution vCenter Update Manager automatically leverages advanced VMware vSphere features like Distributed Resource Scheduler (DRS). If you make sure that your ESX/ESXi hosts are configured in a DRS cluster, then vCenter Update Manager will leverage VMotion and DRS to move virtual machines to other ESX/ESXi hosts, avoiding downtime, in order to patch one host.

Apply patches to Windows guests. Even though you deal with virtual machines in a VMware vSphere environment, you must still manage the installations of Windows in those virtual machines. These Windows installations need security patches and bug fixes, like the installations on physical systems. vCenter Update Manager has the ability to apply patches to the Windows operating system and select applications within Windows in order to keep both the guest operating system and these select applications updated.

Master It You are having a discussion with another VMware vSphere administrator about keeping hosts and guests updated. The other administrator insists that in order to use vCenter Update Manager to keep ESX/ESXi hosts updated, you must also use vCenter Update Manager to keep guest operating systems updated as well. Is this accurate?

Solution No, this is not accurate. vCenter Update Manager can be used to patch just ESX/ESXi hosts, just guest operating systems, or both. There is no requirement to use all the functionality of vCenter Update Manager in order to use a subset of the functionality. vSphere administrators should use whatever portions of vCenter Update Manager that make sense for their environment.

Chapter 5: Creating and Managing Virtual Networks

Identify the components of virtual networking. Virtual networking is a blend of virtual switches, physical switches, VLANs, physical network adapters, virtual adapters, uplinks, NIC teaming, virtual machines, and port groups.

Master It What factors contribute to the design of a virtual network and the components involved?

Solution Many factors contribute to a virtual network design. The number of physical network adapters in each ESX/ESXi host, using vSwitches vs. Distributed Virtual Switches, the presence or use of VLANs in the environment, the existing network topology, and the connectivity needs of the virtual machines in the environment are all factors that will play a role in the final network design. These are some common questions to ask while designing the network:

- Do you have or need a dedicated network for management traffic, such as for the management of physical switches?
- Do you have or need a dedicated network for VMotion traffic?
- Do you have an IP storage network? Is this IP storage network a dedicated network? Are you running iSCSI or NAS/NFS?
- Is there a need for extremely high levels of fault tolerance for VMs?
- Is the existing physical network comprised of VLANs?
- Do you want to extend the use of VLANs into the virtual switches?

Create virtual switches (vSwitches) and distributed virtual switches (dvSwitches). vSphere introduces a new type of virtual switch, the vNetwork Distributed Virtual Switch, as well as continuing to support the host-based vSwitch (now referred to as the vNetwork Standard Switch) from previous versions. vNetwork Distributed Switches bring new functionality to the vSphere networking environment, including private VLANs and a centralized point of management for ESX/ESXi clusters.

Master It You've asked a fellow VMware vSphere administrator to create a vNetwork Distributed Virtual Switch for you, but the administrator is having problems completing the task because he or she can't find the right command-line switches for `esxcfg-vswitch`. What should you tell this administrator?

Solution vNetwork Distributed Virtual Switches can be created only using the vSphere Client. Although the `esxcfg-vswitch` command does have a few options for modifying an existing dvSwitch, creating a new dvSwitch will need to be done from the vSphere Client.

Install and perform basic configuration of the Cisco Nexus 1000V. The Cisco Nexus 1000V is the first third-party Distributed Virtual Switch for VMware vSphere. Running Cisco's NX-OS, the Nexus 1000V uses a distributed architecture that supports redundant supervisor modules and provides a single point of management. Advanced networking functionality like quality of service (QoS), access control lists (ACLs), and SPAN ports are made possible via the Nexus 1000V.

Master It A VMware vSphere administrator is trying to use the vSphere Client to make some changes to the VLAN configuration of a dvPort group configured on a Nexus 1000V, but the option to edit the settings for the dvPort group isn't showing up. Why?

Solution The Cisco Nexus 1000V Virtual Supervisor Module (VSM) controls the creation, modification, and deletion of dvPort groups on the Virtual Ethernet Module (VEM) on each host. All changes to the dvPort groups must be made via the VSM; the dvPort groups cannot be modified in any way from the vSphere Client.

Create and manage NIC teaming, VLANs, and private VLANs. NIC teaming allows for virtual switches to have redundant network connections to the rest of the network. Virtual switches also provide support for VLANs, which provide logical segmentation of the network, and private VLANs, which provide added security to existing VLANs while allowing systems to share the same IP subnet.

Master It You'd like to use NIC teaming to bond multiple physical uplinks together for greater redundancy and improved throughput. When selecting the NIC teaming policy, you select Route Based On IP Hash, but then the vSwitch seems to lose connectivity. What could be wrong?

Solution The Route Based On IP Hash load-balancing policy requires that the physical switch is also configured to support this arrangement. This is accomplished through the use of link aggregation, referred to as *EtherChannel* in the Cisco environment. Without an appropriate link aggregation configuration on the physical switch, using the IP hash load-balancing policy will result in a loss of connectivity. One of the other load-balancing policies, such as the default policy titled Route Based On Originating Virtual Port ID, may be more appropriate if the configuration of the physical switch cannot be modified.

Configure virtual switch security policies. Virtual switches support security policies for allowing or rejecting promiscuous mode, allowing or rejecting MAC address changes, and allowing or rejecting forged transmits. All of the security options can help increase Layer 2 security.

Master It You have a networking application that needs to see traffic on the virtual network that is intended for other production systems on the same VLAN. The networking application accomplishes this by using promiscuous mode. How can you accommodate the needs of this networking application without sacrificing the security of the entire virtual switch?

Solution   Because port groups (or dvPort groups) can override the security policy settings for a virtual switch, and because there can be multiple port groups/dvPort groups that correspond to a VLAN, the best solution involves creating another port group that has all the same settings as the other production port group, including the same VLAN ID. This new port group should allow promiscuous mode. Assign the virtual machine with the networking application to this new port group, but leave the remainder of the virtual machines on a port group that rejects promiscuous mode. This allows the networking application to see the traffic it needs to see without overly compromising the security of the entire virtual switch.

Chapter 6: Creating and Managing Storage Devices

Differentiate and understand the fundamentals of shared storage, including SANs and NAS.   VMware vSphere depends on shared storage for advanced functions, cluster-wide availability, and the aggregate performance of all the virtual machines in a cluster. Designing high-performance and highly available shared storage infrastructure is possible on Fibre Channel, FCoE, and iSCSI SANs and is possible using NAS; in addition, it's available for midrange to enterprise storage architectures. Always design the storage architecture to meet the performance requirements first, and then ensure that capacity requirements are met as a corollary.

Master It   Identify examples where each of the protocol choices would be ideal for different vSphere 4 deployments.

Solution   iSCSI would be a good choice for a customer with no existing Fibre Channel SAN and getting started with VMware. Fibre Channel would be a good choice for a customer with an existing Fibre Channel infrastructure or for those that have virtual machines with high-bandwidth (200MBps+) requirements (not in aggregate, but individually). NFS would be a good choice where there are many virtual machines with a low-bandwidth requirement individually (and in aggregate) that is less than a single link's worth of bandwidth.

Master It   Identify the three storage performance parameters and the primary determinant of storage performance and how to quickly estimate it for a given storage configuration.

Solution   The three factors to consider are bandwidth (MBps), throughput (IOps), and latency (ms). The maximum bandwidth for a single datastore (or RDM) for Fibre Channel is the HBA speed times the number of HBAs in the system (check the fan-in ratio and number of Fibre Channel ports on the array). The maximum bandwidth for a single datastore (or RDM) for iSCSI is the NIC speed times the number of NICs in the system up to about 9Gbps (check the fan-in ratio and number of Ethernet ports on the array). The maximum bandwidth for a single NFS datastore for NFS is the NIC link speed (across multiple datastores, the bandwidth can be balanced across multiple NIC). In all cases, the throughput (IOps) is primarily a function of the number of spindles (assuming no cache benefit and no RAID loss). A quick rule of thumb is that the total number of IOps = IOps × the number of that type of spindle. Latency is in milliseconds, though can get to tens of milliseconds in cases where the storage array is overtaxed.

Understand vSphere storage options. vSphere has three fundamental storage presentation models: VMFS on block, NFS, and RDM. The most flexible configurations use all three, predominantly via a "shared container" model and selective use of RDMs.

Master It Characterize use cases for VMFS datastores, NFS datastores, and RDMs.

Solution VMFS datastores and NFS datastores are "shared container" models; they store virtual disks together. VMFS is governed by the block storage stack, and NFS is governed by the network stack. NFS is generally (without use of 10GbE LANs) best suited to large numbers of low bandwidth (any throughput) VMs. VMFS is suited for a wide range of workloads. RDMs should be used sparingly for cases where the guest must have direct access to a single LUN.

Master It If you're using VMFS and there's one performance metric to track, what would it be? Configure a monitor for that metric.

Solution The metric to measure is queue depth. Use ESXtop to monitor. A good "nonperformance" metric is the "datastore availability" or "used capacity" managed datastore alerts.

Configure storage at the vSphere ESX 4 layer. After a shared storage platform is selected, the VMware vSphere ESX/ESXi 4 cluster needs a storage network configured. The network (whether Fibre Channel or Ethernet based) must be designed to meet availability and throughput requirements, which is influenced by protocol choice and vSphere fundamental storage stack (and in the case of NFS, network stack) architecture. Proper network design involves physical redundancy and physical or logical isolation mechanisms (SAN zoning and network VLANs). With connectivity in place, configure LUNs and VMFS datastores and/or NFS exports/NFS datastores using the predictive or adaptive model (or a hybrid model). Use Storage VMotion to resolve hot spots and other nonoptimal virtual machine placement.

Master It What would best identify an oversubscribed VMFS datastore from a performance standpoint? How would you identify the issue? What is it most likely to be? What would be two possible corrective actions you could take?

Solution An oversubscribed VMFS datastore is best identified by evaluating the queue depth and would manifest as "slow VMs." The best way to track this is with ESXtop, using the QUED (the Queue Depth column). If the queue is full, take any or all of these courses of action: make the queue deeper, and increase Disk.SchedNumReqOutstanding advanced parameter to match; vacate virtual machines (using Storage VMotion); and add more spindles to the LUN so that it can fulfill the requests more rapidly or move to a faster spindle type.

Master It A VMFS volume is filling up. What are three possible nondisruptive corrective actions you could take?

Solution The actions you could take are as follows:

◆ Use Storage VMotion to migrate some virtual machines to another datastore.

◆ Grow the backing LUN, and grow the VMFS volume.

◆ Add another backing LUN, and add another VMFS extent.

Master It   What would best identify an oversubscribed NFS volume from a performance standpoint? How would you identify the issue? What is it most likely to be? What are two possible corrective actions you could take?

Solution   The workload in the datastore is reaching the maximum bandwidth of a single link. The easiest way to identify the issue would be using the vCenter performance charts and examining the VMkernel NIC's utilization. If it was at 100 percent, the only options are to upgrade to 10GbE or to add another NFS datastore, add another VMkernel NIC, follow the load-balancing and HA decision tree to determine whether NIC teaming or IP routing would work best, and finally use Storage VMotion to migrate some virtual machines to another datastore (remember that the NIC teaming/IP routing works for multiple datastores, not for a single datastore). Remember that the step of Storage VMotion adds additional work to an already busy datastore, so consider scheduling it during a low I/O period, even though it can be done live.

Configure storage at the virtual machine layer.   With datastores in place, create virtual machines. During the creation of the virtual machines, place VMs in the appropriate datastores, and employ selective use of RDMs, but only where required. Over time, monitor for excessive space consumption due to VMware native snapshots, and consider collapsing snapshots for very significant space consumption cases.

Master It   Without turning the machine off, convert the virtual disks on a VMFS volume from thin to eagerzeroedthick and back to thin.

Solution   Use Storage VMotion and the new Target Virtual Disk configuration radio button.

Master It   Identify where you would use a physical compatibility mode RDM, and configure that use case.

Solution   One use case would be a Microsoft cluster (either W2K3 with MSCS or W2K8 with WSFC). You should download the VMware Microsoft clustering guide and follow that use case. Other valid answers are a case where virtual-to-physical mobility of the LUNs are required or a Solutions Enabler virtual machine is needed.

Master It   Take a series of ESX snapshots with and without memory snapshots. Then, without using the storage views and only using the datastore browser, determine from the file structure how much space the snapshots are consuming. Predict the result of deleting snapshots. Delete the snapshots, and match the result with your expectations.

Solution   This reinforces the virtual machine file structure and its "unpredictability" from a capacity-planning standpoint. You should note that each snapshot generated a new VDMK with a `-000x.vmdk` postfix and a `-Snapshotx.vmsn` if they are snapshot-running virtual machines. You should note that the vmdks are small relative to the base—unless they made a lot of changes to the disk and the `.vmsn` is in the order of the size of the memory of the VM, which may be less depending on the degree of memory oversubscription. Deleting a snapshot removes the `.vmsn` but not the `.vmdk` until the last snapshot is deleted (at which point all the VMDKs are collapsed into the first one).

Leverage new vSphere storage features.   Use managed datastore alerts to manage and optimize utilization. Leverage the new thin provisioning options independently or together with array thin provisioning to drive a higher asset utilization of your shared storage infrastructure. Use the storage views and maps to pinpoint a single point of failure and report on the overall asset use. Use Storage VMotion to not only resolve nonoptimal storage configuration but to transform between thin and thick virtual disk configurations. Leverage the paravirtualized SCSI adapter with the new Virtual Machine 7 format to drive higher I/O performance with lower CPU utilization. If you are using ESX 3.5 with iSCSI using the software iSCSI initiator, use the new initiator's multiple sessions per target to drive higher throughput (and configure it this way to start if using vSphere 4 for the first time). Enable the Round-Robin path selection policy on LUNs manually. Consider a third-party multipathing plug-in (MPP) as an option to simplify the vSphere storage configuration while improving performance and availability.

Master It   Configure an iSCSI target, and then configure multiple iSCSI VMkernel connections to a single iSCSI target. (If you don't have an iSCSI array, you can always download the freely available EMC Celerra VSA from `http://virtualgeek.typepad.com`.)

Solution   There are a wide variety of actions you could do here—the ultimate "Master it" answer is that you get the Storage Adapter Properties screen to show multiple paths and that in the Storage Views tab's report, the datastore shows as "fully redundant."

Leverage best practices for SAN and NAS storage with vSphere 4.   Read, follow, and leverage key VMware and storage vendors' best practices/solutions guide documentation. Don't oversize up front, but instead learn to leverage VMware and storage array features to monitor performance, queues, and back-end load—and then nondisruptively adapt. Plan for performance first and capacity second. (Usually capacity is a given for performance requirements to be met.) Spend design time on availability design and on the large heavy I/O VMs, and use flexible pool design for the general-purpose VMFS and NFS datastores.

Master It   Quickly estimate the minimum usable capacity needed for 200 virtual machines with an average VM size of 40GB. Make some assumptions about ESX snapshots. What would be the raw capacity needed in the array if you used RAID 10? RAID 5 (4+1)? RAID 6 (10+2)? What would you do to nondisruptively cope if you ran out of capacity?

Solution   Using "rule of thumb" math, 200 × 40GB = 8TB × 25 percent extra space (snapshots, other VMware files) = 10TB. Using RAID 10, you would need at least 20TB raw. Using RAID 5 (4+1), you would need 12.5TB. Using RAID 6 (10+2), you would need 12TB. If you ran out of capacity, you could delete snapshots (use the Storage Views tab's report to quickly find big offenders). You could add capacity to your array and then add datastores and use Storage VMotion. If your array supports dynamic growth of LUNs, you could grow the VMFS or NFS datastores, and if it doesn't, you could add more VMFS extents.

Master It   Using the configurations in the previous question, what would the minimum amount of raw capacity need to be if the VMs are actually only 20GB of data in each VM, even though they are provisioning 40GB and you used thick on an array that didn't support thin provisioning? What if the array *did* support thin provisioning? What if you used Storage VMotion to convert from thick to thin (both in the case where the array supports thin provisioning and in the case where it doesn't)?

Solution   If you use thick virtual disks on an array that doesn't support thin provisioning, the answers are the same as the previous question. If you use an array that *does* support thin provisioning, the answers are cut down by 50 percent: 20TB for RAID 10, 6.25TB for RAID 5 (4+1), and 6TB for RAID 6 (10+2). If you used Storage VMotion to convert to thin on the array that doesn't support thin provisioning, the result is the same, just as it is if you do thin on thin.

Master It   Estimate the number of spindles needed for 100 virtual machines that drive 200 IOps each and are 40GB in size. Assume no RAID loss or cache gain. How many if you use 500GB SATA 7200 RPM? 300GB 10K Fibre Channel/SAS? 300GB 15K Fibre Channel/SAS? 160GB consumer-grade SSD? 200GB Enterprise Flash?

Solution   This exercise highlights the foolishness of looking just at capacity in the server use case. $100 \times 40\text{GB} = 4\text{TB}$ usable. $\times 200$ IOps = 20,000 IOps. With 500GB 7200 RPM, that's 250 drives, which have 125TB raw (ergo nonoptimal). With 300GB 10K RPM, that's 167 drives, which have 50TB raw (ergo nonoptimal). With 15K RPM, that's 111 drives with 16T B raw (getting closer). With consumer-grade SSD, that's 20 spindles and 3.2TB raw (too little). With EFD, that's 4 spindles and 800GB raw (too little).

The moral of the story is that the 15K RPM 146GB drive is the sweet spot for this workload. Note that the "extra space" can't be used unless you can find a workload that doesn't need any performance at all; the spindles are working as hard as they can. Also note that the 4TB requirement was usable, and we were calculating the raw storage capacity. Therefore, in this case, RAID 5, RAID 6, and RAID 10 would all have extra usable capacity in the end.

It's unusual to have all VMs with a common workload, and 200 IOps (as an "average") is relatively high. This exercise also shows why it's efficient to have several tiers and several datastores for different classes of virtual machines (put some on SATA, some on Fibre Channel, some on EFD or SSD), because you can be more efficient.

Chapter 7: Creating and Managing Virtual Machines

Create a virtual machine.   A virtual machine is a collection of virtual hardware pieces, like a physical system—one or more virtual CPUs, RAM, video card, SCSI devices, IDE devices, floppy drives, parallel and serial ports, and network adapters. This virtual hardware is virtualized and abstracted from the underlying physical hardware, providing portability to the virtual machine.

Master It   Create two virtual machines, one intended to run Windows Server 2003 and a second intended to run Windows Server 2008. Make a list of the differences in the configuration that are suggested by the Create New Virtual Machine Wizard.

Solution   vCenter Server suggests 1GB of RAM, an LSI Logic parallel SCSI controller, and an 8GB virtual disk for Windows Server 2003; for Windows Server 2008, the recommendations are 2GB of RAM, an LSI Logic SAS controller, and a 40GB virtual disk.

Install a guest operating system.   Just as a physical machine needs an operating system, a virtual machine also needs an operating system. VMware ESX and ESXi support a broad range of 32-bit and 64-bit operating systems, including all major versions of Windows Server,

Windows Vista, Windows XP, and Windows 2000, as well as various flavors of Linux, FreeBSD, Novell NetWare, and Solaris.

Master It What are the three ways in which a guest operating system can access data on a CD/DVD, and what are the advantages of each approach?

Solution The three ways to access a CD/DVD are as follows:

- Client device: This has the advantage of being very easy to use; VMware administrators can put a CD/DVD into their local workstation and map it into the virtual machine.

- Host device: The CD/DVD is physically placed into the optical drive of the ESX/ESXi host. This has the advantage of keeping the CD/DVD traffic off the network, which may be advantageous in some situations.

- Use an ISO image on a shared datastore. This is the fastest method and has the advantage of being able to have multiple virtual machines access the same ISO image at the same time. A bit more work may be required up front to create the ISO image.

Install VMware Tools. For maximum performance of the guest operating system, it needs to have virtualization-optimized drivers that are specially written for and designed to work with the VMware ESX/ESXi hypervisor. VMware Tools provides these optimized drivers as well as other utilities focused on better operation in virtual environments.

Master It A fellow administrator contacts you and is having a problem installing VMware Tools. This administrator has selected the Install/Upgrade VMware Tools command, but nothing seems to be happening inside the virtual machine. What could be the cause of the problem?

Solution There could be any number of potential issues. First, a guest operating system must be installed before VMware Tools can be installed. Second, if the virtual machine is running Windows, AutoPlay may have been disabled. Finally, it's possible—although unlikely—that the source ISO images for VMware Tools installation have been damaged or deleted and need to be replaced on the host.

Manage and modify a virtual machine. Once a virtual machine has been created, the vSphere Client makes it easy to manage and modify the virtual machine. Virtual hardware can be added to or removed from the virtual machine, network adapters can be modified, and CD/DVD drives can be mounted or unmounted as necessary. Some types of virtual hardware can be "hot-added" while the virtual machine is turned on, while other types require that the virtual machine is powered off.

Master It Which method is preferred for modifying the configuration of a virtual machine—editing the VMX file or using the vSphere Client?

Solution Although it is possible to edit the VMX file to make changes, that method is error-prone. Using the vSphere Client is the recommended method.

Create templates and deploy virtual machines. vCenter Server's templates feature provides an excellent way to quickly and easily deploy consistent virtual machines. With options to clone or convert an existing virtual machine to a template, vCenter Server makes it easy to create templates. Then, once a template has been created, vCenter Server can clone virtual machines from that template, customizing them in the process to ensure that each one is unique. The customization specifications that vCenter Server uses to customize the cloned virtual machines can be saved and reused numerous times.

Master It Of the following tasks, which are appropriate to be performed on a virtual machine running Windows Server 2008 that will eventually be turned into a template?

a. Align the guest operating system's file system to a 64KB boundary?
b. Join the virtual machine to Active Directory?
c. Perform some application-specific configurations and tweaks?
d. Install all patches from the operating system vendor?

Solution

a. Yes. All virtual machines then cloned from this template will also have their file systems properly aligned.
b. No. This should be done by the vSphere Client Windows Guest Customization Wizard or a customization specification.
c. No. Templates shouldn't have any application-specific files, tweaks, or configurations unless you are planning on creating multiple, application-specific templates.
d. Yes.

Chapter 8: Migrating and Importing Virtual Machines

Use vCenter Server Guided Consolidation. vCenter Guided Consolidation is integrated into vCenter Server. Guided Consolidation analyzes physical computers, gathers performance statistics and configuration information, and makes recommendations around how those physical computers should be consolidated as virtual machines. This functionality helps organizations figure out how to convert their infrastructure and take advantage of VMware vSphere.

Master It What requirement is there for user accounts with vCenter Guided Consolidation?

Solution The Windows services that support Guided Consolidation run in the background in the context of a specific user account. This user account is used to connect to remote systems to gather inventory and performance information. The user account under which Guided Consolidation is running should have administrative permissions on the remote systems. If this is not possible, then you will need to specify alternate credentials to connect to remote systems with the correct permissions and rights.

Perform physical-to-virtual migrations of running computers. VMware vCenter Converter has the ability to perform P2V conversions on running physical computers. This allows organizations to convert systems with a minimum of downtime. This type of P2V conversion process is best suited for physical computers with relatively static data sets.

Master It During the process of performing a P2V conversion on a physical system running Windows Server 2003, the wizard fails about halfway through with an error regarding name resolution. How can you resolve this issue?

Solution The physical computer that is being converted must be able to resolve the network name of the vCenter Server from which the conversion is being initiated. Double-check the DNS and WINS settings; if name resolution is still not working, add an entry to the local hosts file temporarily to allow the migration to complete. However, be sure to remove the hosts file entry after conversion to avoid potential problems later.

Perform physical-to-virtual migrations of computers that are powered off. In addition to conversions of running physical systems, vCenter Converter can use a boot CD to perform cold migrations, for example, conversions of physical systems when the installed operating system is not running. This type of conversion involves greater downtime but is best suited for applications with very dynamic data sets, such as email systems or database servers.

Master It List two advantages and two disadvantages of using vCenter Converter's cold migration functionality.

Solution Two of the advantages of using the cold migration functionality of vCenter Converter include the ability to convert workloads with dynamically changing data, such as email servers and database servers, and a streamlined cutover from the physical machine to the virtual machine.

Two of the disadvantages of cold migration are increased downtime and a lack of ability to perform remote cold migrations. You must have console access in order to perform a cold migration.

Import virtual appliances. Virtual appliances are virtual machines that have been packaged with a pre-installed guest operating system and tuned for a specific purpose. Often, the guest operating system is stripped down to only those components necessary to support its intended function; this helps improve performance and reduce the footprint. Virtual appliances are typically distributed in Open Virtualization Format (OVF, formerly referred to as Open Virtual Machine Format). VMware also provides an online marketplace where virtual appliances can be distributed.

Master It A vendor has given you a ZIP file containing a virtual machine they are calling a virtual *appliance*. Upon looking inside the ZIP file, you see several VMDK files and a VMX file. Will you be able to use vCenter Server's import functionality to import this as a virtual appliance? If not, how can you get this virtual machine into your infrastructure?

Solution You will not be able to use vCenter Server's import feature; this requires that the virtual appliance be provided with an OVF file that supplies the information that vCenter Server is expecting to find. However, you can use vCenter Converter to perform a V2V conversion to bring this virtual machine into the VMware vSphere environment, assuming it is coming from a compatible source environment.

Chapter 9: Configuring and Managing VMware vSphere Access Controls

Manage and maintain ESX/ESXi permissions. VMware ESX and VMware ESXi provide a structured approach to permissions based on users, groups, roles, and privileges. This approach provides granular access to virtual machines and related resources.

Master It You've granted permission to one of your administrators on an ESX host by adding this administrator's account to the Administrator role. Now this administrator is trying to manage a couple of virtual machines on another host but can't. You've verified this administrator does have an account on the other host. What could be the problem?

Solution The most likely problem is that the account on the second host has not been added to the Administrator role. Role assignments must be handled on a per-host basis when you are not using vCenter Server.

Manage and maintain vCenter Server permissions. vCenter Server centralizes the management of users and groups for permissions by integrating with Active Directory. In addition, vCenter Server extends the structured approach using users, groups, roles, and privileges not only to ESX/ESXi hosts and virtual machines but also to datastores, networks, resource pools, vCenter Update Manager, vApps, and host profiles, to name a few.

Master It A group of administrators needs full access to a specific subset of virtual machines. All these virtual machines have been placed within a resource pool. This resource pool also contains some other virtual machines to which this group of administrators should *not* have access. Without having to move the extra VMs out of the resource pool, what is the best way to grant permissions to this subset of virtual machines?

Solution If you don't already have a role that grants full access to virtual machines, create a new role to do that. Then create a group and assign it to that role. Create a second group that is assigned to the No Access role. Apply the full access role to the resource pool, and apply the No Access role to the specific virtual machines to which these administrators should not have access.

Manage virtual machines using the web console. In addition to using the vSphere Client, vCenter Server also provides web-based access to perform basic management tasks, such as changing power states, managing snapshots, or viewing the virtual machine console.

Master It With vCenter Server Web Access, is it possible to provide a URL to view the console of a specific virtual machine? If so, how?

Solution Yes. When viewing the details of a specific virtual machine within vCenter Server Web Access, scroll down the list of commands on the right side until you see the Generate Virtual Machine Shortcut. Use that link to create a URL that can be passed to others in order to directly access the console of a specific virtual machine. Remember that correct authentication and permissions are still required.

Chapter 10: Managing Resource Allocation

Manage virtual machine memory and CPU allocation.   In a VMware vSphere environment, the ESX/ESXi hosts control virtual machine access to physical resources like RAM and CPU. To effectively manage and scale VMware vSphere, administrators must understand how to allocate memory and CPU resources to virtual machines, including how to use reservations, limits, and shares. Reservations provide guarantees to resources, limits provide a cap on resource usage, and shares help adjust the allocation of resources in a constrained environment.

> **Master It**   To guarantee certain levels of performance, your IT director believes that all virtual machines must be configured with at least 2GB of RAM. However, you know that many of your applications rarely use this much memory. What might be an acceptable compromise to help ensure performance?

> **Solution**   One way would be to configure the virtual machines with 2GB of RAM and specify a reservation of only 512MB. VMware ESX/ESXi will guarantee that every VM will get 512MB of RAM, including preventing additional VMs from being powered on if there isn't enough RAM to guarantee 512MB of RAM to that new VM. However, the RAM greater than 512MB is not guaranteed and, if it is not being used, will be reclaimed by the host for use elsewhere. If plenty of memory is available to the host, the ESX/ESXi host will grant what is requested; otherwise, it will arbitrate the allocation of that memory according to the shares values of the virtual machines.

Create and manage resource pools.   Managing resource allocation and usage for large numbers of virtual machines creates too much administrative overhead. Resource pools provide a mechanism for administrators to apply resource allocation policies to groups of virtual machines all at the same time. Resource pools use reservations, limits, and shares to control and modify resource allocation behavior.

> **Master It**   Your company runs both test/development workloads and production workloads on the same hardware. How can you help ensure that test/development workloads do not consume too many resources and impact the performance of production workloads?

> **Solution**   Create a resource pool and place all the test/development virtual machines in that resource pool. Configure the resource pool to have a CPU limit and a lower CPU Shares value. This ensures that the test/development will never consume more CPU time than specified in the limit and that, in times of CPU contention, the test/development environment will have a lower priority on the CPU than production workloads.

Configure and execute VMotion.   VMotion is a feature that allows running virtual machines to be migrated from one physical ESX/ESXi host to another physical ESX/ESXi host with no downtime to end users. To execute VMotion, both the ESX/ESXi hosts and the virtual machines must meet specific configuration requirements. In addition, vCenter Server performs validation checks to ensure that VMotion compatibility rules are observed.

> **Master It**   A certain vendor has just released a series of patches for some of the guest operating systems in your virtualized infrastructure. You request an outage window from your supervisor, but your supervisor says to just use VMotion to prevent downtime. Is your supervisor correct? Why or why not?

Solution   Your supervisor is incorrect. VMotion can be used to move running virtual machines from one physical host to another, but it does not address outages within a guest operating system due to reboots or other malfunctions. If you had been requesting an outage window to apply updates to the host, the supervisor would have been correct—you could use VMotion to move all the virtual machines to other hosts within the environment and then patch the first host. There would be no end user downtime in that situation.

Create and manage clusters.   Clusters provide the basic building block for a number of advanced VMware vSphere features, including VMware Distributed Resource Scheduler, VMware High Availability, and Enhanced VMotion Compatibility. Clusters are collections of ESX/ESXi hosts and can contain resource pools for more efficient allocation of resources within the cluster.

Master It   What features discussed thus far are dependent upon clusters? What features discussed so far are not dependent upon clusters?

Solution   Out of the features discussed so far in this book, only VMware Distributed Resource Scheduler, Enhanced VMotion Compatibility, vNetwork Distributed Switches, and the Cisco Nexus 1000V third-party distributed virtual switch are dependent upon clusters. All other features, including VMotion, templates, deploying from templates, snapshots, and so forth, do not require using an ESX/ESXi cluster.

Configure and manage VMware Distributed Resource Scheduler.   VMware Distributed Resource Scheduler enables vCenter Server to automate the process of conducting VMotion migrations to help balance the load across ESX/ESXi hosts within a cluster. DRS can be as automated as desired, and vCenter Server has flexible controls for affecting the behavior of DRS as well as the behavior of specific virtual machines within a DRS-enabled cluster.

Master It   You want to take advantage of VMware DRS to provide some load balancing of virtual workloads within your environment. However, because of business constraints, you have a few workloads that should not be automatically moved to other hosts using VMotion. Can you use DRS? If so, how can you prevent these specific workloads from being affected by DRS?

Solution   Yes, you can use DRS. Enable DRS on the cluster, and set the DRS automation level appropriately. For those VMs that should not be automatically migrated by DRS, configure the DRS automation level on a per-VM basis to Manual. This will allow DRS to make recommendations on migrations for these workloads but will not actually perform the migrations.

Chapter 11: Ensuring High Availability and Business Continuity

Understand Windows clustering and the types of clusters.   Windows clustering plays a central role in the design of any high availability solution for both virtual and physical servers. Microsoft Windows clustering gives us the ability to have application failover to the secondary server when the primary server fails.

Master It   Specifically with regard to Windows clustering in a virtual environment, what are three different types of cluster configurations that you can have?

Solution The first is a cluster in a box, which is mainly used for testing or in a development environment where both nodes of a Windows cluster run on the same VMware ESX/ESXi host.

The second is the cluster across boxes, which is the most common form of clustering in a virtual environment. In this configuration, you have the ability to use Windows clustering on virtual machines that are running on different physical hosts.

The third is the physical to virtual configuration where you have the best of both the physical and virtual worlds by having a Windows clustering node on both a physical server and a virtual server.

Understand built-in high-availability options. VMware Virtual Infrastructure has high-availability options built in and available to you out of the box. These options help you provide better uptime for our critical applications.

Master It What are the two types of high-availability options that VMware provides in vSphere?

Solution VMware provides two forms of high availability in vSphere. VMware HA provides a form of high availability by having the ability to restart any virtual machines that were running on a host that crashes. VMware Fault Tolerance (FT) uses vLockstep technology to record and replay a running virtual machine on another host in the cluster. Failover from the primary virtual machine to the secondary virtual machine is without any downtime.

Understand the differences between VCB and VCDR. VMware has provided some disaster recovery options via backup and restore capability. First there was VMware Consolidated Backup (VCB), and now VMware has introduced VMware Data Center Recovery (VCDR), giving you different options for backing up and restoring your virtual machines.

Master It What are the main differences between VCB and VCDR?

Solution VCB is run on a proxy server that could be a physical or virtual server, while VCDR comes in the form of a provided appliance.

VCB is a framework that will allow you to back up directly to the backup software vendor of your choice, and VCDR will allow you to back up to disk only via the VCDR virtual appliance. VCDR has the ability to use the new vSphere storage APIs.

Understand data replication options. There are other methods to keep continuity in your businesses. Replication of your data to a secondary location is a must to address a company's needs during a real disaster.

Master It What are three methods to replicate your data to a secondary location as well as the golden rule for any continuity plan?

Solution First, you have the backup and restore method from tape. It is a best practice to send out backup tapes off-site and, when they are needed for a disaster, have them shipped to the secondary site.

Second, you have the ability to replicate your data by using block-level replication at the SAN level. This gives you the ability to replicate data over both short and long distances.

Third, you have the ability to think out of the box and with virtualization can create an office environment running on a single physical host that can be shipped to give you an "office in a box."

Finally, the golden rule for any successful continuity design is to test, test, and test again.

Chapter 12: Monitoring VMware vSphere Performance

Use alarms for proactive monitoring. vCenter Server offers extensive alarms for alerting vSphere administrators to excessive resource consumption or potentially negative events. You can create alarms on virtually any type of object found within vCenter Server, including datacenters, clusters, ESX/ESXi hosts, and virtual machines. Alarms can monitor for resource consumption or for the occurrence of specific events. Alarms can also trigger actions, such as running a script, migrating a virtual machine, or sending a notification email.

Master It What are the questions a vSphere administrator should ask before creating a custom alarm?

Solution You should ask several questions before you create a custom alarm:

◆ Does an existing alarm meet my needs?

◆ What is the proper scope for this alarm? Do I need to create it at the datacenter level so that it affects all objects of a particular type within the datacenter, or at some lower point?

◆ What are the values this alarm needs to use?

◆ What actions, if any, should this alarm take when it is triggered? Does it need to send an email or trigger an SNMP trap?

Work with performance graphs. vCenter Server's detailed performance graphs are the key to unlocking the information necessary to determine why an ESX/ESXi host or virtual machine is performing poorly. The performance graphs expose a large number of performance counters across a variety of resource types, and vCenter Server offers functionality to save customized chart settings, export performance graphs as graphic figures or Excel workbooks, or view performance graphs in a separate window.

Master It You find yourself using the Chart Options link in the Advanced view of the Performance tab to frequently set up the same graph over and over again. Is there a way to save yourself some time and effort so that you don't have to keep re-creating the custom graph?

Solution Yes. After using the Customize Performance Chart dialog box to configure the performance graph to show the desired counters, use the Save Chart Settings button to save these settings for future use. The next time you need to access these same settings again, they will be available from the Switch To drop-down list on the Advanced view of the Performance tab.

Gather performance information using command-line tools.   VMware supplies a few command-line tools that are useful in gathering performance information. For VMware ESX hosts, `esxtop` provides real-time information about CPU, memory, network, or disk utilization. For both VMware ESX as well as VMware ESXi, `resxtop` can display the same information. Finally, the `vm-support` tool can gather performance information that can be played back later using `esxtop`.

Master It   Compare and contrast the `esxtop` and `resxtop` utilities.

Solution   The `esxtop` utility can be used only with VMware ESX, because it relies upon the Linux-based Service Console supplied with ESX. On the other hand, `resxtop` works with both VMware ESX as well as VMware ESXi. Both utilities can display CPU, memory, disk, network, and CPU interrupt information in near real-time.

Monitor CPU, memory, network, and disk usage by both ESX/ESXi hosts and virtual machines.   Monitoring usage of the four key resources—CPU, memory, network, and disk—can be difficult at times. Fortunately, the various tools supplied by VMware within vCenter Server can lead the vSphere administrator to the right solution. In particular, using customized performance graphs can expose the right information that will help a vSphere administrator uncover the source of performance problems.

Master It   A junior vSphere administrator is trying to resolve a performance problem with a virtual machine. You've asked this administrator to see whether it is a CPU problem, and the junior administrator keeps telling you that the virtual machine needs more CPU capacity because the CPU utilization is high within the virtual machine. Is the junior administrator correct, based on the information available to you?

Solution   Based on the available information, not necessarily. A virtual machine may be using all of the cycles being given to it, but because the overall ESX/ESXi host is CPU constrained, the virtual machine isn't getting enough cycles to perform acceptably. In this case, adding CPU capacity to the virtual machine wouldn't necessarily fix the problem. If the host is indeed constrained, then migrating virtual machines to other hosts or changing the shares or the CPU limits for the virtual machines on this host may help alleviate the problem.

Chapter 13: Securing VMware vSphere

Manage local users on ESX/ESXi hosts.   Despite that vCenter Server eliminates most of the uses for local accounts created and managed on each ESX/ESXi host, there is still a small but critical need for local accounts. You can use Linux-based tools like `useradd`, `userdel`, `groupadd`, and `groupdel` to create and delete local users and groups on ESX hosts. For both ESX and ESXi hosts, the vSphere Client also offers the ability to manage local users and groups.

Master It   You've asked an administrator on your team to create some accounts on an ESX host. The administrator is uncomfortable with the Linux command line and is having a problem figuring out how to create the users. Is there another way for this administrator to perform this task?

Solution   Yes, the administrator can use the vSphere Client and connect directly to the ESX hosts on which the accounts need to be created.

Configure authentication on ESX hosts. vCenter Server centralizes the authentication of users through integration with Active Directory, but that authentication support does not extend to user accounts that exist directly on ESX hosts. To provide more centralized authentication for ESX hosts you can use the `esxcfg-auth` command to enable integration with Active Directory. This provides a single point of administration for accounts accessing both vCenter Server as well as ESX hosts directly.

Master It You've just installed a new ESX host into your VMware vSphere environment and used the `esxcfg-auth` command to enable integration with your Active Directory environment. For some reason, though, you can't authenticate to this new host. You've compared the configuration of this new host to the configuration of other working hosts but can't pinpoint any differences. What could be the problem?

Solution Most likely, the problem is that you haven't created local user accounts on that ESX host. Although `esxcfg-auth` centralizes the authentication of user accounts, the ESX hosts must still have actual user accounts created locally in order for that authentication to operate properly. Use the `useradd` command to create local ESX accounts that match the Active Directory usernames you want to be allowed to log into the new ESX host.

Control network access to services on ESX hosts. VMware ESX allows you to leverage the Linux-based Service Console to control access to network services, like SSH, through a couple of different means. First, VMware supplies an iptables-based firewall configured using the `esxcfg-firewall` command. Second, you can use TCP Wrappers to control access to a variety of network services. Third, and finally, you can leverage functionality native to SSH to control what user accounts are allowed to log in via SSH. All of these tools are complementary to one another.

Master It Describe how the Service Console firewall and TCP Wrappers are complementary to each other and where their functionality overlaps.

Solution Both the Service Console firewall and TCP Wrappers have the ability to control access to network services based on information like TCP or UDP port, so there is overlap in their functionality in that regard. However, TCP Wrappers provides a bit more granularity than the Service Console firewall in that it permits you to specify specific clients or groups of clients that are allowed to connect. Although iptables, the firewall engine that powers the Service Console firewall, has this ability, this functionality is not exposed to end users via the `esxcfg-firewall` command.

Provide secure network zones. VMware vShield Zones provides a network-based security solution designed to eliminate a key problem with virtualized environments: the lack of visibility and control over the network access layer. Using a modular approach consisting of vShield Manager for configuration and management and multiple vShield virtual appliances for policy enforcement, vShield Zones enables administrators to both see and control the traffic flowing through their virtual switches. This makes vShield Zones a key component in a defense-in-depth strategy that also includes traditional physical network security appliances.

Master It Your CIO believes that it is not safe to use VMware vSphere in environments with multiple trust zones. How can the functionality provided by vShield Zones help you convince her otherwise?

Solution vShield Zones provides a distributed virtual firewall that is centrally controlled and centrally managed but that will apply network security policy globally in the virtualized environment. This will allow you to create rules to control traffic flow between the different trust zones to ensure that your organization's security policies are maintained even after the move to a virtualized environment.

Chapter 14: Automating VMware vSphere

Identify some of the tools available for automating VMware vSphere. VMware offers a number of different solutions for automating your VMware vSphere environment, including vCenter Orchestrator, PowerCLI, an SDK for Perl, an SDK for web service developers, and shell scripts in VMware ESX. Each of these tools has its own set of advantages and disadvantages.

Master It VMware offers a number of different automation tools. What are some guidelines in helping to choose what automation tool to use?

Solution One key factor is prior experience. If you have prior experience with creating scripts using Perl, then you will likely be most effective in using the vSphere SDK for Perl to create automation tools. Similarly, prior experience or knowledge with PowerShell will mean you will likely be most effective using PowerCLI.

Configure vCenter Orchestrator. vCenter Orchestrator is installed silently with vCenter Server, but before you can use vCenter Orchestrator, you must configure it properly. The vCenter Orchestrator Configuration interface provides a web-based interface to configuring the various portions of vCenter Orchestrator.

Master It How can you tell whether some portion of the vCenter Orchestrator configuration is incomplete or incorrect?

Solution The status indicators in the vCenter Orchestrator Configuration interface will show a red triangle for any configuration item that is incorrect or incomplete and will show a green circle for items that have been successfully configured.

Use a vCenter Orchestrator workflow. After vCenter Orchestrator is configured and is running, you can use the vCenter Orchestrator Client to run a vCenter Orchestrator workflow. vCenter Orchestrators comes with a number of pre-installed workflows to help automate tasks.

Master It A separate administrator in your environment configured vCenter Orchestrator and has now asked you to run a couple of workflows. However, when you log into the vCenter Server where vCenter Orchestrator is also installed, you don't see the icons for vCenter Orchestrator. Why?

Solution The vCenter Server installer creates the vCenter Orchestrator Start menu icons in the user-specific side of the Start menu, so they are visible only to the user who was logged on when vCenter Server was installed. Other users will not see the icons on the Start menu unless they are moved to the All Users portion of the Start menu.

Create a PowerCLI script for automation. VMware vSphere PowerCLI builds upon the object-oriented PowerShell scripting language to provide administrators with a simple yet powerful way to automate tasks within the vSphere environment.

> **Master It**   If you are familiar with other scripting languages, what would be the biggest hurdle in becoming familiar with PowerShell and PowerCLI, other than syntax?
>
> **Solution**   Everything in PowerShell and PowerCLI is object-based. Thus, when a command outputs results, those results are objects. This means you have to be careful to properly match object types between the output of one command in the input of the next command.

Leverage shell scripts on VMware ESX. For tasks that are host-centric, shell scripts on VMware ESX hosts can help provide automation. Some of these shell scripts may also work with slight modifications on the vSphere Management Assistant, which provides a CLI that you can use for managing ESXi hosts.

> **Master It**   What is the biggest drawback of using shell scripts with VMware vSphere?
>
> **Solution**   There are two significant drawbacks. First, shell scripts are inherently limited to per-host configuration tasks because the scripts execute on a host. Second, shell scripts are limited, for all intents and purposes, to run only on VMware ESX hosts. Although you may be able to modify some scripts to run on the vSphere Management Assistant, this is not necessarily guaranteed.

Appendix B

Frequently Used Commands

Being able to use the command-line interface (CLI) provided by VMware ESX and the vSphere Management Assistant (vMA) is an important skill for all VMware vSphere administrators. The frequently used commands described in this appendix focus on basic proficiency, such as navigating around the VMware ESX Service Console, using the esxcfg-* and vicfg-* commands, and managing files and directories.

Navigating, Managing, and Monitoring Through the Service Console

Getting around the ESX Service Console is a critical skill for troubleshooting and managing ESX hosts when the traditional graphical tools are not available. The following commands are some of the common commands for moving around a Linux-based operating system. In all of the following examples, the hash sign (#) represents the shell prompt.

cd   Used to change directories.

Example: # cd /vmfs/volumes

ls   Used to list files and folders in the current directory.

Example: # ls

ls -l   Used to list files and folders in a long format with rights and owners.

ls -s   Used to list files and folders in a short format.

ls -R   Used to list files and folders with the ability to scroll.

whoami   Used to identify the effective user.

who am i   Used to identify the currently logged-on user.

logout   Used to log out the current user.

reboot   Used to reboot a system.

useradd   Used to add a new user.

Example: # useradd newaccount

passwd   Used to update a user account password.

Example: # passwd newaccount

ifconfig   Used to obtain information about network interfaces. You can use the -a parameter to show all network interfaces.

Example: # ifconfig -a

Managing Directories, Files, and Disks in the Service Console

Without a graphical interface available, you will have to use the ESX CLI to create, manage, and delete files and directories. The following commands provide basic instructions for moving, copying, creating, and deleting files and directories. In all these examples, the hash sign (#) represents the shell prompt.

mv   Used to move or rename files. By default, mv defaults to an interactive setting (equal to mv -i), which confirms each operation.

> Example 1: # mv oldfile newfile

> Example 2: # mv file1 /newfolder/file1

cp   Used to copy directories or files. You can rename a file during the copy process. Use the -f parameter to force the copy, the -p parameter to preserve the permissions, and the -R parameter to recursively copy all subdirectories. The cp command defaults to interactive mode (equal to cp -i), which confirms each operation.

> Example 1: # cp file1 /newdocs/file1

> Example 2: # cp file1 /newdocs/file2

rm   Used to remove files and directories. Use the -f parameter to force the removal, and use the -R parameter to recursively delete. As with cp and mv, rm defaults to an interactive mode (equal to using rm -i).

> Example: # rm -f /olddirectory

rmdir   Used to remove empty directories.

> Example: # rmdir

touch   Used to create a new file or change file access and modification time.

> Example: # touch mynewfile.txt

fdisk   Used to manage disk partitions.

mount   Used to mount CD-ROM or floppy drives.

> Example: # mount /mnt/cdrom

Using the esxcfg-* Commands

In addition to the standard Linux commands I've covered so far, VMware has implemented a specific set of commands directed toward ESX-specific tasks. The following list of commands shows how to manage various components of the ESX host configuration. Again, the hash sign (#) represents the shell prompt.

esxcfg-auth   Used to configure an ESX server host to support network-based authentication methods. One such authentication method would be Active Directory. When used to configure Active Directory authentication, this command uses the following parameters:

--enablead to configure Service Console for Active Directory authentication

--addomain to set the domain the Service Console will authenticate against

--addc to set the domain controller to authenticate against for Active Directory authentication

--usecrack to enable the pam_cracklib library for managing password complexity

Example: # esxcfg-auth --enablead --addomain vmwarelab.net --addc vmwarelab.net

esxcfg-firewall   Used to query, enable, and disable services on the Service Console firewall. The following parameters are commonly used:

-q to query the current firewall settings

-q servicename to query the status of a specific service

-q incoming/outgoing to query the status of incoming and outgoing ports

--blockIncoming to block all incoming connections on ports not required for system function

--blockOutgoing to block all outgoing connections on ports not required for system function

--allowIncoming to allow incoming connections on all ports

--allowOutgoing to allow outgoing connections on all ports

--e servicename to enable a specific service

--d servicename to disable a specific service

Example: # esxcfg-firewall -e swISCSIClient

esxcfg-info   Used to review the hardware information for Service Console and VMkernel. Some of the supported parameters include the following:

-w to print hardware information

-s to print storage and disk information

-n to print network information

Example: # esxcfg-info -s

esxcfg-mpath   Used to view and configure the multipathing settings for an ESX host's Fibre Channel or iSCSI storage devices. Some frequently used parameters include the following:

-l to list all paths with their detailed information

-L to list all paths in compact form

-b to list all devices with their paths

-P to define a path to operate on

-s with active or off to enable or disable a specific path

Example: # esxcfg-mpath -L

esxcfg-nas   Used to configure network-attached storage (NAS) file systems on an ESX host. Some frequently used parameters include the following:

-l to list all NAS

-a to add a new NAS datastore on a specified host

-o to provide the name of the NAS host

-s to provide the name of the NAS share

-d to delete a NAS datastore

Example: # esxcfg-nas -a -o 192.168.31.10 -s /vol/isoimages DatastoreName

esxcfg-nics   Used to obtain information about and configure the physical network adapters installed in an ESX host. Some frequently used parameters include the following:

-l to list all the installed NICs and their settings

-s to set the speed of a card to 10, 100, 1000, or 10,000

-d to set the duplex to half or full

Example: # esxcfg-nics -s 1000 vmnic5

esxcfg-route   Used to configure the VMkernel routing table. Some frequently used parameters include the following:

-a to add a route to the VMkernel

-d to delete a route from the VMkernel

-l to list routes configured in the VMkernel

Example: # esxcfg-route -a 192.168.31.0/24 192.168.31.254

esxcfg-swiscsi   Used to configure the software iSCSI initiator in an ESX host. Some frequently used parameters include the following:

-e to enable software iSCSI

-d to disable software iSCSI

-q to query to see whether software iSCSI is enabled

-s to scan for new LUNs using software iSCSI

Example: # esxcfg-swiscsi -q

esxcfg-vmknic   Used to configure the VMkernel NIC. You must already have a port group created to which the VMkernel NIC is attached or will be attached. Some frequently used parameters include the following:

-a to add a VMkernel port group

-d to delete a VMKernel

-e to enable the VMkernel NIC

-D to disable the VMkernel port

-i to set the IP address of the VMkernel NIC

-n to set the network mask for the IP of the call

Example: # esxcfg-vmknic -a -i 192.168.28.105 -n 255.255.255.0 PortGroupName

esxcfg-vswif   Used to set the parameters of the Service Console network interface. You must already have a port group created to which the Service Console interface is attached or will be attached. Some frequently used parameters include the following:

-a to add a Service Console NIC (this option is predicated on having IP information and port group names)

-d to delete the Service Console NIC

-e to enable the Service Console NIC

-D to disable the Service Console NIC

-p to set the port group name for the Service Console NIC

-i to set the IP address to be used for the Service Console NIC

-n to set the network mask for the Service Console NIC

Example: # esxcfg-vswif -a -i 192.168.29.150 -n 255.255.255.0 -p ServiceConsole2 vswif1

esxcfg-vswitch   Used to add, remove, or modify a virtual switch. Limited operations are available for vNetwork Distributed Switches. Some frequently used parameters include the following:

-a to add a new virtual switch

-d to delete a new virtual switch

-l to list all existing virtual switches

-L to link a physical network adapter as an uplink

-U to unlink a network adapter currently connected as an uplink

-v to set the VLAN ID for a port group

-A to add a new port group

-D to delete a port group

-C to query for the existence of a port group name

Example: # esxcfg-vswitch -v 2 -p VLAN2-Production vSwitch1

esxcfg-volume   Used to work with Virtual Machine File System (VMFS) volumes. Some frequently used parameters include the following:

-l to list volumes detected as snapshots/replicas

-m to mount a snapshot/replica volume if the original copy is not online

-r to resignature a snapshot/replica volume

Example: # esxcfg-volume -l

Using the vicfg-* Commands

The lack of a Service Console in ESXi has driven the development of a set of remote command-line utilities. In VMware vSphere, the vSphere Management Assistant provides a set of commands similar to the esxcfg-* commands but designed to work remotely with ESXi hosts. These commands are the vicfg-* commands.

vifp   Used to manipulate servers in FastPass. FastPass streamlines the authentication process when using vMA and remote commands. Some frequently used parameters include the following:

addserver followed by <host> to add a server to FastPass

`listservers` to list the servers current in FastPass

`removeserver` followed by `<host>` to remove a server from FastPass

Example: # `vifp addserver esx01.vmwarelab.net`

vifpinit   Used to initialize FastPass. Some frequently used parameters include the following:

Example: # `vifpinit esx01.vmwarelab.net`

vicfg-nas   Used to manipulate NAS/NFS datastores. Some frequently used parameters include the following:

`--add` or `-a` to add a new NAS file system

`--delete` or `-d` to delete a NAS file system

`--help` to display help text

`--nasserver` or `-o` followed by `<n_host>` to add the hostname of the new NAS file system

`--share` or `-s` used with `-a` to provide the name of the directory that is exported on the NAS device

`--vihost` or `-h` followed by `<host>` to direct the command to a particular ESX/ESXi host

Example: # `vicfg-nas --delete nfsvolume --vihost esx01.vmwarelab.net`

vicfg-mpath   Used to manipulate multipathing. Some frequently used parameters include the following:

`--help` to display help text

`-d` or `--device` to filter list commands to display only a specific device

`-l` or `--list` to list all paths with their detailed information

`-L` or `--list-compact` to list all paths in compact form

`-b` or `--list-paths` to list all devices with their paths

`-P` or `--path` to define a path to operate on

`-s` or `--state` with `active` or `off` to enable or disable a specific path; requires a path with `--path`

Example: # `vicfg-mpath --list-compact --vihost esx01.vmwarelab.net`

vicfg-rescan   Used to perform a rescan for discovering new LUNs. Some frequently used parameters include the following:

`--help` to display help text

`--vihost` or `-h` followed by `<host>` to direct the command to a particular ESX/ESXi host

`<VMkernel_SCSI_adapter_name>` to provide the name of the adapter to rescan (i.e., vmhba1)

Example: # `vicfg-rescan --vihost esx01.vmwarelab.net vmhba1`

vicfg-nics   Used to report on and manage physical network adapters. Some frequently used parameters include the following:

`--help` to display help text

--auto or -a to set the given adapter to autonegotiate the speed and duplex settings

--duplex or -d followed by [full | half] <nic> to set the duplex value for a given NIC

--speed or -s followed by <speed><nic> to set the speed value for a given NIC

--list or -l to list the physical adapters in the system

--vihost or -h followed by <host> to direct the command to a particular ESX/ESXi host

Example: # vicfg-nics --speed 1000 vmnic0 --vihost esx01.vmwarelab.net

vicfg-vmknic Used to configure virtual network adapters. Some frequently used parameters include the following:

--help to display help text

--add or -a to add a virtual network adapter to the system (an IP address and port group name must be specified)

--delete or -d followed by <port_group> to delete the virtual network adapter on the specified port group

--enable-vmotion or -e to enable VMotion on this VMkernel port

--ip or -i followed by [<IP address>| DHCP] to set the virtual network adapter to a given IP address or to obtain an address from a DHCP server

--list or -l to list virtual network adapters on the system

--netmask or -n followed by <netmask> to set the network mask for the assigned IP address

--vihost or -h followed by <host> to direct the command to a particular ESX/ESXi host

Example: # vicfg-vmknic --add --ip 192.168.69.100 --netmask 255.255.255.0
--portgroup VMotion --vihost esx01.vmwarelab.net

vicfg-vswitch Used to configure virtual switches. Some frequently used parameters include the following:

--help to display help text

--add or -a followed by <vswitch_name> to add a new virtual switch

--add-pg or -A followed by <portgroup> <switch> to add a port group to the specified switch

--check or -c followed by <virtual_switch> to check for the existence of a virtual switch

--check-pg or -C followed by <port_group> to check for the existence of a port group

--delete or -d followed by <vswitch_name> to delete the specified virtual switch (this command will not work if any of the virtual switch ports are in use)

--del-pg or -D followed by <portgroup> to delete the specified port group (this command will not work if the port group is in use)

--link or -L followed by <pnic> to add a physical adapter to a virtual switch

--list or -l to list all virtual switches and port groups

--mtu or -m to set the maximum transmission unit (MTU) of the virtual switch

--pg or -p followed by <port_group> to provide the name of a port group when using the --vlan option (use the ALL parameter to set VLAN IDs on all port groups of a virtual switch)

`--vlan` or `-v` to set the VLAN ID for a specific port group (using the parameter 0 disables all VLAN IDs; using `--vlan` requires the `--pg` option)

`--vihost` or `-h` followed by `<host>` to direct the command to a particular ESX/ESXi host

Example: # `vicfg-vswitch -A VLAN31-Finance vSwitch2 --vihost esx01.vmwarelab.net`

vicfg-route Used to configure the routing table for the VMkernel. Some frequently used parameters include the following:

`--help` to display help text

`-add` or `-a` to add a route to the VMkernel

`-del` or `-d` to delete a route from the VMkernel

`-list` or `-l` to list routes configured in the VMkernel

`--vihost` or `-h` followed by `<host>` to direct the command to a particular ESX/ESXi host

Example: # `vicfg-route --add 192.168.31.0/24 192.168.31.254 --vihost esx01.vmwarelab.net`

vicfg-ntp Used to configure NTP settings. Some frequently used parameters include the following:

`--help` to display help text

`--add` or `-a` followed by `<server>` to add an NTP server

`--delete` or `-d` followed by `<server>` to delete an NTP server

`--list` or `-l` to list the configured NTP servers

`--vihost` or `-h` followed by `<host>` to direct the command to a particular ESX server host

Example: # `vicfg-ntp --add 0.us.pool.ntp.org --vihost esx01.vmwarelab.net`

Appendix C

VMware vSphere Best Practices

This appendix serves as an overview of the many design, deployment, management, and monitoring concepts discussed throughout the book. You can use it as a quick reference for any phase of your virtual infrastructure deployment. The appendix is also meant as a review of the material I covered, with a focus on the concepts of VMware vSphere that are commonly discussed in the world of virtualization management. By reviewing this appendix, you can gauge your level of fluency with the concepts I've discussed. If you're unsure of any of the best practices outlined here, you can revisit the various sections of the book for more details about that particular best practice.

ESX/ESXi Installation Best Practices

The following best practice suggestions are derived from the full details outlined in Chapters 2 and 13:

- ◆ Review your architecture needs to determine whether ESX or ESXi is the right foundation for your virtual infrastructure. Identify the answers to these questions:

    - ◆ Do you need the console operating system?

    - ◆ Do you need to minimize the footprint on the physical server?

    - ◆ Do you want to install any third-party applications that require the Service Console?

- ◆ Always consult the ESX/ESXi compatibility guides before purchasing any new hardware. Even if you are successful at installing on unsupported hardware, be aware that using hardware not listed on the Hardware Compatibility List (HCL) will force any support calls to end abruptly. Ensure that you review the appropriate compatibility guide for the product you have chosen to install.

- ◆ Plan the Service Console management methods before installing. Identify the answers to these questions:

    - ◆ Will the Service Console be on a dedicated management network or on the same network as virtual machines?

    - ◆ Will you be using VLANs or physical hardware to segment the Service Console?

    - ◆ How will you provide redundancy for the Service Console communication?

◆ If you're installing ESX and not ESXi, construct a Service Console security plan. Ensure limited access to the Service Console by minimizing the number of administrators with local user accounts or knowledge of the root password.

◆ Create user accounts for each administrative user who requires direct access to an ESX/ESXi host.

◆ For VMware ESX, establish strong user account policies in the Service Console by utilizing Active Directory or by deploying a Linux-based security module.

◆ Establish growth projections, and plan the ESX Service Console partition strategy accordingly:

  ◆ Increase the /root partition size to provide ample room for growth and/or the installation of third-party applications. If the root of the file system runs out of space, there will most certainly be issues to address.

  ◆ Increase the /swap partition size to address any projected increases in the amount of RAM provided to the Service Console. /swap should be twice the amount of RAM that will be allocated to the Service Console.

  ◆ Change /var/log to /var and increase partition size to provide ample room for logs and the ESX patch management process that writes to the /var directory.

◆ Unless performing a boot from SAN, detach ESX/ESXi hosts from the external storage devices during installation to prevent overwriting existing data. At a minimum, don't present LUNs to a new ESX/ESXi host until the installation is complete.

◆ When reinstalling ESX/ESXi on a physical server, be careful not to initialize LUNs with existing data. Once again, disconnecting a host from the SAN during the reinstall process will eliminate the threat of erasing data.

◆ Configure a time synchronization strategy that synchronizes all ESX/ESXi hosts with the same external time server.

◆ Ensure the security of console access by guaranteeing the physical security of the box. If the server is configured with a remote console adapter, such as the HP iLO, ensure that the default password has been changed and that the iLO network is accessible only from appropriate network segments. For example, Distributed Power Management (DPM) requires that vCenter Server is able to access the iLO/Intelligent Platform Management Interface (IPMI) port of the ESX/ESXi host.

vCenter Server Best Practices

The following vCenter Server best practices are taken from the full recommendations provided in Chapters 3, 9, 10, and 13:

◆ Uninstall IIS prior to installing vCenter Server.

◆ Use the Service applet in the Windows Control Panel to configure the VMware vCenter Server Service for autorestart.

◆ Design a strong high availability solution for the vCenter Server database server (for instance, Microsoft Clustering or consistent database backups).

◆ Installing vCenter Server with an SQL Server back-end database requires a user account with membership in the db_owner database role and ownership of the vCenter Server database. After the installation of vCenter Server is complete, the db_owner database role membership can and should be removed.

◆ The db_owner role is also required on the MSDB database in SQL Server during the installation of vCenter Server. This access should be removed after installation is complete.

◆ Carefully monitor the transaction logs of the vCenter Server database. To eliminate transaction log growth, configure SQL Server databases in Simple Recovery mode. For maximum recoverability, configure SQL Server databases in Full Recovery mode.

◆ Create a high availability plan for vCenter Server. You can configure vCenter Server in an active/passive server cluster with Microsoft Clustering Services, use VMware vCenter Heartbeat, or install vCenter Server into a virtual machine and perform a copy of the virtual machine at regular intervals.

◆ Create a vCenter Server hierarchy to support your management model. If your organization manages resources by location, then create management objects (datacenters, clusters, folders) based on location. On the other hand, if your organization manages by department, then create objects accordingly. In most organizations the vCenter Server hierarchy will reflect a hybrid approach that combines location, department, server function, server type, and so forth.

◆ Use host profiles within ESX/ESXi clusters to ensure consistent configuration and VMotion compatibility.

◆ Apply the principle of least privilege to permission assignment policies in vCenter Server. Employees who use vCenter Server as a common management tool should be granted only the permissions required to perform their job.

◆ Use Windows groups in the vCenter Server security model. Assigning Windows groups to a vCenter Server role that is assigned privileges and permissions will facilitate the application of similar settings in the future. For example, create a Windows group called DomainControllerAdmins that is a member of the VC role called DCAdmins, which has the privilege to power on and power off and has been granted the permission on a folder containing all domain controller virtual machines. When a new user is hired to administer the domain controller virtual machines, the user can simply be added to the DomainControllerAdmins Windows group and will inherit all the necessary permissions.

◆ Identify a systematic approach to LUN creation and management. Identify either the adaptive or the predictive scheme as the LUN management process. Keep in mind that your overall storage management may involve a combination of larger LUNs with several virtual machine files and smaller LUNs for individual virtual machine files.

◆ Configure DRS to perform VMotion based on comfort level. Some VMotion will be necessary to ensure balance and fairness of resource allocation.

◆ Disable the automated VMotion for critical virtual machines that you do not want to be VMotion candidates based on the DRS algorithm.

◆ Apply the recommendation if the DRS algorithm suggests a VMotion migration of four or five stars. The algorithm takes into account many factors for offering recommendations that result in increased system performance.

Virtual Networking Best Practices

You can find the configuration details regarding the virtual networking best practices shown in the following list in Chapter 5:

◆ Plan the virtual-to-physical networking integration.

◆ Maximize the number of physical network adapters (Ethernet ports) to provide flexibility in the virtual networking architecture.

◆ Separate Service Console, iSCSI, NAS, VMotion, Fault Tolerance (FT), and virtual machine traffic across different physical networks pending the availability of network adapters, or use a VLAN architecture to segment the traffic.

◆ Create port groups with VLAN IDs to provide security, segmentation, and scalability to the virtual switching architecture.

◆ Construct a virtual networking security policy for virtual switches, ports, and port groups.

◆ Create port groups for security, traffic shaping, or VLAN tagging.

◆ For optimal security, configure the virtual switch properties with the following settings:

  ◆ Promiscuous mode: Reject

  ◆ MAC Address Changes: Reject

  ◆ Forged Transmits: Reject

◆ Avoid VLAN tags used by common third-party hardware devices, like VLAN 1. Virtual switches do not support the native VLAN as physical switches do.

◆ Define traffic shaping to reduce the outbound bandwidth available either to the virtual machines that do not require full access to the bandwidth of the physical adapter or to the virtual machines that inappropriately monopolize bandwidth. Weigh the options of micro-managing virtual machine bandwidth against the configuration of NIC teams with the installation of additional network adapters.

◆ Construct NIC teams on a physical adapter connected to separate bus architectures. For example, use one onboard network adapter in combination with an adapter from an expansion card. Do *not* use two adapters from the same expansion card in the same NIC team or two onboard adapters in the same NIC team. The exception to this recommendation would be in the case of multiple onboard adapters that are actually on separate I/O buses, like in the HP DL380 G6.

◆ To eliminate a single point of failure at the physical switch, connect network adapters in a NIC team to separate physical switches that belong to the same broadcast domain. You will need physical switches that support cross-switch link aggregation in order to provide physical switch redundancy when using IP-hash-based load balancing on your vSwitches. An example of such a switch is the Cisco Catalyst 3750G.

◆ Consider creating a NIC team for the service console. Otherwise, consider providing multiple vswif ports on different networks for redundant Service Console access.

◆ Construct a dedicated Gigabit LAN for VMotion. All physical network adapters in the server must offer support for Gigabit Ethernet.

◆ Provide a dedicated Gigabit Ethernet or 10 Gigabit Ethernet network interface card (NIC) for fault tolerance logging traffic.

◆ Create separate networks for test and production virtual machines.

Storage Management Best Practices

You can find the configuration details regarding the virtual networking best practices shown in the following list in Chapter 6:

◆ When booting from SAN, mask each bootable LUN to be seen only by the ESX host booting from that LUN.

◆ Build a dedicated and isolated storage network for iSCSI SAN storage to isolate and secure iSCSI storage-related traffic.

◆ Build a dedicated and isolated storage network for NAS/NFS storage to isolate and secure NAS/NFS storage-related traffic.

◆ Perform all masking at the storage device, not at the ESX/ESXi host.

◆ Separate disk-intensive virtual machines on different LUNs carved from separate physical disks.

◆ Provide individual zoning configurations for each ESX/ESXi host.

◆ Allow the SAN administrators to manage LUN sizes. VMFS extents might help immediate needs but might lead to loss of data in the event that an extent becomes corrupted or damaged.

◆ Spread the storage communication workload across the available hardware devices. For example, if the ESX/ESXi host has two Fibre Channel adapters, ensure that the VMkernel is not sending all traffic through one adapter while the other remains dormant.

◆ Use separate storage locations for test virtual machines and production virtual machines.

◆ Build LUNs in sizes that are easy to manage yet can host multiple virtual machines. For example, create 300GB or 400GB LUNs to host five or six virtual machines. Be prepared to use Storage VMotion to move disk-intensive virtual machines.

◆ Use Storage VMotion to eliminate downtime when needing to migrate a virtual machine between datastores.

◆ Use Raw Device Mappings (RDMs) for Microsoft Clustering scenarios or to provide virtual machines with access to existing LUNs that contain data on NTFS-formatted storage.

◆ Implement a solid change management practice for the deployment of new LUNs. Identify a standard-sized LUN, and stray from the standard only when the situation calls for it.

Virtual Machine Best Practices

The following virtual machine best practices are collected from the full recommendations found in Chapters 7, 8, 10, and 13:

- ◆ Construct virtual machines with separate drives for operating systems and user data, and use separate virtual SCSI adapters for drives that have higher I/O requirements.

- ◆ Always install VMware Tools to provide the optimized SCSI drivers, enhanced virtual NIC drivers, the balloon driver, and support for quiescing the file system during the VMware snapshot process.

- ◆ Use the VMware Tools to complement the Windows Time Services to synchronize the time on a virtual machine. The Windows Server computer functioning as the PDC emulator operations master should be configured to synchronize time with the same time server used by the ESX/ESXi hosts.

- ◆ Where possible, use the Paravirtualized SCSI (PVSCSI) driver for improved disk performance with lower ESX/ESXi host utilization.

- ◆ Where possible, use the VMXNET3 network driver for improved network performance with lower ESX/ESXi host utilization.

- ◆ Avoid special characters and spaces in the display names of virtual machines. Create virtual machine display names with the same rules you apply when providing DNS hostnames.

- ◆ During a physical-to-virtual (P2V) migration, adjust the size of the hard drives to prevent excess storage consumption of the target datastore.

- ◆ After a P2V migration, reduce the amount of memory to a more appropriate level. In most physical server environments, the amount of RAM is drastically overallocated. In virtual environments, resource allocation must be carefully considered.

- ◆ After a P2V migration, reduce the number of vCPUs to one. Increase only as needed by the virtual machine. Additional vCPUs can cause unwanted contention with the scheduling of multiple vCPUs onto pCPUs. The number of vCPUs in a virtual machine should be less than the number of pCPUs in the server to prevent the virtual machine from consuming all pCPUs.

- ◆ After a P2V migration of a Windows-based server, use Device Manager to remove devices for hardware that no longer exist in the virtual environment.

- ◆ Maintain virtual machine templates for several different operating system installations. For example, create and maintain templates for Windows Server 2003 Service Pack 2, Windows Server 2008 32-bit, Windows Server 2008 64-bit, and so forth.

- ◆ When templates are brought online, place them onto isolated networks away from access by standard end users.

- ◆ Use CPU and memory reservations to guarantee resources to critical virtual machines, and use share values to guarantee appropriate resources to critical virtual machines during periods of increased contention.

Disaster Recovery and Business Continuity Best Practices

The best practices in the following list are taken from the detailed recommendations found in Chapter 11:

◆ Implement Microsoft Clustering Services to achieve the high availability of individual virtual machines.

◆ Implement VMware High Availability (HA) to provide the automatic restart of virtual machines residing on an ESX/ESXi host computer that fails.

◆ Use strict admission control for HA clusters unless virtual machine performance is not as important as simply having the virtual machine powered on.

◆ Prioritize virtual machines for startup after server failure. Prepare a contingency plan for powering off unnecessary virtual machines in the event of server failure, resulting in reduced computing power.

◆ For the highest levels of availability, configure VMware Fault Tolerance (FT).

◆ Limit the number of FT-protected primary VMs on a host.

◆ Implement a backup strategy that involves a blend of full virtual machine backups with file-level backups.

◆ Purchase enough backup agents to ensure minimal recovery times for servers with critical production data. Schedule the backups to ensure that recovery times are appropriate for the data type. For example, for data with greater value and a requirement for quicker restore, backups should be scheduled more often than usual.

◆ Do not use virtual machine snapshots as long-term solutions to disaster recovery or business continuity. Snapshots are meant as a temporary means of providing an easy rollback feature and are used primarily for short-term recovery purposes. An example of when a snapshot would be used is during a software upgrade in a virtual machine.

◆ Test the full and virtual machine backups regularly by restoring to a test or development network.

◆ Store a copy of virtual machine backups in an off-site location. Otherwise, use tools to perform virtual machine replication to distant datacenters. Virtualization offers significant advantages in the realm of disaster recovery because virtual machines are encapsulated into a discrete set of files.

◆ Purchase licenses for Windows Server 2008 Datacenter to achieve a greater return on investment and achieve less stringent VMotion restrictions. Datacenter licenses allow for the installation of an unlimited number of virtual machines per ESX/ESXi host. Windows Server 2008 Datacenter can also be "downgraded" to run earlier versions of Windows Server and lesser editions of Windows Server such as Standard or Enterprise.

Monitoring and Troubleshooting Best Practices

The following best practices will help you troubleshoot a problematic VMware vSphere deployment. Chapter 10 provides additional information on monitoring your VMware vSphere environment.

◆ Monitor virtual machine performance with a combination of tools inside the virtual machine and the tools in vSphere. For example, use Task Manager inside a virtual machine and the performance reports from vCenter Server to monitor CPU utilization and to identify bottlenecks.

◆ Regularly review the levels of the CPU Ready and Ballooning counters in the performance charts provided by vCenter Server. Abnormally high values of either counter would indicate an issue with CPU or memory, respectively.

◆ Create virtual machine benchmarks as a standard of comparison when changes are made.

◆ Create email-based performance alarms for key virtual machines. Allow administrators to be notified of system problems for virtual machines that provide core network services such as mail, databases, and authentication.

◆ Identify the root of any problem and then attempt fixes based on monitoring results, feature dependencies, and the company's documented change management process. For example, if VMware HA is not failing over properly, review the DNS configuration for the affected hosts because HA relies on name resolution across ESX/ESXi hosts.

◆ Engage in a systematic approach to identifying and fixing problems with ESX/ESXi hosts and virtual machines.

◆ To troubleshoot CPU-related issues, check the guest operating system CPU usage and %RDY on the ESX/ESXi host. High guest CPU usage and low %RDY on the host indicates the need to add an additional vCPU. High guest CPU usage and high %RDY indicates a physical contention issue.

◆ To troubleshoot memory-related issues, check the guest operating system for swapping first, and then check the ESX/ESXi host for ballooning and virtual machine swap. High guest OS memory usage with no ballooning or virtual machine swap indicates the need to add more memory to the virtual machine. High balloon usage or high virtual machine swap usage indicates a physical contention issue.

Index

Note to the reader: Throughout this index **boldfaced** page numbers indicate primary discussions of a topic. *Italicized* page numbers indicate illustrations.

Symbols and Numbers

(hash sign), for shell prompt, 637
%ACTV counter, 542
%ACTVF counter, 542
%ACTVN counter, 542
%ACTVS counter, 542
%WAIT counter, 541–542
/ (slash), for Linux root, 23
000#.vmdk file, 273

A

access port, 140, 160
acknowledged alarm, 529
active/active storage array,
227–228
Active Directory, **571–572**
domain, 59
domain controllers
and hot migrations, 373
as LDAP server, 591
integration, **559–561**
settings, 99
user accounts, 77
Active Directory Users And
Groups snap-in, 393
user account for management
cluster, 466
active/passive storage array,
227–228
adaptive scheme, planning best
practices, 313
Add Adapter Wizard, Adapter
Selection, 167
Add Hardware Wizard
Advanced Options page, 463
Create a Disk page, 279
Device Type page, 341
Network Type page, 341
Add Host To Distributed Virtual
Switch Wizard
Ready to Complete, 186
Select host and physical
adapters, 185
Add Network Wizard, 149–150, 158
Connection Type, 150
Service Console - Network
Access, 151

Add New Role dialog, 388
Add Nodes Wizard, Analyzing
Configuration, 469
Add Storage dialog, 252
Disk/LUN - Formatting, 253
Ready to Complete, 253
Add To Analysis dialog box,
368–369, 369
Add Virtual Adapter Wizard, 195
Address Resolution Protocol (ARP),
456
Administration menu
Roles command, 100
Sessions menu, 100
vCenter Server Settings
command, 95
administrator password, 35
Administrator role
in ESX/ESXi host, 387
in vCenter Server, 398
Administrators group, 571
Advanced Options (HA) dialog
box, **489–490**
Advanced Settings dialog, 269
aggregate capacity, 7, 8
aggregates, 223
Alarm Settings dialog box, Triggers
tab, 524
alarms, **520–529**
built-in, 527
creating, **522–528**
editing or deleting, 528
email for sending, 99
managing, **528–529**
multiple trigger conditions,
527, 527
resetting status to green, 529,
529
scopes, **521–522**
Alarms privilege, 399
Alarms tab
for dvPort group, 191
in vSphere Client window, 87
in Web Console, 406
alerts, 299, 300
aligning
virtual disks, 276–277

virtual machine file systems,
346–347
volumes in VMFS, 256
allocation size, of file systems, 252
AllowGroups attribute, for SSH,
562
AllowUsers attribute for SSH, 562
TCP wrappers and, 564
ALUA (Asymmetrical Logical Unit
Access), 227
PSP for, 306
AMD, eXecute Disable (XD), 437
AMD-V, 437
answer script for unattended
install, location for, 37
anti-affinity rule, creating DRS,
445–446
Apache Tomcat web service,
76, 406
application-level security, 555
arbitrated loop (FC-AL) mode, for
Fibre Channel protocol, 229–230,
230
ARP (Address Resolution Protocol),
456
array integration, vStorage APIs
for, 308–309
array software, 221
Assign Permissions dialog box, 389
Asymmetrical Logical Unit Access
(ALUA), 227
PSP for, 306
asynchronous mode (SRDF/A),
516
attributes, custom, **94–95**
as search criteria, 95, 96
auditing, Service Console files,
567–569
authentication, **556–561**. *See also*
Windows authentication
for connection to vCenter
Server, 6
of users, centralizing, **59–60**
automated data movement, by
array software, 221
Automatic Availability Manager
(AAM), 473–474, 486

automation. *See also* vCenter
  Orchestrator
    with PowerShell and
      PowerCLI, **597–605**
    reasons to use, **587–588**
availability
  planning best practices, 313
  storage infrastructure design
    and, 216
  of vCenter Server, planning,
    64–65
  of virtual machine, 218
average bandwidth, 177

B

back-end database, 62
  for vCenter Orchestrator, 589
    setup, **592–593**
  for vCenter Server, 4
    configuring, **67–73**
    retention policy, 99
backup strategy, 10
balloon driver, 413, 414, 418
bandwidth, 217
  for large I/O sizes, 265
  for shared storage, 222
  for virtual machines, 146
  for virtual network adapter,
    177
bare-metal hypervisors, 2
baseline groups, 115–117, *116*
baselines
  for remediation, attaching and
    detaching, **121–123**
  for VUM, 114
beacon probing failover detection
  setting, 172–174, *173*, *174*
best practices
  published, 218
  for security, 583
  vendor, storage timeouts and,
    269
  VMware vSphere, **645–652**
    disaster recovery and
      business continuity, **651**
    ESX/ESXi installation,
      645–646
    monitoring and
      troubleshooting, **652**
    storage management, **649**
    vCenter Server, **646–647**
    virtual machines, **650**
    virtual network, **648–649**
bidirectional CHAP, 235
binding
  iSCSI initiator to multiple
    interfaces, **293–297**
  physical network adapter, to
    vSwitch, 159

blade form factor
  and limits on network interface
    cards, 21
  physical memory constraints,
    546
block-centric storage arrays, queues
  for, 257
block storage devices, 266
Blocked policy option, *193*, 193
blue screen of death (BSOD), 25
boot CD for VMware Converter,
  downloading, 378
Boot Options command, 39
/boot partition, 24
booting, from CD/DVD drive, 333
Broadcom BNX2 Gigabit Ethernet
  network ports, 147
Broadcom TG3 Gigabit Ethernet
  network ports, 147
"building bet-the-business
  Ethernet", 243–244
burst size, 177
business continuity
  back-end database and, 68
  best practices, **651**
  planning for, 64
BusLogic parallel SCSI controller,
  325
BusyBox, 556

C

C#, 588
cache memory, for array software,
  222
calculator, online TCO, 14
capacity
  in design process, 309
  planning best practices, 312
case sensitivity, of port group
  names, 436–437
Cat6a cables, for iSCSI network, 243
cd command, 637
CD/DVD
  ISO image as, *333*
  mounting drive in Linux, 338
Celerra Create Filesystem Wizard,
  262
centralized restore, 508, *508*
Challenge Authentication Protocol
  (CHAP), 235–236
CHAP (Challenge Authentication
  Protocol), 235–236
Chart Options link, 532, 533
CIFS (Common Internet File
  System), 509
Cisco, on Private VLANs, 199
Cisco Nexus 1000V distributed
  virtual switch, 199, **200–206**
  configuring, **204–206**

installing, **201–204**
  ISO image for, *201*
  major components, 200
  support for multiple uplink
    groups, 204
  updating, 103
Cisco switches, virtual switches on,
  176
cisco_nexus_1000v_extension.xml
  file, 202
Citrix, 408
Citrix XenServer, 2
  vs. VMware vSphere, **11**
Client Device option, for mapping
  disk to virtual machine, 331
client-server architecture, 57
Clone To Template feature, 351,
  352–354, *353*
Clone Virtual Machine Disk Format
  wizard, *280*
Clone Virtual Machine to Template
  Wizard
  Disk Format page, *353*
  Name and Location page, *353*
clones
  of roles in vCenter Server, 399
  of server, 66
  virtual disk behavior change
    from, 279–280
  of virtual machines, 358
cluster across boxes, 458
  configurations, **460–469**, *462*
    first cluster node creation,
      462–465
    management cluster
      creation, **466–467**, *468*
    second cluster node
      creation, **465–466**
    second node added to
      management cluster,
      468, 468–469
cluster feasibility analysis, 466
cluster in box, 458
  scenarios, *459*, **459–460**
cluster objects, Virtual Machine tab,
  performance summary, 519–520
Cluster Resources custom chart
  setting, 540
Cluster Services resource type, 538
cluster-wide rescan, **300**
clustered file system, 250
clusters, 7, **441–442**
  attaching baselines, 122
  CPU affinity and, 424
  HA-enabled, for VMware Fault
    Tolerance, 492
  limiting number of hosts in,
    441
  resource distribution within,
    538

and resource pools, *442*, 442
of virtual machines, **455–470**
   for Windows Server,
      458–459
cold migrations, 371, **378–379**
Common Internet File System
   (CIFS), 509
community secondary VLAN, 198
comparing files, diff command for,
   569, *569*
compliance, with baseline, 124
Computer Management, *465*
confidence level for analyzed
   systems, *370*
config.js file, 507–508
Configuration tab, in vSphere
   Client window, 87
Configure Management Network
   menu, 156, *157*
Connect-VIServer command, 599
connection
   between iSCSI target and
      initiator, pinging, 239–240
   between PowerCLI and
      vSphere environment, 599
   to remote server with resxtop,
      543
   to vCenter Converter with
      vCenter Server, *363*
   for vCenter Orchestrator,
      590–591
   between vSphere Client and
      vCenter Server instance, 558
console operating system (COS), 23.
   See also Service Console
Console tab, in Web Console, 407,
   408
consolidated backup, *10*, **10**
Consolidation Wizard, 370
   Review Recommendations, *371*
continuous ping, 435
controllers, 226
converged enhanced Ethernet
   (CEE), 244
conversion tools, **361–367**
   Guided Consolidation service,
      361
      confidence level for
         analyzed systems, *370*
      dedicated user account for,
         366
      domain and, 367
      installing, **364–367**, *366*
      integrating into vSphere
         Client, *367*
      permissions and privileges,
         365–366
      using, **367–371**
   vCenter Converter, 361,
      371–379

cold migrations, **378–379**
hot migrations, **373–378**,
   374, *375*
installing, **361–364**, *362*
Convert To Template feature, 351,
   352
copy run start command, 203
copying kickstart file, 40
COS (console operating system), 23.
   See also Service Console
counters, 547. *See also* Customize
   Performance Chart dialog box
   descriptions, 534
   variations in values, 523–524
cp command, 638
CPU
   allocation, **420–425**
      assigning custom shares
         value, **423–425**
      default allocation, **421**
      setting custom limit,
         422–423
   cores, 63
   esxtop to view interrupts, 542
   graph for virtual machine,
      544–545
   performance monitoring,
      543–546
   point of diminishing returns
      for adding, 20
   requirements for VMotion, 437
CPU affinity
   avoiding settings, 425
   clusters and, 424
CPU Identification Mask dialog
   box, *450*
CPU masking, per-virtual machine,
   448–450
CPU Ready counter, 545
CPU Reservation, in resource pool,
   430
CPU Used (%Used) counter, 541
"crash consistent" behavior, 256
Create A New Certificate Database
   And Server Certificate link, 593
Create a New Data Source Wizard,
   107
Create Distributed Virtual Port
   Group Wizard, 188–189, *189*
   for dvPort group using
      PVLANs, *199*, 199
Create New Data Source To SQL
   Server dialog box, 72–73
Create New Virtual Machine
   Wizard
   Advanced Options page, *327*,
      327, *328*
   Configuration page, *321*
   CPUs page, *324*
   Datastore page, *322*

Guest Operating System, *323*
   launching, *320*
   Memory page, *324*
   Name and Location page, *321*
   Network page, *325*
   Ready to Complete page, *328*
   Select a Disk page, *327*
   Virtual Machine Version page,
      322
Create Resource Pool dialog box,
   426, *427*, *428*
CREATE TABLESPACE statement,
   69
CREATE USER statement, 69, 70
Create vNetwork Distributed
   Switch Wizard, 182
   Add hosts and physical
      adapters, *183*
   General Properties, *183*
   Ready to Complete, *184*
Critical Host Patches baseline, 115
Critical VM Patches baseline, 115
cross-stack EtherChannel, for NFS,
   246
custom attributes, **94–95**
   as search criteria, 95, *96*
custom drivers, installing, 28, *29*
Customize Performance Chart
   dialog box, 533, *533*, 545
   chart settings, 538, 540
   choosing resource type,
      533–534
   CPU performance objects and
      counters, 534, 535
   disk performance objects and
      counters, 535, 537, 550–552
   memory performance objects
      and counters, 534, 535
   network performance objects
      and counters, 535, 538
   setting custom interval, 534
   system performance objects
      and counters, 535, 539

D
Data Center High Precedence rules,
   580
Data Center Low Precedence rules,
   580
data protection, vStorage APIs for,
   308
data transfers, balancing for large,
   170
database retention policy, for
   back-end database, 99
database server
   configuring, for vCenter
      Update Manager, **104–107**
   recovery plan and, 65

for vCenter Server data, 62, *62*
choosing, **63–64**
databases
estimated size change, 98
ownership by account for
vCenter Server connection,
72
for VUM, location, 105, *107*
Datacenter Bridging (DCB), 244
Datacenter Consumer sample role,
399
datacenter Ethernet (DCE), 244
datacenter objects, 83
adding, 84
in vCenter Server hierarchy,
394
Virtual Machine Operations
resource type, 538
Virtual Machine tab,
performance summary,
519–520
Datacenter privilege, 399
datacenters, 80, 81
attaching baselines, 122, 123
Datastore Consumer sample role,
privileges, 403
Datastore ISO file option, for
mapping disk to virtual machine,
331
datastore objects, **299–300**, *300*
Datastore privilege, 399
datastores, **249–251**, **258–270**
creating, **252–258**
moving storage for running
virtual machine between, 7
name for, 265
NFS (Network File System)
adding to ESX server,
263–265
choices for configuring
highly available, *267*
creating, **260–265**
for server cluster, 456–457
DB2, and VUM support, 105
dd command, 50
decentralized restore, 508
Decision Support System Business
Intelligence database,
performance, 217
dedicated user account, for Guided
Consolidation service, 366
deduplicated destination storage,
515
Default Credentials dialog (Guided
Consolidation), *368*
default gateway, assigning to
VMkernel port, 156
Default option, for DRS, 447
default permissions, in vCenter
Server installation, 393

default roles
in ESX/ESXi host, 387
privileges for, 402–403
in vCenter Server, 397
default security profile, for
vSwitches, *207*, 207
"delayed write error", 270
delegating ability to create virtual
machines, 401
deleting
alarms, 528
dvPort groups, 191
local groups, 558
port profiles, 205–206, *206*
snapshots, 349
user accounts, from ESX host,
557–558
delta disk, 348
demilitarized zone (DMZ), 196
DenyGroups attribute, for SSH, 562
DenyUsers attribute, for SSH, 562
Deploy OVF Template Wizard, 575
Network Mapping page, *382,
575*
Source page, *381*
Deploy Template Wizard
Datastore page, *356*
Name and Location page, *355*
deploying
VMware ESX, **23–40**
installing from DVD,
27–37
partitioning Service
Console, **23–27**
unattended install, **37–40**
VMware ESXi Embedded, **43**,
44
VMware ESXi Installable,
40–43
deterministic replay, 490
DHCP server, virtual machine for,
411
dictionary (.vmsd) file, 273
diff command, for comparing files,
569, *569*
directory
home, of user, deleting, 558
for VCB proxy backup, 500
dirty memory, 433
disaster recovery, **495–496**
best practices, **651**
Office in a Box and, 516
planning, 64
remote storage replication for,
221
disks
for array software, 222
performance monitoring,
550–552

seek times, and VMkernel
swap performance, 415
snapshot space requirements,
348
alarm to monitor, 522–525
Disk.SchedNumReqOutstanding
ESX setting, 257, *258*
Display Template Wizard, Guest
Configuration page, *354*
distributed locking mechanism,
250–251
Distributed Virtual Port Group
privilege, 399
Distributed Virtual Switch
privilege, 400
distributed virtual switches. *See also*
Cisco Nexus 1000V distributed
virtual switch
DMZ (demilitarized zone), 196
DNS server, editing settings in host
profile, *93*, 93
domain, for Guided Consolidation
service, 367
Domain Admins group, removing
default permissions, 571–572
domain controllers, accessing, 560
Domain Name Service (DNS), and
host configuration for HA, 476
downloading
ESXi installation files, 40
latest vCenter Server version,
73
settings for patches,
configuring for VUM, *118*,
118
VMware Converter boot CD,
378
downstream VLAN, 196
downtime
after server failure, 471
from remediation, planning
for, 132
drag-and-drop, to reconfigure
virtual machine networking, 187
drivers, within virtual machine, 318
DRS. *See* VMware Distributed
Resource Scheduler (DRS)
dual drive failure, mitigating risk
of, 225
dual-vCPU virtual machines, 421
DVD, installing VMware ESX from,
27–37
dvPort groups, 139
assigning virtual adapter to,
195, 195
changing access VLAN of, 206
changing name, 206
configuring, **188–193**
deleting, 191
editing configuration, *191*, 191

editing security profile, 212
getting information about, 190
modifying NIC team and
    failover policies for, 192
modifying VLAN settings, 192
traffic shaping policy for, 193,
    193
Virtual Machine Properties
    dialog, *190*
dvSwitch. *See* vNetwork
    Distributed Switches (dvSwitch)
dvSwitch Properties dialog,
    Security page, *207*
dvUplinks port group, adding
    physical network adapter,
    195–196
dynamic baselines, 114
    creating, 115, *116*
dynamic discovery, configuring,
    240
Dynamic Host Configuration
    Protocol (DHCP), 30, 41
Dynamic Trunking Protocol (DTP),
    143

E
e1000 adapter, 140
eagerzeroedthick disk format, *275*,
    275–276
    converting thin disk format to,
        280–281
    vs. thin provisioning, 278–279
Edit Annotations dialog, *95*
editions, 12
effective MAC address, for virtual
    machine, 209, *210*
efficiency of storage capacity, 248
eliminating resource excess, 377
email notifications
    configuring vCenter Server for,
        525
    SMTP server for, 119
embedded hypervisor, 43
EMC Celerra, 238
    LUN masking on, 241, *242*
EMC CLARiiON, LUN masking on,
    241, *242*
EMC PowerPath/VE, 307
EMC Rainfinity, 286
end of line, Linux vs. Windows, 38
Enhanced VMotion Compatibility
    (EVC), 5, **450–451**, *451*
enterprise flash disks, 222
enterprise storage arrays, 226
enterprise storage design, **226–228**
ESX/ESXi hosts
    adding to vCenter Server, 84,
        474
    attaching baselines, 122

attaching host profile to, 93
clusters, 441, *472*
configuration maximums for
    networking components, 181
default maximum number of
    datastores, 260, *261*
default permission
    assignments, 387
dvSwitch and, 184
high availability components,
    473, *473*
        Automatic Availability
            Manager (AAM),
            473–474
importance of patching, 129
installation, best practices,
    645–646
management tool. *See* vCenter
    Server
maximum number per vCenter
    Server, 78
Performance tab, *531*, 531
    Storage view, *532*
permissions, **385–393**
remediation, **127–128**
removing from dvSwitch, 186,
    187
Resource Allocation tab, 520
roles, 387
    creating custom, **387–389**,
        388
    granting permissions, **389**
security for, **556–570**
    auditing Service Console
        files, **567–569**
    authentication, **556–561**
    patches, **570**
    Secure Shell access,
        561–563
    Service Console firewall,
        564–567
    TCP wrappers, **563–564**
security-related patches,
    dynamic baseline for, 115,
    116
system running on. *See also*
    virtual machines
upgrading, **133–136**
vSphere Client for logging on,
    60
VUM maintenance settings, 119
Web Access page, installing
    vSphere Client from, 44–45
ESX host firewall, iSCSI and, 237
ESX iSCSI software initiator,
    enabling, 239
ESX kickstart file, vs. Red Hat
    kickstart file, 38
ESX server
    adding NFS datastore, 263–265

root access to NFS export, *261*
    storage options, 219
esxcfg-auth command, 559–560,
    638–639
esxcfg-firewall command, 52,
    564–567, 639
esxcfg-info command, 639
esxcfg-mpath command, 639
esxcfg-nas command, **607**, 639–640
esxcfg-nics command, *47*, 47, 640
esxcfg-route command, 156, 640
esxcfg-swiscsi command, 640
esxcfg-vmknic command, 155, 156,
    640
    shell script using, 606
esxcfg-volume command, 641
esxcfg-vswif command, 152,
    640–641
    output, *152*
esxcfg-vswitch command, 47, *48*,
    48, 142, 148, 151, 152, 155, 156,
    159
    to display dvSwitch, 184
    options, 641
    output, *151*
    for ports or port groups VLAN
        settings, 164
    shell script using, 606
esxcli nmp satp list command, 304
esxcli swiscsi nic add command,
    296
ESXi. *See* VMware ESXi
ESXi Embedded, 18
ESXi Free, 12
ESXi host, security for, **569–570**
ESXi Installable, 18
esxtop tool, *541*, **541–543**
/etc/hosts file, 85, 479–480
/etc/hosts.allow file, 562
/etc/hosts.deny file, 562, 563
/etc/krb5.conf file, 560
/etc/resolv.conf file, 479
/etc/vmware/esx.conf file, 568
Ethernet, 221
    lossless, 244
Ethernet adapter, adding to virtual
    machine, 340, *341*
Ethernet frames, iSCSI
    encapsulation in, *234*
EVC (Enhanced VMotion
    Compatibility), 5, **450–451**, *451*
Events tab, in Web Console, 406
Events view, in vCenter Server, **89**,
    90
Exchange, web resources, 218
expandable CPU reservation, 430
expectations of performance, 544
exporting vCenter Server events to
    text file, *90*
ext3 (Linux), VMFS vs., 250–251

Extension privilege, 400
extents, VMFS file systems
    spanning, 256–257, 284
external connectivity, between
    storage array and hosts, 221

F

failover
    of array, 228
    modifying policies for dvPort
        group, 192
    for NAS device, vs. block
        storage device, 268
    storage choices and handling,
        248
failover clustering, 455
fan-in-ratio, for iSCSI, 235
FastSCP, 510, 510
fault and error domains, zoning
    for, 232
fault tolerance. See also VMware
    Fault Tolerance
    turning on, 491
FC-AL (arbitrated loop) mode, for
    Fibre Channel protocol, 229–230,
    230
FC-P2P (point-to-point) mode, for
    Fibre Channel protocol, 229–230,
    230
FC-SW (switched) mode, for Fibre
    Channel protocol, 229–230
FCoE (Fibre Channel over
    Ethernet), 244–245
fdisk command, 638
feasibility check, stall from error,
    469
Fibre Channel, 221, 228–233, 229
    bandwidth aggregation, 297
    disks for, 222
    vs. iSCSI, 234, 234–235, 247
    most common configuration,
        231
    vs. NFS, 247
    performance envelope, 248
    VCB for, 498
    worldwide name (WWN), 231
    zoning, 232
Fibre Channel multimode duplex
    LC/LC/ fiber-optic cable, 230
Fibre Channel over Ethernet
    (FCoE), 244–245
file-level backups, VCB for,
    505–506, 506, 508
file-level locking, NFS vs. VMFS,
    259
file system, multiroot, 23
fileserver centric storage, queues
    for, 257

firewall. See Service Console
    firewall
Firewall Properties dialog box, 52,
    53
fixed baselines, 114
Fixed PSP module, 304–305
floppy disk images, 388
floppy drives, 342
Flow Control, for iSCSI network,
    243
.flp file extension, 388
Folder privilege, 400
folders
    attaching baselines, 122
    name in VMFS volume, 329
    in vCenter Server hierarchy,
        394–396, 395
forged transmits, 208–212, 210
fragmentation, in VMFS, 255
FreeBSD, VMware tools for, 335
Frequency parameters for alarms,
    525–528
FTP server, for kickstart file, 40
full virtual machine backups
    restoring, 509–511, 511
    VCB for, 498–502, 499
        results, 502
        steps, 501–502

G

Get- commands (PowerCLI), 601
Get-Help command (PowerCLI),
    599
Get-NetworkAdapter command
    (PowerCLI), 600
Get-ResourcePool command
    (PowerCLI), 604
Get-VM command (PowerCLI),
    599, 603
Get-VMHost command
    (PowerCLI), 599, 603
Gigabit Ethernet
    adapters, 147
    bandwidth aggregation, 297
Global privilege, 400
graphical user interface (GUI),
    vSphere Client and, 6
graphics hardware, acceleration for
    console session performance,
    336, 336
graphs, 529–540
    layout
        CPU performance
            information, 534, 535
        custom interval, 534
        disk performance, 535, 537
        memory performance
            information, 534, 536

network performance
            information, 535, 538
        overview, 530, 530–531
        resource type, 533–534
        system performance
            information, 535, 539
    printing, 532
    real-time, for host's memory
        usage, 547
    saving, 540
groupadd command, 558
groupdel command, 558
groups
    granting access control to
        virtual machine, 389
    local management, 557–559
    permissions, interaction,
        404–405
growth, planning for, 412
guaranteed admission control, 482,
    483
guaranteed memory, 416
guest I/O devices, bypassing
    virtualization layer, 301
guest operating systems, 317
    allowing customization of
        Windows Server 2003, 354,
        355
    assigning permission to install,
        404
    and disk timeout, 269
    failure, VMware Fault
        Tolerance and, 494
    to force non-VMware-assigned
        MAC address, 209, 210
    installing, 330–332, 401
    installing VMware tools,
        335–336
    memory seen by, 412, 413
    performance monitoring, 552
    powering off vs. shutting
        down, 342
    remediating, 129–131
    security, 573
    shutdown for VM hardware
        upgrade, 132
    upgrading VMware tools,
        339–340
Guided Consolidation service, 361
    beginning analysis with, 368
    confidence level for analyzed
        systems, 370
    configuring Service and
        Default credentials, 368
    dedicated user account for, 366
    domain and, 367
    installing, 364–367, 366
    integrating into vSphere Client,
        367

permissions and privileges, **365–366**
using, **367–371**

H

hard drive, for ESXi install, 40–41, *41*
hardware
  downtime for upgrades, 14
  sizing for vCenter Server, **61–63**, *62*
Hardware Compatibility List (HCL), 19, *20*, 21
hardware iSCSI initiators, 235
  vs. software initiators, 237, *237*
Hardware Status tab, in vSphere Client window, 88
hash sign (#), for shell prompt, 637
heartbeat of cluster service, 269, 456
  AAM responsibility for, 473
  connecting network adapter for, 464
  loss of, 458
high availability (HA), 455. *See also* VMware High Availability
  in NFS, *266*, 266–270, *267*
  real world scenario, 471–472
  testing for, 475
  and vCenter Server, 473
  VMotion and, 440
high-throughput (IOps) workloads, 265–266
home directory of user, deleting, 558
host baseline group, in orchestrated upgrade, 136
host baselines, 114
Host Device option, for mapping disk to virtual machine, 331
host operating system, for Type 2 hypervisors, 2
Host privilege, 400
Host Profile privilege, 400
host profiles in vCenter Server, 5, **92–94**, *93*
  attaching to ESX/ESXi hosts, 93
hosts. *See* ESX/ESXi hosts
Hosts And Clusters inventory view, 81–82, 122, 395
  based on departmental management style, 83, *83*
  based on geographic management style, *82*, 82
  to create cluster, 441
  navigating, 126
  for scan, 124
Hosts tab, for dvPort group, 190
hot-add of memory, 418

hot migrations, 371, **373–378**, *374*, *375*
  performing, 372
hot spares, 223, 225
hot virtual disk, expansion, **284**, *285*
HTTP over Secure Sockets Layer (HTTPS), 79
hybrid storage designs, 226
Hyper-V (Microsoft), 2
  vs. VMware vSphere, **11**
hyperlinks, in Events view, 89
hypervisors, 2, 18, 301, 544
  embedded, 43
  and memory allocation, 418
  memory pages for, 414
  Type 1 and Type 2, 2

I

I/O error, 270
IBM DB2 v.9.5, 63
IDE disks, in virtual machines, 327
idle page reclamation, 413
IEEE 802.1Q standard, 160
ifconfig command, *152*, 152, 637
IGMP (Internet Group Management Protocol), 144
Import Wizard
  Source Data page, 374, *375*
  Source Login page, *374*
  Source Type page, *374*
importing
  vCenter Server license, **593–594**
  virtual appliances, **380–381**
  virtual machines, into VMware vSphere, 372–373
in-guest iSCSI initiators, 244
inflating, 413
InfinBand-like CX cables, 244
initiator, 229
  for iSCSI, 235, **293–297**
installing
  Cisco Nexus 1000V distributed virtual switch, **201–204**
  custom drivers, 28, *29*
  guest operating systems, **330–332**, 401
  Guided Consolidation service, **364–367**, *366*
  PowerCLI, **597–598**
  vCenter Converter, **361–364**, *362*
  vCenter Orchestrator, **595**
  vCenter Update Manager (VUM), **104–113**
    database server configuration, **104–107**
    download service, 104
    install process, **108–110**

ODBC data source name, **107–108**
  plug-in, **113**, *113*
  proxy settings, *110*, 110
  VMware tools, **335–340**
    on Linux, 338, *339*
  vShield zones, **574–579**
  vSphere Client, **44–45**
integrating Guided Consolidation, into vSphere Client, *367*
Intel I/O Acceleration Technology (Intel I/O AT), 301
Intel NoExecute (NX), 437
Intel Virtualization Technology (VT), 437
intelligent placement, 443
  by DRS, 7
internal-only vSwitch, 145
  virtual machines communicating through, *146*
  and VMotion, 146
International Organization for Standardization (ISO) 9660 file system standard, 332
Internet Group Management Protocol (IGMP), 144
Internet Information Services (IIS), vCenter Server and, 76
Internet Relay Chat (IRC), Data Center High Precedence rule to block, 580–581
Internet time server, 51
intrusion detection system, and Promiscuous mode, 208, *208*
inventory
  logical vs. physical, 321
  of vCenter Server
    adding and creating objects, **83–86**
    views and objects, **81–83**
inventory objects, limiting map scope to, *92*
IP address
  for cluster management, 467
  for Service Console port, 150
  for time server, 53
  for VMkernel port, 155
  for vShield Manager, 575
IP-based storage, using failback with, 174
IP hash load balancing, **170–176**, *171*
IPsec (IP Security), 236
IPv4, for VM networks, 244
IPv6, for VM networks, 244
iSCSI, **233–244**, *234*
  elements, *236*
  encapsulation in TCP/IP and Ethernet frames, *234*
  vs. Fibre Channel or NFS, 247

LUN configuration, **237–242**
maximum number of links, 296
multipathing and availability, **243–244**
qualified name, *240*
VCB support for, 498
iSCSI initiator, binding to multiple interfaces, **293–297**
iSCSI initiator properties page, Dynamic Discovery tab, 240
iSCSI Naming Service, 236
iSCSI software initiator, enabling, 239
iSCSI-VMkernel Properties dialog, NIC Teaming tab, *294*
ISO files, 388
  for installing guest operating system, 332
ISO image, 332
  as CD/DVD, *333*
  for VMware tools, 335
isolated secondary VLAN, 198
isolation response address, 486
  configuring, **488–490**
IT staff, experience with ESX and ESXi, 19

J

Java, 588
JavaScript, 588
JPEG graphic, exporting chart as, 532
jumbo frames
  and creating VMkernel interfaces, **606–607**
  for iSCSI network, 243

K

kdc.conf file, 559
Kerberos, 559
  configuration file, 560
  time synchronization and, 337–338
keyboard layouts, *28*, 28
kickstart file, 37–38
  copying, 40
  customization with, 40
  example, 38–39
  location for, 39–40

L

LACP (Link Aggregation Control Protocol), 170
LAN mode, and consolidated backup, 498
Layer 2 bridging software, 144
LDAP connection, for vCenter Orchestrator, **591–592**

LeftHand Networks, 26
license key, for vCenter Server, 75
licensing
  assigning to ESX/ESXi host, *85*
  for backups, 497
  configuring in vCenter Server, 96, 97
  importing to vCenter Orchestrator, **593–594**
  from Microsoft for virtual machines, **334–335**
  VMware vSphere, **12–13**
Link Aggregation Control Protocol (LACP), 170
link state tracking, 172
linked mode group, installing vCenter Server in, **77–79**, *79*
Linux
  disk partitions, 23, *24*
  installing VMware tools, 338, *339*
  shell scripting, 587
  single-root file system for, 23
  vCenter Server for, 4
  VMware tools for, 335
live migration, 6
load balancing
  across NIC team, 167
  Ethernet stack for, 243
  IP hash, **170–176**, *171*
  with multiple uplinks, *165*
  for NFS, 246
  policy, on vSwitches, **168–169**
  source MAC, **169**, *169*
  storage choices and, 248
  virtual switch policies for Microsoft network, 211
  VMotion and, 432
local disks, 26–27
  on vCenter Server, 62
local domain controllers, accessing, 560
local groups, managing, 558
local host file, 474
local storage, 219
  absence of, 219–220
  making use of, 26
local user accounts
  creating, from Service Console command-line interface, 557
  managing, 392
lock, in multiextent VMFS configurations, 255
log files, partition for, 25
Logging Options page, 99, *100*
logical inventory, vs. physical inventory, 321
logical units (LUNs), 216
  2TB boundary, 254

changing count maximums, 258
configuring, **237–242**
connecting to ESX iSCSI initiator, 241
identifying as Unknown and Unreadable, 503
in iSCSI, 235
masking, 232
name in ESX configuration, 232, *233*
properties dialog box, 305–306
for spanned VMFS configurations, 255
login, to web console, 406
logout command, 637
lossless Ethernet, 244
ls command, 637
LSI Logic parallel SCSI controller, 325
LUN ID, 282
LUN queues, **257–258**

M

MAC address
  changes for virtual adapters, **208–212**, *210*
  for virtual machine
    initial, *209*
    manually setting, 209
maintenance mode, for remediation, 128
Maintenance Mode on host, 444
man-in-the-middle security attacks, 236
Manage Physical Adapters dialog, *196*
Manage Plug-Ins dialog box, *364*
Manage Virtual Adapters dialog, *194*, 194–195
managed objects, 299
Management Agent resource type, 538
management networking, configuring of ESXi, **156–157**
Maps tab, in vSphere Client window, 88
Maps view, 298–299, *299*
masking, 232
  on iSCSI target, 241
  per-virtual machine CPU, **448–450**
memory
  allocation, **412–420**, *413*
    addressing overhead, **419–420**
    controlling, **414**
    overcommitment, **417**
    reclaiming pages, 413

setting custom limit, **417–418**

setting custom reservation, **415–417**

setting custom shares value, **419**

for cold migration, 378

configuring virtual machine with, 323–324

hot-add of, 418

including in snapshot, 347

performance monitoring, **546–548**

with esxtop, 542

point of diminishing returns for adding, 20

for Service Console, adjusting, **49–51**, *50*

speed of, **415**

memory bitmap, 433

Memory Swap Used (Average) counter, 547

message of the day (MOTD), 100

metadata

adding to objects, *95*

updates, 251

metas, 223

Microsoft, licensing for virtual machines, **334–335**

Microsoft ADAM, 78

Microsoft Cluster Services (MSCS), 271, **455–458**

Microsoft clustering guide, 276

Microsoft Exchange Server 2007, and clusters, 469

Microsoft Hyper-V, 2

vs. VMware vSphere, **11**

Microsoft Network Load Balancing, 176

virtual switch policies for, 211

Microsoft PowerShell, 588

Microsoft SQL Server

and clusters, 469

for vCenter Orchestrator back-end database, 589

for vCenter Server data, 63, **70–73**

Microsoft Windows clusters, 271

midrange storage design, **226–228**

Migrate Virtual Machine Networking tool, 196, *197*

Migrate Virtual Machine tool, **438–440**

Select Datastore, *287*

Select Destination, *439*

migration. *See also*

physical-to-virtual (P2V) operations; VMware VMotion

of virtual machine, script for, 603

"mirrored" RAID, 223–224, *224*

mirrored VM, 9

Mixed Mode authentication, vCenter Server 4.0 support for, 71

mkswap command, 51

Monad, 597

monitoring. *See* performance monitoring

MOTD (message of the day), 100

mount command, 638

mount point, 23

mounting

CD/DVD drive, in Linux, 338

NFS datastores, **607**

mountvm command (VCB), 511

for file-level backups, 505, *506*

Move-ResourcePool command (PowerCLI), 602

Move-VM command (PowerCLI), 602

MRU PSP module, 304

MSCS (Microsoft Cluster Services), 271, **455–458**

MSDB database, permissions for VUM, 108

multi-vCPU virtual machines, 421

multipathing

Ethernet stack for, 243

for NFS, 246

vStorage APIs for, **303–307**

Multipathing plug-in (MPP), 307

Multiple Connections Per Session, 236–237

multiroot file system, 23

mv command, 638

MySQL, 589

N

naa (Network Address Authority) ID, 305

name resolution

high availability and, 474

testing, 84–85

nano editor, 53

NAS. *See* network attached storage (NAS)

NAS/NFS access, VMkernel ports for, 153

Native Multipathing plug-in (NMP) module, 303

native VLAN, 162

navigation bar, in vSphere Client, **81**

NetApp FAS arrays, 238

LUN masking on, 242

NetWare, VMware tools for, 335

Network Address Authority (naa) ID, 305

network attached storage (NAS), 216

best practices, **309–314**

configuring file system on, 216

Network Consumer sample role, 399

privileges, 403

Network File System. *See* NFS (Network File System)

network interface card team, 140

network interface cards (NICs)

blade form factor and limits on, 21

breakdown of traffic by, 549

changing association, 48

changing for Service Console, **45–49**

for Cisco Nexus 1000V, 201

deciding number to use, 22

PCI addresses of, 47

selecting wrong during installation, 36–37

for system tasks, selecting during install, 30

for VMware VMotion, 22, 438

network load balancing (NLB) clusters, 455

architecture, *456*

network portals, in iSCSI, 235, 236

Network privilege, 400

network security policies, **573–574**

Network Time Protocol (NTP), 34

configuring on ESX, 337

manually enabling client traffic through firewall, 52

Networking view, 82, 187

networks

actions to minimize delays, 176

basic hygiene, 263

configuring VUM for connectivity, 117

integrating infrastructure, **21–22**

performance monitoring, **548–550**

alarms for, 526

with esxtop, 542

reconfiguring virtual machine, with drag-and-drop, 187

storage for kickstart file, 39–40

Test Management Network option to verify connection, 49

New Baseline Group Wizard, *117*

New Baseline Wizard, *116*

New-Cluster command (PowerCLI), 602

New Cluster Wizard, 441

New-HardDisk command (PowerCLI), 602

New-NetworkAdapter command (PowerCLI), 602

New-ResourcePool command (PowerCLI), 602

New Server Cluster Wizard
Analyzing Configuration, *466*
Creating the Cluster, *467*

New-Snapshot command (PowerCLI), 602

New-VM command (PowerCLI), 602

NFS (Network File System), **245–247**, *246*
configuring export, 263, *264*
datastores, **258–270**
choices for configuring highly available, 267
creating, **260–265**
ESX server root access to export, *261*
vs. Fibre Channel or iSCSI, 247
high availability (HA) design, *266*, 266–270, *267*
mounting datastores, **607**
server, for kickstart file, 40
supporting large bandwidth (MBps) workloads, 265
supporting large throughput (IOps) workloads, 265–266

NFS.HeartbeatFrequency setting, 269

NIC team, 147, *166*, 179, *180*
configuring, **164–176**
configuring Failover Order policy, *175*, 175
constructing, 166
creating, 166–167
failover and failback of uplinks, 172
modifying policies for dvPort group, 192

NICs. *See* network interface cards (NICs)

NMP (Native Multipathing) plug-in module, 303

No Access role
in ESX/ESXi host, 387
in vCenter Server, 397–398

Non-Critical Host Patches baseline, 115

Non-Critical VM Patches baseline, 115

noncompliance, with baseline, 124

nondeterministic events, 490

Notepad, 38

Notify Switches option, turning off, *176*, 176

NTFS, VMFS vs., 250–251

NTP Daemon (Ntpd) Options dialog, 51, *52*

NTP (Network Time Protocol), 34
configuring on ESX, 337
manually enabling client traffic through firewall, 52

ntp.conf file, configuring for NTP time synchronization, 52–54

.nvram (virtual machine BIOS configuration) file, 272

NX-OS, 204, 206

O

objects
in PowerShell, **599–601**
commands to manipulate, 602
commands to retrieve, 601
in vCenter Server
alarms, 520–521, *521*
naming strategy, 82

ODBC Microsoft SQL Server Setup dialog box, 108

Office in a Box, **515–516**

Online Transaction Processing (OLTP) databases, performance, 217

Open Connection To Cluster dialog box, 466

Open Database Connectivity (ODBC) data source name (DSN), 68, 75
for VUM, **107–108**

Open Virtual Machine Format, 380

Open Virtualization Format (OVF), 380, 575

/opt partition, 26

optical disks, virtual machines' access to, 331

Oracle, **68–70**
JDBC driver, 69
multiple vCenter Server instances with, 78
patches needed for 10G release 2, 68
for vCenter Orchestrator back-end database, 589
for vCenter Server data, 63
web resources, 218

Oracle VM, 2

orchestrated upgrade, **136–137**

original equipment manufacturer (OEM), VMware ESXi installation, 43

out-IP policy, 170

"out-of-space" conditions, thin provisioning and, 281

over-subscription, of storage resources, 270

overcommitment of memory, **417**

overflows, of queue, 257

P

PAgP (Port Aggregation Protocol), 143, 170

pam.d file, 559

paravirtualize driver, 140

paravirtualize vSCSI, **290–291**

parity RAID, 224, 224–226

partitioning Service Console, **23–27**
custom, host upgrade baselines and, 136

partitions
aligning, 276
custom VMware ESX scheme, 26
customizing, 30

passwd command, 557, 637

passwords
enforcing policies, 559
for Service Console, 557
for vCenter Orchestrator authentication, 592

patch baselines, 114

patch metadata, database server to store, 104

patch repository, **120–121**, *121*

patches, 103
download settings, configuring for VUM, 118, *118*
for ESX/ESXi hosts, **570**
location for storing, 110, *111*
staging, **126–127**, *127*

Path Selection plug-in (PSP), 304–305

peak bandwidth, hard-coded limits for, 177

per-virtual machine CPU masking, **448–450**

per-virtual machine swap files, 415

performance
decline with growth, 423
determining requirements, 217–218
DRS cluster, 444–445
NFS vs. VMFS, 259
planning best practices, 311–312
snapshots and, 348
and storage choices, 248
storage infrastructure design and, 215
thin provisioning and, 282

performance-centered planning dynamic, 310–311

Performance Chart Legend, 532

performance monitoring
alarms, **520–529**

creating, **522–528**
managing, **528–529**
scopes, **521–522**
best practices, **652**
capturing data, 542–543
command-line tools, **541–543**
esxtop tool, *541*, **541–543**
resxtop tool, **543**
CPU usage, **543–546**
disk usage, **550–552**
graph layout
CPU performance
information, 534, 535
custom interval, 534
disk performance, 535, 537
memory performance
information, 534, 536
network performance
information, 535, 538
overview, *530*, **530–531**
resource type, 533–534
system performance
information, 535, 539
graphs, **529–540**
from inside and outside, 552
memory usage, **546–548**
network usage, **548–550**
overview, **519–520**
saving graphs, **540**
Performance privilege, 400
Performance tab, in vSphere Client
window, 87
Perl, 587
permissions
on back-end database server,
68
for changing virtual media, 388
combining with privileges and
roles, in vCenter Server,
401–405
default assignments for
ESX/ESXi hosts, 387
in Guided Consolidation
service, **365–366**
identifying usage, **391–392**
interaction in vCenter Server,
404–405
removing, **391**
resource pools to assign, **390**,
391
for roles, in ESX/ESXi host, **389**
for SQL login to Microsoft SQL
Server, 71
SQL Server 2005, 71
in vCenter Server, **393–405**
for VUM, on MSDB database,
108
Permissions privilege, 400
Permissions tab
for dvPort group, 191

in vSphere Client window, 88
PermitRootLogin attribute, for SSH,
561
Physical compatibility mode
(pRDM), for raw device
mapping, 270, 460–461
physical computers, analyzing,
370
physical ESX/ESXi hosts, migration
between. *See* VMware VMotion
physical host failure, VMware Fault
Tolerance and, 9
physical infrastructure, redundancy
in, *488*
physical inventory, vs. logical
inventory, 321
physical network adapter
assigning to vSwitch, 153
binding to vSwitch, 159
connecting multiple to single
vSwitch, 164–165, *165*
connecting to port in
dvUplinks port group, 195
information on those connected
to dvUplinks port, *196*
vSwitch configured to use, 146,
147
physical switch ports, as trunk
ports, *163*
physical switches
to support IP-based hash
load-balancing policy, *171*
vs. virtual switches, **143–144**
physical to virtual clustering, 458,
469–470, *470*
physical-to-virtual (P2V)
operations, **361–367**
eliminating resource excess,
377
importing virtual appliances,
380–381
with vCenter Converter,
371–379
pinging
after missing heartbeat, 486
continuous, 435
iSCSI target from initiator,
239–240
to test vShield Manager
connection, 576
between VMkernel IP address
and NFS server, 263
piping commands, 599
planning
for downtime from
remediation, 132
for growth, 412
performance-centered
dynamic, 310–311

vCenter Server deployment,
61–66
availability, **64–65**
VMware vSphere, **17–22**
Plug-in Manager dialog box, *202*,
363
plug-ins, in vCenter Orchestrator,
594
Pluggable Storage Architecture
(PSA), 296, 303
point-to-point (FC-P2P) mode, for
Fibre Channel protocol, 229–230,
230
pool, 281
Port Aggregation Protocol (PAgP),
143, 170
port-based zoning, 232
port flapping, 174
port groups, 139, **144**
dvPort, configuring, **188–193**
editing security profile, 211
names for, 436
port-profile vm-access-ipstorage
command, 206
port profiles
configuring, 206
deleting, 205–206, *206*
for Nexus 1000V, 204–205
PortFast mode, for Cisco devices,
176
ports, 139, **144**
for dvSwitches, 185
opening with esxcfg-firewall
command, 566–567
vSwitches configuration with,
143
Ports tab, for dvPort group, *190*,
190
post-backup.bat file, 507
PostgreSQL, 589
power-capping, 494
PowerCLI
commands, 601
installing, **597–598**
objects in, **599–601**
running scripts, **601–605**
for migrating virtual
machines, 603
moving virtual machines
between resource pools,
604–605
for snapshot manipulation,
603
virtual machine
networking
configuration, 603–604
startup screen, *599*
powering off guest system, vs.
shutting down, 342
PowerPC, 221

PowerShell (Microsoft), 588, **597–605**
  installing PowerCLI, **597–598**
  resources, 600–601
  working with objects, **599–601**
PowerShell Execution policy, 598
pre-backup.bat file, 507
Preboot Execution Environment (PXE) boot server, 37
predictive scheme, planning best practices, 313
primary VLAN, 196
printing graphs, 532
priority setting, for virtual machine, 419
Private VLANs, 189
  setting up, **196–200**, *197*
privileged EXEC mode, 205
privileges
  combining with roles and permissions, in vCenter Server, **401–405**
  for default roles, 402–403
  in Guided Consolidation service, **365–366**
  in vCenter Server, **399–401**
progress meter, for ESX installation, *36*
Promiscuous mode, **207–208**, 573–574
promiscuous port, 199
Propagate To Child Objects option, for roles, 389
Protected port group, for vShield appliance, 577
protocols for shared storage, **228–247**
  Fibre Channel, **228–233**, *229*
  Fibre Channel over Ethernet, **244–245**
  iSCSI, **233–244**, *234*
    elements, *236*
    LUN configuration, **237–242**
    multipathing and availability, **243–244**
  NFS (Network File System) protocol, **245–247**, *246*
  support for Storage VMotion, 287
proxy settings, configuring, during VUM install, *110*, 110
PSA (Pluggable Storage Architecture), 296, 303
purple screen of death (PSOD), 26

Q
quad-core CPUs, for servers, 63

Qualified Name (IQN), in iSCSI, 235
queues, 257

R
RAID technologies, **223–226**
  downside to RAID 5, 225
  for installing ESX, 27
  RAID 6 (RAID-IP), 225–226, *226*
RAM. *See* memory
Range parameters for alarms, 525–528
RARP (Reverse Address Resolution Protocol), 176, 433
raw device mapping (RDM), **270–272**, 460
RDM. *See* raw device mapping (RDM)
read cache, 222
Read-Only role
  in ESX/ESXi host, 387
  in vCenter Server, 398
Ready Time (%RDY) counter, 541
reboot command, 637
rebuild periods, minimizing, 225
recovery point objectives (RPOs), 221
Red Hat kickstart file, vs. ESX kickstart file, 38
red triangles, in vCenter Orchestrator Configuration interface, 590
redundancy
  eliminating during snapshot streaming, 515
  from multiple uplinks, *165*
  for paths to VCB server, 502–503, *503*
  in physical infrastructure, *488*
reference architecture, web resources, 218
relaxed coscheduling algorithm, 421
reliability statistics, for hard disks, 223
Remediate dialog box, 127, *128*
Remediate Wizard, *135*, 135
remediation, **121–133**
  attaching and detaching baselines, **121–123**
  performing scan, **124–126**, *125*
  planning for downtime, 132
  remediating guest operating systems, **129–131**
  remediating hosts, **127–128**
  rollback, 130, *131*
  staging patches, **126–127**, *127*

remote computer, accessing server from, *36*
remote console URLs, 409
Remote Desktop, 408
remote domain controllers, accessing, 560
remote management tools, 408
Remote Registry service, 365–366
remote server, connection with resxtop, 543
Remove All Snapshots workflow, 596
Remove-Snapshot command (PowerCLI), 602
removing permissions, **391**
replicating storage area network (SAN), **516–517**
Reports view, 298–299
Rescan Datacenter HBAs workflow, 596
reservation of memory, editing, 414
resource allocation
  automatic distribution of, 7
  CPU capacity, **420–425**
    assigning custom shares value, **423–425**
    default allocation, **421**
    setting custom limit, **422–423**
  memory, **412–420**, *413*
    addressing overhead, **419–420**
    controlling, **414**
    overcommitment, **417**
    setting custom limit, **417–418**
    setting custom reservation, **415–417**
    setting custom shares value, **419**
  resource pools, **425–431**
    configuring, **426–429**
  for virtual machine, **411–412**
resource consumption alarm, creating, **522–525**
Resource Pool Administrator sample role, 398
  privileges, 402
resource pools, **425–431**, *429*
  to assign permissions, **390**, *391*
  and clusters, 442, *442*
  configuring, **426–429**
  creating, *426*, 426
  moving virtual machines between, script for, 604–605
  Resource Allocation tab, 520
  in vCenter Server hierarchy, **396**
Resource privilege, 400
resources, eliminating excess, 377

Restart Management Network
    option, *158*
restart priority, for VMware High
    Availability, **484–486**, *485*
Restart-VMGuest command
    (PowerCLI), 602
restoring with VMware
    Consolidated Backup (VCB), *508*,
    508–513
resxtop tool, 541, **543**
Reverse Address Resolution
    Protocol (RARP), 176, 433
reverting to snapshot, 349, 351
rm command, 558, 638
rmdir command, 638
roles
    combining with privileges and
        permissions, in vCenter
        Server, **401–405**
    editing and removing, **392**
    in ESX/ESXi host, 387
        creating custom, **387–389**,
        388
        granting permissions, **389**
    in vCenter Server, **397–399**, *398*
Roles command, 100
rollback
    after failure, *134*, 134
    of remediation operations, 130,
    131
root account, and SSH, 561
root (/) partition, 24–25
root password, 34–35, *35*, 84
    for ESX/ESXi host, 386
root permissions, 151
root squash command, 260
root username, for ESX/ESXi host,
    386
Round-robin PSP module, 305
running physical computer,
    migration. *See* hot migrations
Runtime Settings, 99

S

SAN. *See* storage area network
    (SAN)
SAP, web resources, 218
SATA, disks for, 222
SATP (Storage Array Type
    plug-in), 296
saving graphs, **540**
scale, 228
scan, performing, **124–126**, *125*
schedule
    for patch downloads, 118
    for remediating virtual
        machines, *130*
Scheduled Task privilege, 400

Scheduled Tasks, in vCenter
    Server, **88–89**
ScratchConfig.ConfiguredScratch
    Location property, 219–220, *220*
scripting. *See* PowerShell
    (Microsoft)
SCSI adapters
    disk I/O statistics for, 542
    paravirtualize, *291*
    virtual, *277*, **277**
    for virtual machine, 325
SCSI devices, 319
    disks in virtual machines, 327
    VMkernel ports for, 153
search criteria, custom attributes as,
    95, *96*
secondary VLAN, 196, 198
Secure Shell (SSH)
    controlling access, **561–563**
    restarting daemon, 562
Secure Sockets Layer (SSL)
    certificate, "untrusted" source of,
    79
security
    best practices, 85
    for ESX/ESXi hosts, **556–570**
        auditing Service Console
        files, **567–569**
        authentication, **556–561**
        model for, 385, *386*
        patches, **570**
        secure shell access,
        561–563
        Service Console firewall,
        564–567
        TCP wrappers, **563–564**
    ESXi and, 18, **569–570**
    overview, **555–556**
    and root login, 151
    for vCenter Server, **570–573**
        Active Directory and,
        571–572
        model, 385, *386*
        vpxuser account, **572–573**
    for virtual machines, **573–574**
    virtualization impact on,
    582–583
    VMsafe, **583–584**
    with vShield zones, **574–582**
        installing, **574–579**
        for virtual machine
            protection, **580–582**
        vShield appliances
            deployment, **576–579**
        vShield Manager
            configuration, **575–576**
        vShield Manager
            deployment, **575**
    for vSwitches, **207–212**

Security Accounts Manager (SAM)
    database, 59, 393
Security Warning dialog box, 79
Select command (PowerCLI), 600,
    600
Select Users And Groups dialog
    box, 389
self-service restore, 508, *508*
    speed of, 509
send targets, adding iSCSI target to,
    241
sender accounts, for notification,
    525
SendTargets command, 236
serial number, for installation, 29
server clusters, 456, *457*, 457
Server Message Block (SMB), 509
server platform, **19–21**
servers, size vs. number of, 8
service account, 366
Service Console, 2
    auditing files, **567–569**
    changing management NIC,
    45–49
    commands
        esxcfg- commands,
        638–641
        for managing directories,
            files and disks, **638**
        for navigating, managing
            and monitoring, **637**
    Configuration tab, Security
        Profile area, 565
    creating port, 149–150, *151*
    custom partitions, host
        upgrade baselines and, 136
    interface configuration, 30
    launching, 112
    memory for, 25, **49–51**, *50*
    networking configuration,
    147–153
    NICs for, 22
    partitioning, **23–27**
        default layout, 32, *33*
    processor 0 for, 545
    reviewing configuration, 47, *48*
    running shell scripts, **605–608**
    storage for, 134
    user accounts, 559
    virtual switch, *46*
    for VMware ESX, 18
Service Console firewall, **564–567**
    and NTP traffic, 52
Service Console port (vswif), 140
    interface, 148
    limits for ESX support, 153
service mgmt-vmware restart
    command, 52, 153
service sshd restart command, 562
"Service Time", of queues, 257

services.xml file, 565
Sessions privilege, *400*, 400
Set Authentication dialog box
    (Guided Consolidation), *370*
Set- commands (PowerCLI), 602
set devmgr_show_nonpresent_
    devices command, 377
Set-ExecutionPolicy RemoteSigned
    command (PowerShell), 598
Set-NetworkAdapter cmdlet, 604
setupcl.exe file, *355*
SHA1 fingerprint, 85
Shadow Copies of Shared Folders,
    513
share system in VMware, 419
    allocations, 430
    editing memory share, 414
shared storage, **216–249**, *217*
    common storage array
        architectures, **220–222**
    midrange and enterprise
        storage design, **226–228**
    protocol choices, **228–247**
    RAID technologies, **223–226**
shares for CPU, 423
shell prompt, hash sign (#) for, 637
shell scripting
    in UNIX/Linux, 587
    using with VMware ESX,
        605–608
    variables in, 608
Shutdown and Destroy VM
    workflow, 596
Shutdown-VMGuest command
    (PowerCLI), 602
shutting down guest system, vs.
    powering off, 342
simple recovery model,
    implications, **75–76**
single host capacity, 7
single-initiator zoning, 232, 233
single point of failure, eliminating,
    170
single-root file system, for Linux,
    23
Single Root I/O Virtualization
    (SR-IOV), 302, *302*
Site Recovery Manager, vStorage
    APIs for, **308**
sizing initial array design, 309
slash (/), for Linux root, 23
"smart reboot", 130
    for vApps, 119–120
SMTP server, for email
    notifications, 119
Snapshot Manager, 349, *350*
snapshots, 14, 66, 221
    and behavior, 348–350
    default settings to enable, 119
    deleting, 349

disk space for, 348
    alarm to monitor, 522–525
eliminating redundancy during
    streaming, 515
reverting to, 349, 351
script for manipulating, 603
space for, 273
VCB use for full backup, *500*,
    500
of virtual machine, 130
    creating, *347*, 347
and VMFS locking, 501
in VShield Manager, 582
SNMP, configuring in vCenter
    Server, 99, 525
software iSCSI initiator
    in ESX 3.x, *292*
    in ESX 4, *292*
    improvements, **291–293**
software patches, 103. *See also*
    patches
Solaris, VMware tools for, 335
source MAC load balancing, *169*,
    169
source machine name resolution,
    for P2V process, 373
Spanning Tree Protocol (STP), 143
    for iSCSI network, 243
"sparse file", 274
sp_changedbowner stored
    procedure, 71
spindle density, 248
spindles, 222
split-brained HA cluster, 486
SQL login, server prompts for, 75
SQL Native Client option, 72
SQL Server
    and cold migrations, 378
    web resources, 218
SQL Server 2005 Express Edition
    limitations, 63–64
    for VUM, 105
SQL Server Agent service, 75
SR-IOV, **301–302**
SRDF (Symmetric Remote Data
    Facility), 516
sshd_config file, 561
    backup of, 562
SSL certificate, for vCenter
    Orchestrator, 593
SSL settings, 100
Stacked Graph chart type, 548–549
stacked views, 550
staging patches, **126–127**, *127*
standby vCenter Server system, 65
static/dynamic discovery in iSCSI,
    236
statistics, in vCenter Server, 97–98,
    98

status indicators, in vCenter
    Orchestrator Configuration
    interface, 590
step-tickers file, configuring for
    NTP time synchronization,
    52–54
Storage Adapter screen, rescanning
    for devices, 242
storage area network (SAN), 216,
    228–229
    best practices, **309–314**
    and disaster recovery, 496
    LUN initialization, and lost
        data, 27
    replicating, **516–517**
Storage Array Type plug-in
    (SATP), 296, 304
storage devices
    for ESX installation, 32
    over-subscription of, 270
storage infrastructure, 21, 215
    basic choices, **247–249**
    best practices, 649
    design, importance, **215–216**
    new features in vSphere 4,
        277–308
    virtual machine-level
        configuration, **272–277**
    for VMware ESX, **249–277**
        core concepts, **249**, *250*
        datastore creation,
            252–258
        datastores, **249–251**
        NFS datastores, **258–270**
        raw device mapping,
            270–272
    vSphere, **277–308**
        binding iSCSI initiator to
            multiple interfaces,
            293–297
        hot virtual disk expansion,
            284, *285*
        management features,
            298–300
        paravirtualize vSCSI,
            290–291
        software iSCSI initiator
            improvements, **291–293**
        Storage vMotion changes,
            284–290
        thin provisioning, **278–282**
        VMDirectPath I/O and
            SR-IOV, **301–302**
        VMFS expansion, **282**, *283*
        VMFS resignature changes,
            282–284
        vStorage APIs for
            multipathing, **303–307**
        vStorage APIs for Site
            Recovery Manager, **308**

storage objects
    best practices, 256
    for virtual machine, *272*,
       272–273
storage processors, 221
storage timeouts, and vendor best
    practices, *269*
Storage Views privilege, *400*
Storage Views tab, in vSphere
    Client window, 88
storage virtualization, defining, 286
Storage VMotion, **6–7**, 551
    changes, **284–290**
    GUI interface, 286, *287*
    internal operations in vSphere
       4, *289*
    internals with VMware
       Infrastructure 3.5, *288*
    limits on simultaneous, 289
    moving parts of virtual
       machine, *288*, 288
    performance impact, 290
streaming SIMD Extensions 2
    (SSE2), 437
strict admission control, 482, *482*
striped disks (RAID 0), 223, *224*
su command, 151, 156
Summary tab
    for dvPort group, 190
    in vSphere Client window, 87
Support and Subscription (SnS), 12
Suspend-VMGuest command
    (PowerCLI), 602
swap file, creating, 50–51
swap partition, 25, 50
    modifying size, 32
    and performance, 415
swapon command, 51
SWCUR (current swap usage)
    counters, 542
switched (FC-SW) mode, for Fibre
    Channel protocol, 229–230
switchport access vlan statement,
    205, 206
switchport trunk allowed vlan
    command, 164, 165, 204
switchport trunk native vlan 999
    command, 162
Symantec Backup Exec 11d, 507
Symmetric Remote Data Facility
    (SRDF), 516
synchronous mode (SRDF/S), 516
sysprep, 354, *355*
System Center Data Protection
    Manager (SCDPM), 513
System Customization menu
    (ESXi), 156, *157*
    Configure Management
       Network, 48

system halt, partition for writing
    information about, 25–26
system tray, VMware logo icon,
    336, *337*
system uplink port profile,
    configuring, 203–204

T

tagging, 160
Take Virtual Machine Snapshot
    dialog, *347*
tape backups, and disaster
    recovery, 496
target in iSCSI, 235
    configuring, *238*, 238
.tar.gz extension, 338
Tasks & Events tab
    for dvPort group, 191
    in vSphere Client window, 87
Tasks privilege, *400*
Tasks tab, in Web Console, 407
TCP/IP frame, iSCSI encapsulation
    in, *234*
TCP/IP stack, network access for
    VMkernel, 153
TCP ports, for vCenter Server, 76
TCP sessions per database, for
    VMware NFS client, *260*, 260
TCP wrappers, **563–564**
template objects, access to, 354
templates, **351–357**, *352*
    deploying virtual machine
       from, 355–357
    virtual disk behavior change
       from, 279–280
Terminal Services, 408
text file, exporting vCenter Server
    events to, *90*
thick virtual disk format, *275*, 275
thin provisioning, 248, 274,
    278–282, 312
    in array or in VMware, 281–282
thin virtual disk format, 274, *275*
    converting to eagerthick, fault
       tolerance and, 490
thin virtualization clients, size of,
    41
third-party companies, additional
    products from, 61
time synchronization, **51–54**
    in virtual environment,
       337–338
    VMware tools for, 337
time zone, 33, *34*
Timeout Settings, 99
timestamps of files, comparing, 568
TNSNAMES.ORA file, 69, 70
Tomcat (Apache web service), 76,
    406

topology maps, 91
touch command, 638
traffic shaping, **177–178**
    policy for dvPort group, 193,
       193
transaction log, back up, 75–76
transparent page sharing, 413
triangles, red, in vCenter
    Orchestrator Configuration
    interface, 590
Triggered Alarms view, *528*,
    528–529
triggers, for alarms, 523
troubleshooting, best practices for,
    652
trunk ports, 140, 160
    physical switch ports as, *163*
    and VLANs, 162
Twinax, 244

U

UDP ports, for vCenter Server, 76
unattended install, VMware ESX,
    37–40
Universally Unique Identifier
    (UUID), of virtual machine, 208
UNIX, shell scripting, 587
unlinking NICs, 48
Unprotected port group, for
    vShield appliance, 577
"untrusted" source, of Secure
    Sockets Layer (SSL) certificate, 79
Update Manager. *See* vCenter
    Update Manager (VUM)
upgrade baselines, 114
    creating, 133–134
    used to upgrade ESX/ESXi
       host, 135
upgrading ESX/EXSi hosts,
    133–136
upgrading virtual machine
    hardware, **132–133**, *133*
upgrading VMware tools, **131–132**
uplink groups, multiple, 204
uplinks, **144–147**, 164
    failover and failback of, 172
upstream failures, detecting, 172
upstream VLAN, 196
URLs
    remote console, 409
    for virtual machines, *409*
USB-based flash device
    for kickstart file, 39
    running ESXi Embedded from,
       18, 43
user accounts
    for administrators, centralizing
       authentication, **59–60**

authentication, against
Microsoft Active Directory,
559
dedicated, for Guided
Consolidation service, 366
deleting, from ESX host,
557–558
ESX/EXSI host authentication
with, 44
granting access control to
virtual machine, 389
local management, **557–559**
for Service Console, 559
for vCenter Collector, 365
for VUM services, 111–112
user data backups, in Windows,
513
useradd command, 557, 637
userdel command, 558
usermod command, 558
username
for Service Console, 557
for vCenter Orchestrator
authentication, 592
for vCenter Server services, 76
UUID (Universally Unique
Identifier), of virtual machine,
208

V

VA Upgrade to Latest baseline, 115
VA Upgrade to Match Host
baseline, 115
vApp privilege, *400*
vApp Settings, for VUM, 119–120
/var/log partition, 25
variables, in shell scripting, 608
vcbExport command, for single
VMDK backups, 504
vcbMounter command (VCB),
499–500
for file-level backups, 505, *506*
for full virtual machine
backups, 502
vcbSnapshot command, for single
VMDK backups, 504
vcbVmName command (VCB), 499
for file-level backups, 505
for full virtual machine
backups, 502
for single VMDK backups, 504
VCDR (VMware Data Recovery),
496, **514–515**
vCenter cluster-level view, 298–299
Storage Views tab, *298*
vCenter Converter, 361, **371–379**
cold migrations, 378–379
hot migrations, **373–378**, *374,
375*

installing, **361–364**, *362*
vCenter Orchestrator, 10, **588–597**
adding vCenter Server host,
594–595
back-end database setup,
592–593
configuring, 77, **588–595**
displaying icons, 590
importing vCenter Server
license, **593–594**
installing and starting service,
595
LDAP connection, **591–592**
missing icons, 74
network connection, **590–591**
plug-ins configuration, **594**
prerequisites, **589**
server certificate configuration,
593
starting configuration service,
590
using workflows, **595–597**, *596*
vCenter Server, **4–5**
adding ESX/ESXi host, 84
alarms, 519
authentication for connection, 6
basics, **57–61**, *58*
centralizing user
authentication, **59–60**
extensible framework, *60,*
60–61
best practices, **646–647**
combining privileges, roles and
permissions, **401–405**
configuring for email and
SNMP notifications, 525
configuring VSM to connect to,
203
creating VSM-specific plug-in,
202, *202*
deployment planning and
design, **61–66**
availability, **64–65**
database server choices,
63–64
sizing hardware, **61–63**, *62*
disaster recovery plan, *66*
downloading latest version, 73
exploring, **79–81**
exporting events to text file, *90*
hierarchy, **394–397**
datacenter objects, **394**
folders, **394–396**, *395*
putting together, **396–397**
resource pools, **396**
home screen, *80,* **80–81**
installing, **67–77**
back-end database server
configuration, **67–73**

in linked mode group,
77–79, *79*
running installer, **73–77**,
74
installing guest operating
system, **330–332**
and Internet Information
Services, 76
inventory
adding and creating
objects, **83–86**
baselines for, 122
views and objects, **81–83**
management features, **86–94**
basic host management,
86–88
Events view, **89**, *90*
host profiles, **92–94**, *93*
maps, *91,* **91–92**
scheduled tasks, **88–89**
maximum number of hosts or
VMs per, 78
navigation bar, **81**
objects, alarms, 520–521, *521*
Performance tab, 520
permissions, **393–405**
interaction, 404–405
pre-installation tasks, 67
privileges, **399–401**
Recent Tasks pane, *376*
Resources pane, Summary tab,
519
roles, **397–399**, *398*
security for, **570–573**
Active Directory and,
571–572
vpsuer account, **572–573**
settings, **94–101**
Active Directory, 99
advanced, *100*
custom attributes, **94–95**
database, 99
database retention policy,
99
licensing, 96, *97*
logging options, 99, *100*
mail, 99
runtime settings, 99
SNMP, 99
SSL settings, 100
statistics, 97–98, *98*
timeout settings, 99
Web service, 99
standby system, 65
Users & Groups tab, 386
on virtual machine
installing, 65–66
running, **66**, *67*
for vNetwork Distributed
Switches, 184

Web Access page, *407*
workgroups for, vs. domain, 393
vCenter Server Essentials, 5
vCenter Server Foundation, 5
vCenter Server objects, Virtual Machine tab, performance summary, 519–520
vCenter Server Standard, 5
vCenter Update Manager (VUM)
    baselines and groups, **114–117**
    calculating limits, 125–126
    Configuration tab, **117–120**
    configuring, **113–121**
        baselines and groups, **114–117**
    Database Information page, *109*
    Events tab, **120**
    installing, **104–113**
        database server configuration, **104–107**
        download service, 104
        install process, **108–110**
        ODBC data source name (DSN), **107–108**
        plug-in, *113*, **113**
        proxy settings, *110*, 110
    object compliance with baseline, *124*
    orchestrated upgrade, **136–137**
    overview, **103–104**
    Patch Repository tab, **120–121**, *121*
    remediation, **121–133**
        attaching and detaching baselines, **121–123**
        performing scan, **124–126**, *125*
        remediating guest operating systems, **129–131**
        remediating hosts, **127–128**
        staging patches, **126–127**, *127*
    schedules for remediating virtual machines, *130*
    services configuration, **111–112**
    support for, 12
    upgrading ESX/EXSi hosts, **133–136**
    upgrading virtual machine hardware, **132–133**, *133*
    upgrading VMware tools, **131–132**
    use only for ESX/ESXi hosts, 118
Veeam fastSCP, 40
VGT (virtual guest tagging), 160

VI Toolkit Community Extensions, 597
vicfg-mpath command, 642
vicfg-nas command, 642
vicfg-nics command, 642–643
vicfg-ntp command, 644
vicfg-rescan command, 642
vicfg-route command, 644
vicfg-vmknic command, *295*, 643
vicfg-vswitch command, 643–644
vifg command, 641–642
vipinit command, 642
virtual adapters
    assigning to dvPort groups, *195*, 195
    MAC address changes, **208–212**
    managing, *194*, 194
Virtual Appliance Marketplace, 380
virtual appliances, importing, **380–381**
virtual clusters, raw device mapping in, 460–461
Virtual Compatibility mode, for raw device mapping, 460–461
virtual disk files, multiple on virtual machine, 329
virtual disks, **274–276**
    adding existing, 326
    aligning, 276–277
    change of behavior from clones and templates, 279–280
    configuration for guest, 274
    naming scheme, 329
    for new virtual machine, 325–326, *326*
    shrinking, 281
    size limits for, 319
virtual environment, time synchronization in, 337–338
Virtual Ethernet Module (VEM), 200
virtual guest tagging (VGT), 160
virtual hard disk (.vmdk) file, 319, 320
virtual hardware, adding to virtual machine, 340
virtual LAN, 140
virtual machine BIOS configuration (.nvram) file, 272
virtual machine configuration (.vmx) file, 272, 319–320
    example, 342–345
virtual machine file system partition, 27
virtual machine link (.vmdk) file, 272
virtual machine lock (.vmx.lck) file, 272
virtual machine memory (.vmem) file, 273

virtual machine monitor (VMM), 18
Virtual Machine Operations resource type, for datacenter objects, 538
virtual machine port group, 140, 157
    configuring, 163, *163*
    creating, 159
Virtual Machine Power User sample role, 398
    privileges, 402
Virtual Machine privilege, 401
virtual machine Properties dialog
    Hardware tab, *464*
    Resources tab, 414
        memory reservation, *416*, *422*
virtual machine suspend (.vmss) file, 273
virtual machine swap, NFS and location, 246
Virtual Machine tab, in vSphere Client window, 87
Virtual Machine User sample role, 398
    privileges, 402
virtual machines. *See also* resource allocation
    adding to virtual hardware, 340
    aggregate performance requirements, 218
    aligning file systems, 346–347
    attaching baseline or baseline group, 122–123
    backup agents in, **497**, *497*
    bandwidth for, 146
    baseline variations, 524
    best practices, **650**
    for Cisco Nexus 1000V, 201
    cleanup tasks after migration, 377
    clones, 358
    clustering, **455–470**
    creating, **317–330**
        from template, 351
    delegating ability to create, 401
    for DHCP server, 411
    display name of, 329
    forcing uniqueness, 354
    generic hardware for, 317–318, *318*, *319*
    granting access control to local user or group, 389
    importing into VMware vSphere, 372–373
    installing vCenter Server on, 65–66
    isolation, 548
    log in to desktop through web console, 408

MAC address, initial, *209*
managing and modifying, **340–350**
maximum number per vCenter Server, 78
memory configuration, 323–324
Microsoft licensing, **334–335**
migration
    to different ESX/ESXi host, 6
    script for, 603
moving between resource pools, script for, 604–605
networking configuration, **157–159**
    script for, 603–604
powering on after migration, 376
priority setting for, 419
provisioning, vs. provisioning physical machines, 330
reconfiguring networking, with drag-and-drop, 187
requirements for VMotion, 437–438
running from previous versions of ESX/ESXi, 323
running when host is isolated, *488*
SCSI adapters for, 325
SCSI and IDE hard disks in, 327
security for, **573–574**
    vShield zones, **580–582**
snapshot to capture status, 119
space requirements, **273–274**
storage objects for, *272*, **272–273**
Universally Unique Identifier (UUID) of, 208
upgrading hardware, **132–133**, *133*
URL generated for, *409*
Web Console for managing, **405–408**
Virtual Machines tab, for dvPort group, 190
virtual media, permissions for changing, 388
Virtual mode (vRDM), of RDMs, 270–271
virtual network
    best practices, **648–649**
    components, 139–140, *141*
    design, **139–142**, 178–180, *179*, *180*
virtual pools, 223
virtual port storage system, 227
virtual SCSI adapters, **277**, *277*
virtual storage appliance (VSA), 26

Virtual Supervisor Module (VSM), 200
virtual switches. *See* vSwitches
VirtualCenter, 347. *See also* VCenter Server
virtualization, and security, 582–583
Vizioncore vRanger Pro, 61, 513
VLAN ID, 30, 150, 160
    for dvPort group, 189
VLAN ID 4095, 160
VLAN Servers Settings dialog
    Teaming And Failover, 192, *192*
    Traffic Shaping, *193*
VLAN trunking, 189
vlance adapter, 140
VLANs
    benefits, 160–161, *161*
    configuring, 160, **160–164**
    modifying settings for dvPort groups, 192
    private, 189
        setting up, **196–200**, *197*
    Service Console and, 160
    type for dvPort group configuration, 189
    vSwitches and uplinks requirements, *162*
vLockstep technology (VMware), 9, 490
VM (Oracle), 2
VM Activity custom chart setting, 540
VM Hardware Upgrade to Match Host baseline, 115, 132
vm-support command, 568
VM/VA baseline group, in orchestrated upgrade, 136
VM/VA baselines, 114
VM wall, 580
VMCapacity Planner, 311
VMDirectPath I/O, **301–302**
VMDK backup, mounting into file system, 511–512, *512*
.vmdk (virtual machine link) file, 272, *345*, 345
    example, 346
.vmem (virtual machine memory) file, 273
VMFS 3 volume, *251*
VMFS file system
    aligning volumes, 256
    datastores, creating, **252–258**
    expansion, **282**, *283*
    name of folder in volume, 329
    partition name, *32*
    partitions or extents for, 254, *255*
    resignature changes, **282–284**
vmkcore partition, 25–26

VMkernel, 2, 18, 143
    load balancing, 546
    networking configuration, **153–156**
VMkernel interfaces
    creating with jumbo frames enabled, shell script for, **606–607**
    enabling for VMotion, **607–608**
VMkernel ports (vmknic), 140, *154*
    creating
        with command line, 156
        on existing vNetwork Distributed Switch, 436
    on ESXi, 155
    for iSCSI, 239, *239*
    for NFS, 262, *263*
    using failback with, 174
VMkernel swap, 415
vmkfstools command, 281
vmknic, 140. *See also* VMkernel ports (vmknic)
VMM. *See* virtual machine monitor (VMM)
VMotion, **6–7**. *See also* Storage VMotion; VMware VMotion
VMotion boundary, 448
VMs and Templates inventory view, 82, 83, 122, *395*, 395
VMsafe APIs, **583–584**
    support for, 12
.vmsd (dictionary) file, 273
.vmsn file extension, 347
.vmss (virtual machine suspend) file, 273
VMware. *See also* vCenter Server
    NLB support from, 456
    website, 19, 64
VMware Capacity Planner, 365
VMware Consolidated Backup (VCB), **10**, *10*, **496–508**
    backup agents in virtual machine, *497*, **497**
    for file-level backups, **505–506**, *506*, **508**
    for full virtual machine backups, **498–502**, *499*
        results, *502*
        steps, 501–502
    restoring with, *508*, **508–513**
    for single VMDK backups, **504**
    with third-party products, **506–508**
    vs. VCDR, 515
VMware Consolidated Backup User sample role, 398
    privileges, 403